The Complete Equipment-Leasing Handbook

The Complete Equipment-Leasing Handbook

A Deal Maker's Guide with Forms, Checklists, and Worksheets

Richard M. Contino

HarperCollins
Leadership

AN IMPRINT OF HarperCollins

The Complete Equipment-Leasing Handbook

Published by HarperCollins Leadership, an imprint of HarperCollins Focus LLC.

Any internet addresses, phone numbers, or company or product information printed in this book are offered as a resource and are not intended in any way to be or to imply an endorsement by HarperCollins Leadership, nor does HarperCollins Leadership vouch for the existence, content, or services of these sites, phone numbers, companies, or products beyond the life of this book.

Bulk discounts available. For details visit:
www.harpercollinsleadership.com/bulkquotes
Email: customercare@harpercollins.com

ISBN 978-0-8144-7379-5

To Penelope, May-Lynne, Matthew,
my mother, and my father

Contents

Chapter 5   Tax Advantages in Lease Transactions   95

Chapter 6   The Minimum Tax's Role in Leasing   105

Chapter 7   How to Cope Successfully with the Tax Lease Rules   119

*Descriptions of the on-CD-only forms are included in the text.

Preface

Equipment leasing is one of the most complex forms of financing in existence today, involving sophisticated concepts often understood only by experts. Many equipment users fail to consider this important alternative when they need equipment because of their lack of understanding of the advantages. Even those who do consider it frequently do not know how to maximize their position. On the other hand, many lessors lenders overlook obvious opportunities for profit because of a limited view of equipment financing. And that's why this book was written.

The Complete Equipment-Leasing Handbook: A Deal Maker's Guide, with Forms, Checklists, and Worksheets is a comprehensive book for lessees and lessors, divided into two parts, a leasing reference section and a forms section. Its purpose is to provide the legal, financial, tax, accounting, and business background and tools essential to evaluate, negotiate, advise on, and document successful equipment lease transactions. Not only does it contain transaction critical information, but it also includes a comprehensive array of over 115 equipment lease and loan business and legal forms, in writing and on computer diskette, for ready reference and drafting guidance. It will assist both leasing novices and those with more experience. The equipment lease transaction is analyzed from start to finish, taking the reader step by step through the ten most important aspects of leasing—the general marketplace, the preliminary evaluation stage, the proposal, the documents, the tax issues, the business aspects, the bankruptcy issues, the security interest issues, the accounting treatment, and the economics. Many prospective lessees, for example, are not aware they can dramatically increase their chances of getting the most favorable available deals by simply eliminating certain type of lessors, those less suited for their particular transactions. The characteristics of the various lessors are explained, as well as the pros and cons of dealing with each. Some prospective lessors, on the other hand, leave themselves needlessly exposed to financial, business, and tax risks.

If you are a prospective or existing lessor, lessee, or equipment lender, or a lease advisor, and you want to have the best available leasing information or documentation, this book is for you. It will address issues such as:

- How does the leasing marketplace really work?
- What are the leasing profit areas?
- How does a leasing company run?
- Do bank leasing companies give the most aggressive rates?
- When is leasing a poor choice?
- What is the best way for a company to solicit lease bids?
- Does a proposal letter really commit a lessor?
- What should a properly written lease cover?
- How can an underwriter protect its fee?
- How good is a legal opinion on questionable issues?
- When should a leveraged lease be used?
- When will a lease meet the IRS requirements?

- How does the alternative minimum tax affect leasing?
- Can a fixed price purchase option be used?
- What advantageous depreciation methods are now available?
- Is the investment tax credit completely gone?
- What tax and economic risks does a lessor have?
- What special risks must a leveraged lease investor consider?
- How should a lease be analyzed financially?
- What impact do the lease accounting rules have?
- What are the bankruptcy issues and concerns?
- What common lease provisions are voided by the bankruptcy rules?
- What are Uniform Commercial Code rules for leasing and secured lending?
- How does UCC Article 2A help both lessors and lessees?
- Can lessors prevent lessees' creditors from getting their leased equipment?
- What is the best document for a particular situation?

In addition, the business of leasing is explained, both domestically and internationally, to provide you, whether you are on the lessor's or lessee's side, with key information on issues such as lessor profit strategies, the establishment and operation of a leasing company, and the leasing of equipment in the growing international market—all with a view to maximizing leasing opportunities and minimizing leasing risks. The equipment leasing rules established under the Uniform Commercial Code, Article 2A, and the secured lending rules under Article 9 of the Uniform Commercial Code, as they affect or impact equipment lending transitions, are handily explained. Finally, the bankruptcy rules, a critical consideration in approaching and managing defaulted equipment lease or secured loan transactions, are simply explained for the businessperson.

Throughout the book the latest and best techniques for dealing with the technical and business issues are explained. Practical suggestions and insights are offered to enable you to gain every advantage and avoid the many legal and financial pitfalls. Following are topics you will find in the leasing reference section.

Proposal stage. In any lease financing arrangement, the proposal stage is the critical point when the parties establish the transaction's business parameters. At this stage, the prospective lessee will be in its strongest negotiating position. By taking advantage of some simple techniques recommended by the author, it can, for example, get a "below market" lease rent. A prospective lessor can, on the other hand, gain some valuable advantages at this time by properly structuring its offer.

Documentation. The documentation stage—where the participant's rights and obligations are defined—is another crucial step in the transaction. To be fully aware of what their risks and obligations will be, all participants must understand the transaction's basic concepts. For example, a lessor may inadvertently assume certain state tax payment obligations that can drastically reduce its profits. A lessee may also unknowingly assume burdensome obligations. This book comprehensively examines the documents to give anyone responsible for negotiating an equipment lease the essentials necessary to avoid the many traps.

Tax issues. Problems often arise because of the lack of understanding complex tax issues. Parties spend time and money on transactions that will not be approved by the IRS. The revised alternative minimum tax is an important consideration in whether to lease or buy equipment. Understanding how it works is essential.

Accounting issues. Lease accountability should always be a foremost consideration. Improper structuring can cause undesirable accounting treatment. The Financial Accounting Standards Board has promulgated an extensive and complicated set of rules on accounting for leases. A chapter summarizes the rules and puts them into a more meaningful context.

Financial issues. Another key consideration is the financial side of a lease decision. There are many apparent—and some not so apparent—economic advantages and disadvantages to leasing. Lease investors, for example, should be aware that incorrect equipment residual assumptions can wipe out profits. A prospective lessee can end up making the wrong financing decision by using an incorrect method of analysis. The economic advantages and disadvantages, as well as the methods of financial analysis, are explained so that a prospective lessor, lessee, lender, or investor can determine a viable position.

Leveraged leasing. An entire chapter explains the specialized field of leveraged leasing—where the lease transaction is financed largely with nonrecourse debt. One of the most sophisticated and competitive forms of leasing, leveraged leasing, can produce many unique benefits, but also pose many dangers. Some lease underwriters, for example, "low ball" rent quotations to eliminate the competition and then later raise the rates. A prospective lease investor can end up making a poor investment by relying on an unrealistic investment analysis.

The business of leasing equipment. How does a lessor reduce its risks and make money in the leasing business? Surprisingly, it is often in ways that are not readily apparent. A successful profit strategy used by some lessors in highly competitive market areas is to target equipment that historically maintains excellent resale value and to aggressively go after lease deals by offering very low rents. Although these low rents often do little more than the lessor's operational overhead, the profit picture brightens when the equipment comes off lease and is sold or re-leased by the lessor. A risk for these lessors is technical obsolescence or reduced buyer demand, but properly approached, these risks can be successfully managed.

International leasing. The business of leasing equipment in the United States is mature and, accordingly, highly competitive. Many lessors with the ability to finance equipment for overseas users are finding a market gold mine. To realize success in the international market, however, requires different skills than those for leasing in the U.S. market. Accordingly, some lessors should avoid this market. For those lessors with the right resources, however, providing they do their homework, the international leasing market may yield attractive new opportunities.

Leasing laws under the Uniform Commercial Code. As a lessor, you cannot protect your equipment under lease from claims of outside lessee creditors unless you have a working knowledge of the technical requirements of the leasing laws adopted by the various states in which your equipment is located, including the secured lending laws. One mistake can eliminate your rights to reclaim your equipment. Although the leasing laws, as embodied in legislation referred to as the Uniform Commercial Code, can vary somewhat from state to state, the issues to be addressed are the same: How do these laws work? Do you need to make a state or local filing to protect your equipment against third-party claims? How do you make any necessary filings? When must any required filings be made? What happens if you fail to make a critical filing? Lessees, on the other hand, must know the impact of these leasing laws, to properly assess if they have unnecessarily committed to a lessor leasing law request that will create problems in the future.

Bankruptcy. One of the most complex laws affecting equipment leasing and secured lending transactions are the bankruptcy laws, in particular the federal bankruptcy laws. The bankruptcy laws can severely impact an equipment lease or loan transaction. If you are a lessor, you will at some point encounter a situation in which your rights are controlled by the bankruptcy rules. If you do not anticipate how these rules can affect your lease, your losses can be far greater than necessary. As a lessee, you must also understand these laws. In particular, you must know your bankruptcy rights in the event it becomes necessary to file for protection under the bankruptcy laws, so your chances of surviving increase.

Many chapters include time-saving checklists that cover the critical stages and aspects of an equipment lease financing. Examples have been incorporated to illustrate many of the financial points discussed. In Chapter 15, the leasing industry's important terms and buzzwords have been compiled and simply defined for ready access.

In summary, the reference text portion of this book gives the reader a complete grasp of the legal, financial, tax, accounting, and business considerations for leasing, including those that are necessary to originate, evaluate, and negotiate the most favorably structured equipment leasing transaction.

In the forms section of *The Complete Equipment-Leasing Handbook: A Deal Maker's Guide with Forms, Checklists, and Worksheets,* you will find examples of virtually every type of document, worksheet, checklist, notification, and letter to assist anyone involved, or intending to become involved, in equipment leasing or lending. In total, there are 115 sample documents. If you are a prospective or existing lessor, lessee, or equipment lender, or a lease or loan advisor, this book will provide a handy and invaluable state-of-the-art document reference for small to multimillion dollar equipment financing, and equipment financing-related transactions. Examples include the following:

- Preparing lessor lease proposals and lessee requests for lease proposals, such as lessor lease proposals and lessee RFQs
- Evaluating lessor proposals or prospective lessee deals, such as transactions summaries
- Documenting equipment lease or loan transactions, such as single deal or master lease and loan agreements
- Starting and operating a leasing business, such as lessee marketing materials, internal deal and operations worksheets, and collection notices
- Setting up equipment vendor financing arrangements, such as vendor program and remarketing agreements

All documents, where relevant, are fully integrated with cross references to other documents, which may be integral with the document being used, thereby enabling you to quickly access these collateral forms. For example, lease agreements are integrated with opinions of counsel, guaranties, corporate resolutions, and various lessee and lessor lease options to provide a complete package. In addition, you receive a computer disk containing the agreements, forms, worksheets, checklists, notifications, and letters (not sold separately).

Each form is preceded by the respective form number, CD file name identification, summary of the form's purpose, identification of the executing parties, and cross references to other pertinent forms. Other than the CD file name identification, that information appears only in this volume, the computer files on the accompanying CD containing only information that is part of the respective document.

Specific Tips on Using Your Form Section

The following tips may help you get the most out of the form section of this book.

Do You Need a Particular Lease or Loan Provision?

The 115 agreements, forms, worksheets, and checklists in this book are based on, and have been honed through, the author's equipment financing experience with hundreds of transactions and situations, both as a legal and business advisor and as a business principal, during his 20-year involvement with the business of equipment leasing and lending. With these documents at your fingertips, you have immediate access to a unique wealth of equipment lease and loan provisions to help you gain every advantage, avoid the many pitfalls, and develop negotiating compromises when necessary. Many form categories provide drafting approach choices to enable you to select the most appropriate provision style for a particular situation. For example, in a small ticket financing, a less detail-specific approach may be the most appropriate. Many provisions also reflect the give-and-take situation of actual deal negotiations. These provisions will provide you with winning insights to increase your bargaining power, help you win profitable business deals or obtain cost-effective equipment financing, enhance your ability to effectively make reasonable negotiating compromises, and assist you in closing beneficial equipment financing deals.

Do You Need a Particular Form?

When you need a particular form, turn to the Contents at the front of the book. When relevant, the author has provided a selection of forms within a particular category. For example, if you are looking for an equipment lease agreement, you will find three lease agreements from which to choose: a long form master lease agreement, a short form lease agreement, and a lease agreement used in a leveraged transaction. If you are involved with a small ticket, nontax-sensitive lease transaction, you will not need, or want, a 50-page document, so the short form lease agreement is the place to start. If, on the other hand, you are involved with a multimillion dollar lease transaction, you should refer to one of the more comprehensive lease agreements which will contain provisions that address the needs found in major equipment financings. If you need assistance with specific lease agreement provisions, refer to the lease agreements for guidance—each document contains valuable deal nuances. In using these documents, keep in mind that no matter what type of equipment is involved, the basic forms can be easily adapted by making the appropriate equipment-type changes.

Are You Putting Together an Entire Transaction?

Equipment lease and loan transactions involve multiple documents which, in many cases, must interrelate. For example, if you are involved with an equipment lending transaction, you will not only need the loan and security agreement, but you will also need the collateral forms typically used in a loan transaction, such as a form legal opinion. By referencing the loan document section of the Contents, you can identify which loan and security agreement forms are packaged specifically to provide fully integrated collateral documents, so important and critical deal aspects and collateral documents are not inadvertently overlooked. Using these fully integrated forms will save you drafting time. Additionally, the description preceding each form has cross references, when relevant, to other documents of interest.

Are You Proposing a Deal?

If you are an equipment lessor or lease underwriter, this book can save you time in assembling the best possible proposal for you and your prospective lessee. The relevant checklists, worksheets, and letters will get you off on the right track—quickly. For example, the book contains forms for single investor and multiple investor proposal formats. Additionally, if you are proposing on an equipment loan, these forms can be readily adapted to loan proposals.

Are You Looking for Equipment Financing Offers?

If you are a prospective equipment lendor or borrower and want financing bids on equipment, the documents available will ensure that you do not miss out on the many possible benefits, that you put together a professional-looking request for bids, and that you are able to quickly analyze financing offers when they come in. For example, there is a time-saving request for lease proposals (RFQ—Deal Sheet Format, Form r-01) developed by the author that sets up the bidding parameters so offer comparisons can be done simply and meaningfully.

Are You Concerned about Missing an Important Deal Point?

Unless you are thoroughly experienced in equipment leasing or lending, it is often difficult, and sometimes impossible, to know what to request and what may be available. Even when you do know, in the rush of a deal it is easy to inadvertently miss an important point. The worksheets and checklists should help guide you away from such situations—whether you are on the lessor's or lessee's side. For example, a handy lease proposal evaluation worksheet, and an invaluable lease negotiation and drafting checklist, gives you expert guidance.

Are You Negotiating a Deal?

In negotiating any equipment lease or loan financing, a ready reference to comprehensive provisions and forms can assist you in documenting or negotiating difficult points, and in formulating possible solutions when transaction impasses occur—and they will. The documents provided in this book come from the negotiating trenches. If you need assistance, they will help you solve difficult problems and gain protection.

Are You Starting or Running a Leasing or Lending Business?

Not only does this book contain the basic agreements needed to document an equipment lease or loan transaction, but it also contains worksheets, checklists, and time-saving form letters to use in the day-to-day running of a leasing business. For example, the lessee marketing materials include a form rate sheet and a form proposal letter, transaction audit worksheets, and collection letters. All are based on documents in actual use by equipment lessors and lenders.

   In summary, whatever your equipment financing needs, the Forms section of this book offers a unique and ready source for invaluable state-of-the-art agreements, forms, worksheets, and checklists that are not available in any other publication.

                                                                             Richard M. Contino, Esq.

About the Author

Richard M. Contino is an internationally known equipment financing expert, as well as a practicing attorney, business consultant, and businessman. He is the Managing Partner of Contino + Partners, an equipment lease and business law firm located in White Plains, New York. Prior to entering private practice, Mr. Contino held the positions, over a five-year period, of Marketing Vice President and Eastern Regional Counsel for GATX Leasing Corporation, a major independent equipment lessor and lease underwriter.

Mr. Contino is the author of five equipment lease financing books, two human potential development books, and the finance author of a business handbook. In addition to his books, he has written numerous articles and conducted seminars throughout the United States for many private corporations, business groups, law associations, and other professional organizations on the legal, financial, business, and marketing aspects of equipment leasing.

Mr. Contino received an LL.M. in corporate law from the New York University Graduate School of Law, a Juris Doctor from the University of Maryland School of Law, and a Bachelor of Aeronautical Engineering from Rensselaer Polytechnic Institute. He is a member of the bars of the states of New York and Maryland, as well as the District of Columbia. Mr. Contino is also a member of the American Bar Association and the New York State Bar Association. He is listed in *Who's Who of American Law, Who's Who of Emerging Leaders, Who's Who in the World,* and *The International Who's Who of Contemporary Achievement.*

The Complete Equipment-Leasing Handbook

Chapter 1

Fundamentals of Equipment Leasing

A. Overview

The concept of the lease as a property right, and the rights and duties of lessors and lessees, has been part of our legal tradition for centuries, particularly with respect to real estate. During the 1950s, leasing began to emerge as a viable alternative for acquiring equipment. Today the equipment leasing industry plays a major role in the financial community. A user can lease virtually any type of equipment on a variety of terms. The drawback to leasing, however, is legal requirements and financial considerations are at times extremely complex. In fact, many transactions involve concepts so sophisticated that even the most experienced people sometimes make mistakes that could cost them or their customers thousands of dollars.

The interest in leasing as an alternative means of acquiring equipment continues to prompt a deluge of questions not only from equipment users, but also from the legal and financial community. For example:

- What are the tax advantages and disadvantages to the lessee?
- What are the tax benefits available to the lessor?
- What is the best business structure for a lease?
- How should lease transactions be analyzed from a financial viewpoint?
- How are leases treated for accounting purposes?
- What are the leasing risks?

For these and many other questions there are no easy answers.

The 1986 Tax Reform Act (1986 TRA) eliminated the investment tax credit (ITC) and expanded the alternative minimum tax (AMT). Safe harbor leases have come and gone. The economic downturn of the late 1980s and early 1990s sparked suggestions of new tax law changes to stimulate business. The economy recovered and these changes never occurred. In the beginning of the new millennium, the economy again dipped, once again giving rise to the possibility of tax law changes that could have a significant positive or negative impact on leasing, and which could create new questions, issues, and business challenges. This ongoing tax law roller coaster, often motivated by political needs and special interests, creates a difficult and uncertain leasing business environment for all parties involved.

Unfortunately, because of the many variables that can be involved in a lease decision, no book could presume to answer all the questions concerning the criteria for, and desirability of, entering into every conceivable transaction. In addition, the desirability of leasing for, and the lease evaluation criteria used by, one company may be totally inappropriate for another company. This book will, however, provide the reader with a comprehensive working knowledge of the fundamental tools necessary to handle competently any lease situation from start to finish. The relevant issues which must be taken into account in developing a solid financing approach will be identified, described, and explained. In addition, this book contains a forms section, which provides, along with the accompanying CD, 115 forms for your use in any type of lease or lease-related transaction.

This chapter sets the stage for the following chapters. After briefly reviewing the tax motivations behind leasing transactions, it describes the major players (the typical lessees and lessors), explains the types of common leases, and then sets out what equipment users should consider when deciding to enter the leasing arena.

B. Tax Motivations of Leasing

1. General Tax Picture

Although any type of equipment can be leased, the critical question to the prospective lessee is at what cost? The answer is complex, but as a threshold matter, leasing often is not the lowest cost way for a company to acquire equipment unless the lessor can take advantage of certain tax benefits and indirectly pass them on, at least in part, in the form of relatively lower lease rents. Consider the following hypothetical example.

> **Illustrative Example**   *The Tax Advantage:* Company Able wants to acquire the use of a $20,000 truck. It can borrow funds from its bank for five years at the prime rate, assumed for this example to be 10% a year. If Company Able were able to borrow 100% of the funds required, its cost to finance the truck would be the cost of the $20,000 loan.
>
> As an alternative, Company Able could lease the truck from Company Baker. Assume that Company Baker also borrowed "at prime" from the same bank as Company Able and that it would fund the truck purchase entirely from its bank borrowing. If there were no truck ownership tax advantages, the only way it could make a profit would be to charge a lease rate greater than its cost of funds. Thus, Company Able would have to pay something over prime rate to Company Baker, a not very attractive arrangement.

Although this example is admittedly oversimplified and not completely realistic, it makes the point: When the lessor and the lessee have the same borrowing rate capabilities, leasing may not be the most economic way for a lessee to acquire equipment it needs unless the lessor is able to use available ownership tax benefits, takes them into account as a lease profit ingredient, and passes them on to a lessee through reduced rental rates. How this process actually works will be explained later in the book.

2. Lessor's Tax Benefit

What tax benefits are available to the lessor? For equipment placed in service before 1986, the lessor could obtain both ITC and depreciation deductions as an equipment owner. With limited exceptions, the 1986 TRA eliminated the ITC for equipment placed in service after 1985. Thus, the tax benefits for the lessor today are the depreciation deductions available under the Modified Accelerated Cost Recovery System (MACRS), introduced by the 1986 TRA. Under recent federal tax law changes, certain qualified property placed in service after September 10, 2001, there is an additional 30% special depreciation allowance for the first year the property was placed in service.

Under MACRS, a lessor generally can write off its equipment costs over a period significantly shorter than the equipment's useful life and at an accelerated rate. For example, a lessor can deduct the cost of leased computer equipment over a six-year period with the percentages for each year as 20%, 32%, 19.2%, 11.52%, 11.52%, and 5.76%, respectively. In a typical lease, the lessor's deductions in the early years will exceed the rental income, permitting the lessor to offset other income with those excess deductions.

➤ **A Word of Caution**   As explained in Chapter 6, if the lessor is subject to the revised corporate and individual AMTs, its depreciation deductions will be deferred significantly. This in turn could have a major impact on what rents should be charged. Therefore, potential lessors must review their AMT exposure when pricing a leasing transaction.

3.   Lessee's Tax Consequences

Basically, an equipment user decreases its tax benefits by becoming a lessee rather than an owner. As lessee, the user can deduct its rental payments, but those will be less than the depreciation it could have deducted in earlier years. Why, then, should leasing be considered? As explained below, there are numerous financial and business reasons for a prospective lessee to lease rather than to buy. Leasing is also particularly attractive to equipment users who cannot take timely advantage of the depreciation deductions. Two types of users fall into this category: First are those who have negative taxable income or carryover losses, so that they have no taxable income to offset; and second, to a lesser extent, are those subject to the AMT, because the AMT would reduce the value of an equipment owner's tax benefits but will not in most cases affect deductions for rent. For those users, the rental payments, charged by a lessor who is taking ownership tax benefits into account in setting its lease rate, can be worth more than the ownership tax benefits.

4.   Importance of Lease Structuring

When the lessor anticipates tax benefits, it will suffer an economic loss if those benefits are unavailable. Those benefits will be available only if the lessor remains the equipment owner for tax purposes; and the lessor will be treated as the tax owner only if the lease is a true lease for tax purposes. To qualify as a true lease for tax purposes, certain tax guidelines must be met. These guidelines are explained in Chapter 7. Although as explained in that chapter, there is the possibility of some variation from the guidelines, it is advisable to comply with the following:

- The lessor must make an economic profit, apart from the tax benefits, on the lease.
- The lessor's equity investment must be at least 20% of the equipment's cost throughout the lease term.
- The lessee cannot, with limited exceptions, make any investment in the property, or make any loan to the lessor.
- Lessee purchase options must be at the equipment's fair market value at the time of purchase.
- The property must be usable by a party other than the lessee after the lease term's end.

Poor lease structuring can lead to disaster. If the transaction does not qualify as a true lease for tax purposes, then the lessee will not be able to deduct the rental payments and the lessor cannot use the ownership tax benefits. For example, if the lease was successfully classified by the Internal Revenue Service as a loan, then the lessee would be deemed the equipment owner and the lessor deemed the lender. If the lessee cannot use any tax benefits and the lessor must have them for the transaction to make economic sense, then everyone loses.

➤ **Observation** All leases must be true leases for the lessor to obtain tax benefits; but for leases in which the lease term is significantly shorter than the equipment's useful life, there will be little risk that the lease will not be treated as a true lease, because the lessor's ownership status will be clear. Generally the closer the lease term comes to matching the equipment's useful life, the more attention that must be paid to the true lease tax rules.

C. Who Are the Prospective Lessees?

Any equipment user is a prospective lessee. The users can range from multinational corporations, to sole proprietorships, to individuals using equipment for personal reasons. Whether the user should lease is another, more complicated question, and depends on factors that vary with each situation. These factors are reviewed in Section F of this chapter.

D. Who Are the Potential Lessors?

In theory, any company in the financing business can be a potential lessor of equipment. Because of the competitive nature of equipment leasing and the expertise required, however, only certain types of organizations are active in the leasing market.

For discussion purposes, it is useful to separate the potential lessors into five categories: individuals, independent leasing companies, lease brokers, captive leasing companies, and banks. Prospective lessees will find the categories helpful in narrowing the field of potential lessors, and prospective lessors may find help in determining their potential competition.

1. Individuals

Prior to the 1986 TRA, the role of the individual as lessor was limited because of the rules restricting an individual from claiming ITCs on leased property. Now that ITC is no longer available to lessors, wealthy individuals can be more rate competitive. This coupled with the fact that they often will take greater business risks than a traditional leasing company can make them a good choice in difficult financing situations. A few innovative equipment leasing companies and investment bankers have begun to develop interesting investment programs for individuals which will make them an increasing part of the equipment financing business. For example, some railcar lessors have set up individual investor programs to provide individuals with opportunities to invest in short-term railcar leases.

An individual considering becoming an equipment lessor must now contend with the passive loss rules. An explanation of those rules is outside the scope of this book, and the reader is generally referred to Internal Revenue Code Section 469 for further information. A prospective lessee receiving a lease proposal from an individual lessor, however, need not be concerned with the passive loss rules, except to be sure that any indemnities do not require the lessee to reimburse the lessor for deductions lost under those rules.

➤ **A Word of Caution** A prospective lessee considering leasing from an individual must look at more than the rent advantage. For example, because individuals often take aggressive tax positions, they may run afoul of the income tax laws. The IRS may then put a lien on all the individual's property, including the leased equipment. Individuals also can be somewhat more arbitrary to deal with when variances from the lease terms are required.

2. Independent Leasing Companies

Independent leasing companies provide a major source of equipment lease financing. Because leasing is their principal source of revenue, independent leasing companies have to be extremely aggressive and, in some cases, willing to bend the rules for the lessee's benefit to win a transaction. For example, some will give a lessee the right to buy the equipment at a low, predetermined fixed price when the lease ends, a practice that can run the risk of adverse tax consequences (see Chapter 7). The two types of independent leasing companies are those that merely buy and lease equipment to the user (so-called finance leasing companies) and those that offer additional services such as maintenance and repair of the equipment (so-called service leasing companies).

a. Finance Leasing Companies

Finance leasing companies—lessors of millions of dollars of equipment each year—operate in much the same manner as banks or other financing companies. They do not maintain an equipment inventory, but, after agreeing on a lease with a lessee, they buy the specific equipment needed for the lease. The lessee orders and receives the equipment from the vendor. When it arrives, the finance leasing company pays for it, takes title, and leases it to the equipment user.

Finance leasing companies typically write leases, called finance leases, that run from 70% to 80% of the equipment's useful life. The total amounts received under these leases, including the rents payable and the equipment residual value proceeds, are usually sufficient to provide lessors with a full return of their equipment investment and a profit. If the equipment purchase is leveraged with third-party debt, then the rents will generally be enough to cover the full repayment of the debt. This type of long-term lease is net to the lessee; that is, the lessee must assume substantially all the equipment ownership responsibilities such as maintenance, taxes, and insurance.

b. Service Leasing Companies

Service leasing companies provide nonfinancial services to lessees in addition to the equipment financing. Services may include equipment maintenance and repair or advice on the equipment's operation and design.

Service lessors typically limit their activity to a single type of equipment, such as computers, or to a single type of industry, such as the mining industry. The intense experience gained through the specialization enables them to reduce many leasing risks. For example, because lessors frequently handle used equipment, they know how to deal efficiently with equipment when it comes off lease, which in turn reduces their re-leasing or sale risk. Because of that reduced risk, they can offer attractive lease termination or equipment exchange privileges.

➤ **Observation** Many industry participants believe that product specialization is less risky for a lessor than industry specialization. The reason is there is a greater likelihood that an industry specialized lessor would suffer more if its industry hit hard times than an equipment specialized lessor would if one of the industries in which its equipment was used hit hard times.

Service lessors typically write leases with much shorter lease terms than finance leases. Nonpayout in nature, those leases do not permit the lessor to recoup its entire equipment investment during the first lease term. Thus, to recover its investment and make a profit, the service lessor must continue to re-lease the equipment. If the equipment becomes obsolete sooner than expected, the lessor may incur a loss. To be compensated for taking that high risk and for providing other services, service lessors will generally charge higher rents than finance lessors.

When should a prospective lessee consider using a service leasing company? Basically, the times is when the lessee needs the specialized services offered by the service lessor or wants a shorter lease term or early termination rights. A user may want the shorter term when, for example, there is a high risk of equipment obsolescence or when the user's industry is in a down cycle.

➤ **Recommendation** A prospective lessee considering leasing equipment that it may want to return early should compare the higher rents typically payable under a shorter term lease offered by service lessors with the lower rents, and early termination penalty, typically payable under a longer term finance lease offered by financial lessors. Frequently the short-term lease is economically preferable, because finance lease termination penalties are often substantial. The reason is financial lessors do not have as strong a remarketing capability as the service lessors.

3. *Lease Brokers*

Also referred to as lease underwriters or syndicators, lease brokers package lease transactions for third-party accounts: They simply match up prospective lessees with prospective lessor-investors. Lease brokers charge a fee for their service, usually ranging from 0.75% to 8.0% of the leased equipment's cost, which is typically paid for by the lessor-investors.

To put the lease broker's role into perspective, it is helpful to understand how a broker normally operates. Generally, a lease broker begins by contacting all types of equipment users and vendors to determine if they have any leasing needs. In the case of a prospective lessee, the lease broker will define the rough parameters through discussions with the prospective lessee. At this juncture, the broker may perform a credit check on the prospective lessee to make sure the credit is marketable. If there are no problems, the broker will formulate a concise lease structure, including rental rate, and offer it to the equipment user generally through a formal proposal letter.

If the user finds the proposed arrangement acceptable, the broker then proceeds to find prospective lessor-investors, commonly referred to as equity participants, or in the case of smaller transactions, a leasing company. If the transaction is to be leveraged with third-party debt, called a leverage lease, it may also put out feelers for prospective lenders, commonly referred to as debt participants, although usually the debt side is handled by an investment banker. Having located the equity and debt participants, the broker proceeds to shepherd the transaction through documentation to completion.

Although generally acting exclusively as a broker, a lease underwriter may occasionally invest some of its own funds in the equipment with other third-party lessor-investors, becoming a part owner. By doing so, the lease underwriter can add credibility to the investment and thus be able to sell the lease transaction to potential investors more readily.

One of the lease broker's major assets is its knowledge of the leasing industry. Because the broker is continually in the market, it will know where to find competitive, cooperative, and realistic equity participants. It will also know how to get the equity participants to agree to what meets the lessee's needs, including, for example, lease rates, overall transaction structure, and documentation.

➤ Recommendations

- A prospective lessee considering a finance lease arrangement should invite a cross section of brokers to quote, in addition to regular lessors. Because of their ability to find aggressive equity participants, lease brokers will add a new dimension to the bidding environment.
- There is a risk in dealing with brokers for a prospective lessee. If they cannot find the funding participants, the prospective lessee must look again for financing. A prospective lessee, therefore, should put realistic performance time limits on any broker arranging the funding, and plan for any nonperformance possibilities by, for example, having a backup leasing company ready in the event of a funding problem.

4. Captive Leasing Companies

In increasing numbers, equipment vendors are setting up their own leasing companies, generally referred to as captive leasing companies, to service their customers. Although the purpose is usually to offer lease financing on equipment sold by an affiliated company, some captive leasing companies also may be willing to buy and lease equipment sold by a nonaffiliated company.

A captive leasing company that is marketing its affiliated company's equipment may offer attractive rates. The reason is when it markets its affiliated company's equipment, that company makes a sale profit, and the captive lessor can then work with a lower financing profit than other types of lessors. Coupled with its knowledge of the equipment's potential residual value, this can result in attractive rents for a lessee.

➤ **Recommendation**   When considering a certain vendor's equipment, a prospective lessee should find out if the vendor has a captive leasing company. If so, the vendor's captive leasing company should be asked to submit a lease quotation.

➤ **Observation**   Although captive leasing companies have a theoretical advantage over other types of lessors because of their connection with the vendor in practice, they often do not know how to take advantage of that position effectively. The reason may be the equipment vendors do not have extensive experience in using leasing as a marketing tool and may not support the leasing operation as fully as they should.

5. Banks

Many banks, particularly national banks, are actively involved in equipment leasing. They usually are lessors in net finance leases because of regulatory requirements and because those leases provide the least risk and most similarity to their lending activity. (Finance leases are explained in Section E.1.)

Banks are not generally inclined to take aggressive equipment residual value positions, thus resulting in potentially higher market lease rates. Their cost of funds, however, in many cases is lower than that of nonbank lessors, frequently offsetting their conservative residual value positions.

The terms and rates offered by bank lessors often vary significantly from one transaction to the next. Internal bank policies may contribute to that variation. Banks are not as dependent as most nonbank lessors on their leasing activities for revenues and so can afford to miss out on many deals. Periodically, however, they can go on major drives for lease business and, at those times, can be extremely rate aggressive.

There is a hidden risk in dealing with banks. Leasing is not considered their main line of business, so if banks experience general financial difficulties, as they have in the late 1980s and early 1990s, their leasing departments are usually the first to go. Management's rationale is that they must go back to basics to get their financial house in order. Chase Manhattan Bank's sale of its profitable leasing subsidiaries in 1991 is a good example of what can happen when a bank experiences general financial problems.

➤ **Recommendation**   Given the unpredictability of bank lessors' responses to potential lease transactions and their commitment to the business, a prospective lessee is well advised to avoid relying exclusively on one to service all its financing needs.

Many bank lessors operate with a limited lease marketing staff. As a result, the transactions they see are fundamentally limited to those coming in through their existing bank customers or lease brokers. There is, however, a significant number of bank lessors with strong marketing organizations that, as a group, comprise a major factor in the equipment leasing marketplace. Banks also participate directly in the leasing market by acting as lenders in leveraged lease transactions.

E.   Types of Leases

Significant differences exist among the various types of leases. Unfortunately, the industry jargon used to label the different types is sometimes vague. Further compounding the problem are many hybrid arrangements that have surfaced that cross over the lines of the standard descriptive terminology. Once the fundamental characteristics of different leases are identified and understood, however, the confusion can be eliminated.

For explanation purposes, it will be helpful to separate all equipment leases into two main categories: financial leases and operating leases. The financial, or finance, lease typically represents a long-term lease commitment in which the sum of the rents due will approximate the equipment's purchase cost. Decisions to enter into a financial lease should be part of a company's financial, as opposed to operating, policy considerations. All equipment leases not fitting within the financial lease category can be put into the operating lease category. Because operating leases involve shorter term financial commitments, decisions as to their use typically come within the scope of a company's operating policy.

Within the two broad categories, are some basic variations: leverage leases, nonleveraged leases, and service leases. These variations are sometimes incorrectly considered to be separate types of leases rather than descriptive forms of the basic types. For example, finance leases can be leveraged leases or nonleveraged leases, and service leases can be financial or operating in nature. They are explained individually, however, to give the reader a working perspective.

Table 1.1 sets out a general overview of fundamental lease characteristics.

Table 1.1 Lease characteristics.

Type of Lease	Lease Term	Typical Type of Transaction	Comments
Finance lease	Substantial portion of asset's economic life	Underwritten and direct lessor	Payout-type lease
Net finance lease	Substantial portion of asset's economic life	Underwritten and direct lessor	Payout-type lease; lessee has basically all ownership responsibilities
Leveraged lease	Usually substantial portion of asset's economic life	Underwritten	Usually net finance lease
Nonleveraged lease	Hours to substantial portion of asset's economic life	Direct lessor	Any lease where no third-party debt is involved
Operating lease	Hours to years	Direct lessor	Usually nonpayout

1. Finance Lease

A common type of equipment lease, finance leases are considered long term leases because the primary lease terms usually run for most of the equipment's useful life. Typically, the total cash flow over the term—from rents, tax savings, and the end-of-lease equipment (residual) resale or re-lease value—will be sufficient to pay back the lessor's investment, take care of the administrative expenses, pay off any equipment-related debt obligations and commissions, and provide a profit. Because they are entered into by lessors as long-term financial commitments, finance lessors usually impose a substantial repayment penalty for a lessee's early lease termination in an amount that will assure the lessor of a return of its investment and a profit, at least up to the date of termination.

Consistent with its financial nature, a finance lease is usually a net lease. A net lease means that the fundamental ownership responsibilities, such as maintaining and repairing the equipment, paying for the necessary insurance, and taking care of property, use, and sales taxes, are placed on the lessee. A net finance lease can be compared with an equipment loan in that the lessor, like a lender, is involved only in asset funding. The lessor's basic responsibilities are to pay for the equipment, lease it to the lessee for the agreed-on term, and not interfere with its use.

Because the term of a finance lease runs for most of the equipment's useful life, the lessee bears the primary risk of the equipment becoming obsolete. The degree of obsolescence risk that the finance lessor assumes depends on the equipment's anticipated residual value. If, for example, a lessor computes the rent based on a zero equipment residual value at the lease term's end, then the lessor has no residual value risk and, thus, no obsolescence risk. This presumes there is no risk of premature equipment return as a result, for instance, of a lessee default. As a practical matter, however, a lessor must generally use a residual value greater than zero to be price competitive. The risk of obsolescence would then be on the lessor to the extent of the value estimated. If its profit is in part dependent on the anticipated residual value, then the greater the risk of obsolescence the greater the chance the transaction will not turn out to be as profitable as anticipated.

One of a financial lessor's principal concerns is the protection of its investment in the event of a lease default or an equipment casualty. Toward this end, finance leases usually include provisions to make the lessor whole if any of these events occur. From a casualty loss standpoint, the lease may include stipulated loss value provisions. These provisions set out the amount the lessee must pay the lessor if an equipment casualty occurs, depending on when it occurs. The amount of the stipulated loss value is intended to guarantee the lessor a return of its investment, reimburse it for any tax benefit losses, and assure it of at least some profit. These stipulated loss values are also sometimes used as a measure of lease default damages, although there are other methods.

Finance leases frequently contain a "hell or high water" rent commitment. Under this type of obligation, a lessee must pay the full rent when due unconditionally and cannot reduce the amount paid even though it has a legitimate claim against the lessor for money owed. This is not as bad as it sounds for a lessee, because it can still bring a lawsuit against the lessor for any claims.

The hell or high water rent provision is critical for a finance lessor to have in a leverage lease transaction, where it wants to borrow money to purchase the equipment on a nonrecourse loan basis. The reason is in a nonrecourse loan, the lender agrees to look only to the lessee's rent payments and the equipment for a return on investment. With a hell or high water provision, the lender need not be concerned that a dispute between the lessor and the lessee will result in the lessee's withholding rent.

2. Operating Lease

When a lease's primary term is significantly shorter than the equipment's useful life, the lease is called an operating lease. Operating leases typically span a few months to a few years, although some are as short as a few hours.

Because the lease terms are relatively short, an operating lessor usually cannot earn much of its equipment investment back through the rents from one lease transaction; thus, it must either sell or re-lease the equipment on attractive terms to be profitable. The danger to an operating lessor, is that the equipment's market value will be inadequate to allow it to sell or re-lease it on economically favorable terms. In other words, it has the risk of equipment obsolescence. As a result, such a lessor will attempt to earn its money back quickly to lessen its investment exposure by charging higher rent than a finance lessor.

Their short lease terms and easy cancellation provisions make operating leases attractive to users in several situations. One example is when the user anticipates using the equipment for a short time, such as with certain types of railcars or aircraft. Another is when the user wants the ability to change equipment if something better comes out. For this reason, users often lease computer equipment under operating leases because of constant technological improvements.

3. Leveraged Lease

In a leveraged lease, a bank or other lender loans a percentage of the funds to buy the equipment, usually 60% to 80%. Because the lessor has put up only a small percentage of the equipment's cost, its investment is said to be leveraged because its return is based on 100% of the cost. Leveraging generally enables a lessor to provide a lessee with relatively lower rents while at the same time maintaining its return. Frequently, net finance leases are structured as leveraged leases.

The debt used to leverage a lease transaction is usually nonrecourse debt. When debt is nonrecourse, the lender has no recourse against the lessor for nonpayment of the loan, but rather must look only to the rental stream, the lessee, and the value of the equipment for its repayment. In such an arrangement, the lessor must assign to the lender its rights under the lease, including the right to the rental payments.

➤ **Observation** Although a lessor has no repayment obligations to a nonrecourse lender if the lessee defaults, it does bear some risk, because its rights against the lessee and the equipment are subordinated to the lender's repayment rights.

4. Nonleveraged Lease

Also referred to as an unleveraged or a straight lease, a nonleveraged lease occurs when the lessor pays for the equipment from its own funds. Leasing companies often enter into nonleveraged leases.

A distinct advantage in using a nonleveraged lease structure is there are usually only two principals involved in the actual financing: the lessee and the lessor. Because of the limited number of parties, the mechanics of putting together a transaction are simpler, saving time and documentation costs such as legal fees. One disadvantage for a lessee, however, is that the rent is usually higher than it would be if the lease were leveraged.

5. Service Lease

Leases in which the lessor assumes equipment ownership responsibilities, such as maintenance, repair, insurance, record keeping, or payment of property taxes, in addition to providing the asset financing, are usually called service leases. Service leases generally have relatively short lease terms.

F. Pros and Cons of Leasing

Leasing is not always the best way for every user to acquire equipment. In some circumstances, it is advisable; in others, buying equipment is the right decision. Deciding whether to lease certain equipment is not always easy, and in each situation the user must weigh the advantages and disadvantages. This section will provide basic considerations that are essential to a comprehensive evaluation.

➤ **Observation** Putting together a lease financing can require less red tape and time than a loan transaction. As a result, in certain situations, the documentation time and expense saved can offset an equipment lease interest rate that is higher than a loan interest rate, particularly when the cost of the equipment involved is relatively low.

1. Advantages of Leasing

a. Minimizes Obsolescence Concerns

When a user is concerned that equipment may become obsolete before the end of its useful life and therefore have little or no resale value, leasing can reduce that concern if the lessor assumes an obsolescence risk by basing part of its investment return on a significant end-of-lease equipment sale or re-lease value. (The greater the residual value assumed by the lessor, the less rent a lessee pays over the lease term.) Typically, computer and other high-technology equipment users face the obsolescence issue, because new, more efficient models quickly outdate their predecessors.

As a practical matter, as long as the equipment does its job, does it really matter if better equipment is available? In some situations, yes. For example, a more efficient item of manufacturing equipment can lower production costs by a sufficient amount, so that the user would have to acquire a new model before the old model has been written off to ensure its price-competitive position in the market. If a user had bought rather than leased the equipment, then the overall cost of replacing it would be expensive; if the old equipment's market value was significantly less than its book value at the time of replacement, then the user could be confronted with a potentially undesirable book loss in addition to the replacement cash outlay.

➤ **Observation**   A lessor also runs the risk of financial loss through equipment obsolescence. Thus, to protect itself, it will undoubtedly build a premium into its rate to compensate for the risk. A prospective lessee may be willing to pay the premium as a form of insurance against a loss through obsolescence. If the equipment does not become obsolete, then the increased rental rate will have reduced the profits it could have made had it owned the equipment.

➤ **Recommendation**   Because it is impossible to determine absolutely if equipment will become obsolete, the obsolescence risk issue can cause a real dilemma. Evaluating the past history of the type of equipment under consideration can be helpful in predicting trends. The user also can estimate the impact on profits when using the older, technologically obsolete equipment.

b.   Is Ideal for Limited Use Needs

If equipment is needed only for a limited time, leasing can be an effective way of acquiring its use. It eliminates the remarketing risks an owner would have at the end of a short use period and it permits a more defined estimate of the effective cost of using the equipment. For example, a public utility that is building its own plant may acquire specialized construction equipment to do the job. Once the plant is finished, the equipment may be of no further use to the utility, but it may still have many years of useful life left. If the equipment cannot be sold for a reasonable price, then the overall cost of its use can be high. Leasing removes the resale risk and allows the utility to determine in advance the total effective usage cost.

c.   Preserves Capital

An advantage of leasing to some users is it helps preserve their existing funds or bank lines for other uses. The absence of a down payment—in effect, 100% financing—can assist high growth rate companies in maximizing their use of funds, particularly during periods when money is tight.

➤ **Observation**   When evaluating whether to lease or to buy equipment, a user must carefully consider the real cost of borrowed funds. For example, a high compensating balance requirement can easily increase the effective cost of a bank loan. As this type of collateral loan cost increases, the attractiveness of leasing usually increases.

d. Obtains Value-Added Technical or Administrative Services

Users lacking the staff or expertise to attend to specialized equipment needs can lease equipment as a way to acquire those necessary technical or administrative services. Through service leases, users can avoid tying up time and manpower in activities that are outside of their normal operations. Usually a charge is built into the rent for the nonfinancial services supplied. Typically, lessors of office equipment, trucks, automobiles, and railcars offer some form of nonfinancial services as a supplement to their financing; for example, railcar lessors frequently offer maintenance services.

e. Avoids Certain Borrowing Problems

Users with credit or borrowing problems may have an easier time getting leasing companies to fund their equipment needs, because these companies often impose less stringent financial requirements than traditional lenders. The reason is leasing companies are willing to take greater risks because they actually own the equipment and they can more readily handle used equipment than can traditional lenders, if they must take possession from a defaulting lessee.

Leasing companies, however, will not provide equipment financing to a user regardless of its financial condition. They still require a reasonable assurance that the user will be able to meet the lease payments.

f. A Way to Trade Tax Benefits for Lower Rent

It is common for a user to be in a situation in which it cannot use the tax benefits (currently depreciation deductions) that would result from equipment ownership. It may, for example, have an excess of accumulated tax benefits or insufficient earnings, either due to poor performance or to major acquisitions, that have used up its tax bill, or the user may be subject to the minimum tax and find the tax benefits deferred (explained in Chapter 6). Such a company can indirectly take advantage of most ownership tax benefits through leasing from a tax-sensitive lessor. Because such a lessor takes these tax benefits into account when calculating the transaction's economic return, in effect it passes these benefits through in the form of a relatively lower rent.

➤ **Observation** A lessor will not pass 100% of the equipment ownership tax benefits on to a lessee through a reduced rental charge. It will make a profit on those benefits by adjusting the rent to reflect only a partial recognition. The rent adjustments vary with each lessor and each situation.

g. Bypasses Capital Budget Restrictions

Decisions to lease equipment are sometimes made to avoid a user's internal capital budget restrictions. For capital equipment purchases above a certain amount, a manager may be required to obtain prior approval, which may be difficult or impossible. If the equipment is leased, management may be able to account for the rental payments as an operating expense, even though the lease represents a long-term financing similar to a capital expenditure, to avoid the approval problem. In this way, it may also be able to maximize its capital budget.

➤ **Observation** Top management personnel in an increasing number of companies have prescribed rules in this area to avoid budget end-running, particularly with finance leases. For example, because long-term equipment leases can have a significant negative future impact on a company's earnings, particularly when cutbacks are necessary, often these transactions require senior management or board of director approval.

h. Hedges Inflation

Leasing equipment can provide a hedge against inflation. An equipment lease, in effect, gives the equipment user the ability to acquire equipment it needs at today's prices, and then pay for it from tomorrow's earnings.

i. Provides Possible Increased Cash Flow

Leasing equipment may be more cost effective than purchasing it entirely with internal funds, or through the use of an equipment loan. Accordingly, the less the user has to pay to acquire necessary equipment, the more cash it has available; that is, its cash flow is increased.

j. Eliminates Off Balance Sheet Benefit

Although no longer a general leasing benefit, an old advantage is worth mentioning that may, to a limited extent, be available in some long-term lease situations. In the early days of leasing, many users leased equipment instead of taking out long-term loans to buy equipment, to avoid burdening their balance sheet with long-term debt liabilities. The lease, regardless of its duration, was basically treated in such a manner that its rent payments were deemed to be an operating expense. As a result, a company's profit to fixed asset ratios were improved that, in turn, generally permitted a greater bank borrowing capability. Today the circumstances have changed. Regardless if significant lease obligations are recorded on the balance sheet, many sophisticated lenders factor them into their evaluation of a company's financial condition. Most importantly, the accounting rules now effectively eliminate the traditional "off balance sheet" benefit. In some situations, however, it is still possible to structure a long-term lease so, for financial reporting purposes, the rent payments due will not be reported as a long-term liability, but rather as an operating expense.

k. Provides Flexible Financing

The ability to obtain flexible financing is an important reason why companies lease equipment. Prospective lessees have the ability to structure the terms and conditions of a lease arrangement to address their specific business needs. For example, lease arrangments can be structured with a variety of lessee options, such as fair market or fixed price equipment purchase options, fair market or fixed price lease term renewal options, early lease termination options, equipment upgrade options, and sublease options. Leases can be set up with varying rent payment structures, such as low/high or high/low rent payments and skipped rent payments during industry down cycles, as well as varying rent periodicity such as payments monthly, quarterly, semiannually or annually, in advance or arrears. Master lease arrangements are available, which permit equipment delivered at varying times in the future to be simply added to an existing lease contract. Leases can include equipment maintenance and repair.

2. *Disadvantages of Leasing*

a. Eliminates Residual Upside

When a user leases equipment, it typically forgoes the possibility of realizing a gain if the equipment appreciates in value during the lease term. Any such gain instead goes to the lessor. For example, through inflation or buyer demand, a ten-year-old river barge may be worth more than it originally cost.

Many leases give lessees the option to buy the leased equipment at the lease term's end for its fair market value at that time. If the fair market value turns out to be high, the purchase price, coupled with the rent paid, can result in an expensive transaction. In such a situation, the lessee would undoubtedly have been better off originally buying the equipment. The problem is that there is no way of predicting the future value.

A prospective lessee can limit its cost exposure, through a fixed-price purchase option, if it is likely it will want to buy the equipment at the end of the term. This also allows the lessee to share in any residual upside. Under this option, a lessee has the right to buy the equipment at the end of a lease at a fixed price, say 25% of original cost, as agreed on at the time the parties entered into the lease. If the equipment's market value at the lease term's end is high, say 75% of cost, the lessee has the option of taking advantage of the favorable market by buying it for 25% of cost and selling it for 75% of cost. There are, however, two problems with fixed-price purchase options: (1) Not all lessors are willing to grant them and give up their residual upside; and (2) fixed-price purchase options can jeopardize a lease's true lease status for tax purposes.

➤ **Recommendation**   If a prospective lessor is willing to grant a fixed-price purchase right at, say, 35% of cost, then the prospective lessee should request it be at 35% of cost or the equipment's fair market value, whichever is less. This way, if the equipment's market value at the time of the option's exercise is lower than the fixed price, the lessee will not have to pay more than the equipment is worth if a purchase is necessary.

Frequently, a prospective lessee's concern over the loss of residual value upside is more emotional than practical. The potential loss must always be kept in the proper economic perspective by attempting to put a realistic value on it, for example, by bringing in a qualified appraiser to give an opinion as to what the equipment is likely to be worth in the future and discounting the value to its present worth.

> **Illustrative Example**   *A Residual Perspective:* Company Able is considering whether to lease or buy a heavy-duty crane. Company Able's financial vice president recommends that it be leased; however, the operational vice president believes that it should be bought because of its favorable market value at the end of the period of use. The facts are as follows:
>
> | | |
> |---|---|
> | Crane cost | $3,000,000 |
> | Lease term | 20 years |
> | Depreciated book value at end of 20 years | $300,000 |
>
> If the market value of the crane is estimated to be $500,000 at the end of the lease term, Company Able would lose the chance at a $200,000 upside gain ($500,000 – $300,00) if it leased the equipment.

What if, the potential loss is considered in terms of current dollars? The present value of such a loss 20 years out, computed using an annual discount rate of 10%, is approximately $30,000. Compared with the original cost of $3,000,000 and considering the fact that the upside gain may not materialize, the residual concern may be overstated, particularly if any down payment that would have been required if purchased was put to productive use.

b. Limits Equipment Control

When a lease ends, so does a lessee's right to use the equipment. This can create problems for an equipment user if suitable replacement equipment is not readily available and the lessor refuses to re-lease or sell it to the lessee. Although purchase or renewal options theoretically eliminate this risk, from a practical standpoint, when a third party owns the equipment there is no guarantee it will abide by the terms of the options voluntarily. The possibility also exists, albeit remote, that a lessor will interfere with the lessee's right to use the equipment during the lease term, even though it may have no legal right to do so. Having the legal right of continued use may be of little consequence to a lessee when equipment essential to its continued operations becomes unavailable.

3. *Key Situations: When to Consider Leasing*

In summary, the following indicators suggest that an equipment user should seriously consider leasing.

- If an equipment user must pay high interest rates for money borrowed, then leasing can be an economically attractive equipment funding alternative. Users whose credit dictates high interest rates, however, may also dictate high leasing rates, because the lessor must offset the increased credit risks by increased returns. The cost of leasing, however, will probably not increase proportionately as high as the cost of borrowing.
- An equipment user who cannot use a significant part or all of the equipment ownership tax benefits may come out ahead by leasing, assuming the tax benefits can be used by the leasing company and the benefits are passed through in the form of a relatively lower rental rate.
- Leasing is desirable when the equipment involved has unusual service problems that cannot be handled by a company internally, for example, because of the technical nature of the equipment or the company's inadequate staffing.
- If implicit lease interest rates are about the same as debt interest rates and there are significant ancillary costs to borrowing, such as high compensating balances or commitment fees, then leasing should be considered.

G.   When-to-Lease Checklist

An equipment user should consider leasing when one or more of the following factors is present.

- There is a high risk that equipment will become obsolete before the end of its useful life.
- The equipment will be needed only for a short time.
- It is desirable to maximize available capital resources.

- Technical, administrative, or other nonfinancial equipment-related services that are not internally available can be easily secured from a leasing company.
- High interest rates must be paid for borrowed money.
- The tax benefits resulting from the equipment ownership cannot be used.
- The equipment will have a poor market value at the end of its term of use.

H. Checklist for Prospective Lessees Approaching Potential Lessors

As the preliminary step in considering a lease transaction, an equipment user should review the following:

What basic type of lease arrangement is to be considered?

- Nonleveraged finance lease (Note: If you want a long-term lease and you need it in a hurry, this may be the best choice.)
  - (1) Net lease (Note: If you do not need the lessor to provide any equipment services, such as maintenance, this is the lease of choice.)
- Leveraged finance lease (Note: This may provide the lowest long-term lease rate, but can take the longest to document because of third-party lender involvement.)
  - (1) Net lease (Note: See same category comment for nonleveraged lease.)
- Operating lease (Note: This is the lease to use when you want equipment for only a short time, or you want lessor-supplied services such as equipment repair.)
  - (1) Long term
  - (2) Short term
  - (3) Nonfinancial services required

What potential sources of lease financing will be invited to submit lease quotations?

- Individuals (Note: This is a good choice if you need an aggressive lessor.)
- Independent nonbank lease companies (Note: They should always be invited to bid, as they are often the most innovative.)
  - (1) Finance lessors
  - (2) Service lessors
- Banks or other financial institutions (Note: They typically offer fair lease documentation, but lease interest rates may vary depending on their internal needs.)
- Captive leasing companies (Note: If your equipment supplier has one, ask its captive lessor to bid on your lease transaction. Although they have the capability to offer the lowest lease rate, they rarely do, but it never hurts to ask.)
- Lease brokers (Note: The good ones can bring solid value-added benefits to your lease situation. Know your broker, because some lack a good sense of business ethics.)

If an individual is under consideration, ask the following:

- Has the individual been involved in lease transactions before?
- Does the individual have experienced lease advisors and management representatives to provide assistance if transaction issues arise in the future?

If an independent nonbank leasing company is under consideration, ask the following:

- Does it have a good reputation in the financial community?
- Have other existing lessees been contacted to determine their experiences with the company in question?
- Is the financial condition sufficient to ensure adequate and timely finding?
- Will the equipment be funded entirely from the lessor's own funds?
- If equipment-related nonfinancial services will be supplied, does it have an adequate staff and facilities to supply these services on a timely basis?
- How tough is the lessor's lease documentation? (A form of the lessor's lease should be reviewed.)

If the prospective lessee's regular bank will be involved, will the lease restrict its future loan availability?

If a lease broker is under consideration, ask the following:

- How many similar transactions has it completed in the last three years?
- What do other companies that have used its service say about its method of operation and its ability to follow through on a proposed transaction?
- Are there any banks or other prospective lessor-investors that should not be approached by the broker?

I. Summary

The concept of leasing equipment is simple: A lessor acquires an asset and leases it to the lessee for an agreed-upon time period. The economic and business decisions, however, on both the lessor's and the lessee's part, are not simple. Each involves many factors that must be understood and assessed before engaging in a lease transactions, including tax, accounting, financial, business, and legal considerations. Most important for the lessor is its creditworthiness assessment of a prospective lessee and how much money it can make by entering into a lease. For the prospective lessee, most important is determining if leasing, as opposed to buying, equipment is an economically attractive alternative, namely, assessing the pros and cons. For the prospective lessee, this cannot effectively be done without understanding the types of lease arrangements available and the best lessors for a given situation.

Chapter 2

The Proposal Stage—Where the Leasing Deal Is Made

A. Overview

Chapter 1 discusses a variety of lessor and lease alternatives open to a prospective lessee in considering a lease financing. All too often, prospective lessees approach these alternatives in an inefficient and disorganized manner. As a result, many pay too much money and miss out on certain benefits. Some prospective lessors, failing to consider the many financing approaches, loose lessee financing opportunities.

This chapter provides guidelines to prospective lessees and lessors on how to set up a lease financing in an efficient and organized manner. The objective for both parties, during what is referred to as the proposal stage, is to enter into a comprehensive outline of the leasing deal through the use of a lease proposal letter. By following the chapter guidelines, a prospective lessee and lessor can achieve maximum results.

B. Obtaining Bids—The Request-for-Bids Letter

Assume we have an equipment user considering the leasing of some equipment. How does this prospective lessee get the best lease deal? First, it must shop the lease market to determine what options are available. This step requires the prospective lessee to secure a meaningful number of specific proposals from potential lessors and lease underwriters. Although there are a number of ways to do this, a prospective lessee typically will get the best results by preparing and circulating a well-thought-out and comprehensive written request-for-bids letter, commonly referred to as a bid letter.

Preparing a bid letter may be time consuming, but it is a worthwhile investment. Such a letter will avoid time lost in handling telephone calls or other inquiries from lessors and underwriters asking for additional information or clarification of facts. A bid letter ensures that the responses will be on a uniform and thus comparable basis, making it easy to select the best offer. Nothing is more frustrating than receiving, say, five proposals, each with a different rental payment mode, such as quarterly, in advance; semiannually, in arrears; semiannually, in advance; monthly, in arrears; and monthly, in advance. Not only is valuable time lost in making comparisons, but even worse, there also is a risk that requotes will be necessary because it may be impossible to make valid comparisons.

Another advantage to using a bid letter is that it will cause everyone on the lessee's side to focus on what they need or would like to obtain from the leasing transaction. Generally if a prospective lessee does not request a particular benefit, it will not be offered.

1.   Key Elements of a Bid Letter

What issues should be covered in a comprehensive bid letter? Because the purpose of a bid letter is to yield proposals, it should address every subject necessary to make a comprehensive lease financing assessment. At bare minimum, a prospective lessee should consider the following issues in putting together a bid letter.

- Equipment type and manufacturer
- Number of equipment units that will be involved
- Equipment's aggregate and per unit cost
- When equipment delivery is anticipated
- Lease type desired (i.e., net financial lease or service lease)
- Lease term and any renewal periods desired
- Rental payment mode (e.g., monthly, quarterly, semiannually, or annually and in advance or in arrears)
- Extent of any acceptable tax indemnifications
- Whether the equipment will be self-insured
- Options that are required
- Request for appropriate casualty and termination values
- Responsible party for the transaction's fees and expenses
- Whether a tax ruling is necessary or desirable
- Whether it is acceptable for a favorable tax ruling to be a prerequisite to execute the lease documents
- Whether a favorable tax ruling should relieve any tax indemnification obligations assumed
- Deadline for submission of lease quotations
- When transaction will be awarded
- Whether underwriting bids are acceptable
- If underwriting proposals are permitted, whether bids may be on a "firm" or "best-efforts" basis
- Potential equity participants and lenders who may be unacceptable if the transaction is to be underwritten

These points will be explained in the text describing the proposal letter.

Additional Sources The following are included to assist the prospective lessee in drafting the bid letter.

- Section H of this chapter sets out a proposal stage checklist for the lessee.
- The forms section and accompanying CD include sample request-for-bids letters.

C.   What Is the Proposal Letter?

After receiving and reviewing the bid letter, interested prospective lessors or underwriters will make their proposals in response to the bid letter's terms. Their response should be written and is referred to as a proposal letter. The proposal letter is significant for several reasons. First, the letter will be the lessee's first opportunity to make preliminary selections from among the respondents to its bid letter. Second, after reviewing the proposal letters received, the lessee may request changes or additions, and the letter forms the focal point for those negotiations. Third, after successful negotiations, the lessee will accept one of the letter offers, and the letter will become the basis for the later deal documentation. It is important that the proposal letter cover all business and major legal points.

1. Proposal Letter's Legal Status

Before reviewing the substance of a typical proposal letter, it is important to understand legally what the proposal letter does and does not do. After the prospective lessee has signed the letter, do the parties have a contract? Yes and no. Although they have a contract—usually the offer, and sometimes the acceptance, are qualified—conditions are imposed that must be satisfied after all parties have signed the lease proposal. Typical examples include the following:

- Necessary governmental or regulatory approvals, licenses, or authorizations
- Favorable opinions of counsel
- Effective placement of the debt, in case of a leveraged lease
- Acceptable financial covenants, such as a minimum debt-to-equity ratio
- Satisfactory audited financial statements
- Mutually satisfactory documentation
- Formal transaction approvals by the prospective equity participants and lenders
- Minimum dollar participation of equity and debt participants
- Detailed equipment list
- Favorable equipment appraisals justifying the equipment residual value

The satisfactory documentation condition gives the transaction's participants the most latitude to find justification to back out if they so desire, because unless the parties can reach agreement on each term and condition contained in the lease documents, they are not obligated to go through with the transaction. This condition leaves room for wide-open discussions on issues not even anticipated in the proposal stage, such as if the lessee should pay for the equipment's return to any location designated by the lessor.

While the accepted proposal letter is usually not legally enforceable because of these conditions, it is important for several reasons that it be comprehensive, detailed, and in writing.

- Although perhaps not legally enforceable, the parties will almost always make significant efforts to complete the deal once the proposal letter has been accepted.
- The proposal letter serves as the guideline and reminder for the parties and their lawyers when they draft the documents.
- Although unlikely, it is possible that if a party unreasonably backs out of the deal after the proposal letter has been accepted, it might form the basis of a legal action, particularly if financial obligations have been incurred on the other side.

A comprehensive and formal proposal letter is beneficial to both parties, and should be used in every transaction.

2. Proposal Stage Negotiating Strategies

Because the major terms are decided and the lessor or underwriter is selected during the proposal stage, that stage is often determinative of the transaction. Besides focusing on specific terms and conditions, the prospective lessee should keep in mind that, during the bidding stage, it has a considerable amount of negotiating leverage, particularly if more than one bidder is involved. One bidder's loss will not jeopardize the transaction, as the bidders are aware. Thus, the lessee's time to press for the tough concessions is before awarding the transaction. Prospective lessors are sometimes willing to concede points just to win the deal. Once the transaction has been awarded, the winning bidder is in a stronger negotiating position merely because the other bidders are no longer involved.

A prospective lessee's negotiating position will also be improved if it plans adequate lead time between a lease award and the equipment delivery. In this way, if problems develop after the award, there may still be time to go elsewhere for the financing. If this is not possible, and the prospective lessor starts to get tough, some balance can be put back into the negotiations by letting it be known that because of the problems, the lessee is considering buying rather than leasing.

From the potential lessor's perspective, the negotiating strategy in the bidding stage is the reverse—the faster it can get a prospective lessee to sign off on a proposal letter, the less likely that the lessee will make a problem request. Once the lease documentation has begun, particularly if there are near-term equipment deliveries, a prospective lessor's negotiating position is improved. Psychologically, a prospective lessee is more reluctant to start over with new people once the document negotiations have started.

D.   What Issues Should the Proposal Letter Address?

Stated simply, the proposal letter should outline the lease "deal." The letter does not have to cover every detail, but it should set the framework for the overall lease arrangement. To do this, however, the parties must know what points should be covered.

➤ **Recommendation**   If an important point comes up after a proposal letter has been accepted by a prospective lessee, but before the lease documentation has begun, the parties should consider amending the letter to include the point and thus help eliminate misunderstandings from arising during documentation.

Typically, although an underwritten leveraged lease situation will be more complex than nonunderwritten transactions, they usually contain similar elements. By understanding the more complex transaction format, then, the others will fall into place. Thus, the following explanation will center on issues that should be addressed in an underwritten leveraged lease proposal.

The forms section includes several proposal letters. You will find one typical of that used by a leasing company acting on its own behalf, a nonunderwritten transaction, and another typical of that used by an underwriter acting on behalf of prospective third-party lessors. Both cover the major topics that should be identified and can be used as guidelines when drafting or reviewing a lease proposal. Because there can be many variables in a particular transaction, however, they should be used only for reference purposes. It may be helpful to review them before reading further, to put the following explanation into an overall perspective.

1.   What Is the Offer?

All proposals will offer to provide equipment financing, but proposals from different types of bidders have different consequences to the lessee. One type of proposal is a direct offer by a prospective lessor to lease the equipment to the prospective lessee; another is an offer by an underwriter to arrange the lease financing of the equipment for the prospective lessee. In the latter case, the underwriter may not have a specific third-party lessor in mind. Even so, the name usually will not be disclosed in the proposal to protect its position as a broker.

> **Illustrative Language** *Lessor Designation:* An unknown or undisclosed lessor may be described by an underwriter in the following manner: The lessor will be a trustee acting as owner trustee pursuant to an owner's trust for the benefit of one or more corporate investors.
>
> In a nonunderwritten transaction, the prospective lessor will make an offer directly as principal to lease the equipment to the prospective lessee. For example, ABC Leasing Company will purchase and lease to XYZ Company the equipment designated in this proposal under the terms and conditions specified herein.

➤ **Recommendations** In an underwriting situation, a prospective lessee is in a better position if it does not make an award to a particular underwriter until the underwriter has disclosed the prospective lessor, and someone with authority to represent the lessor has been contacted by the prospective lessee to confirm its interest. If there is going to be a problem, the time to find out is when the remaining bidders are still available.

An underwriter should make sure its proposal is only an offer to arrange the proposed financing, unless it is fully prepared to step in as lessor in the event a third-party investor cannot be found.

There are many types of offer combinations. A direct lessor could offer to purchase and lease equipment using in part its own funds and in part funds from a nonrecourse loan, a simple form of leveraged lease. An underwriter may offer to develop a leveraged lease using one or more lessor-investors and one or more third-party lenders. Another alternative is that the underwriter may propose to bring in a single source investor to act as lessor, such as a regional bank, which would pay for the equipment entirely from its own funds.

To the prospective lessee, the choice among the different variations represents a trade-off between delivery and price. A prospective lessee seeking a near-term equipment delivery situation may be well advised to limit its consideration to a direct lessor transaction, because dealing with one party directly will lessen the risk that the financing cannot be done within the short time frame. If there is plenty of time, the best approach may be to pursue a syndicated leveraged lease transaction. This type of transaction will certainly be more involved, but it can provide the best rental rate for a prospective lessee.

All parties must keep in mind that the amount of lead time available before the equipment will be delivered may dictate the type of transaction used. Table 2.1 is a general guide for planning the timing of a proposed lease financing.

2. Best Efforts or Firm Offer

Typically, in its proposal, a lease underwriter will state if the offer is made on a best efforts or firm basis. A best efforts proposal is nothing more than an offer to try to arrange the lease financing on the stated terms and conditions. There are no performance guarantees, and the underwriter is generally not liable to the prospective lessee if it cannot perform.

Table 2.1 Recommended transaction lead time.

Type of Transaction	Anticipated Number of Lessor-Investors	Anticipated Number of Lenders	Recommended Lead Time[1](Months)
Underwritten leveraged lease	2+	2+	6
Underwritten leveraged lease	2+	1	6
Underwritten leveraged lease	1	2+	5
Underwritten leveraged lease	1	1	4
Underwritten single investor[2]	1	0	3
Direct lease[3]	1	1+	3
Direct lease	1	0	2

[1]*Lead time* is defined as the time between the proposal's due date and the first equipment delivery. The estimates assume an allowable proposal analysis time of one month.
[2]An underwritten single investor transaction is defined as one in which the underwriter brings in only one lessor-investor who puts up 100% of the funds required.
[3]A direct lease transaction is defined as one in which the prospective lessee will deal directly with the prospective lessor.

Illustrative Language *Best Efforts Commitment:* ABC Leasing Company proposes to use its best efforts to arrange an equipment lease according to the terms and conditions set forth in this proposal.

A firm underwriting bid is simply one in which the underwriter states that it can deliver the financing under the proposed terms and conditions.

Illustrative Language *Firm Commitment:* ABC Leasing Company proposes to arrange on a firm commitment basis an equipment lease for XYZ Inc., according to the terms and conditions set forth in this proposal.

From the prospective lessee's viewpoint, whether to go with a best efforts or firm offer is like the choice among bidders—a trade-off between delivery time and price. Underwriters usually offer a better price on a best efforts bid because that way they do not have to market the transaction to potential lessors until it has been awarded to them. Marketing an awarded deal saves the underwriter time, and also may make the potential lessors more willing to offer a better price. They will know the transaction is theirs if they accept the underwriter's bid, and so are more willing to invest time evaluating the transaction than if the transaction has not been awarded.

The best efforts offer, however, has a downside to the lessee, that of time. If the underwriter cannot, after having been awarded the deal, rapidly find a lessor, it loses valuable documentation time. In fact, if the underwriter takes an extended period to market the deal, the possibility becomes greater that no lessor will accept the deal, because prospective lessor-investors become suspicious when a transaction has been around the marketplace for a while and may refuse to consider it for that reason alone.

▶ **Recommendation** If a prospective lessee has adequate lead time, a best efforts underwriting should be permitted. If the winning underwriter cannot perform quickly, the prospective lessee can move on to the second choice underwriter without creating a timing problem.

As described previously, even an accepted firm offer will not usually be a binding agreement because of the various conditions such as satisfactory documentation of the proposal letter terms. As a practical matter, however, some firm offers may be more likely to go ahead to a completed transaction than others. For example, in certain situations an underwriter will firmly commit to do the transaction, even though it does not have a commitment from any lessor prospects, and is agreeing to buy and lease the equipment itself if it cannot broker it. This type of arrangement can be risky for a prospective lessee, because if the underwriter cannot sell the deal, it may not want to go ahead itself, and may seek an excuse to justify a way out. For example, offers conditioned on mutually satisfactory lease documentation can provide an underwriter with an opportunity to create a document disagreement and, thus, a basis to refuse to go forward.

➤ **Recommendation**   A prospective lessee should carefully investigate the financial situation of a lease underwriter offering a firm underwriting bid. If the underwriter does not have the financial resources to stand behind the transaction in the event it cannot deliver a lessor-investor, the fact that the offer is firm may be worth nothing.

If the offer is made directly by a prospective lessor instead of an underwriter, the situation will be different. Because the prospective lessor will use its own money to fund the transaction, the chances of the lessor looking for an excuse to back out are greatly reduced.

> **Illustrative Language**   *Direct Commitment: ABC* Leasing Company, as lessor, offers to purchase and lease to XYZ Inc. the equipment described below under the stated terms and conditions.

3.   *Specifying the Exact Cost*

The proposal letter should identify total equipment cost. Frequently, a prospective lessor will put a limit on, or cap, the amount of money it is willing to commit to a transaction. For example, it may agree to buy and lease an oil tanker at a cost not to exceed $40 million. Without a cap, it runs the risk that unexpected cost escalations will cause it to invest outside of its comfort zone. An unanticipated cost increase thus may give a prospective lessor who no longer finds the transaction desirable an excuse to back out.

➤ **Recommendation**   A prospective lessee entering into a lease agreement covering equipment to be delivered in the future must make sure the lessor's cost commitment is adequate. For example, will it cover any allowable manufacturer price escalations? If there is a problem with determining an exact price, a dollar cushion can be built into the estimate.

➤ **A Word of Caution**   If a fee has been imposed by the prospective lessor for the failure to use all the committed funds (commonly referred to as a nonutilization fee), a prospective lessee should be careful not to build in an excessive cushion, because any fee paid on the excess over the amount used will increase the effective cost of the financing.

4.   *Identify the Real Lessee*

The proposal letter will identify the lessee responsible for the rent, but sometimes the *real* lessee is not identified. For example, the proposal letter may name XYZ Inc. as lessee, but XYZ Inc. plans to have a subsidiary lessee. The lessor will do a credit review and approval based on XYZ Inc.'s statements. If the subsidiary is the lessee, the check on the parent will not be sufficient, and there may not be enough time to make any necessary adjustments. Getting the parent company's guarantee may be enough, but it may be difficult to obtain at the last minute.

5.   *Rent Payments and Rental Adjustment Clauses*

The proposal should specify how often, how much, and for how long rent will be paid. For example, a five-year lease may provide for 20 consecutive level quarterly payments, in arrears, each payment to equal 3% of the equipment cost, beginning at the start of the primary term.

When a leveraged lease is involved, the rent calculation becomes more complicated. The amount of rent a lessor charges is in part determined by the debt interest rate. The lessor generally will not secure the debt until after the award, however, because it would not be practical to spend the time and money necessary until there is a deal. Thus, to calculate the rent, the lessor will use an assumed debt interest rate and calculate the rent accordingly. Then, to protect its return in case the actual interest rate varies from the assumed rate, the lessor will often want a rental adjustment clause.

> **Illustrative Example**   *The Need for a Rent Adjustment Clause:* Company B proposes to lease to Company A a $10,000 item of mining equipment. The transaction will be leveraged with 80% debt at an assumed interest rate of 6% per annum. The terms are as follows:
>
> | | |
> |---|---|
> | Lease term | 10 years |
> | Loan term | 10 years |
> | Annual rent | $1,200 |
> | Annual debt service (level, in arrears) ($8,000 @ 6%) | $1,087 |

The annual rent will cover the annual debt service by $113 ($1,200 − $1,087). Assume that when Company B goes into the debt market the best available annual interest rate is 10%. The annual debt service, assuming level payments, will be approximately $1,302. In this case not only will the increased debt service expense erode the lessor's return, but the lessor also will have to invest an additional $102 a year ($1,302 − $1,200) to make up for the shortfall.

The rental adjustment clause enables the lessor to be protected against an increased interest rate, and this provision should be stated in the proposal letter.

> **Illustrative Language**   *Proposal Rent Adjustment:* Lessee shall make 20 consecutive level quarterly payments, in arrears, each equal to 3.0% of equipment cost, commencing on January 1, 20-. The rental percentage factor is based on the assumption that the interest rate on the leveraged debt will be 9.5% per annum. If the interest rate is other than 9.5%, the rental factor will be adjusted, upward or downward, accordingly so that the Lessor's economic return shall be maintained.

➤ Recommendations

- If a prospective lessor has the right to protect its return by adjustments upward if the actual debt interest rate is higher than assumed, then a prospective lessee should require a downward rent adjustment if the debt comes in lower than assumed.

- A prospective lessee should determine what criteria the prospective lessor will use to make any rent adjustment so the accuracy of the calculation can be independently confirmed.
- Any time a rental adjustment is permitted, the parties should also provide for appropriate adjustments in values that relate to the rent, such as casualty and termination values.

6. Primary and Interim Lease Terms

The proposal letter must specify the equipment's lease term and, if more than one item of equipment is to be leased, identify each item's lease period. When numerous items of equipment are involved, using an interim term in addition to the main or primary lease will simplify rental payment mechanics. The interim term covers the period from the time the equipment is accepted for lease to the start of the primary term. The interim term concept is commonly used when many items of equipment are involved and deliveries are scattered over many months. By consolidating the start of the primary lease terms to, for example, calendar quarters, the rent payment and processing mechanics are simplified.

> **Illustrative Example**   *The Interim Technique for Rent Consolidation:* Company B wants to lease 120 trucks from Company A. The trucks will be delivered over a 12-month period at a rate of 10 trucks a month. Company B wants to pay the lease rent in quarterly, in arrears, payments. Company A proposes the following solution.
>
> 1. There shall be four primary lease terms starting as follows:
>   a. First primary term—April 1, 20-
>   b. Second primary term—July 1, 20-
>   c. Third primary term—October 1, 20-
>   d. Fourth primary term—January 1, 20-
> 2. All trucks delivered and accepted for lease in the calendar quarter preceding the nearest primary term start date shall be on interim lease until the start date, at which time the primary term shall begin for such trucks.
>   Without the interim arrangement, Company A could end up with as many as 120 different primary lease term start dates and, thus, 120 different rental payment dates.

7. Credit Support for Lease Obligations

The prospective lessor should evaluate the prospective lessee's financial strength, and if the prospective lessee is not financially strong enough to support a particular leasing financing, then the prospective lessor should require, in the proposal letter, some form of credit support. In that event, prospective lessors prefer to get a full and unconditional guarantee of all the lease obligations from a creditworthy entity, such as a parent company, a bank, or possibly an underwriter. Other acceptable forms of credit support include a manufacturer's deficiency guarantee or a "take or pay" contract assignment. Different forms may be acceptable in different situations. An experienced leasing company or underwriter should be able to offer some viable alternatives to meet the needs of a particular transaction.

▶ **Recommendation** If the proposed lessee is a corporate subsidiary and credit support is required, the parent company should pursue a structure that will have the least impact on its future borrowing capabilities. For example, an assignment of a take or pay contract between the subsidiary and an outside entity may have little impact on the parent company, but, a full, unconditional guarantee could have a substantial impact.

8. *Structure of Owning Entity*

In structuring a typical underwritten leveraged lease transaction, an underwriter may propose one of several alternative entities to own the equipment, for example, a trust, partnership, or corporation. The underwriter's choice of entity should be decided in the proposal stage.

Concern for tax issues and limited liability issues will be of greatest concern to a prospective lessor, particularly when two or more are brought together to act as the lessor. On the tax side, the chosen structure should permit a direct flow-through of all the available tax benefits. As to limited liability, the lessors may want protection against direct liability on a specific transaction in the event of a lawsuit.

▶ **Recommendation** Trust arrangements can be a useful equipment ownership structure for prospective lessor-investors. If set up properly, it is generally agreed that they will be treated, for tax purposes, as a partnership and, for liability purposes, as a corporation.

The ownership vehicle form can also be important to a prospective lessee. For example, if the equipment ownership is not centralized in a multiple lessor-investor situation, then the lessee may have to deal individually with each investor throughout the lease. The lessee may then have to issue separate prorated rent checks and, if a lease variance is necessary, obtain separate consents. This entire process would be a substantial inconvenience.

▶ **Recommendation** In a multiple lessor-investor situation, a prospective lessee should insist on a single representative with the authority to handle the day-to-day issues.

9. *Debt Arrangement*

If the lessor proposes a leveraged lease, the debt arrangement mechanics and terms should be outlined in the proposal letter. Consider the following points regarding debt.

- Who will find the debt?
- What is the debt repayment schedule?
- What is the anticipated per annum interest charge?
- What is the anticipated principal amount as a percentage of equipment cost?
- What is the form of lender representative?
- Will the debt be recourse or nonrecourse to the lessor?

The lessor may need the ability to make changes in the proposal if the debt structure eventually obtained varies from that stated therein.

Illustrative Language   *Debt Structure: ABC* Leasing Company (ABC), or an investment banker acceptable to the lessee and to ABC, shall arrange for the private placement of a note (Indebtedness) to be issued by the lessor for a principal amount of approximately 80% of the total cost of the equipment to certain institutional investors (Lenders). The Lenders may be represented by an indenture trustee or agent bank.

This proposal assumes that the Indebtedness shall be amortized in 20 payments of principal and interest at 9.5% per annum, payable quarterly, in arrears, over five years. The Indebtedness shall be secured by a lease assignment and a security interest in the equipment, but otherwise shall be without recourse to the lessor. Any variance from the debt assumptions, other than interest rate which is provided for in the rent adjustment clause, will relieve the offeror from its commitment thereunder, if so elected.

The proposal letter should address which party will handle the debt placement and pay the placement fees. Typically, the underwriter or lessor will pay those costs. If the lessor or underwriter places the debt itself, it will save the debt placement fee and thereby increase its profit. Keep in mind that when the underwriter or lessor handles the debt placement, and there is a rent adjustment provision, it may have little incentive to obtain the rock-bottom rate.

➤ **Recommendations**

- When the prospective underwriter or lessor is arranging the debt, the lessee should require the right to exclude any potential lender for the following reasons. First, it should be able to protect itself against a lessor obtaining an unreasonably high interest rate and passing it along through the rental adjustment clause. Second, a lessee may not want any of its line banks to become involved because of potential future borrowing restrictions. Third, some lenders are difficult to deal with and so should be brought in only as a last resort.
- If a prospective lessor or underwriter must pay the debt placement fee, it should have an equal say in the selection of the party that will place the debt. This will prevent it from being stuck with an inappropriately high placement fee.

➤ **Documentation Suggestion**   Many documents used in a leveraged transaction will be subject to lender approval. Some lenders can be difficult to negotiate with and slow responders. To avoid last-minute problems, the relevant papers should be sent to them as soon as possible and monitored carefully as to their review progress.

10. Tax or Business Reasons May Require a Narrow Equipment Delivery Time Frame

In some instances, the equipment's delivery date may significantly affect the economic benefits to the lessor. Most lessors will be taking depreciation deductions on the equipment, and *when* the equipment is placed in service determines the first-year deduction. Different dates can substantially affect the lessor's deduction. For example, a lessor may want the deduction in a current year because it has substantial income to offset; it may want it in its next tax year because it cannot use the benefits in the current year; or it may want it before or after its last quarter to avoid the midquarter depreciation convention treatment (see Chapter 5).

Business concerns can similarly dictate a narrow delivery time. For example, the lessor may not want to be obligated to provide lease financing at a particular fixed economic return beyond a certain date. The prospective lessor also may need to anticipate its cash needs for funding equipment purchases. Late deliveries can particularly be a problem when a long-term lease commitment involves many equipment items and the likelihood of delays is increased.

A solution to that problem is to use a commitment period, which limits the lessor's obligation to fund to a designated period, for example, six months after the last expected delivery date. From a lessee's viewpoint, however, this may have a cost. The longer the commitment period, the more likely it is that a prospective lessor will impose a fee for holding the funds available. Such a fee, commonly referred to as a commitment fee, is usually based on a percentage of equipment cost; for example, a lessor may charge a fee equal to 0.5% of the total funds committed.

➤ **Observation**   Lessors are often willing to hold funds available for up to six months without charging a commitment fee.

➤ **Recommendation**   A commitment fee should be included in a prospective lessee's cost-to-lease computation. A transaction with a lower rent and a commitment fee may be less attractive than one with a higher rent and no fee. This is not, however, always the case, so, a prospective lessee should not automatically exclude a proposal just because it involves a commitment fee.

11. *Equipment Location*

The proposal letter should specify where the lessee intends to use the leased equipment. The lessor may want to make security interest filings to protect its ownership interest against a lessee's creditors. To do so, it must know the equipment's location. The lessor's potential tax benefits also may depend on the equipment's location; for example, if the equipment is used outside the United States, the lessor will generally have less attractive depreciation deductions.

Another consideration is the equipment's location may have psychological benefits that affect a lease underwriter's marketing effort. Certain lessor-investors or lenders may be more willing to participate in situations involving equipment used in the local area. For example, if the equipment is to be used in Maryland by a division of a California corporation, Maryland regional banks may be interested because of the possibility of doing future business with a company they normally may not be involved with.

12. *Purchase or Renewal Options*

To have the option to continue to use the equipment, a lessee may want the right to buy the equipment, or renew the lease, under certain conditions, at the primary lease term's end. To accomplish this, the lessee must have purchase or renewal options.

> **Illustrative Language**   *Purchase and Renewal Options: At* the end of the primary lease term, the lessee may (with 180 days written notice prior to the end of such term do one of the following):
>
> 1. Renew the lease with respect to the equipment for an amount equal to its then fair market rental value.
> 2. Purchase the equipment for a price equal to its then fair market value.

➤ **Recommendation** From a lessee's viewpoint a purchase option should be exercisable not only at the end of the main lease term, but also at the end of each renewal term. Renewal term rights also should adequately cover potential periods of extended use.

An alternative is a right of first refusal option. Basically, this option gives the lessee the right to buy or renew the equipment under the same terms as offered to the lessor by an unrelated third party.

> **Illustrative Language** *Right of First Refusal: At* the end of the primary lease term, the lessee will have a right of first refusal as to any sale or re-lease of the equipment.

➤ **Observation** A right of first refusal can create a potential problem for a lessee. It is conceivable that a competitor would bid for equipment essential to a lessee's operations merely to attempt to interfere with its business.

In some situations prospective lessors want the right to require a lessee to buy the equipment at the lease's end. This type of right is commonly referred to as a "put" and should, as with the other options, be identified in the proposal. However, because of potential tax problems, puts are not generally used.

In recent years, a new purchase option has surfaced, called an early buyout option. There are certain tax risks in incorporating such an option into a lease arrangement, but, carefully structured, some lessors are willing to grant them. Typically, the lessor requires the lessee to pay a premium at the time the purchase option is exercised.

➤ **Recommendation** Lessors and lessees should seek the advice of experienced tax counsel before incorporating an early buyout option in a lease agreement. The wrong structure can result in adverse tax consequences for both the lessor and the lessee.

13. Early Termination Right

A prospective lessee may want an early termination option, which is the right to end the lease prematurely as to any equipment that becomes obsolete or surplus to its needs. Some lessors do not like to grant termination options because they cut off future earnings. Thus, when granted, the lessee usually must pay a substantial premium to exercise the option, a premium referred to as a termination value payment.

> **Illustrative Language** *Termination Right:* At the expiration of each year during the primary lease term, the lessee shall have the right, as its option, to terminate the lease. The lessee will be required to give the lessor 90 days prior written notice of its intention to terminate and, during the period from giving notice until the termination date, the lessee shall use its best efforts to obtain bids from unaffiliated third parties for the equipment's purchase. On the termination date, the lessor shall sell the equipment for cash for the highest bid received. The total proceeds of such sale shall be retained by the lessor, and the lessee will pay to the lessor the difference, if any, by which the sale proceeds are less than the appropriate termination value indicated on the attached schedule.

➤ **Recommendation** If a prospective lessor is willing to grant a termination right, then the prospective lessee should ensure that the termination values and the right are incorporated into the lease proposal. These values are not standard and can vary significantly depending on the competition and the lessors. Too many times, the values are not seen until after the award, and sometimes they are seen only a few days before the anticipated lease document closing. If they turn out to be excessive, it may be too late to go elsewhere for the financing.

14. Upgrade Financing Right

In some situations a prospective lessee will want the ability to have a lessor finance additions or changes, commonly referred to as upgrades, to equipment on lease with a lessor during the lease term. If the upgrade has no stand-alone value or utility, such as an internal modification to an existing computer system to enhance its performance, there would be only one lessor to which the lessee can turn for the financing—the incumbent lessor. If it is not willing to provide the financing, a lessee would have two alternatives, either to pay for the upgrade itself, a cost which it typically cannot recover when it returns the leased equipment, or to forgo the upgrade. To avoid this problem, some prospective lessees negotiate an upgrade financing right, which is the right to require an incumbent lessor to finance all equipment upgrades to its leased equipment during the lease term at a predetermined lease financing rate, or a rate to be determined by a set of guidelines fair to both parties.

➤ **Recommendation**   Prospective lessees contemplating equipment upgrades should always require an upgrade financing right; and the right should incorporate a formula for determining the upgrade financing interest rate, to avoid being forced into accepting an arbitrarily high rate offer from the incumbent lessor.

15. Equipment Damage or Loss

The proposal letter should identify the lessee's basic financial responsibilities in the event of a casualty loss. Typically, to protect its equipment investment, the lessor requires the lessee to pay a defined casualty value. How the casualty value amount will be determined should be set out in the proposal letter.

➤ **Recommendation**   Lessees required to insure equipment against casualty losses for the lessor's benefit should make sure any insurance proceeds received by the lessor will be credited against any casualty value due.

16. Tax Assumptions and Indemnification

A prospective lessor generally anticipates receiving certain tax benefits, such as depreciation, as a result of owning the leased equipment, and incorporates the assumed tax benefits into the rental computation. Those benefits thus become critical to the lessor's transaction economic return. When that is the case, the prospective lessor's lease proposal should spell out exactly what tax benefits are expected, as well as any responsibility a prospective lessee may have if benefits are lost.

Because of the adverse impact the loss of anticipated tax benefits can have for tax-oriented lessors, prospective lessees are frequently asked to provide indemnifications against any loss of expected tax benefits. Lessees, for their part, will usually agree to some indemnification, but will want to limit the circumstances triggering the indemnity as much as possible. Whereas the precise terms of the indemnification will be negotiated during the documentation, the basic terms should be determined at the proposal stage.

17. Tax Law Changes

When a lessor is anticipating tax benefits, a change in tax laws can affect the lessor's economic return. For example, changes in the tax laws affecting the equipment's depreciation life, the equipment depreciation method, or the federal tax rate on corporate income can have a substantial positive or negative impact.

➤ **Observation** Because of the intense ongoing governmental focus on the federal tax laws in the equipment and the corporate tax rate area, lessors and lessees should pay particular attention to the implications of anticipated changes.

One way to handle this risk is to quote the rent subject to an appropriate adjustment to reflect any tax law change affecting the lessor's expected economic return. The parties may agree, for example, that the rent will be adjusted to maintain the lessor's net return.

➤ **Recommendation** The particular parameter that will serve as a guide for any rent adjustment should be defined precisely to prevent a calculation disagreement. Net return, for example, can mean different things to different people. If a lessee does not know how to check a tax law change adjustment, it may pay more than necessary if the lessor tries to squeeze a little higher return. By the same token, a lessee may incorrectly object to a legitimate adjustment.

18. Tax Rulings

In response to a taxpayer's request, the IRS will rule on a transaction's tax consequences by delivering a tax letter ruling. Provided the taxpayer's request is complete and accurate, the IRS letter (called a private letter ruling) will be dispositive of the tax consequences (see Chapter 7). When a leasing transaction is particularly complex, or involves uncertain tax law issues, a lessor may require a private letter ruling on a transaction's tax consequences before entering into it. Or, if the lease is signed before a ruling is made, a lessor may agree to release a lessee from required indemnifications on issues addressed favorably in a requested ruling. If such a ruling is considered necessary, the prospective lessor must make that a condition of its offer.

> **Illustrative Language** *The Use of a Private Letter Ruling:* The lessor plans to obtain a private IRS ruling with respect to the assumptions stated in this proposal letter. The lessee shall agree to indemnify the lessor for the tax assumptions that are the subject of the ruling request. Such indemnity shall remain in effect until a favorable ruling has been obtained on each of these points.

19. Transaction Expenses

The proposal letter should address who will pay what transaction expenses, particularly in deals involving an underwritten leveraged lease. When the lease is not an underwritten leveraged lease, the primary expense is legal fees, and the party incurring the expense usually pays for it. The matter is more complex in underwritten transactions. These types of transactions can involve many parties—equity participants, lenders, trustees, and an underwriter—and possibly a variety of substantial expenses. For example:

- Fees and disbursements of special counsel for the lenders and their representative
- Acceptance and annual fees of the lenders' representative, usually found in a trust arrangement

- Special counsel fees and disbursements for the equity participants and their representative
- Acceptance and annual fees of the equity participants' representative, usually found in a trust arrangement
- Fees and disbursements related to the filing for a private letter ruling
- Documentation expenses such as reproduction and printing expenses
- Fees related to the placement of the debt

In practice, the expense allocation is not as great a problem as it may appear, because often the underwriter agrees to pay substantially all the expenses. An underwriter can, however, cap these expenses by agreeing to pay only up to a specified percentage, usually 0.75% to 1.25% of the equipment cost, and the lessee must then pay the excess. Because an underwriter makes its money by charging the lessor-investors a set fee for bringing them the transaction, the more it can limit its expense responsibility, the less it has to worry about fees and expenses eroding its profit. In a competitive market, however, many underwriters are willing, particularly if pushed a little, to assume the entire expense responsibility.

Illustrative Example   *The Underwriter Expense Problem:* Company A, an underwriter, arranged for Company C and Company D to participate as the equity investors in the leveraged lease financing of one oceangoing tugboat to be leased to Company B. Companies C and D agreed to pay Company A a brokerage fee equal to 2% of the equipment's cost for bringing in the transaction. As a condition of the transaction award, Company A had to commit to Company B that Company B would not have to pay any expenses, except its own counsel fees. At the closing, the following costs were incurred.

```
Tugboat cost  . . . . . . . . . . . . . . . . . . . . . . . . . . . . . . . . . . . . . . $6,000,000
Fees for the lender's counsel  . . . . . . . . . . . . . . . . . . . . . . . . . . . 20,000
Counsel fees for Companies C and D . . . . . . . . . . . . . . . . . . . . . . 50,000
Counsel fees for Company A  . . . . . . . . . . . . . . . . . . . . . . . . . . . . 2,000
Counsel fees for Company B  . . . . . . . . . . . . . . . . . . . . . . . . . . . . 35,000
Printing expenses . . . . . . . . . . . . . . . . . . . . . . . . . . . . . . . . . . . . 21,000
```

What does Company A's profit picture look like? Company A's gross fee from the transaction is $120,000 (2% × $6,000,000). All fees and expenses, excluding Company B's counsel fees, total $93,000 ($20,000 + $50,000 + $2,000 + $21,000). Therefore, Company A nets $27,000 ($120,000 – $93,000). If Company A had a 1% cap, its expense responsibility would have been limited to $60,000 (1% × $6,000,000) and it would have made $60,000 ($120,000 – $60,000) instead of $27,000.

a. What If the Deal Collapses?

The difficult expense question is, who must pay what expenses if a proposed underwritten transaction collapses? The lenders and the prospective lessor-investors will refuse to be responsible if the transaction does not go through, which leaves the underwriter and the prospective lessee as responsible parties. Some underwriters attempt to put the responsibility for all expenses incurred in such a situation on the prospective lessee by inserting an appropriate clause in the proposal letter. Typically, the clause provides that the prospective lessee must pay all expenses if the transaction is not consummated for any reason. This position can be dangerous for a prospective lessee, particularly when the underwriter's poor performance may be the reason why the transaction failed.

➤ **Recommendation**   In a major underwritten lease financing, the expenses can be substantial. For example, it is not unheard of for the legal fees and other expenses in a complicated $10,000,000 leveraged lease financing to run anywhere from $200,000 to $400,000. Thus, underwriters and prospective lessees should each carefully evaluate their potential expense exposure and clearly define the responsibilities in all events.

20. Lease Type

Of the variety of different lease types described in Chapter 1, each imposes different responsibilities for the lessor and lessee. Care must be taken to ensure that the cost responsibilities are fully defined and understood. A typical net finance lease requires the lessee to pay all fixed expenses relating to the equipment during the lease term, such as maintenance, insurance, and certain taxes. Without, for example, a lessee understanding what the equipment-related expense obligations will be, the overall costs cannot be properly assessed. And it can be an expensive surprise for a lessee to discover after the equipment is on lease that a substantial sales tax is owed.

E.   Agreement to the Proposal Letter

Following any proposal letter negotiations, a prospective lessee accepts the proposal offer by acknowledging its willingness to proceed on the basis of the terms presented. If the proposal is written it can be accepted by an appropriate officer, either by signing the acceptance directly on the letter or in a separate writing by properly referencing the proposal letter. Any acceptance condition should be clearly a part of the acceptance and identified as such. For example, if the acceptance is made by signing in a designated space on a proposal letter, the condition should precede the signature.

➤ **Recommendation**   If a proposal letter is used, a prospective lessee should accept directly on the proposal letter, not in a separate writing, particularly if the acceptance is conditioned. Separate papers can easily be lost or misplaced.

F.   Prospective Lessee's Obligations after a Proposal Is Accepted

Because a proposal letter is generally not a contract, it may have no more than a psychological hold on the transaction because of various stated conditions, such as mutually satisfactory documentation, which are usually imposed. Thus, except for any obligation to pick up a collapsed transaction's expenses, the prospective lessee's obligations may be minimal or nonexistent at the time of the proposal acceptance. As a result, prospective lessors may be unable to require a prospective lessee to go through with a transaction or recover damages for its failure to proceed.

➤ **Recommendation**   Inasmuch as a prospective lessee's obligations to go forward may be nonexistent after the acceptance of the offer, prospective lessors and underwriters must make sure transactions are completed quickly and efficiently.

G. Prospective Lessor's Obligations after a Proposal Is Accepted

Because the lease proposal is conditioned, the offeror's obligations after the prospective lessee accepts the proposal will probably be limited. For example, if the offer is conditioned on acceptable documentation, a prospective lessor may have no trouble finding "unacceptable" points and walking away from the transaction. Of course, there may be an ethical obligation to go forward, but this will be of little value to a prospective lessee when left standing at the last minute without the essential financing.

➤ **Recommendation** If a proposal is conditioned on certain lessor committee approvals, a prospective lessee should request written verification once the approvals have been given. Psychologically, this step will bring the prospective lessor further into the transaction.

H. Proposal Stage Checklist for the Lessee

The following lists are issues that a prospective lessee must address during the proposal stage. The prospective lessee will want to review the lists in preparing its bid letter and again to ensure that issues are addressed in the proposal letter.

Equipment Description

- What type will be involved?
- Who is the manufacturer?
- What is the model?
- How many units will be involved?

Equipment Cost

- What is the total cost involved?
- What is the cost per item?
- Is the cost per item fixed? If not, what is the probable cost escalation?

Equipment Payment

- When must the equipment be paid for?
- Must the entire purchase price be paid at once?

Equipment Delivery

- What is the anticipated delivery date?
- How long should the lease commitment run past the last anticipated delivery date?

Equipment Location

- Where will the equipment be located?
  1. At the lease inception
  2. During the lease term

Equipment Lease

- What type of lease is desired?
  1. Net finance lease
  2. Service lease
  3. Other

Lease Period

- How long must the lease run?
- Will an interim lease period be acceptable? If so, what is the latest date on which the primary term can begin?
- How long a renewal period is desired?
- How will the renewal right be structured (e.g., five one-year periods, one five-year period)?

Rent Program

- When should the rent be payable?
  1. Annually
  2. Semiannually
  3. Quarterly
  4. Monthly
  5. Other
- Should the payments be in advance or in arrears?
- If there is an interim period, how should the interim rent be structured?
  1. Based on the primary rent (e.g., the daily equivalent of the primary rent)
  2. Based on the long-term debt interest rate
  3. Other
- If there will be a renewal period, how should the renewal rent be structured?
  1. Fixed
  2. Fair rental value

Options

- What type of options are desired?
  1. Fair market value purchase right
  2. Fixed price purchase right
  3. Fair market rental value renewal right
  4. Fixed price renewal right
  5. Right of first refusal
  6. Termination right
  7. Upgrade right
  8. Other
- Is a right of first refusal specifically unacceptable?

Casualty and Termination Values

- If a termination right is required, will the termination values be a primary factor in the lease decision?
- Must the termination and casualty values be submitted at the time of the proposal?

Maintenance and Repair

- Who will have the equipment maintenance and repair obligations?

Tax Indemnifications

- What tax indemnifications will be acceptable, if any?

Insurance

- Is the right of self-insurance desired?

Taxes

- What taxes will be assumed?
  1. Sales
  2. Rental
  3. Other

Transaction Expenses (usually only a concern in underwritten transactions)

- What expenses other than lessee's legal fees, if any, will be assumed if the transaction is completed?
  1. Counsel fees for any lenders and their representative
  2. Acceptance and annual fees of any lender's representative (trust arrangement)
  3. Counsel fees for the lessor-investors and any representative
  4. Acceptance and annual fees of any lessor-investor's representative (trust arrangement)
  5. IRS private ruling letter fees
  6. Documentation expenses
  7. Debt placement fee
  8. Other
- What expenses, if any, will be assumed if the transaction collapses?

Tax Ruling

- Is an IRS private letter ruling necessary or desirable?
- Can a favorable letter ruling be a prerequisite to any of the lessor's obligations?
- Should a private letter ruling relieve any tax indemnification obligations?

Submission Date

- What is the latest date on which the proposal can be submitted?

Award Date

- On what date will the transaction be awarded?

Type of Proposals

- Is an underwritten transaction acceptable? If so:
  1. Will best efforts or firm proposals be accepted?
  2. Is a leveraged or single source transaction preferred?
- If best efforts proposals are acceptable, how long after the award will the underwriter have to firm up the prospective lessor-investors and any lenders?

Prospective Lessors—Underwritten Transaction

- Are any prospective lessors-investors not to be approached?

I. Proposal Stage Checklist for the Lessor

The following checklist will serve as a guide to the prospective lessor in identifying issues and in preparing and negotiating a proposal letter.

Offer

- Will an underwritten or direct lessor proposal be involved?
- If an underwritten offer is involved,

    1. Will it be on a best efforts or firm basis?
    2. Must there be more than one equity participant?
    3. If it can be on a best efforts basis, is there a deadline when the equity participants must give their formal commitment?
    4. Will the transaction be leveraged with third-party debt?

Lessee

- Has the lessee been accurately identified?
- Has the lessee's financial condition been reviewed?

Credit Support

- Can the lessee's financial condition support the entire lease obligation?
- If the lessee's credit is not sufficient, what additional credit support alternatives are available?
    1. Parent company guarantee
    2. Affiliated company guarantee
    3. Unrelated third-party guarantee
    4. Deficiency guarantee
    5. Bank support
    6. Other
- If credit support is necessary, has the financial condition of the entity giving the support been reviewed?

Equipment Description

- What type will be involved?
- Who is the manufacturer?
- What is the model?
- How many units will be involved?

Equipment Cost

- What is the total cost involved?
- What is the cost per item?
- Is the cost per item fixed? If not, what is the probable cost escalation?

Equipment Delivery

- What is the anticipated delivery date?
- Must the lease commitment run past the anticipated delivery date? If so, for how long?
- Will a fee be charged for the commitment to lease future delivered equipment?

Equipment Location

- Where will the equipment be located?
  1. At the lease inception
  2. During the lease term

Rent Program

- What is the primary rent payment program structure?
  1. Will the rent be payable in advance or in arrears?
  2. Will the rent be payable annually, semiannually, quarterly, monthly, or other?
- Will interim rent be involved? If so:
  1. Will it be based on the primary rent, the long-term debt interest rate (if leveraged), or other?
  2. When will the payments be due?

Term of the Lease

- How long will the lease run?
  1. Primary lease term
  2. Renewal period
- Will an interim lease term be involved? If so:
  1. When will the interim lease term start?
  2. When will the primary lease term start?

Lessor

- How will the equipment be owned?
  1. Directly
  2. Indirectly through a partnership, trust, or corporation
- Will the ownership structure satisfy any tax and liability criteria?
  1. Flow-through of tax benefits
  2. Corporatelike liability protection
  3. Other

Debt If Transaction Is Leveraged

- What is the loan repayment program?
  1. In advance or in arrears
  2. Debt service to be payable annually, semiannually, quarterly, monthly, or other
- Who will be responsible for arranging for the placement of the debt?
- Will the rent be quoted on the basis of an assumed debt principal amount, per annum interest charge, etc.? If so, will the rent quoted be subject to adjustment if other than assumed?
- If the rent is subject to a debt assumption adjustment, what adjustment criteria will be used?
  1. After-tax yield
  2. Cash flow

      3. Net return
      4. Other
- Who will be responsible for fees related to the debt?
      1. Placement fee
      2. Lender's commitment fee
      3. Other

Options

- What special rights will the lessee have?
      1. Fixed price purchase right
      2. Fair market value purchase right
      3. Fixed price renewal right
      4. Fair market rental value renewal right
      5. Right of first refusal
      6. Termination right
      7. Upgrade right
      8. Other
- What special rights will the lessor have?
      1. Fixed price sale right
      2. Fixed price renewal right
      3. Termination right
      4. Other

Casualty Loss

- What financial responsibilities will the lessee have in the event of a casualty loss?

Casualty and Termination Values

- What amounts are to be used?

Tax Aspects

- What are the relevant tax assumptions?
- For what tax assumptions, if any, will the lessee have to indemnify the lessor in the event of loss or inability to claim?
- If there are lessee tax indemnifications, what events that result in tax benefit unavailability will trigger an indemnification payment?
      1. Any reason
      2. Acts or omissions of lessee
      3. Acts or omissions of lessor
      4. Change in law
      5. Other

Tax Ruling

- Will a tax ruling be involved?
- If so, will a *favorable* ruling:
      1. Relieve the lessee from any tax indemnifications?
      2. Be a prerequisite to the lessor's obligation to lease the equipment?

Transaction Expenses

- Who must pay for the expenses if:
  1. The transaction goes through without problems?
  2. The transaction collapses before the lease documents are executed?
  3. The transaction collapses after the lease documents are executed but before the equipment is delivered?

Type of Lease

- What type of lease will be involved?
  1. Net finance lease
  2. Service lease
  3. Other

Conditions

- What conditions must be satisfied before the lessor is committed?
  1. Governmental or regulatory approvals
  2. Licenses or authorizations
  3. Favorable opinions of counsel
  4. Maintenance or achievement of certain financial tests
  5. Satisfactory audited financial statements
  6. Acceptable documentation
  7. Approvals by prospective lessor or equity participants
  8. Minimum dollar participation by equity and debt participants
  9. Favorable equipment appraisals justifying equipment residual value
  10. Other

Form of Proposal

- Will a written proposal be used? If so, how should acceptance be acknowledged?

Submission and Award Dates

- When is the latest date on which the proposal can be submitted?
- What is the anticipated transaction award date? Is there adequate time to do the deal?

Offer Termination Date

- How long will the prospective lessee have to accept the offer?

J. Summary

Critical to getting the best possible lease arrangement for a lessee is understanding what to ask for and how to evaluate what a lessor is offering. This begins by the lessee putting together a clear and effective request for bids letter, one that gives the lessor enough information about a possible upcoming lease transaction, and then making a informed assessment of any offer it receives from a lessor. For a lessor, getting an attractive lease deal begins by accurately assessing the lessee's needs, and then setting out the deal aspects of its lease offer in a clear and comprehensive proposal letter. By doing so, not only will the lessor save time, but it also will avoid last-minute misunderstandings that can result in costly failed transactions.

Chapter 3
Negotiating the Lease Document

A. What Is the Lease's Central Purpose?

Although a lease agreement can involve many complex, highly technical, and sometimes overwhelming concepts, its central purpose is very simple: A lease agreement is a contract in which a property owner, the lessor, transfers the right to use the property to another, the lessee, for a period of time. The lessor retains title.

A lease differs from a conditional sale, an outright sale, or a mortgage type of transaction. Under a conditional sale, the property owner sells the property, not merely its use, to the buyer. At the time the agreement is reached, the seller transfers the property to the buyer, but retains title until the buyer performs certain conditions, usually the payment of the purchase price in installments. Following satisfaction of the conditions, the seller transfers title to the buyer.

In an outright sale, the property owner unconditionally transfers the property, including title, to the buyer and, at the same time, the buyer pays the seller the full purchase price. In a mortgage situation, a buyer of property borrows from a third-party lender some or all of the money necessary to buy the property. The lender, or mortgagee, as security for the repayment of its loan, requires the borrower, or mortgagor, to give it a security interest in the property. The borrower has possession of, and title to, the property subject to the lender's right to foreclose on the property in the event of a loan default.

B. Common Lease Forms

Leases fall into one of two basic formats—the single transaction lease format and the master lease format. Although both follow the same fundamental structure, the lessor's format choice is dictated by the type of financing transaction, the relationship the lessor anticipates, and its document negotiation strategy. If the lessee has its own lease forms, the format choice is typically dictated by which is more cost-effective for a given relationship or transaction.

1. Single Transaction Lease

Lessors, particularly in small transactions and vendor programs, frequently use a standard, preprinted single transaction lease. The standard lease form has fill-in blanks for aspects such as rent that typically vary with each transaction. Although this type of lease format can be tailored to meet certain required variations, too many changes squeezed into the document margins or attached as riders can result in a unreadable document. Traditionally, this type of lease is used in small-ticket lease financings.

The preprinted lease format, whether it is the lessor's or the lessee's, is particularly attractive in small-dollar lease transactions because it reduces drafting and negotiation and thus helps keep documentation costs, such as legal fees, to a minimum. Both parties benefit because the greater the expenses, the less the profit to a lessor, and the greater the overall cost to the lessee. However, using a lessor's preprinted form lease can be risky for a lessee. They are often one sided, giving few benefits to the lessee and containing many traps hidden in the fine print. Lessors use preprinted leases to create the false impression that their document is standard in the industry. Unfortunately, that is not true. Preprinted lease terms and conditions vary widely among lessors.

A few sophisticated lessees have recently begun to use lessor document strategies, developing and requiring the use of their preprinted standard form lease as a condition of a lease award. This approach not only saves documentation costs, but also eliminates the potential for falling into lessor document traps.

➤ **Recommendation**   The parties should always consider the estimated costs involved in documenting a lease in determining the transaction's economic attractiveness. Documentation expenses can be the same regardless of the dollar amount of equipment involved. A $10,000 legal fee may be reasonable for a $500,000 transaction but not for a $20,000 transaction.

2. *Master Lease*

A lease format set up to permit future delivered equipment to be easily added is commonly referred to as a master lease. It may be in a preprinted form or specifically typed for a particular transaction (a custom lease approach). Traditionally, master lease formats are used in medium-sized (middle market) and large-ticket lease transactions.

A master lease has two parts: The main, or boiler plate, portion contains the provisions that will remain the same from transaction to transaction (such as basic representations, warranties, tax obligations, and maintenance responsibilities); the second part, sometimes called the schedule, contains the items that will vary among transactions (such as equipment type, rent, and options). Typically, the schedule will be short—often only one or two pages—while the main portion may be 40 to 50 pages. The advantage to using a master lease format is the parties can document future transactions with a minimum amount of time and expense by merely adding a schedule containing the information pertaining to the specific transaction. A master lease has been included in the forms section.

➤ **Observations**
  • Strategically, a lessor with a master lease in place with a particular lessee has a competitive advantage over other prospective lessors in any new bidding situation. Because documenting new equipment additions on an existing master lease is simpler than negotiating an entire new lease, companies having master leases frequently go out of their way to let an existing lessor win by, for example, giving the lessor the last opportunity to match a lower offer.
  • Companies that frequently lease large-ticket items of equipment have increasingly developed their own master lease format and require that a prospective lessor agree to use it as a condition of a lease award. When multimillion dollar financings are concerned, this can substantially reduce legal fees and other documentation and negotiation costs.

C. Subjects to Address in Negotiating the Lease

Before starting and during lease negotiations, the parties must understand the legal, financial, and practical aspects of a lease. Without that understanding, a party may inadvertently give up on an issue that is important, be too adamant about a point of little consequence, or miss an issue altogether. The following explanation identifies and describes issues that can arise in a major equipment lease and suggests ways that the parties may resolve them. In preparing for the negotiations, the parties must weigh the relative values of different alternative approaches to effectively make the necessary trade-offs.

➤ **Reminder** Besides the transaction's participants, another party must be considered in negotiating a tax-oriented lease—the IRS. Although the parties may find that a particular approach is in their business interests, the approach may jeopardize the lease's status as a true tax lease. The tax lease rules are explained in Chapter 7, and particular issues that may give rise to tax problems are noted in this chapter.

The following explanation uses a net finance lease as an example because it is generally the most comprehensive and complex form. Having an understanding of the issues arising in a net finance lease will enable an individual to deal with virtually any kind of equipment lease.

➤ **Note** The forms section includes a sample net finance lease. The reader is urged to read it in conjunction with the following explanation.

➤ **Recommendation** In drafting a lengthy lease document, the parties should compile an index of the topic headings and page numbers to help the participants of the negotiation process locate relevant provisions.

1. Identify Parties to the Lease

The lease should begin by clearly stating each party's full legal name, the jurisdiction in which each is organized, and the mailing address of their principal places of business. This documentation will prevent disputes as to who is intended to be bound by the contract.

> **Illustrative Language** *The Proper Name Designations:* This lease made as of the 25th day of February, 20XX, by and between ARROW CORPORATION, a Delaware corporation, having its principal place of business at 200 Curtis Street, New York, New York (hereinafter called "Lessor") and THE HARRIS CORPORATION, a Missouri corporation, having its principal place of business at 100 Barkley Street, St. Louis, Missouri (hereinafter called "Lessee").

➤ **Recommendation** Sometimes a corporation leases equipment to be used exclusively by one of its divisions. When such a division has been organized as a profit center, the corporation frequently wants it to be the named lessee. However, if the division is not a separate legal entity, it cannot be bound by a contract. If the division is a corporate subsidiary, however, this problem will not be present, because it will have a separate legal existence. A prospective lessor should therefore ensure that the lessee entity has been properly identified and is capable of being legally bound in the capacity indicated in the lease.

2. Factual Summary

When the lease document is typed specifically for the transaction, and not a preprinted form, it's always a good idea for it, at the outset, to summarize the basic facts surrounding the transaction. Writing the summary helps each party focus on the overall transaction, and provides a valuable future reference for individuals not involved at the time the lease was negotiated. For example, the summary might describe the equipment purchase contract into which the lessee entered prior to the lease transaction and state that it has been assigned to the lessor as part of the transaction.

Typically, the factual summary is incorporated into "whereas" clauses. The factual summary is often followed by a statement of the consideration for the lease, generally stated as the mutual obligations of the lessor and the lessee under the agreement. This is usually done in a "now, therefore" clause following the "whereas" section. Stating the consideration for the transaction in this manner is not legally necessary, but many lawyers consider it good form.

> **Illustrative Language**   *A Factual Summary:* Whereas, pursuant to a purchase agreement (the "Purchase Agreement") dated January 2, 20XX between White Aircraft Corporation (the "Manufacturer"), a Delaware corporation, and the Lessee identified above, the Manufacturer has agreed to manufacture and sell to the Lessee, and the Lessee has agreed to purchase from the Manufacturer, one White Model A-14 aircraft, that is to be financed pursuant to this Lease; and
>
> Whereas, the Lessee and the Lessor will enter into an assignment of the Purchase Agreement simultaneously with the execution of this Lease whereby the Lessee assigns to the Lessor all the Lessee's rights and interests under the Purchase Agreement, except to the extent reserved therein.
>
> Now, therefore, in consideration of the mutual agreements contained in this Lease, the parties hereto agree as follows:

3. Definitions of the Key Terms

The lease should define the fundamental terms used repeatedly in the lease agreement that have special meaning in one section, preferably at the document's beginning. For example, terms such as "fair market purchase value," "fair market rental value," "manufacturer," "purchase contract," "stipulated loss value," and "termination value" will usually have certain meanings in a particular transaction, and the parties must agree on their meaning to prevent future ambiguities. Using such a definition section makes the text clearer, permits the parties to locate definitions more readily, and lessens the risk that an important term will accidentally be left undefined.

➤ **Recommendation**   If a preprinted lease does not have such a section incorporated and the definitions are scattered throughout the text, it is advisable to include a rider that lists all key terms and the page number and lease section where they are first defined.

4. Dealing with Future Delivered Equipment

Often the parties will want to enter into the lease well before the equipment's delivery date. Coming to terms on the lease in advance of the equipment's delivery can often benefit both parties: The prospective lessee can then be assured no insurmountable problems will arise before it is too late to find another lessor; and an equally anxious prospective lessor may want to be assured the lessee does not change its mind.

a. Putting the Equipment Under the Lease

When a lease transaction is documented before the equipment's delivery, the parties must prescribe a method for putting the equipment under lease when it arrives. Usually the arrangement is for the lessee to notify the lessor in writing of the equipment's delivery and its acceptability for lease. The notification is usually in an *acceptance supplement*, a written statement that lists the equipment delivered and states that the lessee accepted it for lease as of a specified date. If the equipment conforms to the agreement, the lessor automatically puts it on lease.

When the lease relates to equipment to be delivered in the future, the lessee's obligation to lease the equipment must be clearly spelled out. For example, the lessee may want the option to accept or reject the equipment when delivered. The lessor also should clearly be aware of the lessee's obligation. An ambiguous phrase, such as "the lessee may accept the equipment when delivered by executing the appropriate acceptance supplement," can cause problems—the lessor may anticipate that the lessee is bound to accept the equipment, but the lessee may not believe it is bound.

b. Nonutilization and Commitment Fees

When the lessee wants the right to reject equipment to be delivered in the future, the lessor has two ways to protect itself: a nonutilization fee and a commitment fee.

A nonutilization fee compensates a lessor for funds committed to future delivered equipment that remain unused at the end of the commitment period. Usually the fee is expressed as a percentage of originally estimated equipment cost and is payable in a lump sum at the end of the commitment period. If all or an agreed-on portion of the funds are used, the lessee owes nothing.

> **Illustrative Example**   *The Nonutilization Fee:* Company Able, a leasing company, has agreed to give Company Baker a lease line of credit for ten river barges. The barges' total cost will be $1,000,000, and they will be delivered over a 12-month period. Company Able, however, has a limited amount of funds available and wants to be assured protection from an opportunity loss if the barges are not delivered or if Company Baker decides not to lease them. Therefore, it imposes a 1% nonutilization fee. If only $400,000 worth of barges are delivered during the commitment period, how much of a fee is due?
>
> Company Baker would owe Company Able $6,000: 1% of the funds remaining unused, $600,000. If none of the equipment was put on lease, Company Baker would owe $10,000 (1% × $1,000,000). If $1,000,000 worth of equipment was leased, Company Baker would owe nothing.

A nonutilization fee arrangement has its risks for a lessee. An unexpectedly high equipment purchase cost (whether from a mistaken estimate or a price escalation) or a delivery delay may give the lessor the right to exclude equipment from the lease. If this happens, a lessee can end up paying a nonutilization fee based on the unused funds remaining at the end of the commitment period. This arrangement is not generally considered unreasonable for the lessee to bear in cases other than when a lessor could arbitrarily choose not to lease certain agreed-on equipment when it arrives.

➤ **Recommendation**   Confronted with a nonutilization fee arrangement, a prospective lessee can lessen the payment impact resulting from equipment exclusions by negotiating a commitment percentage leeway. For example, the lease can provide for the fee to be payable only to the extent that greater than 10% of the committed funds are not used.

The other approach, a commitment fee, is more commonly used. Under this arrangement, a lessee pays a flat fee at the time the lease is entered based on the total equipment cost involved for the lease funding commitment. Generally the fee is expressed as a percentage of total cost, commonly ranging from 0.375% to 1%. Because the commitment fee pays a lessor for holding funds available, the lessee can freely elect not to put equipment on lease.

➤ **Observation**   In a competitive lease market, lessors may find it difficult to make a lessee accept nonutilization and commitment fees, because many other lessors may be willing to hold funds available without a fee to win business.

c.   Minimum Grouping Requirements

When a lease involves many less-expensive equipment items to be delivered over an extended period, a lessor can require a minimum equipment acceptance grouping to reduce its administrative handling expenses. For example, a lessee may not be able to accept equipment for lease in aggregate cost groups of less than $100,000.

An equipment grouping requirement can cause serious problems for a lessee. For example, if the dollar minimum was set high, the lessee may have to manipulate deliveries to avoid having to pay for equipment for which it does not yet have lease funding until the specified amount is accumulated.

➤ **Recommendation**   When confronted with a minimum dollar amount equipment grouping requirement, the prospective lessee should seek a best efforts qualification. Under this provision, if, after using its best efforts to assemble the required minimum, it becomes impractical to do so, the lessee will be permitted to have a smaller amount accepted.

5.   Lease Terms

The parties must clearly define the period of permitted use, called the term of lease. Generally, there are two basic periods: (1) a main lease term, referred to as the base lease term, the primary lease term, or the initial lease term; and (2) a renewal term. Some transactions also call for an interim lease term, beginning when the equipment becomes subject to lease until the start of a predetermined base term. The interim term concept is frequently used when many equipment items will go on lease at various times. For example, the base term may start on January 1, 20XX for all equipment delivered during the prior three-month period. By consolidating the start of the primary lease term to one date after which all equipment will be delivered, administrative work and rent payment mechanics are simplified.

In setting up the renewal term options, from the lessee's viewpoint, generally the more the alternatives the better. For example, one four-year renewal term is less preferable than four one-year terms, because the lessee can compare market prices at more intervals. For the lessor, a longer renewal period will generally be preferable because it will want to have a longer period during which its rents are predictable and it does not have to undertake to remarket the equipment.

6. Rent Payment Structure

Because such facts as when the rent payments are due and how much the lessee must pay are key elements of every lease transaction, the lease must precisely detail those terms. For example, a ten-year lease may call for rent to be payable in 20 consecutive, level, semiannual in arrears payments, each payment to be equal to 2% of the total cost of the equipment.

a. Payment Mechanism

To avoid problems, the lease should specify (1) where the rent is payable, such as at the lessor's place of business; (2) the form of payment, such as in immediately available funds; and (3) when payment is to be deemed received by the lessor, such as when deposited in a U.S. mailbox. Unless the lease specifies those terms, a lessee runs the risk of a lessor claiming a technical default based on what the lessor deems to be an incorrect or late payment, and a lessor runs the risk of losing interest it could have earned had the rent been paid in a manner that would have permitted an earlier use of the money. For example, a lessor will lose interest if payment is made by a bank check which would take time to clear, as opposed to immediately available funds through, for example, an electronic wire funds transfer.

➤ **Recommendation** Lessees should establish appropriate internal rent payment procedures to avoid technical defaults through, for example, accidental late payments. If the rent must be sent to a special P.O. box number, all individuals responsible for handling the payments should be separately advised so that the rent does not instead get sent to the lessor's regular business address.

b. Fixing the Rental Amount

Besides using fixed dollar amounts, the lease may express the rent in different ways. One way is as a percentage of equipment cost. The parties frequently use this method when equipment is to be delivered after the lease is signed because then the rent does not have to be recalculated if the purchase price varies from that anticipated. For example, if the annual rent is expressed as 2% of equipment cost, changes in cost will not require a lease adjustment. If, on the other hand, the lease sets rent at $2,000 a year based on a $100,000 item of equipment and the price later turns out to be $105,000, a lease amendment is needed to incorporate the proper rent.

When the rent is based on a percentage of equipment cost, the lease should define what expenses may be included, or capitalized, in the cost term. If a prospective lessor has ample funds available, it may be eager to include more expenses into the rent computation cost base. For example, it may readily pay for sales taxes, freight charges, and installation cost and thereby increase the rent. If, however, its money supply is limited, it will probably want to exclude the extras. Also, when "soft" costs, such as installation costs, are substantial in relation to the raw equipment purchase price, a prospective lessor may not be willing to exceed a certain dollar amount on such costs because to do so would lessen its collateral value protection. For example, if a lessor financed the installation costs, which ran 25% of the raw equipment cost, the lessor's collateral position would be diluted. In other words, 25% of the total amount financed would relate to installation charges that would have no remarketing value.

➤ **Recommendation** The equipment-related cost items that a prospective lessor is willing to finance can vary with each transaction. A prospective lessee should therefore define the ground rules in the proposal letter stage to eliminate potential misunderstandings or misconceptions.

c. Tax Law Rental Adjustment

When a prospective lessor's economic return depends in part on anticipated equipment ownership tax benefits, it may want the option to make rent adjustments if unexpected tax law changes occur that adversely affect return. For example, the lease can incorporate a provision that would allow the lessor to adjust the rent to maintain its "yield and after-tax cash flow." Instead of a yield and after-tax cash flow, leases sometimes use a maintenance of earnings or net return standard.

➤ **Recommendations**

- A prospective lessor with the right to make rent adjustments in the event of adverse tax law changes should also have the ability to make appropriate adjustments to values based on the rent, such as termination or stipulated loss values. Without being able to adjust these rent-related values, the financial integrity of the transaction may not be maintained in the event, for example, of an early termination or a casualty loss.
- A prospective lessee should ensure that the lease clearly defines any lessor rent adjustment criterion. Terms such as yield or earnings, for example, do not have standard meanings and can be subject to many interpretations. The lease must set out the exact formula to be used in making any adjustment to enable an independent verification of any of the lessor's computations.
- If a lessor has the right to increase the rent in the event of an adverse change in the tax laws to compensate for any loss, then a lessee should request the right to have the rent decreased if there is a tax law change economically favorable to the lessor.
- If a specific tax law change looks likely during lease negotiations, it may be advisable to determine in advance the rents and rent-related values should the change occur and incorporate them into the lease agreement. This way everyone knows exactly what to expect before a final commitment is made.

d. Conditions on Payment

In many equipment leases, particularly finance leases, the lessee's rent obligation is absolute and unconditional; that is, the lessee must pay the rent in full and on time regardless of any claim the lessee may have against the lessor. Commonly referred to as a hell or high water obligation, the provision at first shocks many new prospective lessees. The provision, however, is not as troublesome as it seems initially, because it does not prevent a lessee from independently bringing a lawsuit against the lessor on any claim.

➤ **Recommendation** Although not technically necessary, a prospective lessee may want to insert a statement in a hell or high water provision to the effect that any rights of action it may have for damages caused by the lessor will exist regardless of the hell or high water rent commitment.

Typically, a lessor will want a hell or high water provision when leveraging an investment through the use of a nonrecourse loan. With this provision, a lender is more likely to lend on a nonrecourse-to-lessor basis, because potential claims against the lessor would not affect the rental stream that is being relied on for the loan repayment.

➤ **Observations**

- Using nonrecourse debt as opposed to recourse debt is the most desirable way for a lessor to leverage a lease transaction. For financial reporting purposes, the nonrecourse nature permits a lessor to disregard the loan obligation on its financial books because the lender may look only to the lessee and the collateral for repayment, not to the lessor's general funds.
- Sometimes a lessor's general lending bank requires a lessor to include hell or high water lease provisions in all leases. If so, the obligation is included in the lending agreement and is usually coupled with a right to require an assignment of all the lessor's rights under each lease, including the right to the rent payments, as an additional form of security for the loans.

7. Lessor's Right to Receive Reports

The lessor, to be able to monitor the transaction, may want the right to receive certain reports from the lessee. The utility of the various possible lessee reports depends on each transaction. It is usually advisable, however, for a prospective lessor to at least require financial reports, accident reports, lease conformity reports, equipment location reports, and third-party claim reports to enable it to stay on top of a transaction.

a. Financial Reports

One of the best methods for a lessor to monitor a lessee's financial condition during the lease term is to require the lessee periodically to submit financial reports, such as current balance sheets and profit and loss statements. Such reports will put a lessor in a good position to spot potential financial problems and take whatever early action may be necessary to protect the investment.

➤ **Recommendations**

- A prospective lessor should require quarterly, as well as annual, balance sheets and profit and loss statements. Each should be certified by an independent public accounting firm.
- A prospective lessee should ensure that the time between the period when the information is gathered and when a financial report is due is adequate for its preparation and submission, to avoid a potential default situation.

b. Accident Reports

A lessor should receive immediate notification of every significant or potentially significant accident involving the leased equipment, whether the damage is to the equipment or to persons or other property. Because it is not uncommon for a lessor to be sued solely on the basis of its ownership interest, lessee accident reports are a must. The reports should be in writing and contain a summary of the incident, including the time, place, and nature of the accident and the persons and property involved. Reviewing all incidents may be a tedious job, particularly when many items of equipment are on lease, but it can prevent some costly surprises.

➤ **Recommendations**

- When an accident could involve major dollar liability, the lease should require the lessee to notify the lessor by telephone immediately in addition to submitting a written report. A lessor's early arrival on the scene can produce facts that would otherwise be lost.
- A prospective lessee should limit accident notification responsibility only to incidents involving serious accidents. Minor accidents can create an unnecessary volume of paperwork. One approach is to set an estimated damage dollar amount below which notification is not required. If there is such a cutoff, the lessor should make the lessee responsible for inaccurate estimates because the lessor may not hear about a major claim until it has received notice of litigation.

c. Lease Conformity Reports

Lessors sometimes require lessees to submit annually an officer's certificate stating if any events of default under the lease have occurred during the reporting year, and if any existing conditions could eventually result in an event of default. If so, an appropriate factual summary must accompany the certificate. From a lessor's viewpoint, this type of report can be a good early-warning technique. Although the reports are somewhat of a burden from a lessee's viewpoint, they are useful in avoiding inadvertent lease default situations. For example, it is not unusual, particularly in larger companies, to discover at the end of the lease that the equipment has been misplaced, sometimes too late to locate it before delinquent return penalties are incurred.

d. Equipment Location Reports

Requiring a lessee to prepare and submit equipment location reports is frequently advisable and sometimes necessary. When practical, a lessor should periodically inspect the leased equipment, particularly when the lessee has an obligation to maintain it. If the location is known, it is easy for the lessor to "drop in" to check on its condition. Location reports may be essential if a lessor intends to keep any security interest or other collateral protection filings up to date, as a location change sometimes necessitates a new filing.

➤ **Recommendation**   When the lessor has filed or intends to file security interests, the lease should require the lessee to notify the lessor at least 45 days before a change of equipment location to give the lessor enough time to make any additional filings or amendments to existing filings.

e. Third-Party Claim Reports

Generally, a lessor has a measure of security because it can take its equipment back if the lessee defaults; however, tax liens or other third-party claims imposed on the equipment, regardless of their viability, can seriously jeopardize this protected position. Thus, the lease should require that the lessee notify the lessor of any events that result, or could result, in such an imposition so that it will have the opportunity to protect its position and equipment.

f. Other Reports

The lessor should request the right to have the lessee submit reports that may be determined necessary in the future, because unforeseeable events may require that the lessor receive certain additional information concerning the equipment. The lessee should seek to qualify any general reporting obligation, however, so that only reasonable information relevant to the lease transaction can be requested.

8. *Equipment Maintenance and Alterations*

a. Equipment Maintenance

The lease must specify which party has the obligation for maintenance and what will be acceptable maintenance. Many types of leases, such as net finance leases, put the normal maintenance responsibilities on the lessee. Regardless of the arrangement, the maintenance issue should be specifically addressed in the lease.

The lease usually will describe the maintenance requirements in terms of the condition in which the equipment will have to be maintained. A common provision requires the lessee to keep the equipment in "good working order, ordinary wear and tear excepted." Unfortunately, such a general requirement may be difficult to apply because it is somewhat vague, and more specific guidelines are difficult to ascertain. Two ways to minimize the difficulties are as follows:

- If the lessee will use the equipment in a manner that may cause extra wear and tear, then the maintenance provision can exclude ordinary wear and tear resulting from the lessee's intended use.
- If the equipment's manufacturer provides maintenance instructions, then the lessee should follow them exactly.

Some types of equipment must be specially maintained. A leased aircraft, for example, must be maintained under standards put out by the Federal Aviation Administration. Failing to meet those standards may mean that the aircraft cannot be flown, or even worse, could result in lawsuits.

➤ **Recommendations**
- The parties should seek expert advice in specialized maintenance situations. Parties negotiating lease agreements frequently do not fully appreciate the cost effect of a proposed maintenance arrangement and, as a result, fail to protect themselves adequately.
- A lessee responsible for maintenance should also be required to keep maintenance records and make them available to the lessor. Keeping records helps both parties: The lessor can determine if the equipment is being properly serviced, and the lessee has greater protection should the lessor raise a claim of inadequate maintenance.
- If the lease permits the lessor access to the lessee's maintenance records, the lessee should limit access to normal business hours.

b. Equipment Alterations

A lessor should have the right to prohibit the lessee from making equipment alterations not related to normal maintenance. As explained in Chapter 7, a lessee making alterations can affect the true lease status of the lease for tax purposes, thereby jeopardizing the lessor's tax benefits. In addition to the tax considerations, an alteration could affect the equipment's market value and impair its value to the lessor following the end of the lease term. Generally this is handled by a lease provision requiring the lessee to get the lessor's prior written consent to a proposed change.

9. The Lessor's Ownership Should Be Specifically Protected

Certain basic possession, use, and operational conditions may be necessary for a lessor to impose to protect its ownership interest in the leased equipment. This section will describe the most essential conditions.

a. Filings Must Be Made

In many cases, filings are necessary to protect the lessor's ownership status. The lessor may want to file security interests under a state's Uniform Commercial Code laws to ensure priority over other creditors, typically called UCC filings. Certain types of equipment require special filings. An aircraft lessor, for example, must make certain filings with the Federal Aviation Administration to protect its ownership interest.

Who should be responsible to make the required filings? It is a matter of negotiation between the parties. If the lessee has that obligation, then the lessor must require the lessee to confirm promptly that the designated action was taken. The lease also should obligate the lessee to pay for any out-of-pocket losses incurred as a result of an improper filing.

b. Equipment Marking Requirement

The lease should require the lessee to mark the leased equipment with the lessor's name and its principal place of business. Marking the equipment has two basic benefits for a lessor: It will help fend off a creditor of the lessee trying to claim the equipment for the lessee's unpaid debts, and it will enable a lessor to identify its equipment more readily during an inspection trip or if a reclaiming action is necessary.

Illustrative Language *Ownership Marking:* White Leasing Corporation, Owner-Lessor, San Francisco, California.

c. Certain Broad Use Prohibitions

The lease should prohibit the lessee from "using, operating, maintaining, or storing the leased equipment carelessly, improperly, in violation of law, or in a manner other than contemplated by the manufacturer." If, for example, improper handling or storing damages the leased equipment, and the lessor becomes responsible to a third party for damages caused through any of these actions, then the lessor may have a basis for making a claim against the lessee.

➤ **Recommendations**
- Because of the scope of some general usage prohibitions, a lessee can easily find itself in technical default for relatively minor violations. A prospective lessee should therefore attempt to define the parameters more specifically, such as pinpointing the exact laws with which it must comply.
- Lessees prohibited from using equipment other than in conformity with the manner contemplated by the manufacturer can unknowingly run into trouble. Frequently, equipment is acquired for a use different from that it was originally built to meet because, for example, nothing else is available. In such a case, a prospective lessee should attempt to get a use exception, a specific authorization to use the equipment as necessary.

10. *The Lessor Should Require Certain Key Assurances*

The lease should require the lessee to make certain key representations on matters related to a lease transaction. The representations should be given as true on the date of the lease document's execution and, when relevant, should also be ongoing during the lease period. The lease should provide that the remedy for the lessee's failure to maintain the representations is that the lessor may declare an event of default and be released of its commitments.

a. The Lessee Is Legally in Existence

The prospective lessor must assure itself through an appropriate lessee representation that the prospective lessee is a legal entity authorized to do business where the equipment will be used. A corporate lessee should, for example, be required to represent that it is properly organized, validly existing, and in good standing under the laws of its state of incorporation and that it is duly authorized to do business in those states where the equipment will be used. If the lessee is not, the lessor may have a difficult time suing the lessee, should it become necessary to do so. Also, any lack of proper legal standing can result in a seizure of the equipment by state authorities. The lessor's secured position could be jeopardized.

b. The Lessee Has the Transactional Authority to Enter into the Lease

A lessor must have the lessee represent that it is authorized to enter into the lease transaction and that the persons executing the lease, by name or official title, are fully authorized to sign on the lessee's behalf. For example, if the lessee is a corporation and it had not been properly empowered by its board of directors to make the lease commitment, then a lessor may be unable to enforce the agreement against the corporation.

The lessor's only recourse may be against the individual executing the lease "on behalf of the corporation." Because it is unlikely that the signing party, in an individual capacity, would have enough personal wealth to satisfy any substantive claim, the lessor would be in a precarious position.

➤ **Observation** Merely because a lessee represents a particular point does not mean it is necessarily true as stated. If, however, a falsehood is deemed an event of default, the lessor would have the ability to reclaim the equipment.

c. There Are No Conflicting Agreements

Existing agreements may restrict a prospective lessee's ability to enter into a lease transaction. A bank credit agreement, for example, could prevent the borrower from taking out additional loans without the lender's consent. If the term *loans* is defined to include lease obligations, then the failure to secure the lender's consent would most likely be treated as a loan default. Typically, if there is a loan default, the lender would have the right to demand an immediate repayment of the outstanding money, which in turn could adversely affect a lessee's financial condition. Any lessening of the lessee's financial strength can jeopardize its ability to meet its lease obligations. The lease should include a provision that by entering into the lease agreement the lessee is not violating any existing credit or other agreements.

d. All Necessary Regulatory Approvals Have Been Obtained

In some situations, a prospective lessee may be required to secure regulatory approval for certain aspects of a lease transaction. For example, a public utility may be required to clear certain lease commitments with the appropriate utility regulatory authority. If they are not cleared, the lease commitments may be unenforceable. It is essential, therefore, that a lessor get a representation from the lessee that all necessary regulatory approvals have been obtained or, if none are needed, a representation to that effect.

➤ Recommendations

- Because of the regulatory complexities existing in certain industries, such as public utilities, it may be wise for a prospective lessor to verify independently that the lessee has complied with all necessary regulatory aspects, rather than relying on the lessee's representation or its counsel's opinion. Failure to comply can result in a major problem. Although the lessor can reclaim the equipment if a misrepresentation is deemed an event of default, the expense and time involved in getting the equipment back, combined with the problem of having to dispose of, for example, 100 heavy-duty used trucks at a reasonable price, can present serious practical problems. Securing a favorable opinion from independent counsel expert in the area is advisable, but not an ironclad solution. The safest course of action, if possible, is to get the appropriate regulatory authority to issue a favorable written opinion on the relevant issues.

- Regulatory approval processes frequently take time. To avoid major delays, a prospective lessee should start the process as soon as possible so that, if necessary, it will be in a position to deliver the necessary assurances at the lease closing, such as supplying certified copies of any approvals obtained.

e. There Are No Adverse Proceedings

A lessor must require the lessee to represent that there are not pending legal, or administrative proceedings that could adversely affect the lessee's operations or financial condition. If such proceedings exist, the lessee should indicate what they are and the lease (or other document) should describe them. For example, it is not inconceivable for an impending lawsuit to be potentially serious enough to bankrupt a company. If it comes to a lessor's attention after the lease is signed, a no adverse proceeding representation would allow a lessor to terminate the transaction.

➤ Recommendations

- It is sometimes impossible for a prospective lessee to be aware of all threatened lawsuits or similar proceedings, particularly those involving minor incidents. Thus, the proceeding representation should be qualified to the effect that there are no proceedings that would have a material adverse impact on the lessee's operations or financial condition of which it is aware.

- A no adverse proceeding representation, from a lessor's viewpoint, should be broad enough to cover not only the lessee but also its subsidiaries and affiliated companies, because a proceeding against a related company could jeopardize the lessee's financial condition.

f. The Lessee's Financial Statements Are Accurate

Because the lessee's financial condition is a critical consideration in a lessor's credit analysis, the lessee should represent that all financial statements delivered to the lessor, including those prepared by the lessee's outside accountants, accurately represent its financial condition. Such a representation should be requested regardless if the statements have been certified by the lessee's independent accountants. If, for example, a mistake was made, the lessor could reassess its willingness to continue with the transaction when the error is discovered.

11. The Lessee Should Require Certain Key Assurances

The lessee should also require that the lessor make certain representations—a point often overlooked by prospective lessees.

a. That the Lessor Has the Transactional Authority to Lease the Equipment

Even though a prospective lessor presents itself to the public as being in the leasing business, there may be restrictions, such as in a credit agreement, prohibiting the lessor from entering into particular types of transactions. A prospective lessor also may have to go through prescribed internal procedures before a lease is in fact an authorized transaction. Violating any restrictions or procedures could jeopardize the lessee's right to continue using the equipment. Of course, an appropriate representation from a lessor will not guarantee there will be no use interference, but it will provide the lessee with another ground on which to base a claim in the event of a problem.

In underwritten transactions, the lessor-investors, or equity participants, are frequently not in the leasing business per se. Many corporations, for example, invest in leases on an irregular basis as equity participants, and if the lessor corporation has not obtained all the appropriate internal approvals for the transaction, a lessee may have some enforceability problems. In such a case, if a lessor backs out, a lessee may try to sue for performance on the basis that the lessor should be held to the contract based on its apparent authority to enter into the lease. If a lessor-investor is involved who is not regularly in the leasing market, this possible ground may be unavailable. Thus, it is important in underwritten transactions for a lessee to secure a representation that the transaction has been duly authorized by the lessor-investor.

b. That the Equipment Will Be Paid for

The lease must include a statement by the lessor, particularly when the lease is executed in advance of equipment deliveries, that the lessor will pay for and lease the equipment to the lessee. Although a firm commitment will not guarantee that funds will be available, it will assist in a legal action for damages in the event the lessor defaults. The lessor, in turn, will want the commitment to be subject to the lessee fulfilling certain obligations, such as equipment inspection and acceptance. As long as those conditions are within the lessee's capability, they should not be of concern.

➤ **Recommendations**

- A lessor payment commitment representation is particularly important when a prospective lessee is dealing with smaller, less well financed leasing companies. It cannot, however, be relied on exclusively if the dollar amount of the equipment involved is significant, or last-minute funding problems could cause a budgeting disruption. Thus, the reputation and financial background of a prospective lessor should be investigated to ensure that funding risk is at a minimum. A cheaper rental rate from a lessor known leasing company, or equity participant in the case of an underwritten transaction, will quickly lose its appeal if the funds are not available when needed.

• The lessor should represent that the equipment will be, and will remain, free of all liens and encumbrances, except those of which the lessee is aware, such as the debt in a leveraged lease. That representation will help ensure no interference with the lessee's equipment use from the lessor's third-party creditors.

c. That There Will Be No Interference with the Equipment's Use

A lessee's right to the quiet enjoyment and peaceful possession of the equipment during the lease period is fundamental, provided, of course, the lessee is not in default under the lease. A prospective lessee should require a representation to that effect.

➤ **Recommendation**   A prospective lessor should limit its representation of quiet enjoyment to its own actions, as opposed to guaranteeing that the lessee will be entitled to quiet enjoyment in all events. If the representative is not so qualified, a lessor can be liable for damages if an unrelated third party, not claiming directly or indirectly through the lessor, interferes with the lessee's use of the equipment.

12. *The Lessor Should Disclaim Certain Product Responsibility*

If the lessor is not the equipment vendor, it will not typically be responsible to the lessee for anything that goes wrong with the equipment. To be certain, however, a lessor should make an appropriate product warranty disclaimer to prevent any possible exposure to a lessee for defects in the equipment's design, suitability, operation, fitness for use, or merchantability. The lessee should be able to accept such a disclaimer because it can rely on the usual manufacturer's, subcontractor's, or supplier's product warranties.

13. *The Lessee Should Obtain an Assignment of Product Warranties*

When equipment is supplied by a manufacturer, subcontractor, or supplier, the lessee may be responsible for defects during or at the end of the lease term even though they were caused by the manufacturer, subcontractor, or supplier. To prevent this problem, a prospective lessee should obtain an assignment of any rights that the prospective lessor would have as equipment owner against any manufacturer, subcontractor, or supplier during the lease term. If these rights are not assignable because of, for example, a warranty restriction, a lessee should have the power to obligate the lessor to sue on its behalf if it deems necessary.

➤ **Recommendations**

• If a prospective lessee finds it necessary to have the right to require the prospective lessor to sue in the name of the lessor because, for example, the product warranty rights cannot be assigned, that right should be coupled with the right to control the action, including the selection of counsel and the grounds of the lawsuit.

- If a prospective lessor agrees to allow the prospective lessee to be able to require it to sue on its behalf, it should also specify the extent of the lessee's obligation to pay the legal expenses. Generally, these will be the lessee's responsibility.

14. The Party with Risk of Loss Should Be Specified

Generally, the lessee will bear the risk of equipment loss, whether due to damage, theft, requisition, or confiscation, because the lessee possesses the equipment. Net finance leases, for example, frequently require the lessee to guarantee that the lessor will receive a minimum amount of money, usually called the stipulated loss value or casualty value, if an equipment loss occurs. The stipulated loss value, which decreases as the lease term runs, is calculated so that the lessor will not have to report a loss on its books. That obligation basically puts the lessee in the position of being the equipment's ultimate insurer.

➤ **Recommendations**

- When the lease imposes a stipulated loss obligation, a prospective lessee should do the following:
  - Request an offset for any insurance proceeds or other awards resulting from the loss.
  - Make sure its obligations, including rent, under the lease as to the affected equipment, terminate as of the loss date.
- When a stipulated loss provision is incorporated, a prospective lessee should insist on a clear definition of the term *loss,* because it can have various interpretations. Generally, unless a defined loss has occurred, the rent must continue with the possible result that the lessee would be paying on unusable equipment. Typically, loss means destruction to the extent the equipment is no longer usable to the lessee. It is also worth noting that loss for the use intended may be somewhat less than actual total destruction. Thus, a prospective lessee should be careful in agreeing to the ground rules.
- If a prospective lessee must repair equipment damaged by a third party at its own expense, it should insist on the right to claim any money received, at least up to the cost incurred, from the party causing the damage.

15. Responsibility for Certain General Taxes

In a typical net financial lease, the lessee is responsible for paying taxes imposed by any local, state, or federal taxing authority. A prospective lessee should take into account any tax payment obligations when determining its effective leasing cost. Note that some taxes can be significant.

➤ **Recommendations**

- Frequently, lease agreements require a lessee to pay equipment-related taxes that, by law, the lessor must pay. If a lessor is improperly assessed by a taxing authority and refuses to institute a proceeding to correct the problem, the lessee may have to pay an incorrect assessment. Thus, a prospective lessee should require a right to have any tax assessment contested or reviewed.
- When the lessee wants to contest a tax imposed on the lessor, the lessor should require that the lessee deliver an opinion from its counsel, setting out the legitimate

basis for the action, and should require the lessee to put up a reasonable amount of money in advance to cover the expenses.
- The lease should require each party to notify in a timely manner the other party of potential or actual imposition of any taxes or similar assessments on the equipment, to allow the interested party to participate at the earliest possible time.

16. *Protecting the Lessor's Tax Benefits*

Generally the parties to a lease will want the transaction to be classified as a *true* lease for federal income tax purposes (see Chapter 7). It is absolutely essential, therefore, that the parties draft the lease to ensure that the desired tax treatment will not be endangered.

If a lease does not qualify as a true tax lease, the lessor would undoubtedly lose ownership tax benefits such as depreciation. Because such a loss can make a favorable transaction highly unfavorable, sophisticated tax lessors try to build protections into the lease documentation in two basic ways—prohibiting inconsistent actions and filings and requiring tax indemnifications.

a. Prohibited Actions and Filings

The lease should prohibit the lessee from taking any action or filing any documents, including income tax returns, that would be inconsistent with the true lease intent. Normally this does not present a problem for lessees, because by doing so they could lose their right to deduct the rent charges as an expense, which is often the reason the transaction was structured as a lease.

b. Tax Indemnifications

The second way that lessors can attempt to protect themselves against tax benefit losses is through tax indemnification provisions. Typically these provisions require the lessee to pay the lessor an amount of money that, after taxes, will put it in the same economic position as before the loss.

Tax indemnification provisions can be extremely complex and, to assess properly their effect and workability, one must know the three ways that ownership tax benefits can be lost: through acts or omissions of the lessor; through acts or omissions of the lessee; or through a change in law. For obvious reasons, lessors would like to put the economic burden of a loss or inability to claim all of the expected tax benefits on the lessees, regardless of the cause. Lessees, however, object to assuming the entire burden, and, as a result, usually reach a compromise.

It is fairly standard in true leases to include a tax indemnity based on the lessee's acts or omissions. An indemnity based on the lessor's acts or omissions is rare and a lessee should agree to such an indemnity only if the transaction provides significant other benefits. The third situation giving rise to potential tax problems, a change in law, can go either way, usually depending on the overall bargaining position of the parties.

c. Tax Law Changes

How significant is assuming the risk of tax benefit losses resulting from changes in tax law? One should first recognize that the risk breaks down into a retroactive risk and a prospective risk, that is, changes that affect equipment already delivered and those that affect equipment to be delivered in the future.

➤ **Observation** There is some logic to the position that a prospective lessee sometimes successfully shifts the burden of a retroactive change in tax laws to a prospective lessor by arguing that it is a "normal" leasing business risk that a lessor should assume.

What about prospective changes in tax law, those affecting equipment that a lessor has made a commitment to lease, but that has not yet been delivered? In this case, the risk does not have to be assumed by either party. For example, the lessor could be given the right to increase the rent an appropriate amount if there is adverse change in the tax benefits before the equipment arrives or have the right to exclude affected equipment. The lessee, in turn, could exclude the equipment if the adjusted rent is too high. Alert prospective lessees usually make sure when a rent adjustment right is given that the lessor will have to make a downward adjustment if there is an increase in the available tax benefits.

➤ **Recommendations**
- Before a prospective lessor agrees to decrease rents, if there is an increase in tax benefits affecting future delivered equipment, it should carefully determine if it can use the increased tax benefits. If not, a downward rent adjustment will merely erode its economic return.
- As explained in the previous section, if the parties agree to provide for a rent adjustment and couple it with a mutual exclusionary right if the adjustment is unfavorable, certain disadvantages must be considered. A lessor can lose alternate investment opportunities if a lessee excludes equipment at the last minute, and a lessee may not have enough time to find substitute lease financing if the lessor exercises its rights.
- If a prospective lessor excludes equipment based on a tax law change, it is possible that a nonutilization fee may be triggered. Thus, a prospective lessee should ensure that any nonutilization fee excludes the cost of equipment not leased as a result of a lessor's change-in-law exclusion right. If this is not provided for, a lessee will have to pay a fee on funds that remain unused as a result of the lessor's exclusion election.

d. Tax Loss Payment Formula

When the lease includes a tax indemnification provision, it must set out a precise formula for determining the amount the lessee must pay. Because the indemnity formula's purpose is to make the indemnified party whole, the formulas are typically broad in scope and provide for a payment that, after deduction of all fees, taxes, and other changes payable as a result of the indemnification payment, will put the indemnified party in the same economic position as before the loss.

Frequently, this will be expressed as paying the lessor enough money to maintain the lessor's "net return." Unfortunately, that term can have many meanings, for example, total earnings, discounted rate of return, or after-tax cash flow. Thus, the lease should define such terms and provide a precise formula determining the amount of the loss.

The formula can become complicated, particularly if the lessor or equity participant is a large multinational corporation, because the payment may affect other aspects of the corporation's tax picture. As a result, when significant sums are involved, it is usually necessary to retain experienced tax lawyers to work out the formulas.

The payment timing has two alternatives: a lump sum or a rent readjustment. Lessors often prefer the lump-sum payment so they can recoup their entire loss as quickly as possible.

e.   Tax Loss Date

The lease must identify the time when the lessee becomes obligated to pay the indemnity. For example, would the lessee become responsible to pay for a tax benefit loss when the lessor discovers the problem or when a court rules on it? In many situations the *loss date* is defined as the time when the tax benefit loss has been established by the final judgment of a court or administrative agency having jurisdiction over the matter.

> **Recommendations**

- A prospective lessee should not agree to any provision that obligates it to make any tax indemnification payment until the lessor has actually incurred, or is about to incur, an out-of-pocket-expense.
- A lessor should have the right under a tax indemnification clause to make justifiable tax adjustments without prompting from the IRS and call on the lessee to pay if it realizes that it may not properly claim a tax benefit. However, it may not always be clear what is a justifiable adjustment, and without some means of making that interpretation, the lessee could be required to pay an indemnity solely at the lessor's discretion. To avoid that problem, the indemnity provision should provide that the lessor will claim a benefit only after receiving the opinion of a jointly chosen lawyer, or under some other similar arrangement in which each party will have some control.
- The lessee should have the right to require a lessor to contest any tax claim that will trigger an indemnification payment. Without it, a lessor could decide not to defend against a claim because it will not be responsible for payment.

f.   Reimbursement for Erroneous Tax Loss Payments

The right to be reimbursed for any money incorrectly paid under a tax indemnification provision is an important concept to include within this arrangement. If the tax loss is determined not to exist, the indemnified party should be required to return any money paid promptly.

> **Recommendation**   When a lessee has the right to force a lessor to contest a tax claim, it should also have a right to the return of any amount that it has had to pay before a final resolution, if the lessor later settles or discontinues the action without justification or consent. The purpose is to make sure the claim will be fully contested.

17.   *Equipment Return*

The condition in which and the place where the leased equipment must be returned to the lessor are important considerations. Overlooking either can result in a costly omission for the lessor or the lessee.

When the equipment is returned, a dispute can arise concerning whether the equipment's condition meets the standards required in the lease. If a lessor determines that the lessee did not properly maintain the equipment, it can insist that the lessee pay for any repairs necessary to restore the equipment. Even if the lessor's claim for repairs is legitimate, a lessee may believe that the maintenance standards in the lease were met and dispute payment. Thus, the lease should provide a means to determine if the lessee has met the standard of care criteria defined in the lease.

The best approach is to set an objective, easy-to-measure external standard, for example, agreeing that an aircraft under lease will be returned with no less than 50% of remaining engine operation time before the next major overhaul. When an easily measurable objective criterion is not available, the parties may agree to use an independent equipment appraiser to assess the equipment's condition. The lease can either identify the equipment appraiser or set out a method to select appraisers if their services become necessary. A selection method can call for each party to pick an appraiser at the appropriate time, and, if the two selected appraisers cannot reach an agreement, the parties will then jointly select a third independent appraiser whose opinion will be final and binding.

The lease should specify where the equipment is to be returned and who will bear the delivery expense. If, at the lease's end, a lessor, for example, unexpectedly had to pay for the transportation of 200 trucks from ten of a lessee's plants scattered along the East Coast to a central sale point in the Midwest, its profit margin could be noticeably affected. Although who pays for shipping expenses varies with each transaction, it is not unusual for a lessee to pay only for shipping charges to a general transportation shipping point near where the equipment is used.

➤ Recommendations

- Prospective lessors without access to inexpensive equipment storage facilities should consider negotiating the right to store equipment on the prospective lessee's premises at the end of a lease until a buyer or new lessee can be found.
- Prospective lessees should be cautious about giving a lessor the right to store equipment on their company premises at the end of a lease until a buyer or new lessee can be found, unless they can do so without, or with minimal, cost. If you, as a prospective lessee, must agree to do so, put a time limit on how long it may be stored, and take no responsibility for insurance or loss while in storage. You may want to consider charging the lessor a storage rent.
- Prospective lessees must carefully consider the potential expense exposure in agreeing to return equipment to a particular return point, particularly when many items are involved. For example, a trucking pickup location may be much closer and, therefore less expensive, than the nearest railhead. Having the right to choose between alternative return locations may also be advisable. Circumstances can change, and it may turn out to be more practical to transport the equipment to, for example, the nearest railhead instead of the nearest truck pickup point.

18. Events of Default

If a problem arises that would jeopardize a lessor's rights or interest in the lease or the equipment, the lessor should be in a position to end the lease and take other action as may be appropriate such as reclaiming the equipment. The various problem situations that could give rise to this type of lessor right should be clearly specified in every lease agreement. Those situations are generally referred to as events of default.

a. Nonpayment of Rent

The lessee's failure to pay the rent, when and in the amount due, should always be an event of default. Rent payment is a fundamental obligation, and a lessor should expect the fullest attention to it, perhaps allowing for a reasonable overdue payment grace period for unavoidable delays.

➤ **Recommendations**

- Prospective lessees should seek both a reasonable overdue rent payment grace period and a lessor notice requirement. For example, the lease could provide that the failure to pay rent will not result in an event of default until a period of time, say five days, after the lessee has received written notice from the lessor of the nonpayment.
- If a lessor agrees to an overdue rent notice provision as described in the previous recommendation, it should make sure the proper controls are instituted to monitor the timeliness of the rent payments.

b.   Unauthorized Transfer

The lease should provide that if the lessee assigns or transfers the lease agreement or the equipment without the lessor's consent, there will be an event of default. The reason is the lessor enters into a lease transaction to a great extent relying on the quality and reputation of the lessee, so if assignments or transfers were freely permitted, the equipment could end up in the hands of an unacceptable third party. A sublease, for example, to someone who intended to use the equipment in a high wear operation could seriously jeopardize the equipment's anticipated residual value. By controlling transfers and assignments, a lessor can protect its investment position.

c.   Failure to Perform an Obligation

It is in the lessor's interest to have an expansive definition of event of default, so it may seek to declare a lease default if the lessee fails to observe or perform any condition or agreement in the lease. Whether a court would allow a lessor to actually terminate a lease agreement, no matter how minor the failure, may be open to discussion; however, the potential threat may keep a lessee in full compliance. Lawsuits are expensive even for the winner.

➤ **Recommendations**

- Many conditions and agreements in a lease may not be fundamental to the essence of the lease transaction, such as the correct marking of the equipment. Therefore, a prospective lessee should attempt to minimize the default risk by requiring that the breach be material before it gives rise to a default event.
- A good way for a lessee to avoid inadvertent lease defaults is to have the lessor obligated to give at least 30 days' prior written notice before a default can be declared. Lengthy notice requirements, however, could hinder a lessor's ability to move quickly to protect its equipment and should be carefully considered before being given.

d.   Material Misrepresentation

As explained, a lessor will often require the lessee to represent certain facts that a lessor deems critical to its decision to enter into the lease. Any misrepresentation of a material nature could subject a lessor to a risk that it would not otherwise have assumed had it known the actual facts. In many cases a lessor will rely on the lessee's representation that there have been no adverse changes in the lessee's financial condition between the date of the latest financial statements and the transaction's closing date. If a lessor discovers the representation was not true after the lease is signed, it should be entitled to declare a default even if the misrepresentation was inadvertent.

e. Bankrupt Lessee

The following should also constitute events of default: a court order or decree declaring the lessee bankrupt or insolvent; the appointment of a receiver, liquidator, or trustee in bankruptcy for a lessee under any state or federal law; any similar action that would expose the leased equipment to a third-party claim or otherwise endanger the lessor's position; or any voluntary act by the lessee that would lead to any of these events.

19. Lessor's Remedies Following an Event of Default

The lease should set out what remedies a lessor can pursue if a lessee defaults under a lease. Although doing so will not necessarily guarantee a lessor that a particular action will be permitted if the parties end up in court, it will put a lessee on notice, and thus may weight against any lessee objection.

Lease agreements incorporate many types of default remedies, usually representing nothing more than a commonsense approach to dealing with the default issue. The various remedies listed in a lease sometimes overlap, but from a lessor's viewpoint it is better to be somewhat redundant than to risk a claim that a certain course of action was waived by implication because of omission.

a. Court Action

The most obvious default remedy is a right to bring a court action to require the lessee to perform any breached obligation or to get money damages for the failure to do so. This standard type of remedy is available in a basic contract action.

b. Termination of the Lease

The lessor's right to terminate a lessee's rights under the lease, including its right to use the equipment, is a basic default remedy. As a part of this right, a lessor usually has the ability to enter the lessee's premises immediately and take possession of the equipment. The reclaiming right is particularly useful when a lessee's creditors are trying to attach assets as security for their claims.

c. Redelivery of the Equipment

Lessors commonly have the right to require a lessee to redeliver the equipment in an event of default. It usually imposes a greater burden than if the lease normally ran its course. For example, the lessee may have to redeliver the equipment at its own expense and risk, to any location that the lessor designates rather than to the nearest general transportation pickup point. In an adversary proceeding, the expanded right may have little more meaning than helping to measure damages because a great deal of cooperation cannot be expected from the lessee.

d. Storage of the Equipment

In a default situation, the lessor may not have a place to store the equipment readily. Thus, the lessor may want to obligate the lessee to store the equipment on its premises, free of charge, until the lessor can dispose of it following a default. Whether it is actually advisable to let a lessee retain control over the equipment is a separate issue that would have to be considered by the lessor when a default occurs. For example, a lessor may run the risk that other creditors would seize the equipment. Even though the creditors have no valid claim, the possible renting time lost and equipment deterioration could endanger the lessor's investment.

➤ **Recommendations**

- To avoid a prolonged storage obligation, a prospective lessee should place a time limit on any lessor storage right. If a time cannot be negotiated, the lessor at least should be committed to proceed to sell, lease, or otherwise dispose of the property diligently.
- Any lessor right to have the lessee store the equipment should be accompanied by a right to enter the storage area for any reasonable purpose, including inspection by a prospective buyer or new lessee.
- When the lessee stores the equipment, there is the issue as to the responsibility for its damage. A prospective lessee, therefore, should specify that the risk of damage through third-party acts during any forced storage period is on the lessor.

e.   Sale of the Equipment

A prospective lessor should insist that, after a lessee defaults, it can sell or otherwise dispose of the leased equipment, free and clear of any of the lessee's rights. However, the lessee should seek the right to have an offset of any proceeds received against any damages it otherwise owes.

➤ **Recommendations**

- The more a lessor receives from an equipment disposition, the less default damages a lessee may owe if it has a right to an offset. To ensure that the lessor undertakes the maximum disposal effort, a lessee should insist on an accounting of the disposition proceeds.
- If a prospective lessor agrees to credit any sale or re-leasing proceeds received from third parties against any amounts that a defaulting lessee would owe, it should limit the credit obligation to the net proceeds actually received. The expenses that the lessor incurs, for example, to lease the equipment should be deducted from the amount that the lessee would be entitled to receive as a credit. Also, until the money is in fact in the lessor's hands, it should not have to recognize any credit.

f.   Right to Hold or Re-Lease the Equipment

Besides being able to dispose of the equipment, a prospective lessor would want the right to "hold, use, operate, lease to others, or keep idle" any equipment that it has reacquired as a result of a lease default. Ideally, then, a lessor could take what action it deems to be in its best interest. If a court finds that the lessor did not act in a manner to minimize the damages suffered, it may limit any recovery that a lessor may be able to get.

g.   Liquidated Damages

A liquidated damage provision should always be included as an alternate default remedy. Under this provision, the parties agree on a method for determining to what damages the lessor is entitled if a default occurs. Generally, courts will uphold a liquidated damage arrangement if it fairly anticipates the losses that may result from the lessee's nonperformance, and is not a penalty.

Although there are no industry standard formulas used to measure the damages that a lessor would suffer because of a lessee's default, two types are frequently used. One provides for the lessee to pay an amount equal to the present worth of the aggregate remaining rentals that the lessor would have received, but for the default, reduced by the equipment's fair market sales value or the present worth of the equipment's fair market rental value over the original remaining lease term. The other calls for the payment of an amount equal to the equipment's stipulated loss value as of the date of default, reduced by the equipment's fair market sales value or the present worth of the equipment's fair market rental value over the original remaining lease term. A prescribed per annum discount rate, such as the prime commercial lending rate in effect at the time of termination, is incorporated into the liquidated damage formula for present worth computation purposes.

➤ **Observation** The discount rate agreed on to compute the present worth of the remaining rental stream can significantly affect what will be owed. Too often parties agree to arbitrary rates without considering the consequences. The higher the rate, the less the offsetting credit and the greater the damage amount payable.

> **Illustrative Example** *Liquidated Damage Formula Computation:* Company Able leased a $1 million aircraft to Company Baker for a ten-year term. As part of the agreement, the parties incorporated a liquidated damage formula that they considered to be a fair measure of the damages Company Able would suffer if Company Baker defaulted. The formula provided that Company Able would be entitled to an amount equal to the present worth of any remaining rents that would otherwise have been due but for the default, offset by the present worth of the aircraft's fair market rental value over the original remaining lease term. The per annum discount rate to be used to compute the present worth was specified as 10%, the current prime lending rate at Company Able's bank. At the end of the fifth year Company Baker defaulted. For simplicity we will assume that the rents are payable annually, in advance. The facts are as follows:
>
> Unexpired lease term . . . . 5 years
> Annual rent $120,000
> Annual fair market rental value $100,000
>
> The present worth of the remaining rents under the lease, calculated using a 10% discount rate, is $500,384. The present worth of the aggregate fair market rental value over a five-year period is $416,986. The amount that the lessee owes is $83,398, the difference between the present worth of the unpaid rents and the fair market value rents.
>
> If the parties had agreed on a discount rate of 8% instead of 10%, the lessee would owe $86,242 instead of $83,392. On the other hand, if the discount rate were 12% instead of 10%, the lessee would owe $80,747. Obviously, the discount rate should not be treated lightly.

➤ **Recommendation** Because the future fair market rental value is an estimate, the actual rentals may be higher or lower, resulting in either an underpayment or overpayment by the lessee. To solve this situation, both parties might consider the possibility of allowing for a future adjustment if the actual amounts vary from the appraisal.

20. *A Lessor May Want Certain Lease Assignment Rights*

Prospective lessors frequently ask for the right to assign their interest in a lease and the equipment at any time during the term. Although a general assignment right sometimes makes prospective lessees uneasy, it should not cause concern if properly negotiated. To help protect its rights, a prospective lessee could insist that any assignment not adversely affect its lease rights.

a. Assignment to a Lender

In many cases, a lessor's lenders will require as part of their credit arrangement that the lessor incorporate in all leases a provision giving the lenders a right to an assignment of the rights, including title to the equipment, if certain loan restrictions are violated. Generally, the purpose of the assignment provisions is to enable a lender to take over the leases as security if there is a loan default. If an assignment requirement exists in a lessor's loan agreement, it must be in each lease agreement, and it is not a negotiable point between the lessor and lessee. In certain situations, a lessor may want to have the ability to borrow a portion of the equipment purchase cost from a lender on a nonrecourse basis. To do that, the lessor usually must assign to the lender all the lessor's lease contract rights, such as the right to receive uninterrupted rentals.

➤ **Recommendation**   Any time a prospective lessee must agree to allow a lessor to assign any or all of its interest in a lease to its lenders, the lessee should require that any such transfer be subject and subordinate to the terms of the lease. Thus, if there is an assignment, the lessee's rights, including the right to use the equipment, will in no way be jeopardized by the lessor's assignment of its rights to the bank. The lease should provide that any transfer will not relieve the lessor from its obligations under the lease, to assure a prospective lessee that it will always have what it originally bargained for.

b. Assignment to an Investor

A lessor will sometimes want the right to sell the lease, including title to the equipment, to a third party. Under this arrangement, the third-party buyer would become the equipment owner, would take subject to the terms and conditions of the lease agreement, and would therefore become the lessor. The original lessor would no longer have rights or duties under the lease.

A broad assignment right can expose a lessee to certain risks. A lease sold to a financially unstable lessor, for example, may endanger the lessee's right to the continued use of the equipment because of potential creditor actions against the new lessor. In addition, an assignment to a lessor who is difficult to deal with can create problems, for example, when the lease must be modified.

➤ **Recommendations**
- A prospective lessor seeking a lease assignment right should also seek the right to require the lessee to execute any documents necessary to effect the assignment. Without that right, a lessee could, intentionally or unintentionally, block the assignment.
- A lessee may want some control over a lease assignment. For example, if the lessor assigned the lease to any of the lessee's banks or lending institutions, that assignment could restrict the lessee's borrowing capability. To prevent this problem, the lessee could request the right to pass on any potential transferees or, if a prospective lessor is unwilling to grant such a right, it could specifically define the limits of who would be acceptable.

21. A Lessee May Want Certain Equipment Sublease Rights

A lessee with the right to sublease equipment is in the best position to lessen or eliminate the impact of having to pay rent on assets that become unproductive because of changes in use needs during the lease term. If there are no restrictions, such as those that would limit transfers to affiliated companies only, a lessee will have the maximum flexibility.

➤ **Recommendations**

- Prospective lessors consenting to a subleasing right should insist that the lessee remain primarily liable under the lease agreement during the sublet period.
- Prospective lessees desiring subleasing rights should avoid agreeing to any exercise conditions, such as having to obtain the lessor's prior written consent. Time wasted waiting for a consent could result in lost revenue.
- From the lessor's perspective, however, it may not be advisable to give a prospective lessee an unrestricted right to sublease the equipment to any party, even though the original lessee will remain primarily liable under the lease. Having the right to pass judgment on any proposed sublessee will prevent knowing transfers to parties who may misuse the equipment or who are financially unstable. Regardless of the original lessee's primary responsibility, misuse can diminish the equipment's value, and a sublessee's bankruptcy could interfere with the equipment's return.

22. Lessor's Options to Renew, Sell, or Terminate

There are a few situations when a prospective lessor will want certain rights that are not usually requested, such as a right to terminate the lease in a non-default situation, a right to force a sale of the equipment to the lessee, a right to force the lessee to renew a lease, or a right to abandon the equipment. These rights can create substantial tax problems or be otherwise undesirable from a lessee's viewpoint. Thus, if proposed, their possible effect should be carefully reviewed.

a. The Right to Terminate the Lease

It is conceivable, although extremely unlikely, that a prospective lessor would want the ability to terminate a lease *for any reason it chooses* during its term without the lessee's consent. For example, if a prospective lessor believes the rental market will rise before the end of the negotiated lease term, it may want the ability to go after a better rate.

➤ **Recommendation**   A prospective lessee should not put itself in a position where a lessor could prematurely terminate the lease without the lessee's prior consent and without reason.

b. The Right to Force a Sale of the Equipment to the Lessee

In certain situations a prospective lessor will insist on having the right (commonly referred to as a put) to force a lessee to buy the equipment under lease at the end of the term. Generally, this right is expressed as a fixed percentage of the original equipment's cost rather than a defined dollar amount. For example, a lessor may have the right to sell the equipment to the lessee for an amount equal to 10% of cost. In effect, a put eliminates any risk that a lessor will not realize the assumed residual value that, in turn, protects its anticipated profit. Transactions involving certain types of store fixtures or equipment that will be difficult or uneconomical to move, such as certain heavy storage tanks, sometimes incorporate a forced sale right.

➤ **Recommendations**

- The use of a put may impair the tax status of a lease transaction (see Chapter 7). Puts should be incorporated only with the advice of tax counsel.
- If a prospective lessor insists on having a put, the prospective lessee should make sure it will not be required to indemnify the lessor for any loss of tax benefits a lessor can suffer if the put causes the lease not to qualify as a true tax lease.

c. The Right to Abandon the Equipment

In the past, equipment abandonment rights were used in leases of equipment that would be difficult and costly, if not totally impractical, to reclaim if the lessee decided not to buy at the end of the term. A good example of the type of leases that involved abandonment rights were those relating to certain kinds of commercial storage tanks that were so large that the only way to move them was to cut them into pieces and then reweld them at the new site. In these situations, the expenses involved could be so great that the lessor could not reasonably recoup them through a re-leasing or a sale.

Lessors sometimes attempt to solve an equipment removal expense problem by requiring the equipment to be delivered to them at the end of the term at the lessee's expense. If the lessee refuses to do so, however, the lessor's only recourse, without a right of abandonment, would be to bring a lawsuit to force the lessee to live up to its agreement or possibly pay for any resulting damages. If the lessee is in financial trouble, a lawsuit may be of little use. Having an abandonment right allows the lessor to drop the property in the lessee's lap and rid itself of any lingering responsibility or expense exposure.

➤ **Recommendation** The lessor's right to abandon the equipment is prohibited under the IRS guidelines and can create serious tax lease treatment problems (see Chapter 7). It should be used only on the advice of tax counsel.

d. The Right to Require a Lease Renewal

In situations when an abandonment right or a put might be considered, a lessor may instead use a forced lease renewal right. Under this right, a lessor could make the lessee re-lease the equipment at a predetermined rental.

➤ **Recommendation** The right of a lessor to require a lessee to renew a lease could also run afoul of the IRS guidelines and can create serious tax lease treatment problems. It should be used only on the advice of tax counsel.

23. *Lessee Options to Buy, Renew, Terminate, or Upgrade the Equipment*

Invariably, a prospective lessee will ask for certain rights, referred to as options, that will enable it to maintain some form of control over the equipment's use, such as an equipment purchase right, a lease renewal right, or a lease termination right. Generally these types of options are willingly granted by prospective lessors.

a. The Right to Buy the Equipment at Fair Market Value

A prospective lessee typically wants the option to buy the leased equipment at the lease's end. In many situations this is done through a fair market value purchase option. Basically, the option gives the lessee the right to buy the equipment for whatever its fair market value is at the time of purchase.

Although the term *fair market value* appears self-explanatory, the parties should agree on a method for its determination. Generally, the fair market value of a piece of equipment is the amount that a willing buyer under no compulsion to purchase would pay a willing seller under no compulsion to sell in the open market. As a practical matter, however, how is the value actually determined between a lessor and a lessee? Typically, it is done through an equipment appraisal. The parties can designate in the lease an independent appraiser who will evaluate the equipment at the appropriate time.

Alternatively, the parties can each select an independent appraiser to make an assessment when necessary. If the two appraisers cannot agree on a satisfactory value, then they must jointly select a third appraiser, whose opinion will be binding.

➤ **Recommendation** A fair market value purchase option can be an expensive way for a lessee to acquire equipment with a typically strong resale value. A purchase price cap is sometimes negotiated to limit how much the lessee would have to pay. For example, the lessee would have the right to buy the equipment at fair market value or 30% of the equipment's original cost, whichever is less. A cap can present tax problems, however (see Chapter 7).

b. The Right to Buy the Equipment at a Fixed Price

When equipment has traditionally maintained a favorable resale value, many companies refuse to lease because a fair market purchase option coupled with the lease rents could result in an economically unfavorable way of acquiring it. As a result, a fixed price purchase option is sometimes given to induce them to lease. Under a fixed price purchase option, commonly referred to as a call, the lessee can buy the equipment at the end of the lease for a predetermined price. The price is usually expressed as a percentage of the equipment's original cost. For example, the lessee may have the right to buy designated equipment for 35% of cost. In this way, the lessee knows the maximum amount of money he will have to spend if he wants to buy the equipment when the lease is over.

➤ **Observation** A lessee fixed price purchase option can cause a lease to fail to be characterized as a lease for federal income tax purposes. If the exercise price is so low that the lessee may, in effect, have a bargain purchase right, the IRS may be able to challenge successfully its status as a true tax lease. Fixed price purchase options therefore should be granted with care, and only with the advice of tax counsel, if it is important that a lease qualify as a true tax lease.

c. The Right to Renew the Lease at Fair Rental Value

Providing a lessee with the right to renew a lease at the equipment's fair market rental value at the time of renewal is acceptable, both from the standpoint of the IRS and, generally, the lessor. The parties can determine the fair rental in a manner similar to that of determining the fair market purchase value, through independent appraisal at the time of the intended renewal.

➤ **Recommendation**   When equipment is vital to a prospective lessee's operations, the lease renewal terms must be adequate to cover anticipated needs. For example, if a four-year renewal is desirable, an option that would allow a selection of two two-year periods, four one-year periods, one one-year period followed by a three-year period, or a four-year period would provide much flexibility as to term and rental rate. Such a structure would give the lessee the ability to limit its renewal costs in a high rental market or to lock in for a longer time in a low rental market. From a lessor's viewpoint, too much latitude on the lessee's side can lessen its chances of maximizing its renewal profits; therefore, any such arrangement should be considered carefully as to the possible future effects.

d.   The Right to Renew the Lease at a Fixed Price

Prospective lessees sometimes request a fixed price renewal option. By knowing in advance the exact dollar amount of the renewal rents, they know where they would stand if they wanted to continue to use the equipment beyond the main lease term. This would not be possible with a fair market renewal option.

➤ **Observation**   A fixed price renewal right may result in adverse tax consequences (see Chapter 7); thus, the amount of fixed renewal option must be carefully considered.

e.   The Right to Terminate the Lease

It is not uncommon for a prospective lessee to have the ability to terminate a lease early, particularly when it believes the equipment could become technically obsolete or surplus to its needs before the lease would normally end. When this right is granted, the lessee frequently will be required to pay the lessor a predetermined amount of money, commonly referred to as the termination value, on exercise. Because most lessors do not like to grant termination rights, the termination amount is usually high.

f.   The Right of First Refusal

A purchase right of first refusal is sometimes used as an alternative to a fair market value purchase option. Under this option, a lessee is given the right to buy the leased equipment at the end of the lease term under the same terms and conditions as offered by an unaffiliated third party. The disadvantage to using it is that a lessee may run the risk that a competitor may bid for the equipment either to push the price up or to acquire it for its own operations.

Illustrative Language   *Right of First Refusal:* Unless an Event of Default shall have occurred and be continuing at the end of the term of this lease, or any event or condition which, upon lapse of time or giving of notice, or both, would constitute such an Event of Default shall have occurred and be continuing at such time, the lessor shall not, at or following the end of the term of this lease, sell any item of equipment (including any sale prior to the end of such term for delivery of such equipment at or following the end of such term) unless:

1. the lessor shall have received from a responsible purchaser a bona fide offer in writing to purchase such equipment;
2. the lessor shall have given the lessee notice (a) setting forth in detail the identity of such purchaser, the proposed purchase price, the proposed date of purchase, and all other material terms and conditions of such purchase, and

(b) offering to sell such equipment to the lessee upon the same terms and conditions as those set forth in such notice; and

3. the lessee shall not have notified the lessor, within 20 days following receipt of such notice, of its election to purchase such equipment upon such terms and conditions.

If the lessee shall not have so elected to purchase such equipment, the lessor may at any time sell such equipment to any party at a price and upon other terms and conditions no less favorable to the lessor than those specified in such notice.

g. The Right to Upgrade Financing

At times, companies lease equipment, such as computer systems, that requires upgrading during the lease term to ensure maximum performance by adding additional equipment or modifying the original equipment. Typically such an upgrade may not be done without the lessor's prior written consent and, in some situations, it may be of such a nature, for example, internal equipment modifications which have no stand-alone value, that no one other than the original lessor would consider financing it. In these situations the incumbent lessor has absolute negotiating control over the financing and can charge the lessee more than the going market rate.

➤ **Recommendation** Prospective lessees—to avoid having to accept whatever rate an incumbent lessor offers for equipment upgrade financing when no other lessor may be willing to finance an upgrade—should insist on having an option to require equipment upgrade financing on reasonable terms. The upgrade financing right should be at a predetermined fixed lease rate, or at a rate which is to be determined in accordance with acceptable standards at the time of financing, such as the original lease rate adjusted for changes in the lessor's debt borrowing rate.

24. A Defaulting Party Should Lose Certain Options

Generally the lease should provide that the party holding an option forfeits its exercise right, if it is in default under the lease. For example, the lessee should lose its right to buy the equipment under a purchase option if the lease is terminated because of default on its part.

25. Designate the Law Governing the Lease

It is always advisable for the parties to specify what jurisdiction's law will apply to their rights and obligations under a lease agreement. For example, the parties can agree that all actions on lease issues will be decided under the laws of New York State, regardless if the proceedings are instituted in a New York court. By doing this, the attorneys are able to draft the documents under the law they believe will give the fairest known outcome.

26. Severability Clause

The lease should include a severability clause, providing that any lease provision determined to be legally unenforceable will be served. Under this clause, the severed provision is treated as though it never existed. This may prevent the entire lease agreement from being held invalid if only certain provisions are unenforceable.

27.   The Interest Penalty for Late Payments

A lease agreement should prescribe the interest rate that will be charged on any overdue payments, such as delinquent rent payments. This will eliminate disputes over late charges and will assist in assessing damages if a lawsuit arises.

➤ **Recommendations**

- When the lease specifies an overdue payment interest penalty, the prospective lessor should also incorporate a qualification that the rate will in no event be higher than the maximum enforceable legal rate to avoid any potential enforceability problems if the legal limit is inadvertently exceeded.
- Prospective lessors will want interest on overdue obligations to run from the date the money is due to the payment date. Prospective lessees, on the other hand, should attempt to get it to run from the date the lessee receives written notice of the overdue obligation from the lessor.

28.   The Lease Should Identify Where and How to Send Any Required Notifications and Payments

Although leases usually provide that all required notifications and payments, such as loss notifications and rent payments, must be promptly made, they sometimes fail to identify exactly where they should be sent. As a result, payments or notifications could be misdirected and money or valuable time lost. The lease should therefore expressly state the appropriate mailing addresses.

In addition to specifying where payments and notifications must be sent, the lease should specify the notification and payment manner. For example, it may be agreed that a notice will be deemed given when it is deposited in a U.S. mailbox, sent by prepaid telegraph, or sent by certified mail.

29.   The Lease Should Be Correctly Signed

All parties to a lease should make sure it is signed in the proper capacities. Leases to be signed by an individual representing himself generally do not present any problems. Leases to be signed by an individual representing a firm, such as a partnership, corporation, or trust, are sometimes troublesome. If, in the latter case, the signature is not made in the correct representative capacity, the represented firm may not be bound. For example, if a vice president intends to sign on behalf of the corporation, the signature block should be set up as follows:

XYZ Corporation

by _____

R. Smith, Vice President

If the signature form is not correct, the signing individual may run the risk of being held *personally* liable on the contract, which is certainly a less than desirable outcome for all parties concerned.

D. Checklist for Drafting and Negotiating a Lease Agreement

In preparing a well-drafted lease agreement, the parties should cover the important issues involved in a transaction. The following checklist pinpoints the issues frequently encountered.

- **What form of lease is appropriate?**
  - Single transaction lease
  - Master lease
- **Should a master lease be used?**
- **Does the lease agreement cover the following issues?**
  - Has a page index of all topic headings been included?
  - Have the parties been properly identified?
    1. Lessor
    2. Lesser
  - Is the lessee a valid legal entity?
  - Has a factual summary of the circumstances giving rise to the transaction been included?
  - Has the consideration for the transaction been stated?
  - Have the following key terms been defined in a definition section?
    1. Affiliate
    2. Business day
    3. Buyer-furnished equipment
    4. Equipment delivery date
    5. Equipment manufacturer
    6. Event of default
    7. Event of loss
    8. Fair market value
    9. Indenture
    10. Interim rent
    11. Lease
    12. Lease period
    13. Lease supplement
    14. Lessor's cost
    15. Lien
    16. Loan certificates
    17. Loan participant
    18. Overdue interest rate
    19. Primary rent
    20. Casualty loss value
  - If equipment will be delivered after the lease is signed, has a procedure for adding it been established?
    1. Can the lessee decide not to lease future delivered equipment when it arrives? If so, will the lessee be obligated to pay other fees?
       a. A nonutilization fee?
       b. A commitment fee?
    2. Can future delivered equipment be accepted for lease as it arrives or must the lessee aggregate a minimum dollar amount?
  - The lease period should be defined.
    1. Will there be an interim lease term? If so, when will it begin and end?
    2. When will the primary term begin?

3. How long will the primary term run?

4. Will the lessee be permitted to renew the lease? If so, what is the renewal period arrangement?

- The rent structure must be defined.
    1. Will a percentage rent factor be used? If so, what may be included in the equipment cost base?
        a. Sales tax
        b. Transportation charges
        c. Installation charges
        d. Other
    2. How much rent must be paid?
    3. When will the rent be due?
    4. How must the rent be paid?
        a. Check
        b. Wire transfer
        c. Other
    5. Where must the rent be paid? Has a post office box or other address been specified?
    6. Can or must the lessor adjust the rent charge if there is a tax law change affecting, favorably or unfavorably, the lessor's economic return?
        a. If a rent adjustment is provided for, has the exact criterion for making it been clearly specified?
        b. If the tax law change applies to future delivered equipment and a rent adjustment is not acceptable, can the party adversely affected elect to exclude the equipment?
    7. Will the rent obligation be a hell or high water obligation?
- What is the lessor's total dollar equipment cost commitment? Will a percentage variance be permitted?
- Will the lessee be required to submit reports? For example:
    1. Financial reports
        a. Profit and loss statements
        b. Balance sheets
        c. Other
    2. Accident reports
        a. Has a minimum estimated accident dollar amount been agreed upon below which a report is not required?
        b. Will the lessee be obligated to immediately telephone if a accident occurs?
    3. Lease conformity reports
    4. Equipment location reports
    5. Third-party claim reports
- Has a time been established for when lessee reports are due?
- Has a general lessee reporting requirement been imposed as to reports that may be deemed necessary by the lessor in the future?
- Equipment maintenance
    1. Who has the responsibility for ensuring proper maintenance?
        a. Lessor
        b. Lessee
        c. Third party

    2. Who must bear the cost of the maintenance?

      a. Lessor

      b. Lessee

    3. Will maintenance records be required? Will the lessor be permitted access to the maintenance records? If so, at what times:

      a. Normal business hours

      b. Any time requested

- Will equipment alterations be permitted?
  1. Will the lessor's consent be required before the following?
     a. An addition that may impair the equipment's originally intended function or that cannot be removed without so impairing such function
     b. Any change
  2. Who will have title to any addition or other alteration?
     a. If it can be easily removed without equipment damage?
     b. If it cannot be removed without function impairment?
     c. What rights will the lessor have to buy the alteration?

- Will certain lessor ownership protection filings be advisable or necessary?
  1. Federal regulatory agencies, such as the Federal Aviation Administration
  2. Uniform Commercial Code
  3. Other

- If lessor ownership protection filings will be made, who has the responsibility for making them and who must bear the expense?
  1. Lessor
  2. Lessee

- If the lessee must make required filings for the lessor, will the lessee have to confirm they have been made?

- Will the equipment be marked with the lessor's name and address? If so, who will have the marking responsibility and expense?
  1. Lessor
  2. Lessee

- Has the lessee been specifically prohibited from using, operating, storing, or maintaining the equipment carelessly, improperly, in violating the law, or in a manner not contemplated by the manufacturer? If the lessee must use the equipment for a purpose other than intended, an exception should be negotiated.

- The lessee must be required to provide certain key representations.
  1. That the lessee is properly organized, validly existing, and in good standing.
  2. That it has proper authorization to do business in the state where the equipment will be located.
  3. That the lessee has the transactional authority to enter into the lease.
     a. That necessary board of director approvals have been obtained covering the transaction *and* the person signing the lease on behalf of the lessee.
     b. That any other required approvals have been obtained.
  4. That there are not conflicting agreements.
     a. Bank credit agreements
     b. Other loan agreements
     c. Mortgages
     d. Other leases
  5. That all necessary regulatory approvals have been obtained.

6. That there are no pending or threatened adverse legal or administrative proceedings that would affect the lessee's operations or financial condition.
7. That there have been no adverse changes as of the lease closing in the lessee's financial condition since the latest available financial statements.

- The lessor must be required to provide certain key representations.
    1. That the lessor has the transactional authority to lease the equipment.
        a. That any necessary board of director approval has been obtained.
        b. That any other approvals have been obtained or, if none are required, a statement that none are required.
    2. That the lessor will pay for the equipment in full.
    3. That the lessor will not interfere with the lessee's use of the equipment. Has an exception when the lessee is in default been negotiated by the lessor?
- The lessee should require product warranties to be assigned if the lessor has no equipment defect responsibility. If the warranties are not assignable, the lessor should be required to act on the lessee's behalf.
- Who has the responsibility for equipment casualty losses?
    1. Lessor
    2. Lessee
- Do the casualty loss values give adequate financial protection to the lessor?
- Are the casualty loss values competitive from the lessee's viewpoint?
- As of what time will a casualty loss be deemed to have occurred—has a loss date been defined? What obligations change or come into effect on the loss date?
- When is the casualty loss value payable and when does interest on the amount payable begin to run?
- What taxes must be paid?
    1. Sales tax
    2. Property taxes
    3. Rental taxes
    4. Withholding taxes
    5. Income taxes
    6. Other
- Who must pay the taxes?
    1. Lessor
    2. Lessee
- For any taxes that a lessee must reimburse a lessor for payment, does the lessee have the right to have the taxes contested? What happens if the lessor does not fully pursue its contest remedies?
- Is each party required to immediately notify the other of any tax imposition for which they will be responsible?
- Do the parties intend a true tax lease? If so,
    1. Inconsistent actions and filings should be prohibited.
    2. Will tax loss indemnifications be required?
    3. Will any tax indemnity cover all lessor tax losses or only those resulting from the lessee's acts or omissions?
- Who has the economic risk of a change in tax law?
    1. For past delivered equipment
    2. For future delivered equipment
        a. Can either party elect not to lease if the economics are no longer favorable?

- Has a formula been agreed on for measuring the amount of any tax benefit loss and the amount of any required reimbursement?
  1. Does the formula make the indemnified party whole?
  2. Is the formula absolutely clear?
- Has the tax loss date been determined?
- Who has the expense responsibility for the equipment return and where must it be returned:
  1. If the lease ends normally?
  2. If the lease ends prematurely?
- May either party designate an alternate return location? If so, what is the expense responsibility?
- The lessor should be able to terminate the lease early or take other protective action in certain situations.
  1. When the rent is not paid
  2. When the lessee makes an unauthorized transfer of the equipment or any of its rights under the lease
  3. When there is a general failure to perform the obligations under the lease
  4. When the lessor discovers the lessee has made a material misrepresentation
  5. When there is a bankruptcy or similar event that would jeopardize the lessor's position
- The actions that the lessor may take in the event of default must be specified.
  1. Court action
  2. Terminate the lease
  3. Cause a redelivery of the equipment
  4. Cause the lessee to store the equipment
  5. Sell the equipment under its own terms
  6. Be able to hold or re-lease the equipment
  7. Be entitled to a predetermined amount of money as damages for a lease default
- Certain lessor assignment rights may be desirable or required.
  1. To a lender as security
  2. To an investor
- Will the lessee be able to sublease the equipment?
  1. Will the lessee remain primarily liable under the lease during the sublease period?
  2. Will the lessor have any control over who the sublessee will be?
- Have all the lessor's options been included?
  1. Right to terminate the lease
  2. Right to force a sale of the lessee
  3. Right to abandon the equipment
  4. Right to force a lease renewal
- Have all the lessee's options been included? For example:
  1. A purchase right
     a. Fair market purchase value
     b. Fixed purchase price
  2. A renewal right
     a. Fair market purchase value
     b. Fixed price rental
  3. A termination right

    4. A right of first refusal
    5. An Upgrade financing right
- Will a defaulting party retain any of its option rights under the lease?
- Has the law of a jurisdiction been specified to control any issues that arise under the lease?
- Is there a severability clause?
- Is there any interest penalty for overdue payments?
- Has each side specified how and where any required notifications and payments will be made?
    1. The address where notifications and payments must be sent
    2. The manner in which notifications and payments must be made
       a. U.S. mail
       b. Other
- Has the signature section been set up properly for the parties?
    1. An individual
    2. A corporation
    3. A partnership
    4. A trust
    5. Other
- Has the signature been made in the proper capacity?

E. Summary

The lease document sets out the business arrangement into which both the lessor and the lessee have agreed to enter their rights and duties. The document must be carefully reviewed and written, covering all aspects that may or should come into play in the lease deal. This cannot be done without understanding each aspect of a typical lease contract and what negotiating leeway is fairly and reasonably available.

Chapter 4

Closing the Lease Financing

A. Overview

Once the terms and conditions of the lease agreement have been negotiated it is time to have it put in final form and prepare for the lease closing. At the closing, all parties will sign the lease agreement and fulfill any closing conditions identified or requested in accordance with the lease or other governing papers, such as the lessee delivering to the lessor any specified collateral documents requested. These collateral, or supplemental, documents range from those that essentially provide comfort on specified issues, such as opinions of counsel, to those that define critical supportive arrangements, such as guarantee agreements. The collateral documents are an integral part of the finance closing: If the lessee, for example, is unable to provide any, the lessor has no obligation to provide the financing.

The leveraged lease closing is the most complex, because of the added participant, the third-party equipment lender (see Chapter 1). Even though the actual leveraged lease agreement does not differ radically from that of a nonleveraged lease, additional supplemental closing documents are usually involved, such as a security and loan agreement, to accommodate the loan arrangement requirements.

Although drafting the supplemental papers will be the responsibility of the transaction's lawyers, the business people should understand the fundamental concepts involved so they can review the papers to ensure they accurately reflect the agreements reached. Having an understanding of the purpose of the collateral documents also will enable the business participants to more readily negotiate compromises when the lawyers reach impasses. The purpose of this chapter is to provide an overview of the closing document so the reader will know in advance what to expect and can facilitate a smooth closing.

One final point before we begin. While this chapter provides a general working knowledge of the typical collateral lease documents, keep in mind that most transactions have their own unique aspects that must also be taken into account.

B. Legal Opinions

1. *Function of Legal Opinions*

In large ticket and, at times, middle market lease transactions, legal opinions are typically required by lessors and, in some cases, by sophisticated lessees. Before going into the various opinions possible and what they might address, let us see what the practical value of such an opinion may be from a business point of view. First it is important to understand what a legal opinion does *not* do. It does not guarantee that the conclusions expressed in the opinion are correct. Regardless of the quality of the lawyer's work in preparing the opinion, a court or administrative agency may interpret the law or facts differently—and their decision, not the legal opinion, will be controlling. A legal opinion, however, provides the recipient with value.

- It provides the participants with a significant degree of comfort, because the lawyer's opinion usually will be correct.
- In drafting the opinion, the lawyer will need access to relevant information; thus, writing it may bring to light transaction trouble spots that can be corrected.
- If a court or agency disagrees with the opinion, having it may help show that the parties exercised due care in entering the transaction and may prevent the imposition of any penalties.

The problem with legal opinions is they are invariably qualified by, for example, stating a specific set of facts on which they are based. To the extent that the relevant facts are not properly conveyed to the lawyer providing the opinion, the opinion may be of little value.

➤ **Recommendations**

- Although legal opinions often make the recipient feel secure on the issues covered, at times more certainty is required. For example, a lessor or lessee concerned about whether a certain lease structure qualifies as a lease for federal income tax purposes is often well advised to consider getting an IRS ruling on the issue.
- The expertness of the lawyer providing an opinion is a critical consideration, particularly when complex legal issues are involved. Therefore, if you need a legal opinion in a lease transaction, choose a lawyer with solid leasing experience.

2. *Opinion from Lessee's Lawyer*

The lessor should ask the lessee to have its attorney deliver a legal opinion on relevant legal issues. The opinion's goal is to provide the lessor with assurances that no legal issues exist that will undermine the lease transaction. Thus, a lessor will typically want the lessee's lawyer to opine whether:

- The lessee has been properly organized, is validly in existence, and is in good standing under the laws of its state of incorporation.
- The lessee has the authority to enter into the lease.
- The lessee has the ability to perform all of its lease obligations.
- All the lessee's lease commitments are legally binding.
- Any consents, such as those of the shareholders or lenders, are necessary and, if so, whether they have been obtained.
- Any regulatory approvals, such as a state public utility commission, are necessary and, if so, whether all the proper action has been taken.
- There are adverse pending or threatened court or administrative proceedings against the lessee and, if so, their probable outcome.
- The lessee would violate any law, rule, or provision of any of its existing agreements by entering into the lease arrangement or complying with any of its terms.

3. *Opinions from Lessor's Lawyer*

a. To the Lessee

In certain situations, particularly in large ticket, underwritten leveraged lease transactions, the lessee should obtain an opinion from the lessor's lawyer concerning the lessor's legal ability to enter into and perform its obligations. That opinion should minimally confirm that the lessor is properly:

- Incorporated or organized, as the case may be, at the time the lease is signed
- Qualified to do business in the state where the equipment will be used, to avoid, for example, any risk that the equipment could be attached by the state authorities for the nonpayment of any taxes that the lessor may owe.

b. To the Lender

An equipment lender should always request a written opinion from the lessor's lawyer on key issues relating to its loan arrangement with the lessor. This type of opinion generally covers the same issues as those covered in the opinion given to the lessee, For example, whether:

- The lessor is duly organized, validly existing, and in good standing in its state of incorporation.
- The necessary transaction authorizations have been secured.
- The lessor's obligations under the loan documents are fully enforceable.

If the equipment loan is to be nonrecourse to the lessor, thus permitting the lender to look only to the lease payments and equipment for repayment, the lender also will want an opinion stating that:

- The lessor has good and marketable title to the equipment covered by the lease.
- The equipment is free and clear of any liens or encumbrances other than those of which the lender is aware.
- The lessor has made no other lease assignments.
- The lender has a free and unencumbered right to receive all payments, such as rent, under the lease agreement.

➤ **Recommendation**   A prospective lessor should consider requiring an opinion from the prospective lender's lawyer confirming that all the necessary action in connection with the loan's authorization has been taken. Because many prospective lessors are grateful to get the loan, they sometimes neglect to determine if it was properly authorized. A loan without proper authorization may be withdrawn.

4. *Opinion from the Guarantor's Lawyer*

In many situations, a third party will guarantee the lessee's lease obligations. For example, the parent company of a financially weak corporate lessee may be asked to guarantee the lease obligations as a condition to the lessor's lease commitment. In that case, the strength and viability of the guarantor's commitment is critical to the lessor and any nonrecourse equipment lender. To help confirm the guarantee's worth, a lessor should request a favorable opinion from the guarantor's lawyer on the applicable aspects.

Such an opinion should address legal issues that relate to the guarantor's ability to fulfill the guarantee. For example, the opinion may be required to state whether:

- The guarantor is duly organized, validly existing, and in good standing.
- Anything exists that could adversely affect the guarantee's quality, such as material litigation.
- The guarantee has been fully and properly authorized.
- The guarantee is a legally enforceable obligation.

5. Opinion from the Vendor's Lawyer

Usually the vendor of the leased equipment is not asked to provide any legal opinion because it has only to deliver clear title to the equipment; and an adequate bill of sale containing proper seller representations and warranties typically gives the necessary comfort. In certain situations, particularly if a substantial dollar amount of equipment is involved, a prospective lessor might want to ask the equipment vendor for its lawyer to provide a legal opinion confirming that the vendor has, upon equipment payment, delivered clear title to the equipment.

C.   Financial Reports

The financial strength of every party to the lease transaction, such as the lessor, the lessee, and any third-party guarantor, is key to the lease financing; thus reliable and up-to-date financial information must be obtained. The degree of information necessary depends on the transaction's size. A lease of a $900 office copier will not warrant the same degree of investigation as that for the lease of a multimillion dollar printing press.

1. Why Financial Information Is Necessary

a.   Of the Lessor

The financial condition of a lessor is an important lessee consideration. A solid lessor contractual commitment to lease is worthless if it has no funds available when the equipment arrives for lease. All too often a prospective lessee fails to check the lessor's financial condition, apparently assuming that a lessor always has adequate funds and that, once the deal has been signed, there is nothing to be concerned about. This may not be true. A financially weak lessor may have no purchase funds available when the equipment is ready for lease. Even if the equipment has been paid for and put on lease—although unlikely—there is a risk that such a lessor's creditors may seize the leased equipment as security for an unpaid obligation.

The availability of adequate funds for equipment purchase is of particular concern if a lease line of credit is involved, that is, when the lessor has committed to buy and lease many items of equipment to be delivered over a long period. Any lack of available lessor financing when equipment arrives could be a serious problem for a would-be lessee.

b.   Of the Lessee

Similarly, the lessee's financial condition is a critical element in the lessor's decision as to whether to enter into a particular lease financing, particularly if a multimillion dollar, long-term lease is involved. So at all times, the lessor, particularly at the lease closing and when it must advance funds, will want to be assured that the lessee has the financial capability to meet its contractual obligations, including payment of rent, for the full lease term.

c. Of a Controlling Corporation

If the lessee is owned by another company, often a lessor will want to review the parent company's financial statements, even if the parent does not guarantee the lease obligations and regardless of the financial strength of the lessee. The weaker the financial condition of an owning company, the greater the possibility that it will drain the lessee's cash to solve any financial problems.

➤ **Recommendation** When there is risk that a controlling corporation could drain a perspective lessee's cash, a lessor must take precautions. One such precaution is to impose a restriction on the amount of dividends that the lessee can declare and distribute to the controlling corporation.

d. Of the Guarantor

If the lessee's financial condition is inadequate, as a condition to going forward with the financing, the lessor may ask for a transaction guarantee from a financially solid entity, such as a parent company or equipment vendor. In this event, the guarantor's financial strength is of primary importance and relevant financial information will be included in the closing.

2. *Type of Financial Information Needed*

Typically, the financial condition of a company can be adequately assessed in a review of its past and present financial statements, including profit and loss statements and balance sheets. A lessor may require bank and trade references to further verify the financial integrity of the company being reviewed. A lessor may also check, particularly in the case of smaller companies, with credit reporting services such as Dunn & Bradstreet for adverse information on file.

Often the lessor's financial review is done prior to its issuing a lease proposal offer, but sometimes it is not done until shortly after the lease award. In any event, it is always well in advance of starting the documentation negotiation. As a result, the lessor will typically ask that the financially reviewed entity, particularly when there is a long time between the review and the lease signing, bring its financial information up to the closing date.

One common way a participant's financial picture is brought up to the transaction's closing date is to require the reviewed entity's financial officer to deliver a certificate at the closing that presents relevant financial information since the last published statements. For example, if the most current financial statements reflect a company's condition as of June 15, 20XX, and the transaction does not close until September 25, 20XX, the certificate must essentially provide that as of the closing date, September 25, 20XX, there have been no materially adverse financial changes since the date of the latest financial statements, June 15, 20XX. Of course, it would be more comforting to get the company's independent accountants to issue the certificate, but is generally not practical.

➤ **Recommendation** It is always wise for any other party concerned to request updates as of the lease signing from any party whose financial condition may affect the transaction's viability. So, for example, a lessee might consider requiring a financial update from a lessor whose financial condition it deemed necessary to review before making an award. This may be done through a financial certificate from the lessor's financial officer.

D.   Corporate Authorization Documents

When a corporation participates in a lease transaction, the other parties generally should require a copy of the corporation's board of directors' resolutions authorizing the transaction. The resolutions should be certified by the corporate or assistant secretary and delivered at the closing. The typical lessee corporate resolution, for example, will state that the lessee has been duly authorized to enter into the transaction for the specified dollar amount and that a certain person has been authorized to execute the documents on behalf of the corporation.

➤ **Recommendations**

- Although lessors and lenders usually require lessees to deliver appropriate board of directors' resolutions at a lease closing, lessees rarely ask for authorizing resolutions from the other parties. They should seriously consider doing so, however, particularly from corporate lessors and lenders not regularly engaged in leasing or lending.
- If the participant is not a corporation, and, for example, is a limited partnership, your attorney should be consulted about what authorization assurances might be advisable.
- If, after the lease has been signed, you discover that a key party failed to get the necessary corporate board of directors' transaction approval, you should immediately request that it deliver appropriate resolutions approving, ratifying, and confirming all actions that have been taken.
- Whereas board of directors' resolutions should be reasonably broad in scope, corporate directors must be careful not to grant more than is necessary. For example, if a lease transaction is to involve a large conveyor system, its cost should be specified with leeway for reasonable changes. Without designating the cost, an individual representing the corporation may be able to bind it to a lease even if unexpected and significant cost increases occur.

E.   Guarantees

When a prospective lessee wants to lease more equipment than its credit capability justifies, it will be asked for additional credit support. Often the lessor will suggest that a financially strong third party be brought in to guarantee the lessee's obligations. The guarantee request may vary anywhere from a full guarantee of all the lease obligations to something significantly less.

The most favorable guarantee for a lessor would be a full lessee guarantee, where the guarantor unconditionally obligates itself to ensure the lessee's full and prompt performance of the lease obligations, covenants, and conditions. For example, if the lessee fails to pay the rent, the lessor could go directly to the guarantor for payment.

Under a partial guarantee, the guarantor may, for example, only be responsible for the repayment of 15% of the total lease payments. Partial guarantees may be acceptable to a lessor when the proposed transaction is financially attractive.

F.   Proof of Insurance Documents

Frequently, the lease agreement will require that the lessee have personal injury and property damage insurance covering the leased equipment. In these cases, the lessor will want the lessee to confirm that the insurance will be in effect when the equipment is accepted for lease. That confirmation should be required to be delivered at the lease closing and will take the form of a certificate of insurance from the lessee's insurance company stating that the necessary coverage will be in effect.

➤ **Recommendations**

- A certificate of insurance should be obtained and carefully reviewed well in advance of the lease closing to verify that the coverage outlined is proper and will be in effect when necessary. A lessor should pay particular attention to any coverage limitations, such as restricted equipment usage; and a prospective lessee should clear the insurance coverage with a prospective lessor in advance of the closing. Finding out at the closing that the insurance certificate is inadequate will not only be embarrassing, but delay the financing. The best approach is to send a draft certificate to the lessor weeks ahead of the closing for its review and acceptance.
- A lessor should insist that the required insurance coverage cannot be canceled without prior written notice, and only after an adequate grace period, to give it an opportunity to take out insurance if the lessee fails to keep it in force. Insurance companies are willing to make such a commitment when asked

G.   Equipment Purchase Agreements

Unless the equipment has been built or is already owned by the lessee, the lessor has to purchase it from a third-party supplier. If the equipment is available at the time the lease is signed and is ready for lease acceptance, the lessor simply buys it at that time. If not, an equipment purchase contract may have to be entered into, ordering the equipment.

At times vendors, knowing the equipment will be put on lease, ask that the lessor enter directly into the purchase agreement. For a variety of reasons this situation is rarely a good idea for the lessor or the lessee. If the lessee, with or without justification, refuses to accept the equipment for lease, the lessor may still be legally obligated to buy the equipment—something it will not want to do if it has no lessee for it. Thus, if a purchase agreement must be executed early, the prospective lessor should insist that the lessee be the signing party.

From a lessee's viewpoint, it is always advisable to enter into the purchase agreement directly with the equipment vendor and then assign only its right to purchase the equipment to the lessor, subject of course to the lessor fulfilling its lease commitment. This is typically done by using a purchase agreement assignment. Under such an assignment, the lessee has direct contract rights with the supplier on warranty or other equipment-related claims and the lessor has what it needs—the right to purchase the equipment directly from the supplier.

Here's how a purchase agreement and assignment might work. The lessee and the equipment supplier enter into the necessary purchase agreement, and then the lessor and the lessee enter into an assignment of this agreement. Under the assignment, the lessor generally acquires the lessee's contract purchase right, but not its obligations. The assignment may also provide that the lessor will acquire additional rights, such as service or training, as well as all buyer warranties or indemnities, as of the time the lease ends and the equipment is returned to the lessor. Further, the assignment often states that the lessee shall remain liable on the purchase contract as if the assignment had not been made and requires the supplier's written consent to the assignment. The supplier is also often asked to specifically acknowledge that the lessor will not be liable for any of the purchase contract duties or obligations.

➤ **Recommendations**

- If a prospective lessor enters into a purchase agreement assignment, it must be careful not to assume any of the buyer's duties or obligations under the purchase agreement. The assignment should specify that the prospective lessee will remain liable on the purchase contract as if the assignment had not been made.
- When a prospective lessor enters into an equipment purchase agreement assignment, it should at the same time get the supplier's written consent to the assignment. The consent should acknowledge the assignment and provide that any rights assigned (such as supplier warranties) will accrue to the lessor's benefit as though it had been originally named as the buyer. The supplier also should be asked to acknowledge that the prospective lessor will not be liable for any of the purchase contract duties or obligations.

H.   An Equipment Bill of Sale

A prospective lessor generally requires that the equipment seller deliver a bill of sale when it pays for the equipment. Typically, the bill of sale is a warranty bill of sale in which the seller not only transfers equipment title, but also warrants that it has delivered to the purchaser full legal and beneficial ownership to the equipment, free and clear of any encumbrances, mortgages, or security interests. Such a bill of sale commonly has a seller representation that it has the lawful right and the appropriate authority to sell the equipment.

➤ **Recommendation**   A prospective lessor should insist that the bill of sale, in addition to typical seller representations and warranties, contain a seller representation that it will defend the lessor's title to the equipment against any person or entity claiming an interest in the equipment.

I.   Waivers from Land Owners or Mortgagees

The leased equipment is often located on real property leased from a third party or that is subject to a mortgage. In this case, statutory lien rights may exist that, for example, permit a landlord to attach any equipment on its land, including leased equipment, if its rent is not paid. Similarly, the holder of a mortgage on a lessee's building may, under a general mortgage claim right, be able to go after leased equipment located in the building. In these situations, the prospective lessor should require as a closing document, a waiver from the landlord or mortgagee of any claim to the leased equipment.

J. Security Interest Filings

Although not technically necessary in a typical equipment lease situation, a lessor will generally want to file appropriate information-only UCC financing statements to provide added insurance that it in fact has priority over other parties who may claim an interest in the equipment, particularly the lessee's creditors. If a UCC financing statement was necessary (for example, because the lease was in fact a conditional sale or other type of loan transaction, secured by the equipment) and is not filed (or not correctly filed), the lessor's claim to the equipment will not be perfected (prior in right) as to the lessee's other creditors. Simple in form, the statement basically requires nothing more than a description of the parties and the equipment. The UCC financing statement filing will be a condition of the lease closing. The filing procedures are routine, and the expenses are nominal.

K. Participation Agreements

A participation agreement—a closing document setting out the lease financing's structural terms and conditions—is frequently used in underwritten lease transactions, particularly leveraged transactions. The parties to such an agreement may include the lessee, the equity participants, the debt participants, and any trust established for the debt or equity participants. The participation agreement states the terms under which the debt participants must make their loans and the equity participants must make their equity investments. It also generally incorporates a method for substituting any defaulting participants, and may include any prescribed tax indemnification provisions.

L. Owner's Trust Agreement

It is not unusual for a trust to be established for equity participants in a leveraged lease transaction, particularly if more than one equity participant is involved. The trust arrangement, referred to as an owner's trust, provides the equity participants with corporatelike liability protection and partnershiplike income tax treatment, and thus can be a desirable ownership vehicle.

To set up a trust, the equity participants enter into a trust agreement with an entity, such as a bank, that will act as the trustee, referred to as the owner trustee. The agreement sets out in detail how and to what extent the trustee will act on behalf of the equity participants.

As part of its trust obligations, the trustee will execute all relevant documents, including the lease, any participation agreement, the indenture, and any purchase agreement assignment, on behalf of each equity participant. The right, title, and interest in the equipment, the lease, any purchase agreement, and any purchase agreement assignment is collectively referred to as the trust estate, and legal title to it is held in the owner trustee's name. The owner trustee is, however, only a figurehead owner, the beneficial interest in the trust estate residing with the equity participants. The equity participant's interests are represented by certificates, referred to as owner certificates, issued by the owner trustee.

M. Lender's Trust Agreement

If the financing is structured as a leveraged lease, the debt participants will typically act through a trust arrangement which enables them to receive favorable tax treatment and liability protection. The arrangement is typically set up through a trust indenture and mortgage agreement entered into between the equity participants and debt participants. A trust indenture and mortgage agreement defines the basic debt financing parameters and provides for issuing loan certificates that set out the debt repayment obligations. The agreement also grants a security interest to the lenders in the equipment and the lease while the loan is outstanding. As with a participation agreement, it will be one of the lease closing documents.

The debt trust structure is similar to the equity trust structure. The debt participants are represented by a trustee, referred to as the loan trustee. (It stands in the same position to the debt participants as the owner trustee to the equity participants.) As the lender's watchdog, the trustee can take any prescribed action that may be necessary to protect the debt participants' interests, such as foreclosing on the lease in case of default.

N. Using a Partnership Instead of a Trust Arrangement

At times, multiple equity or debt participants find it undesirable or impractical to act through a trust arrangement. Instead, they frequently use a partnership structure. Here, the "lessor" or "lender," as the case may be, is the partnership, with the equity or debt participants as partners in the partnership. It's usually advisable for a formal partnership agreement to be entered into that defines each partner's rights and obligations. The agreement will be a part of the lease closing.

O. Underwriter's Fee Agreement

In underwritten transactions, the lease underwriter will be responsible for bringing together the equity participants, the lessee, and, if the transaction is leveraged, the debt participants. For its services, the underwriter will be entitled to a fee, typically varying with each transaction and each broker, and typically payable by the equity participants. To protect itself and prevent later misunderstandings as to the payment terms, the underwriter may ask that the equity participants enter into a formal fee agreement clearly defining the fee arrangement, which will also be included as a closing document

P. Supplemental Lease Document Closing Checklist

Although the type of additional closing documents required in a lease transaction will vary with each situation, the following checklist can be used as a general guideline.

Legal Opinions

- Is the lawyer who is rendering the legal opinion thoroughly experienced in the area to be covered by the opinion? Fox example, if an opinion is required on complex tax issues, is the lawyer fully knowledgeable on all relevant aspects?
- How much has the legal opinion been conditioned? In other words, has the lawyer left so many outs as to his or her position that he or she really has provided little comfort?
- To the extent that the legal opinion is based on facts supplied to the lawyer, are the facts accurate and complete?

Does the opinion of the lessee's lawyer, to be delivered to the lessor, address the following issues?

- Proper organization, valid existence, and good standing of the lessee
- The lessee's full authority to enter into the lease
- The lessee's complete and unrestricted ability to perform all obligations
- Whether all the lessee's lease commitments are legally binding
- Whether all necessary consents have been obtained
- Whether all necessary regulatory approvals have been obtained
- Whether there are any pending or threatened adverse court or administrative proceedings and their potential impact
- Whether any law, rule, or collateral agreement will be violated by the lessee entering the lease transaction

Does the opinion of the lessor's lawyer, to be delivered to the lessee, address the following issues?

- Whether the lessor is properly organized, validly existing, and in good standing
- Whether the lessor is properly authorized to do business in the jurisdiction where the equipment will be located
- Whether the transaction has been fully authorized by the lessor. For example, have all necessary committee and board of director approvals been secured?
- Whether the lessor's commitments are binding
- Whether the lessor's ability to perform its obligations is unrestricted
- Whether any shareholder, lender, etc., consents are necessary. If so, have they been obtained?
- Whether the transaction will violate any law, rule, or collateral agreement as to the lessor

Does the opinion of the lessor's lawyer, to be delivered to a third-party lender, address the following issues?

- Whether the lessor is properly organized, validly existing, and in good standing
- Whether all necessary authorizations, both as to the lease financing and the loan financing, have been obtained
- Whether the loan obligations are fully enforceable against the lessor
- Whether the lessor has good and marketable title to the leased equipment
- Whether the equipment has any liens or encumbrances on it
- Whether the lessor's rights under the lease are unencumbered, including its right to receive the rent payments

Does the opinion of the guarantor's lawyer, to be delivered to the lessor, address the following issues?

- Whether the guarantor is properly organized, validly existing, and in good standing
- Whether all necessary authorizations as to the lease financing have been obtained
- Whether the lease obligations are fully enforceable against the guarantor

Does the opinion of the vendor's lawyer, to be delivered to the lessor, address the following issues?

- Whether the title of the equipment will be delivered free and clear to the lessor
- Whether all necessary internal authorizations have been obtained

Has the lessor been supplied with the required lessee, lessee controlling corporation, and guarantor financial statements?

- Profit and loss statements
- Balance sheets
- Officer's certificate updating the prior financial statements to the closing

Have adequate lessor financial statements or information been obtained?

- Profit and loss statements
- Balance sheets
- Officer's certificate updating the prior financial statements to the closing

Have all the critical financial statements been certified by an independent certified public accounting firm?

Has a certified copy of any relevant corporate board of director resolutions been delivered?

If the lease obligations will be guaranteed by a third party, will it be a full and unconditional guarantee? If not, is the limited extent of the guarantee understood?

If personal injury and property damage insurance is required, does the insurance company's certificate of insurance properly represent the required insurance?

If the lessor must enter into an equipment purchase agreement directly with the vendor, is it prepared to buy the equipment if the lessee backs away? If not, can a purchase agreement assignment be used?

- Does any equipment purchase agreement assignment specifically provide that only the rights, not the obligations, will be transferred to the lessor?
- Under an equipment purchase agreement assignment, will the lessor be entitled to all vendor-supplied services, training, information, warranties, and indemnities?
- Has the vendor's consent been obtained as to the purchase agreement assignment?
    1. Does it acknowledge the assignment?
    2. Does it acknowledge that the lessor will not have to buy the equipment if the lessee backs out before the lease is executed?

Has an equipment bill of sale been included?

- Is it a warranty bill of sale?
- Does it contain a representation that the seller has the lawful right and authority to sell the equipment?

If the equipment will be located on leased or mortgaged property, has the landowner or mortgagee supplied a written waiver of any present or future claim to the leased equipment?

Have appropriate UCC financing statements (UCC-1) been prepared for filing?

If the transaction is underwritten:

- Has a participation agreement been prepared?
- Will the lenders and the equity participants each act through:
  1. Trust arrangement
  2. Partnership arrangement

Has a fee agreement been prepared to formalize the underwriter's fee arrangement?

Q. Summary

The ancillary documents that accompany the closing of a lease transaction are often overlooked until the last minute, and then given little thought because of their supplemental nature. These documents, however can give rise to problems, concerns, or issues that can prevent or unduly delay a lease transaction closing. Understanding what they are and how they work will facilitate avoiding costly closing issues.

Chapter 5

Tax Advantages in Lease Transactions

Introduction

A lessor's ability to write off, or depreciate, the cost of the leased equipment is crucial to the economic viability of many equipment lease transactions. Prior to 1986, there was another important tax benefit often available to an equipment lessor: an equipment investment tax credit. The investment tax credit (ITC) offered a taxpayer a big reward for buying new equipment—a 10% credit. Like other credits, the ITC did not merely reduce taxable income, but rather offset, dollar for dollar, the equipment owner's federal income tax liability. The 1986 Tax Reform Act (TRA) dramatically changed the ITC picture. Except for certain transition property—generally property in the works before 1986—the ITC was eliminated by the TRA. It should be noted that, at the time of this writing, there have been numerous proposals for various changes to the tax laws to stimulate the U.S. economy to enhance or otherwise change the equipment ownership tax attributes. Of particular importance to both equipment lessors and users is a recent enactment into federal tax law; the provision for an additional 30% first-year special depreciation allowance for certain qualified property placed into service by the taxpayer after September 10, 2001, referred to as "bonus" depreciation.

A.   Investment Tax Credit

Because ITC is not at this time a generally available tax benefit, a detailed discussion about how ITCs work is beyond the scope of this book. In the government's on-again, off-again pursuit of economic stimulus, however, it is still possible that the ITC will again appear, so a brief explanation may be of use.

Basically, the ITC's purpose was to encourage investment in new equipment to stimulate economic growth. The tax writers also used ITCs to encourage the growth, development, and stabilization of a business area that the federal government sought to promote.

The ITC rules implemented that purpose by permitting an equipment owner to claim a tax credit in an amount equal to a specified percentage of the cost of equipment bought in a particular tax year against its potential tax liability for that same year. Generally, for equipment placed in service before January 1, 1986, a taxpayer could claim a maximum investment tax credit equal to 10% of the cost of equipment acquired during a tax year. Thus, for example, a taxpayer buying an equipment item in a particular tax year that cost $1,000,000 could reduce its federal income tax liability by an amount equal to $100,000 (10% x $1,000,000 = $100,000) for that year. If a taxpayer would have owed

$250,000 in federal income taxes for the purchase year apart from the ITC, it would actually have to pay only $150,000 ($250,000 – $100,000 = $150,000) after claiming the ITC. Given that tax reduction, the ITC played a major role in equipment leasing.

As stated, the TRA virtually eliminated ITCs, thus magnifying the importance of equipment depreciation benefits to equipment owners. The TRA was not all bad from an equipment lessor's point of view, because it enhanced depreciation deductions for most equipment. It stands to reason, therefore, that a prospective lessor must have a thorough understanding of the depreciation rules to evaluate a leasing transaction. These rules are also important to a prospective lessee for two reasons:

- Unless the benefits available are fully understood and evaluated, an intelligent lease versus purchase analysis cannot be made.
- If a prospective lessor requires depreciation indemnities, the lessee cannot properly assess the potential risks without a clear appreciation of the technical intricacies.

➤ **Note**   If a transaction that purports to be a lease in fact does not qualify as a true lease for federal income tax purposes, the lessor is not entitled to depreciate the leased asset. See Chapter 7 for an explanation of the guidelines that determine if a transaction will qualify for true lease classification under the tax rules.

We now examine the depreciation rules for equipment (personal property).

➤ **Caution**   The depreciation rules explained in this chapter may be altered if the alternative minimum tax applies, so Chapter 6 must be read in conjunction with this chapter.

B.   Equipment Depreciation—An Overview

Among the wide-reaching changes introduced by the 1986 TRA was Section 168 Modified Accelerated Cost Recovery System (MACRS)—a revised depreciation system discussed in Chapter 1. Replacing the existing Accelerated Cost Recovery System (ACRS) depreciation rules, the MACRS rules generally apply to property placed in service by a taxpayer on or after January 1, 1987, with certain exceptions.

Although MACRS incorporates some of the ACRS concepts, substantial and fundamental differences exist. MACRS, for example, retains the concept of property classes, but reclassifies certain assets into different property classes (also called recovery classes), and adds more classes. There were also changes in depreciation methods and in depreciation conventions.

Under MACRS, three depreciation methods, six recovery periods, and two averaging conventions apply to equipment, depending on a variety of factors.

C.   Property Eligible for MACRS

Besides meeting the MACRS requirements, to be depreciable, equipment must pass muster under Section 167(a). Section 167 establishes the basic rule authorizing an equipment owner to a deduction, in computing federal income tax liability, for the exhaustion, wear, and tear of property used in a trade or business or held for the production of income. All depreciation deductions under MACRS and previous systems must fulfill those threshold requirements: The property must be depreciable (for example, land is considered not to wear out and so is not depreciable) and must be used in a business or income-producing activity.

Generally, property qualifying under Section 167(a) may be depreciated under MACRS. The following types of property, however, are excluded:

- Intangible property (e.g., copyrights, licenses). This property also does not qualify for ACRS and is amortized under other rules
- Property classified as public utility property (unless the taxpayer uses a normalization method of accounting)
- Certain property that a lessor has elected to apply a depreciation method not expressed in terms of years (such as the unit of production method)
- Motion picture films, video tapes, sound recordings (such as music tapes)
- Property covered by MACRS antichurning or transition rules

When property is transferred in a nonrecognition transaction under Sections 332, 351, 361, 371(a), 374(a), 721, or 731, MACRS may be used for only a portion of the equipment's basis. Certain property also must be depreciated under an alternative MACRS method, described later in this chapter.

D. MACRS Deduction Computations

Four steps determine the annual MACRS depreciation deduction amount for any leased equipment: (1) Determine the total amount to be depreciated; (2) determine the applicable MACRS recovery class from among the six classes; (3) apply the appropriate depreciation method; and (4) incorporate the applicable convention.

1. Total Amount to Be Depreciated

The total amount a lessor can write off for acquired equipment, and thus the annual deduction amount, depends on the lessor's basis in the equipment. For MACRS purposes, basis is determined under general Internal Revenue Code rules for determining the gain or loss on the sale or other disposition of an asset, and includes not only what the lessor paid for the equipment but also the costs incurred in acquiring the equipment. A lessor must reduce the basis so calculated by any amount expensed under Section 179, and if the lTC is available because of a grandfathering provision, a lessor must account for that ITC. There is, however, no reduction for salvage value.

2. MACRS Recovery Classes

MACRS continues, with modifications, the recovery class concept instituted by ACRS. The recovery class concept represents the current solution to the long-standing tax question: Over how long a period should depreciation deductions be spread? Before 1971, the lessor took depreciation deductions over an estimate of the equipment's useful life, determined by the facts and circumstances. While having the virtue of potential accuracy, the facts and circumstances method was cumbersome and difficult for both taxpayers and the IRS to administer.

In 1971, the IRS simplified matters by promulgating the Class Life Asset Depreciation Range System (ADR). ADR set out a list of prescribed asset classes. Generally, an asset's useful life was determined by referring to the list.

In 1981, the Economic Recovery Tax Act (ERTA) introduced ACRS. ACRS grouped assets based on their ADR class lives into recovery classes. For example, property with an ADR class life of more than 4 years, but less than 10, was put into the 5-year class. Under ACRS, all personal property fell into one of four personal property recovery classes. ERTA also replaced the various optional depreciation methods with statutory write-off periods.

MACRS continues the recovery class concept, grouping equipment into one of six recovery classes. Like ACRS, the MACRS recovery class grouping is based on the equipment's class life, assigned by the ADR tables. The ADR class lives for MACRS purposes are set forth in Revenue Procedure 87-57 (IRB 1987-42).

MACRS also assigns certain equipment to particular recovery classes notwithstanding their ADR classification. Property neither assigned to an ADR class life, nor specifically assigned by MACRS falls within the seven-year class. The Treasury has, within certain restrictions, the authority to shift the property assigned by MACRS from one class to another.

Following are the six recovery classes applicable to equipment:

- **3-Year Property** The 3-year MACRS class generally includes property with an ADR class life of four years or less (for example, special tools and devices for the manufacture of rubber products and special handling devices for the manufacture of food and beverages). Automobiles and light general-purpose trucks that have ADR lives of less than four years have been expressly assigned to the 5-year class.

➤ **Note** There are certain depreciation restrictions and requirements placed on passenger automobiles used for business. See Internal Revenue Code Section 280F for details.

- **5-Year Property** The 5-year property class generally includes equipment with an ADR class life of greater than 4 years and less than 10 years. Heavy general-purpose trucks, computer equipment, trailers and trailer-mounted containers, duplicating equipment, and typewriters are examples of types of equipment that come within the 5-year classification. Certain equipment is assigned to the 5-year class notwithstanding its ADR classification: automobiles; light general-purpose trucks; computer-based telephone central office switching equipment; semiconductor manufacturing equipment; qualified technological equipment; equipment used in connection with research and experimentation; certain specified biomass properties that qualify as small power production facilities under the Federal Power Act; and ocean thermal, geothermal, wind, and solar energy properties.
- **7-Year Property** The 7-year MACRS class generally includes property with an ADR class life of 10 years or greater but less than 16 years, for example, office furniture, fixtures, and equipment, and equipment used in the manufacture of tobacco and food products (other than those listed in the 10-year class). Railroad track and single-purpose agricultural and horticultural structures are specifically assigned by MACRS to the 7-year class.
- **10-Year Property** The 10-year MACRS property class generally includes property with an ADR class life equal to 16 years or greater but less than 20 years. This class includes equipment used in the manufacture of grain and grain mill products, sugar and sugar mill products, and vegetable oils and vegetable oil products, and equipment used in petroleum refining.
- **15-Year Property** The 15-year MACRS property class includes property with an ADR class life of 20 years or greater but less than 25 years. This class includes municipal sewage treatment plants, telephone distribution plants, and comparable equipment that is used for two-way exchange of voice and data communica-

tions. Cable television equipment that is used primarily for one-way communication is not considered "comparable equipment" for the purposes of this asset classification.
- **20-Year Property** The 20-year MACRS property class includes property with an ADR class life of 25 years and greater. Specifically included in this class by statute are municipal sewers.

3. Depreciation Methods

Under MACRS, the lessor recovers the equipment's cost over the number of years in the recovery class plus one, for example, three-year property yields deductions over a four-year period. For equipment in the 3-, 5-, 7-, or 10-year class, the lessor uses the 200% declining balance method of depreciation, with a switch to straight-line depreciation at the time that maximizes the deduction. For property in the 15- and 20-year classes, the lessor uses the 150% declining balance method with a switch to the straight-line method at a time that maximizes the deduction.

Under the declining balance method, the equipment owner calculates the depreciation deduction for any year by multiplying the asset's basis, reduced by any prior years' depreciation deductions, by the declining balance rate, and then multiplying by the percent available each year. Thus, an asset with a $100 basis and a five-year recovery period, the first year's depreciation is $40 (ignoring the averaging conventions):

$$\$100 \text{ basis} \times 2 \times 20\% = \$40$$

For the second year, the MACRS deduction would be $24:

$$\$100 \text{ basis} - \$40 \text{ first-year deduction} = \$60$$

$$\$60 \times 2 \times 20\% = \$24$$

And so on, for three more years.

At the point when the declining balance method yields smaller deductions than straight-line depreciation, the method switches to straight-line. The 200% balance method resulted in more accelerated deductions than had been available under ACRS. The IRS has calculated and published, in Revenue Procedure 87-57 (IRB 1987-42), the appropriate annual deductions applying the 200% and 150% methods for each MACRS recovery class (set out in the appendix).

A lessor can elect to use the straight-line depreciation method instead of the prescribed MACRS accelerated method established for MACRS property classes. If the election is made, it is irrevocable and applies to all MACRS eligible property within the same asset class that is placed in service during the relevant tax year. The assets within the class for which a straight-line method is elected are to be written off over the recovery period prescribed under the applicable regular recovery period.

➤ **Note** For certain depreciable computer software that has been acquired after August 10, 1993, and which is not an amortizable Section 197 intangible, the taxpayer may depreciate it using the straight-line method of depreciation over a 3-year period (see Internal Revenue Code Section 167 [f]). Prior to August 11, 1993, if the taxpayer received computer software with its computer and the cost of the software was bundled with the computer hardware cost (not separately stated), the taxpayer depreciated it with the computer hardware under MACRS over the specified 5-year recovery period. If the software cost was separately stated (unbundled), its cost had to be amortized over a 5-year period on a straight-line basis. If the software had a useful life of less than one year, it was simply expensed.

4. MACRS Averaging Conventions

In determining how to handle depreciation deductions under any system, there is an issue of how to handle placements in, and retirements from, services that occur during the year.

Generally under MACRS, a lessor recovers equipment costs using the half-year convention. Under that convention, equipment is deemed to have been placed in service at the midpoint of the year in which it was placed in service, regardless of when during the year it was placed in service. Similarly, an asset is deemed to have been disposed of or retired from service at the mid-point of the year during which it was disposed of or retired, regardless of when it was disposed of during the year. Thus, a lessor is entitled to one-half a full year's permitted depreciation in the year it places an eligible asset in service, and one-half a full year's depreciation in the year it disposes of or retires the asset from service. When there is a short tax year (a year less than 12 months), an asset is deemed to have been placed in service for a period of time equal to one-half the number of months in the short tax year.

To prevent taxpayers from abusing the half-year convention by bunching purchases at year's end, MACRS includes a mid-quarter convention, which kicks in if a taxpayer places in service, in the tax year's last quarter, over 40% of the aggregate bases of property placed in service during the tax year. Under the mid-quarter convention, all property placed in service (or disposed of) during a tax-year quarter is treated as though placed in service (or disposed of) in the middle of such quarter.

Author's Note

At the time of this writing, there have been governmental discussions of changes to this mid-quarter convention, as well as certain other write-off aspects.

---

5. Applying MACRS

To summarize: Find the appropriate recovery class and check the averaging convention. Then refer to Revenue Procedure 87-57 to find the MACRS deduction annual percentage. (Note: 3-, 5-, 7-, and 10-year classes are based on 200% declining method; 15- and 20-year classes use 150% method.)

E. Alternative MACRS Depreciation Approach

The 1986 TRA established an alternative depreciation system (ADS) that the lessor must use in certain select cases and can elect in other situations. Under ADS, a taxpayer generally is to compute its permitted depreciation allowance by applying the straight-line method, without making a basis reduction for salvage value, over a recovery period typically longer than that specified under the other MACRS approaches. The applicable averaging conventions—the half-year or mid-quarter convention—apply in the same situations as under the regular MACRS.

1. When Must ADS Be Used?

A taxpayer must use ADS to depreciate the following:

- **Equipment used predominantly outside the United States** This is equipment located for more than 50% of the time during a tax year outside the United States. To determine U.S. use, the rules relating to the ITC have been deemed to apply. Under the 1986 TRA rules, an additional special exception applies to the predominant use outside of the U.S. classification for property that qualifies as a satellite or other spacecraft or interest therein held by a U.S. person and that is launched within the United States.
- **Tax-exempt bond-financed property** This is equipment that has been financed out of the proceeds of tax-exempt bonds that were issued after March 1, 1986. It includes any property to the extent that it is financed directly or indirectly by an obligation, if the interest from that obligation is tax exempt.
- **Tax-exempt use property** This includes equipment that is leased to a tax-exempt entity under certain types of leases that do not fit specified Internal Revenue Code requirements (known as "disqualified" leases). A lease is considered to be a disqualified lease if, for example, its lease term exceeds 20 years.
- **Imported property** This is equipment produced or manufactured in a foreign country and is the subject of an executive order issued by the U.S. President. It is considered made outside the United States if it is completed outside the United States or 50% or more of its basis is attributable to value added outside of the United States. The president has the authority to issue an executive order for property brought in from a foreign country that either maintains burdensome trade restrictions that are not consistent with trade agreements or engages in discriminatory or other acts that unjustifiably restrict U.S. commerce.
- **For alternative minimum tax depreciation preference computation purposes** (Section 56[g][4]).
- **To figure the earnings and profits of a domestic corporation or a controlled foreign corporation** (Section 312[k][3]).
- **For listed property,** if the property's business use does not exceed 50% for the year.

2. When Can ADS Be Elected?

A lessor can elect to use ADS regarding any MACRS property for any MACRS-eligible tax year. The election, once made, is irrevocable and applies to all property in the class that the taxpayer has placed in service during the election year.

3. ADS Recovery Periods

Under ADS, the lessor will generally depreciate the equipment over the ADR class life period. The following are assigned specific recovery periods notwithstanding their ADR class lives:

- **5 years** Automobiles, light general-purpose trucks, semiconductor manufacturing equipment, computer or peripheral equipment, any high-technology telephone station equipment installed on the customer's premises, and any high-technology medical equipment
- **9.5 years** Any computer-based telephone central office switching equipment
- **10 years** Any railroad track

- **12 years** Personal property with no class life
- **15 years** Single-purpose agricultural or horticultural structures
- **24 years** Any municipal waste water treatment plant and any telephone plant and comparable equipment used for two-way exchange of voice and data communications

4. *Applying ADS*

Revenue Procedure 87-57 sets out tables to find the annual deduction percentage amount for equipment depreciated under ADS with a recovery period of 2.5 to 50 years.

F. Antiabuse Rules Under MACRS

Because MACRS generally permits more rapid deductions than prior systems, Congress was concerned that certain taxpayers might try to use MACRS on equipment previously placed in service through transfers not resulting in substantive ownership changes. To address this concern, MACRS incorporates antichurning provisions that precluded specified property from qualifying under MACRS rules. As a result, the 1986 TRA incorporated into law special provisions to prevent the improper churning so as to obtain enhanced benefits under the MACRS method. If one of the antichurning provisions applies, the taxpayer cannot use MACRS; thus, MACRS cannot be used if the equipment was any of the following:

- Owned or used at any time during 1986 by the taxpayer or a related person
- Acquired from a person who owned the property at any time during 1986 and, as part of the transaction, the property user remained the same
- Leased by the taxpayer to a person, or any person related to such person, who owned or used the property at any time during 1986
- Acquired in a transaction where the property user did not change, and it was not MACRS-eligible property in the transferor's hands

➤ **Caveat** These antichurning rules do not apply if, by using them, a taxpayer would receive a more generous write-off for the year the property was placed in service than under the MACRS method. These rules also do not apply to property, used for personal use before 1987, that first was used for business purposes after 1986, so that the property is deemed to have been placed in service when it is first used for business.

G. Special Depreciation Rules for Automobiles and Listed Property

Section 280F specially limits MACRS deductions available for automobiles and certain other equipment. MACRS deductions available for automobiles are limited to $2,560 for the first tax year; $4,100 for the second tax year; $2,450 for the third tax year; and $1,475 for each succeeding tax year. A lessor also must use ADS, rather than regular MACRS, for automobiles and other listed property costs, if the business use of the property fails to exceed 50% of its use. Listed property includes the following:

- Any property used as a means of transportation
- Any property of a type generally used for purposes of entertainment, recreation, or amusement

- Any computer or peripheral equipment (unless used exclusively at a regular business establishment and owned or leased by the person operating that establishment)

If the business use exceeds 50% of annual usage, and then, in a later year, drops below 50%, the lessor must recapture the excess of accelerated depreciation over the straight-line amount claimed in earlier years.

H.   Recapture

Generally, on disposition of MACRS equipment, the equipment owner must recapture, as ordinary income, the MACRS deduction—including any Section 179 deduction—up to the amount realized on the equipment disposition.

I.   Expensing

Under Section 179, an equipment owner can elect to deduct currently up to $17,500 of MACRS property used in the active conduct of its business. (The $17,500 limit is the total per taxpayer, not for each equipment item.) However, if a taxpayer places in service over $200,000 of Section 179 property in a year, the amount that can be expensed is reduced dollar-for-dollar by the excess over $200,000. Expensing is available to noncorporate lessors only if they meet the requirements of Section 46(e)(3), which describes when a noncorporate lessor may be eligible for ITC.

J.   MACRS Effective Dates

The 1986 TRA depreciation rules are generally effective for property placed in service on or after January 1, 1987, for tax years that end on or after that date. A lessor can elect to use the MACRS rules for property placed in service after July 31, 1986, and before January 1, 1987, if the property is not transition property. That election can be on an asset-by-asset basis and is irrevocable.

1.   Transition Rules

The general effective dates do not apply to property subject to transitional rules. Under the general transitional rules, MACRS does not apply to property placed in service after December 31, 1986, and pre-MACRS rules apply if the property:

- was constructed or acquired by the taxpayer under a written contract binding on March 1, 1986;
- was an equipped building (including equipment and machinery to be used in or incidental to the building), or a plant facility not housed in a building, on which construction began no later than March 1, 1986 under a specific written plan and greater than 50% of the cost was either incurred or committed no later than March 1, 1986; or
- was self-constructed property (constructed or reconstructed by the taxpayer) where that the construction or reconstruction started by, and at least the lesser of 5% of the property's cost or $1 million was incurred or committed by, March 1, 1986.

Transition property with an ADR class life of at least 7 years but less than 20 years must be placed in service before January 1, 1989. Transition property with a class life of 20 years or greater must be placed in service before January 1, 1991.

Special transition property rules apply to certain specified property. These include property that is an integral part of a qualified urban renewal project, certain projects that qualify under the 1978 Public Utility Regulatory Policies Act, property that is integral to carrying out certain supply or service contracts, and certain solid waste disposal facilities. The lessor writes off property that comes within the special transitional rules under pre-1987 depreciation rules.

2. Sale-Leaseback Rule

Property that qualifies as transition property in a lessee's hands, or that was originally placed in service by the lessee before January 1, 1987, may come within the pre-1987 depreciation rules if it meets certain sale-leaseback date requirements: The lessee must have placed the property in service by January 1, 1987, or the property must be covered by one of the transition rules described previously; and the property must be sold and leased back by the lessee no later than the earlier of the applicable transition dates or three months after it was placed in service.

K.   Bonus Depreciation

As mentioned at the start of this chapter, at the time of this writing there has been a federal tax law change of particular importance to both equipment lessors and users that allows for an additional 30% first-year special depreciation allowance for certain qualified property placed into service by the taxpayer after September 10, 2001. This "bonus" depreciation is available for the first taxable year specified qualified property is placed in service by the taxpayer and is computed by multiplying the depreciable basis of the qualifying property by 30%, and then adding to that the depreciation amount otherwise available, using for this calculation the property's original depreciable basis reduced by the 30% claimed as bonus depreciation. The rules are complex, and beyond the scope of this chapter. Therefore, the reader is referred to the federal tax rules [Internal Revenue Code Section 168(k)] for details. It is of use, however, to point out that one item of "qualified property" is tangible property depreciated under MACRS with a recovery period of 20 years or less.

L.   Summary

Before the enactment of the 1986 TRA, an equipment owner had available two key tax benefits: equipment depreciation and equipment investment tax credit for, generally, new equipment. The ITC offered an equipment purchaser an attractive tax benefit: the ability to offset dollar-for-dollar the equipment owner's federal income tax liability in an amount equal to the available ITC. The TRA, however, generally eliminated available equipment ITCs, but kept in place and enhanced the equipment owner's ability to write off (depreciate) the cost of its equipment.

Chapter 6

The Minimum Tax's Role in Leasing

A.   Introduction

The 1986 Tax Reform Act (TRA) enacted a tax applicable to corporations, an alternative minimum tax (AMT), replacing the previous add-on minimum tax. The 1986 TRA also expanded the coverage of the AMT applicable to noncorporate taxpayers. At the time of this writing there has been governmental talk of a repeal of, or adjustment to, the AMT.

The key to understanding the AMT is to understand that it is an "alternative" tax system. Essentially, it sets up a separate system of taxation that runs parallel with the regular tax system, with its own rules for deductions, credits, and income inclusion.

In the leasing community, the revised AMT has given rise to questions for both the prospective lessee and lessor.

- For equipment users, the key question is what effect any potential AMT liability may have on their decision to lease or buy equipment.
- For prospective lessors, the question is how to take account of the AMT in making their lease pricing decisions.

To answer these questions, it is necessary to understand the overall AMT. This chapter discusses the AMT in three parts. The first part explains the corporate AMT, in general. The second part summarizes the individual AMT, and the final part discusses the AMT implications for equipment leasing transactions.

PART I: THE CORPORATE AMT

A.   Overview

Before the 1986 TRA, corporations were subject to an add-on minimum tax—simply, a tax corporations had to pay in addition to their regular tax under certain conditions. A corporation became subject to that additional tax, computed at a 15% rate, if it reduced its tax liability through the use of certain tax preference items. For example, the amount by which accelerated depreciation, claimed on real property the corporation owned, exceeded straight-line depreciation could give rise to add-on tax liability.

The existing AMT alters the tax picture for many more corporations than had the prior add-on tax. Congress's intent in enacting the AMT was to stop profitable corporations from excessively reducing their tax liability through deductions, credits, and exclusions, in effect ensuring that corporations pay their "fair" share of federal income taxes.

This chapter will present an overview of the AMT rules so that the leasing implications can be addressed.

B. The AMT's General Approach

The conceptual approach under the corporate income tax rules is straightforward. The corporation first computes its income tax liability under the regular method prescribed by the Internal Revenue Code. It then calculates its AMT "tentative" tax under the AMT rules (referred to as tentative minimum tax, or TMT). If the TMT exceeds the "regular" income tax liability, the taxpayer must pay the TMT excess in addition to its regular tax liability. If there is no excess, only the regular tax is paid.

> **Illustrative Example**   White Corporation determines that its federal income tax liability computed under the prevailing "regular" rules is $120,000. Under the AMT tax system, White Corporation calculates that its TMT is $150,000. What is White Corporation's federal tax liability?
>
> Because the TMT is greater than the tax liability computed under the regular rules, White Corporation must pay its regular tax liability of $120,000 and, in addition, pay another $30,000, the excess of the TMT ($150,000) over the regular tax liability ($120,000). If its TMT were $110,000, White Corporation would pay only $120,000, its tax liability computed under the regular tax rules.

To determine its AMT, a corporation first calculates its regular taxable income. To the taxable income, the corporation adds preferences, adds or subtracts adjustments, and subtracts the AMT net operating losses (NOLs), resulting in its alternative minimum taxable income (AMTI). From that amount, the corporation subtracts an exemption, if available, up to $40,000.

The corporation then multiplies the result by the AMT rate (currently 20%) and subtracts any allowed foreign tax credits (FTCs) and investment tax credits (lTCs). This total is the corporation's TMT. The excess over the regular tax liability is the corporation's AMT.

➤ **Observation**   At first glance it may seem that the TMT would always be lower than the regular corporate tax liability because the AMT rate (currently at 20%) is much lower than the regular corporate income tax rate. This is often not the case because the AMT's income base, the AMTI, is significantly greater than the regular corporate tax income base.

The following shows the steps involved in computing the AMT, explained further in the following pages.

AMT Road Map

Regular Taxable Income

\+ AMT Tax Preferences
± AMT Adjustments (Other Than ACE Adjustment)

\= Tentative AMTI
± AMT ACE Adjustment
– AMT NOL

\= AMTI

                         – AMT Exemption
                         × 20% AMT Rate
                         – AMT FTCs and AMT ITCs

                         = TMT
                         – Regular tax liability (after allowable tax credits)

                         = AMT

➤ **Note** For tax years beginning after 1986, and before 1996, corporations are required to pay an environmental tax equal to $12 for every $10,000 of AMTI. See Internal Revenue Code Section 59A for more details on the environmental tax.

1. The AMT Tax Preferences

In determining if it has any AMT liability, a corporation's first step is to calculate the amount of its AMT tax preferences. The tax preferences that must be added to taxable income include the following:

a. Tax-Exempt Interest

Tax-exempt interest on certain "private activity bonds" issued after August 7, 1986, is an item of AMT tax preference. A "private activity bond" is essentially one issued by a state or local authority in which (1) more than 10% of the proceeds are to be used for private business use, and (2) either (a) more than 10% of the bond proceeds are secured with private business activity property or (b) more than 10% of the principal or interest on the bond is to be repaid from private business activity revenue.

There are certain exceptions to the tax-exempt interest inclusion rule. For example, tax-exempt interest on certain bonds issued to benefit specified charitable organizations is not a preference.

b. Charitable Contributions

For contributions of appreciated capital gain tangible personal property in a tax year beginning after 1986, and before 1991, and contributions of appreciated other capital gain property after 1986, and before 1993, there is an AMT preference in the amount that the donated property's fair market value exceeds the property's adjusted basis. The preference does not apply to carryovers arising from charitable contributions made before August 16, 1986. There is no tax preference for contributions of appreciated tangible personal property in tax years beginning after 1990, nor for contributions of appreciated other capital gain property after 1992.

c. Percentage Depletion

Under the percentage depletion method of determining deductions for certain natural resource reserves, corporations can take percentage depletion deductions exceeding the property's basis. When a corporation does that, it gives rise to a preference in the amount by which percentage depletion deductions exceed the property's adjusted basis. This was also a tax preference item under the prior tax law.

d. Intangible Drilling Costs

Intangible drilling costs (IDCs) were an item of tax preference for individuals under the prior tax law, and they are an AMT tax preference for corporations under the 1986 TRA. The portion treated as a preference item is the amount by which the excess of

(1) deductions determined by expensing IDCs over (2) deductions that would result from 10-year straight-line amortization of such costs is greater than 65% of the net income from oil, gas, and geothermal properties for such year.

➤ **Note**   Beginning after 1992, subject to certain restrictions, independent producers are not subject to this tax preference.

e.   Bad Debt Reserves for Financial Institutions

The amount by which reasonable bad debt reserve deductions exceed the deductions that would be computed based on the prior year's actual bad debt loss of certain financial institutions is deemed to be an item of AMT tax preference. The bad debt reserve preference was an item of preference under the prior tax law.

f.   Pre-1987 Real Property Depreciation

The amount by which the accelerated depreciation deductions on real property placed in service before 1987 exceeds the straight-line depreciation deductions on such property is an item of AMT tax preference. For personal holding companies, the same rule applies to leased personal property.

g.   Pre-1987 Pollution Control Facilities

The excess of the allowable rapid amortization deductions (generally over 5 years), on certified pollution-control facilities placed in service before 1987 over otherwise permitted depreciation deductions (usually 15 years), must be included as an item of tax preference.

2.   *AMT Adjustments*

In determining a corporation's AMT liability, certain specified adjustments must be made to its regular taxable income in computing its AMTI. The concept of adjustments evolved to address items that are actually deferral preferences—items where the timing of the deduction or income, as opposed to its amount, is the basis for its being treated as a tax preference. For an equipment item that a taxpayer depreciates on an accelerated basis, for example, the adjustment will be positive (added to regular taxable income in computing AMTI) in early years and negative (subtracted from regular taxable income in computing AMTI) in later years. The aggregate of the adjustments made over the item of equipment's depreciable life will net to zero.

➤ **Further Explanation**   Before the 1986 TRA, the AMT (applicable only to individuals) did not fully address a tax preference resulting from a timing difference. For example, for a deferral preference resulting from the excess of accelerated over straight-line depreciation, the later years AMT liability calculations did not consider that the regular tax deductions would be less than if the equipment had been depreciated on a straight-line basis over the equipment's depreciable life.

The corporate AMT includes numerous tax adjustments. The following briefly describes the most important ones, and lists adjustments of more limited application.

a.   Depreciation on Personal Property Placed in Service After 1986

A corporation must make an AMT adjustment for personal property placed in service after 1986, in the amount of the difference between the regular accelerated depreciation deduction and the AMT depreciation deduction. The AMT alternative depreciation deduction uses the 150% declining balance method (switching to a straight-line method at the time to maximize the allowance) over a specified AMT recovery period. The AMT recovery period for personal property is the period used for the Alternative Depreciation System: With certain exceptions, it is the ADR class life (see Chapter 5). The regular tax depreciation averaging conventions apply to AMT depreciation deductions (see Chapter 5).

The AMT depreciation deductions result in slower write-offs than the regular MACRS deduction. The result being a positive adjustment in the earlier years of an equipment's depreciation, and a negative adjustment in the later years.

▶ **Note** To determine gain or loss on an asset's disposition for AMT purposes, the asset's basis is adjusted using the AMT depreciation rules. As a result, the AMT basis may often be higher than the regular tax basis, causing any gain for regular tax purposes to be larger than the gain for AMT purposes.

b. Post-1986 Real Property Depreciation

For real property placed in service after 1986, the Alternative Depreciation System deduction, generally computed by using the straight-line method of depreciation over a 40-year period, must be used instead of the more regular accelerated depreciation deduction.

c. Post-1986 Pollution Control Facility Depreciation

For certified pollution-control facilities placed in service after 1986, a corporation must substitute, in calculating its AMTI, the straight-line method of depreciation over the facility's Alternative Depreciation System life for the 60-month amortization period permitted under the regular tax rules.

d. Mining Exploration and Development Costs

Mining exploration and development costs, which otherwise may be currently deducted, must be amortized over a 10-year period. Only costs that have been incurred or paid after 1986 come within this rule.

e. Long-Term Contracts

Long-term contracts that have been entered into by a corporation on or after March 1, 1986, can give rise to an AMT adjustment. A corporation must use the specified "percentage of completion" method of accounting for these contracts in computing its AMTI if any other accounting method, such as the completed contract or cash basis, had been used.

f. Dealer Installment Sales

Generally, a corporation that sells property in the regular course of business must report for AMT purposes all gains on property sales in the year the property is actually sold. In other words, a dealer is not permitted to recognize profits on the sale of dealer property for AMT purposes on the installment method. Property that is disposed of on or after March 1, 1986, is subject to this rule.

g. Other Adjustments

Other adjustments pertaining in more limited circumstances are as follows:

- Merchant marine capital construction fund deposits and earnings
- Blue Cross/Blue Shield special deductions

- Passive activity losses (applicable to closely held corporations and personal service corporations only)
- Farm losses (applicable to personal service corporations only)
- Circulation expenses (applicable to personal holding companies only)

3. *Book Income and Adjusted Current Earnings Adjustments*

The 1986 TRA prescribed that corporations make a book income adjustment, defined below, to AMTI for tax years beginning in 1987, 1988, and 1989. This adjustment required an addition to tentative AMTI of 50% of the difference between a corporation's book profits or loss and its tentative AMTI.

The book income adjustment worked this way: All other preferences and adjustments were to be computed and added or subtracted from taxable income to arrive at tentative AMTI. The tentative AMTI was to be compared with the corporation's "adjusted net book income," and if that book income was greater, then 50% of the excess was added to the tentative AMTI. (There was no required adjustment if the book income was less than the tentative AMTl.)

The "adjusted net book income" was defined as the corporation's income or loss reported on its "applicable financial statement", subject to adjustments. The first step, then, in determining the adjusted book net income was identifying the corporation's applicable financial statement from which the book income was taken. As different corporations have different types of statements, the IRS had issued priority rules to be followed. Financial statements filed with the Securities and Exchange Commission were given the highest priority. The tax regulations can be consulted for additional guidelines on the relative priorities of other statements.

Once the corporation had selected its applicable financial statement, it had to make the required adjustments. Taxpayer guidance for these complex adjustments were found in the tax regulations. In summary, adjustments were required for the following reasons.

- For certain taxes
- To prevent omission or duplication
- For footnote disclosure or other supplementary information
- To take account of related corporations

Other special rules applied when the corporation's tax and financial years differed.

The book income adjustment applied to all regular corporations. S corporations, regulated investment companies (RICs), real estate investment trusts (REITs), and real estate mortgage investment companies (REMICs) were excluded. It presented corporations with numerous planning possibilities and raised other issues not directly affecting leasing. A more detailed explanation of these is outside the scope of this book.

For tax years starting in 1990, the book income adjustment has been replaced by an adjustment based on the corporation's earnings and profits, referred to as its "adjusted current earnings," or simply its "ACE." A corporation's ACE is basically its earnings and profits, adjusted by certain specified items. Determining the ACE is a complex process for many corporations. Generally, ACE is a concept used to determine the tax status of corporate distributions to shareholders.

This particular preference is not geared toward recapturing a tax *benefit* that a corporation derives from the use of a specific tax deduction or exclusion, such as that available through using the depletion deduction described in Part 1 B.1.c of this chapter. Rather, the purpose of the ACE adjustment is to recapture some of the tax *savings* a corporation would enjoy in cases when large earnings are reported to its shareholders and creditors, but, because of the availability of tax benefits, has to pay little or no taxes.

The ACE adjustment is an amount equal to 75% of the difference between the corporation's adjusted current earnings and its tentative AMTI. If the adjusted current earnings exceed the tentative AMTI amount, then the corporation must add 75% of the excess to its tentative AMTI. If the tentative AMTI exceeds the adjusted current earnings, then 75% of that excess is subtracted, within certain limitations. The corporation cannot decrease its AMTI over a period of years by an amount greater than the amount which the ACE increased its AMTI over that same period of time.

> **Illustrative Example** White Corporation has a tentative AMTI equal to $200,000 before taking into account adjustments for its AMT NOL or ACE. White Corporation's ACE for its current tax year is $400,000. As a result, it has an ACE preference of $150,000 ($400,000 – $200,000 = $200,000 × 75% = $150,000), which increases its AMTI to $350,000.

➤ **Observation** The AMT book income adjustment could not reduce tentative AMTI; if the adjusted net book income was lower than the tentative AMTI, there was simply no change. By contrast, the ACE adjustment can, within certain limitations, either add to tentative AMTI or reduce it.

4. AMT Net Operating Losses

After taking into account its preferences and adjustments, the next step in computing the AMT is to subtract any AMT Net Operating Losses (NOLs). A corporation computes this in the same way it computes its regular tax NOL, with certain exceptions. To compute its AMT NOL, the corporation must add back its loss year tax preferences and adjustments to its regular tax NOL. The AMT NOL may not be used to offset more than 90% of tentative ATMI (determined without taking into account the AMT NOL deduction).

> **Illustrative Example** White Corporation's taxable income for its current tax year is $250,000. It had tax losses equal to $300,000, of which $40,000 were attributable to tax preference items. White Corporation's NOL for regular tax purposes is $50,000 ($250,000 – $300,000 = $50,000). In computing its AMTI, however, tax preference items cannot be used. As a result, only $260,000 of the losses can be used to offset income ($300,000 – $40,000 = $260,000), leaving White Corporation with an AMT NOL equal to $10,000 ($250,000 – $260,000 = $10,000).

A special transition rule permitted corporations to carry forward for AMT purposes all pre-1987 law regular tax NOLs as AMT NOLs. Although such NOLs had to be applied to the corporation's first tax year to which the AMT applied, they then could be carried forward until they were used up. If, however, the corporation had a pre-1987 deferral of add-on minimum tax liability, a reduction was required on the loss amount carried forward to the first tax year beginning after 1986 for any preferences that gave rise to the deferred AMT liability. See the Internal Revenue Code and related regulations for greater detail on the carryforward and carryback rules.

➤ **Observation** The AMT NOL rules often keep a corporation's tax department busy, because a corporation must track its AMT NOLs separately from its regular tax NOLs.

5. *Corporate AMT Exemption*

After a corporation subtracts its AMT NOL, the next step is to subtract any exemption amount. A corporation is permitted a $40,000 exemption.

6. *Applying AMT Rate*

After subtracting any exemption from the AMTI, the corporation multiplies the result by the AMT tax rate (currently at 20%).

7. *Foreign and Investment Tax Credits*

A corporation then subtracts any AMT Foreign Tax Credits (FTCs), which are computed by making AMT substitutions to the regular tax FTC calculation. The reader should consult the FTC rules in making the determination. To the extent there are any available Investment Tax Credits (ITCs), generally limited after 1986 (see Chapter 5), they can be used within certain restrictions to reduce AMT.

8. *Tentative Minimum Tax*

After credits are subtracted, the result is the corporation's Tentative Minimum Tax (TMT). The corporation must pay the amount that the TMT exceeds its regular tax liability.

9. *AMT Credit*

A corporation having to pay the AMT may be able to obtain a credit, called the AMT credit, for use in future years. Designed to prevent double taxation, the AMT credit is the amount of the TMT that exceeds the regular tax liability (reduced by certain nonrefundable credit). In tax years that begin after 1989, the credit earned by corporate taxpayers is based on their total AMT liability, not, as in the case of earlier tax years, on deferral-type AMT adjustments and preferences.

The AMT credit can only be used to reduce a corporation's regular, not AMT, tax liability. It can be carried forward indefinitely, but cannot be carried back to earlier tax years.

PART II: THE INDIVIDUAL AMT

A. Overview

The 1986 TRA expanded the prior version of the individual AMT. Because its format is the same as the corporate AMT, this section will only summarize its provisions.

B. Computing the Individual AMT

The individual AMT is calculated as follows: The taxpayer starts with taxable income. To that, preferences are added, adjustments added or subtracted, and the AMT NOL is subtracted, resulting in AMTI. The AMT exemption, if available, is then subtracted, and the result is multiplied by the AMT tax rate. AMT foreign tax credits are subtracted. The result is compared with the taxpayer's regular tax liability, and the taxpayer must add any AMT excess to the tax liability.

1. AMT Preferences

Many of the individual AMT preferences are the same as those for corporate AMT. They include the following:

- Charitable contributions of appreciated capital gain property
- Intangible drilling costs
- Interest on private-activity bonds
- Percentage depletion

Two additional preferences are as follows:

- For most property placed in service prior to 1987, the excess of accelerated depreciation on leased personal property over its straight-line depreciation
- For most property placed in service prior to 1987, subject to certain guidelines, the excess of the ACRS deduction for lease recovery property over its straight-line depreciation deduction

2. AMT Adjustments

Many of the individual AMT adjustments are the same as those for the corporate AMT. They include the following:

- Excess depreciation on personal property placed in service after 1986
- Excess depreciation on real property placed in service after 1986
- Long-term contracts
- Installment sales
- Mining exploration and development costs
- Passive-activity losses
- Farm losses
- Circulation expenses

Additional individual AMT adjustments not applicable to corporations are as follows:

- Certain gains on incentive stock options
- Research and experimentation expenses (For AMT purposes, these expenses are amortized over ten years.)
- Certain itemized deductions (An individual must add back the standard deduction, consumer interest, and certain state, local, and foreign taxes. The deductions for medical expenses, investment interest, and qualified residence interest are subject to certain adjustments.)

➤ **Note** There is no book income adjustment or ACE adjustment for noncorporate taxpayers, even if they are doing business as partnerships or in other forms.

After taking into account the preferences and adjustments, the AMT NOL is subtracted. The result is the taxpayer's AMTI.

3. AMT Exemption

The next step is to apply the AMT exemption. The exempt amounts are as follows:

- For married couples filing joint returns, the exemption is $45,000. It begins to be phased out when AMTI exceeds $150,000 and is completely phased out at $330,000.
- For singles or heads of households, the exemption is $33,750, phased out at AMTl between $112,500 and $247,500.
- For married taxpayers filing separately, the exemption is $22,500, phased out at AMTI between $75,000 and $165,000.

After subtracting the applicable exemption, the result is multiplied by the AMT rate for noncorporate taxpayers, currently 26% for the first $175,000 of a taxpayer's AMTI over the exemption amount, and 28% for the AMTI in excess of $175,000 over the exemption amount.

4. AMT Foreign Tax Credit

The taxpayer then can subtract the AMT foreign tax credit. The result is the TMT liability. This is compared with the taxpayer's regular tax liability, and the taxpayer must pay the amount by which the TMT exceeds the regular tax liability, in addition to the regular tax liability.

5. AMT Credit

Taxpayers who have AMT liability may be able to use the AMT credit in later years. The AMT credit is the amount by which AMT exceeds regular tax (subject to certain specified adjustments) for a tax year. The AMT credit can offset regular tax liability, but not reduce AMT liability, in later years.

PART III: THE AMT CONSIDERATIONS FOR LEASING

A.   Working with the AMT

It is apparent that the AMT rules are complex. Corporate and noncorporate taxpayers must consider their entire tax and financial situations to assess their AMT liability and its implications. Because of their complexity, it has taken a long time to understand the ramifications for equipment leasing. In a nutshell, the AMT is a sneaky and punitive tax. It takes away with one hand the tax benefits that had been given by Congress with the other hand. The only chance against what can result in a significant tax problem is foresight. Proper planning can help avoid or at least reduce its impact.

Lessors and lessees had many initial concerns, both unfounded and founded. Companies and their advisers struggled frantically to get a handle on what the AMT law changes meant, how they actually worked, and how to deal with any vagueness or ambiguities. Even today there are questions and difficulties in working with the AMT rules.

One aspect, however, is clear: The AMT rules have made it more difficult to assess whether purchasing or leasing an item of equipment is the best choice.

➤ **Observation** The AMT for individuals was ostensibly aimed at wealthy people who were taking advantage of tax shelter-type benefits, such as accelerated depreciation, to reduce their taxable income below what was felt to be a politically acceptable amount. In fact it has had an adverse impact on people who are not so wealthy. For example, in 1991, 244,000 not so wealthy people had to pay an AMT, which cost them, in the aggregate, approximately $1 billion more in taxes than they would have otherwise had to pay.

B. Overview

It should be apparent from the preceding material that the current corporate and individual AMTs have an effect on equipment leasing for both lessors and lessees. From the prospective lessee's standpoint, the issue is whether the AMT makes leasing equipment more desirable than buying it. To the potential lessor, the question is how the AMT will alter the tax benefits that the lessor may receive by owning the leased equipment, and thus what lease rate it can profitably charge a lessee.

A taxpayer's first step in answering both questions is to review the AMT steps as described, as applied to its overall tax position. If the taxpayer determines that it may be subject to the AMT, then it must analyze the leasing deal by taking that possibility into account.

There are no general guidelines which, if followed, provide all the answers for a particular lessee or lessor. The following discussion will assist lessees and lessors in putting a quick perspective on the impact the AMT has on equipment leasing transactions.

C. The Deferral Effect

Keep in mind that, from an equipment leasing standpoint, the AMT generally defers, rather than eliminates, certain tax benefits. The deferral effect is achieved by means of the AMT credit. As described, a credit in the amount of the AMT paid, within certain restrictions, may be used to offset regular tax liability in later years. Thus, the amount lost through the AMT, as described below, may be recouped through the use of the AMT credit.

The recouping, however, involves two caveats. First, the AMT credit can be used only to offset regular tax liability. Thus, a taxpayer subject to the AMT in many or most years may not receive the AMT credit benefit for many years, or not at all. Second, depending on how long it is before the taxpayer can use the credit, the taxpayer is losing the time value of money. Funds that the taxpayer does not have as a result of the deferral could be earning other money; if nothing else, interest could have been earned if the unavailable funds were invested in attractive investment instruments.

➤ **Important** In summary, when the AMT reduces a tax benefit, it is usually merely deferring it; thus, the taxpayer's loss is, for the most part, the loss of the time value of money.

D. The AMT and the Lessee

1. AMT's Impact on a Lessee

When a lessee leases equipment and pays rentals, those payments are not preferences or adjustments under the AMT. Thus, assuming the lease is a true lease and the lessee is not the equipment owner, the lessee may deduct its lease payments without increasing its AMTI.

2. Purchasing Equipment

If the lessee instead bought the equipment, there would be greater AMT consequences. For AMT computation purposes, a taxpayer must depreciate equipment it owns and places in service after 1986 by using the prescribed 150% declining balance method over a longer recovery period. As compared with the regular MACRS depreciation, the AMT write-off period is generally long, and the rate of depreciation is slow. The reason is the regular MACRS depreciation method is the 200% declining balance method. Thus, if for AMT calculation purposes (1) the depreciation rate is less than for regular tax purposes (150% rather than 200% declining balance method) and (2) the required write-off period is longer than for regular tax purposes, then the ownership of the equipment under consideration will result in a relative increase in a corporation's potential AMT as a result of the AMT depreciation preference adjustment.

> **Illustrative Example**   Assume John Jones buys and places in service a $10,000 printing press for use in his company. For regular MACRS purposes, the press is seven-year property. He is, however, subject to the AMT. The press has an 11-year ADR class life. Assuming the mid-quarter convention did not apply, the depreciation deductions under the regular MACRS and AMT are as follows:

Year	Regular MACRS	AMT
1	$1,429	$ 662
2	2,449	1,271
3	1,749	1,097
4	1,249	948
5	893	818
6	892	798
7	893	797
8	446	798
9		797
10		798
11		797
12		399

E.   The Lessor and the AMT

The lessor's decision in considering its equipment lease rent pricing is to determine how any potential AMT liability will impact the lessor's lease economic return. As the lease rate will be determined in large part by the transaction's tax benefits, and when they will be fully available, the lessor must decide if the tax benefits, and their timing of receipt, will be sufficient, if the AMT applies, so that it can make an attractive offer to a prospective lessee.

Both corporate and noncorporate lessors will be affected by the adjustment on depreciation of personal property. As described, this means the lessor must use the slower AMT depreciation method. It will thus have lower write-offs in earlier years and larger write-offs in later years, for AMT computation purposes.

F. Summary

The alternative minimum tax, existing under the 1986 Tax Reform Act, is a complex and, at times, burdensome tax. As its name suggests, AMT is an alternative tax system that runs parallel to the regular tax system, with its own set of rules. For lessors and prospective lessees, AMT brings into play tax uncertainties that make it difficult and, at times, impossible to properly assess the economic integrity of entering into a lease transaction. At the time of this writing, there has been governmental talk of modifying or eliminating the AMT.

Chapter 7

How to Cope Successfully with the Tax Lease Rules

A. The True Lease

When the parties sign a document entitled a "lease," and the document is a lease under state and local law, is it a lease for federal income tax purposes? Not necessarily. The financing transaction, under the federal tax laws, must be considered a "true" lease—a lease for federal income tax purposes. And that means that the lessor must be deemed to be the lease asset's owner. Failure to so qualify as the tax owner will cause the lessor to lose the available ownership tax benefits (and even possibly be subjected to penalties) and the lessee to forfeit rent deductions. Result: The leasing transaction sinks into a pool of red ink.

What, then, characterizes a "true" lease? The term is not specifically defined as such in the Internal Revenue Code or its underlying regulations. Two U.S. Supreme Court cases, however, established basic definitional rules—*Helvering v. F. & R. Lazarus & Co.*, 308 U.S. 252 (1939) and *Frank Lyon Company v. United States,* 435 U.S. 561 (1978). The *Helvering* case is noted for setting down the substance over form rule: The tax nature of what is purported to be a true lease depends on whether the lessor can be determined to have sufficient property ownership of the asset involved, taking into account all the surrounding facts and circumstances, to be accorded the tax attributes available to an asset owner, or whether the purported lessor is really a conditional seller, an option holder, a lender, or some other type of transaction participant. The case's decision, although very general in nature, was the basic guidance looked to until, in 1978, the advent of the *Frank Lyon* case, when the U.S. Supreme Court, for the first time since the 1939 *Lazarus* decision, took another look at the leasing tax ownership issue. The bottom line of the *Frank Lyon* case decision—as summarized by the Supreme Court—in considering tax ownership, and therefore true lease status, is to determine whether the lessor, rather than the lessee, is the equipment's tax owner, having "significant and genuine attributes of the traditional lessor status. What those attributes are in any particular case will necessarily depend upon its facts."

Although the ultimate "true" lease test is based on the transaction's facts and circumstances, the IRS, in 1975, provided guidelines for leveraged lease transactions which, if followed, will help ensure they stay afloat. In the form of four published revenue procedures (Revenue Procedure 75-21, 75-28, 76-30, and 79-48) collectively called the *Guidelines,* the IRS sets out the formal criteria that must be met if the parties to a transaction want to obtain a ruling (referred to as a private ruling) from the IRS that the transaction qualifies as a lease for federal income tax purposes. Although nominally limited to ruling requests, the *Guidelines* provide helpful advice on achieving true lease status even when the parties to the transaction do not request an IRS private ruling. Prior to the issuance of the *Guidelines,* the parities to a lease transaction found some guidance in Revenue Ruling 55-540 (1955-2 CB 39), discussed later in this chapter. Revenue Ruling 55-540, which still has guidance applicability, focuses primarily on describing aspects of a transaction that would cause it to fail to qualify as a true lease. It has applicability to *all* purported lease transactions, not just the *leveraged* lease transaction.

B.   Procedural Alternatives

How do the parties maximize their chances of obtaining true lease status? The best two alternatives are to obtain an IRS private letter ruling or to proceed without one while following the *Guidelines* and Revenue Ruling 55-540.

1.   *Private Letter Ruling*

As a general matter, if a taxpayer submits a ruling request to the IRS concerning a transaction, the IRS, after reviewing the request, will rule on some or all of the transaction's tax consequences. Then, provided the information submitted was accurate and complete, the IRS's position on the issues on which it has ruled is considered final. In case of leveraged leasing transactions, the *Guidelines* not only prescribe the criteria that must be met for a transaction to receive a favorable true lease ruling, but also sets out the specific submission procedures that the submitting taxpayer must follow when making a request. If the transaction parties receive a favorable ruling from the IRS, they can rest assured that the transaction's anticipated tax results will not be challenged.

Although the safest route is to obtain a ruling, it is not always the optimum alternative for a number of reasons. First, it is costly. Preparing and submitting the request involves a significant amount of legal work, resulting in a higher transaction cost and a several-hundred-dollar fee paid to the IRS. Second, submitting a request takes time, both to prepare the request and for the IRS to rule. Third, if the IRS ruling is unfavorable and the transaction has been closed, there is a risk that this will draw attention to an issue that may otherwise have gone unnoticed.

a.   When to Consider an IRS Private Letter Ruling

Weighing the downside factors of asking the IRS for a private letter ruling discussed in the previous section against the increased certainty, a request should be considered when the following occurs.

*   The lessor will not go ahead without a ruling.
*   There is considerable doubt as to the lease's true lease status or other tax issues.
*   The overall costs of the deal are substantial enough to sustain the added costs.
*   The lessee has time to wait for the ruling to be issued before closing the deal.

2.   *Proceeding Without a Ruling*

When a ruling is not practical for one or more reasons presented here, the next safest approach is to structure the lease financing so it complies with the IRS *Guidelines.* As mentioned, the *Guidelines* tells taxpayers what criteria a transaction must minimally meet to obtain an advance ruling on a leveraged leasing deal. They do not establish as a matter a law whether a transaction will or will not qualify as a true lease. In addition, the IRS does not promise that compliance with the *Guidelines* will guarantee favorable treatment on audit. As a practical matter, however, it is highly unlikely that a transaction meeting the *Guidelines* would have IRS audit problems. *So,* compliance with the *Guidelines* can provide good comfort to parties to a purported leveraged lease transaction that the arrangement will in fact qualify as a true lease.

Keep in mind that although following the *Guidelines* does not guarantee true lease treatment, failure to comply precisely with each provision does not necessarily doom a lease. The reasons are as follows: (1) The *Guidelines* states the IRS's position only on advance rulings. They do not necessarily reflect the IRS's view of the law, so a slight variation may not raise a problem on audit. (2) If the transaction goes to court, the *Guidelines* will carry less weight; under *Frank Lyon,* the court will look at all the facts and circumstances and may well find, on balance, that a true lease exists.

➤ **Observations**

- As the equipment leasing industry and its advisors have gained experience working with the *Guidelines* rules, there has been an increasing number of transactions put together that do not fully comply. For example, some lessors may make less than a 20% equity investment, or grant fixed price purchase options, something that would violate the favorable *Guidelines* ruling requirements, as discussed in the following material. Certain *Guidelines* requirements, however, are generally never deviated from; in particular, the anticipated residual value test and the remaining useful life requirement, also discussed later in this chapter.
- Another reason why the leasing industry and its advisors have increasingly varied from the *Guidelines* is competition. Because the leasing market has matured, and due to the economic downturn of the late 1980s and early 1990s, there are too many lessors, with too much money, chasing too few lease deals. To win business, let alone survive, lessors have chosen to become more tax aggressive, taking chances that they may have not otherwise chosen to take.

When a ruling will not be sought, an advisable course of action, particularly in situations where there will be variation from the *Guidelines,* is to obtain a written opinion from experienced lease tax counsel that the arrangement will have the desired lease treatment. Although this increases costs, it may provide some beneficial support if a transaction is audited or when defending an IRS litigation challenge.

C.   The *Guidelines*

As briefly mentioned, the following revenue procedures comprise the *Guidelines.*

- Revenue Procedure 75-21 [1975-I CB 715] generally sets out conditions that must be met for there to be an advance ruling on a leveraged lease.
- Revenue Procedure 75-28 [1975-1 CB 752] sets out information and representations required to be furnished by taxpayers in a leveraged leasing transaction ruling request.
- Revenue Procedure 76-30 [1976-2 CB 647] supplements Revenue Procedure 75-21 on issue of limited use property.
- Revenue Procedure 79-48 [1979-2 CB 529] supplements Revenue Procedure 75-21 on improvements to leased property.

Keep in mind that the *Guidelines* is expressly designed to tell taxpayers what they must do to obtain an advance ruling. And that following the rules, even where no ruling is sought, is advisable to help assure true lease treatment. It should also be noted that, although the *Guidelines* applies only to leveraged leases, the parties to a nonleveraged transaction should consider those portions of the *Guidelines* that do not apply to the transaction debt aspects.

In addition to following the *Guidelines*, prospective lessors and lessees will want to comply with Revenue Ruling 55-540 (1955-2 CB 39), explained below, which provides general guidance on all types of leasing transactions, leveraged and nonleveraged.

➤ **Observations**

- Syndicators must be careful when deviating from the *Guidelines* in structuring a lease financing, even though each party initially states a private ruling will not be required. Invariably, when the parties, particularly the equity investors, hear about the theoretical risks from their lawyers, they get nervous and frequently ask for a favorable opinion from tax counsel as to the true lease nature. In many situations, when there is a *Guidelines* variance, counsel is reluctant to give an opinion because of the uncertainty as to the variance's effect. Coming at the last minute, this can lead to a serious roadblock to completing the deal.
- When a private ruling will not be involved, the *Guidelines* rules are sometimes stretched to keep all the parties satisfied. For example, a company may not be willing to lease equipment without a low fixed price purchase option. Although prohibited under the rules, a prospective lessor may grant such a right just to win the transaction.

At first glance, the *Guidelines* rules do not appear complex, but in structuring a particular transaction, it is easy to violate them inadvertently. The best protection against a violation is having a thorough understanding of the concepts. Toward this end, let us examine the various *Guidelines* aspects.

1. *The Lessor Must Make and Maintain a Minimum Investment*

Under the *Guidelines*, the lessor must initially make an unconditional equity investment in the equipment equal to at least 20% of its cost. This can be done in a number of ways: with cash, with other consideration, or by personally assuming the obligation to buy the equipment. Typically the lessor makes a cash payment from its own funds. The 20% equity investment is referred to as the "minimum investment."

The IRS requires the unconditional nature of the initial investment to prevent the lessor from arranging to receive, either from the lessee or certain lessee-related parties, all or any part of its equity back once the equipment is put into service. This is in keeping with the IRS's position that if a lessor wants to be treated as an equipment owner for tax purposes, and thus be entitled to claim the tax benefits, there must be an ownership risk.

When a lessor intends to meet the minimum equity test by personally assuming the obligation to purchase the equipment, its net worth must be sufficient to make the assumption in fact meaningful.

➤ **Observation**   It is generally felt that the 20% equity investment requirement is higher than actually necessary to survive an IRS true lease challenge. In the pre-*Guidelines* era, the

IRS would issue a favorable true lease ruling even when the equity investment was as low as 15% of equipment cost. Many leveraged lease transactions are structured today with less than a 20% equity investment when a favorable private letter ruling will not be sought.

The lessor must also maintain this 20% "minimum investment" in the equipment during the lease term. The test for determining if the minimum investment rule has been met during the term is complicated; follow it carefully. The test will be met if the excess of (1) the cumulative payments that the lessee is obligated to pay over (2) the cumulative disbursements that the lessor is obligated to pay as a result of the equipment ownership is never greater than the *sum* of (a) any excess of the initial equity investment over 20% of the equipment cost and (b) the cumulative pro rata portion of the transaction's projected profit, not considering tax benefits. Simply, this means that the excess of the amounts coming in to the lessor over the amounts going out must never be more than the sum of any equity investment amount greater than 20% of equipment cost and the pro rata portion of the anticipated profit. The tax benefits accruing from ownership cannot be considered as profit in the computation.

➤ **Recommended Computation**   In Revenue Procedure 7-28, the IRS provides a mechanical formula to establish the 20% investment during the lease term. It may be useful to run the following test on a computer and retain it for audit purposes.

Verify that throughout the lease term the items designated as (1), (2), (3), and (4) below comply with the formula "(1) – (2) never exceeds (3) + (4)."

1. The projected cumulative payments required to be paid by the lessee to or for the lessor.
2. The projected cumulative disbursements required to be paid by or for the lessor in connection with the ownership of the property, excluding the lessor's initial equity investment, but including any direct costs to finance the equity investment.
3. The excess of lessor's initial equity investment over 20% of the cost of the property.
4. A cumulative pro rata portion of the projected profits from the transaction (exclusive of tax benefits). Profit for this purpose is the excess of the sum of (a) the amounts required to be paid by the lessee to or for the lessor over the lease term plus (b) the value of the residual investment referred to in Section 4(1)(C) of Revenue Procedure 75-21, over the aggregate disbursements required to be paid by or for the lessor in connection with the ownership of the property, including the lessor's initial equity investment and any direct costs to finance the equity investment.

Also, the minimum investment test must be met at the end of the lease term. It consists of two basic parts:

* The lessor must show that the leased equipment's estimated fair market residual value is equal to at least 20% of its original cost.
* The lessor must show that a reasonable estimate of the equipment's useful life at the end of the lease term is the longer of one year or 20% of the equipment's originally estimated useful life.

Illustrative Example   *At-Risk Residual Test:* Company A wants to lease a $10,000 steel shipping container from Company B for an 11-year lease term. The container has an estimated useful life of 12 years and an estimated fair market value at the end of 11 years of $2,300. Will the end of the lease term "at risk" investment test be met?

   The estimated fair market residual value test has been met; that is, the $2,300 residual meets the first test (20% of $10,000 = $2,000, the minimum).

   The useful life test has not been met. Twenty percent of 12 years is 2.4 years. When the lease term is over, only 1 year of useful life will be left, and the second test says the remaining useful life must be the longer of 1 year or, in our example, 2.4 years.

In making the fair market residual value determination, no weight can be given to any inflationary increases or deflationary decreases during the lease term—the determination must be made as to future value base on current dollars. The estimated residual amount also must be reduced by any anticipated costs that may be incurred by the lessor in removing and reacquiring the property at the end of the lease term.

➤ **Observation**   There is an express exception to the *Guidelines* rule requiring the lessor to take into account anticipated removal and redelivery costs in determining if the estimated residual value test is met: The lessor generally need not account for such cost when the lessee is obligated under the lease to pay for the removal and redelivery costs. This leads to an implied exception that if the lessor could realize the equipment's residual value without equipment removal by either the original lessee, another lessee, the lessor, or a purchaser, then these estimated removal costs also would not have to be taken into account in determining if the estimated residual test has been met.

These calculations cannot be made without first figuring out what the "lease term" will be for a particular transaction. The lease term is not merely the "primary term" designated by the lease document. By definition, the "term" must include all renewal and extension periods other than those that are at fair market rental value and are at the lessee's option. For example, the lessor would have to include any period for which it could require the lessee to continue to lease the equipment even though it would be at fair market rental value. This rule prevents a lessor from avoiding its "residual risk" through a forced renewal of the lease, which would in effect run until the lessor had no residual value risk. This again reinforces the *Guidelines* intent that if an equipment owner wants to be a "lessor" it must incur real ownership risks.

2.   *The Transaction Must Produce a Profit*

The *Guidelines* provides that the lessor must make a profit on the transaction. At first this statement seems ridiculous. What businessperson would be involved in a situation in which he or she did not make a profit? None, so what is the IRS getting at? Simply, that the lessor must make money on the deal aside from the return generated by the tax benefits. In other words, the lessor must be able to show that the lease transaction makes economic sense without considering the tax benefits. The IRS wants to make sure that lease deals are not merely tax avoidance devices.

   How does a lessor know if the profit requirement has been met? By meeting the following *Guidelines* test: The total rent and other amounts that the lessee is obligated to pay over the lease term, when added to the equipment's estimated residual value, has to be greater than the amount of money that the lessor is obligated to pay out for the equipment, such as debt service and equity investment, including any related direct equity financing costs. Simply, the lessor must anticipate having money left over, when adding in the estimated residual value, at the end of the lease term after repaying any transaction debt, the money it took out of its own pocket to acquire the equipment, and any other direct equity investment financing costs.

➤ **Observation** Under the *Guidelines,* the profit test would be met even if the profit is as little as $1.

➤ **Recommended Computation** Run the following profit test calculation from Revenue Procedure 75-28.

Demonstrate that the items identified as (1), (2), and (3) below will solve the formula "(1) + (2) exceed (3)."

1. The projected aggregate payments required to be paid by the lessee to or for the lessor over the lease term.
2. The value of the residual investment described in Section 4(1)(C) of Revenue Procedure 75-21.
3. The projected sum of the aggregate disbursements required to be paid by or for the lessor in connection with the ownership of the property, including the lessor's initial equity investment, and any direct costs to finance the equity investment.

Illustrative Example *The Profit Test:* Company B has leased a new $100,000 barge to Company A under the following facts.

Lease term	10 years
Barge residual value	$ 20,000
Equity investment	$ 20,000
Debt principal	$ 80,000
Debt interest rate	10%
Loan term	10 years
Total aggregate rentals	$125,000
Legal fees	$ 5,000
Miscellaneous fees	$ 1,000

For simplicity, assume that the debt repayments are based on an average outstanding principal of $40,000 over the ten-year period. Based on the previous data, the deal evolves as follows:

Total debt interest due	$ 40,000
Total principal payment	$ 80,000
Total fees ($5,000 + $1,000)	$ 6,000

Does the lessor pass the IRS profit test? The formula is:

Aggregate rentals + Residual value must exceed cash out

Aggregate rentals + Residual = $125,000 + $20,000 = $145,000

Equity investment + Debt service + Fees = Cash out =
$20,000 + $80,000 + $40,000 + $6,000 = $146,000

The lessor fails the test. The net result is the rents must be increased to pass the test.

Not only must a lessor anticipate a profit, it also must demonstrate that the transaction will produce a positive cash flow that is "reasonable" in amount. That is, the aggregate rents and other required lessee payments must comfortably exceed the aggregate outflows, which are basically the debt service and the direct equity financing costs.

➤ **Observations**

- Although the *Guidelines* does not spell out what will be a reasonable cash flow amount, historically the IRS has ruled favorably when the cash flow amount is in the range of 2% to 4% of the equity investment per annum, computed on a simple interest basis.
- The *Guidelines* does not explicitly state that the positive cash flow must be on an even basis over the lease term; however, it is generally considered prudent to avoid situations in which the positive cash only exists for one or two lease periods.

➤ **Recommended Computation**   Run the following positive cash flow test calculation from Revenue Procedure 75-28.

Demonstrate that the lessor will have a projected positive cash flow from the lease transaction. This analysis must contain the following information to show that the items identified as (1) and (2) will solve the formula "(1) exceeds (2) by a reasonable minimum amount."

1. The projected aggregate payments required to be paid by the lessee to or for the lessor over the lease term.
2. The projected aggregate disbursements required to be paid by or for the lessor in connection with the ownership of the property, excluding the lessor's initial equity investment, but including any direct costs to finance the equity investment.

3. *No Lessee Investment*

Generally, the lessee cannot invest in the equipment by providing funds necessary to buy, add to, modify, or improve the equipment. There are several exceptions. The lessee may make "severable improvements," additions or improvements that can easily be removed without causing material damage—so long as they are not necessary for the equipment's intended use, and the lessor does not have the right to buy them at below market price.

The lessee generally cannot make nonseverable improvements—those that cannot readily be removed by the lessee without causing material damage. However, the lessee can make nonseverable improvements if they (1) are not required to complete the property for the lessee's intended use, (2) do not constitute a lessee or lessee-related party equity investment (e.g., if the lessor is required to buy the improvement), and (3) do not cause the property to become limited use property (property of use only to the lessee). The lessee also can be permitted or required to make nonseverable improvements provided they are necessary to comply with health, safety, or environmental standards as required by governmental law or regulation (including industry standards which have government recognition) or do not substantially increase the original property's productivity or capacity (essentially more than 25% of original performance, or, if so, do not cost, when added to other noncompliance leasehold improvement costs, in excess of 10% of the original cost, adjusted for inflation). The rules governing severable and nonseverable improvements are extensive, and an in-depth explanation is beyond the scope of this chapter. See Revenue Procedure 79-48 for a full explanation.

Ordinary maintenance and repairs that the lessee must make at its expense are not deemed "additions or improvements" and are thus excluded from the rule. The problem with this exception is that the *Guidelines* do not set up any parameters for determining what is considered "ordinary maintenance and repairs." If the IRS successfully challenges any expenses as not "ordinary," there may be a risk that the true lease nature will be lost.

Under the same basic concept, the lessee cannot pay for any equipment cost overruns. Usually this becomes a problem only when equipment with a long construction period is involved. In many of these situations, the purchase contracts have price escalation clauses. Some prospective lessors committing to lease such equipment before completion limit their cost exposure by specifying they will not pay for equipment if it exceeds a certain amount. If a lessor had this type of "cap," a prospective lessee runs the risk of having to negotiate a new lease deal at the last minute or buy the equipment.

4. The Lessee Cannot Be a Lender

Before the IRS issued Revenue Procedure 75-21, some lessees and parties related to them loaned money to the lessor to be used toward buying the equipment. For example, a prospective lessee may want to lease equipment manufactured by its parent company. The parent company would offer to sell the equipment to the lessor on a favorable installment basis. The payment delay would "pump up" a lessor's time value yield over a non-delayed payment, and at least part of the benefit would be reflected in a more attractive rental rate.

Under the *Guidelines*, the lessee and members of the lessee group are specifically prohibited from lending funds to the lessor to assist in the equipment financing. Thus, direct loans and other credit-extending techniques similar to that described in the previous paragraph will transgress the *Guidelines* and prevent the issuance of a favorable private ruling on the transaction.

5. Certain Guarantees Cannot Be Used

The lessee and certain lessee-associated parties, such as its parent company or sister subsidiary, cannot guarantee any equipment debt. For example, a lessee's parent company cannot guarantee the repayment of a leveraged lease third-party loan. In most cases this will not be a great loss; however, it was a handy technique for lessors to use when, for example, third-party, nonrecourse lenders wanted added security.

The *Guidelines* permits lessee-related parties to guarantee certain conventional obligations found in a net lease, such as rent, maintenance, or insurance premium obligations. This takes some of the sting out of the debt guarantee prohibition.

6. Lessee Purchase Options Must Be at Fair Market Value

To ensure that the lessee is not the equipment owner, the *Guidelines* prohibits any arrangement granting a lessee or lessee-related party the option to buy the leased equipment at a price below its fair market value. The lessee may have a purchase option only if the price is no less than the equipment's fair market value at the time of purchase under the option.

That rule eliminates all fixed price purchase options, including so-called nominal purchase options. A typical nominal purchase right is one in which the lessee can buy the equipment at the end of the lease term for $1. In the past, some lessors had used this option to induce a prospective lessee to take their deal by claiming that lessees could have the best of both worlds: a rental deduction during the lease term and, in effect, an equipment purchase credit for the rent paid.

➤ **Observation**   Although the IRS will refuse to issue a favorable true lease ruling when a transaction contains a fixed price purchase option, many tax advisors believe that by following pre-*Guidelines* case law (which upheld as true lease transactions those that contain fixed price purchase options that were not so low that it was "reasonably certain" the lessee would exercise such option), the transaction would be entitled to true lease treatment. Fixed price purchase options are particularly attractive to companies that are aware certain equipment will have a "high residual" at the end of the term. With a fair market value purchase option, they run the risk that their cost to buy will be substantial in relation to the original price. This would, in turn, relatively increase their effective leasing cost. Therefore, the lower the option's exercise price, the less the overall cost.

> **Illustrative Example**   *The Purchase Cost Is Critical:* Company A wants to lease a barge from Company B. The facts are as follows:
>
> Original barge cost $100,000
> Estimated residual value . . . . $ 20,000
>
> If the lessee, Company A, had an option to buy the barge at the lease term's end for $20,000, its cost for leasing could be easily determined in advance. The rents and the purchase price are known. Assume instead that the lessee was granted only a fair market value purchase option under the *Guidelines.* If, at the end of the lease term, the barge was actually worth $50,000 because of the current demand, the lessee would have to pay out an additional $30,000, thus increasing the overall cost.

This example is not unrealistic. In many cases items such as barges or private aircraft have a market value after years of use equal to or greater than the original cost. Leasing that equipment, therefore, can be expensive if the lessee wants to buy it at the end of the term and must pay the fair market value.

7.   *Lessor Cannot Have Right to Require Sale*

A lessor is specifically prohibited from having any initial right to require "any party" to buy the leased equipment for any reason, except when there are nonconformities with written supply, construction, or manufacture specifications. The lessor's investment in the equipment would, therefore, be said to be subject to the "risks of the market."

Thus, a lessor cannot have the right, called a "put"—to force an equipment sale at a predetermined price at the lease term's end to, for example, the lessee, a manufacturer, or a dealer. What does this mean for a lessor concerned about whether certain equipment will have any residual value? Simply, that a zero residual value may have to be assumed in calculating the rent to ensure that the transaction's economic return will be maintained. If "puts" were permitted, a lessor could base its investment return analysis on an anticipated residual value equal to the "put." As a result, a lessee could then be charged a relatively lower rent amount during the lease term on potentially poor residual value equipment. If the equipment could be sold at the end of the lease for an amount equal to or greater than the "put" amount, the lessee would have had a rent savings, because the lessor would not need to force the lessee to buy the equipment to get its required economic return.

The right of a lessor to abandon the property is considered to be a right to require a purchase and, therefore, is also prohibited. The *Guidelines* provides some leeway in that, after the equipment goes on lease, the IRS may, depending on the particular facts and circumstances, permit an arrangement in which the lessor could require someone to buy the equipment.

➤ **A Word of Caution** Parties can be tempted to elude this rule by entering into a side agreement before the lease is closed, giving the lessor a sale right. After the equipment is placed in service, the side agreement is to be submitted to the IRS for approval as a proposed arrangement, without mention that it had been agreed to during the prohibited period. This practice is dangerous and clearly not recommended. Private letter rulings are granted strictly on the basis of the facts submitted in the ruling request, and if the facts actually vary from those presented, the IRS may not adhere to the tax treatment stated.

8. *Uneven Rent Programs Must Meet Certain Tests*

"Step rentals," such as "low-high" or "high-low" rent structures, had been a valuable lessor marketing tool. Particularly attractive to lessees were rents that started low and increased during the lease's term, for a variety of reasons, including showing higher profits in early years, anticipating inflation, or increasing cash flow.

The *Guidelines* asks a taxpayer submitting a ruling request to submit certain information on any rent payment variations during the lease term. It should be noted, however, that uneven rent payments, under the *Guidelines*, will not impact the IRS's ruling on whether the lease is a true lease. Rather, under the *Guidelines*, uneven rents can result in a portion of the uneven rent being treated as prepaid or deferred rent.

The *Guidelines* sets out two safe harbor tests, so that if the rent payments satisfy either test there will be no issue as to prepaid or deferred rent. If the lease fails to meet either test, then the ruling request must also contain a request for a determination of whether any portion of the uneven rent payments will be deemed by the IRS as prepaid or deferred rent.

a.   Ten Percent Variation Test

Under the first test, rent payments come within the safe harbor if the rent for each year varies less than 10% above or below the average annual rent payable over the lease term. The average annual rent is computed by dividing the aggregate rent payable over the entire lease term by the number of years in the term. As a practical matter, this does not permit a lessor to offer anything significant, when compared with some pre-*Guidelines* uneven rent programs.

> **Illustrative Example**   *Uneven Rent Test:* Company A wants to lease a fuel truck for ten years for a start-up operation, but anticipates that its cash flow will allow only a $1,000 annual rent expense for the first three years. Company B, the prospective lessor, proposes the following rent program.
>
> | | |
> |---|---|
> | Lease term | 10 years |
> | Annual rent for years 1–3 | $1,000 |
> | Annual rent for years 4–10 | $2,000 |

Company A finds the rent to be within its cash flow projections. Is there a deferred rent issue?

Let us examine the numbers. The rule says the rent for each year cannot be above or below 10% of the average annual rent. The average annual rent is computed by dividing the total of the ten-year rents (3 × $1,000 + 7 × $2,000 = $17,000) by the number of years in the lease.

$$\text{Annual average rent} = \$17,000/10 = \$1,700$$

Because 10% of $1,700 is $170, the rent per year cannot be above $1,870 ($1,700 + $170) or below $1,530 ($1,700 – $170). Therefore, this rent program does not meet the test, and the issue of deferred rent must be addressed.

b. Initial Period Test

The second safe harbor is designed to permit, to some degree, rental payments that fluctuate during the lease term. Lease payments satisfy that test if, during at least the initial two-thirds of the lease term, the yearly rent is not more than 10% higher or lower than the average annual rent for such selected initial portion, and the remaining individual yearly rent is not greater than the highest annual rent payable during the initial portion and not less than one-half of the initial term average yearly rent. There is somewhat more flexibility in using this alternative, but it is still limited.

Illustrative Example   *Initial Period Test:* Assume the following rent program.

Lease term . . . . 9 years
Annual rent for years 1–3 . . . . $1,000
Annual rent for years 4–6 . . . . $1,200
Annual rent for years 7–9 . . . . $ 600

Will this rent structure pass the IRS alternative test?

First the average rent must be computed for the initial two-thirds of the lease term as follows:

$$\text{Average rent} \frac{(3 \times \$1,000 + 3 \times \$1,200)}{6 \text{ years}} = \$1,100$$

The yearly rent cannot be greater than $1,210 ($1,100 + 10% × $1,100) or less than $990 ($1,100 – 10% × $1,100). The test is met for the initial two-thirds of the lease.

What about years 7 through 9? The annual rent ($600) cannot be greater than the highest rent payable during the initial two-thirds of the lease term ($1,200) and less than one-half of the initial term average annual rent (1/2 × $1,100 = $550). This program just meets the test, so the IRS under the *Guidelines* would not object to the steps as presented.

➤ **Tax Law Observation**   Section 467, added by the 1984 Deficit Reduction Act, may require certain lessors and lessees to accrue uneven lease rental income and deductions in a level manner. Section 467 applies to an equipment lease totaling over $250,000 in rental payments under which either (1) at least one amount is allocable to the use of property during a calendar year or (2) there are increases in the amount of rent to be paid over the lease term. Accrual will not be required when the lease payments satisfy a presumptive tax avoidance test. Parties to a leasing transaction should review Section 467 when considering an uneven rent structure.

9. Limited Use Property

Limited use property is not expected to be useful to or usable by the lessor except for purposes of continued leasing or transfer to the lessee or a member of the lessee group. According to the IRS, then, at the lease term's end, there will probably be no potential lessees or buyers other than the lessee or members of the lessee group. As a result, the lessor will probably sell or rent the property to the lessee or a member of the lessee group, so that, in effect, the lessee will receive the equipment's ownership benefits for substantially its entire useful life. To obtain a favorable ruling, it is necessary to establish that it is commercially feasible for a party, not the lessee or a member of the lessee group, to lease or buy the property from the lessor, demonstrating that it is not limited use property.

D. Ruling Request Submission Requirements

In submitting a ruling request, the taxpayer must present the information the *Guidelines* require in the manner prescribed by Revenue Procedure 75-28, as modified by Revenue Procedure 79-48.

Generally all the parties to the transaction, including the lessor and the lessee, must join in the ruling request. The request must contain a summary of the surrounding facts, and be accompanied by certain relevant documents such as the lease or, in the case of a brokered transaction, any economic analysis, prospectus, or other document used to induce the lessor to invest.

The request must include the following information.

- Type and quality of the leased equipment
- Whether the equipment is new, reconstructed, used, or rebuilt
- When, how, and where the equipment will be, or was, first placed in service or use
- Whether the equipment will be permanently or temporarily attached to land, buildings, or other property
- Flow of funds among the parties

The request must disclose the lease term, any renewals or extensions, and any purchase and sale options. This includes any right the lessor has to force a purchase or to abandon the equipment, and any intention to give this right in the future.

If the lessee, or any related party, must pay for cost overruns or will invest in the equipment, by, for example, contributing to its cost or paying for an improvement, modification, or addition, then this must be disclosed. The request must also identify any unrelated parties who will provide funds.

Information covering any lessee-related guarantees, regardless if the profit and positive cash flow tests have been satisfied, and any uneven rent structure must be presented. An economic analysis has to be submitted, showing that the minimum at risk investment rules will be satisfied. A detailed description must be sent out indicating the debt and the repayment terms; any lease provisions relating to indemnities, termination, obsolescence, casualty, or insurance; and the party who is to claim any investment credit. The request must include representations that the property is not limited use property. The parties must submit an expert's opinion on the equipment's residual value, setting out the manner in which the conclusion was determined, any removal or delivery costs at the end of the lease term, and the useful life of the equipment remaining at the term's end.

E.   Foundation Tax Rules

Two decades before issuing the *Guidelines,* the IRS issued Revenue Ruling 55-540 (1955-12 CB 39), setting out the factors that it considers in deciding whether a leasing transaction is really a conditional sale for tax purposes. Unlike the Guidelines, Revenue Ruling 55-540 sets out the IRS audit position rather than dealing with what is required to obtain a ruling. The ruling is, however, much less useful than the Guidelines, because it is less precise; but by checking its tests you will help ensure a leasing transaction's viability.

In that ruling, the IRS stated generally that whether:

> an agreement, which in form is a lease, is in substance a conditional sales contract depends upon the intent of the parties as evidenced by the provisions of the agreement, read in the light of the facts and circumstances existing at the time the agreement was executed.

In addition, it provided that in "ascertaining such intent no single test, or any special combination of tests, is absolutely determinative," no "general rule, applicable to all cases can be laid down," and that each "case must be decided in the light of its particular facts." The IRS then went on to state that an intent causing an arrangement to be treated as a sale instead of a lease for tax purposes is found if one or more of the following factors exist.

- Portions of the periodic payments are specifically made applicable to an equity interest to be acquired by the lessee.
- The lessee will acquire title to the property under lease on the payment of a stated amount of "rentals" that the lessee under the contract must make.
- The total amount that the lessee must pay for a relatively short period of use constitutes an inordinately large proportion of the total sum required to acquire title.
- The agreed "rental" payments materially exceed the current fair rental value.
- The property may be acquired by the lessee under a purchase option at a price that is nominal in relation to the property's value at the time the option may be exercised (determined at the time the agreement was entered into) or which is relatively small when compared with the total payments that the lessee must make.
- Some portion of the periodic payments is specifically designated as interest or is otherwise readily recognizable as the equivalent of interest.

➤ **Observation**   Revenue Ruling 55-540 provides guidelines for determining if a conditional sale contract exists. The assumption is, if a conditional sales contract does not exist and the parties structured the transaction as a tax lease, everyone is on safe ground. If the transaction is structurally complex, experienced tax leasing counsel may be necessary to get adequate assurances.

F.   Potential Penalties

Not only do the parties risk losing their tax benefits if a transaction fails to qualify as a true lease, but they also run a risk of incurring penalties. The 5% negligence penalty is possible if the parties fail to exercise reasonable care. In addition, in several tax court cases, the Section 6659 overvaluation penalty has been imposed on lessors when the court found no reasonable expectation that the lessor could make an economic profit apart from tax benefits—from the leasing transaction. The Section 6659 penalty is 30% of the amount of the understatement attributable to the overvaluation (here, the equipment's basis). Applying only to individuals (including partnerships) and closely held or personal service corporations, Section 6659 is not applicable to all lessors, but is a potential risk in certain leasing transactions.

G.   Quick True Lease Checklist

The following checklist can be used as a guide to determine if a lease transaction's basic features comply with *Guidelines* requirements. If you answer no to any questions, there may be a problem.

	Yes	No
1. Has the lessor made an initial equity investment equal to at least 20% of equipment cost?	☐	☐
2. Is the initial equity investment unconditional in nature?	☐	☐
3. Will the lessor's minimum investment remain equal at least to 20% of equipment cost during the lease term?	☐	☐
4. Is the estimated residual value of the equipment at least equal to 20% of equipment's original cost?	☐	☐
5. Will the useful life of the equipment remaining at the end of the lease term be equal to the longer of one year or 20% of the originally estimated useful life?	☐	☐
6. If there is a lessee purchase option, is it at fair market value as of the time of exercise?	☐	☐
7. Is the lessor without any rights to force a sale of the equipment to any party?	☐	☐
8. Is the lessor without any specific right to abandon the equipment?	☐	☐
9. Has the lessor furnished all the equipment cost other than any third-party debt?	☐	☐
10. Will the lessor have to bear the cost of any permanent equipment improvement, modification, or addition?	☐	☐
11. If the lessee pays for a severable improvement, could the equipment be used for its intended use without it?	☐	☐
12. If the lessee pays for a severable improvement, can the lessor buy it only at a price at least equal to its fair market value?	☐	☐
13. If the lessee pays for a nonseverable improvement, could the equipment be used for its intended use without the improvement?	☐	☐
14. If the lessee pays for a nonseverable improvement, will someone other than the lessee be able to use the equipment?	☐	☐
15. Does every nonseverable improvement that is paid for by the lessee not constitute a lessee investment?	☐	☐
16. Will the lessor pay for any equipment cost overruns?	☐	☐
17. Are all the equipment loans from lenders unrelated to the lessee?	☐	☐
18. Is the transaction devoid of any indebtedness guarantees by the lessee or related parties?	☐	☐

	Yes	No
19. Will the lessor make a profit on the lease without considering the tax benefits?	☐	☐
20. Will the transaction generate a positive cash flow for the lessor?	☐	☐
21. Will the equipment have a use at the end of the lease term to someone other than to the lessee?	☐	☐
22. Have the required backup information and material been submitted with the request for ruling?	☐	☐

H. Summary

If the parties to a lease transaction intend to have the lease characterized for tax purposes as a lease, they must know the tax rules governing whether a transaction will in fact be considered by the applicable taxing authorities as a "true" lease for tax purposes. If a lease is so considered, the lessor will be deemed to be the lease asset's owner and thus be able to claim the available equipment ownership tax benefits. The lessee, on the other hand, will be entitled to deduct the lease rent payable as an expense of its income tax returns. Failure of the lease to so qualify can result in an unfortunate rearranging of the tax attributes assumed to be available—and the potential of an economic loss for the lessor and a less attractive arrangement for the lessee. To avoid this problem, the rules governing the tax characterization must be understood. Unfortunately, doing this is often an art, because the tax rules are not always precise or clearly discernable.

Chapter 8

Advantages and Risks of Leveraged Leasing Decisions

A. What Is the Concept of Leveraged Leasing?

The leveraged lease can be one of the most complex and sophisticated vehicles for financing capital equipment in today's financial marketplace. The individuals and firms in the leveraged leasing industry are aggressive and creative. As a result, the environment is one of innovation and intense competition.

Is the concept of a leveraged lease complex? Not really. It is simply a lease transaction in which the lessor puts in only a portion, usually 20% to 40%, of the funds necessary to buy the equipment and a third-party lender supplies the remainder. Because the benefits available to the lessor are generally based on the entire equipment cost, the lessor's investment is said to be "leveraged" with third-party debt.

Generally the third-party loan is on a nonrecourse-to-the-lessor basis and ranges from 60% to 80% of the equipment's cost. The nonrecourse nature means the lender can only look to the lessee, the stream of rental payments that have been assigned to it, and the equipment for repayment. The lessor has no repayment responsibility even if the lessee defaults and the loan becomes uncollectible.

The fact that a nonrecourse lender cannot look to the lessor for the loan repayment if there is a problem is not as bad as it seems for two reasons:

- The lender will not make a nonrecourse loan unless the lessee is considered creditworthy.
- The lender's rights to any proceeds coming from a sale or re-release of the equipment comes ahead of any of the lessor's rights in the equipment and lease.

The lessor's equity investment is subordinated to the loan repayment obligation. If a lender only contributed, for example, 70% of the funds necessary, then the subordination arrangement would put it in an overcollateralized loan position that, in turn, would decrease its lending risk.

Although the third-party loan is usually made on a nonrecourse basis, if the lessee's financial condition is weak, a lender may only be willing to make a recourse loan. Under this type of loan, the lender can look to, or has recourse against, the lessor for repayment if it cannot be satisfied through the lessee or the equipment. The lessor still has the economic advantage of a leveraged investment, however.

Although the concept of leveraging a lease investment is simple, the mechanics of putting one together is often complex. Leveraged lease transactions, particularly ones involving major dollar commitments, frequently involve many parties brought together through intricate arrangements. The "lessor" is typically a group of investors joined together by a partnership or trust structure. The partnership or trust is the legal owner, or titleholder, of the equipment. The "lender" is often a group of lenders usually acting through a trust arrangement. This situation is further complicated by the fact that each participant will be represented by counsel with varying views. As a result, the job of organizing, drafting, and negotiating the necessary documents is usually difficult.

➤ **Observation**   Because the expenses involved in documenting a leveraged lease can be substantial, transactions involving less than $2 million worth of equipment can be economically difficult to structure as a leveraged lease. If, however, documentation fees (such as counsel fees) can be kept within reason, smaller equipment amounts can be financed in this manner. In many cases a prospective lessor or underwriter has an in-house legal staff with the ability to originate and negotiate the required documents. If so, this will help minimize costs.

Generally leveraged lease financings are arranged for prospective lessees by companies or individuals who specialize in structuring and negotiating these types of leases. These individuals and firms are referred to as lease underwriters. Essentially, their function is to structure the lease economics, find the lessor-investors, and provide the necessary expertise to ensure that the transaction will get done. In a limited number of situations, underwriters also find the debt participants. They do not generally participate as an investor in the equipment. Because the vast majority of leveraged leases are brought about with the assistance of lease underwriters, lease underwriting has become synonymous with leveraged leasing.

The premise on which lease underwriting services are provided by an underwriter (i.e., on a "best efforts" or "firm" basis) varies significantly. It is therefore worthwhile at this stage to explore the two types of underwriter offers: best efforts and firm commitment underwriting arrangements.

1. A "Best Efforts" Underwriting Arrangement Can Be Risky

Lease underwriting transactions are frequently bid on a best efforts basis. This type of bid is an offer by the underwriter to do the best it can to put a transaction together under the terms set out in its proposal letter. There are no guarantees of performance. As a result, a prospective lessee accepting the offer may not know for some time whether it has the financing.

In practice, a best efforts underwriting is not as risky as it appears. Most reputable underwriters have a good feel for the market when bidding on this basis and usually can deliver what they propose. Thus, there is a good chance they will be able to get firm commitments from one or more prospective lessor-investors to participate on the basis offered.

➤ **Recommendations**
*   A prospective lessee must always keep in mind that a best efforts underwriting proposal gives no guarantee the transaction can be completed under the terms proposed. Thus, it must give careful consideration to the experience and reputation of an underwriter proposing on this basis before awarding a transaction to it. An inability to perform as presented can result in the loss of valuable time.
*   When there is adequate equipment delivery lead time, a prospective lessee may be inclined to award a transaction to an unknown underwriter who has submitted an unusually low bid. There is, however, a risk that must be considered. If the

transaction is so underpriced that it cannot be sold in the "equity" market, it may meet resistance when it is reoffered on more attractive investor terms. This can happen merely because it has been seen, or "shopped," too much. It is an unfortunate fact that when an investor is presented with a transaction that it knows has been shopped, even if the terms are favorable, it may refuse to consider it. Therefore, a prospective lessee should not be too eager to accept a "low ball" best efforts bid unless it has taken a hard look at the underwriter's ability to perform.

- Best efforts underwriters sometimes submit proposals that are substantially below the market. At times this happens by mistake. For example, transactions may have been priced in good faith based on acceptable investor market yields, but by the time the award is made, the market has moved upward. At other times, an underwriter may intentionally underprice a transaction to ensure the win. If it cannot be placed as proposed, the underwriter will go back and attempt to get the prospective lessee to agree to a higher rental rate. With its competitors no longer involved, it may be in a good bargaining position. A prospective lessee with near-term deliveries must be particularly careful in recognizing this possibility; otherwise, it may have little choice but to be pushed into a less favorable deal.

- A prospective lessee can control the risk of nonperformance under a best efforts proposal by putting a time limit on the award, for example, by requiring the underwriter to come up with, or "circle," interested parties within one week following the award and securing formal commitments by the second week.

- It is not unheard of for a prospective lessee to make a time limit award to an unusually low bidding, or unknown, underwriter without telling the remaining bidders. The purpose is to try to keep them around just in case the underwriter cannot perform. This practice can be unfair to an underwriter who, in good faith, is continuing to spend time and money on the transaction in the hope of winning it. Doing this can also hurt a prospective lessee in the long run, because it is likely that the other underwriters will find out that this happened. Once the word gets around that a company does business in this manner, reputable underwriters may refuse to participate in future biddings. Even if they do participate, they may quote rates that have not been as finely tuned as possible, because they will not spend the time or money necessary in situations where they may not be treated fairly. Thus, this tactic is not recommended because a prospective lessee may, as a result, not see the best possible market rates.

2. A "Firm Commitment" Underwriting Arrangement Is Often the Best

From a prospective lessee's viewpoint, a firm commitment underwriting proposal is generally the preferred type of offer. When an underwriter has said to have "come in firm," it is guaranteeing to put the proposed lease financing together. Typically, before an underwriter submits this type of proposal, it has solid commitments from lessor-investors to enter into the transaction on the terms presented. Beware, however, that the underwriter's firm bid may only represent its willingness to be the lessor if it cannot find a third-party lessor.

➤ Recommendations

- If an underwriter proposing on a firm basis does not have "committed equity" at the time its proposal is submitted, a prospective lessee may be subject to certain risks. Unless the underwriter is in a strong financial position, its commitment may be worthless if a third-party lessor cannot be found. Thus, a prospective lessee must always investigate whether an underwriter has lined up one or more lessor-investors. If not, the underwriter's financial condition must be reviewed to determine, before making the award, whether it has the financial ability to stand behind it.

- Underwriters sometimes state they have firm "equity" even though they have nothing more than a verbal indication from a prospective lessor-investor's contact that it will recommend the transaction to its approving committee. Thus, a prospective lessee must ask to be put in touch with each lessor-investor to confirm its position. Doing this will also ensure that there are no misunderstandings as to the transaction terms.

B. Leveraged Lease Participants Have Unique Characteristics

Generally a leveraged lease transaction will involve more parties than a nonleveraged one. At a minimum, the participants will include an equity participant (lessor-investor), a debt participant, a lessee, and an equipment supplier. In the event the equity or debt participant acts through a trust arrangement, a trustee will also be a party. Often these participants have certain unique characteristics.

1. The Equity Participants

An investor in a leveraged lease is referred to as an "equity participant." Generally more than one investor is involved on the "equity side" of a leveraged lease. These equity participants, or owners, often act together through a trust arrangement. A trust provides partnershiplike tax treatment, while at the same time giving corporatelike liability protection. The equity participants are deemed the beneficial owners of the equipment. Legal title is held by the representative (the trustee) of the trust.

It is possible when more than one lessor-investor is involved for them to act through a partnership arrangement, rather than a trust. Here, the partnership is the lessor. Legal title to the equipment is held in the partnership name.

➤ **Recommendation**   The actual form of equipment owning entity (trust or partnership) will depend on the particular needs of each transaction and the participants. Counsel must be used to select the best form for a particular situation.

The typical leveraged lease equity participant is an "institutional investor." Banks, for example, fall within this category. Because a leveraged lease can be an attractive investment, many "regular" corporations and, in a limited number of situations, wealthy individuals also are potential lessor-investor candidates.

Some prospective leveraged lease investors have their own leasing companies actively looking for lease investment opportunities. But many do not. Those that do not, often referred to as "passive" investors, usually rely exclusively on the lease underwriting community to locate leveraged lease investments for them. Typically, the passive-type investor depends heavily on underwriters for advice on the structure and documentation of these investments.

2. The Lessee

A leveraged lease transaction, as with any lease transaction, does not begin to come into existence until an equipment user, the prospective lessee, decides to consider leasing as a

way to finance the acquisition of equipment it needs. Thus, the lessee is the key participant in any lease financing.

Because documenting a leveraged lease transaction tends to be expensive, this type
of lease usually makes economic sense only for financings involving a significant dollar
amount of equipment. As a result, the type of potential lessee is usually a large equipment
user who has the financial strength to support the obligations involved.

3. The Debt Participants

A lender in a leveraged lease transaction is generally referred to as a debt participant. It
is common for there to be more than one debt participant involved in a particular lease.
When this is the case, they frequently form a trust through which they will act. The document setting out the trust's terms is referred to as the trust indenture. The amount of
money each debt participant intends to loan is transferred to the trust, which in turn lends
it to the lessor. The loan made to the lessor is generally nonrecourse in nature. It is represented by a note or series of notes payable over the lease term from the rent proceeds the
lessor receives.

If properly organized, the lender's trust will receive partnershiplike income tax
treatment and corporatelike liability protection. Each participant, as a beneficial owner of
the trust estate, is treated for income tax purposes as though it made its loan directly to
the lessor and will not have a direct exposure to any third-party claim.

Leveraged lease third-party debt is often supplied by banks or insurance companies;
however, because a leveraged lease loan is no different from any other loan secured by
personal property, generally any lender able and willing to make a secured loan is a
potential loan source. The one limiting factor is the prospective lender's ability to offer
competitive market interest rates. The debt interest rate is a critical factor in the rent computation. A leveraged lease rent quotation is usually premised on an assumed debt interest rate, so the lower the interest rate the more profit a lessor makes and vice versa. This
is so, unless the prospective lessee gets the benefit or bears the risk of interest rate variations. In the latter case the underwriter's proposal will provide that if the debt interest
rate comes in other than assumed, the rent will be adjusted upward or downward to
appropriately reflect the variance. As a result, only the most rate-aggressive lenders (such
as, banks and insurance companies) are usually able to compete, particularly in the better credit transactions.

4. The Underwriter

The lease underwriting business has a relatively low capital entrance requirement.
Because of this there is an overabundance of "packagers" offering lease underwriting services. These packagers run the gamut from individuals operating out of telephone booths
to investment bankers to specialized lease underwriting firms. Some are well versed in
leveraged leasing economics and documentation and others know little more than the
basics. The choice of an underwriter is critical to the success of a transaction. Those who
have a solid understanding of the business and who are continually active in the underwriting market are more likely to better structure and ensure leveraged lease financing
success.

➤ **Recommendation** Prospective lessees entertaining leveraged lease proposals must
make sure before awarding a transaction that the intended underwriter has the qualifications to do the job necessary, both from an experience and a technical standpoint.

5.   The Equipment Manufacturer

The equipment manufacturer or distributor involved in a leveraged lease transaction usually does nothing more than sell the agreed on equipment to the lessor at the negotiated price. Once the full price has been paid, its only obligation is to stand behind its product for any warranty period.

In some situations, the vendor's role is not limited to merely selling the equipment to the lessor. It sometimes provides various inducements to a lessor to assist in selling its equipment. For example, it may be willing to guarantee some of the lessee's lease obligations in situations when the lessee's financial condition is weak.

6.   The Investor's Representative—The Owner's Trustee

In the event equity participants act through a trust, a trustee will be appointed to be the trust's representative. The trustee is sometimes referred to as the owner's trustee and is usually a commercial bank or trust company.

The owner's trustee is considered the mechanical arm of the trust, because the trust arrangement specifically defines the trustee's responsibilities. For example, one of its prescribed duties will be to allocate and disburse the lease funds among the various equity participants under a predetermined formula. As the equity participants' representative, it makes sure their investment is protected by monitoring their rights under the lease.

7.   The Lender's Representative—The Indenture Trustee

When a trust arrangement is established for the debt participants, a trustee, referred to as the indenture trustee, is employed to represent the trust. The trust agreement clearly defines the indenture trustee's duties. For example, the indenture trustee collects the money to be loaned from the debt participants and then turns it over to the lessor. As a part of the loan transaction, the indenture trustee takes an assignment of the lease and a security interest in the equipment as security for the loan repayment. Typically, a commercial bank or trust company is selected to act as the indenture trustee.

C.   How Different Is the Leveraged Lease Document?

The format of a typical leveraged lease document is essentially the same as that of any other finance lease. However, the terms and provisions are usually more detailed, because the major dollar commitments involved usually dictate that greater attention be paid to each aspect.

What about the collateral, or supplemental, documents? There are typically a greater number involved in a leveraged lease than in a "straight" lease transaction. For example, in addition to those found in nonleveraged lease situations, such as the lease, opinions of counsel, and board of director resolutions, the leveraged transaction documentation will at a minimum usually include trust agreements, a participation agreement, promissory notes, and a security and loan agreement.

D.   Three Advantages to the Lessee in a Leveraged Lease

In certain situations, a leveraged lease transaction offers many benefits for a prospective lessee. It may in some cases be the only economically viable approach.

1. The Rent Can Be More Attractive

As a rule of thumb, a competitively bid leveraged lease transaction will provide a lower cost to a lessee than a comparable term nonleveraged lease. Logically, if a company can borrow at a more favorable interest rate than a lessor, it stands to reason that if the lessor pays part of the equipment's cost with a loan based on the lessee's credit, it can lower its rents without sacrificing economic return. There are, of course, exceptions to this rule, and each situation must be examined on its own. For example, if the dollar amount of equipment financed is small, then the documentation expenses involved can offset the economic benefits gained through leveraging.

2. The Market Is Better for Large Transactions

Major dollar equipment lease financings can generally be arranged more readily by using a leveraged lease structure, because a lessor-investor only has to come up with a portion of the required equipment investment, the remainder being provided by a third-party lender. Because many investors and lenders are unwilling to make a major dollar investment in one transaction, a number of lessor-investors and lenders must frequently be brought together. Forming investor and lender syndicates can keep the dollar exposure for each within desired limits.

Bringing together more than one investor and lender can be beneficial for a lessee. When the investment risk is spread among a greater number of participants, it increases the likelihood that a large dollar lease financing can be done at more reasonable rates. No one party has such a great exposure that it believes it must charge a premium for the risk. The disadvantage is the added paperwork; however, a competent and experienced underwriter will be able to successfully usher everyone through the documentation tangle—another reason why the choice of the underwriter is a critical factor.

➤ **Observation** There are a small number of prospective lessor-investors willing to act as the sole equity participant in major equipment lease financings. The advantage to using such an investor is the necessary approvals and potential complications will be kept to a minimum. Generally, however, this type of investor realizes not many others are willing to take an entire major transaction and their rent charge will usually be high. Whether the extra rate is worth the reduced risks of a simpler transaction is a matter of judgment. An experienced underwriter should be of great assistance in evaluating the trade-off.

3. The Lessors Can Be More Competitive

The type of lessor interested in pursuing a leveraged lease investment is often most concerned over the available equipment ownership tax benefits. As a result, such a lessor may be willing to be more aggressive on those aspects of a lease transaction not impacting the lease's tax consequences.

E. Investment Pitfalls and Recommendations for Prospective Lessors

A prospective lessor must consider many factors before deciding to enter into a particular lease transaction, leveraged or not. These considerations, however, are particularly crucial for leveraged lease investors, because the transactions can be highly competitive and the investment economics finely tuned. A slight mistake or change in the investment assumptions can thus have a major adverse impact.

For a prospective lessor-investor to evaluate the risks involved, it must know what they are. The following explanation provides fundamental points that must be considered by every lease investor before entering into a lease transaction.

1. Equipment Delivery Delays Can Destroy Profits

The date when the equipment is delivered determines when the ownership tax benefits will be available to a lessor. When these benefits are available is a critical factor in a prospective lessor's analysis of its anticipated economic return. An unexpected delivery delay can have a serious negative impact. Consider, for example, a transaction entered into by a calendar year taxpayer-investor based on the assumption that the equipment will be delivered no later than the end of the current year. A following year delivery could jeopardize its contemplated return, because the equipment ownership tax benefits would not be available until the next year. If the transaction had been priced in a competitive market, that slippage could easily make the transaction's economics completely unacceptable to the investor.

➤ **Recommendations**

- A prospective lessor-investor can protect itself against a potential yield deterioration because of equipment delivery delays in two ways. The first is by establishing a commitment cutoff date, that is, setting a point in time after which it will no longer be obligated to buy and lease delivering equipment. A second way is to provide for a rent adjustment that preserves the transaction's economics if a certain delivery date is passed.

- From a lessee's viewpoint, either of the lessor delivery delay solutions explained in the last recommendation can create problems. The first solution, however, is generally considered the more dangerous. When a delivery cutoff date is imposed, a prospective lessee could end up without a lease financing source for the late equipment. When a rental adjustment is permitted, a lessee may be confronted with an undesirably high rent. In the latter situation, however, it at least knows that lease financing will be available regardless of the delay.

- A prospective lessor should be careful when establishing the rental adjustment criterion to apply to equipment delivered late. For example, if the rental analysis is based on certain yield and after-tax cash flow standards, the prospective lessor should make sure the adjustment provision will permit it to maintain both criteria, because they will not run parallel. In other words, maintaining yield will not necessarily maintain after-tax cash flows and vice versa.

2. The Lessee's Financial Condition Is Crucial

The financial strength of a prospective lessee is an important lessor consideration in any lease transaction. It should be of prime concern to a passive type lessor-investor with limited equipment knowledge and remarketing capability. A lease default could easily endanger its invested capital and anticipated economic return. It is of utmost importance, therefore, for the prospective lessee's financial standing to be thoroughly reviewed.

3. Changes in Tax Law Can Eliminate Profits

If the tax benefits anticipated by investing in an equipment lease are eliminated or reduced because of a change in tax law, a lessor-investor could be confronted with an extremely unfavorable investment. The possibility of a tax law change is difficult, if not impossible, to predict. It is not, however, generally considered an unreasonable risk to assume in certain situations.

In major leveraged leases, lessees are sometimes "forced" to indemnify the lessor against any adverse change in the tax law that causes loss of a tax benefit. The tax indemnification provisions are usually incorporated directly in the lease agreement.

➤ Observations

- Prospective lessees have become increasingly successful in placing the tax benefit loss risks from changes in law on the lessor. It usually depends on who has the most negotiating strength. A favorite lessee argument is that the burden properly belongs on the lessor, because the prospective lessor is better able to assess the risk through its experience. The argument has some validity as to "regular" leasing companies. It may not be true, however, as far as the typical leveraged lease investor is concerned. In its passive role it may not have the type of exposure necessary to make the appropriate evaluation.
- A prospective lessor-investor can hedge against the change-in-tax-law risk by having the right to appropriately adjust the rental rate or to exclude equipment that will be affected but has not yet been delivered. The danger to a prospective lessee with these lessor solutions is that it may have to pay too high a lease rate or may be without financing at the last minute.

4. Income Variations Can Be Dangerous

A typical leveraged lease transaction may not be economically viable for a lessor-investor unless it can use all of the available equipment ownership tax benefits in a timely manner. If the investor had, for example, an unexpected net loss for the year the equipment was placed in service, it would have no taxable income against which to apply the tax benefits. The inability to use the tax benefits when anticipated would reduce the transaction's expected time value return. The time value concept says $1 received today is worth more than $1 received a year from today because of its earning capability. Thus, a lease investment must be looked at by a prospective lessor-investor in light of a careful and realistic appraisal of its present and future earning situations.

5. Tax Rate Variations—Consider the Possibility

How valuable the tax benefits that are available from owning equipment are to a lessor-investor depends to a large extent on its overall effective income tax rate: The greater its effective tax rate the more tax savings it will realize from the tax benefits. Any decrease in its tax rate will reduce the favorable impact of the available write-offs. Thus, a prospective lessor-investor must consider any potential income tax rate change in light of the future tax benefits coming from a lease investment.

➤ **Observation**   A prospective lessor-investor can protect itself against an adverse tax rate change by getting the prospective lessee to agree to indemnify it in the event it occurs. In today's market, however, it is unlikely that any prospective lessee would agree to provide this type of indemnity.

6.   Incorrect Residual Value Assessment—An Easy Trap

The value of the equipment at the end of a lease, referred to as its residual value, can have a dramatic impact on the profitability of the transaction. If a prospective lessor's residual value estimate is too high when it analyzes a lease investment, its return will be adversely affected. For example, if a prospective investor makes its investment analysis assuming a certain return based on selling the equipment at the end of the lease for 20% of its original cost, the transaction's profitability is reduced if the equipment sells for only 5% of its original cost. The overall effect of the diminished value depends on its importance in the investor's analysis. Very often it is a significant factor.

➤ **Recommendation**   It is advisable for a prospective lessor-investor to consult an equipment appraiser for assistance in making a reasonable residual value estimate. Remember, however, that an appraiser's opinion as to future value is nothing more than a professional guess. It does not assure the investor of the equipment's future worth, but it does provide a degree of comfort that would otherwise not exist.

7.   An Early Lease Termination Must Be Considered

A prospective lessor-investor must ensure that a permitted early lease termination will have little, if any, impact on its lease investment economics. Consider, for example, a 20-year full payout lease that is terminated at the end of 2 years. To begin with, the investor's future lease profits will be cut off. Depending on how the rents have been reported for income purposes, an early termination can cause a "book" loss. For example, if the rent income was reported faster than actually received, the early termination might make it necessary to report as a loss the difference between what was reported on the income statement and what has actually been taken in.

   If the equipment cannot be favorably re-leased in a timely manner, the lessor may be forced to sell it immediately. An unplanned sale situation can make it difficult for a lessor to realize the best price, particularly when large amounts of equipment are scattered across the country. Having adequate and inexpensive storage space can ease the problem, because then the lessor may be better able to afford to wait the market out. Lessors sometimes negotiate the right to store it on the lessee's premises free of charge, but this solution may not be a good one if the parties are in an adversary situation.

   Having to sell equipment early may also create another problem—a recapture of tax benefits claimed. If the tax benefits are an important part of the lessor's yield, a recapture can further destroy the already faltering lease economics.

   Incorporating a "termination value" concept into the lease can solve the early termination economic and tax recapture risks. Essentially a termination value is an amount a lessee would be obligated to pay to the lessor to help protect its investment and anticipated return.

8.   Casualty Loss—Are There Protections?

The types of problems confronting a lessor if there is an equipment casualty loss are similar to those that must be addressed if a lease termination occurs; that is, future profits will be unavailable, tax benefit recapture may result, and a "book" loss may have to be reported. There is, however, an important difference—the equipment will have little if any value. When a casualty loss occurs, therefore, the lessor is left without its collateral protection and must look to the lessee and any insurance proceeds for loss repayment. This is a good reason why prospective lessor-investors must ensure that the lessee is a creditworthy entity and that adequate insurance is secured and maintained.

► **Recommendation**   If a prospective lessee will be obligated to insure the leased equipment, the prospective lessor should require evidence at the time of the lease closing that the appropriate insurance coverage has been secured. Arrangements also should be made for the insurance company to notify the lessor if the lessee does anything, such as neglecting to pay the premiums, that could cause the policy to lapse. In this way, the lessor will have the opportunity of taking over any lapsed obligations to assure continued coverage.

Even though the lessee must maintain casualty loss insurance, prospective lessors should also incorporate a "casualty loss value" concept. Casualty values, sometimes referred to as "stipulated loss values," are calculated in much the same manner as termination values. Their purpose is to protect the lessor's investment position in the event of a casualty loss. Under this concept, the lessee in effect guarantees that the lessor will receive a certain amount of money if an equipment casualty occurs. The amount decreases after each rent payment is made, to reflect an appropriate recognition of the lessor's decreased financial exposure. It typically will be sufficient to repay the lessor's outstanding investment and any remaining equipment loan obligations. It also will provide the lessor with its profit, at least to the date of the loss. Typically, the lessee is given a credit for any insurance money received as a result of the loss against the amount owed. In effect, the lessee becomes an insurer of the lessor's investment and profit.

9. The Economic Analysis—A Critical Aspect

When a lease underwriter presents a lease investment to a prospective lessor-investor, it generally submits an economic analysis showing the return the investor can expect. If the method of analysis is incorrect, or unrealistic, a prospective investor can end up with a disastrous investment. It is not uncommon, for example, for an underwriter to incorporate a sinking fund arrangement in its analysis calculations. The sinking fund simply improves the investor's economics by assuming that cash available over the lease term will earn a certain amount of interest. If for some reason the interest rate assumption is too high, the return analysis will be misleading. Thus, a prospective investor must always verify any economic presentation on which it intends to base its investment decision.

► **Recommendation**   If a prospective lessor-investor cannot independently analyze the resulting economics of investing in a lease submitted by an underwriter, it should bring in an independent expert to review the presentation.

10. A Long-Term Commitment Can Present a Problem

Frequently, an equipment lease agreement is entered into well before the equipment actually delivers. This is done for a number of reasons. From a lessor's viewpoint, the faster it gets the lease "signed up," the less risk there will be that the prospective lessee will change its mind. Prospective lessees also are generally interested in proceeding as quickly as possible to avoid last-minute documentation problems.

When a lease agreement is signed well in advance of equipment delivery, particularly if it calls for the lessor to hold a substantial amount of money available, an unexpected decision by the lessee not to lease the equipment when it arrives will result in an alternate investment opportunity loss for the lessor during the commitment period. To avoid this risk, prospective lessors frequently require prospective lessees to agree to pay commitment or nonutilization fees. These fees guarantee that they will be compensated for holding funds available.

11. *Documentation Expenses Can Ruin a Lease Investment*

Expenses, such as legal fees, involved in documenting a lease transaction can be substantial. Depending on the transaction's complexity, it is not unheard of for the expenses to run into the hundreds of thousands of dollars. A $30,000 expense for a $3,000,000 lease investment may be acceptable; a $500,000 expense will no doubt be unacceptable. If an investor must pay these expenses, a substantial bill could ruin its investment economics. Thus, it is essential for a prospective lease investor to know who is responsible for the various charges and what the estimated amounts will be. Of particular concern will be who is responsible for the expenses if the transaction falls apart before the lease is signed.

➤ Recommendations

- In an underwritten leveraged lease transaction, the responsibility for the various documentation expenses is frequently outlined in the underwriter's proposal letter. In many cases, the underwriter will offer to pay most of the expenses. It is, however, an area of negotiation between the parties. A prospective investor must make sure it has not inadvertently assumed any expense responsibility that has not been considered. The more the expense burden can be shifted to someone else, the less the risk the economic integrity of the investment will be endangered.
- Frequently, a lease underwriter will place the burden for expenses incurred in a collapsed lease transaction on the prospective lessee. It is recommended, however, that a prospective lessee at least require a sharing of the expenses with any other party contributing to the failure.

F. Checklist for the Leveraged Lease Investor

Before making a commitment to invest in a leveraged lease, a prospective lessor-investor must consider the following points.

If the equipment will not be put on lease at the time the lease commitment is signed, does it matter when the equipment actually delivers? If so:

- Does the lease agreement provide for a cutoff date beyond which the lessor will not be obligated to buy and lease the equipment?
- If there is no equipment delivery cutoff date, does the lease permit the lessor to appropriately adjust the rents if its economics are affected?
- Can the lessee substitute equipment if specific equipment delivers late or never arrives? If so, are there controls on the type that will be acceptable?

Has the prospective lessee's financial condition been thoroughly reviewed?

If any credit support for the lessee's lease obligations will be provided, has the financial condition of the supporting party been carefully reviewed?

Has tax counsel been consulted as to any near-term possibility of the tax laws changing so as to affect the anticipated equipment ownership tax benefits?

In the event of a tax law change affecting the equipment ownership tax benefits, will the lessee have to indemnify the lessor for any resulting adverse effect?

Can the entire future tax benefits generated by a lease investment be used? That is, will the lessor's taxable income be sufficient to cover the available write-offs?

Has tax counsel been consulted as to any future federal income tax rate changes? If there is a change adversely affecting the leased equipment, who must bear the burden?

Is the residual value of the equipment an important factor in the lessor's economic analysis? If so:

- Has it been properly assessed?
- Has a qualified equipment appraiser been consulted?

Will the lessor's economics be protected if there is an early lease termination?

- If it results from a lease default?
- If it results from a permitted termination?

If a termination value concept has been incorporated to protect a lessor's investment position, have the values been verified?

Will the lessor's investment position be protected if there is an equipment casualty loss?

- If a stipulated loss value (also referred to as casualty loss value) concept has been incorporated in the lease, has each value been verified?

Will an underwriter's economic analysis of a proposed lease investment be relied on? If so:

- Has it been independently checked?
- Are all the investment criteria assumptions, such as sinking fund interest rate, realistic from the prospective lessor's standpoint?

Must the prospective lessor make a long-term commitment to buy and lease equipment? If so, will the lessee be able to decide at the last minute not to lease the equipment without a penalty? If not, has a proper commitment fee or nonutilization fee been incorporated?

Have the expenses for documenting the lease and the responsibility for payment been clearly defined?

- If the transaction actually goes through?
- If the transaction collapses before the lease documents are signed?

G. Summary

A leveraged lease is typically a complex and sophisticated vehicle for financing capital equipment. The basic concept, however, is not complex—it is simply a lease transaction in which the lessor puts in only a portion, usually 20% to 40%, of the funds necessary to buy the equipment and a third-party lender supplies the remainder. Generally, the third-party loan is on a nonrecourse-to-the-lessor basis and ranges from 60% to 80% of the equipment's cost. The nonrecourse nature means the lessor has no repayment responsibility even if the lessee defaults and the loan becomes uncollectible. Keep in mind, however, that the mechanics of putting a leveraged lease transaction together are generally complex, often involving many parties brought together through intricate document arrangements. The complexity can be offset by the transaction structure benefits to both the lessor and the lessee.

Chapter 9

Financial Analysis of Leases

A. Overview

As described in Chapter 1, there are a variety of factors to be considered when a prospective lessee or lessor decides to enter into an equipment lease. The lease's financial consequences are always important and often decisive.

A prospective lessee, therefore, should not choose to lease before making a financial comparison with the other available methods of financing the equipment's acquisition. The extent of the analysis will of course depend on the level of commitment involved. Similarly, a prospective lessor should not commit to a lease until it has been reviewed for investment soundness.

This chapter explains the financial concepts involved in the analysis of a finance lease, both from a prospective lessee's and a prospective lessor's viewpoint. Although not every possible method of financial lease analysis is explored, the explanation provides a concise foundation in lessee and lessor financial lease analysis.

B. Importance of Cash Flow and Timing for a Lessee

In making a financial assessment of whether to lease or buy equipment, a prospective lessee must take the varying cash flows, and their timing, into account for each alternative. Stated simply, how much are the cash inflows and outflows, and when do they occur? The timing of the cash inflows and outflows is critical because of the principle of time value of money, that money received earlier is worth more than money received later.

The following example illustrates simplistically how taking cash flow and its timing into account alters the result of an analysis.

> **Illustrative Example**   *Cash Flow and Time Value:* An equipment user is considering two options: Leasing equipment over a seven-year period with an annual rent of $990 payable at the beginning of each year; and buying the equipment using a seven-year loan with $1,000 annual payments due at each year's end. By choosing to lease, the company would pay out $990 one year earlier than it would have to pay the required $1,000 loan payment. If the company could earn, say, 6% a year after taxes on its available funds, giving up the $990 in advance would result in a "loss" of $59.40 (6% × $990 = $59.40) the first year. In

149

this case, the advance payment could be said to cost $1,049.40 ($990 + $59.40 = $1,049.40). Putting other considerations aside, the $1,000 loan payment would have been less expensive. If the company were able to earn only 1% a year after taxes, paying the $990 would result in only a $9.90 "loss" (1 % × $990 = $9.90). That is, the effective cost of paying the $990 would have been $990.90, instead of $1,049.40. In the latter case, the $1,000 loan payment could be said to be more expensive.

C.   Prospective Lessee's Analysis

Once a company has decided it needs certain equipment, it must determine how to finance its acquisition. The following discussion will address three alternatives:

- The user leases the equipment (the Leasing Alternative).
- The user draws on its general funds to buy the equipment (the Purchase Alternative).
- The user takes out a specific loan to buy the equipment (the Financing Alternative).

This section will compare the three financial alternatives by using a common method for taking cash flows and their timing into account, sometimes called the discounted cash flow—or present value—analysis method. The first step will be to compute the periodic costs and tax savings for each alternative. The next step will be to factor in the timing of those cash flows so there is a basis for comparison by calculating the present value of each alternative's cash flows. To compute the present value of a series of future cash flows, an interest rate, called the discount rate, must be selected to discount the flows back to their present worth. The result will be the present value cost of the alternatives.

Because getting to these results involves many computations, the following analysis will center around one hypothetical equipment acquisition situation.

➤ **Note** The financial analysis computations from which the examples in this chapter were developed were done on SuperTRUMP, a lease analysis computer software program, by Ivory Consulting Corporation, Orinda, California. The information from the computer analysis results was at times summarized by the author to aid in the explanation of the concepts described in the text material.

1.   Typical Equipment User's Financial Alternatives

White Industries wants to acquire a new computer and can use all available tax benefits. For ease of illustration, "bonus" depreciation currently allowed will be ignored. White is considering three financing alternatives—the Lease Alternative, the Purchase Alternative, and the Financing Alternative. Additional facts include the following (assumed for ease of illustration without regard to whether any applicable tax or other rules will be satisfied):

General Data

Computer cost	$1 million
Depreciable period	5 years
Residual value	$0
ITC	0%

White Industries income tax rate 35%
White Industries tax year .... Calendar year
Delivery date .... January 1, 2003
Depreciation method .... MACRS (Half-year, DB/SL 200%)

Proposed Financial Lease

Lease term .... 7 years
Rental payments .... $200,000, payable in 7 annual payments in arrears
Lease simple interest rate 9.1961%
Commencement date .... January 1, 2003

Proposed Bank Loan

Loan amount .... $1 million, repayable in 7 equal annual payments of $205,405.50 in arrears
Loan term .... 7 years
Long-term interest rate 10.0%
Commencement date .... January 1, 2003

2. Cost of the Leasing Alternative

The first step is to compute the after-tax cost of the various alternatives. Table 9.1 sets out those costs for the Leasing Alternative.

Table 9.1 is computed as follows:

- The Rental Payments are the annual payments the lessee must make. These begin in 2004 because the rent is payable in arrears.
- The Tax Savings from Rent Deductions represents the federal income tax savings White Industries would realize from the rent deductions, computed at White Industries's assumed 35% bracket.

Table 9.1 Cost of Leasing Alternative.

Year Ending	Rental Payments	Tax Savings from Rent Deductions	After-tax Cost	Cumulative After-tax Cost
Dec. 30, 2003	$ 0	$ 70,000	$(70,000)	$(70,000)
Dec. 30, 2004	200,000	70,000	130,000	60,000
Dec. 30, 2005	200,000	70,000	130,000	190,000
Dec. 30, 2006	200,000	70,000	130,000	320,000
Dec. 30, 2007	200,000	70,000	130,000	450,000
Dec. 30, 2008	200,000	70,000	130,000	580,000
Dec. 30, 2009	200,000	70,000	130,000	710,000
Dec. 30, 2010	200,000	0	200,000	910,000
TOTAL	$1,400,000	$490,000	$910,000	n/a

- The After-tax Cost is derived by subtracting the Tax Savings from the Rent Deductions from the Rental Payments.
- The Cumulative After-tax Cost represents the transaction's total after-tax cost as of each year end.

The result is a total after-tax cost of $910,000, if White Industries leases the computer.

3. Cost of the Purchase Alternative

The next step is to compute the after-tax cost of an outright purchase using internal funds. The Annual Depreciation Expense indicated in Table 9.2 is the amount White Industries would be entitled to deduct under MACRS as the computer owner over a five-year period. The other columns are computed as in the leasing example (see Table 9.1).

4. Comparing Cash Flows

At this point in the analysis, the Purchase Alternative seems substantially less expensive than the Lease Alternatives as its total after-tax cost is only $650,000 compared with $910,000 for leasing. However, this ignores the leasing cash flow advantage because, as shown in Table 9.3, the total cost of the lease is less until the seventh year.

Plainly, leasing does conserve money in the early years, and those available funds could be put to use elsewhere. The resulting earnings on those funds would offset the disparity in total cost between the two alternatives. Thus, it cannot be concluded that leasing is more expensive until the present value of the two alternative's cash flows is compared.

Table 9.2 Cost of Purchase Alternative.

Year Ending	Equity	Annual Depreciation Expense	Tax Savings	After-tax Cost	Cumulative After-tax Cost
Dec. 30, 2003	$1,000,000	$ 200,000	$ 70,000	$930,000	$930,000
Dec. 30, 2004	0	320,000	112,000	(112,000)	818,000
Dec. 30, 2005	0	192,000	67,200	(67,200)	750,800
Dec. 30, 2006	0	115,200	40,320	(40,320)	710,480
Dec. 30, 2007	0	115,200	40,320	(40,320)	670,160
Dec. 30, 2008	0	57,600	20,160	(20,160)	650,000
TOTAL	$1,000,000	$1,000,000	$350,000	$650,000	n/a

Table 9.3 Cash flow comparison.

Year	Lease Cumulative After-tax Cost	Purchase Cumulative After-tax Cost	Lease Cash Advantage
2003	$(70,000)	$930,000	$1,000,000
2004	60,000	818,000	758,000
2005	190,000	750,000	560,000
2006	320,000	710,000	390,000
2007	450,000	670,000	220,000
2008	580,000	650,000	70,000
2009	710,000	650,000	(60,000)
2010	910,000	650,000	(260,000)

To calculate the present value of the leasing and buying cash flows, White Industries must discount both alternatives' cash flows to their present worth. Choosing a 10% annual discount rate and assuming White Industries pays its estimated taxes on April 15, June 15, September 15, and December 15 of each year, the after-tax cash flows for the Leasing and Purchase Alternatives are shown in Table 9.4.

The discounted cash flow analysis clearly reverses the outcome. The Leasing Alternative's present worth is $611,253.72, whereas the Purchase Alternative's worth is $720,947.55. Based on this analysis, leasing the computer would be less expensive than buying with internal funds.

5. The Financing Alternative

The next step is to calculate the Financing Alternative's cash flow in the same manner. The computation is the same as the Purchase Alternative (Table 9.2) with the additional factors being the payment of the 10% interest and the tax savings on deducting the interest. The after-tax cost calculations are shown in Table 9.5.

The present worth calculations, again using a 10% discount rate, are shown in Table 9.6 (again assuming estimated federal income tax payments are made on April 15, June 15, September 15, and December 15 of each tax year).

6. Comparison of Cash Flows

As Table 9.6 shows, the Financial Alternative results in a present value cost of ($598,599.23), the least expensive of the three alternatives. This result is not intended to mean that financing with borrowed funds is always the best alternative because the specific result was based on the assumed facts. Rather it is intended to show how dramatically the present value cash flow analysis alters the result. The Financing Alternative, with the highest cumulative cost, results in the lowest present worth cost; and Purchase Alternative, with the lowest cumulative cost, results in the highest present worth cost.

D. Lessor's Lease Investment Analysis

The prospective lessor, in making its financial analysis, wants to know how much its return will be on the leased equipment. The concepts of cash flow and present value also play important parts in the lessor's analysis.

This section will analyze two types of leases: the nonleveraged lease, in which the lessor uses its own funds entirely to buy the equipment, and the leveraged lease, in which the lessor borrows to pay for a portion of the equipment cost.

1. Nonleveraged Lease

As explained earlier, in a nonleveraged lease, the lessor supplies all the money necessary to buy the equipment from its own funds. Whether this type of investment will make economic sense depends on how profitable the transaction will be to the lessor. Thus, determining the profit—commonly referred to as the rate of return (usually computed on an after-tax basis)—is a threshold issue in any financial lease investment evaluation.

Traditionally, an after-tax lessor's rate of return has been defined as the interest rate, or discount rate, that will discount a lease's after-tax cash flows back to a value equal to the initial cash outlay. Or, looking at it another way, it is the rate that, when applied to the

Table 9.4 Present value comparison.

	Lease		Purchase	
Year	After-tax Cost	Present Value	After-tax Cost	Present Value
Jan. 01, 2003	0.00	0.00	1,000,000.00	1,000,000.00
April 15, 2003	(17,500.00)	(17,008.64)	(17,500.00)	(17,008.64)
June 15, 2003	(17,500.00)	(16,729.81)	(17,500.00)	(16,729.81)
Sept. 15, 2003	(17,500.00)	(16,321.77)	(17,500.00)	(16,321.77)
Dec. 15, 2003	(17,500.00)	(15,923.67)	(17,500.00)	(15,923.67)
	70,000.00	65,983.89	930,000.00	934,016.11
Jan. 01, 2004	200,000.00	181,179.00	0.00	0.00
April 15, 2004	(17,500.00)	(15,408.09)	(28,000.00)	(24,852.95)
June 15, 2004	(17,500.00)	(15,166.50)	(28,000.00)	(24,245.80)
Sept. 15, 2004	(17,500.00)	(14,785.85)	(28,000.00)	(23,657.37)
Dec. 15, 2004	(17,500.00)	(14,425.22)	(28,000.00)	(23,080.38)
	130,000.00	121,404.92	112,000.00	95,639.47
Jan. 01, 2005	200,000.00	164,130.23	0.00	0.00
April 15, 2005	(17,500.00)	(13,958.16)	(16,800.00)	(13,399.83)
June 15, 2005	(17,500.00)	(13,729.34)	(16,800.00)	(13,180.16)
Sept. 15, 2005	(17,500.00)	(13,394.47)	(16,800.00)	(12,858.70)
Dec. 15, 2005	(17,500.00)	(13,067.78)	(16,800.00)	(12,545.07)
	130,000.00	109,980.48	67,200.00	51,983.76
Jan. 01, 2006	200,000.00	148,685.24	0.00	0.00
April 15, 2006	(17,500.00)	(12,644.67)	(10,080.00)	(7,283.33)
June 15, 2006	(17,500.00)	(12,437.38)	(10,080.00)	(7,163.93)
Sept. 15, 2006	(17,500.00)	(12,134.03)	(10,080.00)	(8,989.20)
Dec. 15, 2006	(17,500.00)	(11,838.08)	(10,080.00)	(8,818.73)
	130,000.00	99,631.08	40,320.00	28,255.19
Jan. 01, 2007	200,000.00	134,693.66	0.00	0.00
April 15, 2007	(17,500.00)	(11,454.78)	(10,080.00)	(6,597.95)
June 15, 2007	(17,500.00)	(11,267.00)	(10,080.00)	(6,459.79)
Sept. 15, 2007	(17,500.00)	(10,992.19)	(10,080.00)	(6,331.50)
Dec. 15, 2007	(17,500.00)	(10,724.09)	(10,080.00)	(6,177.08)
	130,000.00	90,255.60	40,320.00	25,598.32
Jan. 01, 2008	200,000.00	122,018.71	0.00	0.00
April 15, 2008	(17,500.00)	(10,376.86)	(5,040.00)	(2,988.54)
June 15, 2008	(17,500.00)	(10,206.75)	(5,040.00)	(2,939.54)
Sept. 15, 2008	(17,500.00)	(9,957.80)	(5,040.00)	(2,867.85)
Dec. 15, 2008	(17,500.00)	(9,714.93)	(5,040.00)	(2,797.90)
	130,000.00	81,762.37	20,160.00	11,593.83
Jan. 01, 2009	200,000.00	110,536.50	0.00	0.00
April 15, 2009	(17,500.00)	(9,400.38)	0.00	0.00
June 15, 2009	(17,500.00)	(9,246.27)	0.00	0.00
Sept. 15, 2009	(17,500.00)	(9,020.75)	0.00	0.00
Dec. 15, 2009	(17,500.00)	(8,800.74)	0.00	0.00
	130,000.00	74,068.36	0.00	0.00
Jan. 01, 2010	200,000.00	100,134.79	0.00	0.00
	200,000.00	100,134.79	0.00	0.00
TOTAL	910,000.00	611,253.72	650,000.00	720,947.55

Table 9.5 Present worth calculations.

Year Ending	Debt Payments	Year-end Principal Balance Outstanding	10% Interest on Principal	Tax Savings (Depreciation & Interest)	Net After-tax Cost
Dec. 30, 2003	$ 0.00	$1,000,000.00	$ 100,000.00	$105,000.00	$(105,000.00)
Dec. 30, 2004	205,405.50	894,594.50	89,459.45	143,310.81	62,094.69
Dec. 30, 2005	205,405.50	778,645.45	77,846.85	94,452.70	110,952.80
Dec. 30, 2006	205,405.50	651,107.80	65,110.78	63,108.77	142,296.73
Dec. 30, 2007	205,405.50	510,813.08	51,081.31	58,198.46	147,207.04
Dec. 30, 2008	205,405.50	356,488.88	35,648.89	32,637.11	172,768.39
Dec. 30, 2009	205,405.50	186,732.27	18,673.23	6,535.63	198,869.87
Dec. 30, 2010	205,405.50	0.00	0.00	0.00	205,405.02
TOTAL	$1,437,838.50	$ 0.00	$ 437,838.50	$503,243.47	$ 934,595.02

original cash investment, will produce the future cash flow amounts generated by the lease.

To explain the investor rate of return analysis approach, we will work through a hypothetical nonleveraged lease example, assuming the following facts.

Equipment Data

Cost	$1 million
Depreciable life	5 years
Residual value	$0
Delivery date	January 1, 2003
Lease commencement date	January 1, 2003
Description	Computer

Lease Investment Data

Lease term	7 years
Rental payments	7 annual payments in arrears, each equal to $200,000
ITC	0%
Investor income tax rate	35%
Depreciation method	MACRS (Half-year, DB/SL 200)

Based on those facts, and the assumption that the lessor is an accrual basis taxpayer, Table 9.7 sets out the lessor's cash flow and federal income reports.

The columns in Table 9.7 are computed as follows:

- Annual Depreciation represents the amount of the annual MACRS deduction available to the lessor on the computer as five-year recovery property and applying the half-year convention.
- The Federal Taxable Income is the result of subtracting the annual depreciation deduction from the rent income. The lessor is an accrual basis taxpayer, so the rent income is accrued for the year ending December 30, 2003, for federal income tax purposes, resulting in no federal taxable income for this year ($200,000 rent income – $200,000 depreciation expense = $0), and there would be no federal tax accrued rent income for the year ending December 30, 2010.

Table 9.6 Present value comparison.

	Lease		Financing	
Year	After-tax Cost	Present Value	After-tax Cost	Present Value
Jan. 01, 2003	$ 0.00	$ 0.00	$ 0.00	$ 0.00
April 15, 2003	(17,500.00)	(17,008.64)	(26,250.00)	(25,512.96)
June 15, 2003	(17,500.00)	(16,729.81)	(26,250.00)	(25,094.71)
Sept. 15, 2003	(17,500.00)	(16,321.77)	(26,250.00)	(24,482.65)
Dec. 15, 2003	(17,500.00)	(15,923.67)	(26,250.00)	(23,885.51)
	70,000.00	65,983.89	105,000.00	98,975.83
Jan. 01, 2004	200,000.00	181,179.00	205,405.50	186,076.43
April 15, 2004	(17,500.00)	(15,408.09)	(35,827.70)	(31,544.94)
June 15, 2004	(17,500.00)	(15,166.50)	(35,827.70)	(31,027.81)
Sept. 15, 2004	(17,500.00)	(14,785.85)	(35,827.70)	(30,271.04)
Dec. 15, 2004	(17,500.00)	(14,425.22)	(35,827.70)	(29,532.72)
	130,000.00	121,404.92	62,094.69	63,699.91
Jan. 01, 2005	200,000.00	164,130.23	205,405.50	168,566.26
April 15, 2005	(17,500.00)	(13,958.16)	(23,613.17)	(18,834.08)
June 15, 2005	(17,500.00)	(13,729.34)	(23,613.17)	(18,525.33)
Sept. 15, 2005	(17,500.00)	(13,394.47)	(23,613.17)	(18,073.49)
Dec. 15, 2005	(17,500.00)	(13,067.78)	(23,613.17)	(17,632.67)
	130,000.00	109,980.48	110,952.80	95,500.68
Jan. 01, 2006	200,000.00	148,685.24	205,405.50	152,703.83
April 15, 2006	(17,500.00)	(12,644.67)	(15,777.19)	(11,399.85)
June 15, 2006	(17,500.00)	(12,437.38)	(15,777.19)	(11,212.97)
Sept. 15, 2006	(17,500.00)	(12,134.03)	(15,777.19)	(10,939.48)
Dec. 15, 2006	(17,500.00)	(11,838.08)	(15,777.19)	(10,672.66)
	130,000.00	99,631.08	142,296.73	108,478.87
Jan. 01, 2007	200,000.00	134,693.66	205,405.50	138,334.09
April 15, 2007	(17,500.00)	(11,454.78)	(14,549.61)	(9,523.58)
June 15, 2007	(17,500.00)	(11,267.00)	(14,549.61)	(9,367.45)
Sept. 15, 2007	(17,500.00)	(10,992.19)	(14,549.61)	(9,138.98)
Dec. 15, 2007	(17,500.00)	(10,724.09)	(14,549.61)	(8,916.08)
	130,000.00	90,255.60	147,207.04	101,388.00
Jan. 01, 2008	200,000.00	122,018.71	205,405.00	125,316.57
April 15, 2008	(17,500.00)	(10,376.86)	(8,159.28)	(4,838.15)
June 15, 2008	(17,500.00)	(10,206.75)	(8,159.28)	(4,758.84)
Sept. 15, 2008	(17,500.00)	(9,957.80)	(8,159.28)	(4,642.77)
Dec. 15, 2008	(17,500.00)	(9,714.93)	(8,159.28)	(4,529.53)
	130,000.00	81,762.37	172,768.39	106,547.27
Jan. 01, 2009	200,000.00	110,536.50	205,405.50	113,524.03
April 15, 2009	(17,500.00)	(9,400.38)	(1,633.91)	(877.68)
June 15, 2009	(17,500.00)	(9,246.27)	(1,633.91)	(863.29)
Sept. 15, 2009	(17,500.00)	(9,020.75)	(1,633.91)	(842.23)
Dec. 15, 2009	(17,500.00)	(8,800.74)	(1,633.91)	(821.69)
	130,000.00	74,068.36	198,869.87	110,119.14
Jan. 01, 2010	200,000.00	100,134.79	205,405.50	102,841.18
	200,000.00	100,134.79	205,405.50	102,841.18
TOTAL	$910,000.00	$611,253.72	$934,595.02	$589,599.23

Table 9.7 Lessor's cash flow and federal income reports.

Year Ending	Rent Income	Annual Depreciation	Federal Taxable Income	Total Taxes Paid	Equity	Pre-tax Cash Flow	After-tax Cash Flow
Dec. 30, 2003	$ 0.00	$ 200,000.00	$ 0.00	$ 0.00	$1,000,000.00	($1,000,000.00)	($1,000,000.00)
Dec. 30, 2004	200,000.00	320,000.00	(120,000.00)	(42,000.00)	0.00	200,000.00	242,000.00
Dec. 30, 2005	200,000.00	192,000.00	8,000.00	2,800.00	0.00	200,000.00	197,200.00
Dec. 30. 2006	200,000.00	115,200.00	84,800.00	29,680.00	0.00	200,000.00	170,320.00
Dec. 30, 2007	200,000.00	115,200.00	84,800.00	29,680.00	0.00	200,000.00	170,320.00
Dec. 30, 2008	200,000.00	57,600.00	142,400.00	49,840.00	0.00	200,000.00	150,160.00
Dec. 30, 2009	200,000.00	0.00	200,000.00	70,000.00	0.00	200,000.00	130,000.00
Dec. 30, 2010	200,000.00	0.00	0.00	0.00	0.00	200,000.00	200,000.00
TOTAL	$1,400,000.00	$1,000,000.00	$400,000.00	$140,000.00	$1,000,000.00	$ 400,000.00	$ 260,000.00

- The Total Taxes Paid represents the dollar savings or cost on the income or loss in the Federal Taxable Income column based on a 35% income tax rate. Where the figure is negative, the lessor reduces the overall tax liability by that amount.
- The After-tax Cash Flow results from adjusting the Pre-tax Cash Flow by the amount of the taxes paid or saved. Thus, where the Total Taxes Paid figure is negative, this amount is added to the Pre-tax Cash Flow; where the Total Taxes Paid figure is positive, this amount is subtracted from the Pre-tax Cash Flow.

Once the after-tax cash flows have been calculated, the after-tax rate of return, or after-tax yield, can be found by finding the interest rate that will discount the after-tax cash flows back to the cost of the computer, which is $1 million. Here, the lessor will receive an after-tax yield equal to 9.1961%.

2. *Lessor's Leveraged Lease Analysis*

The prospective lessor's goal in analyzing a leveraged lease is the same as with a non-leveraged lease, but the addition of the loan makes the analysis much more complex. As a result, the investment analysis is frequently done on a computer.

➤ **Recommendation** Prospective lessees should consider using a lessor computer software analysis program to estimate a proposing lessor's yield on a transaction. Such a program will also enable prospective lessees to compute other lease-related information. Stipulated loss values, for example, are based on the lessor's anticipated return, and so a program will enable lessees to reasonably verify those values. Unless this is done, there is no way to know if they have been properly computed. Because a prospective lessee will typically not have access to a lessor's computer yield analysis input information and, thus, a simulated lessor "run" may not be exact, a fair approximation can be obtained that will be helpful in negotiations.

To show the lessor's analysis in a leveraged lease, this section will use an illustrative example. Because a computer run is often used, the example's assumed facts and analysis, shown in Table 9.8, are set out in the manner of a computer run that is typical of one a prospective lessor would receive.

The Table 9.8 reports present the transactions facts as follows:

- The Summary Report Cash Flows section shows the equipment's total cost is $1 million ("asset cost"). The funds to buy the equipment will come from a $200,000 equity investment ("equity") representing 20% of the total cost, and a $800,000 third-party loan ("loan[s]"). This section also sets out other relevant information such as pretax and after-tax cash flows.
- The Summary Statistics section list various investment return information, on a pre-tax and after-tax basis. It indicates the method of lease analysis used as the multiple investment sinking fund, or MlSF method. The implicit lease interest rate is 9.1961% ("implicit lease rate").
- The Summary Report Asset(s) section specifies the equipment delivery date as January 1, 2002 ("delivery"), and that a $0 residual value ("residual") was assumed.
- The Summary Report Depreciation section shows that depreciation was assumed to begin on January 1, 2002 ("start date") and that the asset will be depreciated over a

period of five years ("term"). It also shows that the method of depreciation, a 200% declining-balance method with a switch to the straight-line method ("method"). A half-year depreciation convention was assumed ("convention").

- The Summary Report Rent(s) section provides the fundamental lease structure information. The lease will begin on January 1, 2002 ("commencement date"). The rent is due annually ("P/Y") and is payable in seven installments ("#") of $200,000 each ("amount"). The annual rent as a percentage of equipment cost is also listed ("% of cost").

- The Summary Report Loan(s) section describes the assumed third-party loan. The principal amount of the loan is $800,000 ("amount") and the annual loan interest rate is 10% ("rate"). The analysis further anticipates that the loan funding date is January 1, 2002 ("Start date") and that the loan is payable in seven installments ("#"). The final payment is due January 1, 2009.

The next component in the prospective lessor's analysis is the federal tax consequences of the proposed transaction. A lessor's lease investment presentation will typically include a tax analysis in the form of Table 9.9.

The preceding shows the steps involved in determining the tax consequences, as follows:

- The "revenue" column shows when the lessor must include the rent payments in income. Although the rent is payable annually in arrears, the taxpayer is an accrual basis taxpayer and it must report for federal income tax purposes the rent income for the year 2002.

- The "interest paid" column shows how much interest may be claimed for federal income tax purposes and when it may be claimed. Although the interest is payable in arrears, the taxpayer is an accrual basis taxpayer and will accrue the interest deduction for the year 2002.

- The "depreciation" column shows how much and when the prospective lessor may take the depreciation deduction. As the equipment will be placed in service in 2002, it is entitled to a $200,000 deduction for 2002. In years 2008 and 2009, the depreciation expense is $0 because the asset has, through 2007, been fully depreciated.

- The amounts in the "taxable income" column are computed by subtracting interest and depreciation deductions from the rent revenue.

- The "federal tax DUE" column shows the amount of tax savings or additional tax payable for each year of the lease. It assumes that the prospective lessor is in the 35% tax bracket. During the first three years, the transaction will reduce the lessor's overall tax liability; then it crosses over and no longer produces a loss, because the depreciation and interest deductions are less than the rental income.

Another frequently included part of an investor presentation is a cash flow report. Table 9.10 presents the lease's cash flow on an annual basis.

The after-tax cash flows are arrived at as follows:

- The "rent & income & residual" column shows the total amount of income received each year.

- The "equity & fees & expenses" column reflects the lessor's initial $200,000 investment in 2002.

- The "debt service" column shows the annual amount of the payment on the third-party loan.

Table 9.8 Summary report.

SUMMARY REPORT

Lessee	White Industries
Lessor	Gold Leasing Corporation
Prepared Nov-02, 2001 12:32 by	R. Contino
Parameter filename	text book: lease, leveraged
Parameter path	c:\ivory\prms\

Cash Flows

Asset cost	1,000,000.00	100.000000
Loan(s)	800,000.00	80.000000
Equity	200,000.00	20.000000
Rent	1,400,000.00	140.000000
Total cash in	1,400,000.00	140.000000
Equity	200,000.00	20.000000
Principal	800,000.00	80.000000
Interest	350,270.80	35.027080
Total cash out	1,350,270.80	135.027080
Pre-tax cash flow	49,729.20	4.972920
Taxes paid	17,405.22	1.740522
After-tax cash flow	32,323.98	3.232398

Statistics

Composite Tax Rate		35.00000
IRS Tests		PASSED

	Pre-tax		After-tax	
	Effective	Nominal	Effective	Nominal
MISF (per)	12.8902	12.4202	8.3787	8.0731
MISF (mon)	12.8961	12.4256	8.3825	8.0767
IRR PTCF (per)	6.0421	5.8810	3.9274	3.8226

Present value at 10.0000% of Rent on Jan-01-02	97.368376	973,683.76
Payback from Jan-01-02		3 yrs 0 mos 0 days
Average-life of loan: borrowing		4.3784 years
Implicit interest rate		9.1961
Effective cost (without residual)		9.1961
(with residual)		9.1961
Implicit cost (without residual)		9.1961
(with residual)		9.1961

160

Asset(s)

#	Cost	Delivery	Funding	Residual	Res. Date	Description
1	1,000,000.00	Jan-01-02	Jan-01-02	0.0000	Jan-01-09	

Depreciation

#	Start Date	Basis	Method	Term	Salv	Convention
1 Fed	Jan-01-02	100.0000	DB/SL 200	5.000	0.000	Half-yr

Rents

Commencement date Jan-01-02
Total payments 1,400,000.00

#	P.Y	Advance / Arrears	Method	Amount	% of cost
1	7 Ann	Jan-01-02 → Jan-01-09	Var Amt	200,000.00	20.000000

Loans

Amount 800,000.00

#	P.Y	Advance / Arrears	Rate	Method	Amount	% of cost
1		Jan-01-02		Funding	–800,000.00	–80.000000
	7 Ann	Jan-01-02 → Jan-01-09	10.0000	Var Amt	164,324.40	16.432440

Taxes/Lessor

Month fiscal year ends . . . . Dec.
Sinking fund rate (AT) 0.0000

Federal

Tax calculation method . . . . Accrual
Tax estimation method . . . . Level

Start date	Rate	Thru	Paid	Percent
Jan-01-02	35.0000	Mar	Apr	25.0000
		Jun	Jun	25.0000
		Sep	Sep	25.0000
		Dec	Dec	25.0000

Table 9.9 Federal tax statement.

FEDERAL TAX STATEMENT

Lessee . . . . White Industries
Lessor . . . . Gold Leasing Corporation
Prepared Nov-02-2001 12:48 by . . . . R. Contino
Parameter filename . . . . text book: lease, leveraged
Parameter path . . . . c:\ivory\prms\

Period Ending	Revenue	Interest Paid	Depreciation	Taxable Income	Federal Tax DUE	Federal Tax PAID
Dec-30-02	200,000.00	80,000.00	200,000.00	−80,000.00	−28,000.00	−28,000.00
Dec-30-03	200,000.00	71,567.56	320,000.00	−191,567.56	−67,048.65	−67,048.65
Dec-30-04	200,000.00	62,291.88	192,000.00	−54,291.88	−19,002.16	−19,002.16
Dec-30-05	200,000.00	52,088.62	115,200.00	32,711.38	11,448.98	11,448.98
Dec-30-06	200,000.00	40,865.05	115,200.00	43,934.95	15,377.23	15,377.23
Dec-30-07	200,000.00	28,519.11	57,600.00	113,880.89	39,858.31	39,858.31
Dec-30-08	200,000.00	14,938.58	0.00	185,061.42	64,771.50	64,771.50
TOTAL	1,400,000.00	350,270.80	1,000,000.00	49,729.20	17,405.22	17,405.22

Table 9.10 Cash flow report.

CASH FLOW REPORT

Lessee . . . . White Industries
Lessor . . . . Gold Leasing Corporation
Prepared Nov-02-2001 12:44 by . . . . R. Contino
Parameter filename . . . . text book: lease, leveraged
Parameter path . . . . c:\ivory\prms\

Date	Rent & Income & Residual	Equity & Fees & Expenses	Debt Service	Pre-Tax Cash Flow	Taxes Paid	After Tax Cash Flow	Cumulative After Tax Cash Flow
Jan-01-02	0.00	2,000,000.00	0.00	−200,000.00	0.00	−200,000.00	−200,000.00
Apr-15-02	0.00	0.00	0.00	0.00	−7,000.00	7,000.00	−193,000.00
Jun-15-02	0.00	0.00	0.00	0.00	−7,000.00	7,000.00	−186,000.00
Sep-15-02	0.00	0.00	0.00	0.00	−7,000.00	7,000.00	−179,000.00
Dec-15-02	0.00	0.00	0.00	0.00	−7,000.00	7,000.00	−172,000.00
	0.00	200,000.00	0.00	−200,000.00	−28,000.00	−172,000.00	
Jan-01-03	200,000.00	0.00	164,324.40	35,675.60	0.00	35,675.60	−136,324.40
Apr-15-03	0.00	0.00	0.00	0.00	−16,762.16	16,762.16	−119,562.24
Jun-15-03	0.00	0.00	0.00	0.00	−16,762.16	16,762.16	−102,800.08
Sep-15-03	0.00	0.00	0.00	0.00	−16,762.16	16,762.16	−86,037.92
Dec-15-03	0.00	0.00	0.00	0.00	−16,762.16	16,762.16	−69,275.75
	200,000.00	0.00	164,324.40	35,675.60	−67,048.65	102,724.25	
Jan-01-04	200,000.00	0.00	164,324.40	35,675.60	0.00	35,675.60	−33,600.15
Apr-15-04	0.00	0.00	0.00	0.00	−4,750.54	4,750.54	−28,849.61
Jun-15-04	0.00	0.00	0.00	0.00	−4,750.54	4,750.54	−24,099.08
Sep-15-04	0.00	0.00	0.00	0.00	−4,750.54	4,750.54	−19,348.54
Dec-15-04	0.00	0.00	0.00	0.00	−4,750.54	4,750.54	−14,598.00
	200,000.00	0.00	164,324.40	35,675.60	−19,002.16	54,677.76	

Date	Rent & Income & Residual	Equity & Fees & Expenses	Debt Service	Pre-Tax Cash Flow	Taxes Paid	After Tax Cash Flow	Cumulative After Tax Cash Flow
Jan-01-05	200,000.00	0.00	164,324.40	35,675.60	0.00	35,675.60	21,077.60
Apr-15-05	0.00	0.00	0.00	0.00	2,862.25	−2,862.25	18,215.36
Jun-15-05	0.00	0.00	0.00	0.00	2,862.25	−2,862.25	15,353.11
Sep-15-05	0.00	0.00	0.00	0.00	2,862.25	−2,862.25	12,490.87
Dec-15-05	0.00	0.00	0.00	0.00	2,862.25	−2,862.25	9,628.62
	200,000.00	0.00	164,324.40	35,675.60	11,448.98	24,226.62	
Jan-01-06	200,000.00	0.00	164,324.40	35,675.60	0.00	35,675.60	45,304.22
Apr-15-06	0.00	0.00	0.00	0.00	3,844.31	−3,844.31	41,459.91
Jun-15-06	0.00	0.00	0.00	0.00	3,844.31	−3,844.31	37,615.60
Sep-15-06	0.00	0.00	0.00	0.00	3,844.31	−3,844.31	33,771.30
Dec-15-06	0.00	0.00	0.00	0.00	3,844.31	−3,844.31	29,926.99
	200,000.00	0.00	164,324.40	35,675.60	15,377.23	20,298.37	
Jan-01-07	200,000.00	0.00	164,324.40	35,675.60	0.00	35,675.60	65,602.59
Apr-15-07	0.00	0.00	0.00	0.00	9,964.58	−9.964.58	55,638.01
Jun-15-07	0.00	0.00	0.00	0.00	9,964.58	−9.964.58	45,673.43
Sep-15-07	0.00	0.00	0.00	0.00	9,964.58	−9.964.58	35,708.85
Dec-15-07	0.00	0.00	0.00	0.00	9,964.58	−9.964.58	25,744.28
	200,000.00	0.00	164,324.40	35,675.60	39,858.31	−4,182.71	
Jan-01-08	200,000.00	0.00	164,324.40	35,675.60	0.00	33,675.60	61,419.88
Apr-15-08	0.00	0.00	0.00	0.00	16,192.87	−16,192.87	45,227.00
Jun-15-08	0.00	0.00	0.00	0.00	16,192.87	−16,192.87	29,034.13
Sep-15-08	0.00	0.00	0.00	0.00	16,192.87	−16,192.87	12,841.25
Dec-15-08	0.00	0.00	0.00	0.00	16,192.87	−16,192.87	−3,351.62
	200,000.00	0.00	164,324.40	35,675.60	64,771.50	−29,095.90	
Jan-01-09	200,000.00	0.00	164,324.40	35,675.60	0.00	35,675.60	32,323.98
	200,000.00	0.00	164,324.40	35,675.60	0.00	35,675.60	
TOTAL	1,400,000.00	200,000.00	1,150,270.80	49,729.20	17,405.22	32,323.98	

- The "pre-tax cash-flow" column reflects the cumulative rent inflow, offset by the equity and loan payment outflows. In 2002, the lessor received no rent payment and made no loan payment, so the only amount in that column is the initial $200,000 equity payment.
- The "taxes paid" column lists the lessor's federal income taxes which will be due.
- The "after tax cash flow" column is the result of adjusting the pre-tax cash flow by the taxes paid. Where the amount in the "taxes paid" column is negative (in the first three years), it is added to the pre-tax cash flow because the tax savings are an inflow of cash that year. Where the taxes paid amount is positive, this amount is subtracted from the pre-tax cash flow.

After the after-tax cash flows are determined, the investment yields are computed in the same manner as in the nonleveraged lease example.

E.   Summary

The key to a proper lessee lease versus purchase analysis, or a lessors' investment return analysis, is determining the various cash inflows and outflows on a present value basis. Because of the complexity of making these determinations, and the risk of human computation error, it is always advisable to use one of the many computer programs available today for these purposes.

Chapter 10

Understanding the Lease Accounting Rules

A. Background

During the early years of the equipment leasing business, the accounting profession devoted considerable time and effort discussing how leases should be accounted for, both from the standpoint of the lessor and the lessee. There were many inconsistencies and substantive disagreements. Finally, in 1973, the subject of accounting for leases was addressed by the accounting profession's standard setting body, the Financial Accounting Standards Board (FASB), with the firm intent of resolving the many problems. After issuing several exposure drafts and considering a multitude of letters of comments, position papers, and oral presentations from interested parties, they adopted, in November 1976, the "Statement of Financial Accounting Standards No. 13-Accounting for Leases." Commonly referred to as FAS No. 13, the rules promulgated therein established the standards to be followed by lessors and lessees in accounting for and reporting lease transactions. The problems were not over, however. Since FAS No. 13 was issued, the FASB has been called on to address a wide variety of issues raised by these financial accounting and reporting guidelines. As a result, various amendments and interpretations have been put out in an effort to clarify or handle many of the guideline's complex issues.

➤ **Observation** Keep in mind that FAS No. 13 is saying that a lease that transfers substantially all of an asset's ownership benefits and risks to the lessee must be treated by the lessee in the same way an asset bought with borrowed money is treated (capital lease treatment). The lessor must account for the lease as a sale or a financing. All other types of leases should be treated as the rental of property (operating lease treatment).

Because of the scope and detail of the lease accounting rules and because the intent of this chapter is to provide the reader with an awareness of the most relevant concepts, every aspect of the rules will not be explained. The material will, however, point out and generally explain the fundamental issues that have an impact on the everyday decisions involved in leasing equipment.

B. Lease Classifications for a Lessee Vary Significantly— A Careful Analysis Is Essential

Under the FAS No. 13, a lessee must account for and report a lease in its financial statements as either a "capital" lease or an "operating" lease, depending on how the transaction is structured. The way the two types of leases are treated varies significantly. In certain cases, it may not be advisable for a company to lease equipment because of the accounting treatment impact.

The criteria for determining if a lease from the lessee's viewpoint must be classified as capital lease or an operating lease have been well defined in FAS No.13. A lease must be treated as a capital lease if, at its inception, it meets one or more of the following criteria.

- The lease arrangement provides for a transfer of the property's ownership to the lessee by the end of the lease term.
- There is a bargain purchase option in the lease. A bargain purchase option is basically one in which the lessee has a right to buy the property for a price that is so far below its anticipated fair value, at the time it can be exercised, that it is likely the lessee will elect to buy the property.
- The term of the lease is for a period equal to or greater than 75% of the property's estimated economic useful life.
- The present value of the "minimum lease payments" at the lease inception (excluding any executory costs included in the payments such as insurance, maintenance, and taxes that the lessor will pay and any profits on those costs) is equal to or greater than 90% of the excess of the fair value of the leased property (determined at the beginning of the lease) over any investment tax credit (ITC) claimed and expected to be realized by the lessor. The present value computation is calculated by discounting the payments at the lower of the lessor's implicit lease interest rate or the interest rate the lessee would have to pay for a loan running the length of the lease term (the lessee's "incremental borrowing rate"). If it is not practicable for the lessee to learn the lessor's implicit lease rate of interest, then the lessee must use its borrowing rate to make the present value computation. FAS No. 13 defines "minimum lease payments" as those payments that the lessee must make or can be required to make. This includes minimum rent payments, residual value guarantees, and payments for failure to renew or extend the lease.

If the lease does not meet any of the above criteria, it is classified as an operating lease.

Illustrative Example   *The Present Value Test:* Company Able is considering leasing a new truck from Company Baker. Will the present value test for capital lease classification be met? Here are the facts:

Noncancelable lease term . . . . 5 years
Monthly rent (in arrears) $180
Fair market value (FMV) at lease inception $10,000
Executory costs . . . . To be paid by Company Able
ITC 0%
Company Able's borrowing rate 10%
Company Baker's implicit lease rate . . . . Company Able unable to
                                                             determine

In this example, the minimum lease payments are the rental payments. The present value of the monthly rental payments computed by discounting the future rent payment stream by 10% per annum is equal to $8,472. Ninety percent of the truck's fair market value at the beginning of the lease is $9,000. Because the present value of the rental stream is less than $9,000, the present value test for capital lease classification is not met.

C. Accounting Requirements Have an Impact on a Lessee

The way a lessee must account for a lease in its financial statements depends on its classification, that is, whether it falls within the capital or operating lease category. If a lease is classified as a capital lease, the lessee must record it both as an asset and an obligation at an amount equal to the present value (at the beginning of the lease term) of the minimum lease payments during the lease term. Executory costs included in the payments, such as insurance, maintenance, and taxes that the lessor must pay, and any profit on these costs, must be excluded before making the present value computation. (If the lessee is unable to determine the executory costs included in the payments, the lessee must estimate such executory costs and exclude such estimated amount prior to making the present value determination.) If the minimum lease payment present value amount turns out to be greater than the property's "fair value" (generally the property's purchase cost) determined at the beginning of the lease, then the fair value is to be recorded.

The lease payment present value calculation is to be made in the same manner as when determining whether a lease meets the present value criteria for capital lease classification. In other words, the payment stream is to be discounted at the lower of the lessee's incremental borrowing rate for a loan of a similar term or the lessor's implicit lease interest rate. If it is not practicable for the lessee to learn the lessor's implicit interest rate, then the incremental borrowing rate must be used.

A lessee must write off (amortize) a capital lease under certain specific rules. Which rule must be followed depends on which of the four capital lease classification criteria is met. If the lease meets the first or second criterion (that is, if the ownership of the property is transferred to the lessee at the end of the lease term or the lessee has a bargain purchase option), the lessee must write it off in a manner consistent with its usual depreciation practice for assets it owns. If the lease does not meet either of these two criteria, the lessee must amortize the property, over a period equal to the lease term, in a manner consistent with its normal depreciation practice down to a value it expects the property to be worth at the end of the lease.

A lessee must account for a lease categorized as an operating lease in a different manner than one that is classified as a capital lease. Generally, the rental payments will be charged to expense as they become due on a straight-line basis, whether they are in fact payable on a straight-line basis. There is, however, an exception to the straight-line reporting rule. If another systematic and rational time pattern method for reflecting the property's use benefit is more representative, that method must be used in reporting the rent expense.

➤ **Recommendation**   The difference in reporting impact between a capital lease and an operating lease is significant. If a prospective lessee does not want a lease obligation to appear as a long-term liability, it must make sure that it will be classified as an operating lease. If it cannot be so treated, and there are no other compelling reasons to lease, the possibility of buying the asset must be carefully considered in view of the effect on its financial picture.

D. Lease Classification Categories for a Lessor Are Extensive

From the standpoint of lessor accounting, FAS No. 13 provides that all leases must be categorized as either sales-type leases, direct financing leases, leveraged leases, or operating leases. Each category has certain attributes that the lessor must carefully take into account when making the classification determination.

A lease will be classified as a sales-type lease if all the following tests are met.

* The lease gives rise to a dealer's or manufacturer's profit, or loss, to the lessor.
* One or more of the lessee criteria for capital lease classification are met.
* The minimum lease payment collectibility is reasonably predictable.
* There are no important uncertainties as to the amount of any unreimbursable costs that the lessor has not yet incurred.

A dealer's or manufacturer's profit, or loss, will exist if the fair value of the leased equipment at the beginning of the lease is greater, or less, as the case may be, than the lessor's cost, or carrying amount if different from the cost. This test is usually met when an equipment manufacturer or dealer leases, instead of sells, its equipment to a lessee. In this case, the fair value of the equipment will typically be greater than its cost or carrying amount.

➤ **Observation**   There are situations under FAS No. 13 when a lessor could accrue a dealer's or manufacturer's type of profit, or loss, without actually being a dealer or manufacturer. The lease accounting rules provide that a sales-type lease can exist if the equipment's fair value at the lease inception is greater, or less, than the lessor's cost or carrying amount, if this amount is different from the cost.

The criteria for determining if a lease will be classified as a direct financing lease is much easier to understand once the governing rules for a sales-type lease and a lessee capital lease have been mastered. Simply, a lease will be a direct financing lease if, at its inception, all of the following five tests are satisfied.

* One or more of the criteria for lessee capital lease classification have been met.
* The lease does not fall within the category of leveraged lease.
* The lease does not give rise to a dealer's or manufacturer's profit, or loss, to the lessor.
* The collectibility of the minimum lease payments is reasonably predictable.
* There are no important uncertainties as to the amount of any unreimbursable costs that the lessor has yet to incur under the lease.

Ascertaining if a lease will be categorized as a leveraged lease is more complex than determining if it is a sales-type lease or a direct financing lease. Basically, if a lease is a direct financing lease *and* meets all of the following criteria, it will be considered a leveraged lease.

* No less than three participants—a lessee, a lessor, and a long-term lender—are involved.
* The long-term debt is nonrecourse as to the lessor's general credit.
* The principal amount of the long-term debt will substantially leverage the lessor's investment.
* The lessor's net investment goes down in the early lease years after it has been competed and goes up in the later lease years before it is entirely eliminated. (The term "net investment" is explained in the following section.)
* Any available ITC that the lessor retains is accounted for as one of the lease cash flow components.

The definition of an operating lease is straightforward. It is simply a lease that does not qualify as a direct financing lease, a sales-type lease, or a leveraged lease.

E. Lessor's Accounting Requirements Are Complex

FAS No. 13 carefully details how lessors must account for sales-type, direct financing, leveraged, and operating leases. The rules are complex, and a lessor must make sure they are clearly understood before committing to a lease transaction, to avoid an undesirable accounting treatment.

1. Sales-Type Lease

If a lease fits within the sales-type lease category, a lessor must determine its gross investment in the lease. The lessor's gross investment is the sum of the lease rents and other minimum lease payments and the equipment's unguaranteed residual value that will accrue to the lessor's benefit. The minimum lease payment sum must be computed net of any executory costs included in the payments, such as insurance, maintenance, and taxes, which the lessor must pay, and any profit on such costs.

The lessor must record the lease's unearned income. Unearned income is the difference between the lessor's gross investment and the sum of the present values of the minimum lease payments, adjusted for certain executory costs, and any profits on such costs, and the equipment's unguaranteed residual value that will accrue to the lessor's benefit. The present value computations are to be made using the lessor's implicit lease interest rate as the discount rate. Generally, the lease's unearned income must be amortized to income over the lease term in such a manner so as to produce a constant periodic rate of return on the lessor's net investment in the lease. Net investment is the difference between the gross investment and the unearned income. The accounting rules require that the lessor's net investment in a lease be treated in the same way as other current or noncurrent assets in a classified balance sheet.

The equipment's sales price, defined as the present value of the minimum lease payments, net of certain executory costs and any profits on those costs, must also be computed and recorded. The equipment's cost (or carrying amount, if different), increased by any initial negotiation and consummation expenses (referred to as initial direct costs), such as legal fees, and reduced by the present value of the lessor's unguaranteed residual value, must be charged against income for the same period. The present value computation is to be made using a discount rate equal to the lessor's implicit lease interest rate.

The leased equipment's residual value is given special attention. The rules require a lessor to review the estimated value used in the required computations on an annual basis. If the value experiences a permanent decline, the reporting criteria must be adjusted accordingly. If, on the other hand, there has been an increase in the expected residual value, no adjustments are permitted.

2. Direct Financing Lease

A lessor must account for a direct financing lease in somewhat the same manner as a sales-type lease. As with a sales-type lease, a lessor must determine its gross investment in the lease. Gross investment is defined in the same way as it is for a sales-type lease.

Unearned income, defined for a direct financing lease as simply the difference between the lessor's gross investment and the equipment's cost, must be recorded. In the event the carrying amount of the equipment is different from its cost, the carrying amount must instead be used in making this computation.

The lessor's net investment in the lease is recorded and is to be classified in the same way as other current or noncurrent assets in a classified balance sheet. Net investment is defined as the gross investment, plus any amortized initial direct costs, minus the unearned income.

The rules require the unearned income and the initial direct costs of putting a lease transaction together, such as commissions or legal fees, to be amortized to income over the lease term in such a way as to show a constant periodic return rate on the lessor's net investment. Other methods of income recognition, however, may be used if the results produced do not differ materially from those obtained by using this suggested method.

The equipment's estimated residual value must be annually reviewed. If a permanent decrease in the value estimate has occurred, the computations incorporating the value must be adjusted accordingly. No adjustments are allowed to reflect an increase in the value estimate.

3. Operating Lease

If a lease is deemed to be an operating lease, the accounting treatment is somewhat simpler for a lessor than if the lease is a sales-type or direct financing lease. Equipment subject to such a lease must be recorded on the lessor's balance sheet in or near the "property, plant, and equipment" category. Also, the equipment must be depreciated under the lessor's usual depreciation policy. The investment in the equipment must be shown reduced by the accumulated depreciation.

The rent received under an operating lease is handled in a straightforward manner. It is reported as income when and as due and is taken in on a straight-line basis, regardless of how the rent is actually to be paid. There is, however, an exception to this reporting method. If any other systematic method for reporting the rent income would more accurately reflect the time pattern reduction in the property's use benefit, then that method must be used.

Any initial direct costs incurred by the lessor in connection with putting the transaction together cannot, in general, be treated as they are in a direct financing lease situation. They must be deferred and allocated over the term of the lease in proportion to how the rent income is recognized. They may, however, be expensed when incurred if the effect would not be materially different than it would be under the deferred treatment.

4. Leveraged Lease

The lessor's investment in a leveraged lease must be stated net of the transaction's nonrecourse debt. The lessor's investment at any point in time is determined by computing (1) the rents receivable, minus the portion going to pay the debt service on the nonrecourse debt; (2) a receivable for any ITC amount to be realized; (3) the equipment's estimated residual value; and (4) the transaction's unearned and deferred income. The unearned and deferred income at any point is defined as the sum of the lease's estimated remaining and unallocated pretax income or loss, adjusted by subtracting any initial direct costs, and any ITC that has not yet been allocated to income over the lease term.

The lessor must also determine the rate of return on its net investment during the years it is positive. The rate of return is defined as the rate that, when applied to the net investment during the years it is positive, will distribute the net income to these years. The lessor's net investment in a leveraged lease is simply the lessor's investment reduced by the deferred taxes arising from the difference between the lessor's pretax accounting income and taxable income.

As with a sales-type lease and a direct financing lease, the lessor must review the estimated residual value of the equipment each year and adjust it downward if it appears that the estimated amount was excessive and that it has undergone a permanent reduction over that originally estimated. If an adjustment is necessary, certain other recalculations are necessary using the new residual assumption. No upward adjustment is permitted if there has been an estimated increase in the residual value.

F. Accounting Rules Governing Sale-Leaseback Situations

Because many leases arise through sale-leaseback transactions, it is worthwhile mentioning the governing lease accounting rules, A "sale-leaseback" is defined as a transaction in which an owner sells equipment to a third party and leases it back. The buyer will then be the lessor and the original owner will become the lessee.

From the lessee's viewpoint, the lease accounting rules are the same as in any lease situation. That is, if the lease would otherwise have to be classified as a capital lease, it will still be considered as a capital lease. If it qualifies as an operating lease, it will still be accounted for as an operating lease. The reporting of the profit or loss from the equipment's sale, however, is specially treated. If the lease is a capital lease, the seller-lessee must defer any profit or loss resulting from the sale to the lessor-buyer and amortize it in proportion to the amortization of the leased equipment. If the lease is classified as an operating lease, generally any profit or loss must be amortized in proportion to the rents charged to expense over the term of the lease.

If the lease would qualify for a lessee as a capital lease, the collectibility of the minimum lease payments is reasonably predictable, and there are no important uncertainties as to the amount of any unreimbursable costs that the lessor has yet to incur under the lease, the transaction must be treated by the lessor as a purchase and a direct financing lease. If it does not, it must be accounted for as a purchase and an operating lease.

G. Lease Classification Checklist for Lessees

The lessee can use the following checklist as general guidelines in classifying its leases for accounting and reporting purposes.

If a lease meets one or more of the following criteria, has it been classified as a capital lease?

- Does the lease transfer the equipment's ownership to the lessee by the end of the lease?
- Does the lessee have the right to buy the leased equipment at a price well below its value at the time the right can be exercised?
- Does the lease run for a term that is equal to or greater than 75% of the equipment's estimated economic useful life?

- Is the present value of the rent and other minimum lease payments, net of certain executory costs and profits on such costs, equal to or greater than 90% of the equipment's fair value as of the lease inception, minus any investment tax credit to be retained by the lessor?

If it is practicable for the lessee to learn the implicit lease rate computed by the lessor and it is lower than the lessee's incremental borrowing rate, has the present value test been computed using this rate?

- If it is not lower, has the value been calculated using the lessee's incremental borrowing rate?

If a lease does not meet any of the previous tests, has it been classified as an operating lease?

H.   Lease Classification Checklist for Lessors

The lessor can use the following checklist as general guidelines in classifying its leases for accounting and reporting purposes. [It should be noted that if a lease does not qualify as a sales-type lease, a direct financing lease, or a leveraged lease, in accordance with the following applicable guidelines, it must be classified as an operating lease. In addition, if the lease arises out of a sale-leaseback transaction, it must, as mentioned in Section F of this chapter, also comply with certain sales-leaseback governing rules.]

A lease must be classified as a sales-type lease if it meets all of the following criteria.

- The lessor incurs a manufacturer's or dealer's type of profit or loss.
- The lease meets at least one of the following criteria.
  1. The lease transfers the equipment's ownership to the lessee by the end of the lease.
  2. The lessee has the right to buy the leased equipment at a price well below its expected fair value at the time the right can be exercised.
  3. The lease runs for a term that is equal to or greater than 75% of the equipment's estimated economic useful life.
  4. The present value of the rent and other minimum lease payments, net of certain executory costs and profits on such costs, is equal to or greater than 90% of the equipment's fair value as of the lease inception, minus any ITC to be retained by the lessor.
- The collectibility of the rent and other minimum lease payments is reasonably predictable.
- There are no important uncertainties concerning the lessor's yet-to-be-incurred unreimbursable costs.

A lease (other than a leveraged lease) must be classified as a direct financing lease if it meets all of the following criteria.

- The lessor does not incur a manufacturer's or dealer's type of profit or loss.
- The lease meets at least one of the following criteria.
  1. The lease transfers the equipment's ownership to the lessee by the end of the lease.
  2. The lessee has the right to buy the leased equipment at a price well below its expected fair value at the time the right can be exercised.

3. The lease runs for a term that is equal to or greater than 75% of the equipment's estimated economic useful life.
4. The present value of the rent and other minimum lease payments, net of certain executory costs and profits on such costs, is equal to or greater than 90% of the equipment's fair value as of the lease inception, minus any ITC to be retained by the lessor.

- The collectibility of the rent and other minimum lease payments is reasonably predictable.
- There are no important uncertainties concerning the lessor's yet to be incurred unreimbursable costs.

A lease must be classified as a leveraged lease if all of the following criteria are met.

- The lease qualifies as a direct financing lease.
- The lease involves at least three parties—a lessee, a long-term lender, and a lessor.
- The long-term debt financing is nonrecourse to the general credit of the lessor.
- The amount of long-term debt will substantially leverage the lessor's invested funds.
- The lessor's "net investment" goes down in the early lease years once made, and rises during the later lease years before eliminated.
- Any available ITC that the lessor retains is accounted for as one of the lease cash flow components.

I. Summary of Accounting Lease Classifications

The chart on the next page summarizes, in a simplified manner, the prominent aspects of each accounting lease classification for lessees and lessors. Only the most salient have been listed. The reader is referred to the earlier text of this chapter for the details of each lease classification.

Lessee/Lessor	Key Characteristics
Lessee Lease Classifications	
Capital lease	A lease that runs for 75% or more of an asset's useful life, automatically transfers ownership at the lease end, has a bargain purchase option, or whose rent's present value to 90% or more of the asset's fair value, adjusted for any ITC. It is treated as a purchase in the lessee's financial statements, the lease recorded as both an asset and an obligation. Most long-term, full payout leases fall into this classification.
Operating lease	Any lease not falling within the capital lease classification. It is generally the most desirable lease classification for lessee financial reporting purposes. The rent payments are charged to expense as they become due.
Lessor Lease Classifications	
Sales-type lease	A lease that gives rise to a dealer's or manufacturer's profit or loss. In certain situations, even a lessor, not a dealer or manufacturer, may have to report a lease as a sales-type lease.
Direct financing lease	A lease that does not fall within the leveraged lease classification and does not give rise to a dealer's or manufacturer's profit or loss, must be classified as a direct financing lease.
Leveraged lease	A direct financing lease that involves a third-party nonrecourse lender.
Operating lease	Any lease that is not classified as a sales-type lease, a direct financing lease, or a leveraged lease.

J. Summary

The "Statement of Financial Accounting Standards No. 13—Accounting for Leases" commonly referred to as FAS No. 13, sets forth the rules to be followed by lessors and lessees in accounting for and reporting lease transactions. FAS No. 13 in effect says that a lease that transfers substantially all of an asset's ownership benefits and risks to the lessee must be treated by the lessee in the same way an asset bought with borrowed money is treated (capital lease treatment). On the other hand, the lessor must account for the lease as a sale or a financing. All other types of leases should be treated by the lessor as the rental of property (operating lease treatment). The rules can be complex, so care must be taken in assessing their impact on an equipment lease transaction.

Chapter 11

The Business of Leasing Equipment

A. Overview

The leasing business in the United States is mature, and competition is intense. There are still many attractive profit opportunities—but you must approach the business knowledgeably, and carefully. If you don't, mistakes are inevitable and devastating losses likely. This has been attested to over and over during the past decade by the many non-bank, and bank-affiliated, leasing company problems, closings, sell-offs, and bankruptcies. A quick review of a typical problem operation invariably shows a variety of historically repetitive and obvious mistakes. Mistakes that frequently went unnoticed for years—ones often resulting from top management's lack of street-wise business expertise, short-sighted attempts to maintain near-term profits, or desire to increase profit-based bonuses. So, if you are considering being in the leasing business, or want to expand, or improve the profitability of, an existing leasing operation, a solid understanding of the basic business strategies successful leasing companies use today to survive and make money is essential. That's what this chapter is about.

The threshold question is why would an individual, or company, set up a leasing operation? There are a number of basic reasons. First, to use available equipment ownership tax benefits to offset, or defer, tax liabilities from unrelated revenues sources—tax shelter. Second, to earn financing profits—the difference between the cost of purchasing and leasing equipment and lease revenues. And third, to assist in marketing products sold by an affiliate of the leasing company. For example, a manufacturer or vendor of telephone systems may establish a captive (in-house) leasing operation to facilitate the sale of its equipment. Having readily available and attractive product financing, particularly when competitors do not, can cinch the product sale. Paying $200 a month, rather than $10,000 upfront, for needed equipment makes the customer's purchase leap of faith much easier.

➤ **Observation**   To assure your chance at success in today's competitive equipment leasing environment, you must have a value-added marketing strategy. One, for example, that fills a niche not already crowded with other lessors. If you can identify such a niche, the opportunity for growth can be great, and the business prospects can be exciting.

B. Key Profit Strategies

Aside from financing profits, equipment leasing offers a leasing company a number of additional benefits. Here are the key ones.

1.   *Valuable Assets Purchased with Someone Else's Money*

How would you react if a wealthy neighbor asked you to lease her an $80,000 BMW? Assume you could borrow the entire purchase price from your local bank at a rate that gave you a $200 monthly profit. And assume the loan could be based solely on your neighbor's credit, having no impact on your future borrowing capabilities. Further, if your neighbor defaulted on her lease payments for any reason, you would not be responsible to pay off any remaining loan balance. Assume also that the lease would be for four years, the rents would pay off the entire bank loan, and when the lease ended, your neighbor would have to return the car to you in excellent condition. The result would be at the end of four years, you would own a cream-puff BMW, free and clear, to do with as you wish. Sell it. Re-lease it. Or simply use it as your personal car. Sound good? Most people would agree that it does. That's the business of equipment leasing.

You might think it's not possible to get a bank to loan you money to invest without holding you responsible for its repayment. But so-called non-recourse equipment loans, discussed in Chapter 8, are available because banks and other lenders will loan money on the strength of a strong lease contract, generally without checking the credit worthiness of the owner-lessor. As discussed in Chapter 3, the lease must contain a hell or high water clause, obligating the lessee to keep sending in the rent payments no matter what happens, even if the lessor-owner fails to live up to the lease obligations to the lessee, or the equipment is destroyed or otherwise unavailable for use. So, if you have a hell or high water lease with a good credit lessee, non-recourse equipment loans are available. The most interesting aspect of non-recourse loans is they, in effect, provide the lessor-owner with an unlimited borrowing capacity.

If this sounds attractive, consider going a step further. What if nine more wealthy neighbors approached you at the very same time to have you lease them BMWs under the same terms, for four-year terms, providing you with a $200 per month profit on each car? Your profit would be $2,000 a month and you would own ten BMWs at the end of their respective four-year lease terms, all free and clear. Not a bad return for a no-money-down investment.

That's one basic strategy of the leasing business: Getting credit-worthy companies to pay for, and maintain, assets which can be sold or re-leased at a profit, all the time making a profit while waiting for their return. All the leasing company has to do, once the lease deals are put together, is to remember to send out the rent bills, and to deposit the payment checks when they come in. And if you, as a lessor, don't want do that, you can sell the lease packages off at a profit equal, or close, to what you would have earned if you had been a patient business person.

2.   *Windfall Profits—A Possibility*

Now let's assume in the prior section example that at the end of the four-year lease each BMW was worth 50% of original cost. In addition to a $200 monthly profit, selling each car at the end of lease would bring in $40,000 in end-of-lease, or residual, revenues.

The residual value revenue expectations—what assets are expected to be worth at the end of their lease periods—are an important part of today's leasing business. It's not unusual for equipment residual values to range from 10% to 100% of the equipment's original cost, and sometimes even higher. The residual values, of course, depend on the type of asset, its return condition, inflation, and market demand. For example, in the mid- to late-1980s, some ten-year-old river barges sold for prices in excess of their original purchase price.

In the early days of the leasing business, when competition was not intense and financing spread profits were high, what an asset was expected to be worth at the end of its lease term was almost irrelevant. When the typical lease was over, a lessor had made all the money it needed from the lease transaction, even if the asset had to be junked. But many quickly augmented their profit objectives when word got around about a few aircraft lessors who made lottery-like windfall profits from selling off their end-of-lease aircraft. Some aircraft sales values after a ten- to fifteen-year lease approached or exceeded original cost. Add to that the fact that these aircraft lessors had returned, through lease term rents, all but a minimal amount (often between 10% and 15% of original cost) of their invested principal repaid, and made a tidy profit, and you had some very happy aircraft lessors. As you might expect, other leasing companies soon caught on to the aircraft residual "end game" and began to stay alert for high residual return possibilities in other types of equipment as well. The residual end game became so profitable that some lessors even adopted a strategy of acquiring millions of dollars of equipment with a high residual value potential, solely for the end-of-lease sale or re-lease profits. They cut their lease term profits to the bare minimum to win business, with rents often covering little more than basic transaction and overhead costs, anticipating profits when the equipment came off lease. Some leasing companies became so aggressive that they wrote leases that produced a loss during the lease term, counting on the fact that once through the initial start-up phase, the cash flow squeeze was over and yearly residual profits would provide solid bottom-line returns. Heavy reliance on residual profits is still a primary objective in leasing today, particularly in "big ticket" lease transactions.

There is risk, however, in placing primary emphasis on residual profit expectations. Lessors that do, run the risk that equipment won't be worth much more than scrap value if there is no market demand for it, or it becomes technologically obsolete. If rents just pay overhead, the potential for loss is great, particularly if unexpected costs are incurred. And if residual revenue expectations are not met, there is little or no economic return for the effort. Some aircraft lessors, for instance, encountering a market demand lull in the 1980s, had to store equipment and wait years for better sale or re-leasing opportunities. Equipment and industry diversification can reduce this type of risk.

3. The Repeat Business Customer Annuity

Developing an extensive customer lease portfolio should be a strategic business objective of every leasing company. Qualified prospects are valuable; customers who lease, often lease again—at times forgetting about getting competitive bids. Noncompetitive bid situations assure lessors of solid returns.

With qualified leasing customer contacts, a leasing company can readily originate new business with little expense: Often a simple letter offering lease financing, with a follow-up telephone call, is enough to identify upcoming leasing opportunities. Doing business with a good-paying existing customer also has far less credit risk than dealing with an unknown customer. Clearly, there is no substitute for firsthand payment experience. All the credit-due diligence in the world may not uncover credit potholes. Financial statements and discussions with trade references and lenders, for example, rarely tell the whole credit story.

a. Low Rate Strategy of Buying Repeat Customers

There is no doubt that approaching leasing customers with whom you have already done business makes the lease financing sale much easier. If rapport and trust have been established through earlier transactions, many of the marketing barriers are removed. So it may make sense, when approaching prospects that regularly lease equipment, to make your first deal very attractive—even at times to consider offering a deal at less than break-even rates to win business, thereby making an investment in a potentially profitable long-term customer relationship. Satisfied lessees often give incumbent lessors exclusive deals from time to time, deals which can often provide better than market lease rates for the lessor.

b. Master Lease Strategy of Tying up Repeat Customers

When dealing with new customers, putting a master lease agreement in place with them will pay dividends. Doing so cuts financing costs for all parties. As explained in Chapter 3, a master lease is a two-part document. The boiler plate portion contains the basic lease terms and conditions, which will remain the same from deal to deal, and an attachment, often called a schedule, which is a short (one- to two-page) document, permits future business to be simply added by specifically incorporating the new equipment under the term of the master, or boiler plate, document portion. Having only to negotiate a one- or two-page document for lease deals allows future financings to be handled with minimal effort and expense on both sides. Lessors with master leases in place are given an edge over competitors not having ones in place because of the ease of documentation, in many situations getting the last opportunity to win by matching the lowest bidder. In some cases, they are awarded deals even when they're not the lowest rate simply because documentation is easy and documentation costs are less.

C. Making Money in the Leasing Business

There are many ways to profit in a lease transaction. To succeed, and sometimes even survive, in the highly competitive business of equipment leasing, a leasing company must take advantage of every possible profit opportunity. The obvious areas for leasing profits are:

- Interest charges
- Tax benefits
- Equipment sales or re-leases

And, to the less experienced lessor, the less obvious ones are:

- Interim rent
- Prepayment penalties
- Casualty occurrences
- Insurance cost markups
- Upgrade financing
- Documentation fees
- Filing fees
- Maintenance charges
- Repair costs
- Excess use charges
- Equity placement fees
- Leveraging a lease investment with third-party debt
- Commitment fees
- Nonutilization fees

- Remarketing fees
- Late payment charges
- Collection telephone charges
- Deal rewrite fees
- Equipment redelivery charges

The profit opportunity areas available to a leasing company may vary depending on the type of transaction, the level of credit risk involved, the dollar size of the lease transaction, and the business practices of its competition. For example, in the case of multi-million dollar leases of typically high residual value equipment, a substantial portion of lease profits come from the equipment ownership tax benefits and the end-of-lease equipment sale, or re-lease, proceeds. In small ticket transactions, such as $10,000 to $50,000 leases, the lessor expects little or no profit from end-of-lease sales. Instead it looks to its lease interest rate spread—the difference between its cost of funds and the interest rate implicit in the lease, and documentation and deal review charges.

The following discussion of lease profit areas has been primarily taken from earlier material throughout this book and summarily provided below to enable the reader interested in looking at involvement in equipment leasing to have all key aspects pulled together for review.

1. Basic Lease Profit Areas

The principal lease transaction profit areas are interest charges, equipment tax benefits, and residual earnings. Not maximizing any one can significantly reduce the potential for transaction profits.

a. Interest Charges

The obvious way to make money in an equipment lease is through financing profits. Financing profit, sometimes referred to as financing spread, is the difference between a leasing company's cost of money and the lease interest rate charged. The higher the interest rate charged, the greater the financing profit.

> **Illustrative Example**   *Financing Profit:* Assume a lessor borrows money at a 9% per annum interest rate and charges a lease interest rate of 11%. Its financing spread is 2% per annum. By increasing the lease interest rate to 12%, its financing profit increases to 3%.

➤ **Lease Marketing Tip**   Prospective lessees, particularly small ticket lessees, are often more sensitive to their monthly rent cash outflow than to the lease interest charged. So, offering a longer lease term (stretching out the period of lease payments from, say, three years to five years) can maintain solid, or increase, financing profits and provide an acceptable lessee rent payment dollar amount. For example, assume that a lessor's cost of money is 9% per annum, and that its desired financing spread is 3% per annum. Assume also that the equipment involved will have a zero end-of-lease value. In this case, the monthly, in arrears, payment on a three-year lease of a $400,000 lathe would be $13,286. If the prospective lessee finds the $13,286 monthly payment too high, stretching the lease term to five years, at the same lease interest rate (9% + 3% = 12%), would drop the monthly lease payment to $8,897. Stretching out the lease term provides an opportunity to build in higher financing profits in a lease, while still keeping periodic cash flow payments relatively lower. For example, increasing the lease interest rate charge to 15% over the same five-year term would result in a monthly lease rent of $9,516.

Market competition, reasonableness, and sometimes state usury laws limit how much financing spread a lessor can build into its lease rate. Typically, the smaller the lease dollar size, the higher the lease interest rate charged. For example, interest rates on $5,000 to $50,000 equipment transactions generally range from 12.5% to 24% per annum. As transactions approach $100,000 and over, simple interest rates are generally in the 10.5% to 13.5% range. Once the deal size hits $1,000,000, rates can run 2% to 4% below the lessee's equivalent long-term borrowing rate. In the latter case, for example, a $4,000,000, 12-year aircraft lease for a lessee that borrows long-term money at 11% per annum could run from 7% to 9% per annum.

➤ **Observations**

- A lower lease rate in a larger equipment transaction is not as bad as it may appear, because greater absolute dollar profits are available. For example, a profit of 2% on a $1,000,000 lease is $20,000, whereas it is $200 on a $10,000 lease.
- The competitive nature of the multimillion dollar lease transaction market often forces lessors to price their lease rates with little or no financing spread profit, making them to look to other transaction aspects, such as tax benefits and equipment residual proceeds, to offset minimal or nonexistent cash flow.

➤ **Recommendation**   Although leasing companies are not generally regulated by federal or state laws, times are changing. Before setting what may be a high lease interest rate, have your lawyer check the governing state laws. A few states have enacted, or are considering implementing, rules which protect lessees. For example, unconscionable profit laws, referred to as usury laws, originally designed to protect individuals have, in Texas, been extended to corporations in installment sale–type financing. Included are low fixed price purchase option leases. If your lease runs afoul of state law, a lessee may be able to cancel the lease agreement and walk away without penalty. If you discover after entering into a lease that you have inadvertently charged a lease rate higher than governing law permits, it's always a good idea to approach the lessee with an offer to reduce it, using a plausible business excuse such as you have decided to make this financing rate adjustment to certain preferred customers.

b.   Equipment Tax Benefits

The tax aspects of equipment leasing are detailed in Chapters 5, 6, and 7. Often, particularly in multimillion dollar equipment leases, the tax benefits available to a lessor are a critical component in computing anticipated transaction profits. In fact, good credit companies considering the multimillion dollar lease transactions typically demand that lease rates reflect—and therefore pass through to a lessee in the form of relatively lower rent charges—at least a portion of the transaction tax benefits. Determining how to take into account the transaction tax benefits is a complex process. Fortunately, the many lessor profit (sometimes referred to as "yield") analysis software programs make the job considerably easier. See Chapter 9 for a discussion of the lessor yield analysis approach.

As explained in earlier chapters, by leasing equipment, a lessor, as equipment owner, has the right to claim equipment ownership tax benefits such as depreciation and any available investment tax credits. In the case of leveraged lease transactions, there are certain other tax write-offs, such as the interest charges on the long-term equipment loans. A lessee, on the other hand, typically cannot claim any equipment ownership tax benefits, but is entitled to deduct for the rent payments as a business expense.

➤ **Observation** By taking into account equipment-related tax benefits, a lessor is able to offer lower rents while maintaining its profit objectives. For example, typically a lessor offering an annual lease rate of 10% could reduce its lease interest rate to 8% without reducing its economic return, by incorporating depreciation benefits into its rent pricing.

c. Residual Earnings

In pricing a lease transaction (setting the lease rents), an ideal lessor objective is to have sufficient lease term rents to return its entire equity investment, repay any equipment loans, and provide a solid profit, with any end-of-lease sale or re-lease (often referred to simply as "residual") earnings simply as windfall profits. In other words, to set the lessee lease rents using a zero equipment residual assumption. In small ticket equipment transactions this is typically possible. In multimillion dollar equipment lease transactions, largely due to market competition, it is typically not possible.

2. Additional Areas of Potential Lease Profit

A leasing company can earn significant profits from less obvious transaction aspects such as interim rent, prepayment penalties, casualty occurrences, insurance cost markups, upgrade financing costs, documentation fees, filing fees, maintenance charges, repair costs, excess use charges, equity placement fees, debt costs and placement fees, commitment fees, nonutilization fees, remarketing fees, late payment charges, collection telephone call charges, deal rewrite charges, and equipment redelivery charges. Paying attention to each potential profit area can produce attractive additional economic returns.

a. Interim Rent

One way many lessors build in extra profit dollars is providing for interim rent. Sometimes called precommencement, or stub period, rent, it is rent that is payable for a period running from the start of the lease to the beginning of its primary, or main, term. For example, a seven-year lease transaction might provide for the primary term to begin on the first day of the month. If the equipment is not delivered and accepted under the lease contract on the first of a month, there will be an interim rent period. If equipment was delivered, for instance, on January 7, the seven-year period would begin February 1, with an interim term running from January 7 through January 31. If the lease rents are computed on the basis of the primary term rents, the stub period rent is a windfall profit.

b. Prepayment Penalties

A typical net finance lease may not be canceled for any reason, thus guaranteeing the lease profits, subject of course to a rent payment default. Some prospective lessees, however, want the right to terminate a lease early if the equipment becomes obsolete or surplus to their needs. This request can be an opportunity for profit. Generally, when a right to terminate a lease early is granted, it is permitted only upon payment of an amount equal to a predetermined termination value. By ensuring that the amount which a lessee must pay upon any lease termination not only makes a lessor economically whole, but also has a premium built in, say 5% of equipment cost, the benefit of the original bargain can be preserved—with a profit.

Generally when an early lease termination right is granted, the lessor incorporates a termination payment schedule into the lease, with each applicable termination payment expressed as a percentage of equipment cost for each rent payment period when a termination could be exercised. Payment of the appropriate termination value amount on any permitted rent date allows the lessee to terminate a lease as of that time. For example, a monthly lease might provide for a termination payment of 85% of equipment cost when the sixth rent payment is made, 83% of equipment cost when the seventh rent payment is made, and so on.

Properly structured, payment of a lease termination value will return the entire remaining equipment investment, with its anticipated profits at least to the date of termination, provide funds to pay off any equipment purchase loans, and add an additional profit, the exercise penalty.

c. Casualty Occurrences

An equipment casualty occurrence brings a lease to its end. In the same manner as an lessee-elected early lease termination, provision must be made for the protection of a lessor's investment and profit, at least to the date of the casualty occurrence.

Typically, leases contain casualty loss provisions that require the lessee to pay a predetermined casualty value payment. These payments are usually prescribed by formula in a lease provision or in a casualty payment schedule. They, like termination payments, are designed to make a lessor economically whole, including payment for loss of anticipated residual profits. For example, a monthly lease might provide, in the event of an equipment casualty occurrence during a specified rent payment period, for the payment of a casualty value amount equal to 98% of equipment cost any time during the second rent payment period, 96% of equipment cost any time during the third rent payment period, and so on.

In structuring an equipment casualty payment obligation, the lessor can build in a reasonable profit to compensate for loss of its long-term investment opportunity. When casualty payments are expressed as a percentage of equipment cost in a casualty payment schedule, one way to do this is to increase rock-bottom casualty loss payments by a small percentage, say 2% of equipment, added on each specified casualty value percentage.

d. Insurance Cost Markups

Equipment insurance is a must in any equipment lease, and generally the lessee is required to provide the coverage through its insurance carrier. Although care must be taken by a lessor not to run afoul of any insurance regulations, providing the insurance itself and passing the cost on to the lessee, with a markup, can create another lease profit opportunity. For example, a lessor might charge $14 a year for a $2,000 casualty insurance policy costing $8 a year, making a $6 profit On a $20,000,000 equipment portfolio, this means $60,000 annually. A lessor with insurance volume purchasing power can offer equipment lease insurance at a markup, while still providing rates equal to or lower than that available to most lessees.

There is another added benefit to a lessor providing the insurance coverage; doing so eliminates the need to administratively track compliance with the insurance coverage requirement of a lessee.

e. Upgrade Financing

Equipment upgrades, when a lessee adds to or modifies existing leased equipment, can provide an opportunity for leasing profit. If the upgrade is not readily removable or has no stand-alone value, generally the existing lessor is the only one willing or able to finance it. In these situations, the lessee has two choices: to purchase upgrade with its own funds or agree to whatever lease rate the lessor offers. If, as is the case in many situations, the upgrade is deemed under the terms of the lease to become the property of the lessor because, for example, it becomes an integral part of the leased equipment and cannot be removed without damage to the existing equipment, then paying a higher financing cost may still be cheaper than purchasing an upgrade which automatically becomes the lessor's property.

f. Documentation and Filing Fees

Many lessees, particularly those leasing small ticket items of equipment such as fax machines and small telephone systems, will pay, with little or no objection, transaction processing, documentation preparation, and security interest filing fees. Small lease transaction documentation fees generally run from $50 to $200 per transaction. Security interest filing fees, such as state Uniform Commercial Code filing fees, are generally nominal, ranging from $15 to $25. The more fees a lessee pays, the less a lessor's profit erosion.

g. Equipment Maintenance and Repair Charges

Requiring a lessee to pay for all normal equipment upkeep, such as maintenance and repairs charges, protects a lessor's investment by ensuring that the lessor's profit is not eroded by unexpected maintenance and repair costs. A lessor able to shift the full cost burden of equipment maintenance and repair to a lessee in effect creates profit by eliminating resale or re-lease rehabilitation expenses when the lease term ends. In a typical finance lease arrangement, the lessee assumes all equipment upkeep expense. In other types of equipment leases it is a matter of negotiation.

Lessors willing and able to provide equipment maintenance and repair service, even in connection with a finance lease, may realize an opportunity for additional profit. Many computer vendors, for example, offer these types of services and have created substantial collateral lease revenues.

Implementing strict equipment maintenance and return provisions is another way to help ensure the highest potential profits. Provisions that require the lessee to return equipment in good operating condition ensure that end-of-lease equipment sale or re-lease values are the highest possible.

h. Excess Use Charges

The better the condition leased equipment is in when returned, the greater the potential for the highest possible end-of-lease sale or re-lease profits. One way to ensure the best possible return condition is to put use restrictions on the equipment, which, if exceeded, call for penalty charges payable at the end of the lease. Automobile lessors typically have annual mileage limitations, which, if exceeded, require the lessee to pay additional rental charges to make up for potentially reduced end-of-lease sale or re-lease value. Leased aircraft are also often subject to use restrictions. Excess use charges can produce extraordinary profits.

i. Equity Placement Fees

A lessor able to sell a portion, or all, of its equity investment in a lease to another equity investor can earn fees for providing the investment opportunity. To ensure this option is available, a lease agreement must explicitly permit the sale of some or all of the lessor's interest in the equipment and the lease without consent by the lessee.

j.   Leveraging a Lease Investment with Third-Party Debt

At times, leasing companies borrow a portion of the funds necessary to purchase the equipment from a third-party lender in transactions referred to as leveraged leases. By properly leveraging a lease investment with third-part debt, a lessor can increase its economic return. The key to being able to do this is to ensure that the lease agreement explicitly permits the assignment of the lessor's interest in the equipment and the lease to a third-party lender without consent by the lessee.

k.   Commitment and Nonutilization Fees

Commitment and nonutilization fees are another area for leasing profits. Lessors frequently ask lessees to pay a commitment or nonutilization fee when equipment is to be delivered in the future.

Commitment fees, nonrefundable in nature, are designed to compensate a lessor for holding funds available. These fees help reduce the risk of lessor yield deterioration through adverse changes in its borrowing cost. Commitment fees are typically imposed when equipment deliveries are more than six months away, but many lessors ask for them when deliveries are not that far off. A fee of this nature must be paid up front and can range anywhere from 0.5% to 2% of equipment cost.

Nonutilization fees are, in effect, a penalty for not using the lease funds that a lessor held available for future delivered equipment. This type of fee can be less onerous, because it is payable only if the equipment is not leased and because it is due when the commitment period is over. For example, a lessor may require that the lessee pay a fee equal to 2% of the available funds unused at the end of, say, five months. If all committed funds are used, the lessee owes nothing.

l.   Remarketing Fees

Equipment remarketing fees are a way for equipment lessors to increase lease profits. For example, a lease may require that a lessee pay a predetermined fee to the lessor if the lessee elects to terminate a lease early, or at the end of the lease, in connection with the lessor's remarketing (the sale or re-lease) of the equipment. These fees are in addition to any other charges which may be payable, such as termination penalties or costs to repair equipment according to the condition required under the lease agreement.

m.   Late Payment Charges

Leases should always incorporate lessee late payment charges. If, for example, rent is not paid when due, there should be a penalty added to the late payment. Lessees often tolerate penalties in excess of the actual time value of money cost. In fact, some late payment penalties run as high as 5% to 10% of the rent charge.

n.   Collection Telephone Charges

Although not strictly a profit opportunity requiring the lessee to pay for any cost of ensuring timely lease payments, many lessors, particularly small ticket lessors, require lessees to pay telephone charges on collection calls. Anything that reduces overhead is indirectly a lessor profit item.

o.   Deal Rewrites

A lessee requesting a change in the structure of a lease, referred to as a deal rewrite, may agree to pay a deal rewrite fee for the privilege, for example, of having its lease extended. This can provide substantial profits, particularly in small lease transactions.

p. Redelivery Charges

Equipment redelivery charges are another area of profit opportunity. It is not unusual for a lessee to agree to return the leased equipment at the end of the lease to a designated return point, free of charge to the lessor. And it is not unusual for a lessor selling or re-leasing the equipment to a third party to obtain a delivery fee from the third party from the lessee's location of use. Some lessors get lessees to agree to pay for all such shipment charges regardless of where the equipment is designated to be shipped by the lessor, and then get the purchaser, or new lessee, to pay a delivery charge as well.

D. Considerations for Setting Up a Leasing Operation

Starting a leasing company is an involved process, and a detailed explanation is beyond the scope of this book. However, if you are considering establishing an equipment leasing activity, the following overview will assist you in determining threshold considerations. In making such a threshold assessment, you should take into account all aspects of leasing that have been discussed earlier in this book, such as the financial, tax, legal, accounting, and business considerations. In addition, you must think about the actual mechanics of starting and running a successful leasing operation, including the day-to-day administrative aspects of running a leasing business, obtaining adequate funding for lease transactions, marketing your financing, credit evaluation, documentation processing, state sales and use tax compliance, equipment appraisal and repossession, handling rent delinquencies, and working with outside counsel in the event a lawsuit is necessary.

The following discussion is a brief overview of the primary start-up and operational considerations necessary for establishing and running a leasing operation. Because of the many individual company variables, it is not possible to address all possible aspects that a particular company should consider.

1. There Must Be a Solid Competitive Reason for Being in the Leasing Business

In determining whether to start a leasing company in today's competitive environment, a company or individual should have a reason to start a leasing company that goes beyond the mere desire to get into the equipment leasing business because it sounds interesting or profitable. And that means that unless you have something unique to offer, such as filling a financing niche that has not been fully addressed by other leasing companies, or your company has a vast appetite for tax shelter offered by depreciation benefits of owning equipment, the road to success can be very difficult. On the other hand, if you or your company has a valued-added reason for entering the equipment leasing business, the story can be different, such as if your company is an equipment manufacturer or vendor looking to make leasing available for your customers. In addition, if you have significant contacts with equipment vendors who do not have effective financing in their marketing package, entering the leasing business may have competitive merit without offering something unique. For companies or banks already in the financial service business, entering the leasing market using the existing customer base can also make sense, even though the financing programs are not market unique.

In a nutshell, before you jump into the leasing business, make sure that you have defined your market and that there is a niche to be filled, or you have a value-added benefit to offer in the traditional market.

2. Are Competitive Interest Rate Loans Available?

Clearly, you must have access to adequate funds at competitive interest rates if you plan to competitively enter the leasing business. Unless you or your company has readily available internal funds, getting the necessary debt and equity funds to purchase equipment for lease may not be easy. Interest rate aggressive equipment lease lenders, such as banks, often require a business track record of as much as two years in the leasing business before they are willing to make loans available. Or they require other justifications for why taking the time to enter into loans arrangements will be worthwhile, such as your company is an equipment vendor with a solid sales and business history.

3. Will Market-Dictated Leasing Profits Be Acceptable?

You must evaluate the lease rates offered by any lessor competition you may encounter. Competition over recent years in the leasing business has forced lease rates down. You may find that your acceptable profit level for lease transactions may not be competitively possible. For example, in the big ticket leasing market, many leasing companies, are accepting after-tax investment yields in the 5% to 6% range. If that is the market you intend to enter, you may not find the economic returns necessary to attract business worthwhile.

4. Residual Assessment

In many transactions, except generally small ticket leases, what you expect the equipment will be worth at the end of the lease term, the estimated residual value, will be an important ingredient in determining your profit expectations. In highly competitive transactions, you may be forced to make high equipment residual estimates in pricing your lease rents to win transactions. If this sounds unacceptable, then find a market area to fit your residual comfort level.

➤ **Observation**   If you are willing to play the residual end game, it's always a good idea to get expert equipment appraisal assistance.

5. Prospective Lessee Credit Evaluations Are Critical

A critical element to survival in the leasing business is having the ability to properly assess the credit risk of entering into long-term leases with prospective lessees. Therefore, if your company doesn't have the internal ability to assess the credit risk of a lease investment, it must acquire the expertise. And you should keep in mind that the credit approach for leasing to small businesses is dramatically different from leasing equipment to Fortune 1000 companies. Someone able to effectively evaluate the credit worthiness of a Fortune 1000 company may be totally unable to make an effective credit evaluation of a small business for lease business purposes.

➤ **Observation**   In order to be competitive in most leasing markets, your company must be able to make credit assessments quickly, that generally means in a matter of days, not weeks.

a. Basic Credit Primer

As mentioned, a prospective lessee's creditworthiness is the most important consideration in the lessor's decision to provide financing. If the prospective lessee's credit is weak, financial support from the vendor or other third party may be the only way for a prospective lessee to secure desired equipment financing.

A discussion of how to evaluate the credit worthiness of a prospective lessee is beyond the scope of this book. In addition, what may create a credit problem to one lessor, may not create a credit problem for another lessor. For example, leasing companies with in-depth equipment and re-marketing expertise may be more willing to overlook the typical credit concerns of a leasing company without this expertise.

Notwithstanding the fact that credit evaluation is beyond the scope of this book, it will be helpful to go over some basic considerations. In reviewing a prospective company's credit strength, there are many factors brought into consideration, including assets and liabilities, cash flows, years in business, management strength, market presence, and the dollar size of the request financing.

Large publicly held companies, particularly the Fortune 1000 companies, are often easiest to evaluate because of the ample and reliable information available from audited financial statements that have been prepared by recognized accounting firms, and from publicly available material on file with the Securities and Exchange Commission. In many cases, these companies have been "rated" for investment purposes by investment rating services such as Moody's and Standard & Poor's. In addition, valuable credit information can be obtained from companies such as Dun & Bradstreet. These reports are invaluable for the equipment lessor.

To give you an idea of the various aspects of the credit evaluation process, let us look at the criteria used in a simple credit evaluation—that for a small business prospective lessee. These "credits" are some of the hardest to evaluate.

The following criteria are actually used by a small ticket lessor whose equipment lease transactions range from $5,000 to $250,000.

- **Minimum time in business** The applicant must have a minimum verifiable time in business of two years; three years is required in the case of applications over $25,000 and four years in the case of applications over $100,000.
- **Existing banking relationship** The applicant must have a business bank relationship of at least two years and the bank account must show a minimum low four-figure average balance. In the case of transactions exceeding $25,000, the minimum average account balance must be in the low five figures. There cannot be any overdrafts or check returns for insufficient funds.
- **Trade references** The applicant must provide three significant trade references, each of whose relationship goes back at least six months. COD trade references will not be acceptable.
- **Good personal credit** Personal credit reports must be forthcoming that contain no derogatory information.
- **Financial statements** Financial statements must be supplied for transactions exceeding $25,000. Current assets must exceed current liabilities and, for transactions in excess of $50,000, a minimum equity of $75,000 must be present.

6. Assessing Leasing Business Risks

As with any other business activity, there are unique business risks in equipment leasing that you must consider. See Chapter 8 for a discussion of investment risk in leveraged lease transactions. The risks are similar in nonleveraged lease transactions. In addition to these risks, you must be prepared to deal with prospective lessee fraud, something that exists, and something that can be minimized with a careful credit and business analysis of each prospective lessee. An experienced leasing credit person will be invaluable in preventing a credit fraud.

7. Administrative Issues

Whether you intend to enter the leasing business as a lease broker or a principal lessor, you must establish the necessary administrative mechanics to carry out all aspects of your leasing operation. And that includes, credit review processing, document processing and review, security interest filings, tracking and payment of state sales and use taxes, rent invoicing, ongoing marketing of existing customers for new business, new prospect marketing, collection, accounting, equipment repossession, and lawsuit initiation and monitoring. The variety of computer software programs available today can facilitate many of the tracking and processing activities, for example, lessor rent pricing and invoicing.

8. Legal, Tax, and Accounting Implications

Every lease transaction has tax and accounting implications to the leasing company, which can vary depending on changes in the business aspects of a lease transaction. For example, offering a $1 purchase option at the end of a lease term changes the lease from a true lease for income tax purposes—where the lessor is entitled to claim equipment depreciation, and, if available, any investment tax credits—to a conditional sale—where the "lessor" is deemed to be an equipment lender and thereby not entitled to the equipment ownership tax benefits.

The characterization of your lease investments for accounting purposes can affect your financial statements. Your accountant must be brought into your early consideration discussions to assist you in understanding the financial reporting effect various lease structures will have on your existing business, or in financial presentations to your shareholders or investors.

There are a variety of legal considerations, in addition to the documentation of a lease transaction. For example, you will have to consider qualifying to do business in the various states you intend to do lease business, otherwise, at a minimum, the courts in the states you did not so qualify, will not be available to you in the event you need to sue a defaulting lessee. And the various state laws must be checked to determine what statutory language, if any, must be included in your lease agreement. Your lawyer will be instrumental in bringing the legal considerations into focus for your particular business.

9. Lease Documentation

The strength of your leasing documentation can make a major business difference in your early success, and in your ability to collect from a defaulting lessee. If, for example, you intend to assign your lease as security for equipment loans, the lease agreement must contain effective assignment clauses, as well as other effective provisions. If the lessee defaults, you will have trouble collecting remaining rents due unless your lease agreement has a hell or high water provision. See Chapter 3 for a discussion of lessor assignment and hell or high water provisions.

Putting a good lease agreement together may take some time and requires an investment for an attorney's advice. Investing thousands or even millions of dollars using a lease you've copied from another lessor can be penny-wise and pound-foolish.

E. Leasing Offers Equipment Vendors a Marketing Edge

Ask any product marketing person and he or she will tell you that the easier it is for a customer to financially acquire a new product, the easier it is for the prospective customer to make an acquisition decision—and the shorter the sale cycle. The shorter the sale cycle, the less chance of losing an equipment sale to a competitor.

Studies show that nine of ten companies now lease equipment. So, if you have lease financing available at the time you make a product sales presentation, your chances of making the sale are increased. The real question, then, for a product vendor is how to set up the most effective customer financing program—and a key aspect of that decision is whether it should work with a third-party lessor or set up its own captive leasing operation.

1. What Are Internal Business Capabilities?

A product vendor's first step in setting up an effective customer equipment financing program is to take into account its equipment leasing management, operational, and financial capabilities, as well as its leasing operation interests. Depending on the answer, the product vendor will pursue establishing its own equipment financing activity, possibly setting up a captive leasing company or entering into a relationship with one or more independent leasing companies (see below). Once that decision is made, the next step is to design a customer financing program that will be responsive to prospective customer financing requirements. For example, the credit considerations when approaching small business customer equipment financings will be considerably different from those when approaching Fortune 1000 business customers. Deciding in advance how to handle the various requirements is a critical element in maximizing the benefits of offering customer equipment financing. Nothing is more damaging to product marketing than having to tell a company it does not meet the financing requirements of a third-party lessor, after offering equipment financing, particularly when the reason for the turndown was something that to another type of lessor would not have been an objection.

2. The Choice Between a Third-Party Lessor and an In-House Financing Setup

As a general rule, having an in-house financing capability, such as a captive leasing company, is the best choice because you control the financing decision and the lease documentation. An in-house leasing capability is also the right choice if you want to be assured that the most effective type of financing program—one tailored to fit the customer's needs—is in place. As a general rule, however, for equipment vendors without financial and operational expertise, good leasing company management, and available competitive funding, the better choice is often to set up an equipment leasing program for prospective customers using outside lessors.

Whether a product vendor's decision is to set up its own internal financing capability or to use outside leasing companies to service its customers' financing needs, for the financing program to work effectively, the funding must be reliable and readily available to every type of prospective vendor customer possible, particularly when working with a third-party leasing company. Merely providing a prospective equipment customer with the name of an equipment leasing company to talk to is not enough. And relying solely on the leasing company to properly put together the equipment financing has its risks. In such a situation, a product vendor must have substantial input into, and understanding of, the credit decisions and documentation processing.

➤ **Observation**   If the decision is to rely on third-party leasing companies to satisfy equipment sales financing needs, one critical point must be kept in mind: If the success of the equipment sales effort depends heavily on customer product financing, then a product vendor cannot rely on one outside funding relationship. There have been many situations in which both bank-affiliated and non-bank leasing companies have closed their funding doors without warning and, at times, with indifference to customer commitments.

3. *Establishing Overall Financing Programs Objectives*

The overall objectives for an effective equipment financing program are obvious, yet time and again they are frequently forgotten in the rush to put business on the books. For example, everyone agrees that maintaining good customer relations is essential, yet many equipment vendors overlook the fact that once a third-party leasing company is involved, the situation may be out of their control. One major U.S. leasing company was well known for aggressively and effectively establishing relationships with equipment vendors. And their customer service/administration department was equally well known for aggressively, and inadvertently, damaging customer relationships through inattention and indifference.

Here are the overall guidelines to follow if you're considering establishing an equipment financing program. A vendor equipment financing program must:

- Preserve at all times good customer relations.
- Allow the product vendor to control its customer relationships.
- Avoid the whims of individual financing sources.
- Give the impression of financing continuity.
- Be totally reliable under all circumstances.

In order to achieve your financing objectives, you'll want to:

- **Consider establishing your own financing company**   Although setting up a financing subsidiary may be difficult, doing this properly can go a long way to providing a significant competitive marketing advantage. This can be done in many ways. For example, if you feel you do not have financial resources or management available to run a leasing operation, or would prefer not to operate a financing company, explore other similar alternatives in which you can maximize control, such as setting up a financing joint venture with an experienced lessor.
- **Establish multiple funding relationships if you decide to work with third-party lessors**   If establishing your own financing company is not feasible or desirable, and you are going to set up a third-party leasing program for your customers, establish relationships with more than one lessor. Relying on one lessor to service all potential customers' needs is unrealistic for many reasons. One lessor's credit standards may not be broad enough to fit your prospective customer profile, which you may not discover until you run into a unanticipated problem, or lessor business changes could put an end to your customer program virtually overnight. Historically, for example, some bank-affiliated and nonbank leasing companies have closed their funding doors without warning and, at times, with indifference to customer commitments. So, establishing multiple funding relationships is essential, and working with at least three lease financing companies is recommended.

In establishing third-party lessor funding relationships, here are some tips.

- **Control the document process** To ensure every transaction that can get done gets done, make sure you control the deal documentation, and that means:
  1. **Develop uniform lease documentation** Developing one set of lease documents generally acceptable to all funding sources is an important marketing step. If a deal is turned down by one lessor, documents do not have to be resigned to use another funding source, thus saving time and possible embarrassment.
  2. **Handle documents** Handling the lease application and documentation process is important. This ensures problems will be properly addressed in a timely manner. For example, your salesperson should prepare the lease application and documents, submit them to the leasing company, and monitor the transaction weekly or, if necessary, every several days.
- **Be wary of funding commitments** Even if you have what appears to be a written commitment to fund customers who meet certain financial and business standards from a third-party leasing company, you may have no assurance of funding reliability. These commitments are typically filled with qualifications, properly so from the lessor's viewpoint, and are rarely legally enforceable.
- **Avoid providing financial guarantees** Be careful about providing financing guarantees for customer leases requested by third-party lessors. It is not unusual, for example, for a leasing company to suggest that if your company would guarantee all your customer leases, deals would always get done. Financial guarantees can adversely affect a product vendor's general growth requirement borrowing capabilities. Worse yet, many lease guarantees permit collection from the guarantor without having first exhausted all remedies against the lessee.
- **Investigate prospective third-party lessor backgrounds thoroughly** The financial backgrounds, years in business, and deal track records of every third-party leasing company you consider must be investigated thoroughly. Not doing so can create avoidable risks. For example, many leasing companies simply don't have the funds available to properly service a vendor's repeated financing needs. An investigation can prevent unfortunate surprises.
- **Use lease brokers cautiously** Lease brokers have no control over whether a deal will be approved or funded. They often send financing packages out to multiple sources hoping someone will approve it. In small transactions, some brokers spend more time sending financing offerings to sources than preparing a good financing package. Improper packaging alone can result in turndown, something that increases the difficulty of finding future funding.
- **If using lease brokers, watch out for fees** Lease brokers often charge a high fee for their services. In large transactions the services generally are worth the fee; in small transactions high fees are generally unwarranted. When questioned about a high fee, brokers often state that the lessor pays the fee, and so it is of no concern. The fact is, a lessor needs a minimum deal profit and the fee is something it pays based on the rent level. The higher the fee, the less competitive the lease financing. And brokers establish a rent level that permits the largest possible fee.
- **Be skeptical about dealing with lease investment funds** Lease investment funds promoted by investment bankers and lessors surface from time to time. They are public or private limited investment partnerships which raise money to invest in equipment leases. Historically, many have had problems as a result of poor management or improper structuring. And when problems arise funding is

cut off. So, if you decide to work with an investment fund, do not rely on it exclusively for customer funding.

- **When working with third-party lessors, conduct preliminary funding reviews**   When using third-party leasing companies to provide customer financing, an equipment vendor should conduct its own preliminary "lease acceptability review" before submitting a transaction to the prospective leasing company to head off problems. Often, issues that could result in a turndown can be addressed to facilitate an approval before the application is submitted. Once a prospective customer is turned down by one leasing company, it is more difficult to get a funding approval from another lessor. The reason may not be logical, but it is a fact of business life: Credit managers at times turn down business they may otherwise accept merely because of fear that another credit manager spotted a problem they could not find.

In summary, there is a customer financing program structure that can work for every equipment vendor, but care must be taken to guarantee that the best possible program is put together. A vendor that works within the financial market realities has the greatest chance of arranging an attractive and reliable financing program.

F.   Summary

Entering the equipment leasing business has benefits, but only if you or your company has a market value-added reason for being in the leasing business. If your company has such a reason, take the time to carefully evaluate all aspects of leasing as it may affect your potential operations.

Chapter 12

Equipment Leasing in International Markets

A.   Overview

The subject of international leasing is complex, and a complete analysis is beyond the scope of this book. However, if you're a part of the leasing business, you should understand the basic issues. And if you believe leasing equipment internationally may be a worthwhile business pursuit, an understanding of key considerations will put the issues you or your company may have to address into a quick business perspective and assist you in assessing whether the subject merits further investigation.

You may have heard that there are many exciting opportunities in the international leasing market. That is true—but only for financially well-qualified and lease transaction-sophisticated entrants, as you'll realize as you read this chapter.

B.   A Complex Market of Growth

There has been a dramatic growth in recent years in the demand for the leasing of equipment overseas, not only in the industrialized countries but also in the industrially developing economies of such countries as China, Korea, and India. This demand has provided unprecedented and major leasing opportunities for U.S. lessors. But, there are many business hurdles to overcome, and risks to address, in what is commonly referred to as "cross-border" leasing.

International leasing brings with it complex tax, accounting, and legal issues. And more. For example, an international lessor must address:

- Business considerations unique to the particular country in which the lease transaction is done, such as restricted availability of local courts for lease enforcement procedures
- Foreign currency exchange risks
- Possible equipment export issues

Accordingly, the lessors best able to take full advantage of the rising equipment financing needs abroad are those with strong financial capabilities and support resources, such as large multinational equipment financing companies with networks of affiliated leasing companies in various international markets.

➤ **Tips**

- Equipment leasing associations exist in many foreign countries, such as the Leasing Associates of Singapore. If you're interested in exploring international leasing in particular markets, they can assist you in identifying local leasing companies to work with, for example, for transaction referrals. They also can provide invaluable advice about local business and legal issues that will impact your company, as well as any lease transactions that you do in their country.
- The *World Leasing Yearbook,* published by Hawkins Publishers, Ltd., Coggeshall, Essex, England, is an excellent source of leasing company information. It provides a list of well over 5,500 lessors operating in over 70 countries. It also provides a handy summary of the leasing business in many foreign countries.

C.   The Foreign Lessee Demand

For a foreign lessee, leasing from a U.S. lessor generally has the same type of traditional lease advantages that a U.S. lessee could expect. A discussion of these traditional lessee leasing advantages is in Chapter 1. There, however, may be additional advantages. In many countries, local circumstances can add substantially to the attractiveness of leasing from an international lessor. For example:

- If available local funding is expensive, or capital is unavailable or in short supply, the ability to obtain a cross-border lease can be the deciding factor in whether to acquire new equipment.
- There are times when a foreign country's lenders are unwilling to provide medium or long-term financing because of economic instability, but international lessors are willing to do so, because they want additional business or their lease investments are more risk diversified, with relatively little local investment concentration in the country in question.

Make no mistake, however, the prospective foreign lessee's decision to enter into a crossborder lease is still primarily a cost decision. There generally must be a clear cost advantage over other financing alternatives. In addition, the lease terms and conditions may have to be better than those available locally.

D.   Advantages for Lessors Leasing Internationally

The United States domestic market, as discussed in Chapter 11, is highly competitive, and currently there is more lessor money available than there are lease deals to do. As a result, some U.S. lessors, in an effort to develop new sources of business, have moved aggressively into the international leasing market for opportunities, finding a particularly high demand for equipment financing in the economically emerging countries, such as China. International leasing interests U.S. lessors for another significant reason: There are possibilities for increased economic lease returns through the use of:

- subsidized export financing
- tax benefits not available to a local foreign financing company

In fact, in some cases, cross-border leases enable lessees and lessors to avail themselves of tax advantages that exist in more than one country, through so-called "double dip" lease transactions. These added tax benefits can either make lease pricing more aggressive or increase a lessor's economic return.

➤ **Observation** Although there may be relatively more opportunities for equipment leasing abroad than in the United States, it is still a competitive market, with large multinational finance companies having a substantial foothold in virtually every significant foreign market.

For U.S. equipment manufacturers and vendors looking for increased export business, the ability to lease internationally has marketing advantages. Being able to provide leasing to prospective customers in foreign countries may facilitate foreign equipment sales.

➤ **Recommendation** Equipment manufacturers not familiar with the business of international equipment leasing should work with multinational third-party leasing companies, at least in beginning stages of leasing internationally. This is the easiest and most cost-effective way to gain the necessary financing knowledge and experience, and to avoid the many pitfalls associated with foreign market leasing.

E. Risks of Operating in Foreign Markets

There are a number of risks that a U.S. lessor faces in cross-border leasing that are not present in domestic leasing. The political risk is the most obvious one, and has wide-ranging ramifications for an international lessor. If, for instance, foreign relations fall apart between the U.S. and the country where the equipment or parties are located, there could be a variety of serious problems, including an inability to collect rent and repossess equipment. In addition, if a lessee pays rent in a foreign currency, there could be a transaction profit deterioration if an adverse change in the currency exchange rate occurs.

Even if political relations remain stable with the country in which the foreign lessee is located, there are risks, such as:

- The long-term nature of the typical equipment lease can subject a lessor to an undue currency exchange fluctuation risk.

➤ **Tip** There are methods to hedge against the currency fluctuation risk. Investment bankers can often provide guidance in how to handle this risk.

- Certain foreign economies are well known for volatile interest rate and economic fluctuations, which may adversely affect the lease transaction.
- Assessing the creditworthiness of a prospective lessee is more difficult, with a possibility of making a credit decision mistake, because company financial statements and presentations may be quite different than that of U.S. companies.
- The business risks are greater than leasing in the U.S. market, if for no other reason than the leased equipment is in a distant land.
- Leasing-related laws in the international environment are constantly changing.
- Foreign laws or judicial systems may make it difficult to repossess equipment from a defaulting lessee.
- The expenses involved in putting together an international lease are typically higher than that of a comparable U.S. lease transaction; thus, the potential for

financial loss is increased if the transaction falls apart during the negotiation stage.

- The language barrier, even with local counsel involved, can create basic misunderstandings that may not be discovered until there is a problem.
- An inadvertent violation of local social customs may result in interpersonnel disharmony and mistrust—and eventual business problems.

Properly evaluating these risks takes considerable work. Experienced assistance is critical in determining the extent to which they exist, and how to best handle them.

1. *Country Risk Management*

Commonly referred to as the "country risk," international lessors must contend with the possibility that events, totally or partially within the control of the foreign lessee's government, such as war; or the government's expropriation of the leased asset, the cancellation of the lessor's export or import license, or the interference with the lessor's ability to repossess equipment in the case of a lessee default, will result in the loss of some or all of their lease investment.

In certain situations, the country risk can be successfully managed. If the leased equipment will be imported into the lessee's country, some form of guarantee or insurance program may be available through a governmental agency. For example, many governments set up an agency to assist in, or support, the export of products manufactured in their country. The Export-Import Bank (Eximbank) of the United States is one such agency set up by the U.S. government to support the exporting of U.S. products. Eximbank directly, and through its agent—the Foreign Credit Insurance Association—offers a number of product export support programs that, for example, can reduce political and commercial risks to which product exporters, lenders, or lessors may be exposed in a foreign locale. The support programs can in effect provide guarantees against loss from specified political and commercial risks, and carry the full faith and credit of the government of the United States.

▶ **Recommendation**   Contact the Export-Import Bank of the United States' Washington, DC office and the Foreign Credit Insurance Association's (FICA) New York City office for information on what support programs they offer and how they work; including to whom they are available and what they cover.

Very briefly, here's what you can generally expect to find in Eximbank and FICA program offerings:

- Guarantees of, or insurance for, equipment residual values are not available.
- Insurance against the expropriation of leased or financed equipment is available.
- New and used equipment can be covered.
- Programs are available for both U.S. and non-U.S. lessors if the equipment under lease is manufactured in United States.
- Guarantees are available for up to 100% of the principal portion of lease payments, and a certain portion of the interest portion of such lease payments.
- Protection against currency fluctuation risk is not available.
- In certain situations, the lessee may be required to make a 15% advance payment to the lessor when the equipment delivers.
- Program coverage is available for specified short-term, as well as long-term, leases.

- The following risks are generally covered.

  1. Political risks, such as war, insurrection, and equipment requisition
  2. The risk of lease nonpayment due to a lessee lease payment default, or insolvency
  3. The inability to repossess equipment following a lease default due to acts of a local government

F. Local Law Considerations

Leasing companies entering a particular foreign market must assess the local law implications for the types of lease transactions in which they intend to participate. Lessors must determine what

- Local laws and regulations govern the leasing operation, including what periodic filing requirements may be necessary.
- Penalties may be imposed for failure to comply with local law and regulations.

In the United States, because there is little regulation, penalties are nonexistent or of minor concern. In many foreign countries, however, the situation can be dramatically different. In some countries, penalties can result in the following:

- An inability to use the country's court system
- A change in a lease transaction's taxation
- Fines
- Imprisonment

Some local laws are quite extensive in their regulation of lease transactions, even going as far as dictating the actual terms and conditions of cross-border lease agreements, including how much interest can be charged, how long or how short the lease term can be, and the required or permitted lease payment grace periods.

An important legal consideration that cannot be overlooked for obvious reasons are the creditor rights laws: The rules that govern what a lessor must do to protect and enforce its rights in the lease collateral within a country's local law. To assess these issues, you will have to be thoroughly versed in the applicable bankruptcy or similar creditor rights laws.

➤ **Recommendation**   There is only one way to adequately protect yourself from local law problems: For each transaction, hire competent local counsel in each jurisdiction in which the equipment and transaction parties are located.

And finally, as part of your local law due diligence, you must also check to see if any treaties exist with the country you intend to do business in that can affect tax or other aspects of the lease transaction.

G. International Lease Documents

The international lease documentation used by U.S. lessors is often based on the documentation used in sophisticated U.S.-style leveraged leases. (For basic provisions in a lease generally, the reader is referred to the lease documentation discussion in Chapters 3 and 4.) However, it should go without saying, the lease documentation must incorporate provisions and protections necessary for doing business in a foreign local.

The one sure way to competently approach proper lease document drafting is to enlist the aid of competent and experienced international U.S. leasing counsel and foreign local counsel. In any event, at a bare minimum, you will want to be particularly careful that:

- You have a noncancelable, or "hell or high-water," lease, one in which the lessee is specifically required to make all the rental payments due under the lease without abatement, reduction, or set-off.
- You have not inadvertently relinquished legal title to the asset under lease. This may require a careful review of applicable laws to ensure that the you, as lessor, have good title at the start of the lease, and that you have adequate protection against the potential claims by any lessee creditor or other third party during the lease term.
- The manner in which rent payments are made, including the currency of payment, fits your currency exchange requirements. This means, for example, inserting provisions that detail what happens if there is a currency exchange rate fluctuation, or the lessee is not permitted by law to make the lease payments as prescribed by the lease agreement.
- You have considered more stringent maintenance and repair duties, and lease reporting requirements (travel costs and distance may make it prohibitive to conduct on-site reviews and inspections). For example, it is often advisable to include in the lease an expanded maintenance provision that details the maintenance standards suggested by the equipment manufacturer.
- There is no necessity for setting up a maintenance reserve account to cover, for example, repairs that the lessee fails to perform, or performs inadequately.
- Comprehensive tax indemnification provisions that cover all expected tax advantages have been incorporated. Typically, the tax aspects of a cross-border lease are crucial to the economic viability of the lease transaction, and very complex. In addition there is the ever-present possibility that the applicable tax laws may change to the detriment of a lessor after the lease is signed. Accordingly, these tax indemnification provisions must spell out in great detail all lessor tax benefits anticipated, and the obligations of the lessee in the event that some or all of these benefits are lost, or otherwise unavailable.
- Whether any applicable commercial laws governing the sale of goods create any implied equipment or other warranties that run to the lessee from you as lessor merely because you are the equipment title holder. In the United States, a lessor is generally able to effectively avoid any such implied warranties by using disclaimer language prescribed by the Uniform Commercial Code laws.
- The method of dealing with any required withholding taxes under local law, such as a requirement that 15% of each rental payment be withheld and remitted to the local taxing authority, is addressed and handled properly. Typically, any required withholding tax payments are responsibility of the lessor, and the lessee is deemed to be the government's agent for their collection and payment. If the lessee fails to make these payments, the government will go after the lessor to collect. And, in this case, without a specific provision in the lease agreement for this, the lessor may have no recourse for reimbursement against the lessee. A lease provision, therefore, that spells out that payment for any such withholding taxes is the lessee's responsibility, exactly how much the lessee must pay, when payment must be made, and to whom it is to be made is essential.

- There are representation and warranties specific to your particular lease transaction, such as that proper equipment import or governmental authorizations have been obtained. If, for example, proper governmental authorizations have not been obtained, and the lease contained a representation that they had been obtained, or none were necessary, then a lessor has the power to move quickly to minimize the potential for loss from potential adverse government actions by calling a lease default and repossessing the equipment.
- The remedies available in the event of a lease default are adequate, and not over-reaching. The area of lease default is one that requires careful attention. As a general rule, at a minimum, the lessor's default remedies should conform with any specific remedies available to a lessor under the applicable foreign law. In addition, care must be taken that any additional ones do not run afoul of accepted rules of fairness, otherwise they, or possibly the lessor's entire rights against the lessee, may be subject to attack under the local laws by lessee's counsel for being unconscionable or against public policy.
- Casualty and third-party insurance provisions provide what you need. Clearly, this is a critical aspect of an equipment lease, and an insurance company thoroughly familiar with insurance coverage available in the foreign local must be consulted.
- There are effective lessor lease assignment rights. Local law must be checked to ensure there are no assignment restrictions, and also to determine if any type of assignment could result in the obligation to pay a transfer or registration fee or tax.
- There are necessary assignment restrictions on the lessee. You, as lessor, do not want the lease to end up in the hands of someone that could jeopardize your lease security or rights.
- You have considered incorporating an arbitration provision to settle disputes to avoid being tied up in local courts. Although an arbitration requirement may not be enforceable under a particular local law if a lessee chooses not to go along with it, having one is recommended. Arbitration is generally a less costly and faster procedure than litigation.
- You have designated which country's law will govern the lease transaction. Care, however, must be taken to ensure that any choice of law will be enforceable under local law.

H. Uniform International Lease Rules

In an attempt to address the many complex issues surrounding equipment leasing in the international market, and in support of the growing interest in this form of financing in various nations, the International Institute for the Unification of Private Law, formerly an affiliate of the League of Nations, but now an independent international organization located in Rome, Italy, caused the formation of a study group in 1977 consisting of legal and financial experts to review international leasing and put together a set of uniform rules that would eliminate many uncertainties. The 1977 study group's efforts ultimately resulted in the unanimous adoption by the representatives of 55 nations gathered in Ottawa, Canada, in May 1988, of a comprehensive set of international leasing rules. The promulgated rules were subject to ratification by all represented nations. The final text of these rules is as follows:

UNIDROIT CONVENTION
ON INTERNATIONAL FINANCIAL LEASING

(Ottawa, 28 May 1988)

THE STATES PARTIES TO THIS CONVENTION,

RECOGNIZING the importance of removing certain legal impediments to the international financial leasing of equipment, while maintaining a fair balance of interests between the different parties to the transaction,

AWARE of the need to make international financial leasing more available,

CONSCIOUS of the fact that the rules of law governing the traditional contract of hire need to be adapted to the distinctive triangular relationship created by the financial leasing transaction,

RECOGNIZING therefore the desirability of formulating certain uniform rules relating primarily to the civil and commercial law aspects of international financial leasing,

HAVE AGREED as follows:

CHAPTER I - SPHERE OF APPLICATION
AND GENERAL PROVISIONS

Article 1

1. This Convention governs a financial leasing transaction as described in paragraph 2 in which one party (the lessor),
    (a) on the specifications of another party (the lessee), enters into an agreement (the supply agreement) with a third party (the supplier) under which the lessor acquires plant, capital goods or other equipment (the equipment) on terms approved by the lessee so far as they concern its interests, and
    (b) enters into an agreement (the leasing agreement) with the lessee, granting to the lessee the right to use the equipment in return for the payment of rentals.
2. The financial leasing transaction referred to in the previous paragraph is a transaction which includes the following characteristics:
    (a) the lessee specifies the equipment and selects the supplier without relying primarily on the skill and judgment of the lessor;
    (b) the equipment is acquired by the lessor in connection with a leasing agreement which, to the knowledge of the supplier, either has been made or is to be made between the lessor and the lessee; and
    (c) the rentals payable under the leasing agreement are calculated so as to take into account in particular the amortization of the whole or a substantial part of the cost of the equipment.
3. This Convention applies whether or not the lessee has or subsequently acquires the option to buy the equipment or to hold it on lease for a further period, and whether or not for a nominal price or rental.
4. This Convention applies to financial leasing transactions in relation to all equipment save that which is to be used primarily for the lessee's personal, family or household purposes.

Article 2

In the case of one or more sub-leasing transactions involving the same equipment, this Convention applies to each transaction which is a financial leasing transaction and is otherwise subject to this Convention as if the person from whom the first lessor (as defined in paragraph 1 of the previous article) acquired the equipment were the supplier and as if the agreement under which the equipment was so acquired were the supply agreement.

Article 3

1. This Convention applies when the lessor and the lessee have their places of business in different States and:

(a) those States and the State in which the supplier has its place of business are Contracting States; or

(b) both the supply agreement and the leasing agreement are governed by the law of a Contracting State.

2. A reference in this Convention to a party's place of business shall, if it has more than one place of business, mean the place of business which has the closest relationship to the relevant agreement and its performance, having regard to the circumstances known to or contemplated by the parties at any time before or at the conclusion of that agreement.

Article 4

1. The provisions of this Convention shall not cease to apply merely because the equipment has become a fixture to or incorporated in land.

2. Any question whether or not the equipment has become a fixture to or incorporated in land, and if so the effect on the rights inter se of the lessor and a person having real rights in the land, shall be determined by the law of the State where the land is situated.

Article 5

1. The application of this Convention may be excluded only if each of the parties to the supply agreement and each of the parties to the leasing agreement agree to exclude it.

2. Where the application of this Convention has not been excluded in accordance with the previous paragraph, the parties may, in their relations with each other, derogate from or vary the effect of any of its provisions except as stated in Articles 8 (3) and 13 (3)(b) and (4).

Article 6

1. In the interpretation of this Convention, regard is to be had to its object and purpose as set forth in the preamble, to its international character and to the need to promote uniformity in its application and the observance of good faith in international trade.

2. Questions concerning matters governed by this Convention which are not expressly settled in it are to be settled in conformity with the general principles on which it is based or, in the absence of such principles, in conformity with the law applicable by virtue of the rules of private international law.

CHAPTER II - RIGHTS AND DUTIES OF THE PARTIES

Article 7

1. (a) The lessor's real rights in the equipment shall be valid against the lessee's trustee in bankruptcy and creditors, including creditors who have obtained an attachment or execution.

(b) For the purposes of this paragraph "trustee in bankruptcy" includes a liquidator, administrator or other person appointed to administer the lessee's estate for the benefit of the general body of creditors.

2. Where by the applicable law the lessor's real rights in the equipment are valid against a person referred to in the previous paragraph only on compliance with rules as to public notice, those rights shall be valid against that person only if there has been compliance with such rules.

3. For the purposes of the previous paragraph the applicable law is the law of the State which, at the time when a person referred to in paragraph 1 becomes entitled to invoke the rules referred to in the previous paragraph, is:

(a) in the case of a registered ship, the State in which it is registered in the name of the owner (for the purposes of this sub-paragraph a bareboat charterer is deemed not to be the owner);

(b) in the case of an aircraft which is registered pursuant to the Convention on International Civil Aviation done at Chicago on 7 December 1944, the State in which it is so registered;

(c) in the case of other equipment of a kind normally moved from one State to another, including an aircraft engine, the State in which the lessee has its principal place of business;

(d) in the case of all other equipment, the State in which the equipment is situated.

4. Paragraph 2 shall not affect the provisions of any other treaty under which the lessor's real rights in the equipment are required to be recognized.

5. This article shall not affect the priority of any creditor having:

(a) a consensual or non-consensual lien or security interest in the equipment arising otherwise than by virtue of an attachment or execution, or

(b) any right of arrest, detention or disposition conferred specifically in relation to ships or aircraft under the law applicable by virtue of the rules of private international law.

Article 8

1. (a) Except as otherwise provided by this Convention or stated in the leasing agreement, the lessor shall not incur any liability to the lessee in respect of the equipment save to the extent that the lessee has suffered loss as the result of its reliance on the lessor's skill and judgment and of the lessor's intervention in the selection of the supplier or the specifications of the equipment.

(b) The lessor shall not, in its capacity of lessor, be liable to third parties for death, personal injury or damage to property caused by the equipment.

(c) The above provisions of this paragraph shall not govern any liability of the lessor in any other capacity, for example as owner.

2. The lessor warrants that the lessee's quiet possession will not be disturbed by a person who has a superior title or right, or who claims a superior title or right and acts under the authority of a court, where such title, right or claim is not derived from an act or omission of the lessee.

3. The parties may not derogate from or vary the effect of the provisions of the previous paragraph in so far as the superior title, right or claim is derived from an intentional or grossly negligent act or omission of the lessor.

4. The provisions of paragraphs 2 and 3 shall not affect any broader warranty of quiet possession by the lessor which is mandatory under the law applicable by virtue of the rules of private international law.

Article 9

1. The lessee shall take proper care of the equipment, use it in a reasonable manner and keep it in the condition in which it was delivered, subject to fair wear and tear and to any modification of the equipment agreed by the parties.

2. When the leasing agreement comes to an end the lessee, unless exercising a right to buy the equipment or to hold the equipment on lease for a further period, shall return the equipment to the lessor in the condition specified in the previous paragraph.

Article 10

1. The duties of the supplier under the supply agreement shall also be owed to the lessee as if it were a party to that agreement and as if the equipment were to be supplied directly to the lessee. However, the supplier shall not be liable to both the lessor and the lessee in respect of the same damage.

2. Nothing in this article shall entitle the lessee to terminate or rescind the supply agreement without the consent of the lessor.

Article 11

The lessee's rights derived from the supply agreement under this Convention shall not be affected by a variation of any term of the supply agreement previously approved by the lessee unless it consented to that variation.

Article 12

1. Where the equipment is not delivered or is delivered late or fails to conform to the supply agreement:

(a) the lessee has the right as against the lessor to reject the equipment or to terminate the leasing agreement; and

(b) the lessor has the right to remedy its failure to tender equipment in conformity with the supply agreement as if the lessee had agreed to buy the equipment from the lessor under the same terms as those of the supply agreement.

2. A right conferred by the previous paragraph shall be exercisable in the same manner and shall be lost in the same circumstances as if the lessee had agreed to buy the equipment from the lessor under the same terms as those of the supply agreement.

3. The lessee shall be entitled to withhold rentals payable under the leasing agreement until the lessor has remedied its failure to tender equipment in conformity with the supply agreement or the lessee has lost the right to reject the equipment.

4. Where the lessee has exercised a right to terminate the leasing agreement, the lessee shall be entitled to recover any rentals and other sums paid in advance, less a reasonable sum for any benefit the lessee has derived from the equipment.

5. The lessee shall have no other claim against the lessor for non-delivery, delay in delivery or delivery of non-conforming equipment except to the extent to which this results from the act or omission of the lessor.

6. Nothing in this article shall affect the lessee's rights against the supplier under Article 10.

Article 13

1. In the event of default by the lessee, the lessor may recover accrued unpaid rentals, together with interest and damages.

2. Where the lessee's default is substantial, then subject to paragraph 5 the lessor may also require accelerated payment of the value of the future rentals, where the leasing agreement so provides, or may terminate the leasing agreement and after such termination:

(a) recover possession of the equipment; and

(b) recover such damages as will place the lessor in the position in which it would have been had the lessee performed the leasing agreement in accordance with its terms.

3. (a) The leasing agreement may provide for the manner in which the damages recoverable under paragraph 2 (b) are to be computed.

(b) Such provision shall be enforceable between the parties unless it would result in damages substantially in excess of those provided for under paragraph 2 (b). The parties may not derogate from or vary the effect of the provisions of the present sub-paragraph.

4. Where the lessor has terminated the leasing agreement, it shall not be entitled to enforce a term of that agreement providing for acceleration of payment of future rentals, but the value of such rentals may be taken into account in computing damages under paragraphs 3 (b) and 3. The parties may not derogate from or vary the effect of the provisions of the present paragraph.

5. The lessor shall not be entitled to exercise its right of acceleration or its right of termination under paragraph 2 unless it has by notice given the lessee a reasonable opportunity of remedying the default so far as the same may be remedied.

6. The lessor shall not be entitled to recover damages to the extent that it has failed to take all reasonable steps to mitigate its loss.

Article 14

1. The lessor may transfer or otherwise deal with all or any of its rights in the equipment or under the leasing agreement. Such a transfer shall not relieve the lessor of any of its duties under the leasing agreement or alter either the nature of the leasing agreement or its legal treatment as provided in this Convention.

2. The lessee may transfer the right to the use of the equipment or any other rights under the teasing agreement only with the consent of the lessor and subject to the rights of third parties.

CHAPTER III - FINAL PROVISIONS

Article 15

1. This Convention is open for signature at the concluding meeting of the Diplomatic Conference for the Adoption of the Draft Unidroit Conventions on International Factoring and International Financial Leasing and will remain open for signature by all States at Ottawa until 31 December 1990.
2. This Convention is subject to ratification, acceptance or approval by States which have signed it.
3. This Convention is open for accession by all States which are not signatory States as from the date it is open for signature.
4. Ratification, acceptance, approval or accession is effected by the deposit of a formal instrument to that effect with the depository.

Article 16

1. This Convention enters into force on the first day of the month following the expiration of six months after the date of deposit of the third instrument of ratification, acceptance, approval or accession.
2. For each State that ratifies, accepts, approves, or accedes to this Convention after the deposit of the third instrument of ratification, acceptance, approval or accession, this Convention enters into force in respect of that State on the first day of the month following the expiration of six months after the date of the deposit of its instrument of ratification, acceptance, approval or accession.

Article 17

This Convention does not prevail over any treaty which has already been or may be entered into; in particular it shall not affect any liability imposed on any person by existing or future treaties.

Article 18

1. If a Contracting State has two or more territorial units in which different systems of law are applicable in relation to the matters dealt with in this Convention, it may, at the time of signature, ratification, acceptance, approval or accession, declare that this Convention is to extend to all its territorial units or only to one or more of them, and may substitute its declaration by another declaration at and time.
2. These declarations are to be notified to the depository and are to state expressly the territorial units to which the Convention extends.
3. If by virtue of a declaration under this article, this Convention extends to one or more but not all of the territorial units of a Contracting State, and if the place of business of a party is located in that State, this place of business, for the purposes of this Convention, is considered not to be in a Contracting State, unless it is in a territorial unit to which the Convention extends.
4. If a Contracting State makes no declaration under paragraph 1, the Convention is to extend to all territorial units of that State.

Article 19

1. Two or more Contracting States which have the same or closely related legal rules on matters governed by this Convention may at any time declare that the Convention is not to apply where the supplier, the lessor and the lessee have their places of business in those States. Such declarations may be made jointly or by reciprocal unilateral declarations.
2. A Contracting State which has the same or closely related legal rules on matters governed by this Convention as one or more non-Contracting States may at any time declare that the Conven-

tion is not to apply where the supplier, the lessor and the lessee have their places of business in those States.

3. If a State which is the object of a declaration under the previous paragraph subsequently becomes a Contracting State, the declaration made will, as from the date on which the Convention enters into force in respect of the new Contracting State have the effect of a declaration made under paragraph 1, provided that the new Contracting State joins in such declaration or makes a reciprocal unilateral declaration.

Article 20

A Contracting State may declare at the time of signature, ratification, acceptance, approval or accession that it will substitute its domestic law for Article 8 (3) if its domestic law does not permit the lessor to exclude its liability for its default or negligence.

Article 21

1. Declarations made under this Convention at the time of signature are subject to confirmation upon ratification, acceptance or approval.

2. Declarations and confirmations of declarations are to be in writing and to be formally notified to the depository.

3. A declaration takes effect simultaneously with the entry into force of this Convention in respect of the State concerned. However, a declaration of which the depository receives formal notification after such entry into force takes effect on the first day of the month following the expiration of six months after the date of its receipt by the depository. Reciprocal unilateral declarations under Article 19 take effect on the first day of the month following the expiration of six months after the receipt of the latest declaration by the depository.

4. Any State which makes a declaration under this Convention may withdraw it at any time by a formal notification in writing addressed to the depository. Such withdrawal is to take effect on the first day of the month following the expiration of six months after the date of the receipt of the notification by the depository.

5. A withdrawal of a declaration made under Article 19 renders inoperative in relation to the withdrawing State, as from the date on which the withdrawal takes effect, any joint or reciprocal unilateral declaration made by another State under that article.

Article 22

No reservations are permitted except those expressly authorized in this Convention.

Article 23

This Convention applies to a financial teasing transaction when the leasing agreement and the supply agreement are both concluded on or after the date on which the Convention enters into force in respect of the Contracting States referred to in Article 3 (1)(a), or of the Contracting State or States referred to in paragraph 1 (b) of that article.

Article 24

1. This Convention may be denounced by any Contracting State at any time after the date on which it enters into force for that State.

2. Denunciation is effected by the deposit of an instrument to that effect with the depository.

3. A denunciation takes effect on the first day of the month following the expiration of six months after the deposit of the instrument of denunciation with the depository. Where a longer period for the denunciation to take effect is specified in the instrument of denunciation it takes effect upon the expiration of such longer period after its deposit with the depository.

Article 25

1. This Convention shall be deposited with the Government of Canada.

2. The Government of Canada shall:

(a) inform all States which have signed or acceded to this Convention and the President of the International Institute for the Unification of Private Law (Unidroit) of:

(i) each new signature or deposit of an instrument of ratification, acceptance, approval or accession, together with the date thereof;

(ii) each declaration made under Articles 18, 19 and 20;

(iii) the withdrawal of any declaration made under Article 21 (4);

(iv) the date of entry into force of this Convention;

(v) the deposit of an instrument of denunciation of this Convention together with the date of its deposit and the date on which it takes effect;

(b) transmit certified true copies of this Convention to all signatory States, to all States acceding to the Convention and to the President of the International Institute for the Unification of Private Law (Unidroit).

IN WITNESS WHEREOF the undersigned plenipotentiaries, being duly authorized by their respective Governments, have signed this Convention.

DONE at Ottawa, this twenty-eighth day of May, one thousand nine hundred and eighty-eight, in a single original, of which the English and French texts are equally authentic.

I. Summary

There is no doubt that in a expanding global economy, cross-border leasing will continue to expand. And, the job of putting together a cross-border lease will become easier as transaction experience is gained. Leasing equipment internationally, however is extremely complex and should not be approached without competent advice.

Chapter 13

The Equipment Leasing Laws under the Uniform Commercial Code

A. Introduction

As an equipment lessor, you must know the state equipment leasing laws, embodied in the various states' Uniform Commercial Code, to properly draft a lease contract, as well as protect your equipment from lessee creditors and claims. One mistake can be costly. Prospective lessees, on the other hand, must understand these laws because they can be turned to for rights and remedies when problems occur. There are no federal leasing law statues.

It will be useful, before beginning this chapter, to give you some historical background. Before these leasing laws came into existence, the courts struggled with whether an equipment financing transaction should be characterized as a lease or as a conditional or installment sale for state law purposes. As a result, there was widespread inconsistency and confusion. To address this problem, a drafting committee, called the National Conference of Commissioners on Uniform State Laws, was organized to assemble the best court interpretations of leasing contract law and, once done, this "model" law was sent to the various states (including the District of Columbia) for consideration and enactment into state law. In most cases, the model law, now known as Article 2A of the Uniform Commercial Code (commonly referred to simply as the "UCC"), was adopted with few changes. Very simply, UCC Article 2A resolved the many issues and inconsistencies over lease chacterization by establishing uniform leasing rules. This has clearly benefited all parties to a lease transaction.

In addition to Article 2A, there are two additional and important UCC sections (known as "Articles") that can impact an equipment financing, Article 2 (Sales), and Article 9 (Secured Transactions; Sales of Accounts and Chattel Paper). These Articles existed prior to the formulation and adoption of Article 2A and were created by the National Conference of Commissioners to provide guidance, in part, for commercial and consumer sales, and general financing of personal property. A detailed analysis of UCC Article's 2 and 9, dealing with the sales of personal property, is beyond the scope of this chapter since they relate to transactions far beyond equipment lease transactions. We will examine, however, their essential elements so you will have a working knowledge of how they may come into play in an equipment lease situation.

UCC Concepts

The overall intent of the various UCC laws is, in effect, to compile, evolve, and, in certain cases, clarify the various laws (such as contract law, as interpreted by the U.S. courts) into one cohesive set of rules to eliminate arbitrary, commercially inequitable, and inconsistent court approaches and decisions.

The drafters of the various UCC Articles intended that the parties to UCC-governed transactions have, with a few exceptions, the freedom to contract as they see fit, permitting the parties to "draft out," for example, UCC Article provisions.

B. UCC Article 2, Sales—An Overview

UCC Article 2 establishes the rights and remedies of the parties to a sale transaction. It imposes, for example, certain implied product warranties that a purchaser can enforce against a seller of goods, something financing companies that are not equipment vendors should not have to fairly assume. The best way to put Article 2 into perspective in relation to Artilce 2A is to understand how it differs from Article 2A, as Article 2A was in part based on Article 2. Both address personal property, basically parting company in the case where the transaction is a lease financing (governed by Article 2A), as opposed to a straight equipment sale (governed by Article 2).

Two important commercial (nonconsumer) differences that Article 2A eliminated from the Article 2 sales rules are:

- Article 2A eliminated implied equipment warranties of merchantability and fitness for use, existing in Article 2.
- Article 2A eliminated implied product infringement warranties when the lease qualifies as a "finance lease," under Article 2A.

C. UCC Article 9, Secured Transactions; Sales of Accounts and Chattel Paper—An Overview

UCC Article 9 governs secured lending transactions, in which the parties intend to create a security interest in the personal property (such as equipment) financed. A security interest is simply an interest in personal property that secures the payment or performance of an obligation. If, for example, a lender loans money to a lessor to enable it to purchase equipment for lease to a lessee (such as in a typical leveraged lease transaction), it will take as collateral for the loan repayment obligations a security interest in the underlying equipment lease and the related equipment. A court would deem this type of lending transaction as governed by the UCC Article 9 rules. UCC Article 9 would also come into play if the lease transaction turns out (even unintended by the parties) to in substance be a secured loan (often referred to as a "financing"), such as when the lessee has a $1 purchase option.

D. Equipment Leasing under UCC Article 2A

1. Overview

As suggested, a major development in the law of personal property leasing was the approval by the National Conference of Commissioners on Uniform State Laws of

Article 2A of the Uniform Commercial Code. Article 2A as proposed by the commissioners has been adopted by the various states (including the District of Columbia), with, in some cases, relatively minor modifications, and sets forth legal guidelines for determining whether a transaction purporting to be a lease is a lease for state law purposes. Very simply, Article 2A is generally intended to govern the formation, construction, and enforceability of equipment lease contracts.

Before Article 2A was enacted by the various states, equipment lease transactions were generally governed under state law by common law principles: UCC Article 2 (Sales) and UCC Article 9 (Secured Transactions). Article 2A has been instrumental in clarifying many personal property leasing issues that had gone unresolved under the various state laws. It has, for example, eliminated ambiguities that arose in determining the rights of equipment lessors and lessees. It established guidelines for determining when an equipment financing transaction was in fact a lease transaction and when it, instead, was a form of conditional sale-type financing (a secured financing transaction that may have looked like a lease transaction, because, for example, the contract was entitled "Equipment Lease Agreement"). Article 2A also spells out the rights an equipment lessor would have against the other lessee creditors.

Key Point

With a few exceptions, the Article 2A provisions can be overridden by agreement between the parties. The exceptions usually relate to matters of public policy, and what would be considered good faith dealings. For issues not addressed by the parties, Article 2A governs. Therefore, you could say in a lease transaction that Article 2A's job is to fill in aspects of the transaction that the parties did not explicitly cover in their contract.

---

2. Lease Distinguished from Security Interest

UCC Article 2A, along with Article 2 and Article 9, specifically defines the characteristics of leases, sales, and security interests. It is often not easy to determine if the transaction purporting to be an lease qualifying under Article 2A is in fact an Article 2A qualifying lease, or should instead be considered, under state law, a nonlease, or secured, financing. Under Article 2A, a lease is essentially defined as a transfer of the right to possession and use of personal property for a period of time (term) in return for consideration (such as money), unless it is a "sale" or a "security interest". Typically, the most difficult part in making an assessment is determining if the transaction is a "security interest." Although the definition of security interest spells out specific factors that will disqualify a transaction as a lease and cause it to be deemed a security interest, and factors that in and of themselves will not cause a purported lease to in fact be deemed a security interest, the definition also provides that the various transaction "facts and circumstances," must be considered. The "facts and circumstances" benchmark is subject to interpretation, and thus can create characterization uncertainty.

Under the UCC, lease disqualifying factors that are:

- The lease term equals or exceeds the remaining useful life of the equipment.
- The lessee is obligated to become the equipment owner at lease end.
- The lessee has the right to purchase the equipment for a nominal amount (such as $1), or can acquire the equipment without cost.

Factors that in and of themselves that will not cause a purported lease transaction to be disqualified as a lease are:

- The lease is a net or full payout lease.
- The lease has equipment renewal or purchase options, nonnominal in amount, even if at a fixed price.

Without getting too technical, however, as a rule of thumb, if the lessor retains a meaningful economic interest in the end-of-lease (residual) value of the equipment, notwithstanding the lessee's right to exclusive use (subject to a lessee lease default) of the equipment during the lease term, it is a lease. Otherwise, it will not be so considered, and must be treated as a secured financing, such as a secured loan or an installment sale financing. For example, if the lessee can become the equipment owner for no additional, or nominal, consideration, the transaction is not a lease under Article 2A.

An Exception—TRAC Leases

Most states have adopted an exception to the foregoing lease/security interest test criteria for motor vehicle leases with terminal rental adjustment clauses (referred to as TRAC leases). Under a TRAC lease, the lessor has no meaningful economic residual interest in the equipment, because the lessee has to pay the lessor for any "shortfall" the lessor incurs in the end-of-lease resale. Under Article 2A, as adopted by those states, the transaction still qualifies as a lease under the state leasing laws, So, for example, a lessor may provide in the lease that its assumed residual is $15,000, and that the lessee must pay the lessor for any shortfall in resale price below $15,000. If the motor vehicle sold for $10,000 at lease end, the lessee would owe the lessor $5,000 ($15,000 − $10,000 = $5,000).

---

3. Protecting the Lessor's Equipment Interest

If the transaction qualifies as a lease under Article 2A, the lessor is deemed the equipment owner and no other creditors can successfully claim superior rights to the equipment. If a transaction does not qualify as a lease under Article 2A, and it is deemed to be an equipment financing, it will typically be governed by Article 9 (Secured Transactions), and possibly Article 2 (Sales). If the transaction fails to qualify as an Article 2A lease, the Article 9 rules will likely govern and the party designated as the lessor has to generally make certain initial and follow-on document filings (referred to as UCC financing statement filings), and possibly take certain other actions to protect its equipment interest against third-party creditors of the lessee. Notwithstanding the fact that the lessors under Article 2A qualifying leases need not take any such protective UCC filing action, most lessors, as a matter of course, make what is referred to as an information-only (precautionary) filing using a UCC-1 Financing Statement form, as indicated earlier in this book. Very briefly, the lessor files a typical UCC-1 financing statement against the lessee, with a notice typed or printed in the body of UCC-1 indicating that it is a information-only filing.

Legal Point

There are no filing requirements provided for under Article 2A if a lease qualifies as a true lease, and not a secured financing. Keep in mind, however, that certificates of title filings may be necessary, such as with automobiles or trucks under the various laws.

4. What Are the Practical Implications of a Lease Being Deemed a Secured Financing?

If a court determines that a transaction purporting to be an equipment lease for state law purposes is in fact a secured financing, UCC Article 9 comes into play. And if the rules of Article 9 are not complied with, a lessor could loose its secured position; that is, its ability to claim a superior right in the equipment over that of other lessee creditors who may have an effective claim to that equipment because of certain security interest rights they have in the lessee's assets. If this occurs, a court may in effect take the position that, notwithstanding that the agreement is labeled a lease, the transaction is the functional equivalent of an equipment installment, or conditional, sale or a loan.

Assume for a moment that Able Leasing Company leases a $1,000,000 computer to Process Company for three years. The lease agreement contains an option in which Process Company, if it chooses, can purchase the computer at the end of the lease for $1, whereupon Able Leasing Company would transfer title to the computer to Process Company. Able Leasing Company determined the lease rental rate by assuming that, at lease end, it would have received a full repayment of its $1,000,000 equipment purchase investment and its profit. It is estimated that the fair market end-of-lease value of the computer would be $175,000. Able Leasing Company made no protective UCC filings. Clearly, here, the lessor did not retain a meaningful economic interest (or risk) in the equipment's residual value, and, undoubtedly, this lease transaction would be interpreted by the courts as a secured financing, subject to UCC Article 9.

Now assume, additionally, that Process Company filed for bankruptcy under Chapter 7 of the federal bankruptcy law (referred to as the Bankruptcy Code), a bankruptcy trustee was appointed, and the assets of Process Company were to be liquidated (known as a Chapter 7 proceeding under the Bankruptcy Code; see Chapter 14 for a discussion of the bankruptcy concepts and rules). Also assume that Process Company's main lending bank, The Big Bank, had given Process Company a general working capital line of credit, and had secured the repayment of this line of credit by taking a security interest in all assets of Process Company, and had legally placed a lien on all existing and future assets. The Big Bank then goes before the trustee and claims that its lien on Processing Company's assets has attached to the Able Leasing Company–owned computer, that the Able Leasing Company lease was in fact a secured financing, and that, since Able Leasing Company did not "perfect" its lien rights to the computer by making an appropriate UCC filing, The Big Bank's "blanket" lien has attached to the computer, thus giving The Big Bank a prior right in the computer. Able Leasing Company states that The Big Bank has no claim because it is the titled owner of the computer. Who wins this case? The answer is The Big Bank.

If Able Leasing Company had made an information-only UCC filing, the outcome would have been different. Able Leasing Company would then have to retain its rights in the computer over the claim of The Big Bank.

So, in effect, if a purported lease is deemed to be a secured financing,

- The lessor's equipment ownership position may be treated as a subordinated security interest assuming the lessor made no Article 9 UCC filings, giving other lessee's creditors who have valid and perfected liens on the lessee's general assets, if a lessee bankruptcy occurs, the opportunity to make a valid superior claim to the equipment.
- A bankruptcy trustee may be able to sell the lessor's equipment free of any lessor rights in the equipment.
- The lessor may come under state usury laws.
- The lessor may subject itself to certain additional equipment product warranties, notwithstanding lease contract warranty disclaimers.

5. *A Key Lease Concept under Article 2A—The Finance Lease*

In order to recognize the economic and business realties in certain types of equipment financings, the UCC drafters came up with a special category of lease, referred to as a "finance lease", which has special lessor benefits. In order for a lease to quality as an Article 2A finance lease, and be automatically entitled to the unique benefits offered under Article 2A, the lease has to meet the following criteria:

- The lessor must not select, manufacture, or supply the equipment.
- The lessor must acquire the equipment in connection with the lease (that means, not out of inventory).
- The lessee has to be provided information, before lease execution, about what equipment warranties are provided, and who stands behind them.

The key advantages for a lessor in having a transaction classified for UCC purposes as an Article 2A statutory finance lease are:

- There are no lessor-implied equipment warranties of fitness and merchantability, as may be provided in other lease transactions.
- The lessee's rent payment obligation is deemed to be an irrevocable commercial lessee obligation to pay rents, i.e., the rent payment obligation under a lease classified as an Article 2A finance lease is automatically deemed to be a statutory hell or high water obligation (rents are noncancelable and absolutely and unconditionally payable, and not capable of being offset or otherwise reduced, even though not specifically stated as such in the lease contract) obligation.

A key advantage to a lessee in a finance lease transaction is that Article 2A automatically passes through the equipment seller's warranties (subject to any warranty exclusions) to the lessee.

Lessor Tips

- If a lease transaction does not meet the Article 2A finance lease criteria, then a lessor can, through proper lease contract drafting, construct the same result by including, for example, equipment warranty disclaimers and a hell or high water lease provision.
- If a hell or high water rent obligation is intended, notwithstanding that the lease transaction apparently qualifies as a Article 2A finance lease, a lessor should NOT reply on the UCC statue to ensure hell or high water rent obligation, in the event that a lessee successfully argues in court that the lease in fact does not qualify under the applicable UCC laws as a statutory finance lease, and, thus, is not entitled to hell or high water rent treatment. So, in drafting a lease, a lessor should always include specific hell or high water language.

Lessee Tips

- If a lease transaction does not meet the Article 2A finance lease criteria, a lessee may be able to pursue, to the extent the lease contract does not make appropriate equipment warranty disclaimers, equipment warranty claims against the equipment lessor, in addition to the actual equipment vendor.
- Even if the lease transaction does not apparently qualify as an Article 2A finance lease, a lessee should raise a defense (if the facts so warrant) against any hell or high water rent payment obligation claim by the lessor.
- Although Article 2A automatically passes through the equipment seller warranties, a lessee should be cautious by contacting the seller to ensure that the lessor/purchaser may not diminish any warranties on which the lessee is relying. If important, a side letter to that effect is always recommended to avoid any future arguments.

---

6. Avoiding Legally Implied Equipment Warranties

An equipment lessor that is not also an equipment seller does not want to take on the responsibility of ensuring that the equipment performs or meets other suitability standards. Prior to the existence of Article 2A, there was a risk under certain circumstances that, say, a pure finance lessor (a lessor that merely provides equipment funding and is not also an equipment vendor) could be subject to certain implied equipment warranties existing under Article 2 (Sales) that an equipment seller would have under the law to an equipment purchaser. Making matter worse, the courts did not take a consistent approach in the implied warranty area.

Under Article 2A, however, there is now consistency. If a lease qualifies as an Article 2A finance lease, implied warranties of fitness for a particular purpose and merchantability are (automatically) excluded by law. All other equipment seller product warranties, however, are extended to the seller to the extent of the lessee's leasehold interest, unless the lease contract arrangement states that these warranties are excluded. Typically, as you can see from the form leases included with this book, financial lessors write leases with warranty disclaimers.

Lease Drafting Tip

The equipment warranty disclaimers must be conspicuous. You're referred to the form leases included with this book for the style of the disclaimers.

---

7. Lessor Lease Remedies under Article 2A

In a lessee lease default situation, the courts had been uniformly inconsistent, and at times incorrect, in determining what damages a lessor was entitled to receive. In keeping with its philosophy, Article 2A addressed this critical issue by allowing the lessors and lessees to generally contractually agree in the lease contract on what default and remedy standards would apply. Article 2A did, however, provide safe harbor provisions that would apply if the lease contract default or remedy provisions were either invalid or omitted. Under Article 2A, unless so stated in the lease contract, the lessor

- Does not have to give notice of default or enforcement action
- Can terminate the lease, repossess the equipment, sell or otherwise dispose of the equipment and recover damages for breach of the contract

Unless otherwise stated in the lease, Article 2A imposes two alternative statutory default damage computation formulas, in addition to allowing claims for past due rent, costs associated with any enforcement, and recovery action, such as court cost, storage changes, and remarketing fees and expenses. The safe harbor damage computations formulas are:

1. The lessor is entitled to claim the present value of any shortfall difference between the future remaining rents due under the original lease at the time of breach and the present value of the rents due under a new and "substantially similar" lease entered into by the lessor with another lessee.
2. If the equipment was not sold or re-leased under a "substantially similar" lease, the shortfall would be calculated using the future remaining rents due under the original lease at the time of breach and what would be considered as existing fair market rentals.

Article 2A further provides that the present value interest rate used to discount the applicable future rents can be the interest rate to which the parties agree in the lease contract, provided, however, that the interest rate stated is not "manifestly unreasonable."

The lease contract also can provide for default liquidated damages, even though the actual damages resulting from a lessee breach can be accurately determined. The liquidated damages may include the loss of such profit aspects as tax benefits or anticipated end-of-lease (residual) value, provided that the liquidated damage amount is reasonable considering the anticipated damages to be suffered by the lessor.

Awareness Tip

Article 2A has not provided any definitive guidance on what a substantially similar lease, a manifestly unreasonable present value discounting interest rate, or a reasonable liquidated damage amount might be, so as you might suspect, there is room for argument in the interpretation of these guidelines.

---

8. Lessee Lease Remedies under Article 2A

Article 2A provides for lessee remedies if the lessor is in default under a lease contract, which, unless otherwise "drafted out" of the lease contract, will apply. Depending on the type of breach, for example, the lessee may seek to cancel the lease contract, seek to recover rents or other payments made (such as a security deposit) or pursue other damages that would typically flow from a contract breach. If the lease, however, is an

Article 2A statutory finance lease, the lessee may not cancel the lease, or offset any amounts which may be due the lessee against the rents payable. Because of this, typically, lessors add a lease provision in which the lessee waives its Article 2A remedies.

9. A Consumer Lease under Article 2A

Although beyond the scope of this chapter, it is important to keep in mind that Article 2A makes a distinction between commercial lease transactions and consumer lease transactions, providing for added protections to a consumer lessee. Generally, a consumer lease is defined as "a lease that a lessor regularly engaged in the business of leasing or selling makes to a lessee who is an individual and who takes under the lease primarily for a personal, family, or household purpose." Under the various state Article 2A enactments, you will typically find that the total lease contract rent payments, excluding equipment purchase or lease renewal option payments, may not exceed a certain legislature-specified amount.

E. Summary

As discussed, over the years the courts have often struggled with whether an equipment financing transaction should be characterized as a lease or as a conditional, or installment, sale for state law purposes. Article 2A of the Uniform Commercial Code was drafted by the National Conference of Commissioners on Uniform State Laws, to resolve the many issues and inconsistencies when it was determined that uniformity in leasing rules would clearly benefit all parties to a lease transaction. The Article 2A "model" law was sent to the various states (including the District of Columbia) for consideration and enactment into state law. In most cases, the model law was adopted with few changes. There are no federal leasing law statues. The overall intent of the various UCC laws is, in effect, to compile, evolve, and in certain cases clarify the various U.S. laws (such as contract law, as interpreted by the U.S. courts) into one cohesive set of rules to eliminate, for example, arbitrary, commercially inequitable, and inconsistent court approaches and decisions. In addition to Article 2A, there are two additional and important UCC Articles that can impact an equipment financing, Article 2 (Sales), and Article 9 (Secured Transactions; Sales of Accounts and Chattel Paper).

Chapter 14

The Bankruptcy Rules for Leasing

A. Introduction

Inevitably, if you're involved in an equipment financing transaction, you will, at some time, be involved in a bankruptcy proceeding with one of the parties of the lease. Highly likely, if you're a lessor. Less likely, but certainly possible, if you're a lessee. And that is why an understanding of the bankruptcy rules is essential for all parties to an equipment lease transaction.

In this chapter we will be examining the basic provisions of the federal bankruptcy law (the law under which most bankruptcies are handled), known as the Bankruptcy Code, as they relate to equipment lease transactions. The Bankruptcy Code is embodied in Title 11 of the United States Code. An examination of similar state laws will not be addressed because they are rarely encountered in an equipment lease situation.

The impact on a lessor, and any equipment lender to the lessor—if the lessee files for protection under, or is involuntarily subjected to, the bankruptcy laws—can be significant. For the equipment lessor, having an understanding of the Bankruptcy Code rules is essential to properly assess whether to enter into an equipment lease, to properly draft the financing contract to facilitate a better potential recovery, and to know what it can and cannot do when a bankruptcy occurs. Mistakes can be costly. The lessor's equipment lender (say, in a leveraged lease transaction) must also understand these rules to properly assess whether to enter into an equipment lease loan, to properly draft the loan contract to facilitate the best possible collateral rights protections, and to know what it can and cannot do as a secured lender when a bankruptcy occurs. A lessee, on the other hand, must understand its rights in the event it, or its lessor, becomes subject to a bankruptcy proceeding. For a lessee, the effect of a lessor bankruptcy, although potentially a problem, is less of a concern, unless, of course, the lessor has ongoing responsibilities such as supplying maintenance or other services over and above simply not interfering with the continued use of the equipment. In the case of a leveraged lease transaction, the bankruptcy of the lessor's equipment lender is generally of little or no practical concern. Typically in all cases, a lessee can expect that its right to the continued use of the equipment will not be interfered with.

Basically, there are two types of proceedings in bankruptcy, reorganization proceedings and liquidation proceedings. A reorganization proceeding is one in which a company in financial difficulty, referred to now in bankruptcy as the debtor, has elected to avail itself of bankruptcy protection to get some breathing room from its creditors to see if it can restructure its business and get financially back on track. A liquidation proceeding is one in which it has been determined that the debtor can no longer continue in business. In a liquidation preceding, the debtor's assets are liquidated (generally sold off) for the benefit of the debtor's creditors. A bankruptcy liquidation or reorganization proceeding can be voluntary, one in which the debtor seeks bankruptcy law protection or assistance, or one in which the debtor is involuntarily forced into bankruptcy by its creditors.

There are, for a lessor, two key Bankruptcy Code provisional concepts that should be highlighted, because they govern two important yet practical aspects of a lessee-in-bankruptcy lease transaction. The first is the automatic stay provision found in Bankruptcy Code Section 362, which puts a hold on important lessor actions once the bankruptcy occurs. The second are the provisions, found in Bankruptcy Code Section 265, which permit the rejection or assumption of an unexpired lease by or on behalf of a lessee in bankruptcy. Also worthy of mention, for aircraft, railroad rolling stock and vessel lessors, there are two additional sections that can be important, Bankruptcy Code Section 1110 and Section 1168, which allow certain preference equipment repossession rights, discussed in greater detail below.

B.   Bankruptcy Liquidation and Reorganization

There are five bankruptcy chapter proceedings, Bankruptcy Code Chapters 7, 9, 11, 12 and 13, that cover the various types of liquidation or reorganization (sometimes referred to as restructuring) proceedings available. Bankruptcy Chapter 7 proceedings govern individual and entity liquidations. Bankruptcy Chapter 11 proceedings govern individual business entrepreneur (as well as certain other individuals) and entity reorganizations. Chapter 7 and Chapter 11 are the ones typically encountered or used when commercial lease transactions are involved. Bankruptcy Chapter 9 governs municipal bankruptcies; Bankruptcy Chapter 12 governs family farmer reorganization proceedings, and Bankruptcy Chapter 13 governs certain limited individual (typically non-business) reorganizations. The later three Chapter proceedings are not typically encounter in the day-to-day business of equipment leasing. They will be left to your reading if such a situation arises.

1.   Chapter 7—Liquidation: An Overview

A Bankruptcy Code Chapter 7 proceeding, in which the business assets are liquidated for the benefit of the business's creditors, is the most difficult to encounter for an equipment lessor for obvious reasons—more likely than not, the lessor will incur an significant economic loss. In a Chapter 7 proceeding, if granted, an individual debtor actually obtains a complete discharge from all debts. Although the substantive effect is the same for an entity liquidation proceeding, technically, when an entity is involved, such as a corporation, an actual formal discharge from all debts is not granted, but the business entity is expected to dissolve its existence under the applicable nonbankruptcy laws, after its assets are liquidated. In general, as mentioned, above, both business entities and individuals can request (a voluntary proceeding initiated by the debtor) or depending on the circumstances be forced into, a Chapter 7 liquidation (an involuntary proceeding initiated by one or more the debtor's creditors).

Once the debtor (such as an equipment lessee) files under Chapter 7, seeking the protection of the bankruptcy laws, an interim bankruptcy trustee is appointed through the bankruptcy court having jurisdiction over the proceeding. In some cases, the interim trustee may be replaced by a bankruptcy trustee that has been elected by the debtor's creditors. If the debtor's creditors do not elect their trustee, the interim trustee will in effect become the final bankruptcy trustee.

The job of the bankruptcy trustee is to determine the proper disposition (liquidation) of the debtor's assets. In some cases, the assets will be sold to third parties and the proceeds distributed to the debtor's creditors in accordance with certain priority rules mentioned below. If the creditor is a secured creditor, such as an equipment lessor or bank with a valid lien on certain assets of the debtor, typically its rights to the secured collateral are retained. Some assets considered inconsequential or burdensome may simply be abandoned by the trustee and returned to the debtor. Certain assets may be exempt, and will be out of the trustee's reach.

2. Chapter 11—Reorganization: An Overview

A Bankruptcy Code Chapter 11 proceeding can be commenced voluntarily by the debtor, or involuntarily against the debtor by certain creditors of the debtor. As suggested, the intent behind a Chapter 11 proceeding is to facilitate the reorganization of the debtor in an effort to put the debtor fully back on its financial feet, and, thus, prevent it from falling into a Chapter 7 liquidation. If a Chapter 11 reorganization is unsuccessful, a Chapter 7 proceeding is assuredly next.

In a Chapter 11 proceeding, it is not unusual for the debtor (such as an equipment lessee), as opposed to a trustee, to retain control over the business assets, in which case the debtor is referred to as the debtor-in-possession, or the DIP. A trustee, however, may be appointed through the bankruptcy court if there are grounds for doing so, typically referred to as "for cause."

The DIP, or trustee, if elected, is required to formulate a plan of reorganization, which must be approved by the governing bankruptcy court (subject to input from the creditors) in which the debtor is to pay its debts in accordance with the reorganization plan. The plan, if approved by the bankruptcy court, will typically, in effect, modify the payment responsibilities of the debtor, thus giving the debtor a new start going forward. As you may suspect, in a Chapter 11 proceeding, typically all the assets are not liquidated, but rather many are retained to facilitate the on-going business operation. Under a Chapter 11 proceeding, however, assets are permitted to be liquidated to the extent necessary to ensure that the business, for example, survives. Equipment leases, as you'll see below, among certain other asset transactions, receive special treatment.

C. Automatic Stay

An important concept within the Bankruptcy Code is something referred to as an automatic stay, provided for in Bankruptcy Code Section 362 (c). Very simply, once bankruptcy is instituted, all actions against the bankrupt (debtor) are prohibited. This, for example, means that once the automatic stay exists (at the time bankruptcy is instituted) the lessor cannot go in and get the leased equipment without the debtor's consent or court authority. The automatic stay also puts a stop to any potential legal proceedings that might be used to recover on any prebankruptcy petition claims against the debtor. The intent of the automatic stay is to protect the debtor and the bankruptcy estate's creditors from the item-by-item dismemberment of the estate's assets. Any knowing violation of the automatic stay rule will subject the lessor to actual and punitive damages.

D.   Equipment Lease Treatment in Bankruptcy

Equipment leases are treated under the bankruptcy rules in a special manner. Section 365 (a) of the Bankruptcy Code allows a bankruptcy trustee or a DIP to assume or reject all executory contracts, which include unexpired equipment lease contracts. Basically, an executory contract, under contract law, is a contract in which the obligations of all parties, in the case of a lease the debtor and the lessor, are so unperformed that it would be considered a material contract breach if any party failed to meets its obligations giving the other party or parties a legal excuse not to perform its obligations.

One additional important point. The general rule under the Bankruptcy Code is that the debtor must fully perform, in a timely manner, all of its equipment lease obligations that come into being starting 60 days following the institution of the bankruptcy proceeding. As you might suspect, the bankruptcy court can reduce these debtor performance obligations if it determines that it is in the best interest of the bankruptcy estate to do so. The lessor must be given notice of this possibility and an opportunity to argue against it before the bankruptcy court can make the change.

1.   *Assumption or Rejection*

If the equipment lease is assumed, the debtor's assets are deemed to available for (technically, the bankruptcy estate becomes bound by) serving the remaining lease obligations assumed. You might wonder whether, if the lessee is in bankruptcy, this is worth anything to a lessor. In fact, it is. To begin with, in order for the trustee or DIP to be able to assume the lease, the bankruptcy estate must do three things:

1. Cure any lease default or provide adequate assurance that the default will be promptly cured.
2. Pay the lessor for any default damages or provide adequate assurance that the default damages will be promptly paid.
3. Give adequate assurance that the future lease obligations will be met.

The real advantage to a lease assumption is that the lease payment obligations become a bankruptcy estate administration expense, giving the lessor a payment distribution priority over the claims of unsecured creditors for any damages arising for lease contract defaults following the assumption. To give you a priority preference perspective, in general, bankruptcy claims are treated in specified categories of priority. The secured claims are paid first, and the unsecured claims are paid next, with the equity owners taking the last recovery position. The assumption of a lease by the debtor requires the approval of the bankruptcy court, after notice, and an opportunity to be heard is given to the unsecured creditors who may be hurt by the payment priority.

Interestingly, as you might suspect, the typical event of default provision found in most lease contracts, such as lessee insolvency, a material adverse change in the lessee's financial condition, the commencement of a lessee bankruptcy proceedings or the appointment of a trustee in bankruptcy for a lessee, are not "defaults" which must be cured as part of the lease assumption.

As stated, the equipment lease can also be rejected, allowing the debtor to abandon any assets that the trustee of the DIP would in its reasonable business judgment consider burdensome to the bankruptcy estate. The decision, however, must be on an all-or-nothing basis (that is, if assumed, all the obligations must be assumed), unless the lease contract contains agreements that can be separated.

If the lease is rejected, however, the rejection is deemed to be a breach of the lease contract and the lessor cannot only reclaim its equipment, but it can also make a claim in bankruptcy for any damages that have been incurred under the lease contract before the filing of the bankruptcy petition. The claim for damages would be a general unsecured claim. Once rejected, the lease cannot be assumed, even if it would be beneficial to the bankruptcy estate to do so.

2. Assumption or Rejection Time Periods

In a bankruptcy liquidation proceeding (Bankruptcy Code Chapter 7), the debtor (through the trustee in bankruptcy, if one is appointed) must decide whether to make the lease assumption or rejection within 60 days following the institution of the bankruptcy proceeding. If the decision to assume or reject is not made within the 60-day period, then the lease contract is deemed to have been rejected. Note that the 60-day period may be subject to extension by the bankruptcy court if it determines there is a valid reason to do so, often referred to as "for cause."

In a bankruptcy reorganization (Bankruptcy Code Chapters 9, 11, 12, or 13), the rule is different. The debtor is allowed (through the trustee in bankruptcy if one is appointed) to determine if it wants to assume or reject an equipment lease at any time, so long as the decision is made before the bankruptcy court puts its stamp of approval (referred to as confirms) the plan of reorganization. This decision time period again is subject to shortening upon notice to, and a hearing by, the bankruptcy court. In certain cases, it is possible for the bankruptcy court to approve a reorganization plan that permits the debtor to assume or reject an equipment lease after the reorganization has been approved by the court and is effective.

One more point. If an equipment lease is assumed in the reorganization proceeding, the general feeling is that it can still be rejected in a subsequent liquidation preceding (if the reorganization is not successful), or possibly if a trustee was appointed if the debtor in possession was later thrown out by the bankruptcy court.

E. Special Treatment for Aircraft, Railroad Rolling Stock, and Vessels

As mentioned, the Bankruptcy Code provides certain additional protections, under Bankruptcy Code Section 1110 and Section 1168, for lessors of aircraft, railroad rolling stock, and vessels. Very simply, if the lessee/debtor wants to continue to use such equipment, it must cure all lease defaults that exist at the time of the filing of the bankruptcy proceeding, within 60 days following its filing; must timely perform all future obligations under the lease contract during the period of continued use; and, if a lease default occurs, must cure the default within 30 days following its occurrence. If these conditions are not met, the lessor can immediately repossess the equipment without regard to the Bankruptcy Code automatic stay provisions, and without regard to any right the lessee would otherwise have under the Bankruptcy Code to use the equipment in the ordinary course of business (say, to assist in its ability to successfully come through a bankruptcy reorganization) or the powers of the bankruptcy court to stop (enjoin) any such repossession. The commitment by the lessee/debtor, if it wants to continue to hold this equipment, to cure past defaults and meet all on-going obligations, however, is nothing more that an exception to the automatic stay, use of equipment, and injunctive rules which would otherwise come into play in a bankruptcy proceeding. It is not deemed to be an assumption of the entire lease contract, with the lessee debtor still able to terminate the lease arrangement when the equipment is no longer required. Whether in fact this right to repossess is worth anything to a lessor, of course, depends on the value of the equipment at the time of repossession. If the value is not there, having the lessee/debtor continue to use the equipment may be the best alternative.

F.   What Happens If the Lease Is Not a True Lease?

If an equipment lease turns out to be a secured equipment financing, for example, a security agreement or an installment (conditional) sale agreement, as discussed in Chapter 13, then the lessor can lose some benefits under bankruptcy. First, the "lease" does not have to be assumed or rejected by the debtor; second, and often of most concern, the debtor may be able to completely ignore the purported security interest in the equipment if the proper Uniform Commercial Code financing statement (a UCC-1) was not filed, was improperly filed, or certain other statutory requirements for "perfecting" the security interest in the equipment were not taken. In a pure bankruptcy liquidation proceeding, this reduces the lessor to an unsecured creditor.

In a bankruptcy reorganization proceeding, there are also adverse consequences. Even if the proper Uniform Commercial Code filings were made, meaning that the equipment at hand was in fact successfully encumbered by the lessor's security interest, there is no requirement under the Bankruptcy Code that any past defaults be cured by the debtor, nor does the debtor have to provide any comfort to the lessor that it can adequately meet its payment or other obligations under the "lease", in order for it to continue to use the equipment. The debtor merely has to give the lessor comfort, called "adequate protection," that the lessor's security interest in the equipment will be secure. Worse yet, for the lessor, is that if the debtor wants to retain the equipment for use in a bankruptcy reorganization, the actual plan of reorganization may reduce the interest rate or payment terms in the original agreement to under the purported lease contract, leaving the lessor with an unrecoverable deficiency. As you can imagine, the "adequate protection" requirement is open for discussion in the bankruptcy court. It may, for example, take of the form a security deposit, the granting of a lien on additional assets the debtor has, or some form of payment preference over other bankruptcy creditors.

For those lessors that package maintenance or other equipment related services with an equipment lease, if the lease is deemed to be, say, a conditional sale agreement, it is possible for the bankruptcy court to separate the two agreement arrangements, determining that the lessor no longer is the equipment owner, but treating the maintenance portion as an executory contract, thus allowing the debtor to assume or reject the equipment services. If the debtor decides to assume the service aspect, and the services were offered below the lessor's cost as part of the lease marketing inducement, the lessor may end up with an ongoing below-cost service responsibility.

G.   Summary

The classification of an equipment lease as a true equipment lease for bankruptcy purposes has benefits. The debtor must decide whether to assume or reject a lease contract within a prescribed period of time, giving the lessor some benefits over those of a typical secured or unsecured creditor in bankruptcy. If rejected, the lessor gets its equipment back, and can file a bankruptcy claim as an unsecured creditor for the damages resulting from the lease rejection, deemed to be a contract breach. If the lease is assumed, the lessor has some assurance that it will be paid what it is owed under the lease contract, subject to adjustment by the bankruptcy court. If a lease contract is not deemed to represent a true lease for bankruptcy purposes, and instead is determined to be, say, a security agreement or a conditional or installment sale arrangement, then, unless the lessor has taken the proper precaution under the Uniform Commercial Code to secure its interest in the equipment, it may lose the equipment collateral to the debtor and become an unsecured creditor.

Chapter 15

Equipment Lease Terminology

When entering into a leasing transaction, you may encounter unfamiliar terms that have developed along with the leasing industry. This chapter defines terms according to their industry usage.

Accelerated cost recovery system (ACRS)   The method prescribed by the Internal Revenue Code that an equipment owner must use in computing depreciation deductions on most equipment placed in service after 1980 and before 1987. Under ACRS, the owner writes off the equipment's cost over a 3-year, 5-year, 10-year, or 15-year period, depending on the recovery period designated for the equipment type.

Acceptance certificate   A document in which a lessee acknowledges that certain specified equipment is acceptable for lease. Generally used in transactions where the parties enter into the lease document well in advance of the equipment's delivery date; it serves to notify the lessor that the equipment has been delivered, inspected, and accepted for lease as of a specified date. The typical form requires the lessee to list certain pertinent information, including the equipment manufacturer, purchase price, serial number, and location.

Acceptance supplement   The same as an acceptance certificate.

Advance rental   Any payment in the form of rent made before the start of the lease term. The term is also sometimes used to describe a rental payment arrangement in which the lessee pays all rentals, on a per period basis, at the start of each rental payment period. For example, a quarterly, in advance, rental program requires the lessee to pay one-fourth of the annual rent at the start of each consecutive three-month period during the lease term.

Alternative minimum tax (AMT)   A system for taxing individuals and corporations that, in effect, prevents taxpayers from otherwise reducing their tax below a formulated level. If the tax liability calculated under the AMT rules is greater than the taxpayer's regular tax, the excess amount has to be paid along with the regular tax. The AMT is basically an attempt to dampen taxpayers' typical motivation to reduce excessively their tax liabilities.

Anti-churning   A concept under the federal tax laws that prevents a taxpayer from taking advantage of more favorable equipment depreciation tax benefits through equipment transaction manipulations that violate the spirit of the tax laws.

Asset depreciation range (ADR) indemnity   A type of tax indemnification given by the lessee to the lessor relating to leased equipment depreciated under the asset depreciation range system method. The lessee, in effect, guarantees the lessor against loss of, or inability to claim, anticipated ADR tax benefits under certain conditions.

Asset depreciation range system (ADR)   A method prescribed by the Internal Revenue Code that could be used in computing depreciation deductions for certain assets placed in service after 1970 and before 1981. ADR provides a range of useful lives for specified assets that serve as the period over which the asset is depreciated. The lives listed are generally shorter than the period over which an asset may be depreciated under the "facts and circumstances" method of depreciation.

Balloon payment   Commonly found in mortgage financings, a balloon payment is a final payment that is larger than the periodic term payments. Usually it results because the debt has not been fully amortized during the repayment period. For example, a one-year financing arrangement providing for interest-only monthly payments during the year, with the principal plus the last interest payment due on the final payment date, is said to have a "balloon payment" or simply a "balloon" due at the end of the term.

Bareboat charter party   A net financial lease relating to vessels. Also sometimes referred to simply as a "bareboat charter." See Net lease.

Base lease term   The primary period of time during which the lessee is entitled to use the leased equipment, without regard to any interim or renewal lease terms. For example the base lease term of a five-year lease is five years.

Base rental   The rental that the lessee must pay during the base, sometimes called primary, lease term.

Beneficial interest holder   A beneficial, as opposed to legal (title), owner. For example, when a trust has been created by the equity participants to act as the lessor, the equity participants are deemed the beneficial interest holders. They hold interests in the trust that has title to the equipment.

Bond   An instrument that represents a long-term debt obligation. The debt instruments, sometimes referred to as loan certificates, issued in a leveraged lease transaction, are referred to as bonds or notes.

Book reporting   The reporting of income or loss for financial as opposed to tax purposes on the financial records of a corporation or other reporting entity.

Book residual value   An estimate of the equipment's residual value that a lessor uses, or "books," to calculate economic return on a lease transaction.

Broker   A person or entity who, for compensation, arranges lease transactions for another's account. A broker is also referred to as a syndicator or underwriter.

Call   The right a lessee may have to buy specified leased equipment for a predetermined fixed price, usually expressed as a percentage of original cost. If provided, such an option commonly does not become exercisable until the end of the lease term; and it lapses if the lessee fails to give the lessor timely notice of its intention to exercise it. For example, a lessee may have a right to buy equipment at the end of the lease term for 30% of original cost, notice of intention to exercise the option to be given not less than 90 days before the lease term's end.

Capital lease   Under the guidelines set out in FAS No. 13 by the Financial Accounting Standards Board, a lessee must classify certain long-term leases as capital leases for accounting and reporting purposes. Capital leases are accounted for in a manner that reflects the long-term repayment obligation of such leases.

Cash flow   In a lease transaction, the amount of cash a lease generates for a lessor.

Casualty value   A predetermined amount of money that a lessee guarantees the lessor will receive in the event of an equipment casualty loss during the lease term. Generally expressed as a percentage of original cost, the value varies according to the point in time during the lease term that the loss occurs. It is also referred to as a "stipulated loss value."

Certificate of delivery and acceptance   The same as acceptance certificate.

Charterer   The lessee of a vessel.

Charter party   A document that provides for the lease (charter) of a vessel or vessels. While the format is basically the same as any other lease, there are certain additions and modifications reflecting the requirements dictated by a vessel transaction.

Chattel mortgage   A mortgage relating to personal property. Thus, a mortgage on equipment is a chattel mortgage.

Collateral   Assets used as security for the repayment of a debt obligation. In a typical leveraged lease, the collateral is the leased equipment.

Commencement date   The date the base, or primary, lease term begins.

Commission agreement   An agreement between a lease broker and a prospective equity participant providing for the payment of a fee to the broker for services in arranging a lease transaction.

Commitment fee   Compensation paid to a lender in return for an agreement to make a future loan or to a lessor for its commitment to lease equipment to a lessee in the future.

Conditional sales agreement   A contract, also referred to as CSA, that provides for the time financing of asset purchases. The seller retains title to the asset until the buyer fulfills all specified conditions, such as installment payments. At that time, title automatically vests in the buyer.

Cost of money   Commonly, the cost that a lessor incurs to borrow money. This includes the interest rate and any additional costs related to such borrowing, such as fees or compensating balances. In pricing a lease transaction, a lessor factors this cost into the computation.

Cost-to-customer   The simple interest rate on a lease transaction.

DDB/SYD/TAN   A technique of switching methods of depreciation to maximize early depreciation write-offs used on property not covered by ACRS or MACRS. Depreciation deductions are initially computed using the double-declining balance (DDB) method with an appropriately timed change to the sum-of-the-years-digits (SYD) method followed by another appropriately timed change to the straight-line method.

Debt participant   A long-term lender in a leveraged lease transaction. Frequently, those transactions have more than one debt participant.

Debt service   The aggregate periodic repayment amount, including principal and interest, due on a loan.

Default   In a lease transaction, when a party breaches certain material lease obligations.

Deficiency guarantee   A guarantee given to a lessor by a third party, such as an equipment vendor or manufacturer, to induce a lessor to enter into a lease that it would not otherwise enter into usually because the prospective lessee may be a poor credit risk, or the future value of equipment may be highly speculative. For example, a deficiency guarantor may agree to pay the lessor for any shortfall below a designated amount, say 20% of original cost, incurred when the equipment is sold at the end of the lease.

Deficit Reduction Act (DRA)   The 1984 Deficit Reduction Act, a federal income tax act.

Delivery and acceptance certificate   The same as an acceptance certificate.

Depreciation indemnity   A tax indemnification given by a lessee against the lessor's loss of anticipated depreciation tax benefits on leased equipment.

Direct financing lease   A classification for a particular type of lease prescribed under the lease accounting guidelines set out by the FASB in FAS No. 13, applicable to lessors. Those guidelines tell lessors how to report direct financing leases for accounting purposes.

Discounted cash flow analysis   The process of determining the present value of future cash flows.

Economic Recovery Tax Act (ERTA)   The 1981 Economic Recovery Tax Act, a federal income tax act.

Equipment certificate of acceptance   The same as an acceptance certificate.

Equity participant   The equity investor in a leveraged lease. Frequently, a leveraged lease transaction has more than one equity participant, who jointly own and lease the equipment. An equity participant is also sometimes referred to as an "owner participant."

Event of default   An event that provides the basis for the declaration of a default. For example, the nonpayment of rent under a lease agreement is typically prescribed as an event of default that gives the lessor the right to declare the lease in default and to pursue permitted remedies, such as terminating the lease and reclaiming the equipment.

Facts and circumstances depreciation   A method of determining the depreciable life of an asset generally usable on assets placed in service before 1981. Under the facts and circumstances method, the useful life determination is based on the owner's experience with similar property, giving due consideration to current and anticipated future conditions, such as wear and tear; normal progress of the art; economic changes, inventions, and current developments within the industry and the taxpayer's trade or business; and climatic and other relevant local conditions that can affect the taxpayer's repair, renewal, and replacement program.

Fair market purchase value   An asset's value as determined in the open market in an arm's length transaction (one in which there is a willing buyer and a willing seller, under no compulsion to act) under normal selling conditions. It is also referred to simply as the "fair market value."

Fair market rental value   The rental rate that an asset would command in the open market in an arm's length transaction (one in which there is a willing lessee and a willing lessor, under no compulsion to act) under normal renting conditions. It is also referred to simply as the "fair rental value."

FASB   Financial Accounting Standards Board, the accounting profession's guideline-setting authority.

FAS Statement No. 13, Accounting for Leases FAS No. 13 sets out the standards for financial lease accounting for lessors and lessees. FAS No. 13 was initially issued by the FASB, in Stamford, Connecticut, in November 1976.

Finance lease (1) The same as a full payout lease. (2) A statutory lease category that would have permitted leases that otherwise would not have qualified as true leases for tax purposes to be so treated. Although enacted by TEFRA in 1982, the finance lease's effective date was postponed, and it was repealed by the 1986 TRA before ever having gone into effect, with limited exceptions.

Financing agreement An agreement commonly entered into by the principal parties to a leveraged lease before equipment delivery. The agreement identifies each party's obligation to the transaction and any conditions that must be satisfied before the obligations are fixed. Typically, it will involve the debt and equity participants, their representatives, and the lessee. It is also referred to as a "participation agreement."

Floating rental rate A form of periodic rental payments that change or "float" upward and downward over a lease's term with changes in a specified interest rate. Frequently, a designated bank's prime rate is the measuring interest rate.

Full payout lease A form of lease that will provide the lessor with a cash flow generally sufficient assure return on equipment investment; pay the principal, interest, and other financing costs on related debt; cover related sales and administration expenses; and generate a profit. The cash flow is determined from the rental payments, the ownership tax benefits, and the equipment residual value. The lessee typically has the right to use the leased equipment for most of its actual useful life.

Gross income tax A tax imposed by a state or local taxing authority on gross income generated from sources within its jurisdiction. The tax is deductible by the taxpayer for federal income tax purposes.

Grossing up A concept that reimbursement for a monetary loss will include sufficient additional monies so that the after-tax amount will equal the loss. The recipient is said to be made whole for his loss because the amount paid must take into account any taxes he will have to pay as a result of the receipt of the payments from the payor.

Guaranteed residual value An arrangement in which, for example, a broker or equipment manufacturer guarantees that a lessor will receive not less than a certain amount for specified equipment when it is disposed of at the end of the lease term. It is also sometimes referred to simply as a "guaranteed residual."

Guidelines **lease** A leveraged lease that meets with the IRS's lease guidelines as set out in Revenue Procedures 75-21, 75-28, 76-30, and 79-48. Although guidelines specifically address only private letter ruling requests, generally a *Guidelines* lease should qualify as a true lease for federal income tax purposes.

Half-year convention A concept under the income tax rules for depreciating equipment under which all equipment placed in service during a tax year is treated as having been placed in service at the midpoint of that year, regardless of when during the year it was in fact placed in service.

Hell or high-water clause A lease provision that commits a lessee to pay the rent unconditionally. The lessee waives any right that exists or may arise to withhold any rent from the lessor or any assignee of the lessor for any reason whatsoever, including any setoff, counterclaim, recoupment, or defense.

High–low rental   A rental structure in which the rent payments are reduced from a higher to a lower rate at a prescribed point in the lease term.

Implicit lease rate   The annual interest rate that, when applied to the lease rental payments, will discount those payments to an amount equal to the cost of the equipment leased.

Indemnity agreement   A contract in which one party commits to insure another party against anticipated and specified losses.

Indenture   In a leveraged lease transaction, an agreement entered into by an owner trustee (the lessor's representative) and an indenture trustee (the lender's representative) in which the owner trustee grants a lien on the leased equipment, the lease rents, and other lessor contract rights as security for repayment of the outstanding equipment loan. It is also referred to as an indenture trust.

Indenture trustee   The representative of the lenders where, in a leveraged lease transaction, the debt is provided through a trust arrangement. As the lender's representative, the indenture trustee may, for example, have to file and maintain a security interest in the leased equipment, receive rentals from the lessee, pay out the proper amounts to the lenders and the lessor, and take certain action to protect the outstanding loan in the event of a loan default.

Installment sale   A sale in which the purchase price is paid in an agree-on number of installment payments over an agreed-on period of time. Typically, title to what is sold does not transfer to the purchaser until, and only when, the last installment has been paid.

Institutional investors   Institutions that invest in lease transactions. They include, insurance companies, pension funds, banks, and trusts.

Insured value   The same as casualty value.

Interim lease rental   The equipment rental due for the interim lease term. Typically, for each day during the interim lease term, a lessee must pay as interim lease rent an amount equal to the daily equivalent of the primary lease term rent. In a leveraged lease transaction, the lease sometimes instead permits the lessee to pay an amount equal to the daily equivalent of the long-term debt interest.

Interim lease term   The lease term period between the lessee's acceptance of the equipment for lease and the beginning of the primary, or base, lease term.

Investment tax credit (ITC)   A credit allowed against federal income tax liability that can be claimed by a taxpayer for certain "Section 38 property" acquired and placed in service by a taxpayer during a tax year. ITC may also be available for certain property under applicable state income tax laws. Under the federal tax laws, ITC is generally not available for property placed in service after 1985.

ITC indemnity   A type of indemnification in which the lessee commits to reimburse the lessor for any financial loss incurred through the loss of, or inability to claim, any or all of the anticipated ITC. If the lessor has "passed through" the ITC to the lessee, the lessor may have to give the indemnity.

ITC "pass-through"   An election made by the lessor to treat, for ITC purposes, the lessee as the owner of the leased equipment. After the election, a lessee can claim the ITC on the equipment covered by the election.

Layoff   The sale by a lessor of its interest in the lease agreement, including the ownership of the leased equipment and the right to receive the rent payments.

Lease agreement   A contract in which an equipment owner, the lessor, transfers the equipment's use, subject to the specified terms and conditions, to another, the lessee, for a prescribed period of time and rental rate.

Lease line   A present commitment by a lessor to lease specified equipment to be delivered in the future. A lease line can cover a variety of types of equipment, at varying rental rates and lease terms. It is also referred to as a lease line of credit.

Lease underwriting   The process in which a lease broker arranges a lease transaction for the account of third parties, a prospective lessor and a prospective lessee. This can be on a best efforts basis or on a firm commitment basis. In a best efforts underwriting, the broker only offers to attempt diligently to arrange the financing on certain proposed terms. In a firm commitment underwriting the broker in effect guarantees to arrange the financing as proposed.

Lessee   The user of equipment that is the subject of a lease agreement.

Lessor   The owner of equipment that is the subject of a lease agreement.

Level payments   Payments that are the same for each payment period during the payment term. Frequently, rent and debt service payments are paid in level payments over the payment period.

Leveraged lease   A lease in which a portion, generally 60% to 80%, of the equipment acquisition cost is borrowed from a bank or other lending institution, with the lessor paying the balance. The debt is commonly on a nonrecourse basis, and the rental payments are usually sufficient to cover the loan debt service.

Limited use property   Leased property that will be economically usable only by the lessee, or a member of the lessee group, at the lease term's end because, for example, of its immobility or unique aspects. The IRS will not rule that a lease is a true lease when the leased equipment is limited use property.

Loan certificate   A certificate that evidences a debt obligation.

Loan participant   A debt participant.

Low–high rental   A rental structure in which the rent payments are increased from a lower to a higher rate at a prescribed point in the lease term.

Management agreement   A contract in which one party agrees to manage a lease transaction during its term, including rental payment processing and equipment disposal.

Management fee   A fee that a lease transaction manager receives for services performed under a management agreement.

Master lease agreement   A lease agreement designed to permit future equipment not contemplated when the lease is executed to be added to the lease later. The document is set up in two parts. The main body contains the general, or boiler plate provisions, such as the maintenance and indemnification provisions. An annex, or schedule, contains the type of items that usually vary with a transaction, such as rental rates and options.

Mid-quarter convention   A concept under the income tax rules for depreciating equipment in which all equipment placed in service during a quarter of a tax year is treated as placed in service at the mid-point of such quarter, regardless of when it was in fact placed in service during the quarter.

Modified Accelerated Cost Recovery System (MACRS)   A method prescribed for depreciating assets that was introduced by the 1986 TRA. It applies to most equipment placed in service after 1986.

Mortgage   An arrangement whereby a lender (mortgagee) acquires a lien on property owned by a taxpayer (mortgagor) as security for the loan repayment. Once the debt obligation has been fully satisfied, the mortgage lien is terminated.

Negative spread   The amount by which a value is below a certain prescribed amount. Generally, in a leveraged lease, a negative spread is the amount by which the transaction's simple interest rate is below the leveraged debt interest rate.

Net lease   A lease arrangement in which the lessee is responsible for paying all costs, such as maintenance, certain taxes, and insurance, related to using the leased equipment, in addition to the rental payments. Typically, finance leases are net leases.

Non-payout lease   A lease arrangement that does not, over the primary term of the lease, generate enough cash flow to return substantially all the lessor's investment, debt financing costs, and sales and administration expenses.

Nonrecourse debt financing   A loan to which the lender agrees to look solely to the lessee, the lease rents, and the leased equipment for the loan's repayment. As security for the loan repayment, the lender receives an assignment of the lessor's rights under the lease agreement and a grant of a first lien on the equipment. Although the lessor has no obligation to repay the debt in the event of a lessee default, its equity investment in the equipment is usually subordinated to the lender's rights.

Nonutilization fee   A fee that a lessor may impose in return for its present commitment to buy and lease specified equipment in the future. The fee is generally expressed as a percentage of the aggregate unused portion of the initial dollar commitment, for example, 1% of the unused balance of a $1 million lease line of credit. Thus, if all the commitment is used, no fee is payable.

Operating lease   A form of lease arrangement in which the lessor generally commits to provide certain additional equipment-related services other than the straight financing, such as maintenance, repairs, or technical advice. Generally, operating leases are non-payout in nature. The term also refers to a lease classification under FAS No. 13.

Option   A contractual right that can be exercised under the granting terms. For example, a fair market value purchase option in a lease is the right to buy the equipment covered by it for its fair market value.

Packager   A person or entity who arranges a lease transaction for third parties. Also referred to as an underwriter, syndicator, or broker.

Participation agreement   The same as a financing agreement.

Payout lease   The same as a full payout lease.

Personal property   The same as Section 38 property. Equipment is considered personal property, but real estate is not so considered.

Portfolio lease   The term commonly refers to a lease that is entered into by a "professional" lessor for its own account and investment.

Present value   The term refers to the present worth of a future stream of payments calculated by discounting the future payments at a desired interest rate.

Primary lease term   The same as base lease term.

Private letter ruling   A written opinion that the IRS issues in response to a taxpayer's request. The letter sets out the IRS's position on the tax treatment of a proposed transaction. In leveraged lease transactions, for the IRS to issue a favorable private letter ruling, the request must comply with the IRS *Guidelines.*

Progress payments   Payments that may be required by an equipment manufacturer or builder during the construction period toward the purchase price. Frequently required for costly equipment with a long construction period, the payments are designed to lessen the manufacturer's or builder's need to tie up their own funds during construction.

Purchase option   The right to buy agreed-on equipment at the times and the amounts specified in the option. Frequently, these options are only exercisable at the end of the primary lease term, although they sometimes can be exercised during the primary lease term or at the end of any renewal term.

Put   A right that a lessor may have to sell specified leased equipment to the lessee at a fixed price at the end of the initial lease term. It is usually imposed to protect the lessor's residual value assumption.

Recourse debt financing   A loan under which the lender may look to the general credit of the lessor, in addition to the lessee and the equipment, for repayment of any outstanding loan obligation. The lender is said to have a "recourse" against the lessor.

Recovery property   Property that can be depreciated under ACRS.

Renewal option   An option frequently given to a lessee to renew the lease term for a specified rental and time period.

Residual sharing   A compensation technique sometimes used by syndicators for arranging a lease transaction. Under this, the equity participants must pay a predetermined percentage of what the equipment is sold for at the end of the lease. For example, a syndicator may get 50% of any amount realized exceeding 20% of the equipment's original cost on sale.

Residual value   The value of leased equipment at the end of the lease term.

Right of first refusal   The right of the lessee to buy the leased equipment, or renew the lease, at the end of the lease term, for any amount equal to that offered by an unaffiliated third party.

Safe harbor lease   A statutory lease category enacted as part of ERTA that permitted a lease to qualify as a true lease for federal income tax purposes, although it would not otherwise ordinarily qualify. It was repealed by the 1984 DRA, with limited exceptions. Under a safe harbor lease, an equipment owner could essentially sell the ownership tax benefits without giving up other ownership rights.

Sale-leaseback   An arrangement in which an equipment buyer buys equipment for the purpose of leasing it back to the seller.

Sales tax   A tax imposed on selling equipment, similar to any other sales tax on property sold.

Sales-type lease   A classification for a particular type of lease prescribed under the lease accounting guidelines that the FASB set out in FAS No. 13, applicable to lessors.

Salvage value   The amount, estimated for federal income tax purposes, that an asset is expected to be worth at the end of its useful life.

Section 38 property   Tangible personal property and certain other tangible property, as defined by Internal Revenue Code Section 38.

Security agreement   An agreement that evidences an assignment by the lessor to the lender, as security for the equipment loan, of the lessor's rights under the lease agreement and a granting of a security interest in the leased equipment.

Sinking fund   A fund frequently established in leveraged lease transactions by the lessor to accumulate funds to pay for future taxes.

Sinking fund rate   The interest rate that a sinking fund is deemed to earn on accumulated funds.

Special-purpose equipment   The same as limited use property.

Spread   The difference between two values. In lease transactions, the term is generally used to describe the difference between the lease interest rate and the interest rate on the debt.

Stipulated loss value   The same as casualty value.

Sublease   The re-lease by a lessee of equipment that is on lease to the lessee.

Take or pay contract   An agreement in which one party commits to buy an agreed-on quantity of goods or material from another at a predetermined price. If the goods or material are not bought, the party making the purchase commitment must pay the party an amount of money equal to the cost of goods or materials it had committed to buy. For example, a public utility can agree to buy 100 tons of coal annually from a mining company, and if it does not buy this amount in any year it will pay an amount of money equal to its sale price.

Tax benefit transfer lease (TBT)   The same as a safe harbor lease.

Tax Equity and Fiscal Responsibility Act (TEFRA)   The 1982 Tax Equity and Fiscal Responsibility Act, a Federal income tax act.

Tax lease   The same as a true lease.

Tax Reform Act (TRA)   The 1986 Tax Reform Act, a Federal income tax act.

Termination option   An option entitling a lessee to terminate the lease during the lease term for a predetermined value, termination value, if the equipment becomes obsolete or surplus to the lessee's needs. The lessor usually requires the lessee to sell the equipment to an unaffiliated third party, and the lessee must pay the lessor any amount by which the sale proceeds are less than the termination value. Typically, any excess sale proceeds go to the lessor.

Termination value   The amount that the lessee must pay the lessor if it exercises a termination option. Typically, the termination value is set as of each rental payment period and is generally expressed as a percentage of equipment cost. For example, the lessee may be permitted to terminate the lease at the end of the third year of a seven-year lease for an amount equal to 60% of cost.

Time sale   An installment sale.

Total earnings   The amount by which the aggregate rentals due the lessor over the entire lease term exceed the total equipment costs, including equity investment and debt financing costs. This concept does not consider the time value of money.

TRAC lease   A lease of motor vehicles or trailers that contains what is referred to as a terminal rental adjustment clause (TRAC). The clause permits or requires the rent amount to be adjusted based on the proceeds the lessor receives from the sale of the leased equipment. TRAC leases qualify as true leases.

Transition rules   Statutory rules enacted when there is a change in the tax laws. The transition rules allow certain transactions to be exempted from the law change. For example, transition rules permitted ITC to be claimed on certain equipment placed in service after 1985.

True lease   An arrangement that qualifies for lease treatment for federal income tax purposes. Under a true lease, the lessee may deduct rental payments and the lessor may claim the tax benefits accruing to an equipment owner.

Trust   An arrangement in which property is held by one party for the benefit of another. It is frequently used in leveraged lease transactions.

Trust certificate   A trust document issued on behalf of a trust to evidence the beneficial ownership in the trust estate.

Trustee   The person or entity appointed, or designated, to carry out a trust's terms. In leveraged lease transactions, the trustee is generally a bank or trust company.

Trustee fees   Fees payable to a trustee as compensation for services performed.

Trustor   An individual or entity who causes the creation of a trust and for whose benefit it is established.

Unleveraged lease   A lease in which the lessor puts up 100% of the equipment's acquisition cost from its own funds.

Useful life   Commonly, the economic usable life of an asset.

Use tax   A tax imposed on the use, storage, or consumption of tangible personal property within a taxing jurisdiction. For example, in most states a lessor purchasing equipment has the option of paying an upfront sales tax equal to a specified percentage of the equipment's purchase price or a use tax equal to a specified percentage of lease rents under the equipment's lease.

Vendor   A seller of property. Commonly, the manufacturer or distributor of equipment.

Vendor program   A program in which an equipment lessor provides a lease financing service to customers of an equipment manufacturer.

Forms

Form: a-01
Disk File Name: a-01.rtf

ACKNOWLEDGMENT OF RECEIPT OF CERTIFICATE OF DEPOSIT

Form Purpose

Acknowledgment for use by an equipment leasing company or equipment lender of the receipt and acceptance of a certificate of deposit as collateral security for equipment lease or loan obligations.

Executing Parties
The equipment leasing company or lender, as applicable.

See:
Assignment of Certificate of Deposit, Form a-02

Acknowledgment of Receipt of Certificate of Deposit

Lessee (or Borrower, as applicable) Name:

Lessee (or Borrower, as applicable) Address:

Lease (or Loan, as applicable) Number:

Certificate of Deposit Identification Number:

To Whom It May Concern:

I hereby certify that I am a duly elected officer of (insert name of leasing company or lender) (the "Company"), and as said officer, I am duly authorized to acknowledge and accept receipt of original Certificates of Deposit on behalf of the Company.

The Certificate of Deposit referenced above has been tendered by the above-referenced lessee (or borrower, as applicable) in accordance with the terms and conditions of the above-referenced lease (or loan, as applicable), and in accordance with the Assignment of Certificate of Deposit, a copy of which is attached hereto as Exhibit A.

This letter is to acknowledge the receipt and acceptance of one original Certificate of Deposit, identified above, issued by (insert name of issuing institution) in the amount of $.

(Insert name of leasing company or lender)

By:

Title:

Date:

Exhibit A

[Copy of Assignment of Certificate of Deposit.]

Form: a-02
Disk File Name: a-02.rtf

ASSIGNMENT OF CERTIFICATE OF DEPOSIT

Form Purpose

Assignment to an equipment leasing company or lender of one or more certificates of deposit as collateral security for equipment lease or loan obligations.

Executing Parties
The equipment lessee or borrower, as applicable (assignor).
The equipment lessor or lender, as applicable (assignee).

See:
Acknowledgment of Receipt of Certificate of Deposit, Form a-01

Assignment of Certificate of Deposit

This Assignment of Certificate of Deposit (the "Agreement"), dated   ,
is entered into by and between   (the "Assignor"),
having its principal place of business at   ,
and   (the "Assignee"), having
its principal place of business at   .

    1. Collateral. As collateral security for the payment of any and all indebtedness and liabilities of Assignor to Assignee, however evidenced or acquired, whether now existing or hereafter arising, whether direct or indirect, absolute or contingent, or joint and several, Assignor hereby assigns, pledges, and transfers to Assignee all of Assignor's right, title, and interest in and to the certificate(s) of deposit (collectively, the "Certificate") described as follows:

Certificate No.	*Institution Name/Address*	*Amount*
		$
		$

    2. Assignor Representations and Warranties. With respect to the Certificate, Assignor represents and warrants that:

    a. Assignor is the lawful owner of the Certificate, free and clear of all loans, liens, encumbrances, and claims, except as disclosed in writing to Assignee on Annex A hereto;

    b. Assignor has full right, power, and authority to enter into this Agreement and to assign the Certificate to Assignee;

    c. The Certificate is genuine and the amount(s) of the Certificate stated above is the true amount(s) of the Certificate as of the date of this Agreement; and

    d. Assignor will not sell, assign, encumber, or otherwise dispose of any of Assignee's rights to the Certificate, except as provided for in this Agreement.

    3. Assignee Rights and Obligations. Assignor hereby appoints Assignee as its true and lawful attorney-in-fact, with full power of substitution, and agrees that Assignee shall have full and irrevocable right, power, and authority, in the name of Assignor or in Assignee's own name, to demand, collect, withdraw, receipt for, or sue for all amounts due or to become due and payable upon the Certificate, including any interest accrued or payable thereon and any renewals, extensions, or reinvestments thereof. Assignee may execute withdrawal receipts respecting the Certificate and endorse the name of Assignor on any or all commercial paper given in payment thereof, and, at Assignee's discretion, take any other action, including without limitation the transfer of the Certificate into its own name or the name of its nominee which it may deem necessary or appropriate to preserve or protect its interest in the Certificate.

    While this Agreement is in effect, Assignee may retain the rights to possession of the Certificate. Assignee may notify the institution that issued the Certificate of this Agreement. Assignor agrees that such institution will not pay any amount on the Certificate, other than to Assignee, so long as this Agreement is in effect. This Agreement will remain in effect until (i) there is no longer any indebtedness owing to Assignee, or (ii) Assignor has received, in writing from Assignee, a release of this Agreement.

Assignor hereby agrees that the Certificate-issuing institution may act, and in doing so shall be fully protected from liability to Assignor when so acting, on any order or direction by Assignee respecting the Certificate without making any inquiry as to Assignee's right or authority to give such order or direction or as to the application of any payment made pursuant thereto; and any payment of the Certificate made to Assignee pursuant to any such order or direction shall satisfy and discharge any liability of such institution to Assignor to the extent of such payment.

In addition to its rights under this Agreement, Assignee shall have all rights of a secured party under the Uniform Commercial Code in effect in the State of _____, and Assignor will execute required financing statements to give notice of such rights.

4. Limitations of Assignee. Assignee shall use reasonable care in the physical preservation and custody of the Certificate, but shall have no other obligation to protect the Certificate or its value, including but not limited to collection or protection of any income on the Certificate or the preservation of rights against issuers of the Certificate or third parties.

5. Events of Default and Remedies. An event of default (an "Event of Default") will exist under this Agreement if Assignor (i) fails to make any payment when due on any indebtedness and/or obligations secured by the Certificate, or (ii) dies (*Author's Note:* Delete "dies" if a corporate Assignor), becomes insolvent, appoints a receiver to any part of Assignor's property, makes any assignment for the benefit of creditors, or commences any bankruptcy proceedings.

Upon the occurrence of an Event of Default, and upon prior notice to Assignor, Assignee may present the Certificate to the issuing institution, obtain all funds deposited or accrued under the Certificate, and apply such funds to the indebtedness. If the Certificate is subject to an early withdrawal penalty, such penalty shall be deducted from the funds prior to application against the indebtedness. Any excess funds remaining after the indebtedness is satisfied will be paid to Assignor.

6. Assignment by Assignee. Assignee shall have the right, upon prior notice to Assignor, to assign its right and interest in the Certificate and to grant an assignee a first security interest in the Certificate.

7. Severability. Any provision of this Agreement which is prohibited or unenforceable in any jurisdiction shall, as to such jurisdiction, be ineffective to the extent of such prohibition or unenforceability without invalidating the remaining provisions hereof, and any such prohibition or unenforceability in any jurisdiction shall not invalidate or render unenforceable such provision in any other jurisdiction.

8. Binding Agreement. This Agreement and all representations and warranties herein contained are binding upon and shall inure to the benefit of the parties hereto and to their respective successors and assigns.

IN WITNESS WHEREOF, the parties hereto have caused this Agreement to be executed
by their duly authorized officers on the date and year first written above.

_____, Assignee

By:

Title:

_____, Assignor

By:

Title:

Annex A

[List any loans, liens, encumbrances, and/or claims affecting the Certificates of Deposit(s).]

Acknowledgment

The undersigned, being the institution referred to in the foregoing Agreement, hereby acknowledges receipt of a copy of, and consents to, this Agreement and certifies that the amount owing on the Certificate listed in the Agreement is not less than the amount(s) set forth above, and that parties executing the Agreement are the only parties having interest in the Certificate as appears on the record of undersigned, and that the undersigned has not received notice of any assignment, other than this Agreement, of the Certificate.

(Insert name of institution)

By:

Title:

Date:

Form: a-03
Disk File Name: a-03.rtf

ASSIGNMENT OF SAVINGS ACCOUNT AND/OR STOCK CERTIFICATE

Form Purpose

Assignment to an equipment leasing company or lender of a savings account and/or stock certificate as collateral security for equipment lease or loan obligations.

Executing Parties
The equipment lessee or borrower, as applicable (assignor).
The equipment lessor or lender, as applicable (assignee).

Assignment of Savings Account and/or Stock Certificate

Date:

[Insert name and address of Assignee.]

Gentlemen:

For value received, I/we (Assignor) hereby assign and transfer to and pledge to [insert name of Assignee] ("Assignee") my/our savings account and/or stock certificate number   , as more specifically identified on Exhibit A hereto (*Author's Note:* Copies of the account statement or stock certificate are recommended), as collateral for my/our obligations ("Obligation") under that certain [insert the identification of the document giving rise to this assignment, such as "that certain equipment lease agreement, dated _____, by and between Assignor and Assignee."].

This assignment shall be a continuing one and shall be effective until canceled, and shall operate as security for payment of any other debts or liabilities of the undersigned to Assignee now in existence or hereafter contracted.

You are hereby authorized to charge against the above savings account and/or stock certificate, for Obligation monies not paid when due, and, in this regard, I/we do hereby irrevocably constitute and appoint Assignee as attorney-in-fact to effect transfers of said stock and/or withdrawals and transfers of said savings account.

Assignor warrants the savings account and/or stock certificate is genuine and in all respects what it purports to be; that Assignor is the owner thereof free and clear of all liens and encumbrances of any nature whatsoever; and that Assignor has full power, right, and authority to execute and deliver this assignment.

, Assignor

By:

Title:

Accepted this   day of   , 20

, Assignee

By:

Title:

Form: a-04
Disk File Name: a-04.rtf

ASSIGNMENT OF LEASE TO LENDER—SINGLE TAKEDOWN

Form Purpose

Assignment to a leasing company's equipment lender of the leasing company's rights under an equipment lease, as collateral security for a loan to be used by the leasing company to pay, at least in part, for the cost of the equipment to be leased. This form contemplates a one-time loan takedown.

Executing Parties
The equipment lessor.
The equipment lender.

See:
Loan and Security Agreements Forms
Promissory Note Forms

Assignment of Lease

This ASSIGNMENT made as of   , [insert name of leasing company], a
corporation, with offices at   (hereinafter referred to as the "Borrower"), to
corporation, with offices at   (hereinafter referred to as the "Lender").

WITNESSETH:

WHEREAS, Borrower and (insert name of lessee) (the "Lessee") are parties to an equipment lease agreement dated as of   , (the "Lease") that   provides for the leasing by Borrower to Lessee of certain equipment (the "Equipment") described in Schedule A attached hereto;

WHEREAS, Borrower desires to borrow from (insert name of lender) (the "Lender") the principal sum of $, such borrowing to be evidenced by a promissory note of Borrower in said principal amount payable to Lender or to its order (the promissory note, together with any extension and renewal thereof, hereinafter referred to as the "Note");

WHEREAS, such borrowing (the "Loan") is to be made at a closing at which Borrower has agreed to deliver to Lender (i) this Assignment (the "Assignment"), and (ii) a Loan and Security Agreement, dated the same date as this Assignment, by and between Borrower and Lender (the "Security Agreement"); and

WHEREAS, this Assignment and the Security Agreement are being delivered to Lender as security for the payment of the Note and the performance by Borrower of its obligations under the Note, the Assignment and the Security Agreement (all such sums and obligations hereinafter referred to as the "Indebtedness").

NOW, THEREFORE, to induce Lender to make the Loan and for other good and valuable consideration, the receipt of which is hereby acknowledged, the parties hereto agree as follows:

1. As security for the Indebtedness, Borrower hereby assigns, transfers, and sets over unto Lender all Borrower's right, title, and interest as lessor under the Lease, together with all rights, powers, privileges, and other benefits of Borrower as lessor under the Lease, including, without limitation, the immediate right to receive and collect all rentals, insurance proceeds, net proceeds from the sale of all the Equipment, profits and other sums payable to or receivable by Borrower under or pursuant to the provisions of the Lease, and the right to make all waivers and agreements, to give all notice, consents, and releases, to take all action upon the happening of a default or an event of default under the Lease, and to do any and all other things whatsoever which Borrower is or may become entitled to do under the Lease. In furtherance of the foregoing assignment, Borrower hereby irrevocably authorizes and empowers Lender in its own name, or in the name of its nominee, if any, or in the name of Borrower or as its attorney, to ask, demand, collect, and receive any and all sums

to which Borrower is or may become entitled under the Lease to enforce compliance by Lessee with all the terms and agreements of the Lease.

2. The assignment made hereby is executed only as security, and, therefore, the execution and delivery of this Assignment shall not subject Lender to, or transfer, or pass, or in any way affect or modify, the liability of Borrower under the Lease, it being understood and agreed that notwithstanding such assignment, or any subsequent assignment, all obligations of Borrower to Lessee under the Lease shall be and remain enforceable by Lessee, its successors and assigns, against Borrower.

3. Borrower covenants and agrees that it will perform all of its obligations to be performed under the terms of the Lease, and hereby irrevocably authorizes and empowers Lender, in its own name, or in the name of its nominee, if any, or in the name of Borrower, or its attorney, on the happening of any failure by Borrower, to perform, or cause to be performed, any such obligation, all at Borrower's expense.

4. Upon (i) the full discharge and satisfaction of the Indebtedness, or (ii) the failure on the part of Lender to diligently exercise any right or remedies to which Lender is entitled by virtue of this Assignment and which arise out of the happening of a default or an event of default under the Lease, the assignment made hereby and all rights herein assigned to Lender shall cease and terminate, and all estate, right, title, and interest of Lender in and to the Lease shall revert to Borrower.

5. Borrower represents, warrants and covenants that: (a) the Lease is valid, is in full force and effect, is not in default, and is enforceable in accordance with its terms (subject only to bankruptcy, insolvency, and reorganization laws and other laws governing the enforcement of lessor's or creditor's rights), (b) the execution and delivery of the Assignment, the Security Agreement and the Note have been duly authorized, and the Assignment, the Security Agreement and the Note are and will remain the valid and enforceable obligations of Borrower in accordance with their terms, (c) Borrower has not executed, and
will not execute, any other assignment of the Lease and its right to receive all payments under the Lease is and will continue to be free and clear of any and all liens or encumbrances created or suffered by any act or omission on the part of Borrower, except as encumbered hereunder, (d) Borrower has delivered to Lender its only executed counterpart of the Lease, and (e) notwithstanding the Assignment, Borrower will perform and comply with each and all of the covenants and conditions in the Lease set forth to be complied with by it.

6. Borrower covenants and agrees with Lender that in any suit, proceeding, or action brought by Lender under the Lease for any sum owing thereunder, or to enforce any provisions of such Lease, Borrower will save, indemnify, and keep Lender harmless from and against all expense, loss, or damage suffered by reason of any defense, setoff, counterclaim, or recoupment whatsoever of Lessee thereunder or its successors, arising out of a breach by Borrower of any obligation in respect of the Equipment covered by the Lease or arising out of any other indebtedness or liability at any time owing to Lessee or its successors from Borrower.

7. Borrower will from time to time execute all such financing statements and supplemental instruments as Lender may from time to time reasonably request in order to confirm or further assure the assignment made hereby and the provisions hereof.

8. Lender may assign, without notice or consent, all or any of its rights under the Lease, including the right to receive any payments due or to become due to it from Lessee. In the event of any such assignment, any such subsequent or successive assignee or assignees shall, to the extent of such assignment, enjoy all rights and privileges and be subject to all the obligations of Lender.

9. Borrower agrees that it will not, without the prior written consent of Lender, enter into any agreement amending, modifying, or terminating the Lease and that any attempted amendment, modification, or termination without such consent shall be void.

10. Borrower hereby constitutes Lender, its successors and assigns, its true and lawful attorney, irrevocably, with full power (in its name or otherwise) to ask, require, demand, receive, and compound any and all rents and claims for money due and to become due under, or arising out of this Assignment, to endorse any checks or other instruments or orders in connection therewith and to file any claims or take any action or institute any proceedings which to Lender or any subsequent assignee seem necessary or advisable, all without affecting Borrower's liability in any manner whatsoever.

11. Borrower shall have no authority, without Lender's prior written consent, to accept payments or other collections, repossess or consent to the return of the property described in the Lease, or modify the terms of said Lease.

12. The Assignment shall be governed by the laws of the State of   .

13. The Assignment shall be binding upon and inure to the benefit of the parties hereto and their respective successors and assigns.

14. Borrower shall cause copies of all notices received in connection with the Lease to be promptly delivered to Lender at   , or at such other address as Lender shall designate in writing.

IN WITNESS WHEREOF, the parties hereto have caused this instrument to be duly executed as of the date first above written.

, Borrower

By:

Title:

Accepted this   day of   , 20

, Lender

By:

Title:

Schedule A

[Insert equipment description.]

Form: a-05
Disk File Name: a-05.rtf

ASSIGNMENT OF LEASE TO LENDER—MULTIPLE TAKEDOWNS

Form Purpose

Assignment to a leasing company's equipment lender of the leasing company's rights under an equipment lease, as collateral security for a loan to be used by the leasing company to pay, at least in part, for the cost of the equipment to be leased. This form contemplates multiple equipment deliveries, and multiple equipment loan takedowns by the leasing company, and has been integrated with a Loan and Security Agreement, Form l-05, a Promissory Note, Form p-02, and an Assignment Amendment, Form a-9.

Executing Parties
The equipment lessor.
The equipment lender.

See:
Loan and Security and Loan Agreement, Form l-05
Promissory Note, Form p-02
Assignment Amendment, Form a-09

Assignment

This ASSIGNMENT made as of   , from   , a   corporation, with   offices   at   (hereinafter   referred   to   as   the   "Company"), to   , with offices at   (hereinafter referred to as the "Lender").

WITNESSETH:

WHEREAS the Company and   (hereinafter referred to as the "Lessee") are parties to a Lease Agreement dated as of   , including as a part thereof, Schedule No.   dated as of   , and the Acceptance Certificate executed between the Company and Lessee, dated as of   , (said Lease, Schedule, and Acceptance Certificate being hereinafter referred to collectively as the "Lease") providing for the leasing by the Company to Lessee of certain newly manufactured equipment (as further described in Schedule A attached hereto and hereinafter referred to as the "Units");

WHEREAS, the Company desires to borrow from Lender an aggregate amount (hereinafter referred to as the "Loan") equal to   % of the purchase price of the Units, said Loan to be evidenced by one or more promissory notes of the Company payable to Lender or to its order (the promissory notes, together with any extension and renewal thereof, are hereinafter referred to as the "Notes");

WHEREAS, the Loan is to be made in a number of installments, each pursuant to a closing prior to which the Company has agreed to deliver to Lender (i) this Assignment (hereinafter referred to as the "Assignment") covering the Lease and (ii) a Loan and Security Agreement (hereinafter referred to as the "Security Agreement") on the Units; and

WHEREAS, the Assignment and the Security Agreement are being delivered to Lender as security for the payment of the Notes and the performance by the Company of its obligations under the Notes, the Assignment and the Security Agreement (all such sums and obligations being hereinafter referred to as the "Indebtedness").

NOW, THEREFORE, to induce Lender to make the Loan and for other good and valuable consideration, the receipt of which is hereby acknowledged, the parties hereto agree as follows:

1. As security for the Indebtedness, the Company hereby assigns, transfers, and sets over unto Lender all the Company's right, title, and interest as lessor under the Lease to receive and collect all rentals, insurance proceeds, net proceeds from the sale of the Units, profits and other sums payable to or receivable by the Company under or pursuant to the provisions of the Lease (except payments and reimbursements by Lessee to the Company for taxes and payments and reimbursements to the Company in the nature of indemnification to the Company, all of which shall be retained by the Company), and the right to make all waivers and agreements permitted under the Security Agreement, to give all notice, consents, and releases permitted under the Security Agreement, to take all action upon the happening of a default or an event of default under the Lease, and to do any and all other things whatsoever which the Company is or may become entitled to do under the Lease; provided, however, that no assignment is hereby made of the rights and options granted to the Lessee in Section _____ of the Lease and, in connection therewith, the Company reserves the right to give all such notices and take all such acts as are required or incident to the exercise of such rights and options, and the Company further reserves the right to receive all financial and other information which the Lessee is required to furnish to the Company pursuant to the Lease, provided that the Company, if requested by Lender, will deliver copies of all such information received by it to Lender. In furtherance of the foregoing assignment, the Company hereby irrevocably authorizes and empowers Lender in its own name, or in the name of its nominee, if any, or in the name of the Company or as its attorney, to ask, demand, collect, and receive any and all sums to which the Company is or may become entitled under the Lease and to enforce compliance by Lessee with all the terms and agreements of the Lease.

2. The assignment made hereby is executed only as security, and therefore, the execution and delivery of this Assignment shall not subject Lender to, or transfer, or pass, or in any way affect or modify, the liability of the Company under the Lease, it being understood and agreed that notwithstanding such assignment, or any subsequent assignment, all obligations of the Company to Lessee under the Lease shall be and remain enforceable by Lessee, its successors and assigns, against the Company.

3. The Company covenants and agrees that it will perform all of its obligations to be performed under the terms of the Lease, and hereby irrevocably authorizes and empowers Lender, in its own name, or in the name of its nominee, if any, or in the name of the Company, or its attorney, on the happening of any failure by the Company, to perform, or cause to be performed, any such obligation, all at the Company's expense.

4. Upon the full discharge and satisfaction of the Indebtedness, the assignment made hereby and all rights herein assigned to Lender will cease and terminate, and all estate, right, title, and interest of Lender in and to the Lease shall revert to the Company. Lender will forthwith execute and file all such termination statements and such other documents as may be necessary or appropriate to make clear upon the public record the termination of such assignment hereunder.

5. The Company represents, warrants and covenants that (a) the Lease is valid, in full force and effect, is not in default, and is enforceable in accordance with its terms against the Company (subject only to bankruptcy, insolvency, and reorganization laws and other laws governing the enforcement of lessor's or creditor's rights), (b) the execution and delivery of the Assignment, the Security Agreement and the Notes have been duly authorized, and the Assignment and Security Agreement are and the Notes will be, the valid and enforceable obligations of the Company in accordance with their terms, (c) the Company has not executed, and will not execute, any other assignment of the Lease and its right to receive all payments under the Lease is and will continue to be free and clear of any and all liens or encumbrances created or suffered by any act or omission on the part of the Company, except as encumbered hereunder, (d) the Company has delivered to Lender the Company's only executed counterpart of the Lease, and notwithstanding the assignment, the Company will perform and comply with each and all of the covenants and conditions in the Lease set forth to be complied with by it, and (e) notice pursuant to Section _____ of the Lease has been given to Lessee. (*Author's Note:* include if Lessor is obligated under the Lease to notify Lessee of a Lease assignment.)

6. The Company covenants and agrees with Lender that in any suit, proceeding, or action brought by Lender under the Lease for any sum owing thereunder, or to enforce any provisions of such Lease, the Company will save, indemnify, and keep Lender harmless from and against all expense, loss, or damage suffered by reason of any defense, setoff, counterclaim, or recoupment whatsoever of Lessee hereunder or its successors, arising out of a breach by the Company of any obligation in respect of the Units covered by the Lease or arising out of any other indebtedness or liability at any time owing to Lessee or its successors from the Company.

7. The Company will from time to time execute all such instruments and supplemental instruments and cooperate in the filing or recording of such documents, as Lender may from time to time reasonably request in order to confirm and perfect the assignment made hereby and the provisions hereof.

8. Lender may assign all or any of its rights under the Lease, including the right to receive any payments due or to become due to it from Lessee. In the event of any such assignment, any such subsequent or

successive assignee or assignees shall, to the extent of such assignment, enjoy all rights and privileges and be subject to all the obligations of Lender.

9 . The Company agrees that it will not, without prior written consent of Lender, enter into any agreement amending, modifying, or terminating the Lease, and any such attempted amendment, modification, or termination without such consent shall be void.

10. The Company hereby constitutes Lender, its successors and assigns, its true and lawful attorney, irrevocably, with full power, (in its name or otherwise) to ask, require, demand, receive, and compound any and all rents and claims for money due and to become due under, or arising out of this Agreement, to endorse any checks or other instruments or orders in connection therewith, and to file any claims or take any action or institute any proceedings which to Lender or any subsequent assignee seem necessary or advisable, all without affecting the Company's liability in any manner whatsoever.

11. The Company shall have no authority, without Lender's prior written consent, to accept payments or other collections assigned to Lender hereunder, or to repossess or consent to the return of the property described in the Lease, or materially modify the terms of said Lease.

12. The Assignment shall be governed by the laws of the State of   .

13. The Assignment shall be binding upon and inure to the benefit of the parties hereto and the respective successors and assigns.

14. The Company shall cause copies of all notices received in connection with the Lease to be promptly delivered to Lender at   , Attn.:   , or at such other address as Lender shall designate in writing.

IN WITNESS WHEREOF, the parties hereto have caused this instrument to be duly executed as of the date first written above.

(Insert name of Company)

By:

Title:

Accepted:

(Insert name of Lender)

By:

Title:

Schedule A

Description of Equipment

Description of Unit and Manufacturer	No. of Units	Location	Supplier or Vendor	Identification or Serial No.

Form: a-06
Disk File Name: a-06.rtf

ASSIGNMENT OF LEASE—SALE BY LESSOR (LIMITED RECOURSE)

Form Purpose

Sale assignment, limited recourse, by one leasing company to another leasing company of an equipment lease and the underlying equipment.

Executing Parties
The selling equipment lessor.
The purchasing equipment lessor.

See:
Bill of Sale, Forms b-01 and b-02

Assignment of Lease

(Limited Recourse)

[Insert name of assigning equipment leasing company] (the "Assignor") hereby sells, assigns, transfers, and conveys to (insert name of purchasing equipment leasing company) (the "Assignee"), its successors and assigns, without recourse except as hereinafter provided, the lease agreement (the "Lease"), covering

(insert equipment description here),

dated   , between Assignor and (insert name and address of Assignor of the lease), and   , as lessee, ("Lessee") and all payments due and to become due thereunder and all right, title, and interest of Assignor in and to the property described in the Lease (the "Property") and all Assignor's rights and remedies thereunder, and the right either in Assignee's own behalf or in Assignor's name to take all such proceedings, legal, equitable, or otherwise, that Assignor might take, save for this assignment.

Assignor represents and warrants that the Lease and all related instruments are genuine, enforceable, and the Lease is the only one executed with respect to the Property; all statements therein contained are true; the Property has been delivered to, and accepted by, Lessee in condition satisfactory to Lessee, and Assignor will comply with all its representations, warranties and other obligations to Lessee.

Assignor hereby agrees to indemnify, hold safe and harmless from and against and covenants to defend Assignee against any and all claims, costs, expenses, damages, and all liabilities arising from or pertaining to the use, possession, or operation of the Property.

Assignor represents and warrants that the Lease is in full force and effect and that Assignor has not assigned or pledged, and hereby covenants that it will not assign or pledge the whole or any part of the rights hereby assigned, to anyone other than Assignee, its successors or assigns.

Assignee shall have no obligations of Assignor under the Lease.

All Assignor's right, title and interest assigned hereunder may be reassigned by Assignee and any subsequent assignee. It is expressly agreed that, anything herein contained to the contrary notwithstanding, Assignor's obligations under the Lease may be performed by Assignee or any subsequent assignee without releasing Assignor therefrom, and that Assignee shall not, by reason of this assignment, be obligated to perform any of Assignor's obligations under the Lease or to file any claim or take any other action to collect or enforce any payment assigned hereunder.

Assignor waives presentment and demand for payment, protest or notice of nonpayment and notice as to the Lease and all related documents now and hereafter assigned or endorsed and subordinate to any rights Assignee may now or hereafter have against Lessee any rights Assignor may now or hereafter have or acquire by reason of payment to Assignee of any payments under the Lease or otherwise.

Assignor hereby constitutes Assignee, its successors and assigns, its true and lawful attorney, irrevocably, with full power (in our name or otherwise) to ask, require, demand, receive, compound, and give acquittance for any and all rents and claims for money due and to become due under, or arising out of this assignment agreement, to endorse any checks or other instruments or orders in connection therewith, and to file any claims or take any action or institute any proceedings which to Assignee or any subsequent assignee seem necessary or advisable, all without affecting our liability in any manner whatsoever.

Assignor shall have no authority, without Assignee's prior written consent, to accept payments or other collections, repossess or consent to the return of the Property described in said Lease, or modify the terms of said contract.

Dated this   day of   , 20____

WITNESS, our hand and seal.

                                                      , Assignor

By:

Title:

Accepted this   day of   , 20____

                                                      , Assignee

By:

Title:

Form: a-07
Disk File Name: a-07.rtf

ASSIGNMENT OF MASTER LEASE—SALE BY LESSOR INTEGRATED (WITHOUT RECOURSE)

Form Purpose

Sale assignment, without recourse, by one leasing company to another leasing company of a master equipment lease, certain specified equipment schedules, and the underlying equipment. This form is integrated with Lease Agreement Form l-03.

Executing Parties
The selling equipment lessor.
The purchasing equipment lessor.

See:
Lease Agreement, Form l-03
Bill of Sale, Forms b-01 and b-02

                                    , Lessor

Home Office Address:

Phone (   )

Assignment and Assumption of Master Agreement to Lease Equipment

ASSIGNMENT AND ASSUMPTION ("Assignment") made this   day of   , between
                          , a   corporation ("Assignor"), and
, a   corporation ("Assignee").

WHEREAS, Assignor has entered into a certain Master Agreement to Lease Equipment ("Master Agreement"), dated as of   , between Assignor, as Lessor, and   , as Lessee ("Lessee"), pursuant to which Assignor has agreed to lease equipment to Lessee by means of Schedules entered into by the parties with respect to certain items of equipment ("Units"); and

WHEREAS, Assignor desires to sell and assign to Assignee the Master Agreement and/or certain Schedules.

NOW, THEREFORE, for good and valuable consideration, the receipt of which is hereby acknowledged, the parties hereto agree as follows:

    1. Assignor hereby assigns, transfers, and sets over unto Assignee all of Assignor's rights and interests in and to the Master Agreement and/or the Schedules identified in Exhibit A hereto (collectively "Assigned Contracts"), including all rights, powers, privileges, and other benefits of Assignor as lessor under the Assigned Contracts. Assignee, for itself and its successors and assigns, hereby expressly assumes and agrees to satisfy all obligations and liabilities existing or arising on or after the date of this Assignment out of or relating to the Assigned Contracts. From and after the date of this Assignment, Assignor shall have no further liability or obligations under the Assigned Contracts as lessor, or otherwise, of any nature whatsoever.

    2. Assignor warrants and covenants that (a) the execution and delivery of this Assignment has been duly authorized, and this Assignment is and will remain the valid and binding obligation of Assignor enforceable against Assignor in accordance with its terms (subject only to bankruptcy, insolvency, and reorganization laws and other laws governing the enforcement of lessor or creditor rights), (b) Assignor has not executed any other assignment of the Assigned Contracts or any of them and any right to receive payments under the Assigned Contracts is free and clear of any and all liens or encumbrances created or suffered by any act or omission on the part of Assignor, and (c) Assignor has delivered to Assignee all executed counterparts of the Assigned Contracts in its possession.

3. Assignee covenants and agrees with Assignor on behalf of itself and its successors and assigns that from and after the date of this Assignment it shall save and hold Assignor harmless from and against and indemnify and defend Assignor with respect to any and all damages, losses, liabilities, claims, and expenses suffered or incurred by Assignor arising directly or indirectly out of or in connection with the Assigned Contracts, the Units and any other matter arising out of or relating to any transaction contemplated by, or effected pursuant to, the Assigned Contracts.

4. Assignor and Assignee agree that each will execute all such supplemental instruments as Assignor or Assignee may from time to time reasonably request in order to confirm or further assure the assignment made hereby and the provisions hereof and to evidence and provide for the specific assumption by Assignee, its successors or assigns, of the obligations and liabilities of Assignor relating to the Assigned Contracts.

5. Assignee may not assign all or any of its rights under the Assigned Contracts, including the right to receive any payments due or to become due to it from Lessee, without the prior written consent of Assignor.

6. This Assignment shall be governed by the laws of the State of   .

7. This Assignment shall be binding upon and inure to the benefit of the parties hereto and their respective successors and assigns.

IN WITNESS WHEREOF, the undersigned have duly executed this Assignment as of the
date first above written.

                              , Assignor

By:

Title:

                              , Assignee

By:

Title:

Exhibit A to Assignment and Assumption of Master Agreement to Lease Equipment

Description of Assigned Contracts

1. Master Agreement Number: _____
2. Schedules:

Schedule No.   *Date of Schedule*

Form: a-08
Disk File Name: a-08.rtf

Assignment of Lease—Sale by Lessor (with Recourse)

Form Purpose

Sale assignment, with recourse, by one leasing company to another leasing company of an equipment lease and the underlying equipment.

Executing Parties
The selling equipment lessor.
The purchasing equipment lessor.

See:
Bill of Sale, Forms b-01 and b-02

Assignment of Lease with Recourse

TO: [Insert name and address of Assignee]

RE: Equipment Lease Agreement ("Lease") by and between [insert name of lessee] (the "Lessee"), and undersigned (the "Assignor"), as lessor, dated   , having aggregate unpaid rentals of $.

FOR VALUE RECEIVED, Assignor hereby sells, assigns, and transfers to [insert name of assignee] (the "Assignee"), Assignor's right, title, and interest in and to the Lease, the property therein leased, and all monies to become due thereunder. In consideration of the purchase of the Lease, Assignor agrees, in the event Lessee defaults in making any payment due under the Lease, at the time and in the manner therein specified, to pay on demand to Assignee such payments due, or to become due under the Lease.

Assignor further agrees to reimburse Assignee for any and all costs and expenses (including reasonable attorney's fees) resulting from any failure or refusal of Lessee to recognize and comply with the conditions of this Lease assignment.

Assignor hereby consents that Assignee, its successors and assigns, may, without notice, extend the time for payment under said Lease, waive the performance of the terms and conditions as it may determine appropriate, and make any reasonable settlement there under without affecting or limiting Assignor's liability hereunder.

Assignor warrants that (i) Assignor is the owner of the property described in the Lease free from all liens and encumbrances except the Lease, (ii) the Lease and any accompanying guaranties, waivers, and/or other instruments are genuine, enforceable, (iii) the Lease is the only lease executed concerning the property described in the Lease, (iv) the Lease rentals and other payments due and to be become due are and will continue to be free from defenses, setoffs, and counterclaims, (v) all signatures, names, addresses, amounts, and other statements and facts contained in the Lease and related documents are true and correct, (vi) the aggregate unpaid Lease rentals shown above is correct, (vii) the property has been delivered to Lessee under the Lease on the date set forth below in satisfactory condition and has been accepted by Lessee, (viii) Assignor will comply with all its warranties and other obligations with respect to the Lease transaction, and (ix) the Lease constitutes and will continue to constitute, as applicable, a valid reservation of unencumbered title to or first lien upon or security interest in the property covered thereby, effective against all persons, and if filing, recordation, or any other action or procedure is permitted or required by statute or regulation to perfect such reservation of title or lien or security interest, the same has been accomplished. If Assignor breaches any of the foregoing, it will, upon Assignee's request, promptly repurchase the Lease for an amount equal to the unpaid rentals thereon, including accrued interest plus any expenses of collection, repossession, transportation, and storage incurred by Assignee, less any customary refund by Assignee of unearned charges. Assignor agrees that Assignee may, in Assignor's name, endorse all remittances received, and Assignor gives express permission to Assignee to release, on terms satisfactory to Assignee or by operation of law or otherwise, or to compromise or adjust any and all rights against and grant extensions of time of payment to Lessee or any other persons obligated on the Lease or on any accompanying guaranty, or to agree to the substitution of a Lessee, without notice to Assignor and without affecting Assignor's obligations hereunder. Assignor shall have no authority to, and will not, without Assignee's prior written consent, accept payments of rents or of option prices, repossess, or consent to the return of the property described in the Lease, or modify the terms thereof or of any accompanying guaranty. Assignee's knowledge at any time of any breach or of noncompliance with any of the foregoing shall not constitute any waiver by Assignee. Assignor waives notice of acceptance hereof.

The property covered by the Lease was delivered to, and accepted by Lessee on   .

Date:

                    , Assignor

By:

Title:

                    , Assignee

By:

Title:

Form: a-09
Disk File Name: a-09.rtf

ASSIGNMENT AMENDMENT—EQUIPMENT LOAN

Form Purpose

Amendment of a loan and security agreement equipment lease assignment. This form has been integrated with Loan and Security Agreement Form l-05.

Executing Parties
The equipment lessor.
The equipment lender.

See:
Assignment of Lease to Lender, Form a-05
Loan and Security Agreement, Form l-05
Promissory Note, Form p-02

Amendment No.   to Assignment

This Amendatory Agreement, dated this   day of   , 20___
("Amendment") by and between   , with a place of business at
                         , (the "Company") and , with a place of
business at   , (the "Lender").

WITNESSETH:

WHEREAS, as security for the repayment of a Note, dated   , in the principal amount of
$, issued by the Company to Lender, the Company and Lender entered into (i) a Loan and Secu-
rity Agreement dated as of   , 20___ (the "Security Agreement") granting to Lender a security
interest in the items of equipment described therein (the equipment being referred to as "Units" in the Security Agreement) and (ii) a related assignment dated as of   , granting a security interest to Lender in
certain rights of the Company as lessor of the Equipment under a Lease Agreement dated as of
                    (the "Lease") by and between the Company and   (the
"Lessee"); and

WHEREAS, pursuant to the Acceptance Certificate referenced below (the "Acceptance Certificate"), Lessee
has leased certain additional items of equipment from the Company under the Lease and the Company
desires to borrow the additional principal amount of $ from Lender to partially finance the purchase
of these additional Units, the borrowing to be evidenced by a promissory note, of even date herewith, to be
issued by the Company to Lender in said principal amount (the "Note") and secured by the additional items
of equipment under the Security Agreement and the Acceptance Certificate under the Assignment.

NOW, THEREFORE, in consideration of the premises and the mutual covenants herein contained, the parties
hereto agree as follows:

　　1. The Note and the Units described in Annex A hereto shall be included as a "Note" and as "Units"
respectively under the Security Agreement and for all purposes thereof be considered a "Note" and "Units"
respectively as defined therein.
　　2. The Acceptance Certificates listed in Annex A hereto shall be included under the Assignment and
shall for all purposes thereof be considered a part of the "Lease" (as defined in the Assignment),

IN WITNESS WHEREOF, the parties hereto have executed this Amendment as of the day
and year first above written.
(Insert name of the Company)

By:

Title:

(Insert name of Lender)

By:

Title:

Annex A

Acceptance Certificate dated

Identification or Description of Unit	*No. of Units*	*Serial Number*

Form: a-10
Disk File Name: a-10.rtf

ASSIGNMENT OF EQUIPMENT PURCHASE CONTRACT

Form Purpose

Assignment by an equipment lessee to an equipment leasing company of the rights, but not the obligations, to purchase equipment from its equipment vendor, which will be the subject of the lease agreement.

Executing Parties
The equipment lessor.
The equipment lessee.

Equipment Purchase Contract Assignment

Equipment Purchase Contract Assignment, dated   , by and between   ("the Assignee"), with a place of business at   and ("the Assignor"), with a place of business at   (the "Assignment").

WHEREAS, the Assignor has entered into certain equipment purchase contracts, copies of which are annexed as Exhibit A hereto (the "Purchase Contracts"), with certain manufacturers, dealers, or distributors (the "Vendors") pursuant to which the Vendors agreed to sell to the Assignor the Equipment described therein (the "Equipment");

WHEREAS, the Assignor wishes to lease said Equipment subject to the Purchase Contracts from the Assignee instead of purchasing the Equipment; and

WHEREAS, the Assignor, as Lessee, and the Assignee, as Lessor, have entered into an Equipment Lease Agreement, dated as of   , (the "Lease") whereby the Assignee will lease, subject to the terms of the Lease, the Equipment described in the Lease as it is delivered to and accepted for lease by the Assignor and the Assignee.

NOW, THEREFORE, in consideration of the premises and the mutual covenants herein contained, the parties hereto agree as follows:

1. For purposes of this Assignment, the terms used hereafter which are not specifically defined herein shall have the meanings that are attributed to them in the Lease, unless the context otherwise requires.

2. The Assignor does hereby sell, assign, transfer, and set over unto the Assignee all of the Assignor's rights and interest in and to the Purchase Contracts as and to the extent that the same relate to such Equipment and the purchase and operation thereof. This Assignment, except to the extent reserved below shall include, without limitation, (a) in respect of the Assignee, the right, upon valid tender by the Vendors, to purchase the Equipment pursuant to the respective Purchase Contracts, and the right to take title to such Equipment and to be named the purchaser in the bills of sale to be delivered by the Vendors in respect of said Equipment, and (b) any and all rights of the Assignor to compel performance of the terms of the Purchase Contracts in respect to the Equipment; reserving to the Assignor, however, so long, and only so long, as such Equipment shall be subject to the Lease (i) the rights to demand, accept, and retain all rights in and to all property (other than the Equipment), data, technical publications, and service which the Vendors are obligated to provide or do provide pursuant to the Purchase Contacts and (ii) the right to any services, training, data, demonstrations, and testing pursuant to the Purchase Contracts.

Notwithstanding the foregoing, so long as the Assignee shall not have declared the Assignor to be in default under the Lease, the Assignee authorizes the Assignor, to the exclusion of the Assignee, to exercise in its own name all rights and powers of the buyer under the Purchase Contracts in respect to said Equipment and to retain any recovery or benefit resulting from the enforcement of any warranty or indemnity under the Purchase Contracts in respect to said Equipment, or otherwise, except that (a) the Assignor may not enter into any change order or other amendment, modification, or supplement to any of the Purchase Contracts without the prior written consent of the Assignee if such change order, amendment, modification, or supplement would result in any rescission, cancellation, termination, or modification of any of the Purchase Contracts.

3. It is expressly agreed that, anything herein contained to the contrary, (a) the Assignor shall at all times remain liable to the Vendors under the Purchase Contracts to perform all the duties and obligations of the buyers thereunder to the same extent as if this Assignment had not been executed and (b) the exercise by the Assignee of any of the rights assigned hereunder shall not release the Assignor from any of its duties or obligations to the Vendors under the Purchase Contracts except to the extent that such exercise by the Assignee shall constitute performance of such duties and obligations.

4. The Assignor does hereby constitute, effective at any time after the time the Assignee has declared the Assignor to be in default under the Lease, the Assignee, its successors and assigns, the Assignor's true and lawful attorney, irrevocably, with full power (in the name of the Assignor or otherwise) to ask, require, demand, receive, compound, and give acquittance for any and all monies and claims for monies due and to become due under, or arising out of, the Purchase Contracts to the extent that the same have been assigned by this Assignment and, for such period as the Assignee may exercise rights with respect thereto under this Assignment, to endorse any checks or other instruments or orders in connection therewith and to file any claims or take any action or institute (or, if previously commenced, assume control of) any proceedings and to obtain any recovery in connection therewith which the Assignee may deem to be necessary or advisable in the premises.

5. Notwithstanding the foregoing Assignment, the Assignee hereby designates the Assignor to perform all obligations and duties of the Assignee under the Purchase Contracts except the purchase of the Equipment and the payment of monies due the Vendors under the Purchase Contracts as of the time of the completion of delivery and acceptance of Equipment and making same subject to the Lease by and between Assignee, as lessor and Assignor, as lessee. The only obligations of the Assignee under this Assignment shall be, on the dates of acceptance of the Equipment by Assignor, as lessee, and Assignor, as lessor, pursuant to the Lease, to purchase said Equipment from the respective Vendors and to pay the Vendors an amount equal to the purchase price due and owing, taking advantage of applicable discounts, subject to the limitations as set forth in the Lease. In the event that any of the Vendors have heretofore required, or may hereafter require, the making of any down payments, progress payments, or other advances, the same shall be (or have heretofore been) made by the Assignor. Any such payments and/or advances shall be reimbursed to the Assignor by the Assignee upon proof of payment therefore when and if the Assignee is required to make payment of the purchase price therefore pursuant to the Lease, including all attachments thereto.

6. In the event that the Assignor or the Assignee determines not to accept for lease any of said Equipment, the Assignee shall reassign to the Assignor the appropriate contract rights governing said Equipment and release the Assignee's interests therein. The Assignee shall thereupon have no further obligations, or liabilities in connection with said contract rights and Equipment, and the Assignor hereby agrees to indemnify the Assignee and hold the Assignee harmless from and against any and all claims, demands, actions, or proceedings arising out of or in any way relating to said contract rights and Equipment, by whomsoever asserted, and any and all losses, damage, obligations, liabilities, costs, expenses (including attorneys' fees) suffered, paid, or incurred by the Assignee in connection therewith.

7. The Assignor agrees that at any time and from time to time, upon written request of the Assignee, the Assignor will promptly and duly execute and deliver any and all such further instruments and documents and take such further action as the Assignee may reasonably request in order to obtain the full benefit of this Assignment and of the rights and powers herein granted.

8. The Assignor does hereby represent and warrant that the Purchase Contracts are in full force and effect and the Assignor is not in default thereunder. The Assignor does hereby further represent and warrant that the Assignor has not assigned or pledged, and hereby covenants that it will not assign or pledge, so long as this Assignment shall remain in effect, the whole or any part of the rights hereby assigned or any of its rights with respect to the Equipment under the Purchase Contracts not assigned hereby, to anyone other than the Assignee.

9. The Assignee agrees that, except as otherwise expressly provided herein, it will not enter into any agreement with any of the Vendors that would amend, modify, supplement, rescind, cancel, or terminate any of the Purchase Contracts in respect to the Equipment without the prior written consent of the Assignor.

10. All notices, requests, demands, or communications to or upon the Assignee and the Assignor shall be deemed to have been given or made when deposited in the U.S. mail, postage for certified mail prepaid, addressed to respective addresses contained in the Lease.

11. The Assignor shall notify the Vendors of this assignment, such notice to be in the form of Exhibit B hereto.

12. Neither this Assignment nor any provision hereby may be changed, waived, discharged, or terminated orally, but only by an instrument in writing signed by the party against whom enforcement of the change, waiver, discharge, or termination is sought.

13. This Assignment shall be binding upon the Assignor and its successors and assigns and shall be binding upon and inure to the benefit of the Assignee and its successors and assigns.

14. This Assignment and the rights and obligations of the parties hereunder shall be construed in accordance with and governed by the laws of the State of   .

IN WITNESS WHEREOF, the parties here to have caused this Assignment to be duly executed this   day of   , 20   .

                              , Assignor

By:

Title:

                              , Assignee

By:

Title:

Exhibit A

[Copies of Purchase Contracts]

Exhibit B

Form of Notification of Assignment
[See Form a-11.]

Form: a-11
Disk File Name: a-11.rtf

Assignment of Purchase Contract Notification to Vendor

Form Purpose

Notification to, and acknowledgment by, an equipment vendor of the assignment by an equipment lessee to an equipment leasing company of the rights, but not the obligations, to purchase equipment, from its equipment vendor, which will be the subject of the lease agreement.

Executing Parties
The equipment lessee.
The equipment vendor.

See:
Assignment of Equipment Purchase Contract, Form a-10

Notification of Purchase Contract Assignment

Date

(Insert name and address of equipment vendor)

Re: Purchase Contract, dated .

(Insert name of assignor) ("Lessee") has assigned its position under the above-referenced purchase contract ("Purchase Contract") to (Insert name of assignee), as lessor, who will lease the equipment which is the subject of the Purchase Contract to Lessee. Notwithstanding such assignment, Lessee hereby guarantees performance of all of buyer's obligations under the Purchase Contract and expects you to permit Lessee to continue to exercise and permit the enforcement of buyer's rights in relation to warranties and/or representations provided by, or through, you the seller.

Please prepare your invoices to show the equipment as billed, and shipped, to Lessor in care of Lessee. Any additional title papers or bills of sale should be prepared to show as owner:

[Insert Lessor's name and address]

We request your written acknowledgment that these changes will be made as requested, by signing and returning to us the enclosed copy of this notification.

Thank you.

(Insert name of Lessee)

By:

Title:

Accepted this   day of   , 20___ .

(Insert name of equipment vendor), Vendor

By:

Title:

Form: a-12
Disk File Name: a-12.rtf

ASSUMPTION AGREEMENT

Form Purpose

When one equipment leasing company sells an equipment lease, and the equipment subject to the lease, to another equipment leasing company, if some or all of the equipment purchase funds have been borrowed from a third-party lender, an assumption agreement can be used to, in effect, transfer the loan obligation to the second leasing company. The following assumption is a recourse assumption, obligating the selling leasing company to pay any transferred obligations not paid by the purchasing leasing company. If the equipment loan had been guaranteed, the guarantor must also consent to the assumption agreement.

Executing Parties
The selling equipment lessor.
The purchasing equipment lessor.
The selling equipment lessor's loan guarantor.
The equipment lender (secured party).

See:
Assignment of Lease, Forms a-06, a-07, and a-08
Assumption Consent—Guarantor, Form a-13

Assumption Agreement

This Assumption Agreement ("Agreement") is made this   day of   , 20___ , by and among
("Transferor"), with a place of business at ;
("Transferee"), with a place of business at   ; and   ("Secured
Party"), with a place of business at   .

WHEREAS, Transferor has entered into a Loan and Security Agreement ("Security Agreement"), dated as of
20___ , with Secured Party covering the following equipment ("Equipment")

[insert equipment description here]

which is subject to an equipment lease (the "Lease"), dated   , by and between Transferor, as lessor, and   , as lessee.

WHEREAS, Transferor wishes to sell, assign, and/or transfer all of its right, title, and interest in and to the Lease, the Equipment, and the Security Agreement thereof to Transferee, and

WHEREAS, the Equipment and the Lease is subject to the security interest of Secured Party, and Secured Party is willing to consent to such sale, assignment, and transfer, subject, however, to the terms and conditions hereinafter set forth.

NOW, THEREFORE, in consideration of the mutual covenants contained herein, this Agreement the parties hereto agree as follows:

1. Transferor hereby sells, assigns, and/or transfers to Transferee all of its right, title, and interest in and to the Security Agreement with respect to the Lease, and the Equipment.
2. Transferee hereby:
    (a) promises to pay to Secured Party all monies due and to become due pursuant to the terms and conditions of the Security Agreement and in the manner set forth therein;
    (b) hereby assumes and covenants to perform all obligations of Transferor under the Security Agreement;

(c) agrees that it shall stand in the place and stead of Transferor and shall be subject to all of the terms and provisions contained in the original Security Agreement, as though it were the original Security Agreement named therein; and

(d) agrees to pay as they become due the remaining monthly rentals numbering   at $ each.

3. In consideration of the consent of Secured Party to the foregoing sale, assignment, transfer, and assumption, Transferor does hereby absolutely, irrevocably, and unconditionally guarantees to Secured Party and its successors and assigns that all warranties and representations made by Transferor to Secured Party to induce Secured Party to consent to this transfer and assumption are true and correct. In addition, upon any default by Transferee hereunder, Transferor shall pay to Secured Party or its successors or assigns the full unpaid amounts of any and all the obligations then owed by Transferee to Secured Party pursuant to the aforementioned Security Agreement.

IN WITNESS WHEREOF, the parties have executed this Agreement on the day and year first above written.

(Insert name of Transferor), Transferor

By:

Title:

(Insert name of Transferee), Transferee

By:

Title:

(Insert name of Secured Party), Secured Party

By:

Title:

Form: a-13
Disk File Name: a-13.rtf

ASSUMPTION CONSENT—GUARANTOR

Form Purpose

When one equipment leasing company sells an equipment lease to another leasing company, if some or all of the equipment purchase funds have been borrowed from a third-party lender, an assumption agreement can be used to, in effect, transfer the loan obligation to the second leasing company. If the equipment loan had been guaranteed, the guarantor must also consent to the assumption agreement. The following agreement provides for such a guarantor consent and should be attached to the assumption agreement as an exhibit.

Executing Parties
The selling equipment lessor's guarantor.

See:
Assumption Agreement, Form a-12

Agreement of Guarantor

Lease Agreement dated:

Selling Lessor:

Lessee:

Purchasing Lessor:

The undersigned, as a guarantor of Selling Lessor's obligations under the Lease, does hereby represent and warrant that the undersigned has read and understands the foregoing Assumption Agreement, does hereby consent to the execution thereof, and covenants and agrees that any obligation or liability, which it may have by virtue of the undersigned's guaranty, will remain in full force and effect upon and after the execution of this agreement and shall secure the full and timely performance of the obligations of both the Selling Lessor and Purchasing Lessor.

, Guarantor

By:

Title:

Form: a-14
Disk File Name: a-14.rtf

AMENDMENT TO LEASE AGREEMENT

Form Purpose

Lease amendment. This form has been integrated with the short form net finance master lease agreement, Equipment Lease Agreement—Short Form l-03.

Executing Parties
The equipment lessor.
The equipment lessee.

See:
Equipment Lease Agreement—Short Form l-03

RIDER   to Schedule No.   dated as of   to Master Agreement to
Lease Equipment, dated as of   , between   , Lessor, and
                              , Lessee.

Amendment to Lease

The terms and conditions of the Schedule designated above are modified and amended as follows:

, Lessor

By:

Title:

, Lessee

By:

Title:

Form: b-01
Disk File Name: b-01.rtf

Bill of Sale—Warranty

Form Purpose

A warranty equipment bill of sale.

Executing Parties
The equipment seller.

Bill of Sale

("Seller"), with a principal place of business at   for and
in consideration of the sum of dollars received from   ("Buyer")
with a principal place of business at   , the receipt and sufficiency of
which is hereby acknowledged as payment in full for the purchase price of the equipment described on
Annex A hereto (the "Equipment"), has bargained, sold, transferred, assigned, set over, and conveyed, and
by these presents does bargain, sell, transfer, assign, set over, and convey unto Buyer, its successors and
assigns forever all of the Equipment.

TO HAVE AND TO HOLD, all and singular the Equipment unto the Buyer, its successors and assigns, for its
and their own use and behoof forever.

Seller shall indemnify, defend, and hold Buyer harmless from and against any and all claims or liabilities
resulting from any misrepresentation by, or breach of warranty, covenant, or agreement of Seller.

Seller, for itself and its successors and assigns, further covenants and agrees to do, execute, and deliver, or to
cause to be done, executed, and delivered, all such further reasonable acts, transfers, and assurances, for the
better assuring, conveying, and confirming unto Buyer and its successors and assigns, all and singular, the
Equipment hereby bargained, sold, assigned, transferred, set over, and conveyed as Buyer and its successors
and assigns shall reasonably request.

Seller hereby represents and warrants to Buyer, its successors and assigns, that at the time of this sale to
Buyer, Seller is the lawful owner of the Equipment; that title to said Equipment is free from all prior claims,
liens, and encumbrances suffered by or through Seller; and that Seller has good right to sell the same as aforesaid. In addition, Seller covenants that it will warrant and defend such title against all claims and demands
whatsoever.

This Bill of Sale and the representations, warranties, and covenants herein contained shall inure to the benefit of Buyer and its successors and assigns, shall be binding upon Seller and its successors and assigns, and
shall survive the execution and delivery hereof.

IN WITNESS WHEREOF, Seller has caused this Bill of Sale to be executed on the day of   , 20____.

                                         , Seller

By:

Title:

Annex A

Form: b-02
Disk File Name: b-02.rtf

Bill of Sale—"As Is, Where Is"

Form Purpose

An "as is, where is" equipment bill of sale.

Executing Parties
The equipment seller.

Bill of Sale

This Bill of Sale, dated the   day of   , 20___, from   ("Seller"), with a place of business at   .

WITNESSETH

In consideration of the receipt of $ and other valuable consideration, the receipt of which is hereby acknowledged, Seller does hereby sell, assign, transfer, convey, and deliver, on an "as is, where is" basis, to   (the "Buyer"), with a place of business at   all the property and equipment of whatsoever kind of character listed, described, or otherwise referred to on its attached invoice, a copy of which is attached hereto and incorporated herein by this reference with the same force and effect as set forth herein full as Annex A.

Seller represents and warrants that:

A. It is the owner of, and has absolute title to, each and every item of said property free and clear of all claims, liens, encumbrances, and all other defects of title, of any kind whatsoever.

B. It has not made any prior sale, assignment, or transfer of any item of said property to any person, firm, or corporation.

C. It has the present power and authority to sell, assign, and transfer each and every item of said property to Buyer.

D. All acts, proceedings, and things necessary and required by law and the articles of incorporation and by-laws of Seller to make this Bill of Sale a valid, binding, and legal obligation of Seller have been done, taken, and have happened; and the execution and delivery hereof have in all respects been duly authorized in accordance with the law, and said articles of incorporation and by-laws.

Seller covenants that it shall forever warrant and defend this sale, assignment, transfer, conveyance, and delivery of each and every item of said property to Buyer and its successors and assigns, against each and every person whomsoever lawfully claiming the same by or through Seller.

This Bill of Sale is binding upon the successors and assigns of Seller and insures to the benefit of the successors and assigns of Buyer.

IN WITNESS WHEREOF, the undersigned Seller has caused this instrument to be executed on the day and year first above appearing, by and through a duly authorized officer.

(Seller):

By:

Title:

Annex A

Form: c-01
Disk File Name: c-01.rtf

CHECKLIST—LESSEE PROPOSAL STAGE

Form Purpose

A lessee proposal stage checklist.

See:
Request for Lease Quotations, Forms r-01 through r-04

NOTE: This form is reproduced on page 36, and is included on the accompanying CD.

Form: c-02
Disk File Name: c-02.rtf

CHECKLIST—LEASE NEGOTIATION AND DRAFTING

Form Purpose

A checklist for drafting and negotiating a lease agreement.

See:
Lease Agreements, Forms l-02 through l-04

NOTE: This form is reproduced on page 75, and is included on the accompanying CD.

Form: c-03
Disk File Name: c-03.rtf

CHECKLIST—LESSOR PROPOSAL STAGE

Form Purpose

A lessor proposal stage checklist.

See:
Lessor Proposal Documents—Forms p-04 through p-05

NOTE: This form is reproduced on page 39, and is included on the accompanying CD.

Form: c-04
Disk File Name: c-04.rtf

CHECKLIST—SUPPLEMENTAL LEASE DOCUMENT CLOSING

Form Purpose

A supplemental lease document closing checklist.

NOTE: This form is reproduced on page 90, and is included on the accompanying CD.

Form: c-05
Disk File Name: c-05.rtf

Collection Notification—Initial Lessee Nonpayment

Form Purpose

A lessee lease payment default notification letter.

Executing Parties
The equipment lessor.

See:
Collection Notification—Follow-up Lessee Nonpayment, Form c-06
Collection Notification—Lawsuit, Form c-07
Collection Notification—Repossession, Form c-08

[Letterhead of Leasing Company]

Date:

(Insert name and address of Lessee)

Re: Equipment Lease Agreement, dated   , 20____ .

Lease Account Number:

Have you forgotten "our date"?

The one on which you promised to make regular payments on your account.

Of course, if you have put your remittance in the mail, please accept our thanks and disregard this reminder. But, if the date merely slipped your mind, won't you send us a check today? Payments made on time avoid additional charges and maintain a good credit record.

If there is some reason you cannot make this payment now, please come into our office or call us.

****

Have you changed your address?

If so, kindly fill in the information requested below. Then, enclose this notice in the envelope with your account statement and payment when mailing to us.

Name:

New Address:

City: State: Zip:

Phone: (   )   Account Number:

Your cooperation is appreciated.

Thank you.

By:

Title:

Form: c-06
Disk File Name: c-06.rtf

COLLECTION NOTIFICATION—FOLLOW-UP LESSEE NONPAYMENT

Form Purpose

A follow-up lessee lease payment default notification letter.

Executing Parties
The equipment lessor.

See:
Collection Notification—Initial Lessee Nonpayment, Form c-05
Collection Notification—Lawsuit, Form c-07
Collection Notification—Repossession, Form c-08

[Letterhead of Leasing Company]

(Insert name and address of Lessee)

Re: Equipment Lease Agreement, dated   , 20   .

Lease Account Number:

Dear

The delinquency on your account has become an extremely serious matter. As of today's date your account remains past due for its   payment of $, plus late charges of $. We very much want to work with you in this matter and understand that these situations do occur. However, you should also be aware that your obligation to us needs to be paid promptly.

If we do not receive your past due payments or work out alternate arrangements within seven days from the date of this letter, you leave us no alternative but to accelerate the entire balance owing under your lease, which totals $. Failure to pay that balance will result in the loss of the leased equipment and a subsequent costly legal action.

We would like to cooperate with you as much as much as we reasonably can, but our cooperation requires immediate attention. Please contact our office immediately upon receipt of this letter.

Sincerely,

Form: c-07
Disk File Name: c-07.rtf

Collection Notification—Lawsuit

Form Purpose

A follow-up leasing company notification letter of intent to file a lawsuit for payment default.

Executing Parties
The equipment lessor.

See:
Collection Notification—Initial Lessee Nonpayment, Form c-05
Collection Notification—Follow-up Lessee Nonpayment, Form c-06
Collection Notification—Repossession, Form c-08

[Letterhead of Leasing Company]

(Insert name and address of Lessee)

Re: Equipment Lease Agreement, dated   , 20___ .

Lease Account Number:

Dear

This letter is to inform you that we are about to file a lawsuit against you due to nonpayment on the above referenced lease. At this time your account balance is $____, plus accrued late charges.

If you wish to avoid this expensive court proceeding, we demand that you forward your check for this balance, or contact our office to make suitable payment arrangements, within the next ten days. The choice is yours. We wish to resolve this with you.

If no action is taken on your part, we will immediately begin to pursue all legal remedies available to us.

Very truly yours,

Form: c-08
Disk File Name: c-08.rtf

COLLECTION NOTIFICATION—REPOSSESSION

Form Purpose

A follow-up leasing company notification letter of intent to repossess leased equipment for payment default.

Executing Parties
The equipment lessor.

See:
Collection Notification—Initial Lessee Nonpayment, Form c-05
Collection Notification—Follow-up Lessee Nonpayment, Form c-06
Collection Notification—Lawsuit, Form c-07

[Letterhead of Leasing Company]

Date:

SENT CERTIFIED AND REGULAR MAIL

(Insert name and address of Lessee)

RE: Notice of Intention to Repossess Equipment

     Under Equipment Lease Agreement, Dated   .

     Lease Account No.:   .

Dear

As of today's date the above referenced lease is past due for $.

We must have the above account brought current immediately. In the event payment is not made within ten days from the date of this letter, it is the intention of the holder of the lease to institute legal action to repossess your leased equipment.

All payments referred to in this notice must be in the form of cash, cashier's check, certified check, or money order, and must be received at our office no later than _____, 20__.

If you wish to cure the default within ten days from the date of this letter you must pay the total amount due as stated above.

If payment is made after ten days from the date of this notice, you will have to pay, in addition to the regular monthly installments then due, all attorney's fees incurred.

Sincerely,

Form: c-09
Disk File Name: c-09.rtf

CERTIFIED CORPORATE GUARANTOR'S RESOLUTIONS

Form Purpose

Secretary's certificate incorporating corporate resolutions for an equipment lessee's guarantor. This form has been integrated with the short form net finance master lease agreement, Lease Agreement Form l-03.

Executing Parties
Corporate secretary, or assistant secretary, of the equipment lessee's guarantor.

See:
Lease Agreement, Form l-03

Form of Guarantor's Resolutions

Secretary's Certificate

I,   , the duly elected and qualified Secretary of   ,
a   corporation (the "Corporation"), hereby certify that set forth below is a true and complete copy of certain resolutions duly adopted by the Board of Directors of the Corporation, at a meeting duly held on   , at which a quorum was present and acting throughout, and such resolutions have not been amended or rescinded, are in full force and effect on the date hereof, and are the only resolutions adopted by said Board which relate to the matters referred to therein:

"RESOLVED, that the form, terms, and provisions of a proposed Guaranty (the "Guaranty") to be made and given by this Corporation to   or its   assignee or designee (collectively "Lessor") in order to induce Lessor to purchase and lease certain equipment to   , a corporation ("Lessee"), pursuant to the (proposed) Master Agreement to Lease Equipment between Lessee and Lessor (the "Agreement"), and proposed Schedule No.   between Lessee and Lessor (the "Schedule"), all as submitted to this meeting and filed with the records of this Corporation, be, and the same hereby are, approved in all respects; and that the   (officer) and   (officer) of this Corporation or any one of them be, and each such officer hereby is, authorized and directed to execute and deliver to Lessor the Guaranty, substantially in the form presented to this meeting, together with such changes, additions, and modifications as may be approved by any such officer, such approval to be conclusively evidenced by an authorized officer's execution of the Guaranty; and

RESOLVED, that the officers of this Corporation be, and each and any such officer hereby is, authorized and directed to execute and deliver all documents and to take or cause to be taken all other action, in the name and on behalf of this Corporation, as may be required by Lessor or otherwise be deemed by such officers or any of them necessary or desirable to fully effectuate the purposes and intent of, and consummate the transactions authorized by, the foregoing resolution and to comply with the terms and provisions of the Guaranty and, if required, the terms and provisions of the Schedule and the Agreement."

IN WITNESS WHEREOF, I have hereunto signed my name this   day of   , 20___.

Secretary

Form: c-10
Disk File Name: c-10.rtf

CERTIFIED CORPORATE RESOLUTIONS—LOAN/LEASE
(WITH INCUMBENCY CERTIFICATION)

Form Purpose

Certified corporate resolutions, with incumbency certification, authorizing the entering into of an equipment lease/loan agreement.

Executing Parties
Corporate secretary, or assistant secretary, of the equipment lessee/borrower.

Resolutions of Corporate Board

Authority to Procure Loans or Leases
(Certified Copy)

I HEREBY CERTIFY that I am the duly elected and qualified secretary, and the keeper of the records and corporate seal, of (insert name of corporation); that the following is a true and correct copy of resolutions duly adopted at a meeting of its Board of Directors held in accordance with its by-laws at its offices at
                          , on the   day of   , 20___ ,
and that the following resolutions are now in full force.

Resolutions

BE IT RESOLVED, that the (insert titles) of this corporation, or their/his/her successors in office, or any (insert number required to sign) of them be and they/he/she hereby are/is authorized for, on behalf of, and in the name of this corporation to:

(a) Negotiate and procure loans or leases from (insert name of lessor or lender) up to an amount not exceeding $ in the aggregate at any one time outstanding (*Author's Note* : If there is no limit, so indicate);

(b) Give security for any liabilities of this corporation to (insert name of lessor or lender) in connection therewith, including the pledge, sale, or assignment, or the granting of a lien, upon any personal property, tangible or intangible, of this corporation; and

(c) Execute in such form as may be required by (insert name of lessor or lender), all notes or lease agreements and other evidences of such loans or lease agreements, all instruments of pledge, assignment or lien, and that none of the same shall be valid unless signed or endorsed by the above-mentioned officers of this corporation; and

RESOLVED FURTHER, that this resolution shall continue in force, and (insert name of lessor or lender) may consider the holders of said offices and their signatures, respectively, to be and continue as set forth in the certificate of the secretary of this corporation accompanying a copy of this resolution shown delivered to (insert name of lessor or lender) or in any similar subsequent certificate, until notice to the contrary in writing is duly served on (insert name of lessor or lender).

I HEREBY FURTHER CERTIFY that the following named persons have been duly elected to the offices set opposite their respective names, that they continue to hold these offices at the present time, and that the signatures appearing hereon are the genuine, original signatures of each respectively (insert name of those with signing authority, such as):

President
Vice President
Secretary
Asst. Secretary
Director

IN WITNESS WHEREOF, I have hereunto affixed my name as secretary and have caused the corporate seal of said corporation to be hereto affixed this   day of   , 20___ .

(CORPORATE SEAL)

Secretary

I hereby certify that I am [a director] of said corporation and that the foregoing is a correct copy of resolutions passed as therein set forth, and that the same are now in full force.

(*Author's Note:* This should be an individual other than the individual who is the Secretary.)

By:

Title:

Form: c-11
Disk File Name: c-11.rtf

CERTIFIED CORPORATE RESOLUTIONS—LOAN (WITH INCUMBENCY CERTIFICATION)

Form Purpose

Certified corporate resolutions, with incumbency certification, authorizing the entering into of an equipment loan agreement.

Executing Parties
Corporate secretary, or assistant secretary, of the equipment borrower.

Certified Copy of Resolutions of Board of Directors of
(Insert name of corporation)

RESOLVED, that the Board of Directors of the Corporation hereby deems it to be in the best interest of the Corporation to borrow money from   ("Creditor") in the principal amount of $ (the "Indebtedness") and issue a note and enter into such other agreements as Creditor may require (collectively the "Agreement"), such Agreement being substantially in the form or forms submitted to the Directors of the Corporation and attached as Annex A to these Resolutions, which form(s) is (are) hereby approved; and it is

FURTHER RESOLVED, that the President, Vice President, Treasurer and/or of this Corporation be and any one of them hereby is authorized, directed, and empowered to execute and deliver the Agreement to Creditor; and it is

FURTHER RESOLVED, that the President, Vice President, Treasurer and/or of this Corporation be and any one of them hereby is authorized, directed, and empowered to execute, issue, and deliver to Creditor, for and on behalf of and in the name of the Corporation, the Corporation's note or notes evidencing the Indebtedness or any part therefore, at such rate(s) of interest and upon such other terms and conditions as are required by Creditor, and any and all other documents, and to do or cause to be done all such further acts and things as shall be deemed necessary, advisable, convenient, or proper in connection with the execution and delivery of any documents or instruments and in connection with or incidental to the carrying of these resolutions into effect, including, but not limited to, the execution, acknowledgment, and delivery of any and all instruments and documents which may reasonably be required by Creditor under or in connection with the Agreement, which acts and things heretofore done to effectuate the purpose or purposes of these resolutions are hereby in all respects ratified, confirmed, and approved as the act or acts of this Corporation; and it is

FURTHER RESOLVED, that the present and future officers of this Corporation are and shall be bound by these resolutions, as too shall this Corporation; and it is

FURTHER RESOLVED, that Creditor is hereby authorized to rely upon these resolutions and the Certificate of the Secretary or Assistant Secretary of this Corporation, and that these resolutions shall be in full force and effect and binding on this Corporation until they shall have been repealed and until written notice of such repeal shall have been delivered to and received by Creditor.

I, (insert name of Secretary), do hereby certify that I am the Secretary of this Corporation; that I am keeper of the corporate records and seal of said Corporation; that the foregoing is a true and correct copy of resolutions duly adopted at a meeting of the Board of Directors of the above-named Corporation duly called and held on (or, where permitted by law, by unanimous written consent of all Directors of the above-named Corporation dated   ); that a quorum was present and acted throughout the meeting; that such resolutions have not been rescinded, annulled, revoked, or modified and are still in full force and effect; that neither the said resolutions nor any action taken or to be taken pursuant thereto are or will be in contravention of any provision or provisions of the Certificate of Incorporation or By-Laws of such Corporation or any agreement, indenture, or other instrument to which such Corporation is a party; and that the Certificate of Incorporation of such Corporation, and all amendments thereto, do not contain any provisions requiring any vote or consent of shareholders of such Corporation to authorize any lease, indebtedness, assignment, or any creation of a security interest in all or any part of such Corporation's property, or any interest therein, or to authorize any other action taken or to be taken pursuant to such resolutions. The persons whose names, titles, and signatures appear on the Incumbency and Signature Schedule of the Corporation hereto attached as Annex B are duly elected, qualified, and acting officers of this Corporation and hold on the date hereof the offices set forth opposite their respective names.

IN WITNESS WHEREOF, I have hereunto set my hand and seal of such Corporation on this   day of   , 20   .

(CORPORATE SEAL)

By:

Secretary

Annex A

(Attach copy of loan agreement)

Annex B

Incumbency and Signature Schedule
of
(Insert name of corporation)

Name	*Title*	*Signature*
	President	
	Vice President	
	Treasurer	
	Secretary	

Form: c-12
Disk File Name: c-12.rtf

CERTIFIED CORPORATE RESOLUTIONS—LEASE (WITH INCUMBENCY CERTIFICATION—ALTERNATE FORM)

Form Purpose

Certified corporate resolutions, with incumbency certification, authorizing the entering into of an equipment lease agreement—Alternate Form.

Executing Parties
Corporate secretary, or assistant secretary, of the equipment lessee.

Secretary's Certificate
Corporate Resolutions

The undersigned,   , Secretary of (insert name of corporation), a (insert state of incorporation) corporation (the "Corporation"), does hereby certify:

1. That he/she is the duly elected, qualified, and acting Secretary of the Corporation and has the custody of the corporate records, minutes, and corporate seal.
2. That the following named person(s) has/have been properly designated, elected, and assigned to the office in such Corporation as indicated below; that such person(s) hold(s) such office at this time and that the specimen signature appearing beside the name of such officer is his/her true and correct signature.

Name	*Title*	*Specimen Signature*

3. That at a meeting of the Board of Directors of the Corporation, duly called, convened, and held on   , at which meeting a quorum was present and voted throughout, the following resolution(s) were duly adopted by said Board and said resolution(s) have not been amended, altered, or repealed, and remain in full force and effect on the date hereof:

RESOLVED, that this Corporation be and hereby is authorized to enter into an equipment lease with   for a period of   months and that (insert below name and/or titles of authorized individuals)

Name	*Title*

of this Corporation be authorized for and on behalf of this Corporation as its corporate act and deed to execute and deliver the lease and such ancillary and supporting documents and instruments as may be necessary or desirable and to do any and all things necessary or desirable to execute the full intent and purpose of this resolution.

4. That he/she is one of the duly authorized and proper officers of such Corporation to make certificates in its behalf and that he/she has caused this certificate to be executed and the seal of the Corporation to be hereunto appended this   day of   , 20___.

(CORPORATE SEAL)

Secretary

Form: c-13
Disk File Name: c-13.rtf

CERTIFIED CORPORATE RESOLUTIONS—LEASE (WITH CHAPTER, BY-LAWS, INCUMBENCY CERTIFICATION)

Form Purpose

Certified corporate resolutions, with charter, by-laws, and incumbency certification, authorizing the entering into of an equipment lease agreement.

Executing Parties
Corporate secretary, or assistant secretary, of the equipment lessee.

Certificate of Corporate Resolutions
Charter, By-Laws, and Incumbency
of
[Insert name of corporation]

I,   , Secretary of (insert name of corporation) hereby certify that:

     1. I am the duly elected and acting Secretary of (insert name of corporation), a corporation duly organized and existing in good standing under the laws of the State of   (insert jurisdiction of incorporation) (hereafter, the "Corporation").

     2. The resolutions set forth on Exhibit A, attached hereto, were duly adopted by the Board of Directors of the Corporation at a meeting duly called and held on   , at which meeting a quorum was present and acting throughout, or by the unanimous written consent of all directors, dated   .

     3. The resolutions set forth on Exhibit A, attached hereto, have not been amended, rescinded, or modified and are in full force and effect on the date hereof.

     4. Attached hereto as Exhibit B is a true, correct and complete copy of the Articles of Incorporation of the Corporation and any amendments thereto as in effect on the date hereof.

     5. Attached hereto as Exhibit C is a true, correct, and complete copy of the By-Laws of the Corporation and any amendments thereto as in effect on the date hereof.

     6. The following persons are the duly elected, qualified, and acting officers of the Corporation in the capacity set forth after their names, are the officers of the Corporation who have been authorized by the Corporation to generally act for and on behalf of the Corporation with respect to the transaction contemplated by these resolutions, and the signatures set forth after their names and titles are their true and genuine signatures.

Title	*Name*	*Signature*

     7. The undersigned further certifies that the following individuals are the directors of the Corporation and that each of the following individuals was duly elected as a director by proper corporate action and is eligible to serve and act as a director until the successor director has been duly elected and has qualified as such.

Name	*Signature*

WITNESS my signature under seal of the Corporation this   day of   , 20___.

(CORPORATE SEAL)

By:

Secretary

I, _____, hereby certify that:
    (a) I am the duly elected, qualified, and acting [President] of the Corporation; and
    (b) _____ is the duly elected, qualified, and acting Secretary of the Corporation, and
    (c) the signature of _____ set forth above is his/her true and genuine signature.

WITNESS my signature this _____ day of _____, 20___.

(CORPORATE SEAL)

By:

[President]

Form: c-14
Disk File Name: c-14.rtf

CERTIFIED CORPORATE RESOLUTION—SHORT FORM

Form Purpose

Certified corporate resolutions, short form, authorizing the entering into of an equipment lease agreement.

Executing Parties
Corporate secretary, or assistant secretary, of the equipment lessee.

Certified Copy of Resolution

This is to certify that a special meeting of the Board of Directors of (insert name of corporation), duly called and held on the   day of   , 20   , at the principal office of the corporation in (insert location where meeting held) at which a quorum was present, the following resolution was unanimously and duly adopted, as shown by the minute book of said corporation, to wit:

"WHEREAS, (insert name and title of individual(s) executing lease agreement) of this corporation has executed or is about to execute an equipment lease agreement with (insert here the name of the leasing company) and approve the terms thereof."

"NOW, THEREFORE, BE IT RESOLVED, that the execution and delivery of said equipment lease agreement for this corporation by its [insert name and title of the individual(s) that will sign or has signed the equipment lease agreement] be and the same are hereby authorized, approved and ratified as the act and deed of this corporation."

IN WITNESS WHEREOF, I have hereunto set my hand and the seal of this corporation this   day of , 20   .

(CORPORATE SEAL)

Corporate Secretary

Form: c-15
Disk File Name: c-15.rtf

CERTIFIED RESOLUTIONS—CORPORATE—INTEGRATED

Form Purpose

Secretary's certificate incorporating corporate resolutions for an equipment lessee. This form has been integrated with the short form net finance master lease agreement, Lease Agreement Form l-03.

Executing Parties
Corporate secretary, or assistant secretary, of the equipment lessee.

See:
Lease Agreement, Form l-03.

Form of Corporate Resolutions

Secretary's Certificate

I,   , the duly elected and qualified Secretary of   , a
corporation (the "Corporation"), hereby certify that set forth below is a true and complete copy of
certain resolutions duly adopted by the Board of Directors of the Corporation, at a meeting duly held
on   , at which a quorum was present and acting throughout, and
such resolutions have not been amended or rescinded, are in full force and effect on the date hereof, and are
the only resolutions adopted by said Board, which relate to the matters referred to therein:

RESOLVED, that the form, terms, and provisions of the proposed Master Agreement to Lease Equipment to
be entered into between this Corporation and   , Lessor (the "Agreement"), and proposed Schedule No.   between Lessee and Lessor (the "Schedule"), all as submitted to this meeting and filed with the records of this Corporation, be, and the same hereby are, approved in
all respects; and that the   (officer) and   (officer) of this Corporation
or any one of them be, and each such officer hereby is, authorized and directed to execute and deliver to
Lessor the Agreement and the Schedule, substantially in the forms presented to this meeting, together with
such changes, additions, and modifications as may be approved by any such officer, such approval to be conclusively evidenced by an authorized officer's execution thereof; and

RESOLVED, that the officers of this Corporation be, and each and any such officer hereby is, authorized and
directed to execute and deliver all documents and to take or cause to be taken all other action, in the name
and on behalf of this Corporation, as may be required by Lessor or otherwise be deemed by such officers or
any of them necessary or desirable to fully effectuate the purposes and intent of, and consummate the transactions authorized by, the foregoing resolution and to comply with the terms and provisions of the Schedule
and the Agreement.

IN WITNESS WHEREOF, I have hereunto signed my name this   day of   , 20___.

Secretary

Form: c-16
Disk File Name: c-16.rtf

CERTIFICATION OF INCUMBENCY

Form Purpose

A secretary's certificate verifying the incumbency of named corporate officers.

Executing Parties
Corporate secretary, or assistant secretary, of the equipment lessee.

See:
Incumbency Certificate, Form l-02e

Incumbency Certificate

Name of Corporation:

Date:

I certify that, as of the date written above, the following are the names and signatures of the duly elected officers of this Corporation:

Name: Signature: Title:

Name: Signature: Title:

Name: Signature: Title:

Name: Signature: Title:

Secretary _____

(CORPORATE SEAL)

Form: d-01
Disk File Name: d-01.rtf

DEFICIENCY AGREEMENT

Form Purpose

To protect a lessor from any loss incurred in the disposition of equipment. Although this form covers aircraft equipment, it may be easily modified to cover any type of equipment.

Executing Parties
The equipment lessor.
The deficiency loss guarantor.

Deficiency Agreement

This Agreement, made and executed as of the   day of   , by and between   , a   corporation, having its principal place of business at   ("Deficiency Guarantor"), and   , a corporation, having its principal place of business at   ("Lessor").

WITNESSETH:

WHEREAS, Lessor and Jet Aircraft Corporation, a   corporation, having a place of business at   ("JAC") contemplate executing a Purchase Agreement of even date herewith (the "Purchase Agreement") bearing JAC Document No.   , whereby Lessor will agree to purchase and JAC will agree to sell two JAC Model TC-60 jet aircraft (the "Aircraft"), together with installed Pratt & White Model RX– 20 jet engines; and

WHEREAS, Lessor and New Airlines, Inc., a   corporation, having its principal place of business at   ("NAI"), as lessee, contemplate executing a lease of even date herewith (the "Lease") whereby Lessor will agree to lease and NAI will agree to hire the Aircraft with such installed engines and in addition two spare Pratt & White Model RX–20 jet engines; and

WHEREAS, Lessor and Deficiency Guarantor desire to enter into this Agreement in order to partially protect Lessor against any loss which may arise out of the disposition of the Equipment (as hereinafter defined) after its delivery to Lessor.

NOW THEREFORE, in order to induce Lessor to enter into the Lease and in consideration of the mutual covenants contained herein, the parties hereto agree as follows:

1. For the purpose of this Agreement, the following terms shall have the following meanings:

1.1 "Equipment" shall mean all equipment subject to the Lease including the Aircraft, installed engines and spare engines, each Aircraft and engine hereinafter separately referred to as an "Item of Equipment."

1.2 "Original Cost" shall mean in respect of each Item of Equipment the purchase price of such Item of Equipment.

1.3 "Receipts" shall mean in respect of each Item of Equipment all amounts received by Lessor from the sale, lease (including the Lease, but excluding all tax benefits arising from ownership of the Equipment) or other disposition, insurance or other contracts relating to the Equipment, but not including any amounts received by Lessor upon the mortgage or other pledge of such Item of Equipment.

1.4 "Expenses" shall mean in respect of each Item of Equipment payments made by Lessor for reasonable attorneys' fees and other expenses incurred and paid by Lessor to third parties arising out of removing, storing and re-leasing, or selling such Equipment and in overhauling, repairing, or modifying such Equipment in condition for such release or sale or other disposition.

1.5 "Unamortized Cost" in respect of each Item of Equipment shall be the sum of (i) the Original Cost of such Equipment, together with interest thereon from the date such Equipment becomes subject to the Lease to the date as of which the computation is made, at the rate of six percent (6%) per annum, compounded quarterly, plus (ii) Expenses in respect of such Equipment, together with interest thereon from the date paid to the date as of which the computation is made, at the rate of six percent (6%) per annum, compounded quarterly, less (iii) Receipts in respect of such Equipment, together with interest thereon from the date received to the date as of which the computation is made, at the rate of six percent (6%) per annum, compounded quarterly.

1.6 "Divestiture" in respect of each Item of Equipment shall mean disposition by Lessor, whether voluntary or involuntary, of all of its right, title, and interest in such Equipment.

2. On the date of Divestiture in respect of each Item of Equipment, provided such Divestiture occurs within fifteen (15) years from the date such Equipment becomes subject to the Lease, Deficiency Guarantor agrees to pay to Lessor the lesser of (i) the Unamortized Cost of such Equipment at the date of Divestiture in respect of such Equipment, or (ii) twenty percent (20%) of the Unamortized Cost of such Equipment at the date of Divestiture in respect of such Equipment excluding from the calculation of Unamortized Cost any Receipts in respect of such Equipment which arise from such Divestiture.

3. Lessor shall have the right to terminate this Agreement at any time prior to Deficiency Guarantor making any payment hereunder. Upon any such termination, neither party shall have any further liability hereunder.

4. This Agreement shall be construed and performance thereof shall be determined according to the laws of the State of   . This Agreement shall not be varied in its terms by oral agreement or representation or otherwise than by an instrument in writing of even or subsequent date hereto, executed by both parties by their duly authorized representatives.

IN WITNESS WHEREOF, the parties have caused this Agreement to be executed as of the date first above written by their officers or agents thereunto duly authorized

, Deficiency Guarantor

By:

Title:

, Lessor

By:

Title:

Form: g-01
Disk File Name: g-01.rtf

Guaranty of Lease—Integrated

Form Purpose

A guaranty for the lessee's obligations under an equipment lease. This form is integrated with the short form net finance master lease agreement, Lease Agreement Form l-03.

Executing Parties
The equipment lease guarantor.

See:
Lease Agreement, Form l-03

Guaranty

GUARANTY, dated as of   , from   , a corporation ("Guarantor")
to   , a   corporation ("Lessor").

WHEREAS, Guarantor desires that   , a   corporation ("Lessee"), pursuant to a Master Agreement to Lease Equipment ("Master Agreement"), dated as of , 20___, between Lessor and Lessee, enter into one or more leases of personal property in the form of Schedule No(s).   , dated as of the date hereof (collectively the "Lease"); and

WHEREAS, as a condition to entering into the Lease, Lessor requires that all the obligations of Lessee under the Lease be guaranteed by Guarantor;

NOW, THEREFORE, in order to induce Lessor to enter into the Lease, Guarantor hereby agrees as follows:

1. Guarantor does hereby acknowledge that it is fully aware of the terms and conditions of the Lease and does hereby irrevocably and unconditionally guarantee, as primary obligor and not as a surety merely, without offset or deduction, the due and punctual payment when due by Lessee of all Rent (as defined in the Lease) which may from time to time become due and payable in accordance with the terms of the Lease and the performance by Lessee of all of its other obligations under the Lease (the payment of Rent and each other obligation of Lessee guaranteed hereby being hereinafter referred to as an "Obligation" and collectively as the "Obligations"). Guarantor does hereby agree that in the event that Lessee fails to perform any Obligation for any reason, Guarantor will perform or otherwise provide for and bring about promptly when due the performance of each such Obligation. This Guaranty of the Obligations shall constitute a guaranty of payment and performance and not of collection. Guarantor specifically agrees that it shall not be necessary or required, and that Guarantor shall not be entitled to require, that Lessor (a) file suit or proceed to obtain or assert a claim for personal judgment against Lessee or any other person for any Obligation, (b) make any effort at collection or other enforcement of any Obligation from or against Lessee or any other person, (c) foreclose against or seek to realize upon any security now or hereafter existing for any Obligation or upon any balance of any deposit account or credit on the books of Lessor or any other person in favor of Lessee or any other person, (d) exercise or assert any other right or remedy to which Lessor is or may be entitled in connection with any Obligation or any security or other guaranty therefore, or (e) assert or file any claim against the assets of Lessee or any other guarantor of other person liable for any Obligation, or any part thereof, before or as a condition of enforcing the liability of Guarantor under this Guaranty or requiring payment or performance of any Obligation by Guarantor hereunder, or at any time thereafter.

2. Guarantor waives notice of the acceptance of this Guaranty and of the performance or nonperformance by Lessee, presentment to or demand for payment or other performance from Lessee or any other person and notice of nonpayment or failure to perform on the part of Lessee. The obligations of Guarantor hereunder

shall be absolute and unconditional and shall remain in full force and effect and shall not be subject to any reduction, limitation, impairment, or termination for any reason.

3. No right, power, or remedy herein conferred upon or reserved to Lessor is intended to be exclusive of any other right, power, or remedy or remedies and each and every right, power, and remedy of Lessor pursuant to this Guaranty now or hereafter existing at law or in equity or by statute or otherwise shall, to the extent permitted by law, be cumulative and concurrent and shall be in addition to each other right, power, or remedy pursuant to this Guaranty, and the exercise by Lessor of any one or more of such rights, powers, or remedies shall not preclude the simultaneous or later exercise by Lessor of any or all such other rights, powers, or remedies.

4. No failure or delay by Lessor to insist upon the strict performance of any term, condition, covenant, or agreement of this Guaranty or to exercise any right, power, or remedy hereunder or consequent upon a breach hereof shall constitute a waiver of any such term, condition, covenant, agreement, right, power, or remedy or of any such breach, or preclude Lessor from exercising any such right, power, or remedy at any later time or times.

5. In case any one or more of the provisions contained in this Guaranty should be invalid, illegal, or unenforceable in any respect, the validity, legality, and enforceability of the remaining provisions contained herein shall not in any way be affected or impaired thereby.

6. This Guaranty (a) constitutes the entire agreement, and supersedes all prior agreements and understandings, both written and oral, among Lessee, Lessor, and Guarantor with respect to the subject matter hereof, (b) may be executed in several counterparts, each of which shall be deemed an original, but all of which together shall constitute one and the same instrument, and (c) shall be binding upon Guarantor and its successors and assigns and shall inure to the benefit of, and shall be enforceable by, Lessor and its successors and assigns.

7. Unless otherwise specifically provided herein, all notices, instructions, requests, and other communications required or permitted hereunder shall be in writing and shall become effective when received or if mailed when deposited in the United States mail, postage prepaid, registered or certified mail, return receipt requested. Notices shall be directed to Lessor at its address set forth in the Lease, and to Guarantor at its address set forth below, or at such other address as such party may from time to time furnish to the other by notice similarly given.

8. This Guaranty shall be governed by, and construed in accordance with, the laws of the State of   .

IN WITNESS WHEREOF, Guarantor has caused this Guaranty to be duly executed as of the date first hereinabove set forth.

                          , Guarantor

By:

Title:

Address:

Telephone:

Form: g-02
Disk File Name: g-02.rtf

GUARANTY OF LEASE—CORPORATE

Form Purpose

Corporate guaranty for lease obligations—short form.

Executing Parties
The equipment lease guarantor.

Corporate Guaranty

Lessee:

Lessor:

Date:

Lease No.:

In consideration of the entering into of the above lease by Lessor, with Lessee, at the request of the undersigned and in reliance on this guaranty, the undersigned (if more than one, then jointly and severally) as a direct and primary obligation, absolutely and unconditionally, guaranties to Lessor and any assignee of Lessor (either of whom are hereinafter called "Holder"), the prompt payment of all rent to be paid and the performance of all terms, conditions, covenants, and agreements of the Lease, irrespective of any invalidity or unenforceability thereof or the security thereof. The undersigned promises to pay all of the Holder's expenses, including reasonable attorney fees incurred by or in enforcing all obligations under the Lease or incurred by the Holder in connection with enforcing this guaranty. The undersigned waives notice of acceptance hereof, presentment, demand, protest, notice of protest, or of any defaults, and consents that Holder may without affecting the obligation hereunder, grant Lessee any extension or indulgence under the Lease, and may proceed directly against the undersigned without first proceeding against Lessee or liquidation or otherwise disposing of any security afforded Holder under the Lease.

This guaranty shall be binding upon the respective heirs, executors, administrators, successors and assigns of the undersigned. This guaranty shall be construed according to the laws of the State of the organization of Lessor.

Witness our hands and seals this   day of   , 20___.

                    , Guarantor

(CORPORATE SEAL)

By:

Title:

Form: g-03
Disk File Name: g-03.rtf

GUARANTY OF LEASE—INDIVIDUAL

Form Purpose

Individual guaranty for lease obligations—short form.

Executing Parties
The equipment lease guarantor.

___

Personal Guaranty

Lessee:

Lessor:

Lease No.:

Date:

In consideration of the making of the above Lease by Lessor with Lessee, the undersigned (if more than one, then "jointly and severally"), as a direct and primary obligation, absolutely and unconditionally guaranties to Lessor and any assignee of Lessor (either of whom are called "Holder"), the prompt payment of all Lease rent to be paid and the performance of all terms, conditions, covenants, and agreements of the Lease, irrespective of any invalidity or unenforceability thereof or security thereof. The undersigned promises to pay all of the Holder's expenses, including reasonable attorney fees, incurred by Holder in enforcing all obligations under the Lease or incurred by Holder in connection with enforcing this Guaranty. The undersigned waives notice of protest or of any defaults, and consents that Holder may, without affecting the obligation hereunder, grant Lessee any extension or indulgence under the Lease, and may proceed directly against the undersigned without first proceeding against Lessee or liquidation or otherwise disposing of any security afforded Holder under the Lease.

This Guaranty shall be binding upon the respective heirs, executors, administrators, successors and assigns of the undersigned. This Guaranty shall be construed according to the laws of the State of   .

Witness my/our hand and seal this   day of   , 20___.

(Insert name of individual), Individual Guarantor	(Insert name of individual), Individual Guarantor
(signature without title)	(signature without title)
Name:	Name:
Home Address:	Home Address:
City: State: Zip:	City: State: Zip:
Home Telephone No.:	Home Telephone No.:
Social Security No.:	Social Security No.:

Form: g-04
Disk File Name: g-04.rtf

GUARANTY—GENERAL OBLIGATION

Form Purpose

General credit extension guaranty. This form is set up for use by an individual or corporate guarantor.

Executing Parties
The credit guarantor.

Guaranty

WHEREAS, (insert name of company asking for a credit arrangement) (hereinafter referred to as "Obligor") desires to transact business and to make credit arrangements with (insert name of company for whose benefit this Guaranty is provided), with a principal place of business at   (hereinafter referred to as "Creditor"); and

WHEREAS, Creditor is unwilling to transact business with Obligor unless it receives the guaranty of the undersigned (hereinafter referred to as "Guarantor") covering the indebtedness of the Obligor to Creditor.

NOW, THEREFORE, in consideration of the premises and of other good and valuable consideration and in order to induce Creditor to transact business with Obligor by providing credit arrangements for the Obligor, Guarantor hereby guarantees, absolutely and unconditionally to Creditor the payment of all indebtedness of Obligor to Creditor of whatever nature, whether now existing or hereafter incurred, whether created directly or acquired by Creditor by assignment or otherwise, whether matured or unmatured and whether absolute or contingent.

The term "credit" is used throughout this guaranty in its broadest and most comprehensive sense and shall include, without limiting the generality of the foregoing (a) all sums of money which Creditor heretofore has advanced or loaned or hereafter advances or lends to Obligor, whether such sums have been or hereafter are drawn from or paid out by Creditor by or on promissory notes, leases or other evidences of indebtedness, made, endorsed, or guaranteed by Obligor, either alone or with others; (b) all other obligations of Obligor, alone or with others, absolute or contingent, joint or joint and several, arising from any other financial accommodation given or continued or from any guaranty, acceptance, or paper discounted, purchased, or held by Creditor or taken as security for any loan or advance of any sort whatever or arising in any other manner; (c) any indebtedness of Obligor to Creditor on account of collections or paper received for collection and all expenses, including attorney fees and costs of collection, incurred by Creditor in connection therewith, and (d) interest, if any, on the foregoing items.

The word "indebtedness" is used throughout this guaranty in its most comprehensive sense and includes any and all advances, leases, debts, obligations, and liabilities of Obligor heretofore, now, or hereafter made, incurred, or created, whether voluntary or involuntary and however arising, whether due or not due, absolute or contingent, liquidated or unliquidated, determined or undetermined, and whether Obligor may be liable individually or jointly with others, or whether recovery on such indebtedness may be or hereafter become otherwise unenforceable.

Guarantor agrees that, with or without notice or demand, Guarantor will reimburse Creditor, to the extent that such reimbursement is not made by Obligor, for all expense (including attorney fees) incurred by Creditor in collection from Obligor of any credit hereby guaranteed or in the enforcement of this guaranty.

Guarantor further agrees that Creditor may renew or extend any indebtedness of Obligor, or accept partial payment thereon, or settle, release, compound, or compromise any of the same or collect on or otherwise liquidate any claims held by Creditor in such manner as Creditor may deem advisable, without impairing the liability of Guarantor. Extensions of the times of payment, renewal of indebtedness, extensions of the times of performance of agreements, and any other compromises, adjustments, or indulgences may be granted to Obligor without notice to Guarantor. Creditor may also release, substitute, or modify any collateral securing any of the obligations of Obligor without the consent of Guarantor.

In the event of any default by Obligor on any indebtedness hereby guaranteed, Guarantor agrees, without Creditor being first required to liquidate any lien or any other form of security, instrument or note held by Creditor, to pay on demand (either oral or written) any and all sums due to Creditor from Obligor. This is a guaranty of payment and not of collection and Guarantor further waives any right to require that any action be brought against Obligor or any other person or to require that resort be first had to any security.

In any right of action which shall accrue to Creditor by reason of indebtedness of Obligor, Creditor at its election may proceed (1) against Guarantor together with the Obligor, (2) against Guarantor and the Obligor individually, or (3) against Guarantor only without having commenced any action against or having obtained any judgment against Obligor. If any claim against Guarantor is referred to an attorney for collection, then Guarantor shall pay such attorney's reasonable fee as determined by state law.

Guarantor hereby waives (a) notice of acceptance of this guaranty and of creations of Obligor to Creditor; (b) presentment and demand for payment of any indebtedness of Obligor; (c) protest, notice of protest, and notice of dishonor or default to Guarantor or to any other party with respect to any of the indebtedness of Obligor; (d) all other notices to which Guarantor might otherwise be entitled; (e) any demand for payment under this guaranty; (f) any defense arising by reason of any disability or other defense of Obligor or by reason of the cessation from any cause whatsoever of the liability of the Obligor; (g) any rights to extension, composition or otherwise under bankruptcy law, or under any state or other federal statute; (h) any rights which the Obligor may assert against Creditor under the Uniform Commercial Code of any state or the laws of the State of   regarding disposition of any collateral, including but not limited to the "commercial reasonableness" of such disposition; and (i) all exemptions and any rights under any homestead laws.

Until all credit and indebtedness hereby guaranteed have been paid in full, Guarantor shall have no right of subrogation and waives any benefit of and any right to participate in the collateral, if any there be.

Any indebtedness of Obligor now or hereafter held by Guarantor is hereby subordinated to the indebtedness of Obligor to Creditor; and such indebtedness of Obligor to Guarantor if Creditor so requests and upon default by Obligor to Creditor shall be collected, enforced, and received by Guarantor as trustee for Creditor and shall be paid over to Creditor on account of the indebtedness of Obligor to Creditor but without impairing or affecting in any manner the liability of Guarantor under the other provisions of this guaranty.

Guarantor declares to and covenants with Creditor, its successors, endorsees, and assigns, that Guarantor now has no defense whatever to any action, suit, or proceeding at law, or otherwise, that may be instituted on this guaranty.

Each reference herein to Creditor shall be deemed to include its successors and assigns, in whose favor the provisions of this guaranty shall also run. The term "Guarantor," as used in this guaranty, shall, if this instrument is signed by more than one party, mean the "Guarantor and each of them" and each undertaking herein contained shall be their joint and several undertaking, provided, however, that in the next succeeding paragraph hereof, the term "Guarantor" shall mean the "Guarantor or any of them." If any party hereto shall be a partnership, the agreements and obligations on the part of Guarantor herein contained shall remain in force and applicable notwithstanding any changes in the individuals composing the partnership and the term "Guarantor" shall include any altered or successive partnerships but the predecessor partnerships and their partners shall not thereby be released from any obligation or liability. The release of any party to this guaranty shall not release any of the others from the obligation of this guaranty.

No exercise, delay in exercising, or omission to exercise any of the rights, powers, remedies, and discretions of Creditor shall be deemed a waiver thereof, and every such right, power, remedy, and discretion may be exercised repeatedly. No notice to or demand on Guarantor shall be deemed to be a waiver of the obligation of Guarantor or of the right of Creditor to take further action without notice or demand as provided herein; nor in any event shall any modification or waiver of the provisions of this guaranty be effective unless in writing nor shall any such waiver be applicable except in the specific instance of which given. Failure of Creditor to insist upon strict performance or observance of any of the terms, provisions, and covenants of any indebtedness of Obligor or to exercise any right therein contained shall not be construed as a waiver or relinquishment for the future of any term, provision, or covenant thereof, but as to Guarantor, the same shall continue to remain in full force and effect. Receipt by Creditor of payment or payments with knowledge of the breach of any provision or any indebtedness of Obligor shall not, as to Guarantor, be deemed a waiver of such breach. All rights, powers, and remedies of Creditor hereunder and under any other agreement now or at any time hereafter in force between Creditor and Guarantor shall be cumulative and not alternative and shall be in addition to all rights, powers, and remedies given to Creditor by law.

This guaranty may be terminated by Guarantor serving written notice upon Creditor, but as to all indebtedness purchased or acquired and all obligations of the Obligor, contingent or absolute, incurred up to the time of the receipt of such notice or such subsequent effective date as may be stated therein. This guaranty shall be continuing and unconditional until the same are fully paid, performed, or discharged. This guaranty shall not be discharged or affected by the death of any party, but shall bind the respective heirs, executors, administrators, successors, and assigns of each party.

Dated this   day of   , 20____.

                                , Guarantor

By:

Address:

WITNESS:

By:

                                , Guarantor

                           (CORPORATE SEAL)

By:

Address:

WITNESS:

By:

Address:

Acknowledgments

[FOR INDIVIDUAL]

STATE OF   )

) ss:

COUNTY OF   )

On the   day of   , 20___, before me personally came
to me known to be the individual described in and who executed the foregoing instrument, and acknowledged that he/she executed the same.

My Commission Expires: Notary Public

[FOR CORPORATE EMPLOYEE]

STATE OF   )

) ss:

COUNTY OF   )

On the   day of   , 20___, before me personally came
to me known, who, being by me duly sworn, did depose and say that he/she resides at   ,
that he/she is the of   ,
the corporation described in and which executed the foregoing instrument; that he/she knows the seal of said
corporation; that the seal affixed to said instrument is such corporate seal; that it was so affixed by order of
the board of directors of said corporation; and that he signed his name thereto by like order.

My Commission Expires: Notary Public

Form: g-05
Disk File Name: g-05.rtf

GUARANTY—VENDOR

Form Purpose

An equipment vendor continuing guaranty to a leasing company purchasing, from time to time, equipment from the vendor that the vendor has put on leases with various customer/lessees. The guaranty provides the leasing company with recourse against the vendor in the event that any of these lessees default in the performance of their lease obligations. This form is set up for use by an individual or corporate guarantor.

Executing Parties
The equipment vendor/guarantor.

Continuing Guaranty

This Guaranty Agreement "Guaranty"), dated this   day of   , 20___, provided by (insert name of equipment vendor), a (insert jurisdiction of incorporation, if applicable) with a principal place of business at (insert address) to (insert name of beneficiary of this Guaranty).

1. In order to induce (insert name of leasing company purchasing equipment and leases from equipment vendor) (the "Creditor") to purchase leases and equipment subject to such leases (the "Equipment") from the undersigned and which the undersigned has entered into with various lessees (each a "Lessee" and collectively the "Lessees"), which shall be fair and sufficient consideration for the execution of this Guaranty, the undersigned, jointly and severally if more than one, hereby unconditionally, directly, and absolutely guarantees to Creditor, its successors and assigns, all present and future obligations (collectively the "Obligations") of Lessees to Creditor under any and all leases of the Equipment, as the same may from time to time be amended, modified, renewed, or replaced (each a "Lease" and collectively the "Leases"), including, without limitation (1) punctual payment (whether upon demand, at stated maturity, upon acceleration, or otherwise) of all sums of money, including renewals, extensions, and refinancings, matured and unmatured, now and hereafter owed to Creditor by each Lessee under each Lease, including, without limitation, rental installments, interest, fees, finance charges, late charges, attorney's fees, and costs and expenses of collection, irrespective of the manner in which such obligations shall arise, whether directly or indirectly, voluntarily or by operation of law; and (2) performance by each Lessee of all present and future covenants, conditions, agreements, and undertakings under each Lease. The undersigned hereby agrees to save harmless and indemnify Creditor from and against all obligations, demands, loss, or liability, by whomever asserted, suffered, incurred, or paid, arising out of or with respect to the Obligations.

2. This shall be a continuing guaranty, terminable only as hereinafter provided. No termination hereof shall be effected by the death, or dissolution, as the case may be, of any or all of the undersigned. No termination shall be effective except by notice sent by the undersigned by certified or registered mail naming a termination date effective not less than 90 days after the receipt of such notice by Creditor; or effective as to any of the undersigned who has not given such notice; or affect the guaranty of the undersigned with respect to the Obligations of any Lessee under any Lease executed prior to the effective date of termination.

3. The undersigned hereby waive(s) notice of acceptance of this Guaranty with regard to each of the Obligations that may now exist or may hereafter come into existence. The undersigned hereby waive(s) presentment, demand, diligence in the enforcement or collection of any of the Obligations, protest, and all notices of any kind whatsoever, including, without limitation, notice of default in the payment of any of the Obligations.

4. The undersigned hereby waive(s) notice of each and every one of the following acts, events, and/or conditions and agree(s) that the creation or existence of any such act, event, or condition or the performance thereof by Creditor (in any number of instances) shall in no way release or discharge any of the undersigned from liability hereunder, in whole or in part (a) the renewal, extension, modification, refinancing, or granting of any indulgence of any nature whatsoever with respect to any or all of the Obligations; (b) the addition of or partial or entire release of any guarantor, maker, surety, endorser, indemnitor, or other party or parties primarily or secondarily liable for the payment and/or performance of any of the Obligations; (c) the assumption of any of the Obligations by any other person, whether by assignment, sale, sublease, conveyance, or oth-

erwise; (d) the institution of any suit or the obtaining of any judgment against any Lessee, any guarantor, maker, surety, endorser, indemnitor, or other party primarily or secondarily liable for the payment and/or performance of any of the Obligations; (e) the sale, exchange, pledge, release, disposition, surrender, loss, destruction, damage to, or impairment of any collateral now or hereafter granted or received to secure any of the Obligations; (f) the obtention, perfection, continuation, amendment, release, waiver, or modification of any security interest or lien with respect to any of the Obligations or the settlement, subordination, compromise, or discharge of same; or (g) any other event, circumstance, or condition which might otherwise constitute a legal or equitable discharge of a surety or a guarantor. It is expressly agreed that Creditor shall have no obligation to obtain, perfect, or continue in effect any security interest or lien with respect to any of the Obligations and that the obligations of the undersigned hereunder shall in no way be diminished, impaired, affected, or released by Creditor's commission of or omission to do any of the above-described acts or by the invalidity, unenforceability, loss or change in priority of any security interest or lien with respect to any of the Obligations.

5. Any money or other property that Creditor may receive in respect of or as security for any of the Obligations of any Lessee from any source whatsoever may be applied to any of the Obligations of such Lessee, whether secured or unsecured, as Creditor shall determine in its sole discretion. Any property that Creditor may receive from a guarantor of any of the Obligations or with respect to which a guarantor of any of the Obligations has granted or shall grant to Creditor a lien or security interest shall secure the payment of the Obligations. In the event that Creditor shall be granted a security interest in or lien upon any real or personal property in respect of or as security for any of the Obligations, the same shall be for the sole and exclusive benefit of Creditor, and not for the benefit, whether direct or indirect, by subrogation or otherwise, of any of the undersigned, unless Creditor shall expressly and in writing grant subrogation or other rights to the undersigned. The undersigned shall not be subrogated to the rights of Creditor against any Lessee or against any property of any Lessee securing any of the Obligations, either in whole or in part, until such time as the Obligations of such Lessee have been paid in full and there is no amount owing to Creditor hereunder with respect to any of the Obligations.

6. If any of the Obligations of any Lessee are not duly paid or performed, as the case may be, all of the Obligations of such Lessee shall at Creditor's option be deemed to be forthwith due and payable for the purposes of this Guaranty and the liability of the undersigned hereunder. If the undersigned shall default in the payment or performance of any of its obligations to Creditor hereunder, all of the Obligations shall at Creditor's option be deemed to be forthwith due and payable for the purposes of this Guaranty and the liability of the undersigned hereunder.

7. The undersigned agree(s) that any suit, action, or proceeding instituted against it with respect to any of the Obligations of this Guaranty may be brought in any court of competent jurisdiction located in the State of (insert appropriate state). The undersigned, by the execution and delivery of this Guaranty, irrevocably waive(s) any objection and any right of immunity on the ground of venue, the convenience of the forum or the jurisdiction of such courts or from the execution of judgments resulting therefrom. The undersigned hereby irrevocably accept(s) and submit(s) to the jurisdiction of the aforesaid courts in any suit, action, or proceeding. The undersigned agree(s) to reimburse Creditor for all attorney fees and other expenses (including stamp taxes and other duties, taxes, filing and other fees and charges) paid or incurred in enforcing this Guaranty. The undersigned further agree(s) that any claim which any of the undersigned may now or hereafter have against Creditor, any Lessee, or any other person for any reason whatsoever shall not affect the obligations of any of the undersigned under this Guaranty and shall not be used or asserted against Creditor as a defense to the performance of said obligations or as a setoff, counterclaim, or deduction against any sums due hereunder. The performance and construction of this Guaranty shall be governed by the laws of the State of   . The use of the singular in this Guaranty shall also include the plural, and vice versa, and the use of any gender or the neuter shall also refer to the other gender or the neuter.

8. In the event that Creditor shall suffer, pay, or be responsible for the payment of any losses, costs, court costs, or attorney fees with respect to any of the Obligations and/or the collection thereof, the undersigned agree(s) to pay and do(es) hereby guarantee payment to Creditor of such amounts in full. Such expenses shall include all attorney fees incurred by Creditor before the filing of any action to enforce this Guaranty, and, in the event of such an action, shall include all attorney fees incurred by Creditor in connection with such action. No delay in making any demand hereunder shall prejudice the right of Creditor to enforce this Guaranty.

9. All of Creditor's rights hereunder shall inure to the benefit of Creditor, its successors and assigns, and all obligations, covenants, and agreements of the undersigned shall be binding upon the undersigned, jointly and severally if more than one, and their heirs, executors, successors and assigns. Creditor may, without notice to, or consent of, any of the undersigned, sell, assign, or transfer to any person or persons all or any part of the Obligations, and each such person or persons shall have the right to enforce this Guaranty as fully

as Creditor, provided that Creditor shall continue to have the unimpaired right to enforce this Guaranty as to so much of the Obligations that it has not sold, assigned, or transferred.

10. The liability of the undersigned shall not be conditioned upon or subject to a defense of reliance upon the guaranty of any other person. In any action to enforce any of the Obligations of this Guaranty, Creditor may, at its option, join the appropriate Lessee, any of the undersigned and any other guarantors in one action, or bring successive actions against any of them in such order as Creditor may elect, in its sole discretion.

11. No waiver by Creditor of any right or remedy shall be effective unless in writing nor, in any event, shall the same operate as a waiver of any other or future right or remedy that may accrue to Creditor. If any part of this Guaranty shall be adjudged invalid, then such partial invalidity shall not cause the remainder of this Guaranty to be or to become invalid, and if a provision hereof is held invalid in one or more of its applications, said provision shall remain in effect in valid applications that are severable from the invalid application or applications. Notwithstanding any partial or entire payment of all or any of the Obligations, this Guaranty shall remain in effect or be reinstated, as the case may be, as though such payment had never been made, with respect to any such payment which is rescinded or recovered from or restored or returned by Creditor under authority of any law, rule, regulation, order of court or governmental agency, whether arising out of any proceedings under the United States bankruptcy laws or otherwise.

12. The undersigned hereby authorize(s) any attorney at law to appear for (it, him/her) them (or any of them) before any court having jurisdiction and, after one or more declarations filed, confess judgment against (it, him/her) them (or any of them) as of any time after any of the Obligations are due (whether by demand, stated maturity, acceleration, or otherwise) for the unpaid balance of the Obligations declared due, together with interest, court costs, and reasonable attorney's fees.

13. The undersigned agree(s) to furnish to Creditor from time to time, upon Creditor's request, current written financial statements of the undersigned.

14. Any notice or other communication in connection with this Guaranty, if by registered or certified mail, shall be deemed to have been given when received by the party to whom directed, or, if by mail but not registered or certified, when deposited in the mail, postage prepaid, provided that any such notice or communication shall be addressed to a party as provided below (or as otherwise specified in writing by such party) (a) if to the undersigned, at the address(es) specified below and; (b) if to Creditor, at:

(insert address)

IN WITNESS WHEREOF, (each of) the undersigned, intending to be legally bound hereby and intending this to be a sealed instrument, has caused this Guaranty to be duly executed under seal the day and year first above written.

Individual Guarantors (*Author's Note:* Individual guarantors must sign without titles. Also, use street addresses, not P.O. boxes.)

        Individually   Home Address

        Individually   Home Address

Corporate Guarantors (*Author's Note:* Use street addresses, not P.O. boxes.)

(Insert name and address of corporation)

(CORPORATE SEAL)

By:

Attest Secretary

Name:

Title:

(CORPORATE SEAL)

By:

Attest Secretary

Name:

Title:

**Form: i-01
Disk File Name: i-01.rtf**

INSURANCE REQUEST LETTER TO LESSEE (FROM LESSOR)

Form Purpose

A leasing company form notification for advising lessees of lease insurance requirements.

Executing Parties
The equipment lessor.

[Letterhead of Leasing Company]

To: , Lessee

Lease No.:

Lease Agreement Date:

Equipment Description:

Important

In accordance with the terms of the above-referenced lease you have with our leasing company, the equipment must be insured. You are required to carry adequate fire, theft, and extended physical damage insurance coverage on the equipment in the amount of $, as well as third-party liability insurance coverage in the amount of $. Your insurance must also conform to any additional requirements set forth in Section   of the above-referenced lease.

Please furnish us with a loss payable endorsement, originated by your agent, showing the above-named lessor as loss payee and additional insured. Be sure to include your customer lease number so that insurance can be applied to the proper account. Normally, your agent will be able to handle this request without any additional charge to your firm.

In the event you have any questions, please feel free to notify this office. Your attention to this matter will be greatly appreciated.

(Insert name of leasing company)

By:

Title:

Form: i-02
Disk File Name: i-02.rtf

INSURANCE REQUEST TO INSURANCE COMPANY (FROM LESSEE)

Form Purpose

An equipment lessee form for requesting that its insurance company provide a certificate of insurance verifying insurance coverage on the specified leased equipment.

Executing Parties
The equipment lessee.

Request for Certificate of Insurance

Lessor: Telephone No.: (   )
Street Address:
City: State: Zip:
Lease No.:

Insurance Agent: Telephone No.: (   )
Street Address:
City: State: Zip:

Insurance Company:
Policy No.:

Gentlemen:

We wish to advise you that we have leased equipment from the above-referenced Lessor, and the conditions of the Lease require that we, as Lessee, carry insurance indemnifying Lessor against any loss, damage, or destruction of the equipment which is valued at $, as well as indemnifying Lessor from and against any claims or actions filed against Lessor as a result of personal injury, death, property damage, or commercial losses in any way claimed to have been sustained by or from the equipment.

A certificate certifying the following limits of liability are requested: $ Bodily Injury Liability, $ Property Damage Liability, and Physical Damage "All Risk" coverage.

The Lessor must be named as additional insured and loss payee under a Certificate of Insurance so indicating. The insurance policy must provide that it may not be canceled for a period of thirty (30) days following written notice by the insurance carrier to the Lessor, and this must be so acknowledged in the Certificate of Insurance.

(Insert name of equipment lessee)

By:

Title:

Date:

Form: i-03
Disk File Name: i-03.rtf

INSURANCE REQUIREMENT NOTICE—INTEGRATED (FROM LESSOR)

Form Purpose

Lessee insurance requirement letter. This form has been integrated with the short-form net finance master lease agreement, Lease Agreement Form l-03.

Executing Parties
The equipment lessor.
The equipment lessee.

See:
Lease Agreement, Form l-03

Lessee:

Address:

Attn.:

Re: Insurance Requirements

Gentlemen:

Reference is made to the proposed lease of equipment ("Lease") between   ("Lessor") and you ("Lessee").

We have set forth below the insurance requirements of Lessor to be complied with by you, as Lessee, in accordance with the Lease. The terms used in this letter shall have the same meanings as in the Lease, unless otherwise defined herein.

You, as Lessee, will as to all Units, at all times commencing when any risk shall pass to Lessor until the return of such Units to Lessor in accordance with the terms of the Lease, at your expense, cause to be carried and maintained with insurers of recognized responsibility acceptable to Lessor (a) property and casualty insurance in respect of such Units and (b) public liability insurance against claims for personal injury, death, or property damage resulting from such Units, including without limitation the ownership, possession, maintenance, use, and operation of such Units, in both cases in at least such amounts and against such risks as are customarily insured against by companies of recognized standing engaged in a business similar to that of Lessee with respect to similar equipment; provided, however, that in no event shall (i) the amount of such property and casualty insurance be less than $ and (ii) the amount of such public liability insurance be less than $ in respect of any one person or $ in respect of any one occurrence; and the benefits thereof shall be payable to Lessor and Lessee, as their respective interests may appear. Each such policy of insurance shall (i) require 30 days prior written notice to Lessor of a material change, cancellation, or nonrenewal, (ii) name Lessor as an additional named insured and loss payee, as its interest may appear, (iii) provide that all provisions of such policy, except the limits of liability, will operate in the same manner as if there were a separate policy governing such additional insured, (iv) include a waiver by the insurer of all claims for premiums, commissions, or similar costs or charges against Lessor, (v) provide that, in respect of the interests of Lessor, such insurance will not be invalidated by reason of any breach of representation or warranty made by Lessee to the insurer in connection with obtaining such policy of insurance or maintaining the same in full force and effect, and (vi) be primary without rights of contribution from any other insurance which Lessor or Lessee may have. Lessee shall deliver to Lessor a certificate of insurance or other evidence of insurance satisfactory to Lessor no later than the execution of the Lease.

Please acknowledge your receipt of the insurance requirements relating to the Units by executing and returning to the undersigned the extra copy of this letter enclosed.

, Lessor

By:

Title:

Received this   day of   , 20___ .

, Lessee

By:

Title:

Form: I-01
Disk File Name: I-01.rtf

LANDLORD WAIVER

Form Purpose

A real estate landlord's waiver to ensure that the landlord of the property on which leased equipment will be located will not exercise any claim against the equipment for obligations due from the lessee to the landlord.

Executing Parties
The real estate landlord.

Landlord's Waiver

The undersigned ("Landlord") is the owner and landlord of the premises at   ,
which Landlord has leased to (insert name of equipment lessee) ("Tenant"). In order to induce (insert name of leasing company) ("Lessor") to extend credit to Tenant, and intending to be legally bound hereby, agrees as follows:

1. The following equipment ("Collateral") in which Lessor is, or will be, the legal owner, will remain personal property and will not be deemed to be fixtures:

2. Lessor may enter the leased premises to remove the Collateral, or any part thereof, at any time in the exercise of its rights as the owner of the Collateral.
3. Landlord waives any right of distraint or execution against the Collateral or any claim to it so long as Lessor owns it.
4. Landlord agrees that it will notify:

   A. Lessor of the termination of the lease between Landlord and Tenant for any reason, and
   B. Any purchaser of the leased premises and any subsequent mortgagee or other encumbrance holder of the lease's premises of the existence of this waiver.

5. This waiver shall be binding upon the successors and transferees of Landlord, and shall inure to the benefit of the successors and assigns of Lessor.

Dated:

(Insert name of landlord), Landlord

By:

Title:

Form: I-02
Disk File Name: I-02.rtf

LEASE AGREEMENT—MASTER (HIGH TECH/GENERAL EQUIPMENT)

Form Purpose

Form of master net finance equipment lease, containing particular business and legal needs in large ticket lease transactions of computer equipment. This form is part of an integrated package, including all key closing documents. Although it contains certain specialized language for leasing computer equipment, it can be readily modified to cover any type of equipment. The master format allows future equipment to be easily added by means of a schedule.

Executing Parties
The equipment lessor.
The equipment lessee.

See:
Equipment Schedule, Form I-02a
Certificate of Acceptance, Form I-02b
Casualty Value Schedule, Form I-02c
Termination Value Schedule, Form I-02d
Incumbency Certificate, Form I-02e
Certified Resolutions, Form I-02f
Opinion of Counsel, Form I-02g
Prohibited Lender Assignee Schedule, Form I-02h

Master Lease of Computer Equipment

dated as of   ,
between
Lessor
and
Lessee

Master Lease of Computer Equipment

Section 1. Definitions
Section 2. Equipment Acquisition and Acceptance
Section 3. Lease Term
Section 4. Net Lease
Section 5. Rent and Usage
Section 6. Identification Marks
Section 7. General Tax Indemnification
Section 8. General Indemnification
Section 9. Payment for Casualty Occurrence
Section 10. Insurance
Section 11. Inspection
Section 12. Disclaimer of Warranties; Compliance with Laws and Rules; Maintenance; Additions
Section 13. Events of Default and Remedies
Section 14. Fair Market Value and Fair Market Rental
Section 15. Assignment, Possession, Liens, Sublease, and Merger
Section 16. Lessee Rights

Master Lease of Computer Equipment, dated as of   , 20___, between   , a
corporation, with a principal place of business located at   (the "Lessor," such
term to include, to the extent permitted hereunder, its successors and assigns), and   ,
a   corporation, with a principal place of business located at
(the "Lessee," such term to include, to the extent permitted hereun-
der, its successors and assigns).

The following terms shall have the respective meanings set forth below for all purposes of this Lease.

   1.1 "Acceptance Date" as to each Item of Equipment shall mean the date on which Lessee determines
that such Item of Equipment is acceptable for lease pursuant to the terms and conditions of this Lease, as
specified by Lessee in the applicable Certificate of Acceptance.
   1.2 "Appraiser" shall mean a qualified independent computer equipment appraiser selected in accordance with the provisions of Section 14 of this Lease.
   1.3 "Basic Lease Commencement Date" as to each Unit shall mean the date on which the Primary Term
shall begin, as specified in the applicable Equipment Schedule.
   1.4 "Basic Lease Rate Factor" as to each Unit shall mean the percentage rental set forth in the applicable Equipment Schedule.
   1.5 "Basic Rent" as to each Unit shall mean the rent due and payable on each Rent Date during the Primary Term, as specified in the applicable Equipment Schedule.
   1.6 "Business Day" shall mean a calendar day, excluding Saturdays, Sundays, and all days on which
banking institutions in [insert jurisdiction(s) of Lessee's and/or Lessor's principal place(s) of business] shall
be closed.
   1.7 "Casualty Occurrence" shall have the meaning set forth in Section 9 of this Lease.
   1.8 "Casualty Value" as to each Unit shall be the amount calculated in accordance with the Casualty
Value provisions of the applicable Equipment Schedule.
   1.9 "Certificate of Acceptance" shall mean a certificate substantially in the form attached as Annex A to
the form of Equipment Schedule attached hereto as Exhibit A.
   1.10 "Code" shall mean the United States Internal Revenue Code of 1986, as amended and in effect from
time to time [if appropriate, insert other relevant governing tax law].
   1.11 "Cut-Off Date" as to each Item of Equipment shall mean the date specified in the applicable Equipment Schedule after which Lessor shall not be obligated to purchase and lease such Item of Equipment to
Lessee in accordance with the terms and conditions of this Lease.

1.12 "Discount Rate" shall mean the per annum interest charge (calculated on the basis of a 360-day year and 30-day month) specified in the applicable Equipment Schedule.

1.13 "Equipment Schedule" shall mean each schedule, substantially in the form of Exhibit A attached hereto, which shall refer to this Lease and which shall become a part hereof as executed from time to time by the parties hereto, covering one or more Items of Equipment that may be leased by Lessee from Lessor hereunder.

1.14 "Event of Default" shall mean any of the events specified in Section 13.1 of this Lease.

1.15 "Fair Market Rental" shall mean the rental value of a Unit determined in accordance with the provisions of Section 14 of this Lease.

1.16 "Fair Market Value" shall mean the sale value of a Unit determined in accordance with the provisions of Section 14 of this Lease.

1.17 "Impositions" shall have the meaning set forth in Section 7.1 of this Lease.

1.18 "Interim Rent" as to each Unit shall mean the rent payable with respect to any Interim Term, as specified in the applicable Equipment Schedule.

1.19 "Interim Term" as to each Unit shall mean the period of time, if any, commencing on the Acceptance Date and ending on the day immediately preceding the Basic Lease Commencement Date.

1.20 "Item of Equipment" shall mean an item of electronic data processing equipment described in an Equipment Schedule. When an "Item of Equipment" becomes subject to this Lease it is thereafter for all purposes of this Lease referred to and defined as a "Unit."

1.21 "Invoice Purchase Price" as to each Unit shall mean the aggregate amount payable by the Lessor to Manufacturer for such Unit, as specified in one or more Manufacturer's invoices for such Unit.

1.22 "Lease" shall mean this Master Lease of Computer Equipment between Lessor and Lessee, including without limitation all Equipment Schedules and all exhibits to this Lease and to all Equipment Schedules. The words "herein," "hereof," "hereunder," and other words of similar import used in this Lease refer to this Lease as a whole and not to any particular Section, Subsection, or other portion of this Lease.

1.23 "Lessor's Cost" as to each Unit shall mean the Invoice Purchase Price plus additional costs and expenses that are assumed and subsequently paid by Lessor pursuant to the applicable Equipment Schedule.

1.24 "Lessor's Lien" shall have the meaning set forth in Section 15.3 of this Lease.

1.25 "Lien" shall have the meaning set forth in Section 15.3 of this Lease.

1.26 "Loss Payment Date" as to a Unit suffering a Casualty Occurrence shall mean the date on which Lessee shall be obligated to pay Lessor the Casualty Value in accordance with provisions of Section 9.1 of this Lease.

1.27 "Manufacturer" as to each Unit shall mean the manufacturer or vendor thereof specified by Lessee in the applicable Equipment Schedule.

1.28 "Overdue Rate" shall mean the per annum interest charge (calculated on the basis of a 360-day year and 30-day month) pursuant to Section 18 as specified in the applicable Equipment Schedule.

1.29 "Primary Term" as to each Unit shall mean that period of time commencing on, and including, the Basic Lease Commencement Date and ending that period of time thereafter, as designated in the applicable Equipment Schedule, unless earlier terminated pursuant to the provisions of this Lease.

1.30 "Purchase Documents" shall mean those documents relating to the purchase of a Unit or Units by Lessor from Manufacturer.

1.31 "Purchase Right" as to each Unit shall have the meaning specified in Section 16.1 of this Lease.

1.32 "Renewal Rent" as to each Unit shall mean the rent due and payable on each Rent Date during a Renewal Term, as specified in the applicable Equipment Schedule.

1.33 "Renewal Right" as to each Unit shall have the meaning specified in Section 16.2 of this Lease.

1.34 "Renewal Term" as to each Unit shall mean that aggregate period of time following the end of the Primary Term for which this Lease is extended.

1.35 "Rent" as to each Unit shall mean and include Basic Rent and any Interim Rent and Renewal Rent payable or to become payable, by Lessee to Lessor.

1.36 "Rent Date" as to each Unit shall mean each date during the Term on which Rent is due and payable, as specified in the applicable Equipment Schedule.

1.37 "Term" as to each Unit shall mean the Primary Term and any Interim Term and Renewal Term.

1.38 "Termination Right" as to each Unit shall have the meaning specified in Section 16.3 of this Lease.

1.39 "Termination Value" as to each Unit shall be the amount calculated in accordance with the Termination Value provisions of the applicable Equipment Schedule.

1.40 "Unit" shall mean an Item of Equipment, and any modifications thereof, or improvements or additions thereto, which is leased by Lessor to Lessee pursuant to the terms and provisions of this Lease.

1.41 "Upgrade Right" shall have all the meaning specified in Section 16.4 of this Lease.

2.1 Lease Commitment. In consideration of the Rent to be paid by Lessee and the other covenants contained in this Lease to be kept and performed by Lessee, Lessor hereby agrees to lease to Lessee each Item of Equipment described in each Equipment Schedule in accordance with the terms and conditions of this Lease.

2.2 Lessor Payment. Lessor shall purchase each Unit from Manufacturer solely for its own investment and account as a principal and not as a broker and promptly pay to Manufacturer the full Invoice Purchase Price for each Unit. In no event shall Lessor make such payment later than the earlier of the due date specified by Manufacturer or thirty (30) days after the Acceptance Date. Lessor shall, immediately upon making such payment, deliver to Lessee reasonably satisfactory evidence of such payment. If the full Invoice Purchase Price for any such Unit is not so paid to Manufacturer as provided in this Section 2.2, Lessee shall have the absolute right, in its discretion, (a) to make such payment to Manufacturer, whereupon all of Lessor's rights in, and title to, such Unit shall automatically vest in Lessee and (b) to withhold any Rent and/or (c) terminate this Lease as to such Unit. In addition to paying the Invoice Purchase Price for each Unit, Lessor shall also pay, no later than the due date, such other costs and expenses as to a Unit as specified as part of the Lessor's Cost for such Unit in the applicable Equipment Schedule.

2.3 Cut-Off Date. Lessor shall have no obligation to purchase and lease any Item of Equipment hereunder which has not been accepted by Lessee in accordance with the provisions of Section 2.5 on or before the Cut-Off Date.

2.4 Installation Location. Each Unit shall be installed at the address set forth in the applicable Equipment Schedule. Lessee may, without Lessor's consent, move any such Unit from such address, or any relocated address, to any other address in the United States of America, provided Lessee has notified Lessor in writing at least thirty (30) days prior to effecting any change of location.

2.5 Lessee Acceptance. Lessee shall acknowledge its acceptance of each Item of Equipment for lease hereunder by executing and delivering to Lessor a Certificate of Acceptance as to each such Item of Equipment, whereupon each such Item of Equipment shall become subject to this Lease as of the Acceptance Date.

3.1 Term of Lease. The Term of each Unit shall be as specified in the applicable Equipment Schedule.

3.2 Lease Termination. This Lease shall not be terminated by Lessor or Lessee with respect to any Unit for any reason whatsoever, except as expressly provided herein.

This Lease is a net lease and Lessee, subject to the provisions of Section 2.2, shall not be entitled to any abatement or reduction of Rent, or setoff against Rent, including without limitation abatements, reductions, or setoffs due or alleged to be due by reason of any past, present, or future claims of Lessee against Lessor under this Lease. Notwithstanding the foregoing, however, nothing shall preclude Lessee from otherwise enforcing any and all other rights it may have against Lessor under this Lease or otherwise.

5.1 Rent Payment. Lessee agrees to pay Lessor Rent for each Unit in accordance with the provisions of this Lease. The Rent for each Unit shall be paid on each Rent Date in the amount set forth in the applicable Equipment Schedule. In accordance with Section 23.1 hereof, if any date on which a Rent payment is due is not a Business Day, the Rent payment otherwise payable on such date shall be payable on the next succeeding Business Day.

5.2 Unlimited Usage. Lessor agrees that there shall be no limit on the number of hours for which any Unit may be used.

Lessee, at its own cost and expense, will cause each Unit to be legibly and permanently marked, in a reasonably prominent location, with the following legend evidencing the fact that such Unit is owned by Lessor and subject to this Lease:

"[Name and Address of Lessor], Owner, Lessor."

Lessee shall, upon at least thirty (30) Business Days prior written notice from Lessor, make such changes and/or additions in such markings specified by Lessor as may be required by law in order to protect Lessor's ownership of such Unit and the rights of Lessor under this Lease. Lessee will promptly replace or cause to be replaced any such markings that are removed, defaced, or destroyed.

7.1 General Tax Indemnity. All Rent and other payments required to be made by Lessee hereunder shall be net of any deductions, charges, costs, expenses, and Impositions with respect to collection or otherwise. Lessee agrees to pay, on written demand by Lessor specifying such Impositions in reasonable detail, any and all Impositions and shall keep and save harmless and indemnify Lessor from and against all such Impositions. "Impositions" shall mean the amount of any local, state, federal, or foreign taxes of any nature whatsoever, assessments, license fees, governmental charges, duties, fines, interest charges, or penalties with respect to any Unit or any part thereof, or with respect to the purchase, ownership, delivery, leasing, possession, use, or operation thereof. The term "Impositions" shall not include (a) federal, state, local, and foreign tax on, or measured by, the net income of Lessor; (b) any tax based on, or measured by, gross income or gross receipts of Lessor as a substitute for and not in addition to taxes based on net income of Lessor; (c) any tax imposed by Section 531 [Accumulated Earnings Tax] or Section 541 [Personal Holding Company Tax] of the Code; (d) taxes, fees, or other charges included in Lessor's Cost; (e) the aggregate of all franchise taxes or other similar taxes up to the amount in the aggregate of any such taxes which would be payable to the states and cities in which Lessor maintains or has maintained places of, or otherwise does, business during the Term of this Lease, except any such tax which is in substitution for or relieves Lessee from the payment of taxes which it would otherwise be obligated to pay or reimburse Lessor for as herein provided; (f) any fines or penalties that are imposed as a result of (A) the misconduct or negligence of Lessor or (B) a failure by Lessor to take reasonable action or to furnish reasonable cooperation to Lessee as a result of which Lessee is unable to diligently fulfill its obligations under this Section 7; (g) any claim made against Lessor for any Imposition that Lessee is obligated to pay hereunder with respect to which Lessor has not notified Lessee in writing pursuant to Section 7.2; (h) any tax imposed on the purchase of a Unit or Units from Manufacturer; and (i) any sales or use tax imposed upon (A) the voluntary transfer or other disposition by Lessor, or any assignee of Lessor, of all or any of the Units, or (B) another obtaining any interest in a Unit by, through, or under Lessor. In this regard it is understood that any transfer or disposition (A) that occurs in the Lessor's exercise of the remedies provided in Section 13.2 after an Event of Default has occurred and while the same is continuing or (B) of a unit which has suffered a Casualty Occurrence, shall not be deemed to be a voluntary transfer or disposition.

7.2 Claim Notification. If a claim is made against Lessor for any Imposition that Lessee is obligated to pay hereunder, Lessor shall promptly notify Lessee in writing.

7.3 Right to Contest. Lessee shall be under no obligation to pay any imposition so long as Lessee is contesting such Imposition in good faith. Lessor hereby agrees to fully cooperate with Lessee, including providing any information Lessee shall request, in connection with any such contest. So long as Lessee is so contesting such Imposition and no final, unreviewable judgment adverse to Lessee has been entered by a court of competent jurisdiction, Lessee shall not be in default hereunder with respect to the nonpayment of any such Imposition.

7.4 Lessor Payment Reimbursement. If any Imposition shall have been charged or levied against Lessor directly and paid by Lessor, Lessee shall reimburse Lessor on presentation of reasonably satisfactory evidence of payment; provided, however, Lessor has obtained Lessee's prior written approval for the payment thereof, which approval shall not be unreasonably withheld.

7.5 Lessor Refund Reimbursement. If Lessee has reimbursed Lessor for any Imposition pursuant to this Section 7 (or if Lessee has made a payment to the appropriate taxing authority for an Imposition which it is required to pay hereunder), Lessee may take such steps (in the name of Lessee or in the name of Lessor) as are necessary or appropriate to seek a refund of such Imposition, and Lessor shall fully cooperate with Lessee in seeking such refund. In the event of a refund of any Imposition for which Lessor has received a payment from Lessee, the amount of such refund shall be immediately paid over to or
retained by Lessee, as appropriate.

8.1 Conflict. The provisions of this Section 8 are in addition to, and not in limitation of, the provisions of Section 7 hereof; provided, however, that in the event of a conflict between the provisions of this Section 8 and the provisions of Section 7, the provisions of Section 7 shall be controlling.

8.2 General Indemnity. Lessee hereby agrees to assume liability for, and does hereby agreed to indemnify, protect, save, and keep Lessor harmless from and against any and all liabilities, obligations, losses, damages, penalties, claims, actions, suits, costs, expenses, or disbursements arising out of Lessee's actions that may be imposed on, incurred by, or asserted against Lessor relating to or arising out of this Lease or the manufacture, purchase, acceptance, rejection, return, lease, ownership, possession, use, condition, operation, or sale of each Unit or any accident in connection therewith. Lessor hereby expressly authorizes Lessee to contest, and agrees to cooperate fully with Lessee in contesting, in the name of Lessee or Lessor as Lessee shall deem appropriate for the benefit of Lessee, any such liability, obligation, penalty, or claim asserted against either Lessee or Lessor. Lessee shall not be required to indemnify Lessor except as specifically set forth in the preceding sentence, including without limitation as to (a) loss or liability in respect of any Unit arising from any act or event which occurs after such Unit has been returned to Lessor pursuant to the provisions of this Lease; (b) loss or liability resulting from the breach of any covenant, representation, or warranty made by

Lessor in this Lease or in any document relating to the transactions contemplated by this Lease; (c) loss or liability resulting from the negligence or misconduct of Lessor (including acts by employees, agents, or other representatives of Lessor); (d) any legal or accounting fees or other expense incurred by Lessor in connection with this Lease and the other documents referred to herein and any amendments or other modifications or additions to this Lease or such other documents; (e) any brokerage fees or similar fees or commissions incurred by Lessor in connection with any transactions contemplated hereby; or (f) any liability, obligation, penalty, or claim indemnified against herein so long as the validity or amount thereof is being contested by Lessee in good faith.

9.1 Casualty Occurrence. In the event that any Unit becomes damaged or otherwise inoperable so as to preclude its use for the purpose intended by Lessee, as determined by Lessee in good faith, or in the event any Unit is lost or stolen or is permanently returned by Lessee to Manufacturer pursuant to the Purchase Documents [*Author's Note:* This relates to when a Unit is permitted to be returned to the manufacturer because it is defective or otherwise fails to meet requirements set forth in the Purchase Documents], or for ninety (90) consecutive days or more is taken or requisitioned by condemnation or otherwise in such a manner as to result in Lessee's loss of possession or use, excluding any permitted sublease (any such occurrence being hereinafter referred to as a "Casualty Occurrence") during the Term of this Lease, Lessee shall promptly so notify Lessor. On the Rent Date next succeeding a Casualty Occurrence (the "Loss Payment Date"), Lessee shall pay to Lessor an amount equal to the Casualty Value of such Unit applicable on the date of such Casualty Occurrence. [*Author's Note:* Casualty Value payments vary in arrangement—each situation must be looked at independently.] Upon, but not prior to, the time when such payment is made by Lessee as to any Unit, Lessee's obligation to pay Rent for such Unit, including without limitation any Rent that would be attributable to any Rent payment period subsequent to the Loss Payment Date, shall cease and the Term of this Lease as to such Unit shall automatically terminate. Lessor hereby appoints Lessee as its sole agent to dispose of any Unit or any part thereof suffering a Casualty Occurrence in the best manner and at the best price obtainable, as determined by Lessee in its sole discretion, on an "as is, where is" basis. If Lessee shall have so paid the Casualty Value to Lessor, unless an Event of Default shall have occurred and be continuing, Lessee shall be entitled to the proceeds of such sale up to an amount equal to the sum of the Casualty Value of such Unit plus all costs, expenses, and damages incurred by Lessee in connection with such Casualty Occurrence and the disposition of such Unit. Lessor shall be entitled to any excess. In the case of the taking or requisition of any Unit by any governmental authority, any payments received from such governmental authority as compensation for such taking or requisition shall, if Lessee has therefore paid the Casualty Value, be immediately paid over to or retained by Lessee, as appropriate, up to an amount equal to the sum of the Casualty Value of such Unit plus all costs, expenses, and damages incurred by Lessee in connection with such Casualty Occurrence, and Lessor shall be entitled to any excess. Lessor shall have no duty to Lessee to pursue any claim against any governmental authority but Lessee may at its own cost and expense pursue the same on its own behalf and on behalf of Lessor, and Lessor shall cooperate fully in Lessee's pursuit of such claim.

9.2 Manufacturer Returned Unit. As to each Unit returned to Manufacturer in the manner described in the first sentence of Section 9.1, Lessee shall be entitled to immediately receive and retain all amounts paid or payable to Lessor by Manufacturer with respect to the return of such Unit, up to the Casualty Value paid by Lessee hereunder plus all cost, expenses, and damages incurred by Lessee in connection therewith. Any excess shall immediately be paid over to or retained by Lessor, as appropriate.

9.3. Return After Requisition. In the event of the taking or requisition for use by any governmental authority of any Unit during the Term of this Lease as to such Unit, unless such taking or requisition shall constitute a Casualty Occurrence, all of Lessee's obligations under this Lease with respect to such Unit shall continue to the same extent as if such taking or requisition had not occurred, except that if such Unit is returned by such governmental authority to Lessee at any time after the end of the Term of this Lease as to such Unit, anything to the contrary contained in this Lease notwithstanding, Lessee shall only be required to promptly return such Unit to Lessor upon such return by such governmental authority, rather than at the end of the Term of this Lease as to such Unit. All payments received by Lessor or Lessee from any governmental authority for the use during the Term of this Lease of such Unit as provided in this Section 9.3 shall be immediately paid over to or retained by Lessee, as appropriate, unless an Event of Default shall have occurred and be continuing, in which case the amount otherwise payable to Lessee may be retained by Lessor and applied to discharge the liabilities of Lessee under Section 13.

10.1 Insurance Maintenance. Lessee will, at all times during the Term of this Lease as to each Unit prior to the return of such Unit to Lessor in accordance with Section 17 of this Lease, at its own expense, cause to be carried and maintained with insurers of recognized responsibility (a) property and casualty insurance for such Unit and (b) public liability insurance against claims for personal injury, death, or property damage resulting from the ownership, possession, maintenance, use, or operation of such Unit, in both cases in at least such amounts and against such risks as are customarily insured against by Lessee on similar equipment; provided, however, that in no event shall (a) the amount of such property and casualty insurance be less than the Casualty Value of such Unit from time to time (except that Lessee may self-insure in an amount up to $) and (b) the amount of such public liability insurance be less than [$] as to any one occurrence. The benefits under such insurance shall be payable to Lessor and Lessee, as their respective interests may appear. Any policy of insurance carried in accordance with this Section 10 shall (a) require thirty (30) days prior written notice to Lessor of a material change or cancellation or nonrenewal; (b) name Lessor as additional insured, as its interest may appear, and provide that all provisions of such policy, except the limits of liability, will operate in the same manner as if there were a separate policy governing such additional insured; and (c) provide that, as to Lessor's interest, such insurance shall not be invalidated by reason of any breach of representation or violation of warranty made by Lessee to the insurer in connection with obtaining such policy of insurance or maintaining the same in full force and effect. Lessee shall deliver to Lessor together with each Certificate of Acceptance a copy of each such policy (or a certificate of insurance relating thereto) with respect to each Unit covered by such Certificate of Acceptance.

10.2 Insurance Proceeds. Any insurance proceeds resulting from insurance carried by Lessee or condemnation payments received by Lessor for each Unit suffering a Casualty Occurrence shall be deducted from the amounts payable by Lessee for a Casualty Occurrence pursuant to Section 9. If Lessor shall receive any such insurance proceeds or condemnation payments after Lessee shall have made payment to Section 9 without deduction for such insurance proceeds or such condemnation payments, Lessee shall immediately pay such insurance proceeds or condemnation payments to Lessee, up to the sum of the Casualty Value amount paid by Lessee plus all costs, expenses, and damages incurred by Lessee in connection with the disposition of each Unit suffering a Casualty Occurrence, unless an Event of Default shall have occurred and be continuing, in which case the amount otherwise payable to Lessee may be retained by Lessor and applied to discharge the liabilities of Lessee under Section 13. The balance of such insurance proceeds or condemnation payments shall be retained by Lessor. All property damage insurance proceeds received by Lessor or Lessee with respect to a damaged Unit not suffering a Casualty Occurrence shall be applied toward the payment, when due, of the cost of repairing such Unit. Any condemnation payments received with respect to a Unit not suffering a Casualty Occurrence shall be the property of Lessee unless an Event of Default shall have occurred and be continuing, in which case the amount otherwise payable to Lessee shall be paid to or retained by Lessor, as appropriate, and applied to discharge the liabilities of Lessee under Section 13.

Lessor shall have the right during the Term of this Lease upon not less than ten (10) Business Days prior written notice to Lessee to inspect any Unit for the purpose of confirming its existence, condition, and proper maintenance, at mutually agreeable times during Lessee's regular business hours. Notwithstanding the foregoing, Lessor may not inspect any Units if it would unreasonably interfere with Lessee's business operations, violate any applicable governmental security laws, regulations rules, or violate the reasonable security regulations or procedures of Lessee.

12.1 Warranty Disclaimer. LESSOR, NOT BEING THE MANUFACTURER OR VENDOR OF THE UNITS NOR A DEALER IN SIMILAR EQUIPMENT, MAKES NO REPRESENTATION OR WARRANTY, EXPRESS OR IMPLIED, AS TO ANY MATTER WHATSOEVER EXCEPT AS EXPRESSLY STATED HEREIN, INCLUDING WITHOUT LIMITATION THE DESIGN OR CONDITION OF THE UNITS, THEIR MERCHANTABILITY, DURABILITY, SUITABILITY OR FITNESS FOR ANY PARTICULAR PURPOSE, INFRINGEMENT, THE QUALITY OF THE MATERIAL OR WORKMANSHIP OF THE UNITS, OR THE CONFORMITY OF THE UNITS TO THE PROVISIONS OR SPECIFICATIONS OF ANY PURCHASE ORDER RELATING THERETO, AND LESSOR HEREBY SPECIFICALLY DISCLAIMS ANY AND ALL SUCH REPRESENTATIONS AND WARRANTIES. [*Author's Note:* This warranty disclaimer should be given to a lessor only when the lessor is not also the vendor], it being agreed that all such risks, as between Lessor and Lessee, are to be borne by Lessee; but Lessor hereby assigns and transfers to Lessee, and hereby irrevocably appoints and constitutes Lessee as its agent and attorney-in-fact to assert and enforce from time to time as Lessee shall deem appropriate, in the name of and for the account of Lessor and/or Lessee, as their respective interest may appear, at Lessee's sole cost and expense, whatever claims and rights Lessor may have as owner of each Unit against Manufacturer (or any subcontractor or supplier of Manufacturer) under the Purchase Documents or otherwise. Lessor agrees to cooperate fully at Lessee's request in Lessee's pursuit of any such claims or rights. If for any reason Lessee is prevented from asserting such claims or rights in the name of and for the account of Lessor and/or Lessee, as their respective interests may appear, Lessor will, at Lessee's expense, promptly upon Lessee's request enforce such claims or rights as directed from time to time by Lessee.

12.2 Compliance with Laws. Lessee agrees to use its best efforts to comply in all material respects with all applicable laws (including without limitation laws with respect to Lessee's use, maintenance, and operation of each Unit) of each jurisdiction in which a Unit is located; provided, however, Lessee shall not be required to comply with any such law so long as Lessee is, in good faith, contesting the validity or application of any such law. Lessor agrees to cooperate fully at Lessee's request in Lessee's contest of any such law or its applicability.

12.3 Maintenance. Lessee shall pay all costs, expenses, fees, and charges (other than those included in Lessor's Cost) incurred in connection with Lessee's use and operation of the Units. Subject to the provisions of Section 9, Lessee, at its own cost and expense, shall maintain, repair, and service, or cause to be maintained, repaired, and serviced, each Unit so as to keep it in the same operating condition and repair as it was when it first became subject to this Lease, ordinary wear and tear for the use intended by Lessee excepted, and within a reasonable period of time shall replace all parts of any Unit that may have become worn out, stolen, confiscated, destroyed, or otherwise rendered permanently unfit for use with appropriate replacement parts, which shall be free and clear from all Liens, other than any Lessor's Lien. Upon replacement, title to the replacement parts shall automatically be vested in Lessee.

12.4 Maintenance Agreement. Lessee shall, upon expiration of the Manufacturer's warranty period applicable to each Unit, enter into and maintain in force for the longest possible period obtainable by Lessee during the Term of this Lease as to such Unit a maintenance agreement (the "Maintenance Agreement") with Manufacturer or with another qualified party covering at least the prime shift maintenance of such Unit; provided, however, if Lessee is unable to obtain Maintenance Agreement reasonably satisfactory to it as to any Unit, Lessee shall have the right to maintain such Unit itself. Charges under the Maintenance Agreement and all other maintenance and service charges, including installation and dismantling charges, shall be borne by Lessee.

12.5 Additions. Lessee may, at its option and at its own cost and expense, make additions, modifications, and improvements to any Unit provided such additions, modifications, and improvements are readily removable without causing material damage to such Unit. All such additions, modifications, and improvements shall remain the property of Lessee and shall be removed by Lessee before such Unit is returned to Lessor. Lessee shall repair all damage to any such Unit resulting from such installation and removal. Lessee shall not, without the prior written consent of Lessor, which consent shall not be unreasonably withheld, alter any Unit, or affix or install any accessories or devices on any Unit, if the same shall materially impair the function or use of such Unit. Except to the extent otherwise provided in the first sentence of this Section 12.5, any and all other additions or modifications and improvements to any Lien (except for any Lessor's Lien), shall immediately be vested in Lessor, any and all warranties of Manufacturer with respect thereto shall thereupon automatically be assigned to Lessee and Lessor shall cooperate fully with Lessee in their enforcement the same extent and on the same basis as provided in Section 12.1.

13.1 Events of Default. During the Term of this Lease the occurrence of any of the following events shall constitute an "Event of Default":

    (a) Nonpayment of all or any part of the Rent provided for in Section 5 (except as otherwise expressly provided in Section 2.2), if such nonpayment shall continue for ten (10) Business Days after Lessee's receipt from Lessor of written notice of such nonpayment;

    (b) Lessee shall make or permit any unauthorized assignment or transfer of this Lease or any interest herein or any unauthorized transfer of the right to possession of any Unit;

    (c) Lessee shall fail or refuse to comply with any other covenant, agreement, term, or provision of this Lease required to be kept or performed by Lessee or to make reasonable provision for such compliance within thirty (30) days after Lessee's receipt from Lessor of a written demand for the performance thereof, which demand shall specify in reasonable detail the nonperformance;

    (d) Any proceedings shall be commenced by or against Lessee for any relief under any bankruptcy or insolvency law, or any law relating to the relief of debtors, readjustment of indebtedness, reorganization, arrangement, composition, or extension, and, unless such proceedings shall have been dismissed, nullified, stayed, or otherwise rendered ineffective (but then only so long as such stay shall continue in force or such ineffectiveness shall continue), all of the obligations of Lessee hereunder shall not have been and shall not continue to be duly assumed in writing, pursuant to a court order or decree, by a trustee or trustees or receiver or receivers appointed (whether or not subject to ratification) for Lessee or its property in connection with any such proceedings in such manner that such obligations shall have the same status as obligations incurred by such trustee or trustees or receiver or receivers, within thirty (30) days after such appointment, if any, or thirty (30) days after such proceedings shall have been commenced, whichever is earlier, or Lessee shall make a general assignment for the benefit of creditors or shall admit in writing its inability to pay its debts generally as they become due;

(e) any representation or warranty made by Lessee in this Lease, or in any certificate or other document delivered by Lessee pursuant hereto, shall be incorrect in any material respect as of the date made and shall remain uncorrected for a period of thirty (30) days after receipt by Lessee of written notice from Lessor specifying in reasonable detail the incorrect representation or warranty.

13.2 Remedies. Upon the occurrence of an Event of Default, and so long as such Event of Default shall be continuing, Lessor may, at its option, declare this Lease to be in default and may exercise in its sole discretion any one or more of the following remedies:

(a) proceed by appropriate court action or actions, either at law or in equity, to enforce performance by Lessee of the applicable covenants of this Lease or to recover damages for the breach thereof; or

(b) by notice in writing to Lessee terminate this Lease with respect to any or all of the Units, whereupon all rights of Lessee to the possession and use of such Unit or units shall absolutely cease and terminate as though this Lease had never been made, but Lessee shall remain liable as hereinafter provided; and thereupon Lessor may, by its agent or agents, enter upon the premises of Lessee or any other premises where any of such Units may be located and take possession of all or any of such Units and thenceforth hold, possess, operate, sell, lease, and enjoy such Unit or Units free from any right of Lessee to use such Unit or Units for any purpose whatsoever and without any duty to account to Lessee for any action or inaction or for any proceeds arising therefrom, but Lessor shall, nevertheless, have a right to recover from Lessee any and all amounts that under the provisions of this Lease and any applicable Equipment Schedule may then be due or which may have accrued to the date of such termination (computing the Rent for any number of days less than a full Rent payment period by multiplying the Rent for such full Rent payment period by a fraction the numerator of which is such number of days and the denominator of which is the total number of days in the full Rent payment period) and also to recover from Lessee as damages for loss of the bargain and not as a penalty, whichever of the following sums, with respect to each such Unit, Lessor, in its sole discretion, shall specify by written notice to Lessee: (a) an amount equal to the excess, if any, computed as of the Rent Date immediately succeeding the date of the Event of Default, of the Casualty Value for such Unit over the present value of the Fair Market Rental of such Unit for the remainder of the Term of this Lease following such Rent Date, such present value to be computed in each case using the Discount Rate specified in the applicable Equipment Schedule [*Author's Note:* This is for an "in advance" rental structure]; or (b) an amount equal to the excess, if any, computed as of the Rent Date immediately succeeding the date of the Event of Default, of the Casualty Value for such Unit over the Fair Market Value of such Unit [*Author's Note:* This is for an "in advance" rental structure]; and any reasonable costs and expenses (including legal and accounting fees) incurred in connection with the recovery, repair, repainting, return, and remarketing of such Unit or other exercise of Lessor's remedies hereunder.

The remedies in this Lease provided in favor of Lessor shall not be deemed exclusive, but shall be cumulative and shall be in addition to all other remedies existing in its favor at law or in equity.

Lessor shall use its best efforts to mitigate any damages suffered by it. IN NO EVENT SHALL LESSEE BE LIABLE FOR ANY INDIRECT, SPECIAL, OR CONSEQUENTIAL DAMAGES OF ANY KIND UNDER THE LEASE.

"Fair Market Value" and "Fair Market Rental," as to each Unit for all purposes in connection with this Lease, shall have the respective meanings and shall be determined in accordance with the procedure set forth in this Section 14. Fair Market Value and Fair Market Rental shall be determined on the basis of, and be equal in amount to, the value which would obtain in an arm's-length transaction between an informed and willing buyer-user (or lessee, if determining Fair Market Rental), other than a lessee currently in possession or a used equipment dealer, under no compulsion to buy (or lease), and an informed and willing seller (or lessor, if determining Fair Market Rental) under no compulsion to sell (or lease), and, in such determination, costs of removal from the location of current use shall not be a deduction from such value.

In the event that a determination of Fair Market Value or Fair Market Rental of a Unit shall be made under any provision of this Lease, the party requesting the determination shall deliver a written notice to the other party so indicating and appointing an Appraiser selected by the requesting party to determine the Fair

Market Value or Fair Market Rental. Within fifteen (15) days after the receipt of such written notice the party receiving such notice shall deliver to the requesting party a written notice appointing an Appraiser of its selection to make such determination. The two Appraisers appointed in such written notices shall meet promptly to determine the Fair Market Value or Fair Market Rental of such Unit as of the applicable date. If within thirty (30) days after the initial written notice the two Appraisers so appointed by Lessor and Lessee shall be unable to agree upon the Fair Market Value or the Fair Market Rental of such Unit, whichever is applicable, such Appraisers shall within five (5) days thereafter appoint a third Appraiser. The decision of the three Appraisers so appointed shall be given within a period of ten (10) days after the appointment of such third Appraiser. Any decision in which any two Appraisers so appointed and acting hereunder concur shall in all cases be binding and conclusive upon Lessor and Lessee. The fees and expenses of the Appraisers shall be borne equally by Lessee and Lessor, unless the Lease shall have been terminated pursuant to Section 13 hereof, in which case Lessee shall pay all such fees and expenses.

15.1 Lessor Assignment. Lessor agrees that it will not assign all or any portion of its rights under, or interests in, this Lease or any of the Units unless such assignment is made pursuant to a security agreement relating to any borrowing by Lessor from one or more institutional lenders. Notwithstanding the foregoing, Lessor agrees that it will not make any such assignment to any entities listed on an Annex to any Equipment Schedule. Lessor agrees that if such a security interest in any Unit is granted, the security agreement covering such Unit shall expressly provide that the rights and interests of Lessee in and to such Unit as provided in this Lease shall remain paramount so long as no Event of Default shall have occurred and be continuing. Lessor shall give Lessee prompt written notice of any such assignment by Lessor. All the rights of Lessor hereunder (including without limitation the right to receive Rent payable under this Lease) shall inure to the benefit of Lessor's permitted assigns to the extent of such assignment. Any payment of Rent or other payment by Lessee to such assignee shall be full satisfaction of Lessee's obligation to make such payment under this Lease and Lessor hereby indemnifies Lessee against any damages, claims, costs, or expenses incurred by Lessee in connection therewith, but Lessee shall be under no obligation to make any payment to any such assignee until Lessor shall give Lessee written notice to make such payment to such assignee. Notwithstanding anything to the contrary herein, any permitted assignee of Lessor can declare an Event of Default hereunder only with respect to one or more Units subject to such assignee's security interest.

15.2 Lessee Possession and Assignment. So long as an Event of Default under this Lease shall not have occurred and be continuing, Lessee shall be entitled to the quiet enjoyment and peaceful possession and use of the Units in accordance with and subject to all the terms and conditions of this Lease, but without the prior written consent of Lessor, which consent shall not be unreasonably withheld, Lessee shall not, except as otherwise permitted herein, lease, assign, or transfer its leasehold interest in any or all of the Units.

15.3 Liens. Except as otherwise provided herein, Lessee, at its own expense, shall promptly pay or discharge any and all sums claimed by, or liabilities in favor of, any person that, if unpaid, would become a mortgage, lien, charge, security interest, or other encumbrance (any of the foregoing being herein referred to as a "Lien"), other than a Lien by, through, or under Lessor on or with respect to any Unit, including any accession thereto, or the interest of Lessor or Lessee therein, which shall include without limitation any Lien resulting from a breach of Lessor's covenant in Section 2.2 or resulting from claims against Lessor not related to the ownership or leasing of any Unit (any of the foregoing being herein referred to as a "Lessor's Lien"), and shall promptly discharge any such Lien that arises. Lessee shall not be required to pay or discharge any such Lien so long as the validity thereof is being contested in good faith. The existence of any Lessor's Lien or any Lien for taxes, assessments, or governmental charges, or levies (in each case so long as not due and delinquent), or inchoate materialmen's, mechanics', workmen's, repairmen's, employees' or other like Liens arising in the ordinary course of business and in each case not delinquent shall not constitute a breach of this covenant.

15.4 Lessee Sublease. So long as no Event of Default under this Lease shall have occurred and be continuing, Lessee shall be entitled without Lessor's consent to sublease any or all of the Units, or any part thereof, to, or permit their use by, any person or entity, including without limitation any subsidiary, affiliate, or parent corporation of Lessee, incorporated in the United States of America or any state thereof, but in all cases only upon and subject to all the terms and conditions of this Lease. No such sublease or other assignment of use by Lessee shall relieve Lessee of its obligations hereunder.

15.5 Merger or Consolidation. Notwithstanding anything herein to the contrary, Lessee may assign or transfer this Lease and its leasehold interest in the Units to any corporation incorporated under the laws of any state of the United States of America into or with which Lessee shall have merged or consolidated or which shall have acquired all or substantially all of the property of Lessee, provided that such assignee or transferee will not, upon the effectiveness of such merger, consolidation, or acquisition and the assignment or transfer of this Lease to it, be in default under any provision of this Lease.

16.1 Purchase Right. Lessee shall have the right to purchase any Units provided in the applicable Equipment Schedule.

16.2 Renewal Right. Lessee shall have the right to renew this Lease as to any Unit as provided in the applicable Equipment Schedule.

16.3 Termination Right. Lessee shall have the right to terminate this Lease as to any Unit as provided in the applicable Equipment Schedule.

16.4 Upgrade Right. Lessee shall have the right to upgrade any Unit as provided in the applicable Equipment Schedule.

As soon as practicable on or after the expiration of the Term of this Lease as to each Unit, Lessee shall prepare the Unit for return to Lessor and deliver possession of such Unit to Lessor at the location of such Unit on the final day of the Term of this Lease. The Units shall be returned in the condition in which they are required to be maintained by Lessee under Section 12.3.

Anything herein to the contrary notwithstanding, any nonpayment of Rent or any other payment obligation with respect to any Unit after the due date shall result in the obligation on the part of Lessee promptly to pay with respect to such Unit, to the extent legally enforceable, interest on such Rent or other payment obligation for the period of time during which it is overdue at the Overdue Rate as specified in the applicable Equipment Schedule, or such lesser amount as may be legally enforceable.

Lessor agrees that it will not, without first obtaining Lessee's written consent, disclose to any person, firm, or enterprise, or use for its benefit, any information not generally available to the public relating to Lessee's business, including without limitation any pricing methods, processes, financial data, lists, apparatus, statistics, program, research, development, or related information concerning past, present, or future business activities of Lessee.

Neither Lessor nor Lessee shall use the name of the other in publicity releases or advertising without securing the prior written consent of the other.

Each of Lessor and Lessee represents and warrants to the other that:

(a) It is a corporation duly organized, validly existing, and in good standing under the laws of the jurisdiction of its incorporation. It has full power and authority to carry on its business presently conducted, to own or hold under lease its properties, and to enter into and perform its obligations under this Lease; and it is duly qualified to do business as a foreign corporation and is in good standing in each jurisdiction in which the location of any Unit requires such qualification.

(b) Its execution, delivery, and performance of this Lease have been duly authorized by all necessary corporate action on its part, do not contravene its corporate charter or by-laws or any law, governmental rule, or regulation, or any order, writ, injunction, decree, judgment, award, determination, direction, or demand (collectively "Order") of which it is aware binding on it or its properties and do not and will not contravene the provisions of, or constitute a default under, or result in the creation of any Lien upon any Unit under, any material indenture, mortgage, contract, or other instrument to which it is a party or by which it or its property is bound.

(c) No consent or approval of, giving notice to, registration with, or taking of any other action by, any [state/province—as appropriate], federal or other governmental commission, agency, or regulatory authority required for the performance by it of the transactions contemplated by this Lease, or if any such approval, registration, or giving of notice is required it has been obtained, so registered, or given, as the case may be.

(d) This Lease has been duly entered into and delivered by it and constitutes a legal, valid, and binding agreement of it enforceable against it in accordance with its terms, except as limited by (i) any bankruptcy, insolvency, reorganization, or other similar laws of general application affecting the enforcement of creditors' or lessors' rights generally, (ii) emergency powers lawfully conferred upon any governmental agency, and (iii) laws or judicial decisions limiting the right to specific performance or other equitable remedies.

(e) To the best of its knowledge there are no actions, suits, or proceedings pending or threatened against or affecting it or any of its property in any court or before any arbitrator or before or by any federal, state, municipal, or other governmental department, commission, board, bureau, agency, or instrumentality, domestic or foreign (collectively "Governmental Body"), except actions, suits, or proceedings of the character normally incident to the kind of business conducted by it as to which any adverse determination in excess of any accruals to reflect potential liability would not materially adversely affect its business, assets, operations, or condition, financial or otherwise, taken as a whole, or materially adversely affect its ability to perform its obligations under this Lease, and it is not in material default with respect to any material Order of any court, arbitrator, or Governmental Body.

(f) As to Lessee only, its consolidated balance sheet as of   , and its related consolidated statements of income, retained earnings and changes in financial position for the two years then ended, heretofore delivered to Lessor, fairly present its consolidated financial position as of such date and its consolidated results of operations and consolidated changes in financial position for the two years then ended, all in conformity with general accepted accounting principles consistently applied during the periods. Since the date of such balance sheet there has not been any material adverse change in its business, assets, liabilities, results of operations, or condition, financial or otherwise.

(g) It is not a party to any agreement or instrument or subject to any charter or other corporate restriction that, so far as it is now aware, materially adversely affects or will, so far as it can now foresee, materially adversely affect, its business, operations, or properties or its ability to perform its obligations under this Lease.

(h) To the best of its knowledge it has filed all required tax returns in all jurisdictions in which such returns were required to be filed and has paid, or made provision for, all material taxes shown to be due and payable on such returns and all other material taxes and assessments that are payable by it, except for any taxes and assessments of which the amount, applicability, or validity is currently being contested in good faith and as to which any adverse determination in excess of any accruals to reflect potential liability would not materially adversely affect its ability to perform its obligations under this Lease.

During the term of this Lease, Lessee agrees to provide Lessor with its consolidated quarterly and annual financial statements promptly as they become available and such other financial information as may be provided to Lessee's shareholders from time to time.

23.1 Postponement of Payment Date. If any date on which a Rent or other payment is due and payable is not a Business Day, the payment otherwise payable on such date shall be due and payable on the next succeeding Business Day.

23.2 Payment Address. All Rent and other payments required to be made by Lessee to Lessor shall be made to Lessor at the address of Lessor set forth in Section 24 or at such other address as may be specified in writing by Lessor at least thirty (30) Business Days prior to the date such notice is intended to become effective.

23.3 Method of Payment. All Rent and other payments under this Lease shall be made in lawful money of the United States of America.

Any notice or document or payment to be delivered hereunder to any of the persons designated below, except as otherwise expressly provided herein, shall be deemed to have been properly delivered if delivered personally or deposited with the United States Postal Service, registered or certified mail, return receipt requested, postage prepaid, to the following respective addresses:

If to Lessor:

Attn.:

If to Lessee:

Attn.:

or such other address as may be furnished from time to time by any of the parties hereto upon at least thirty (30) days prior written notice.

It is expressly understood and agreed by and between the parties hereto that this instrument constitutes a lease of the Units, and nothing herein shall be construed as conveying to Lessee any right, title, or interest in the Units except as a lessee only. Neither the execution nor the filing of any financing statement with respect to any of the Units or the execution or filing of any financing statement with respect to this Lease or the recording hereof shall in any manner imply that the relationship between Lessor and Lessee is anything other than that of lessor and lessee. Any such filing of financing statements or recordation of this Lease is solely to protect the interests of Lessor and Lessee in the event of any unwarranted assertions by any person not a party to this Lease transaction.

26.1 Severability. Any provision of this Lease that is prohibited or unenforceable by any applicable law of any jurisdiction shall as to such jurisdiction be ineffective to the extent of such prohibition or unenforceability without invalidating the remaining provisions hereof, and any such prohibition or unenforceability in any jurisdiction shall not invalidate or render unenforceable such provision in any other jurisdiction.

26.2 Complete Statement of Rights. This Lease exclusively and completely states the rights of Lessor and Lessee with respect to the leasing of the Units and supersedes all other agreements, oral or written, with respect thereto.

26.3 Section Headings. All Section headings are inserted for convenience only and shall not affect any construction or interpretation of this Lease.

The terms and provisions of this Lease and all rights and obligations hereunder shall be governed in all respects by the laws of [   ].

Each of Lessor and Lessee agrees that at any time and from time to time, after the execution and delivery of this Lease, it shall, upon request of the other party, promptly execute and deliver such further documents and do such further acts and things the requesting party may reasonably request in order fully to effectuate the purposes of this Lease.

Any modification or waiver of any provision of this Lease, or any consent to any departure by Lessee or Lessor, as the case may be, therefrom, shall not be effective in any event unless the same is in writing and signed by the party to be charged, and then such modification, waiver, or consent shall be effective only in the specific instance and for the specific purpose given.

This Lease shall be binding upon and shall inure to the benefit of the respective successors and permitted assigns of Lessee and Lessor.

This Lease may be executed in any number of counterparts, each of which shall constitute an original and which taken together shall constitute one and the same Lease.

IN WITNESS WHEREOF, the parties, pursuant to due authority, have caused this Lease to be signed in their respective names by duly authorized officers or representatives as of the date first above written.

                                        as Lessor

By:

Title:

                                        as Lessee

By:

Title:

Form: I-02a
Disk File Name: I-02a.rtf

EQUIPMENT SCHEDULE

Form Purpose

Form of master net finance equipment lease schedule. This form is integrated with a master lease agreement, Lease Agreement Form I-02.

Executing Parties
The equipment lessor.
The equipment lessee.

See:
Lease Agreement, Form I-02

Exhibit A

Equipment Schedule No.   ("Schedule")
Dated as of   ,
to Master Lease of Computer Equipment ("Lease")
Dated as of   ,
between
("Lessor")
and
("Lessee")

1. Equipment Description

Quantity	Manufacturer	Model	New/Used	Description	Estimated Invoice Purchase Price Per Unit	Aggregate

****
[Insert Equipment Description]

Total Estimated Invoice Purchase Price $

2. Basic Lease Commencement Date
   The Basic Lease Commencement Date for each Unit shall commence on [insert relevant time, such as the first day of the month immediately following the Unit's Acceptance Date if the Acceptance Date does not fall on the first day of a month].
3. Cut-Off Date
   Lessor shall be obligated to purchase and lease each Item of Equipment specified in Section 1 of this Schedule to Lessee provided such Item of Equipment has been accepted by Lessee for lease in accordance with the provisions of Section 2.5 of the Lease on or before   .
4. Discount Rate
   The Discount Rate applicable to each Unit shall be equal to an interest charge of   % per annum.
5. Lessor's Cost
   The Lessor's Cost for each Item of Equipment subject to this Schedule shall be an amount equal to the Invoice Purchase Price for such Item of Equipment plus all sales taxes in connection with the purchase from Manufacturer of such Item of Equipment, transportation charges in connection with the delivery of such Item of Equipment from the Manufacturer to Lessee and [insert other relevant charges which are to be included].

6. Overdue Rate

The Overdue Rate for each Unit shall be equal to an interest charge of   % per annum.

7. Rent Date

The Rent Date as to each Unit shall be the   day of each   during the Primary
Term and the   day of each   during any Renewal Term.

8. Unit Location

Each Unit shall be located at Lessee's place of business at   .

9. Lessor Commitment

Lessor shall be obligated to purchase and lease Items of Equipment pursuant to the terms of the
Lease and this Schedule with an aggregate Lessor's Cost of not less than $.

10. Lease Term

(a) The Primary Term for each Unit shall commence on the Basic Lease Commencement Date of
such Unit and shall end on the anniversary date thereof that number of years indicated below
opposite the relevant Unit thereafter.

Unit Description   *Primary Term in Years*

(b) The Renewal Term for each Unit shall be as specified in Section 13 of this Schedule.

11. Unit Rent

(a) The Interim Rent for each Unit as to any Interim Term shall be payable on the Basic Lease
Commencement Date of such Unit and shall be an amount equal to the Basic Rent multiplied
by a fraction, the numerator of which is that number of days in the Interim Term and the
denominator of which is that number of days in a Primary Term Rent payment period.

(b) The Basic Rent shall be an amount equal to the product of the Basic Lease Rate Factor indicated
below for the relevant Unit times the Lessor's Cost of such Unit.

Unit Description   *Basic Lease Rate Factor as a % of Lessor's Cost*

(c) The Renewal Rent for each Unit shall be payable on each Rent Date during the Renewal Term
in the amounts specified in Section 13 of this Schedule.

12. Casualty Value

The Casualty Value of each Unit shall be that percentage of the Lessor's Cost for such Unit as specified on Annex B attached hereto opposite the Rent Date through which Lessee has paid Rent.

13. Purchase and Renewal Right

Provided that the Lease has not been terminated earlier and no Event of Default has occurred and
is continuing not earlier than one hundred eighty (180) days and not later than ninety (90) days
before the end of the Primary Term or each year of any Renewal Term of each Unit, Lessee may
deliver to Lessor a written notice (a) tentatively electing either to purchase such Unit at the end of
the Primary Term or each year of any Renewal Term for an amount equal to the Fair Market Value
of such Unit at the end of such Term, or to extend the Term of this Lease at the end of the Primary
Term or each year of any Renewal Term as to such Unit on a year-to-year basis (but such aggregate
Renewal Term shall not exceed   years) at the Fair Market Rental at the end of such Term; and
(b) appointing an Appraiser selected by Lessee to determine the Fair Market Value or the Fair Market Rental thereof, whichever is applicable, in accordance with the provisions of Section 14 of the
Lease. If no such written notice is delivered by Lessee to Lessor within such period, Lessee shall be
deemed to have waived any right to purchase or extend the Term with respect to such Unit. At any
time within the fifteen (15) day period following the determination of Fair Market Value or Fair
Market Rental, as appropriate, of such Unit, Lessee may deliver to Lessor a further written notice
finally electing to purchase or extend the Term with respect to such Unit. If no such further notice
is delivered by Lessee to Lessor within such fifteen (15) day period, Lessee shall be deemed to have
waived any right to purchase or extend the Term with respect to such Unit. At the end of the Term,
if Lessee has finally elected to purchase such Unit, Lessee shall purchase from Lessor, and Lessor
shall sell to Lessee, such Unit for a cash consideration equal to the Fair Market Value of such Unit,
and Lessor shall transfer title to such Unit to Lessee without recourse or warranty, except that
Lessor shall represent and warrant that it owns such Unit free and clear of any Lessor's Lien.

14. Early Termination Right

(a) Provided an Event of Default shall not have occurred and be continuing, Lessee shall have the
right at its option at any time with not less than ninety (90) days prior written notice to Lessor

to terminate the Lease with respect to any or all of the Units on the   Primary Term Rent Date or any Primary Term Rent Date thereafter for any one or more such Units (hereinafter called the "Termination Date"), provided that Lessee shall have made a good faith determination that such Unit or Units are obsolete or surplus to Lessee's requirements. During the period from the giving of such notice until the Termination Date Lessee, as agent for Lessor, shall use its best efforts to obtain bids for the purchase of such Unit or Units by a person other than Lessee or an affiliate of Lessee. Lessee shall promptly certify in writing to Lessor the amount and terms of each bid received by Lessee and the name and address of the party submitting such bid. Subject to Lessor's right to retain such Unit or Units as provided in Subsection (b) below, on the Termination Date Lessor shall sell such Unit or Units for cash to the bidder or bidders who shall have submitted the highest bid for each such Unit prior to such date and shall transfer title to such Unit or Units to such purchaser or purchasers without recourse or warranty, except that Lessor shall represent and warrant that it owns such Unit or Units free and clear of any Lessor's Lien. The total sale price realized upon such sale shall be retained by Lessor and, in addition, on the Termination Date, Lessee shall pay to Lessor the amount, if any, by which the Termination Value of such Unit or Units as provided in Subsection (d) below, computed as of the Termination Date, exceeds the proceeds of such sale, whereupon the Lease shall terminate as to such Unit or Units except as herein otherwise expressly provided. Subject to the provisions of Subsection (c) below, in the event no bids are received by Lessee, Lessee shall pay to Lessor the Termination Value of such Unit or Units, computed as of the Termination Date, and deliver such Unit or Units to the Lessor in accordance with the provisions of Section 17 of the Lease, whereupon the Lease shall terminate as to such Unit or Units, except as herein otherwise expressly provided.

(b) Notwithstanding the provisions of Subsection (a) above but subject to the provisions of Subsection (c) below, Lessor shall have the right at any time up to and including thirty (30) days prior to the Termination Date, within its sole discretion, to elect not to sell such Unit or Units to any prospective purchaser obtained by Lessee ("Third Party Purchaser"). In the event Lessor elects not to sell such Unit or Units to the Third Party Purchaser, Lessee shall return such Unit or Units to Lessor in accordance with the provisions of Section 17 of the Lease, and Lessor thereupon may retain such Unit or Units for its own account without further obligation under the Lease. If no sale shall have occurred on or as of the Termination Date because the Third Party Purchaser fails to consummate a proposed sale and Lessor shall not have requested the return of such Unit or Units pursuant hereto, the Lease shall continue in full force and effect as to such Unit or Units. In the event of any such sale or the return of such Unit or Units to Lessor pursuant hereto, and provided no Event of Default has occurred and is continuing, all obligations of Lessee to pay Rent and otherwise with respect to such Unit or Units for any period subsequent to the Termination Date shall cease.

(c) If the Termination Value exceeds the highest bidder in the event no bids are received by Lessee, or if Lessor should exercise its election under Subsection (b) above, Lessee may, at its option, upon written notice given to Lessor not less than fifteen (15) days prior to the Termination Date, elect to (i) rescind and cancel Lessee's notice of termination with respect to any one or more of such Units, whereupon the Lease shall not terminate with respect to such Unit or Units pursuant to this Section 14 but shall continue in full force and effect as though no notice of termination had been given by Lessee with respect to such Unit or Units, or (ii) pay Lessor the applicable Termination Value with respect to any one or more of such Units, whereupon Lessor shall transfer title to such Unit or Units to Lessee without recourse or warranty, except that Lessor shall represent and warrant that it owns such Unit or Units free and clear of any Lessor's Lien. In the event Lessee fails to pay Lessor an amount of money equal to the applicable Termination Value on the Termination Date, the Lease as to such Unit or Units shall continue in full force and effect.

(d) The Termination Value of any Unit shall be that percentage described on Annex C attached hereto of Lessor's Cost set forth opposite the Rent Date through which the Lessee has paid Rent.

15. Upgrade Right

[*Author's note:* This must be negotiated on a case-by-case basis. There is no one standard form.]

16. Representations and Warranties

Each of Lessor and Lessee represents and warrants to the other that:

(a) Its representations and warranties contained in Section 21 of the Lease are true and accurate on and as of the date of this Schedule as though made on and as of such date.

(b) It is not in default under any of the terms, covenants, agreements, or other provisions of the Lease.

(c) Simultaneously with the execution and delivery hereof it has delivered to the other its Incumbency Certificate, Certified Resolutions, and Opinion of Counsel substantially in the respective forms of Annexes D, E, and F attached hereto, with such changes as the receiving party shall reasonably request.

17. Term Definitions

The terms used in this Schedule, where not defined in this Schedule to the contrary, shall have the same meanings as defined in the Lease.

, as Lessor

By:

Title:

, as Lessee

By:

Title:

Form: I-02b
Disk File Name: I-02b.rtf

CERTIFICATE OF ACCEPTANCE

Form Purpose

Form of master net finance equipment lease equipment lessee certificate of acceptance. This form is integrated with a master lease agreement, Lease Agreement Form l-02.

Executing Parties
The equipment lessee.

See:
Lease Agreement, Form l-02

Annex A
Certificate of Acceptance

Date

Certificate of Acceptance No.

to Equipment Schedule No.   ("Schedule")

dated as of   ,

to Master Lease of Computer Equipment ("Lease")

dated as of   ,

between

                              ("Lessor")

and

                              ("Lessee")

Lessee hereby confirms that the Acceptance Date of the Unit or Units described in Exhibit A attached hereto shall be the date of this Certificate.

Lessee confirms that (a) such Unit or Units have been examined by duly appointed and authorized representatives of Lessee, (b) such Unit or Units have been duly accepted by Lessee as Units for Leasing under the Lease, (c) such Unit or Units have become subject to and governed by the terms of the Lease, and (d) Lessee has become obligated to pay to Lessor the Rent provided for in the Lease and the Schedule with respect to such Unit or Units.

The terms used herein shall have the respective meanings given to such terms in the Lease.

                    , as Lessee

By:

Title:

Form: I-02c
Disk File Name: I-02c.rtf

CASUALTY VALUE SCHEDULE

Form Purpose

Form of master net finance equipment lease casualty value schedule. This form is integrated with a master lease agreement, Lease Agreement Form l-02.

See:
Lease Agreement, Form l-02

Annex B
Casualty Value Scedule

After Rent Date No.   *Percentage of per Unit Cost*

**Form: l-02d
Disk File Name: l-02d.rtf**

TERMINATION VALUE SCHEDULE

Form Purpose

Form of master net finance equipment lease termination value schedule. This form is integrated with a master lease agreement, Lease Agreement Form l-02.

See:
Lease Agreement, Form l-02

Annex C
Termination Value Schedule

After Rent Date No.   *Percentage of Lessor's Cost*

Form: I-02e
Disk File Name: I-02e.rtf

INCUMBENCY CERTIFICATE

Form Purpose

Form of master net finance equipment lease incumbency certificate. This form is integrated with a master lease agreement, Lease Agreement Form l-02.

Executing Parties
The equipment lessee's secretary or assistant secretary.

See:
Lease Agreement, Form l-02

Annex D
Incumbency Certificate

This Certificate is delivered by the undersigned pursuant to the Master Lease of Computer Equipment (the "Lease") dated as of   , between   (the "Lessor"), and   (the "Lessee"):

The undersigned hereby certifies that the following persons are on the date hereof, and have been at all times since   , duly elected or appointed, qualified, and acting officers of the undersigned holding the offices set forth opposite their respective names below and that the signatures set forth opposite their respective names and offices below are their genuine signatures:

Name   *Title*   *Signature*

_____

Secretary

Form: I-02f
Disk File Name: I-02f.rtf

CERTIFIED RESOLUTIONS

Form Purpose

Form of lessee's certified corporate resolutions authorizing the entering into of an equipment lease transaction. This form is integrated with a master lease agreement, Lease Agreement Form I-02.

Executing Parties
The equipment lessee's secretary or assistant secretary.

See:
Lease Agreement, Form I-02

Annex E
Certified Resolutions

The undersigned, being the   of
a   corporation ("   "), does hereby certify
that the following is a true and correct copy of certain resolutions duly adopted by the
of   on   , and that such resolutions have not been modified
or rescinded and remain in full force and effect on the date hereof:

RESOLVED, that the proposed Master Lease of Computer Equipment (the "Lease"), including the proposed Equipment Schedule attached as Annex A thereto (the "Schedule"), between as
and this Corporation as   , in the form of the draft of   ,
filed with the records of this Corporation, be, and it hereby is, approved in all respects; and further

RESOLVED, that the officers of this Corporation be, and each and any of them hereby is, authorized and empowered, in the name and on behalf of this Corporation, to execute and deliver the Lease and any Schedule substantially in the form approved in the preceding resolution, together with such changes therein as such officers or any of them, in conjunction with counsel to this Corporation, shall from time to time in their discretion deem necessary or desirable and shall approve, such approval to be conclusively evidenced by their execution and delivery thereof, and to enforce all rights and perform all obligations of this Corporation thereunder; provided, however, that without further action by this Board of Directors the aggregate cost of equipment to become subject to the Lease and all Schedules shall not exceed $; and further

RESOLVED, that the officers of this Corporation be, and each and any of them hereby is, authorized and empowered, in the name and on behalf of this Corporation, to execute, deliver, file, and record any and all such further agreements, undertakings, instruments, certificates, letters, and documents, and to perform any and all such further actions, as such officers or any of them, in conjunction with counsel to this Corporation, shall from time to time in their discretion deem necessary or desirable to fully effectuate the Lease and the purposes of the foregoing resolutions.

IN WITNESS WHEREOF, the undersigned has made and executed this Certificate as of this   day
of   , 20___.

Secretary

Form: I-02g
Disk File Name: I-02g.rtf

OPINION OF COUNSEL

Form Purpose

Form of master net finance lease lessee's counsel opinion. This form is integrated with a master lease agreement, Lease Agreement Form I-02.

Executing Parties
The equipment lessee's counsel.

See:
Lease Agreement, Form I-02

Annex F
Opinion of Counsel

[Date]

Gentlemen:

As counsel to   ("   ")
I have examined the Master Lease of Computer Equipment dated as of   (the "Lease"), between   and   and Equipment Schedule No.   to the Lease dated of even date herewith, such other documents and corporate records, and such questions of law as I have deemed relevant for purposes of the opinions expressed below. The terms used herein have the same meanings as defined in the Lease. Based on such examination, I am of the opinion that:

1.   is a corporation duly organized, validly existing, and in good standing under the laws of the   ; has full power and authority to carry on its business as presently conducted, to own or hold under lease its properties and to enter into and perform its obligations under the Lease; and is duly qualified to do business as a foreign corporation and is in good standing in each jurisdiction in which the location of any Unit requires such qualification.

2. The execution, delivery, and performance by   of the Lease have been duly authorized by all necessary corporate action on the part of   , do not materially contravene any law, governmental rule, regulation, or Order binding on   or its properties or the corporate charter or By-Laws of   , and to the best of my knowledge do not contravene the provisions of, or constitute a material default under, or result in the creation of any Lien upon the Units under, any material indenture, mortgage, contract, or other instrument to which is a party or by which   or its property is bound.

3. No consent or approval of, giving of notice to, registration with, or taking of any other action by, any state, federal, or other governmental commission, agency, or regulatory authority is required for the performance by   of the transactions contemplated by the Lease; or, if any such action is required, it has been obtained, performed, or registered.

4. The Lease has been duly entered into and delivered by   , and constitutes a legal, valid, and binding agreement of   enforceable against in accordance with its terms, except as limited by (a) bankruptcy, insolvency, reorganization, or other similar laws of general application affecting the enforcement of creditors' or lessors' rights; (b) emergency powers lawfully conferred upon any governmental agency; and (c) laws or judicial decisions limiting the right to specific performance or other equitable remedies, and the Lease creates a valid leasehold interest in the Units.

5. To the best of my knowledge there are no actions, suits, or proceedings pending or threatened before any court, administrative agency, arbitrator, or Governmental Body which would, if determined adversely to   , have a material adverse effect on the business, assets, operations, or condition, financial or otherwise, of   , or materially adversely affect the ability of   to perform its obligations under the Lease; and to the best of my knowledge   is not in material default with respect to any material Order of any court, arbitrator, or Governmental Body.

6. No recorded Lien other than the Lease of any nature whatsoever which now covers or affects, or which will hereafter cover or affect, any property (or interests therein) of   now attaches or hereafter will attach to any of the Units, or materially adversely affects or will affect   right, title and interest in or to any of the Units.

Very truly yours,

Form: I-02h
Disk File Name: I-02h.rtf

PROHIBITED LENDER ASSIGNEE SCHEDULE

Form Purpose

Form of master net finance lease prohibited lender assignees. This form is integrated with a master lease agreement, Lease Agreement Form 1-02.

See:
- Lease Agreement, Form 1-02

Annex G

Prohibited Lender Assignees

Form: I-03
Disk File Name: I-03.rtf

LEASE AGREEMENT—SHORT FORM (GENERAL)

Form Purpose

Short form, net finance master equipment lease agreement. The master format allows future equipment to be easily added by means of a schedule. This form is set up so that each schedule is a lease, making it easy to enter into loan arrangements with various lenders that provide equipment purchase funds, and is part of an integrated package, including all key closing documents.

Executing Parties
The equipment lessor.
The equipment lessee.

See:
Schedule, Form l-03a
Acceptance Certificate, Form l-03b
Casualty Value Table, Form l-03c
Amendment, Form a-14
Automatic Transfer of Title, Form o-16
Insurance Notification, Form i-02
Representation and Warranties, Form l-03d
Opinion of Counsel—Lessee, Form l-03e
Opinion of Counsel—Guarantor, Form l-03f
Purchase—Fair Market Value, Form o-11
Purchase—Fixed Price, Form o-12
Put, Form o-17
Renewal—Fair Market Value, Form o-13
Renewal—Fixed Price, Form o-14
Sublease Right, Form o-15
Secretary's Certificate—Lessee Resolutions, Form c-14
Secretary's Certificate—Guarantor's Resolutions, Form c-09

Master Agreement No.

Master Agreement to Lease Equipment

(Insert name of leasing company), Lessor

Home Office: Address:

      Phone: (   )

and   , Lessee,
a   corporation, hereby agree as of this   day of
                              , as follows:

     1. Agreement to Lease. This Agreement sets forth the basic terms and conditions upon which Lessor shall lease to Lessee and Lessee shall lease from Lessor items of equipment ("Units") specified in Schedules to be entered into from time to time. Each Schedule shall incorporate the terms and conditions of this Agreement and shall constitute a lease as to the Units specified in such Schedule. The term "Lease" as to each Unit as used in this Agreement shall mean the applicable Schedule which incorporates the terms and conditions of this Agreement.

2. Acceptance. Lessee shall accept each Unit for lease by delivering to Lessor an executed Acceptance Certificate in the form provided by Lessor whereupon such Unit shall be deemed accepted by Lessee and become subject to the Lease on the Acceptance Certificate Execution Date.

3. Rent and Lease Term. Lessee shall pay Lessor Rent for each Unit in the amounts and at the times specified in the Lease. The Lease Term for each Unit shall commence on the Acceptance Certificate Execution Date and shall continue for the period specified in the Lease. The Lease Term as to any Unit may not be terminated by Lessee unless otherwise expressly provided in the Lease.

4. Payment Obligation. All Rent and other payments under each Lease shall be made to Lessor at its address shown above, or at such other address as Lessor may designate, in immediately available funds in such coin or currency of the United States of America which at the time of payment shall be legal tender for the payment of public and private debts. EACH LEASE SHALL BE A NET LEASE, AND LESSEE'S OBLIGATION TO PAY ALL RENT AND OTHER SUMS THEREUNDER SHALL BE ABSOLUTE AND UNCONDITIONAL, AND SHALL NOT BE SUBJECT TO ANY ABATEMENT, REDUCTION, SETOFF, DEFENSE, COUNTERCLAIM, INTERRUPTION, DEFERMENT, OR RECOUPMENT, FOR ANY REASON WHATSOEVER.

5. Statement of Lease. Each Lease shall constitute a lease of personal property and Lessee agrees to take all actions necessary or reasonably requested by Lessor to ensure that each Unit shall be and remain personal property, and nothing in any Lease shall be constituted as conveying to Lessee any interest in any Unit other than its interest as a lessee. Lessee shall, at its expense, protect and defend the interests of Lessor in each Unit against all third party claims; keep each Unit free and clear of any mortgage, security interest, pledge, lien, charge, claim, or other encumbrance (collectively, "Lien"), except any Lien arising solely through acts of Lessor ("Lessor's Lien"); give Lessor immediate notice of the existence of any such Lien; and indemnify and defend Lessor against any claim, liability, loss, damage, or expense arising in connection with any of the foregoing.

6. Use. Each Unit shall be used and operated by Lessee only in the ordinary conduct of its business by qualified employees of Lessee and in accordance with all applicable manufacturer and vendor instructions as well as with all applicable legal and regulatory requirements. Lessee shall not change the location of any Unit from that specified in the Lease without obtaining Lessor's prior consent.

7. Maintenance and Alterations. Lessee shall, at its expense, repair and maintain each Unit so that it will remain in the same condition as when delivered to Lessee, ordinary wear and tear from proper use excepted. Such repair and maintenance shall be performed in compliance with all requirements necessary to enforce all product warranty rights and with all applicable legal and regulatory requirements. Lessee shall enter into and keep in effect during the Lease Term those maintenance agreements with respect to each Unit required by the Lease. Lessee shall, at its expense, make such alterations ("Required Alterations") to each Unit during the Unit's Lease Term as may be required by applicable legal and regulatory requirements. In addition, Lessee may at its expense, without Lessor's consent, so long as no Event of Default, or event which with the passage of time or giving of notice, or both, would constitute an Event of Default ("Incipient Default"), has occurred and is continuing, make alterations ("Permitted Alterations") to any Unit which do not impair the commercial value or originally intended function or use of such Unit and which are readily removable without causing material damage to such Unit. Any Permitted Alterations not removed by Lessee prior to the return of such Unit to Lessor, and all Required Alterations, shall immediately without further action become the property of Lessor and part of such Unit for all purposes of the Lease. Other than as provided in this Section 7, Lessee may make no alterations to any Unit. Any prohibited alterations to a Unit shall, at Lessor's election, immediately become the property of Lessor without further action and without Lessor thereby waiving any Incipient Default or Event of Default.

8. Return. At the expiration or earlier termination of the Lease Term as to each Unit, Lessee shall, at its expense, return such Unit to Lessor at the location in the continental United States specified by Lessor.

9. Identification. Lessee shall, at its expense, place and maintain permanent markings on each Unit evidencing Ownership, security and other interests therein, as specified from time to time by Lessor. Lessee shall not place or permit to be placed any other markings on any Unit which might indicate any ownership or security interest in such Unit. Any markings, on any Unit not made at Lessor's request shall be removed by Lessee, at its expense, prior to the return of such Unit in accordance with Section 8.

10. Inspection. Upon reasonable prior notice, Lessee shall make each Unit and all related records available to Lessor or its agents for inspection during regular business hours, at the location of such Unit.

11. No Lessee Sublease or Assignment. Lessee shall not, unless, expressly permitted in the Lease, sublease or otherwise, relinquish possession or control of, or assign, pledge, hypothecate, or otherwise transfer, dispose of, or encumber, any Unit, this Agreement or any Lease or any part thereof or interest therein, or any right or obligation with respect thereto.

12. Lessor Assignment. Lessor may from time to time without notice to Lessee sell, grant a security interest in, assign, or otherwise transfer (collectively "Transfer"), in whole or in part, this Agreement, one or more Leases, any or all Units, or any of its interests, rights, or obligations with respect thereto, including without limitation all Rent and other sums due or to become due under any Lease, to one or more persons or entities ("Assignee"). Each Assignee shall have, to the extent provided in any Transfer document, Lessor's rights, powers, privileges, and remedies with respect thereto, but shall not be obligated to Lessee, except to the extent expressly provided in any Transfer document, to observe or perform any duty, covenant, or condition required to be observed or performed by Lessor. Except to the extent expressly assumed by an Assignee in any Transfer document, no Transfer shall relieve Lessor from any of its obligations to Lessee. Lessee shall, upon receipt of notice of a Transfer from Lessor, be bound by such Transfer. Lessee shall not assert against any Assignee any claim, defense, counterclaim, or setoff that Lessee may at any time have against Lessor.

13. Liens. Lessee shall not directly or indirectly create, incur, assume, or suffer to exist any Lien on or with respect to any Unit or Lease, Lessor's title to any such Unit, or other interest or right of Lessor with respect thereto, except Lessor's, Liens. Lessee, at its expense, shall promptly pay, satisfy, and take such other action as may be necessary or reasonably requested by Lessor to keep each Unit and Lease free and clear of, and to duly and promptly discharge, any such Lien.

14. Risk of Loss. Lessee shall bear all risk of loss, damage, theft, taking, destruction, confiscation, or requisition with respect to each Unit, however caused or occasioned, which shall occur prior to the return of such Unit in accordance with Section 8. In addition, Lessee hereby assumes all other risks and liabilities, including without limitation personal injury or death and property damage, arising with respect to each Unit (unless arising solely through Lessor's willful misconduct), including without limitation those arising with respect to the manufacture, purchase, ownership, shipment, transportation, delivery, installation, leasing, possession, use, storage, and return of such Unit, howsoever arising, in connection with any event occurring prior to such Unit's return in accordance with Section 8.

15. Casualty. If any Unit shall become lost, stolen, destroyed, or irreparably damaged from any cause whatsoever, or shall be taken, confiscated, or requisitioned (any such event herein called an "Event of Loss"), Lessee shall promptly notify Lessor of the occurrence of such Event of Loss, and shall pay Lessor, within 15 days after the date of such Event of Loss (but in no event later than the Rent payment date next following such Event of Loss), an amount equal to the applicable Casualty Value of such Unit as specified in the Lease. Upon Lessor's receipt of such payment in full, the Lease shall automatically terminate as to such Unit, and Lessor's right, title, and interest in such Unit shall immediately without further action pass to Lessee, on an as-is, where-is basis, without recourse or warranty.

16. Insurance. Lessee shall, at its expense, cause to be carried and maintained for each Unit, commencing at the time any risk shall pass to Lessor as to such Unit and continuing until the return of such Unit in accordance with Section 8, insurance against such risks, in such amounts, in such form, and with such insurers, all as may be satisfactory to Lessor. If any insurance proceeds are received with respect to an occurrence which does not constitute an Event of Loss, and no Incipient Default or Event of Default has occurred and is continuing, such proceeds shall be applied to payment for repairs. If any insurance proceeds are received by Lessor with respect to an occurrence which constitutes an Event of Loss, and no Incipient Default or Event of Default has occurred and is continuing, such proceeds shall be applied toward Lessee's obligation to pay the applicable Casualty Value for such Unit. If an Incipient Default or Event of Default has occurred and is continuing, any insurance proceeds received shall be applied as Lessor in its sole discretion may determine. At the time each Schedule is executed and thereafter on a date not less than 30 days prior to each insurance policy expiration date, Lessee shall deliver to Lessor certificates of insurance or other evidence satisfactory to Lessor showing that such insurance coverage is and will remain in effect in accordance with Lessee's obligations under this Section 16. Lessor shall be under no duty to ascertain the existence of any insurance coverage or to examine any certificate of insurance or other evidence of insurance coverage or to advise Lessee in the event the insurance coverage does not comply with the requirements hereof. Lessee shall give Lessor prompt notice of any damage, loss, or other occurrence required to be insured against with respect to any Unit.

17. Taxes and Fees. Lessee hereby assumes liability for, and shall pay when due, and on a net after-tax basis shall indemnify and defend Lessor against, all fees, taxes, and governmental charges (including without limitation interest and penalties) of any nature imposed upon or in any way relating to Lessor, Lessee, any Unit (including without limitation the manufacture, purchase, ownership, shipment, transportation, delivery, installation. leasing, possession, use, operation, storage, and return of such Unit) or any Lease, except state and local taxes on or measured by Lessor's net income payable to each state and locality in which Lessor maintains one or more places of business immediately prior to the date of the applicable Lease (other than any such tax which is in substitution for or relieves Lessee from the payment of taxes it would otherwise be obligated to pay or reimburse Lessor as provided), and federal taxes on Lessor's net income. Lessee shall

at its expense file when due with the appropriate authorities any and all tax and similar returns and reports required to be filed with respect thereto (with copies to Lessor) or, if requested by Lessor, notify Lessor of all such requirements and furnish Lessor with all information required for Lessor to effect such filings, which filings shall also be at Lessee's expense.

18. Indemnification. Lessee hereby assumes liability for, and shall pay when due, and shall indemnify and defend Lessor against, any and all liabilities, losses, damages, claims, and expenses in any way relating to or arising out of any Lease or any Unit, including without limitation the manufacture, purchase, ownership, shipment, transportation, delivery, installation, leasing, possession, use, operation, storage, and return of such Unit. Lessee shall give Lessor prompt notice of any occurrence, event, or condition in connection with which Lessor may be entitled to indemnification hereunder. The provisions of this Section 18 are in addition to, and not in limitation of, the provisions of Section 17.

19. Limited Warranty. Lessor warrants to Lessee that, so long as no Incipient Default or Event of Default has occurred and is continuing, Lessor will not interfere with Lessee's use and possession of the Units. LESSOR, NOT BEING THE MANUFACTURER OR VENDOR OF THE UNITS NOR A DEALER IN SIMILAR EQUIPMENT, MAKES NO OTHER REPRESENTATION OR WARRANTY, EXPRESS OR IMPLIED, AS TO ANY MATTER WHATSOEVER, INCLUDING WITHOUT LIMITATION THE DESIGN OR CONDITION OF THE UNITS, THEIR MERCHANTABILITY, DURABILITY, SUITABILITY OR FITNESS FOR ANY PARTICULAR PURPOSE, INFRINGEMENT, THE QUALITY OF THE MATERIAL OR WORKMANSHIP OF THE UNITS, OR THE CONFORMITY OF THE UNITS TO THE PROVISIONS OR SPECIFICATIONS OF ANY PURCHASE ORDER RELATING THERETO, AND LESSOR HEREBY SPECIFICALLY DISCLAIMS ANY AND ALL SUCH REPRESENTATIONS AND WARRANTIES. LESSEE ACKNOWLEDGES THAT IT HAS MADE THE SELECTION OF EACH UNIT BASED UPON ITS OWN JUDGMENT AND EXPRESSLY DISCLAIMS ANY RELIANCE ON STATEMENTS MADE BY LESSOR AND AGREES THAT LESSOR SHALL NOT BE LIABLE FOR ANY CONSEQUENTIAL DAMAGES ARISING OUT OF THE USE OF OR INABILITY TO USE THE UNITS. LESSEE AGRESS THAT THE UNITS ARE LEASED "AS IS." Lessor hereby appoints Lessee as Lessor's agent, so long as no Incipient Default or Event of Default has occurred and is continuing, to assert at Lessee's expense any right Lessor may have against any manufacturer or vendor to enforce any product warranties with respect to each Unit during such Unit's Lease Term; provided, however, Lessee shall indemnify and defend Lessor against all claims, expenses, damages, losses, and liabilities incurred or suffered by Lessor in connection with any such action taken by Lessee.

20. Events of Default. An "Event of Default" shall occur if (a) Lessee fails to make any Rent or other payment under any Lease when due and such failure continues for a period of 5 days thereafter; (b) Lessee violates any covenant set forth in Section 8, 11, or 16 or the last sentence of this Section 20; (c) Lessee violates any other provision of this Agreement, any Lease or any document furnished Lessor in connection herewith or therewith and such violation shall continue unremedied for a period of 20 days after notice from Lessor; (d) Lessee or any guarantor of Lessee's obligations under any Lease ("Guarantor") or any material subsidiary of Lessee or Guarantor ("Subsidiary") shall be in default with respect to any other agreement with Lessor or any other obligation for the payment of borrowed money or rent; (e) Lessee, any Guarantor or any Subsidiary shall commit an act of bankruptcy or become or be adjudicated insolvent or bankrupt or make an assignment for the benefit of creditors or become unable or admit in writing its
inability to pay its debts as they become due, or a trustee receiver or liquidator shall be appointed for Lessee, any Guarantor or any Subsidiary, or for a substantial part of its property, with or without its consent, or bankruptcy, arrangement, reorganization, composition, readjustment, liquidation, insolvency, dissolution, or similar proceedings under any present or future statute, law, or regulation shall be instituted by or against Lessee, any Guarantor, or any Subsidiary, or Lessee, any Guarantor, or any Subsidiary shall file an answer admitting the material allegations of a petition filed against it in any such proceeding, or any execution or writ or process shall be issued under any proceeding whereby any Unit may be taken or restrained, or Lessee, any Guarantor, or any Subsidiary shall cease doing business as a going concern; or Lessee, any Guarantor, or any Subsidiary shall, without Lessor's prior consent, sell, transfer, pledge, or otherwise dispose of all or any substantial part of its assets, or consolidate or merge with any other entity; or (f) any representation or warranty made by Lessee, any Guarantor, or any Subsidiary in any document furnished Lessor under or pursuant to this Agreement or any Lease shall be incorrect or incomplete at any time in any material respect. Lessee shall promptly notify Lessor of the occurrence of any Incipient Default or Event of Default.

21. Remedies. If one or more Events of Default shall have occurred and be continuing, Lessor, at its option, may (a) proceed by appropriate court action or actions, either at law or in equity, to enforce performance by Lessee of the applicable covenants of each Lease or to recover damages for the breach thereof, including without limitation net after-tax losses of federal, state, and local income tax benefits to which Lessor would otherwise be entitled as a result of owning any Unit or leasing such Unit to Lessee, or (b) by notice to Lessee terminate any or all Leases with respect to any one or more of the Units covered thereby, whereupon

all rights of Lessee to the possession and use of such Units shall absolutely cease and terminate as though each such Lease as to such Units had never been entered into; provided, however, Lessee shall nevertheless remain liable under each such Lease; and thereupon Lessor may, by its agent or agents, enter upon the premises of Lessee or any other premises where any of such Units may be located and take possession of all or any of such Units and from that point hold, possess, operate, sell, lease, and enjoy such Units free from any right of Lessee, its successors and assigns, to use such Units for any purposes whatsoever without any duty to account to Lessee for any action or inaction or for any proceeds arising therefrom; provided, however, Lessor shall nevertheless have a right to recover from Lessee any and all amounts which under the terms of each such Lease may be then due or which may have accrued to the date of such termination and also to recover immediately from Lessee (x) as damages for loss of the bargain and not as a penalty, whichever of the following sums, with respect to each such Unit, Lessor in its sole discretion shall specify by notice to Lessee: (i) an amount equal to the excess, if any, of the Casualty Value for such Unit, in effect for the Rent payment period during which the specified Event of Default occurred, over the present value (computed as of the Rent payment date next following the date of such notice) of the rent which Lessor reasonably estimates will be realized for such Unit for the remainder of the initially specified Lease Term of such Unit following the termination of the Lease, such present value to be computed by discounting such estimated rent payments at a 5% per annum rate of interest (based on a 360-day year and 30-day month), or (ii) an amount equal to the excess, if any, of the Casualty Value for such Unit in effect for the Rent payment period during which the specified Event of Default has occurred over the amount Lessor reasonably estimates to be the sales value of such Unit as of the date of the estimate specified in such notice and (y) all damages, losses, liabilities, claims, and expenses (including without limitation expenses incurred in connection with the recovery, repair, repainting, return, and remarking of any Unit or other exercise of Lessor's remedies hereunder and reasonable attorneys' fees) which Lessor shall sustain in connection with any Event of Default. No remedy referred to in this Section 21 shall be deemed exclusive, but all such remedies shall be cumulative and shall be in addition to all other remedies in Lessor's favor existing under this Agreement, any Lease or otherwise at law or in equity.

22. Financial Information. Lessee agrees to furnish Lessor (a) as soon as available, and in any event within 120 days after the last day of each fiscal year of Lessee, a copy of the financial statements of Lessee as of the end of such fiscal year, certified by an independent certified public accounting firm of recognized standing reasonably satisfactory to Lessor, (b) within 45 days after the last day of each fiscal quarter of Lessee a copy of its financial statements as of the end of such quarter certified by the principal financial officer of Lessee, and (c) such additional information concerning Lessee, any Guarantor, and any Subsidiary as Lessor may reasonably request.

23. Lessor's Qualified Obligation. Lessor shall not be obligated to lease any Unit specified in a Lease to Lessee if (i) such Unit is not accepted by Lessee on or before the Acquisition Expiration Date specified in such Lease or (ii) the Acquisition Cost of such Unit, when added to the Acquisition Cost of the Units specified in such Lease previously accepted for lease, is in excess of the Aggregate Acquisition Cost set forth in such Lease. In addition, anything in this Agreement or any Lease to the contrary notwithstanding, Lessor shall not be obligated to acquire or lease to Lessee any Units not already subject to a Lease if Lessor determines Lessee's financial or business condition (or that of any Guarantor or any Subsidiary) has suffered any material adverse change from the condition existing or represented to Lessor as at the date of such Lease. In such event, Lessee shall promptly pay Lessor and indemnify and defend Lessor against all amounts which Lessor has expended or may be or become obligated to expend with respect to each such Unit and the transactions contemplated under the Lease and shall assume, undertake, and relieve Lessor of, and indemnify and defend Lessor against, all damages, losses, claims, liabilities, obligations, and duties under any related requisition, purchase order, purchase contract, or otherwise with respect thereto.

24. Late Charges; Security Deposit; Advance Rentals. Any nonpayment of Rent or other amounts payable under any Lease shall result in Lessee's obligation to promptly pay Lessor as additional Rent on such overdue payment, for the period of time during which it is overdue (without regard to any grace period), interest at a rate equal to the lesser of (a) the Late Charge set forth in the Lease, or (b) the maximum rate of interest permitted by law. Lessor may apply any security deposit required under any Lease toward any oblig-

ation of Lessee thereunder; shall return any unspoiled balance to Lessee, without interest, unless otherwise required by applicable law, upon satisfaction of Lessee's obligations thereunder; and may, unless otherwise required by applicable law, commingle such security deposit with its other funds. In the event that Lessor applies a security deposit to satisfy an obligation of Lessee under any Lease, Lessee shall immediately replace any portion of the security deposit so applied by Lessor. Lessee shall pay any advance rental payments provided for in any Lease at the time Lessee executes such Lease. All such advance rental payments shall (i) be deemed earned by Lessor immediately upon their receipt by Lessor, (ii) be applied immediately in satisfaction of Lessee's advance rental payment obligations under such Lease, and (iii) not be refundable to Lessee for any reason, including in connection with any premature termination of such Lease.

25. Lessor's Right to Perform for Lessee. If Lessee fails to duly and promptly pay, perform, or comply with any of its obligations, covenants, or agreements under any Lease, Lessor may itself pay, perform, or comply with any of such obligations, covenants, or agreements for the account of Lessee without thereby waiving any Incipient Default or Event of Default. In such event, any amount paid or expense incurred by Lessor in connection therewith shall immediately on demand, together with interest as provided in Section 24, be paid to Lessor as additional Rent, and Lessee shall indemnify and defend Lessor against any damage, loss, claim, liability, or expense suffered or incurred by Lessor in connection therewith.

26. Notices. Any consent, instruction, or notice required or permitted to be given under any Lease shall be in writing and shall become effective when delivered, or if mailed when deposited in the United States mail with proper postage prepaid for registered or certified mail, return receipt requested, addressed to Lessor or Lessee, as the case may be, at their respective addresses set forth herein or at such other address as Lessor or Lessee shall from time to time designate to the other party by notice similarly given.

27. Miscellaneous. Lessee shall, at its expense and upon Lessor's demand, promptly execute, acknowledge, deliver, file, register, and record any and all further documents and take any and all other action reasonably requested by Lessor from time to time, for the purpose of fully effectuating the intent and purposes of each Lease, and to protect the interests of Lessor, its successors and assigns. Any provision of any Lease which is prohibited or not fully enforceable in any jurisdiction shall, as to such jurisdiction, be ineffective only to the extent of such prohibition or unenforceability without otherwise invalidating or diminishing Lessor's rights thereunder or under the remaining provisions thereof in such jurisdiction, and any such prohibition or unenforceability in any jurisdiction shall not invalidate or render unenforceable such provision in any other jurisdiction. To the extent permitted by applicable law, Lessee hereby waives its rights under any provision of law now or hereafter in effect which might limit or modify or otherwise render unenforceable in any respect any remedy or other provision of any Lease. No term or provision of any Lease may be amended, altered, waived, discharged, or terminated except by an instrument in writing signed by a duly authorized officer of the party against which the enforcement of the amendment, alteration, waiver, discharge, or termination is sought. No delay by Lessor in exercising any right, power, or remedy under any Lease shall constitute a waiver, and any waiver by Lessor on any one occasion or for any one purpose shall not be construed as a waiver on any future occasion or for any other purpose. Except as otherwise specifically provided in any Lease, each Lease shall be governed in all respects by, and construed in accordance with, the laws of the State of   , without regard to its choice of laws principals. All of the covenants and agreements of Lessee contained in each Lease shall survive the expiration or earlier termination of such Lease and the Lease Term of the Units leased thereunder. Subject to all of the terms and provisions of each Lease, all of the covenants, conditions, and obligations contained in such Lease shall be binding upon and inure to the benefit of the respective successors and assigns of Lessor and Lessee. Each Lease, and any documents executed and delivered in connection therewith, shall constitute the entire agreement of Lessor and Lessee with respect to the Units leased thereby, and shall automatically cancel and supersede any and all prior oral or written understandings with respect thereto. This Agreement and each Lease may be executed in any number of counterparts, each of which, when so executed and delivered, shall be an original (except that to the extent, if any, this Agreement or any Lease constitutes chattel paper, no security interest therein may be created except through the transfer or possession of the original counterpart, which shall be identified by Lessor), but all

such counterparts taken together shall constitute one and the same instrument. The headings in this Agreement and each Lease shall be for convenience of reference only and shall form no part of this Agreement or such Lease.

IN WITNESS WHEREOF, the parties hereto have caused this Agreement to be duly executed by their authorized representatives as of the date first above written.

(Insert name of leasing company), Lessor

By:

Title:

                        , Lessee

By:

Title:

Address:

Phone: (   )

Form: I-03a
Disk File Name: I-03a.rtf

SCHEDULE

Form Purpose

Schedule to short form, net finance master equipment lease agreement. This form is integrated with Lease Agreement Form l-03. The Schedule sets forth those terms and conditions that will vary from time to time with respect to equipment identified in the Schedule.

Executing Parties
The equipment lessor.
The equipment lessee.

See:
Lease Agreement, Form l-03

Master Agreement No.

Schedule No.   ("Lease"),

Dated as of   , to Master Agreement to Lease

Equipment, Dated as of   , between

                          , Lessor

Home Office: Address:

Phone: (   )

and   , Lessee

Address:

Phone: (   )

1. Equipment Description:

Manufacturer or Vendor	Unit Description	New/ Model Used	Acquisition Cost Per Unit	Total	Qty.

Aggregate Acquisition Cost $

2. Equipment Location:

Unit Description	Street Address	City	County	State	Zip

3. Acquisition Cost:
The "Acquisition Cost" of each Unit shall mean the sum of the actual purchase price of such Unit plus the additional expenses listed below (not to exceed in the aggregate % of the actual purchase price of such Unit):

4. Acquisition Expiration Date: _____

5. Lease Term:
The "Lease Term" of each Unit shall be that period specified below:

Unit Description	Primary Term

plus a period of time ("Interim Term"), if any, from the Acceptance Certificate Execution Date to, but not including,

6. Rent:
The daily Rent for each Unit for the Interim Term, if any, shall be equal to the daily equivalent (based on a 30-day month and a 360-day year) of the Rent specified below.

The Rent for each Unit during the Primary Term shall be payable in that number of consecutive, level payments indicated below, in _____ on the _____ day of each _____ and each Rent payment shall be in an amount equal to the indicated percentage of Acquisition Cost of such Unit.

Unit Description	*Number of Rent Payments*	*Percentage of Acquisition Cost*

7. Late Charge:
   _____ % per annum.

8. Casualty Value:
   The Casualty Value from time to time of each Unit shall be as specified on Annex A to this Lease.

9. Maintenance Agreement Requirements:
   (If none, so state.)

10. Identification:
    Lessee shall place the following identification marking prominently on each Unit:

    (Insert name of leasing company), Lessor/Owner, (Insert City of Lessor) (Insert State of Lessor)

11. Special Terms:
    The following Riders attached hereto shall constitute a part of this Lease:

12. Definitions:
    The terms used in this Lease which are not otherwise defined herein shall have the meanings set forth in the Master Agreement to Lease Equipment identified above.

13. Terms of Schedule:
    Lessor and Lessee agree that this Lease shall constitute a lease of each Unit described in Section 1 of this Lease, upon the execution and delivery to Lessor by Lessee of an Acceptance Certificate with respect to such Unit in the form of Annex B to this Lease, and of which each such Unit shall be subject to the terms and conditions of this Lease and of the Master Agreement to Lease Equipment, the terms and conditions of which are hereby incorporated by reference in full in this Lease and made a part of this Lease to the same extent as if such terms and conditions were set forth herein.

IN WITNESS WHEREOF, Lessor and Lessee have caused this Lease to be duly executed by their authorized representatives as of the date first above written.

       , Lessor

By:

Title:

       , Lessee

By:

Title:

Annex A to Schedule No.

[See Casualty Value Table, Form l-03c]

Annex B to Schedule No.

[See Acceptance Certificate, Form l-03b]

Form: I-03b
Disk File Name: I-03b.rtf

ACCEPTANCE CERTIFICATE

Form Purpose

Lessee equipment certificate of acceptance. This form is integrated with a master equipment lease agreement, Lease Agreement Form l-03.

Executing Parties
The equipment lessee.

See:
Lease Agreement, Form l-03

Annex B to Schedule No.

Acceptance Certificate No.   under Schedule No.   , dated as of   , to Master Agreement to Lease Equipment dated as of   , between   , Lessor, and   , Lessee

Acceptance Certificate Execution Date:

This Acceptance Certificate is issued pursuant to the Master Agreement to Lease Equipment and Schedule designated above.

Lessee acknowledges that each Unit specified on Exhibit A (i) has been delivered to, inspected by, and accepted as of this date for lease by Lessee, (ii) is of a size, design, capacity, and manufacture acceptable to Lessee and suitable for Lessee's purposes, (iii) is in good working order, repair, and condition, and (iv) has been installed to Lessee's satisfaction or located, as the case may be, at the location specified on Exhibit A.

Lessee confirms and agrees that (i) no Incipient Default or Event of Default under any Lease entered into pursuant to the Master Agreement to Lease Equipment has occurred and is continuing and (ii) the representations and warranties in the Officer's Certificate dated   executed and delivered in connection with the Lease are correct and complete as though made on and as of the date hereof and shall continue to be correct and complete throughout the Lease Term of each Unit accepted hereby.

The person signing this Acceptance Certificate on behalf of Lessee hereby certifies that such person has read and acknowledges all terms and conditions of the Lease, and is duly authorized to execute this Acceptance Certificate on behalf of Lessee.

The terms used in this Acceptance Certificate shall have the same meanings defined in the Master Agreement to Lease Equipment and the Schedule designated above.

                , Lessee

By:

Title:

Exhibit A to

Acceptance Certificate No.   , dated   , to Schedule No.   ,
dated   , to Master Agreement to Lease Equipment, dated   ,   between
                              , Lessor and ,   Lessee

Qty.	Mfr. or Vendor	Unit Descrip. Model	Term	Periodic Primary Rent (in Dollars)	New/ Used	Location	I.D. or Ser. No.	Acquisition Cost Per Unit	Total

Aggregate Acquisition Cost of Units subject to this Acceptance Certificate $

Form: I-03c
Disk File Name: I-03c.rtf

CASUALTY VALUE TABLE

Form Purpose

Equipment casualty value table. This form is integrated with a master equipment lease agreement, Lease Agreement, Form l-03.

Executing Parties
The equipment lessee.

See:
Lease Agreement, Form l-03

Annex A
to Schedule No.

The Casualty Value of any Unit shall be an amount equal to the product of the Acquisition Cost of such Unit times the percentage below corresponding to the number of the last Rent payment received by Lessor, plus any unpaid Rent with respect to the Rent payment period during which the applicable Event of Loss occurred. [See table on next page.]

After Rent Payment No.	Percentage	After Rent Payment No.	Percentage	After Rent Payment No.	Percentage
0					
1		41		81	
2		42		82	
3		43		83	
4		44		84	
5		45		85	
6		46		86	
7		47		87	
8		48		88	
9		49		90	
10		50		90	
11		51		91	
12		52		92	
13		53		93	
14		54		94	
15		55		95	
16		56		96	
17		57		97	
18		58		97	
19		49		99	
20		60		100	
21		61		101	
22		62		102	
23		63		103	
24		64		104	
25		65		105	
26		66		106	
27		67		107	
28		68		108	
29		69		109	
30		70		110	
31		71		111	
32		72		112	
33		73		113	
34		74		114	
35		75		115	
36		76		116	
37		77		117	
38		78		118	
39		79		119	
40		80		120	

Acknowledged by Lessee this   day of , <u>20   </u>.

                              , Lessee

By:

Title:

Form: I-03d
Disk File Name: I-03d.rtf

Representation and Warranties

Form Purpose

Lessee representation and warranty Rider integrated with a master equipment lease agreement, Lease Agreement, Form l-03.

Executing Parties
The equipment lessee.

See:
Lease Agreement, Form l-03

RIDER   to Schedule No.   dated as of   , to Master Agreement to
Lease Equipment, dated as of   , between   , Lessor, and
                                                  Lessee.

Lessee's Representations and Warranties

The undersigned ("Lessee"), in connection with the execution and delivery of the Equipment Leasing Agreement ("Lessee") dated as of the date hereof, entered into between   ("Lessor") and Lessee, hereby represents and warrants to you, and agrees with you, as follows:

(a) Lessee is a corporation duly organized, validly existing, and in good standing under the laws of the State of   ; Lessee has full power and authority and all necessary licenses and permits to carry on its business as presently conducted, to own or hold under lease its properties and to enter into the Lease and to perform its obligations under the Lease; and Lessee is duly qualified to do business as a foreign corporation and is in good standing in each jurisdiction in which the character of its properties or the nature of its business or the performance of its obligations under the Lease requires such qualifications.

(b) The execution and delivery by Lessee of the Lease and the performance by Lessee of its obligations under the Lease have been duly authorized by all necessary corporate action on the part of Lessee; do not contravene any law, governmental rule or regulation, or any order, writ, injunction, decree, judgment, award, determination, direction, or demand (collectively "Order") binding on Lessee or its properties or the corporate charter or by-laws of Lessee, and do not and will not contravene the provisions of, or constitute a default (either with or without notice or lapse of time, or both) under, or result in the creation of any security interests in or lien, charge, claim, or encumbrance upon, the Equipment or any property of Lessee under any indenture, mortgage, contract, or other instrument to which Lessee is a party or by which Lessee or its properties is bound.

(c) No consent or approval of, giving of notice to, registration with, or taking of any action by, any state, federal or other governmental commission, agency, or regulatory authority or any other person or entity is required for the consummation or performance by Lessee of the transactions contemplated under the Lease.

(d) The Lease has been duly entered into and delivered by Lessee, and constitutes a legal, valid, and binding agreement of Lessee enforceable against Lessee in accordance with its terms, except as limited by any bankruptcy, insolvency, reorganization, or other similar laws of general application affecting the enforcement of creditor or lessor rights.

(e) There are no actions, suits, or proceedings pending or threatened against or affecting Lessee or any property of Lessee in any court, before any arbitrator of any kind or before or by any federal, state, municipal, or other governmental department, commission, board, bureau agency, or instrumentality (collectively "Governmental Body"), which if adversely determined, would materially adversely affect the business, assets, operations, or conditions, financial or otherwise, of Lessee, or adversely affect the ability of Lessee to perform its obligations under the Lease; and Lessee is not in default with respect to any Order of any court, arbitrator, or Governmental Body.

(f) Each financial statement of Lessee furnished to Lessor by Lessee fairly presents the financial information set forth therein with respect to Lessee as of and for the period ended on each date specified therein in conformity with generally accepted accounting principles and practices consistently applied, and since the latest such date of each type of financial statement furnished to Lessor by Lessee, there has not been any material adverse change in the information set forth therein, in the business or condition, financial or otherwise, of Lessee.

(g) Lessee is not a party to any agreement or instrument or subject to any charter or other corporate restriction which materially adversely affects or, so far as Lessee can now foresee, will materially adversely affect the business, operations or properties of Lessee or the ability of Lessee to perform its obligations under the Lease.

(h) Lessee has filed all required tax returns in all jurisdictions in which such returns were required to be filed and has paid, or made provision for, all taxes shown to be due and payable on such returns and all other taxes and assessments which are payable by it, except for any taxes and assessments of which the amount applicability or validity is currently being contested in good faith by appropriate proceedings and which in the aggregate do not involve material amounts.

(i) Lessee is not in default in the payment of the principal or interest on any indebtedness for borrowed money or in default under any instrument or agreement under or subject to which any indebtedness for borrowed money has been issued; no event has occurred and is continuing under the provisions of any such instrument or agreement which with the lapse of time or the giving of notice, or both, would constitute a default or an event of default thereunder; Lessee is not in violation of any provision of its corporate charter or by-laws or of any term of any material agreement, lease of real or personal property, including any term providing for the payment of rent, or other instrument; and no Event of Default has occurred and is continuing with respect to the Lease as of the date hereof.

(j) Lessee has not taken and will not take any action or maintain any position inconsistent with treating the Lease as a valid leasehold interest in the Equipment.

The terms used herein which are defined in the Lease shall have the respective meanings set forth in the Lease, unless otherwise defined herein.

Dated:

                                        , Lessee

By:

Title:

Attest:

Clerk/Secretary, if corporate Lessee

Form: I-03e
Disk File Name: I-03e.rtf

OPINION OF COUNSEL—LESSEE FORM

Form Purpose

A Lessee's counsel form of legal opinion. The form opinion is integrated with master lease agreement, Lease Agreement, Form l-03.

Executing Parties
Counsel for the equipment lessee.

See:
Lease Agreement, Form l-03

[Form of Opinion to Be Delivered by Counsel for Lessee]

Dated

    [Insert name and address of leasing company]

    Re: Equipment Lease dated   ,
    by and between (insert name of lessor),
    and (insert name of lessee)

Dear Sirs:

We have acted as counsel for   , a   corporation ("Lessee"), in connection with the execution and delivery of a lease between you, as Lessor, and Lessee, in the form of a Schedule, dated   . ("Lease"), relating to the lease of certain equipment described therein, entered into pursuant to a Master Agreement to Lease Equipment, dated   , between you, as Lessor, and Lessee ("Agreement"). The Lease incorporates the terms and provisions of the Agreement.

This opinion is furnished to you in connection with Lessee's execution and delivery to you of the Lease. The terms used herein which are defined in the Lease shall have the meanings set forth in the Lease, unless otherwise defined herein.

In connection with this opinion, we have examined executed counterparts of the Agreement and the Lease and such corporate documents and records of Lessee, certificates of public officials and of officers of Lessee, and such other documents and questions of fact and law as we have deemed necessary or appropriate for the purposes of this opinion.

Based upon the foregoing, we are of the opinion that:

    (1) Lessee is a corporation duly organized and validly existing in good standing under the laws of the State of   and is duly qualified and authorized to do business and is in good standing in every other jurisdiction where the nature of Lessee's business or activities and the transactions contemplated by the Agreement and the Lease require such qualification;

    (2) Lessee is duly authorized to lease the Units, execute and deliver the Agreement and the Lease, and to perform its obligations under the Lease;

    (3) The execution and delivery of the Agreement and the Lease by Lessee, and the performance by Lessee of its obligations under the Lease, do not and will not conflict with any provision of law or any provision of the charter or by-laws of Lessee or of any indenture, mortgage, deed of trust, or other agreement or instrument binding upon Lessee or its properties or to which Lessee is a party;

(4) The execution and delivery of the Agreement and the Lease by Lessee, and the performance and consummation by Lessee of the transactions contemplated thereunder, do not require the consent, approval, or authorization of, or giving of notice to, or registration or filing with, any federal, state, or local governmental authority or public regulatory body or any other person or entity;

(5) The Lease is a legal, valid, and binding obligation of Lessee enforceable against Lessee in accordance with its terms, except as limited by any bankruptcy, insolvency, reorganization, or other similar laws of general application affecting the enforcement of creditor or lessor rights;

(6) There are no pending or threatened actions or proceedings before any arbitrator, court, or administrative agency which will, if adversely determined, adversely affect to a material extent the financial condition or operations of Lessee or its ability to perform its obligations under the Lease; and

(7) There exists no person, partnership, corporation, or other entity which is or will as a result of Lessee's execution, delivery, and performance of the Lease be entitled to a Lien (except Lessor's Liens) with respect to any Unit.

Very truly yours,

Form: I-03f
Disk File Name: I-03f.rtf

OPINION OF COUNSEL—GUARANTOR FORM

Form Purpose

A lessee guarantor's counsel form of legal opinion. The form opinion is integrated with the master lease agreement, Lease Agreement, Form I-03.

Executing Parties
Counsel for the equipment lessee's guarantor.

See:
Lease Agreement, Form I-03

[Form of Opinion to Be Delivered by Counsel for Guarantor of Lessee's Obligations]

Dated

[Insert name and address of leasing company]

Re: Equipment Lease dated   ,
by and between (insert name of lessor), and
(insert name of lessee).

Dear Sirs,

We have acted as counsel for   , a   corporation ("Guarantor"), in connection with the execution and delivery of the Guaranty, dated   ("Guaranty"), made by the Guarantor in your favor. The Guaranty relates to the performance by   , a   corporation ("Lessee"), of its obligations under a lease in the form of a Schedule, dated   , between you, as Lessor, and Lessee ("Lease"), relating to the lease of certain equipment described therein, entered into pursuant to a Master Agreement to Lease Equipment, dated   , (the "Agreement").

This opinion is furnished to you in connection with Guarantor's execution and delivery of the Guaranty.

In connection with this opinion, we have examined executed counterparts of the Agreement, the Lease and the Guaranty, and such corporate documents and records of Guarantor, certificates of public officials and of officers of Guarantor, and such other documents and questions of fact and law as we have deemed necessary or appropriate for the purposes of this opinion.

Based upon the foregoing, we are of the opinion that:

   (1) Guarantor is a corporation duly organized and validly existing in good standing under the laws of the State of   and is duly qualified and authorized to do business and is in good standing in every other jurisdiction where the nature of Guarantor's business or activities and the performance of its obligations under the Guaranty require such qualification;

   (2) Guarantor is duly authorized to execute and deliver the Guaranty and to perform its obligations thereunder;

   (3) The execution and delivery of the Guaranty by Guarantor, and the performance by Guarantor of its obligations thereunder, do not conflict with any provision of law or any provision of the charter or by-laws of Guarantor or of any indenture, mortgage, deed of trust, or agreement or instrument binding upon Guarantor or its properties or to which Guarantor is a party;

(4) The execution, delivery, and performance of the Guaranty by Guarantor do not require the consent, approval, or authorization of, or giving of notice to, or registration or filing with, any federal, state, or local governmental authority or public regulatory body or any other person or entity;

(5) The Guaranty is a legal, valid, and binding obligation of the Guarantor enforceable against Guarantor in accordance with its terms, except as limited by any bankruptcy, insolvency, reorganization, or other similar laws of general application affecting the enforcement of creditor or lessor rights; and

(6) There are no pending or threatened actions or proceedings before any arbitrator, court, or administrative agency which will if adversely determined, adversely affect to a material extent the financial condition or operations of Guarantor or its ability to perform its obligations under the Guaranty.

Very truly yours,

Form: I-04
Disk File Name: I-04.rtf

LEVERAGED LEASE (AIRCRAFT/GENERAL)

Form Purpose

A comprehensive equipment lease agreement, part of a leveraged lease financing transaction. The transaction contemplates the sale of an aircraft by the manufacturer to an airline, and then the entering into of a sale/leaseback between the airline (lessee) and the aircraft lessor. Although the form contemplates the lease of an aircraft, modifications can be made for any type of equipment. This form is integrated with typical documents found in a leveraged lease transaction. (*Author's Note:* The capitalized terms, which are not defined in the lease agreement, or the other transaction documents [see below], are defined in the Participation Agreement, Form l-04b, as is customary; specifically in Appendix A to the agreement. This form, although it covers the lease of an aircraft, is an excellent reference for a wide variety of leasing concepts and provisions.)

Executing Parties
The equipment lessor.
The equipment lessee.

See:
Assignment of Rights Under Purchase Agreement, Form l-04a
Participation Agreement, Form l-04b
Trust Indenture and Security Agreement, Form l-04c
Trust Agreement, Form l-04d
Tax Indemnity Agreement, Form l-04e

FORM ON CD ONLY

Form: I-04a
Disk File Name: I-04a.rtf

ASSIGNMENT OF RIGHTS UNDER PURCHASE AGREEMENT

Form Purpose

An assignment of rights under an equipment purchase agreement in which the parties set forth the terms and conditions of the equipment purchase. This form is part of a leveraged lease transaction and is integrated with a Participation Agreement, a Trust Indenture and Security Agreement, a Trust Agreement, and a Lease Agreement.

Executing Parties
The equipment lessee.
The owner participant.

See:
Participation Agreement, Form l-04b
Trust Indenture and Security Agreement, Form l-04c
Trust Agreement, Form l-04d
Leveraged Lease, Form l-04
Tax Indemnity Agreement, Form l-04e

FORM ON CD ONLY

Form: I-04b
Disk File Name: I-04b.rtf

PARTICIPATION AGREEMENT

Form Purpose

A leveraged lease participation agreement in which all parties to the leveraged lease transaction set forth the terms and conditions of their participation in the financing transaction. This form is integrated with a Leveraged Lease Agreement, an Assignment of Rights Under Purchase Agreement, a Trust Indenture and Security Agreement, a Trust Agreement, and a Tax Indemnity Agreement.

Executing Parties
The equipment lessee.
The equipment lessor.
The equipment lenders.
The lender trustee.

See:
Leveraged Lease, Form l-04
Assignment of Rights Under Purchase Agreement, Form l-04a
Trust Indenture and Security Agreement, Form l-04c
Trust Agreement, Form l-04d
Tax Indemnity Agreement, Form l-04e

FORM ON CD ONLY

Form: I-04c
Disk File Name: I-04c.rtf

TRUST INDENTURE AND SECURITY AGREEMENT

Form Purpose

A leveraged lease trust indenture and security agreement in which all parties to the leveraged lease transaction set forth the terms and conditions of lending arrangement. This form is integrated with a Participation Agreement, a Trust Agreement, an Assignment of Rights Under Purchase Agreement, a Lease Agreement, and a Tax Indemnity Agreement.

Executing Parties
The owner trustee.
The indenture trustee.

See:
Assignment of Rights Under Purchase Agreement, Form l-04a
Leveraged Lease, Form l-04
Participation Agreement, Form l-04b
Trust Agreement, Form l-04d
Tax Indemnity Agreement, Form l-04e

FORM ON CD ONLY

Form: I-04d
Disk File Name: I-04d.rtf

TRUST AGREEMENT

Form Purpose

A leveraged lease trust agreement in which the lending party in the leveraged lease transaction sets forth the terms and conditions of trust arrangement. This form is integrated with a Participation Agreement, a Trust Indenture and Security Agreement, an Assignment of Rights Under Purchase Agreement, a Lease Agreement, and a Tax Indemnity Agreement.

Executing Parties
The owner participant.
The indenture trustee.

See:
Assignment of Rights Under Purchase Agreement, Form l-04a
Leveraged Lease, Form l-04
Participation Agreement, Form l-04b
Trust Indenture and Security Agreement, Form l-04c
Tax Indemnity Agreement, Form l-04e

FORM ON CD ONLY

Form: I-04e
Disk File Name: I-04e.rtf

TAX INDEMNITY AGREEMENT

Form Purpose

A leveraged lease tax indemnity agreement in which the lessor sets forth the terms and conditions of the tax indemnity arrangement. This form is integrated with a Participation Agreement, a Trust Indenture and Security Agreement, a Trust Agreement, an Assignment of Rights Under Purchase Agreement, and a Lease Agreement.

Executing Parties
The owner participant.
The equipment lessee.

See:
Assignment of Rights Under Purchase Agreement, Form l-04a
Leveraged Lease, Form l-04
Participation Agreement, Form l-04b
Trust Indenture and Security Agreement, Form l-04c
Trust Agreement, Form l-04d

FORM ON CD ONLY

Form: I-05
Disk File Name: I-05.rtf

LOAN AND SECURITY AGREEMENT—SHORT FORM

Form Purpose

A short form equipment loan and security agreement setting forth a nonrecourse loan arrangement between a lender and an equipment leasing company, the proceeds of which are to be used by the leasing company to pay for equipment subject to lease. By deleting the nonrecourse limitation, the form can be used to document a recourse loan arrangement. This form references a promissory note and an assignment, both of which have been integrated with this form.

Executing Parties
The borrower (equipment lessor).
The lender.

See:
Promissory Note—Integrated, Form p-02
Assignment of Lease to Lender—Multiple Takedowns, Form a-05

Loan and Security Agreement

This Loan and Security Agreement, dated   , (the "Agreement") by and between
                              , a (insert jurisdiction of incorporation) (the "Borrower"),
with a place of business at   , and   ,
a (insert jurisdiction of incorporation) (the "Lender"), with a place of business at   .

Subject to the terms and conditions of this Agreement, Lender agrees to lend to Borrower on or before
              , an aggregate amount (the "Loan") equal to   % of the purchase price of certain newly
manufactured equipment, as described in Exhibit A hereto (the "Units") which are subject to an Equipment
Lease Agreement dated as of   between Borrower, as lessor, and   ,
as lessee (the "Lessee") (said lease together with its (two) equipment schedules, hereinafter referred to as the
"Lease").

    1. Use of Loan Proceeds. The proceeds of the Loan shall be applied toward the cost to Lessor of the
Units (the "Purchase Price") which are the subject of the Lease.

    2. Closing; Conditions Precedent. It is anticipated that the Loan will be made in (two) installments. The
first will be made on (insert appropriate date) with respect to Units accepted for lease by Lessee prior to such
date. The second installment will be made on (insert appropriate date) with respect to all other Units leased
by Lessee. On each such date that an installment is made (a "Closing Date"), Borrower will deliver to Lender
a promissory note substantially in the form annexed hereto as Exhibit A [*Author's Note:* For promissory note
integrated with this Loan and Security Agreement, see Form p-02], in the principal amount of the loan being
made on such Closing Date (a "Note"). The obligation of Lender to make the Loan hereunder is subject to the
performance by Borrower of all of its respective covenants, agreements, and other obligations required to be
performed under this Agreement, and to the following further conditions:

        (a) On or prior to the first Closing Date, Lender shall have received:

           (i) an assignment executed by Borrower in substantially the form annexed hereto as Exhibit B
[*Author's Note:* For assignment agreement integrated with this form, see Form a-05] (the "Assignment);

           (ii) an opinion of counsel for Borrower, in form and substance satisfactory to Lender, to the effect
that (A) Borrower is a corporation duly organized and existing and in good standing under the laws
of the jurisdiction of its incorporation, with adequate power to enter into and perform this Agreement and the Lease and (B) this Agreement, the Lease, the Assignment, and the Notes have been duly
authorized, executed, and delivered by Borrower and are (or will be in the case of the Notes) legal,
valid, and binding instruments enforceable in accordance with their respective terms (which opinion
of counsel may be subject to appropriate qualifications as to applicable bankruptcy law and other
similar laws affecting creditors' rights generally);

(iii) Lessor's original, executed copy of the Lease; and

(iv) such other documents as Lender shall reasonably request.

(b) In respect of each Closing Date Lender shall have received:

(i) notice of Lessee's acceptance of Units for lease, the date of such acceptance and the amount of the Purchase Price of the Units to be paid by Borrower for such Units, and (ii) a Note in the principal amount of the Loan being made on such Closing Date and payable to Lender.

(c) The first Closing shall be held at the offices of   or as otherwise agreed to by the parties. Each Loan shall be made by a bank wire transfer or by a certified or official bank check in New York Clearing House funds payable to the order of Borrower. On each Closing Date Borrower shall execute and deliver to Lender a single Note in the principal amount of the Loan being made on such date.

3. Repayment. The principal amount of each Note shall be repaid by Borrower to Lender in such number of installments and on such dates ("Payment Dates") as are specified in the Note. The unpaid balance of the Note shall bear interest from the Closing Date in respect thereof at the rate of   % per annum. Interest shall be payable on each Payment Date and on such other dates as are set forth in the Note. The principal amount of the Note payable on each Payment Date shall be calculated so that the aggregate of the principal and interest payable on each of the Payment Dates shall be substantially equal and the aggregate of all such payments will completely amortize the Loan. Interest under the Notes shall be determined on the basis of a 360-day year of twelve 30-day months. Borrower will pay Lender interest, computed at a rate per annum equal to   %, on all installments of principal and, to the extent legally enforceable, interest remaining unpaid after the same shall have become due and payable. All payments shall be made in immediately available and lawful money of the United States of America. Lender agrees to furnish Borrower as a schedule to each Note, an amortization table showing the respective amounts of principal and interest payable on each Payment Date and the unpaid principal amount outstanding ("Loan Schedules").

It is anticipated that once all Units have been accepted for lease, Borrower and Lessee will consolidate the various (quarterly) rental payment schedules with respect to all Units. In such event, Borrower and Lender will consolidate the Notes based on the amount of unamortized principal into a single Note which shall be amortized with Payment Dates concurrent with the consolidated lease payment dates.

In the event that Lessee shall pay amounts in respect of a casualty occurrence or condemnation or seizure of any Units as set forth in the Lease, a sum equal to such payment shall be applied to the prepayment without penalty of the applicable Note secured by such Units. Each such prepayment shall be applied, first, to the payment of all accrued and unpaid interest under such Note to the date of such prepayment and, second, to the pro rata reduction of the respective principal amounts of the remaining unpaid installments of the Note, and the amount of interest included in each future installment shall be correspondingly reduced to reflect such reductions in principal amount. Borrower shall pay such amounts together with an amount equal to interest at   % per annum compounded monthly from the date said accelerated payments are due to and including the date of receipt.

Upon acceleration of a Note as provided in this Agreement, Borrower shall pay an amount equal to interest at a rate of   % per annum compounded monthly from the date said amounts are due and payable to the date of receipt, not to exceed the maximum interest rate permitted by law.

Borrower hereby authorizes Lender (i) to collect all payments to be made by Lessee under the Lease and (ii) to separate and retain for Lender's account the applicable payments as and when due to Lender. Borrower agrees to direct Lessee to make all payments to be made by it under the Lease, directly to Lender. Borrower agrees that should it receive any such payments with respect to the Units or the Lease that have been assigned to Lender pursuant to the Assignment; it will promptly forward such payments to Lender for disbursement in accord with the terms hereof. Lender agrees to apply amounts from time to time received by it (from Lessee, Borrower, or otherwise) with respect to the Lease or the Units, to the extent such amounts have been assigned to Lender pursuant to the Assignment, first to the payment of the principal of and interest on any Note then due and any other amounts then due and payable under this Agreement, and then, if no event of default hereunder shall have occurred and be continuing, promptly to pay any balance to Borrower no later than the day after receipt of such payment by depositing such payments to the account of Borrower in Borrower's account at   or such other account as Borrower may designate in writing. Any payments Lender receives with respect to the Lease or Units that have not been assigned to Lender shall be remitted by Lender to the said account of Borrower.

4. Security. Borrower hereby grants to Lender a security interest in the Units (subject to the rights to the use of the Units by Lessee pursuant to the Lease) and in the Lease, and for such purpose, assigns to Lender the Lease and all payments due or to become due thereunder pursuant and subject to the terms of the Assignment, to secure obligations of Borrower hereunder and under the Notes. Borrower hereby authorizes Lender to file or record this Agreement, the Assignment or financing statements with respect to Lender's security interest in the Units and the Lease with any appropriate governmental office in order to perfect such security interest. The security interest created thereunder will terminate when all obligations of Borrower hereunder and under the Notes are discharged, and Lender, at the request of Borrower, will then execute termination statements and such other documents as may be necessary or appropriate to make clear upon the public records the termination of such security interest.

Borrower hereby appoints Lender its true and lawful attorney, with full power of substitution, to enforce Borrower's rights as Lessor under the Lease, and to take any action which Lender may deem necessary or appropriate to protect and preserve the security interest of Lender.

5. Limitation on Liability. The liability of Borrower with respect to the payments specified in Section 3 hereof shall be nonrecourse to the Buyer and shall be limited to the Units, the Lease, and "income and proceeds therefrom," but Borrower's liability hereunder shall not be so limited in respect of any breach or inaccuracy of the covenants, warranties, and agreements contained in Section 6 hereof. As used herein the phrase "income and proceeds therefrom" shall mean:

(i) all Rent (as defined in the Lease) and any other sums due or to become due under the Lease which have been assigned to Lender, including but not limited to all proceeds of insurance, or payments due as a result of a casualty occurrence or condemnation, and

(ii) any and all payments or funds received by Borrower or Lender for or with respect to the Units as a result of the sale or other disposition thereof.

Notwithstanding the limitation on liability of Borrower otherwise herein contained, the obligation of Borrower to pay the principal of and interest on the Loan and all other amounts payable to Lender hereunder shall be fully enforceable (by appropriate proceedings against Borrower in law or in equity or otherwise) against Borrower's right, title, and interest in the Units, the Lease, the Rent, and any other assigned sums due or to become due under the Lease, and nothing contained herein limiting the liability of Borrower shall derogate from the right of Lender to enforce its security interest in the Units or the Lease for the unpaid principal of and interest on the Loan and all other amounts payable to Lender hereunder and under the Notes, including, without limitation, the right to accelerate the maturity of payments on the Loan as provided herein upon an event of default hereunder and to proceed against Lessee under the Lease and to realize upon the Units.

6. Covenants, Warranties, and Agreements of Borrower.

Borrower covenants, warrants, and agrees that:

(a) it will not, except with the prior written consent of Lender, agree to modify any material provision of the Lease or give any consent thereunder;

(b) on each Closing Date Borrower will have good and marketable title to the subject Units and the interest of Borrower in the Units, the Lease, the Rent, and any other assigned sums due or to become due under the Lease will continue to be held free and clear of security interests, liens, claims, encumbrances, and rights of others (excepting only the rights of Lender hereunder and of Lessee under the Lease);

(c) this Agreement, the Assignment, and the Loan have been duly authorized by Borrower;

(d) the execution and delivery of this Agreement, the Assignment, the Notes, the Lease, and the carrying out of the transactions contemplated hereby and thereby do not and will not constitute a default under, or result in the creation of any lien, charge, encumbrance, or security interest upon any assets of Borrower under, any agreement, (except this Agreement) or instrument to which Borrower is a party or by which its assets may be bound or affected;

(e) Borrower, at its expense, will fulfill all its obligations under the Lease and, upon default, will, upon the request of Lender, enforce all its rights as Lessor under the Lease or such other rights as Lender shall request;

(f) Borrower will maintain, preserve, and keep in full force and effect its corporate existence and all rights and qualifications necessary for the enforcement of the Lease by Borrower or Lender; and

(g) except for the Lease and this Agreement, Borrower will not sell, loan, pledge, mortgage, assign, or otherwise dispose of, or create or suffer to be created any levies, liens, or encumbrances on the Units, the Lease, or any interest or part thereof.

7. Representations of Lender. Lender represents that except as heretofore disclosed in writing to special counsel for Lender, it is acquiring the Notes for its own account for investment and not with a view to, or for sale in connection with, any distribution thereof, but subject, nevertheless, to any requirement of law that the disposition of its property shall at all times be within its control. Lender understands that the Notes to be issued hereunder have not been registered under the Securities Act of 1933, as amended.

Lender hereby agrees that any transfer or assignment of the Notes or of all or any part of its interest hereunder shall be on the express condition that the transferee or assignee shall be bound by the terms of this Agreement.

8. Default.

(a) Any of the following events shall constitute an event of default hereunder:

(i) payment of any part of the principal of or interest on the Note shall not be made when and as the same shall become due and payable (irrespective of the limitations contained in Section 5 hereof), and such default shall continue unremedied for 10 days;

(ii) Borrower shall default in the due observance or performance of any other covenants, conditions, or provisions hereof or of the Assignment or the Lease and such default shall continue for more than 10 days after written notice from Lender specifying the default and demanding the same to be remedied;

(iii) Borrower shall cease doing business as a going concern, make an assignment for the benefit of creditors, admit in writing its inability to pay its debts as they become due, file a voluntary petition in bankruptcy, be adjudicated a bankrupt or an insolvent, file a petition seeking for itself any reorganization, arrangement, composition, readjustment, liquidation, dissolution, or similar arrangement under any present or future statute, law, or regulation or file an answer admitting the material allegations or a petition filed against it in any such proceeding, or consent to or acquiesce in the appointment of a trustee, receiver, or liquidator of it or all or any substantial part of its assets or properties, or if any of them shall take action looking to its dissolution or liquidation or if any, within 30 days after the commencement of any proceedings against Borrower seeking reorganization, arrangement, readjustment, liquidation, dissolution, or similar relief under any present or future statute, law, or regulation, such proceedings shall not have been dismissed, or if within 30 days after the appointment without Borrower's consent or acquiescence of any trustee, receiver, or liquidator of it or of all or any substantial part of its assets or properties, such appointment shall not be vacated; and

(v) an Event of Default (as the term is defined in the Lease) shall have occurred and be continuing under the Lease.

In case an event of default shall have occurred and be continuing hereunder, Lender may declare the entire unpaid principal amounts of the Notes outstanding and unpaid interest thereon and any other sums owed hereunder immediately due and payable, subject, however, to the limitations as to the liability of Borrower contained in Section 5 hereof, and Lender shall have all the rights and remedies of a secured party under the Uniform Commercial Code. If an Event of Default shall have occurred and be continuing under the Lease, Lender may exercise all rights and remedies of Borrower, as Lessor under the Lease and apply any amounts realized in consequence thereof against the unpaid principal amount of the Note and unpaid interest thereon.

(b) Notwithstanding the foregoing, an Event of Default under the Lease resulting from nonpayment of Rent due thereunder on a specific Payment Date shall not be an event of default hereunder provided that (i) Borrower shall have paid the full amount of such defaulted Rent within ten days of notification to Borrower of such nonpayment (notwithstanding the limitation of Borrower's obligation set forth in Section 5 hereof), (ii) Lender shall have reasonably determined that the delaying of a declaration of such an event of default would not have a materially adverse effect on the exercise or realization of Lender's rights hereunder with respect to the Units or (iii) Lessee shall have made the next preceding payment of Rent when due, together with the payment of Rent then in arrears.

9. Notes. Lender, upon payment to it of all amounts payable to it hereunder and under the Notes, will surrender the Notes to Borrower. Lender shall be entitled to all payments due hereunder and under the Notes without being required to surrender the Notes. However, Lender agrees to make appropriate notation on the Notes before any transfer thereof to reflect all payments of principal and interest theretofore received.

10. Notice. All notices required or permitted to be delivered hereunder shall be in writing and shall be deemed given when delivered or when deposited in the United States mails, certified, postage prepaid and addressed with the full name and address of the appropriate party set forth below:

If to Borrower:

If to Lender:

    11. Execution; Controlling Law; Successors and Assigns. This Agreement may be executed in one or more counterparts, each of which, when so executed, shall be deemed to be an original, and such counterparts, together shall constitute one and the same agreement, which shall be sufficiently evidenced by one of such original counterparts. This Agreement shall be governed by and be construed in accordance with the laws of the State of   and shall inure to the benefit of and be binding upon, Borrower and Lender and the permitted successors and assign.

Borrower:

(Insert name of borrower)

By:

Title:

Lender:

(Insert name of lender)

By:

Title:

Exhibit A

[Insert equipment description.]

Exhibit B

[See Form p-02.]

Exhibit C

[See Form a-05.]

Form: I-06
Disk File Name: I-06.rtf

LOAN AND SECURITY AGREEMENT—LONG FORM (RAILCARS/GENERAL)

Form Purpose

A comprehensive long form loan and security and loan agreement for railcar lending. This form contemplates a nonrecourse loan arrangement with respect to two separate equipment lease transactions. With minor modifications, the form may be used for any type of equipment, as well as cover a recourse loan arrangement. Collateral documents necessary to complete the loan transaction are integrated with this form (see below).

Executing Parties
The borrower.
The lender.

See:
Form of Note, Form l-06a
Form of Guaranty, Form l-06b
Form of Bill of Sale, Form l-06c
Form of Certificate of Acceptance, Form l-06d
Form of Certificate of Cost, Form l-06e
Form of Legal Opinion in General, Form l-06f
Form of Legal Opinion for Lessee—Special Counsel, Form l-06g

FORM ON CD ONLY

Form: I-06a
Disk File Name: I-06a.rtf

FORM OF NOTE

Form Purpose

A promissory note for use in connection with an equipment loan transaction. This form is integrated with Loan and Security Agreement, Form l-06.

Executing Parties
The borrower.

See:
Loan and Security Agreement, Form l-06

FORM ON CD ONLY

Form: I-06b
Disk File Name: I-06b.rtf

FORM OF GUARANTY

Form Purpose

A form of borrower guaranty for use with an equipment loan transaction. This form is integrated with Loan and Security Agreement, Form l-06.

Executing Parties
Borrower's guarantor.

See:
Loan and Security Agreement, Form l-06

FORM ON CD ONLY

Form: I-06c
Disk File Name: I-06c.rtf

FORM OF BILL OF SALE

Form Purpose

An equipment bill of sale for use in connection with an equipment loan transaction. This form is integrated with Loan and Security Agreement, Form l-06.

Executing Parties
The equipment vendor.

See:
Loan and Security Agreement, Form l-06

FORM ON CD ONLY

Form: I-06d
Disk File Name: I-06d.rtf

FORM OF CERTIFICATE OF ACCEPTANCE

Form Purpose

An equipment certificate of acceptance for use in connection with an equipment loan transaction. This is integrated with Loan and Security Agreement, Form l-06.

Executing Parties
The equipment lessee.

See:
Loan and Security Agreement, Form l-06

FORM ON CD ONLY

Form: I-06e
Disk File Name: I-06e.rtf

FORM OF CERTIFICATE OF COST

Form Purpose

A certificate of equipment cost for use in connection with an equipment loan transaction. This form is integrated with Loan and Security Agreement, Form l-06.

Executing Parties
The borrower.

See:
Loan and Security Agreement, Form l-06

FORM ON CD ONLY

Form: I-06f
Disk File Name: I-06f.rtf

FORM OF LEGAL OPINION—GENERAL

Form Purpose

A form of legal opinion for use by counsel for borrower and its guarantor in connecton with an equipment loan transaction. This form is integrated with Loan and Security Agreement, Form l-06.

Executing Parties
Counsel for borrower and guarantor.

See:
Loan and Security Agreement, Form l-06

FORM ON CD ONLY

Form: I-06g
Disk File Name: I-06g.rtf

FORM OF LEGAL OPINION—SPECIAL COUNSEL

Form Purpose

A form of legal opinion for use by special counsel for borrower in connection with an equipment loan transaction. This form is integrated with Loan and Security Agreement, Form l-06.

Executing Parties
Special counsel for borrower.

See:
Loan and Security Agreement, Form l-06

FORM ON CD ONLY

Form: I-07
Disk File Name: I-07.rtf

LOAN AND SECURITY AGREEMENT—MASTER FORMAT

Form Purpose

Form of master equipment security and loan agreement. The master format allows future equipment loans to be easily added by means of a schedule, and is integrated with all collateral closing documents (see below).

Executing Parties
The borrower.
The lender.

See:
Loan Supplement, Form l-07a
Promissory Note, Form l-07b
Acknowledgment and Consent to Assignment of Equipment Lease, Form l-07c
Supplement, Form l-07d

Master Loan and Security Agreement

dated as of

between

[   ]

Lender

and

[   ]

Borrower

Master Loan and Security Agreement

Table of Contents

Sections
1. Definitions
2. Loan Request
3. Loan
4. Place of Payment
5. Loan Prepayment
6. Payment Lease Amounts Due; Limitation of Liability
7. Lender Application of Amounts Received
8. Late Payments; Other Charges
9. Assignment and Grant of Security Interests
10. Lender Appointment as Attorney-in Fact
11. Assignments; Encumbrances; Transfers
12. Borrower's Representations and Warranties
13. Covenants of Borrower
14. Indemnity
15. Events of Default

16. Remedies
17. Lessee Quiet Enjoyment Right
18. Receipt of Funds by Borrower
19. Notices
20. Payment of Expenses and Taxes
21. Performance by Lender of Borrower's Obligations
22. Loan Request Right Termination
23. Miscellaneous

Exhibit A. Loan Supplement, See Form l-07a
Exhibit B. Promissory Note, See Form l-07b
Exhibit C. Acknowledgment and Consent to Assignment of Equipment Lease, See Form l-07c
Exhibit D. Supplement, See Form l-07d

MASTER LOAN AND SECURITY AGREEMENT (the "Master Agreement") entered into
as of the   day of   , 20   , by and between   ,
a   corporation having its principal place of business at
                                ("   Lender")   and   ,
                                   a corporation having its principal place of business at
                  ("Borrower").

WHEREAS, Borrower will be entering into arrangements from time to time for the purchase of certain equipment, which equipment will be, at the time of purchase, subject to various equipment leases between Borrower and various lessees;

WHEREAS, Borrower desires to obtain, from time to time, loans to finance a portion of the purchase price of certain Borrower specified equipment it will be purchasing and which will be subject to certain Borrower specified equipment leases; and

WHEREAS, pursuant to, and in accordance with, the terms of this Master Agreement Lender is willing to make loans, which loans meet Lender's lending criteria, to Borrower to purchase such equipment.

NOW, THEREFORE, In consideration of the foregoing and of the mutual covenants and conditions contained herein, Lender and Borrower hereby agree as follows:

The following terms shall have the respective meanings set forth below for all purposes of this Master Agreement (Terms defined in the singular shall have a comparable meaning when used in the plural and vice versa.):

1.1 Specific Definitions

"Business Day" shall mean a calendar day, excluding Saturdays, Sundays, and all days on which banking institutions in the State of   are authorized or required to be closed.
"Code" shall mean the Uniform Commercial Code, or comparable law, as now or hereafter in effect in any applicable jurisdiction.
"Collateral" with respect to a Loan shall have the meaning set forth in Section 9 of this Master Agreement.
"Cut-Off Date" shall mean the date specified in a Loan Supplement after which Lender shall not be obligated to make a Loan.
"Default" shall have the meaning set forth in Section 16 of this Master Agreement.
"Documents" shall have the meaning set forth in Section 23.1 of this Master Agreement.
"Equipment" shall mean the equipment described on a Loan Supplement together with all attachments, accessories, additions, parts, and equipment whenever affixed thereto.
"Equipment Lease" shall mean each equipment leasing agreement identified in a Loan Supplement, including without limitation all equipment schedules or supplements and all exhibits, and documents related to the equipment lease.
"Event of Default" shall mean any of the events or conditions specified in Section 15 of this Master Agreement.
"Event of Loss" shall have the meaning set forth in a Loan Supplement.
"Governmental Body" shall have the meaning set forth in Section 12.8 of this Master Agreement.
"Item of Equipment" shall mean an item of equipment described in a Loan Supplement.

"Interim Loan Term" as to any Loan shall mean the period of time, if any, commencing on the Loan Closing Date and ending on the day immediately preceding the date that the Primary Loan Term begins.

"Lessee" shall mean the Lessee identified in a Loan Supplement, and any and each guarantor of such Lessee obligations under the applicable Equipment Lease.

"Lessee Consent" shall mean an Acknowledgment and Consent to Assignment of Equipment Lease, as Lender may require a Lessee to execute and deliver on a Loan Closing Date.

"Lien" shall mean any mortgage, pledge, hypothecation, assignment, security interest, lien, charge, or encumbrance, priority, or other security agreement or arrangement or other claim or right of any kind or nature whatsoever created by Borrower (including any conditional sale or other title retention agreement, any lease, and the filing of, or agreement to give, any financing statement under the Uniform Commercial Code or comparable law of any jurisdiction), other than the rights of Lessee under an Equipment Lease and the rights of Lender under a Loan Agreement.

"Loan" shall mean the amount of money which Lender lends Borrower on the Loan Closing Date pursuant to a Loan Agreement.

"Loan Agreement" shall mean a Loan Supplement and all documentation attached thereto or delivered pursuant thereto, together with the Master Agreement made a part thereof as the same may from time to time be amended, supplemented, or otherwise modified. Each Loan Supplement shall be considered a separate and enforceable agreement incorporating the terms and conditions of this Master Agreement.

"Loan Closing Date" shall mean the date on which Borrower shall have received Loan proceeds.

"Loan Commencement Date" with respect to each Loan shall mean the date on which the Loan Term shall begin, as specified in a Loan Supplement.

"Loan Fee" shall be that fee, if any, specified as such in a Loan Supplement.

"Loan Interest Rate" with respect to a Loan shall mean that per annum interest rate specified in a Loan Supplement.

"Loan Request" shall have the meaning set forth in Section 2.2 of this Master Agreement.

"Loan Supplement" shall mean each supplement, substantially in the form of Exhibit A hereto, which shall refer to this Master Agreement and which shall become a part hereof as executed from time to time by the parties hereto, covering one or more Loans.

"Loan Term" with respect to a Loan shall mean the Primary Loan Term and any Interim Loan Term.

"Manufacturer" as to each Item of Equipment shall mean the manufacturer or vendor thereof specified in a Loan Supplement.

"Note" shall mean each secured promissory note, substantially in the form of Exhibit A hereto, including any amortization schedule attached thereto, issued and delivered by Borrower to Lender in connection with a Loan and which evidences the Loan repayment obligation of Borrower to Lender.

"Order" shall have the meaning set forth in Section 12.3 of this Master Agreement.

"Overdue Rate" shall mean the per annum interest charge specified in a Loan Supplement.

"Permitted Early Equipment Lease Termination" shall have the meaning set forth in Section 7.3 of this Master Agreement.

"Primary Loan Term" with respect to a Loan shall mean that period of time commencing on, and including, the date specified in a Loan Supplement on which the Primary Term shall begin, and ending that period of time thereafter, as designated in the applicable Loan Supplement, unless earlier terminated pursuant to the provisions of the applicable Loan Agreement.

"Prime Rate" shall mean the rate publicly announced from time to time by [insert name of financial institution to be sued] as its prime lending rate to its commercial customers. The Prime Rate for purposes of a Loan Agreement shall be determined at the close of business on the 15th day of each calendar month and shall become effective as of the first day of the calendar month succeeding such determination and shall continue in effect to, and including, the last day of said calendar month.

"Principal Amount" shall mean the principal amount of a Loan, as set forth in a Loan Supplement.

"Purchase Cost" as to each Item of Equipment shall mean the amount paid, or payable, by Borrower to Manufacturer for such Item of Equipment, and evidenced by one or more Manufacturer's invoices for such Item of Equipment, plus any additional cost so identified in a Loan Supplement, all as set forth in a Loan Supplement.

"Secured Obligations" with respect to a Loan shall have the meaning set forth in Section 9 of this Master Agreement.

"Term" shall mean the term of this Master Agreement which shall commence on the date of first execution and delivery of this Master Agreement by the parties hereto and continue in effect until all Notes have been paid in full and all other obligations, responsibilities, and liabilities, including Secured Obligations, of Borrower pursuant to this Master Agreement and all Loan Agreements have been fully satisfied and discharged.

"Total Equipment Cost" shall mean the aggregate Equipment Purchase Cost, plus additional costs and expenses, all as specified in a Loan Supplement.

1.2 General Word Definitions

"Hereof," "herein," and *"thereunder"* and words of similar import when used in this Master Agreement or in any Loan Supplement, Note, or other agreement shall refer such agreement as a whole and not to any particular portion or provision thereof.
"Including" when used in this Master Agreement or in any Loan Supplement, Note, or other agreement shall mean including but not by way of limitation.
"Original" when used in this Master Agreement or in any Loan Supplement, Loan Agreement, or other agreement shall mean the execution copy of such document or, when executed in counterparts the counterpart of a document designated as such by Lender for collateral, security interest, filing, and/or any other purpose.

2.1 General Borrowing

Borrower may request equipment loans from time to time during the Term of this Master Agreement in accordance with the procedure in Section 2.2 hereof.

2.2 Loan Request Procedure

In the event Borrower shall desire to obtain equipment loan financing, Borrower shall make a loan request by delivering to Lender a written request for a loan pursuant to the terms of this Master Agreement (hereinafter referred to as a "Loan Request") at least thirty (30) days prior to the Borrower's requested loan closing date, supplying such information as Lender shall require, including satisfactory-to-Lender financial statements and other credit information of the equipment lessee(s), a complete copy of the equipment lease agreement(s) and related documents, a detailed description of the type of equipment involved, and specifying the proposed Principal Amount, Loan Term, Loan repayment schedule, and Loan Closing Date.

3.1 Equipment Loans

Subject to the terms and conditions of this Master Agreement, and each applicable Loan Supplement, Lender agrees to make one or more Loans to Borrower which will be used to finance a portion of the Purchase Cost of the Items of Equipment.

3.2 Loan Term and Principal Amount

Each Loan shall be for a Loan Term, and Principal Amount, as set forth in the applicable Loan Supplement.

3.3 Loan Repayment and Note

Each Loan shall be repayable in that number of consecutive periodic installments as set forth in the applicable Loan Supplement. Borrower's obligation to repay each Loan shall be evidenced by a Note. The Principal Amount of each Note will be repaid, together with interest accruing thereon at the Loan Interest Rate on the unpaid balance thereof, in that number of consecutive periodic installments set forth in the Note, in such amounts and at such times as specified in the Note.

3.4 Conditions Precedent

The obligation of Lender to make a Loan shall be subject to the following conditions:

3.4.1 Loan Request

Lender shall have received from Borrower a Loan Request in accordance with Section 2 of this Master Agreement, along with such additional information as Lender shall request to evaluate the Loan Request.

3.4.2 Lending Criteria Satisfied

The loan requested by Borrower pursuant to the Loan Request shall satisfy all lending criteria adopted from time to time by, and governing, Lender, as determined within its sole discretion.

3.4.3 Formal Notice

Lender shall have notified Borrower in writing that the loan as requested in the Loan Request has been approved by Lender.

3.4.4 Security Interest

Each Loan shall be based on, among other things, a satisfactory-to-lender and its legal counsel continuing first priority security interest in the applicable Equipment and Equipment Lease as specified in the applicable Loan Supplement.

3.4.5 No Financial Change

No material adverse change in the business or the financial condition of Borrower or any Lessee under the applicable Equipment Lease shall have occurred and be continuing since the respective dates of the most recent financial statements and other credit information furnished by each of them to Lender.

3.4.6 Approvals and Filings

All acts, conditions, and actions (including, without limitation, the obtaining of any necessary regulatory approvals and the making of any required filings, recordings, or registrations) required to be done or performed or to have happened prior to the execution, delivery, and performance of the Master Agreement and the Loan Agreement, and Note and Equipment Lease shall have been done and performed to the satisfaction of Lender and its legal counsel.

3.4.7 Corporate Authorization

All corporate and legal proceedings, and all documents and instruments, in connection with the authorization of the Master Agreement, Loan Agreement, Note, and Equipment Lease shall be delivered to Lender and shall be satisfactory in form and substance to Lender and its legal counsel, and Lender shall have received all other Lender requested and related documents and instruments, including records of corporate proceedings, which Lender and its legal counsel may reasonably have requested in connection therewith, such documents and instruments, where appropriate, to be certified by proper corporate or government authorities.

3.4.8 Equipment Lease

With respect to a Loan, Lender shall have received the sole original of each applicable Equipment Lease satisfactory in form and substance to Lender and its legal counsel, and related documents, and the duly executed originals of the Loan Agreement and the Note and all ancillary documentation related thereto and delivered in connection therewith and shall have received all other documents, agreements, and instruments relating to any aspect of the transactions contemplated hereby, including the Supplement, substantially in the form of Exhibit C hereto, and the Acknowledgment and Consent to Assignment of Equipment Lease, substantially in the form of Exhibit D hereto (hereinafter referred to as the "Lessee Consent").

3.4.9 Insurance

Lender shall have received evidence of insurance as to the Equipment, satisfactory in form and amount to Lender and its legal counsel.

3.4.10 Counsel Opinion for Borrower

Lender shall have received, in form and substance satisfactory to Lender and its counsel, the written opinion addressed to it of legal counsel for Borrower, as to matters contained in Section 12, Subsections 12.1

through 12.4 inclusive and 12.7 through 12.11 inclusive, and as to such other matters incident to the transactions contemplated by this Master Agreement as Lender may request.

3.4.11 Counsel Opinion for Lessee

Lender shall have received, in form and substance satisfactory to Lender and its counsel, a written opinion addressed to it of counsel for Lessee, as to matters incident to the transactions contemplated by the Loan Agreement as Lender may request.

3.4.12 Equipment Ownership

Borrower shall own the Equipment free and clear of all Liens (except for the first priority security interest of Lender created by the Loan Agreement, and the rights of the Lessee created by the applicable Equipment Lease) and Lender shall have received such lien searches, consents, waivers, releases, or the like as it shall deem necessary or desirable to establish the same and shall have received, in form and substance satisfactory to it, copies of such invoices, bills of sale, and evidence of payment, as it shall deem necessary or desirable as evidence of Borrower's ownership of the Equipment.

3.4.13 Transaction Matters Satisfactory

All legal, financial, and documentation matters, and all documents executed, in connection with the contemplated transaction shall be satisfactory in form and substance to Lender and its legal counsel.

Section 4. Place of Payment

Payment of principal, interest, and other sums due or to become due with respect to each Loan and all the Secured Obligations are to be made at the office of Lender referred to in Section 19 of this Master Agreement, in lawful money of the United States of America in immediately available funds.

Section 5. Loan Prepayment

Borrower may not prepay any Note unless otherwise specifically provided for in, and then only in accordance with the terms and conditions of, the applicable Loan Supplement.

Section 6. Payment from Lease Amounts Due; Limitation of Liability

6.1 Payment from Lease Amounts Due

Lender and Borrower agree that, except as otherwise provided in Section 16 hereof, payment due under each Note shall be made by the Lessee's payment of the rentals and other amounts due or to become due (including, without limitation amounts due as Equipment casualty or purchase payments, or as to any early lease termination permitted under the applicable Equipment Lease) under the applicable Equipment Lease, assigned as collateral security for such Note, directly to Lender; provided, however, that nothing contained herein shall be deemed to alter or diminish the Borrower's absolute and unconditional obligation to make the payments to Lender required under the terms of the Note.

6.2 Limitation of Borrower's Liability

Notwithstanding anything to the contrary in Section 6.1, and subject to the succeeding sentence, with respect to each Loan, Lender agrees that it will look solely to the Collateral for such Loan for repayment for the Loan, without recourse against Borrower, and that Borrower shall not be personally liable to Lender for any amounts payable under such Loan; *provided, however,* Borrower expressly agrees that Borrower shall have personal recourse liability to Lender for any damages suffered by Lender in the event any representation, covenant, or warranty made by Borrower contained in this Master Agreement, Loan Agreement, Note, or Equipment Lease shall prove to be untrue in any material respect when made or has been breached in any material respect; including any representation, covenant, or warranty as to the indemnity made in Section 14.3 hereof, any representations and warranties made in Section 12 hereof, any covenants made in Sections 11.1, 13, 18, 20, and 21 hereof, and for its own gross negligence or willful misconduct. The foregoing limitation of recourse liability shall not limit, restrict, or impair the rights of Lender to accelerate the maturity of

any Note upon any Event of Default, or to exercise all rights and remedies provided under this Master Agreement, any Loan Agreement, Note, or Equipment Lease, or otherwise realize upon the Collateral.
Section 7. Lender Application of Amounts Received

7.1 Rent Payments

So long as no Default or Event of Default or event which with notice, lapse of time, or the happening of any further condition, event, or act would constitute an Event of Default shall have occurred and be continuing, each payment of an installment of rent under each Equipment Lease (including each payment of interest on overdue installments of rent) received by Lender shall be applied (i) *first,* to the payment of the installments of principal and interest (including interest on overdue principal) on the applicable Note(s) which have become due or which become due on or before the day on which such installment of rent is due from the applicable Lessee, and (ii) *second,* the balance, if any, of such installment of rent shall be paid by Lender to Borrower.

7.2 Casualty Payments

So long as no Default or Event of Default or event which with notice, lapse of time, or the happening of any further condition, event, or act would constitute an Event of Default shall have occurred and be continuing, any amounts received by Lender as a result of an Event of Loss with respect to an Item of Equipment (including, without limitation, any payment of casualty or stipulated loss value, insurance or condemnation, or similar, proceeds) shall be applied (i) *first,* to the prepayment amounts required to be paid by any mandatory prepayment requirement in a Loan Agreement, (ii) *second,* to the payment in full of all other Secured Obligations which are then due and payable, and (iii) *third,* the balance, if any, shall be paid by Lender to Borrower for distribution in accordance with the terms of the applicable Equipment Lease.

7.3 Permitted Early Lease Termination

So long as no Default or Event of Default or event which with notice, lapse of time, or the happening of any further condition, event, or act would constitute an Event of Default shall have occurred and be continuing, any amounts received by Lender as a result of an early equipment lease termination permitted under an Equipment Lease with respect to an Item of Equipment ("Permitted Early Equipment Lease Termination"), including, without limitation, any payment of early termination value, or similar, proceeds, shall be applied (i) *first,* to the prepayment amounts required to be paid by any mandatory prepayment requirement in a Loan Agreement, (ii) *second,* to the payment in full of all other Secured Obligations which are then due and payable, and (iii) *third,* the balance, if any, shall be paid by Lender to Borrower for distribution in accordance with the terms of the applicable Equipment Lease.

7.4 Other Amounts

So long as no Default or Event of Default or event which with notice, lapse of time, or the happening of any further condition, event, or act would constitute an Event of Default shall have occurred and be continuing, all amounts from time to time received by Lender (other than amounts specified in Section 6 or Sections 7.1, 7.2, or 7.3), (i) if due to Lender pursuant to the terms of a Loan Agreement, shall be applied by Lender to the purpose for which such payment was made, (ii) if provision as to its application is made in this Master Agreement or in an Equipment Lease, Lender shall, in its sole discretion, either apply such payment to the purpose for which it was made or pay it to Borrower, which shall so apply it, and (iii) if due to Borrower or Lessee, pay it to Borrower for distribution by Borrower in accordance with the terms of the applicable Equipment Lease.

7.5 Application After Declaration

All payments received and amounts realized by Lender after an Event of Default or event which with notice, lapse of time, or the happening of any further condition, event, or act would constitute an Event of Default shall have occurred and be continuing and after Lender has either declared (as assignee from Borrower of the Equipment Lease) the Equipment Lease to be in default pursuant to the provisions thereof or declared the Notes to be due and payable pursuant to Section 16 hereof, as well as all payments or amounts then held by Lender as part of the Collateral, shall be applied pursuant to said Section 16.

7.6 Application After Event of Default

All payments received and amounts realized by Lender after an Event of Default or event which with notice, lapse of time, or the happening of any further condition, event, or act would constitute an Event of Default shall have occurred and be continuing, but prior to the declaration of an Equipment Lease to be in default or the acceleration of the Notes, which funds would, but for the provisions of this Section 7.6, be paid to Borrower, shall be held by Lender as part of the Collateral until such time as no Events of Default or event which with notice, lapse of time, or the happening of any further condition, event, or act would constitute an Event of Default shall be continuing thereunder (at which time such funds shall be paid to Borrower) or until such funds are applied pursuant to Section 16 hereof.

Section 8. Late Payments; Other Charges

If any installment or other amount due with respect to the repayment of a Loan or any portion of the Secured Obligations is not paid when the same shall be due, Borrower shall pay interest on any such overdue amount at the applicable Overdue Rate.

Section 9. Assignment and Grant of Security Interests

As collateral security for the prompt and complete payment when due (whether at the stated maturity, by prepayment, by acceleration, or otherwise) of all indebtedness and other obligations of Borrower to Lender under or arising out of each Loan Agreement and/or evidenced by each Note, including any extensions or renewals thereof, and for the payment of all obligations of each Lessee under each Equipment Lease (all of which are referred to collectively herein as the "Secured Obligations"), the Borrower hereby: (a) assigns, pledges, and hypothecates to Lender, its successors and assigns, and grants to Lender, a continuing first priority security interest in and to, all of its present and future right, title, and interest in, to and under each Equipment Lease identified in each applicable Loan Supplement (including any extensions or renewals thereof) and all rentals, other sums payable thereunder (including without limitation any amounts payable in connection with an Equipment casualty or Permitted Equipment Lease Early Termination), and any and all cash and non-cash proceeds (including proceeds of insurance) thereof, and all rights, powers, and remedies (BUT NONE OF THE DUTIES OR OBLIGATIONS, IF ANY) of Borrower, as lessor, including without limitation the rights to give and receive any notice, consent, waiver, demand, or approval under or in respect to each applicable Equipment Lease, to exercise any election or option thereunder or in respect thereof, to accept a surrender of any of the applicable Equipment and to do all other things which the Borrower is entitled to do as lessor under each applicable Equipment Lease, and (b) assigns, pledges, and hypothecates to Lender, and grants to Lender a continuing first priority security interest in and to all Equipment and any and all accessories and additions thereto, substitutions and replacements therefor, and proceeds (including without limitation, insurance proceeds or condemnation awards) thereof. All of the property, rights, benefits, and interests referred to in clauses (a) and (b) of this Section 9 are referred to collectively herein as the "Collateral").

Section 10. Lender Appointment as Attorney-in-Fact

10.1 Lender Appointment

Borrower hereby irrevocably constitutes and appoints Lender and any officer or agent thereof, with full power of substitution, as its true and lawful attorney-in-fact with full irrevocable power and authority in the place and stead of Borrower and in the name of Borrower or in its own name, from time to time in Lender's discretion, for the purpose of carrying out the terms of each Loan Agreement, to take any and all appropriate action and to execute any and all documents or instruments which may be deemed necessary or desirable by Lender to protect and preserve, and/or exercise its rights and remedies with respect to, the Collateral and, without limiting the generality of the foregoing, hereby gives Lender the power and right, on behalf of Borrower and without notice to or assent by Borrower, to do the following: to demand, enforce, collect, receive, receipt, and give release for any monies due or to become due under or arising out of or with respect to, any of the Collateral, and to endorse all checks and other instruments, and to do and take all such other actions relating to any of the Collateral, to file any claims or institute any proceedings with respect to any of the foregoing which Lender deems necessary or desirable, and to compromise any such demand, claim or action.

10.2 Borrower Ratification

Borrower hereby ratifies all that Lender as attorney-in-fact shall lawfully do or cause to be done by virtue of this Section 10. This power of attorney is a power coupled with an interest and shall be irrevocable.

10.3 Right to Extend

Borrower consents and agrees that any of the liabilities of each Lessee under each Equipment Lease may be extended by Lender in whole or in part, without notice to Borrower and without affecting the liability of Borrower thereunder.

10.4 No Lender Duty

The powers conferred on Lender thereunder are solely to protect its interest in the Collateral and shall not impose any duty upon it to exercise any such powers. Lender shall be accountable only for amounts that it actually receives as a result of the exercise of such powers and neither it nor any of its officers, directors, employees, or agents shall be responsible to Borrower for any act or failure to act, except for its gross negligence or willful misconduct.

Section 11. Assignments; Encumbrances; Transfers

11.1 No Borrower Assignment

Borrower will not, without the prior written consent of Lender, assign, convey, transfer, sell, exchange, further lease, or otherwise dispose of any of its right, title, or interest in, to or under any of the Collateral, or this Master Agreement, any Loan Agreement, or any Note, or create, incur, or suffer to exist any Lien upon any of the Collateral (except the security interests and the assignments created by the applicable Loan Agreement).

11.2 Permitted Lender Assignment

Lender may, without notice to, or the written consent of, Borrower, assign, convey, transfer, sell, exchange, or otherwise dispose of any of its right, title, or interest in, to or under any of the Collateral, or this Master Agreement, any Loan Agreement, or any Note, or create, incur, or suffer to exist any Lien upon any of the Collateral; provided, however, any such action shall be subject to each applicable Lessee's right of quiet enjoyment as set forth in Section 17 of this Master Agreement.

Section 12. Borrower's Representations and Warranties

Borrower represents and warrants to Lender that as of the date of this Master Agreement, and (with respect only to the Loan being made as of such date) each Loan Closing Date as follows:

12.1 Not Insolvent

Borrower is not insolvent within the meaning of applicable state or federal law.

12.2 Good Standing

Borrower is a corporation duly organized and validly existing in good standing under the laws of the jurisdiction of its incorporation, (i) is duly qualified to do business and is in good standing in each jurisdiction (x) in which the location of its properties and any Equipment requires such qualification, and (y) where failure to qualify would materially and adversely affect Lender's ability to enforce its rights under any Equipment Lease or Loan Agreement, and (ii) has full power, authority, and legal right to purchase, own, and hold under lease its properties, and to transact the business in which it is engaged.

12.3 Loan Transaction Power and Authority

The (i) acquisition of the Equipment and the leasing of the Equipment to each Lessee pursuant to the applicable Equipment Lease(s), and (ii) execution, delivery, and performance by Borrower of this Master

Agreement, and as of the applicable Loan Closing Date, each Loan Agreement, Note, and Equipment Lease, and any related documents and the transactions contemplated hereby and thereby have been duly authorized by all necessary action on the part of Borrower and do not, and will not, as the case may be, contravene any provisions of law applicable to Borrower or the certificate of incorporation or by-laws of Borrower, and do not conflict or are not inconsistent with, and will not result (with or without the giving of notice) in a breach of or constitute a default or require any consent under, or result in the creation of any Lien upon the Collateral pursuant to, the terms of any judgment, award, order, injunction, determination, direction, demand, writ, or decree of any court or Governmental Body (collectively "Order"), credit agreement, indenture, mortgage, purchase agreement, deed of trust, security agreement, guarantee, or other instrument to which Borrower is a party or by which Borrower may be bound or to which any of its property may be subject.

12.4 Transaction Document Binding Nature

This Master Agreement, and, as of each Loan Closing Date when executed and delivered by Borrower, each Note, and Loan Agreement is a legal, valid, and binding obligation of Borrower enforceable in accordance with its respective terms, except as limited by bankruptcy, insolvency, reorganization, moratorium, or other similar law or equitable principles relating to or affecting the enforcement of creditor's rights in general and subject to general principles of equity.

12.5 Binding Equipment Lease

As of the applicable Loan Closing Date, each Equipment Lease constitutes the legal, valid, and binding obligation of the respective Lessee, enforceable against such Lessee in accordance with its terms thereof, except as limited by bankruptcy, insolvency, reorganization, moratorium, or other similar law or equitable principles relating to or affecting the enforcement of creditor's rights in general and subject to general principles of equity.

12.6 No Financial Change

No material adverse change in the business or the financial condition of Borrower, or as of the applicable Loan Closing Date with respect to the applicable Lessee, shall have occurred and be continuing since the respective dates of the most recent financial statements and other credit information furnished by each of them to Lender.

12.7 No Adverse Proceedings

There is no action, suit, investigation, or proceeding (whether or not purportedly on behalf of Borrower) pending or, to Borrower's knowledge, threatened against or affecting Borrower or any of its assets in any court or before any arbitrator or before and/or by any federal, state, municipal, or other governmental department, commission, board, bureau, agency, or instrumentally, domestic or foreign (collectively, "Governmental Body"), (a) which involves any of the Equipment or any of the transactions contemplated by this Master Agreement, any Loan Agreement, Note, or Equipment Lease or (b) which, if adversely determined, would have a material adverse effect upon the financial condition, business, or operations of Borrower or upon the transactions contemplated by this Master Agreement, any Loan Agreement, Note, or Equipment Lease, and Borrower is not in material default with respect to any material Order of any Court, arbitrator, or Governmental Body.

12.8 Sales, Use, Property Taxes

All sales, use, property or other taxes, licenses, tolls, inspection or other fees, bonds, permits, or certificates which were or may be required to be paid or obtained in connection with the acquisition by Borrower of the Equipment or its subsequent lease to each applicable Lessee will have been, or when due will be, paid in full or obtained, as the case may be.

12.9 Good, Valid, and Marketable Title

Borrower has good, valid, and marketable title to the Collateral free and clear of all liens, claims, and encumbrances, except for (i) the rights of the Lessee as user of the applicable Equipment in accordance with the terms of each applicable Equipment Lease, and (ii) the liens, claims, and encumbrances in favor of Lender created by each Loan Agreement.

12.10. Perfected Security Interest

At the time each Loan is made, Lender will have a perfected continuing first priority security interest in and to all of the applicable Loan Collateral.

12.11 Tax Return Filings

Borrower has as of the date of execution of this Master Agreement, and as of each Loan Closing Date will have, filed all required tax returns in all jurisdictions in which such returns were required to be filed and has paid, or made provision for, all material taxes shown to be due and payable on such returns and all other material taxes and assessments that are payable by it, except for any taxes and assessments of which the amount, applicability, or validity is currently being contested in good faith and as to which any adverse determination in excess of any accruals to reflect potential liability would not materially adversely affect its ability to perform its obligations under this Master Agreement, any Loan Agreement, Note, or Equipment Lease.

12.12 Equipment Lease Counterparts

Any counterpart of any Equipment Lease which has not been delivered to Lender bears the following legend on the face and signature pages thereof: "Counterpart No.   of   manually executed counterparts. Only the manually executed counterpart numbered 1 is sufficient to transfer Lessor's interest, or to grant a security interest herein." Each such counterpart also bears a legend on the face and signature pages thereof specifying Lender as the assignee of the Equipment Lease.

12.13 Equipment Lease Statements Correct

All amounts, statements, and conditions of fact stated in each Equipment Lease are true and correct.

12.14 Lease Performance

As of each applicable Loan Closing Date, Borrower, and to the best of Borrower's knowledge, each Lessee, have performed and observed each term, provision, covenant, and condition contained in the applicable Equipment Lease to be performed or observed by Borrower, as lessor, and as lessee, respectively, up to and including such Loan Closing Date.

12.15 Entire Lease Agreement

As of each Loan Closing Date, each applicable Equipment Lease constitutes the entire agreement of Borrower and the applicable Lessee with respect to the Equipment and the lease thereof, and has not been amended, supplemented, or otherwise modified in any manner, and Borrower has not entered into any understanding or agreement (oral or in writing), relating to the Equipment, or to such Equipment Lease, the transactions contemplated thereby, or any other transactions contemplated or permitted by this Master Agreement or any applicable Loan Agreement, or Note, with any person or entity.

12.16 No Assignment

As of each Loan Closing Date Borrower has not theretofore alienated, assigned, granted a security interest in, or otherwise disposed of any interest in each applicable Equipment Lease, amounts due Lender or to become due Lender thereunder, Borrower's leasehold interest or the applicable Equipment.

12.17 No Defense; Setoff

As of each Loan Closing Date, there are no defenses, setoffs, or counterclaims which each applicable Lessee has, or may have, in connection with the applicable Equipment Lease, or, any such defense, claim, or setoff on the part of any entity in connection with any of the obligations set forth in such Equipment Lease, or of any event which with the passage of time or giving of notice or both would constitute a default with respect to any of the foregoing.

12.18 Borrower's Place of Business

The chief place of business and the chief executive office of Borrower and the office where Borrower keeps its records relating to the Collateral, is located at the address set forth in Section 19 hereof.

Section 13. Covenants of Borrower

Borrower covenants and agrees that from and after the date hereof and so long as any of the Secured Obligations are outstanding:

13.1 Loan Proceeds Use

The proceeds of each Loan will be used exclusively for commercial or business purposes to finance the acquisition of Equipment for which the Loan has been provided under a Loan Agreement.

13.2 Notices

Borrower will promptly give written notice to Lender of (i) the occurrence of any Event of Default or of any event which with notice, lapse of time, or both would constitute an Event of Default, of which it has knowledge, (ii) the occurrence of any Event of Loss of which it has knowledge, and (iii) the commencement or threat of any material litigation or other proceedings affecting Borrower or any Lessee or any other entity that involves any of the Collateral that might materially interfere with the normal business operations of Borrower or any Lessee.

13.3 Lessee Communications

Borrower will promptly deliver, no later than five (5) days after receipt thereof, to Lender a copy of each communication received from each Lessee with respect to each Equipment Lease or the transactions contemplated thereby.

13.4 Compliance with Laws; Corporate Existence; Governmental Approvals

Borrower will (i) duly observe and conform to all valid requirements of governmental authorities necessary to the performance of its obligations under this Master Agreement and each Loan Agreement, Note, and Equipment Lease, (ii) maintain its corporate existence and obtain and keep in full force and effect all rights, franchises, licenses, and permits which are necessary to the proper conduct of its business, and (iii) obtain or cause to be obtained as promptly as possible any governmental, administrative, or agency approval and make any filing or registration therewith which shall be required with respect to the performance of its obligations under this Master Agreement, and each Loan Agreement, Note, and Equipment Lease.

13.5 Performance of Equipment Leases

Borrower will duly observe and perform all covenants and obligations to be performed by it under each Equipment Lease and, subject to Section 13.10 hereof, will promptly take any and all action as may be necessary to enforce its rights under each such Equipment Lease or to secure the performance by the applicable Lessee of such Lessee's obligations under such Equipment Lease.

13.6 Equipment Location Change

Borrower shall cause the Equipment to be used solely by each Lessee in accordance with the terms of the applicable Equipment Lease, and shall not consent to a change in the location of any Item of Equipment as specified in the applicable Equipment Lease, without the prior written consent of Lender.

13.7 Equipment Insurance

Borrower shall cause each Lessee to provide insurance coverage with respect to the applicable Equipment in accordance with the terms of the applicable Equipment Lease; shall further cause each such Lessee to cause such insurance to be endorsed to provide that losses, if any, shall be payable to Borrower, Lender, and such Lessee, as their interest may appear; shall further cause it to be further endorsed to provide that such insurer will give Lender thirty (30) days' prior written notice of the effective date of any material alteration or cancellation or nonrenewal of any such policy; shall further cause it to provide that all provisions of such policy, except the limits of liability, will operate in the same manner as if there were a separate policy governing such additional insured; shall further cause it to provide that as to Lender's interest, such insurance shall not be invalidated by reason of any breach of representation or violation of warranty by Lessee to the insurer in connection with obtaining such policy to insurance or maintaining the same in full force and effect; and shall further cause such insurance to meet such other reasonable requirements as Lender may request from time to time.

13.8 Security Interest Filing Costs

Borrower will pay, or reimburse Lender for, any and all fees, costs, and expenses of whatever kind or nature incurred in connection with the creation, preservation, and protection of Lender's security interests in the Collateral, including, without limitation, all fees and taxes in connection with the recording or filing of instruments and documents in public offices, payment or discharge of any taxes or Liens of any nature upon or in respect of the Collateral, premiums for insurance with respect to the Collateral and all other fees, costs, and expenses in connection with protecting, maintaining, or preserving the Collateral and Lender's interests therein, whether through judicial proceedings or otherwise, or in defending or prosecuting any actions, suits, or proceedings arising out of or related to the Collateral; and all such amounts that are paid by Lender shall, until reimbursed by Borrower, constitute Secured Obligations of Borrower secured by the Collateral.

13.9 No Liens

Borrower will not create, assume, or suffer to exist any Lien of any kind upon any of the Collateral, of or by any individual (or association of individuals), entity or governmental instrumentality, claimed or asserted against, through or under Borrower, except the interest granted hereby to Lender, and any Liens expressly permitted by Lender pursuant to Section 11 hereof, and Borrower shall promptly notify, no later than five (5) days after the receipt thereof, Lender upon the receipt of any Lien, or judicial proceeding affecting any Equipment in whole or in part, and Borrower shall cause Lessee to maintain the Equipment free from all Liens, and legal processes of Lessee.

13.10 Restriction on Equipment Lease Actions

Borrower will not, without the prior written consent of Lender, declare a default under any Equipment Lease, exercise any remedies under any Equipment Lease or enter into or consent to or permit any cancellation, termination, amendment, supplement or modification of or waiver with respect to any Equipment Lease, and any such attempted declaration, exercise, cancellation, termination, amendment, supplement, modification, or waiver shall be void and of no effect.

13.11 Change in Office Location

Borrower will not change its principal place of business or chief executive office or remove its books and records concerning the Collateral from the address set forth in Section 19 hereof unless it shall have given at least thirty (30) days' prior written notice of such change or removal to Lender, specifying the new address.

13.12 Further Assurances

Borrower will promptly, at any time and from time to time, at its sole expense, execute and deliver to Lender such further instruments and documents, and take such further action, as Lender may from time to time reasonably request in order to carry out the intent and purpose of this Master Agreement, and each Loan Agreement, Note, and Equipment Lease and to establish and protect the rights, interests, and remedies created, or intended to be created, in favor of Lender hereby and thereby, including, without limitation, the execution, delivery, recordation, and filing of financing statements and continuation statements with respect to the Collateral. Borrower hereby authorizes Lender, in such jurisdictions where such action is authorized or permitted by law, to effect any such recordation or filing without the signature of Borrower thereto, and Lender's expenses with respect thereto shall be payable by Borrower on demand.

13.13 Indemnification

Without limiting the generality of any other provision hereof, Borrower shall indemnify, protect, save, and keep harmless Lender from and against any reduction in the amount payable out of the Collateral to Lender with respect to the Secured Obligations, or any other loss, cost, or expense (including legal fees) incurred by Lender, as the result of Borrower's breach of Section 13.9 hereof.

Section 14. Indemnity

14.1 Fees, Assessments, and Taxes

Borrower agrees to pay when due, and to indemnify and hold Lender harmless from all license, filing and registration fees and assessments, and all sales, use, property, excise, and other taxes and charges (other than those measured by Lender's net income) now or hereafter imposed by any Governmental Body upon or with respect to (i) this Master Agreement, or any Loan Agreement, Note, or Equipment Lease, or the creation and continued perfection of the security interest created hereby or thereby, and (ii) any of the Collateral, including without limitation the use, possession, ownership, and operation of any of the Equipment.

14.2 Equipment Operation and Use Expenses

Borrower hereby assumes liability for, and indemnifies and holds Lender harmless against, all claims, costs, expenses (including reasonable legal fees), damages, and liabilities arising from or pertaining to the manufacture, assembly, installation, use, operation or sale, or disposition of, or in any way relating to, the Equipment or any interest therein.

14.3 Lawsuit Costs

Without limiting the generality of the foregoing, Borrower hereby agrees that in any suit, proceeding, or action brought by Lender under any Equipment Lease for any sum owing thereunder, or to enforce any provision thereof, Borrower will save, indemnify, and keep Lender harmless from and against all expense, loss, or damage suffered by reason of any defense, setoff, counterclaim, recoupment, or reduction of liability whatsoever of Lessee, arising out of a breach by Borrower of any obligation under such Equipment Lease or arising out of any other agreement, indebtedness, or liability at any time owing to or in favor of Lessee from Borrower.

14.4 Survival

The indemnities set forth in this Section 14 shall survive the expiration or earlier termination of this Master Agreement and each Loan Agreement, Note, and Equipment Lease with respect to acts or events occurring or alleged to have occurred prior to such expiration or earlier termination.

Section 15. Events of Default

During the Term of this Master Agreement, the occurrence of any of the following events shall constitute an "Event of Default":

15.1 Nonpayment

Borrower fails to pay, or cause to be paid, any amount owing pursuant to this Master Agreement, any Loan Agreement, or Note, including, but not limited to the principal or interest of any Note, when due (whether at the stated maturity, by acceleration or otherwise), and such failure shall continue for a period of ten (10) days.

15.2 Nonperformance

Borrower disaffirms or fails to perform or observe any other covenant, agreement, obligation, or under-taking under this Master Agreement or under any Loan Agreement, Note, or any Equipment Lease, or under any agreement contemplated hereby or thereby to which Borrower is a party, or under any other agreement or document given to evidence or secure any of the Secured Obligations, and such failure shall continue for a period of thirty (30) days.

15.3 Event of Default Occurrence

If an event of default (as therein defined) occurs under any Equipment Lease or a default by any Lessee of its obligations under its Lessee Consent occurs.

15.4 Breach of Representation or Warranty

Any representation or warranty, made by Borrower in connection with any transaction contemplated by this Master Agreement, any Loan Agreement, or any Note, whether contained in any Equipment Lease, any related document, in this Master Agreement, in any Loan Agreement, in any Note, or in any certificate or other related document delivered to Lender in connection herewith or therewith, shall prove to be incorrect or untrue in any material respect.

15.5 Bankruptcy Proceedings

Borrower institutes proceedings to be adjudicated a bankrupt or insolvent, or consents to the institution of bankruptcy or insolvency proceedings against it, or commences a voluntary proceeding or case under any applicable federal or state bankruptcy, insolvency, or other similar law, or consents to the filing of any such petition or to the appointment of or taking possession by a receiver, liquidator, assignee, trustee, custodian, or sequestrator (or other similar official) of Borrower or of any substantial part of its property, or makes any assignment for the benefit of creditors or the admission by it of its inability to pay its debts generally as they become due or becomes willing to be adjudicated a bankrupt or fails generally to pay its debts as they become due or takes any corporate action in furtherance of any of the foregoing or Borrower shall file any such proceeding, or any execution or writ of process shall be issued under any proceeding whereby any Item of Equipment may be taken or restrained.

15.6 Entered Decree or Order

A decree or order is entered for relief by a court having jurisdiction in respect of Borrower adjudging the Borrower a bankrupt or insolvent, or approving as properly filed a petition seeking a reorganization, arrangement, adjustment or composition of or in respect of Borrower in an involuntary proceeding or case under any applicable federal or state bankruptcy, insolvency, or other similar law, or appointing a receiver, liquidator, or assignee, custodian, trustee, or sequestrator (or similar official) of Borrower or of any substantial part of its property, or ordering the winding-up or liquidation of its affairs, and the continuance of any such decree or order unstayed and in effect for a period of thirty (30) days.

15.7 Business Cessation

Borrower shall cease doing business as a going concern or shall be dissolved.

Section 16. Remedies

Upon the occurrence of an Event of Default, and so long as such Event of Default shall be continuing, Lender may, at its option, declare this Master Agreement and/or any or all Loan Agreements in default (herein referred to as a "Default") and may exercise, at its option, one or more of the following remedies:

16.1 Right of Acceleration

Lender may accelerate the full amount of any or all of the then outstanding Secured Obligations in which event such amounts will become immediately due and payable by the Borrower without presentment, demand, protest, or other notice of any kind, all of which are hereby expressly waived, and Lender may thereafter pursue any or all of the rights and remedies with respect to the Collateral accruing to Lender thereunder or by operation of law as a secured creditor under the Code or other applicable law, as it may elect in its sole discretion, and all such available rights and remedies, to the full extent permitted by the law, shall be cumulative and not exclusive.

16.2 Additional Remedies

If an Event of Default shall occur and be continuing, Lender may exercise in addition to all other rights and remedies granted to it in this Master Agreement, in any Loan Agreement, Note, or Equipment Lease and in any other instrument or agreement securing, evidencing, or relating to the Secured Obligations, all rights and remedies of secured parties under the Code or under any other applicable law. Without limiting the generality of the foregoing, Borrower agrees that in any such event, Lender, without demand of performance or other demand, advertisement, or notice of any kind (except the notice specified below of time and place of public or private sale) to or upon Borrower or any other person (all and each of which demands, advertisements, and/or notices are hereby expressly waived), may forthwith collect, receive, appropriate, and realize upon the Collateral, or any part thereof, and may take possession of (subject to the right of quiet enjoyment with respect to any Lessee pursuant to Section 17 hereof) any or all Equipment or any part thereof and/or may forthwith sell, lease, assign, give option or options to purchase, or otherwise dispose of and deliver the Collateral (or contract to do so), or any part thereof, in one or more parcels at public or private sale or sales, at any exchange or broker's board or at any of Lender's offices or elsewhere at such prices as it may deem best, for cash or on credit or for future delivery without assumption of any credit risk. Lender shall have the right upon any such public sale or sales, and, to the extent permitted by law, upon any such private sale or sales, to purchase the whole or any part of the Collateral so sold, free of any right or equity of redemption in Borrower, which right or equity is hereby expressly waived or released to the extent permitted by law. Borrower further agrees (subject to the right of quiet enjoyment with respect to any Lessee pursuant to Section 17 hereof), at Lender's request, to assemble the Collateral, make it available to Lender at places which Lender shall reasonably select, whether at Borrower's premises or elsewhere. Lender shall apply the net proceeds of any such collection, recovery, receipt, appropriation, realization, and/or sale (after deducting all costs and expenses of every kind incurred therein or incidental to the care, safekeeping, or otherwise of any or all of the Collateral or in any way relating to the rights of Lender thereunder, including attorney's fees and legal expenses) to the payment in whole or in part of the Secured Obligations, in such order as Lender may elect and only after so applying such net proceeds and after the payment by Lender of any other amount required by any provision of law, need Lender account for the surplus, if any, to Borrower. To the extent permitted by applicable law, Borrower waives all claims, damages, and demands against Lender arising out of the repossession, retention, or sale of the Collateral, including any costs of evaluation and or appraisal of the Collateral or any part thereof. Borrower agrees that Lender need not give more than ten (10) days' prior written notice (which notification shall be deemed given when mailed, postage prepaid, addressed to Borrower at its address set forth in Section 19 hereof) of the time and place of any public sale or of the time after which a private sale may take place and that such notice is reasonable notification of such matters.

16.3 Lease Action

If an Event of Default referred to in Section 15.3 shall occur and be continuing, Lender (as assignee of Borrower) may declare the applicable Equipment Lease to be in default and may exercise all rights, powers, and remedies of Borrower under the applicable section of such Equipment Lease, either in Lender's own name or in the name of Borrower for the use and benefit of Lender.

16.4 Waiver of Presentment

Borrower hereby waives presentment, demand, protest, and (to the extent permitted by applicable law) notice of any kind in connection with this Master Agreement, each Loan Agreement, each Note, or any Collateral.

16.5 Rights, Powers, and Remedies Cumulative

All rights, powers, and remedies herein specifically given to Lender shall be cumulative and shall be in addition to all other rights, powers, and remedies herein specifically given or now or hereafter existing at law, in equity or by statute, and all rights, powers, and remedies whether specifically given herein or otherwise existing may be exercised from time to time and as often and in such order as may be deemed expedient by Lender and the exercise or the beginning of the exercise of any power or remedy shall not be construed to be a waiver of the waiver of the right to exercise at the same time or at any other time any other right, power, or remedy. No delay or omission by Lender in the exercise of any right, remedy, or power, or in the pursuance of any right, remedy, or power shall impair any such right, power, or remedy or be construed to be a waiver of any Event of Default on the part of Lender.

16.6 Discontinuance of Proceeding

In case Lender shall have proceeded to enforce any right, power, or remedy under, or arising out of, or in connection with, this Master Agreement, any Loan Agreement, Note, Equipment Lease or any other related agreement, document, by foreclosure, entry, or otherwise, any such proceeding or any portion thereof shall have been discontinued or abandoned for any reason or shall have been determined adversely to Lender, then and in every such case Borrower and Lender shall be restored to their former position and rights hereunder or thereunder with respect to the Collateral subject to such proceeding or portion thereof, and all rights, remedies, and powers of Lender shall continue as if no such proceeding or portion thereof had been taken.

Section 17. Lessee's Quiet Enjoyment Right

So long as a Lessee is not in default of its obligations under the applicable Equipment Lease or of its obligations to Lender under the applicable Lessee Consent, Lender will not interfere with the Lessee's peaceful use and enjoyment of the applicable Equipment for its intended purposes as provided for by the terms of such Equipment Lease.

Section 18. Receipt of Funds by Borrower

Should Borrower, notwithstanding the assignment of the Equipment Leases and the granting to Lender of a first priority security interest in and to the Collateral, at any time while any of the Secured Obligations remain unsatisfied, receive any amount representing funds due, or proceeds of, any of the Collateral, such sums shall be held by Borrower in trust for Lender, shall be segregated from other funds of Borrower, and shall be immediately paid by Borrower to Lender in the form so received, together with any necessary endorsement thereon.

Section 19. Notices

Any notice or document or payment to be delivered thereunder to any of the persons designated below, except as otherwise expressly provided herein, shall be deemed to have been properly delivered if delivered personally or deposited with the United States Postal Service, registered or certified mail, return receipt requested, postage prepaid, to the following respective addresses:
If to Borrower:

If to Lender:

or such other address as may be furnished from time to time by any of the parties hereto upon at least thirty (30) days' prior written notice.

Section 20. Payment of Expenses and Taxes

Borrower agrees, whether or not the transactions contemplated by this Master Agreement and each Loan Agreement shall be consummated, to pay (i) all costs and expenses of Lender in connection with the negotiation, preparation, execution, and delivery of this Master Agreement, and the other documents relating hereto, including, without limitation, the reasonable fees and disbursements of counsel to Lender; (ii) all fees and taxes in connection with the recording of this Master Agreement and any Loan Agreement or Note or any other document or instrument required hereby; and (iii) all costs and expenses of Lender in connection with the enforcement of this Master Agreement, and each Loan Agreement and each Note, including all legal fees and disbursements arising in connection therewith. Borrower also agrees to pay, and to indemnify and save Lender harmless from any delay in paying, all taxes, including without limitation, sales, use, stamp, and personal property taxes (other than any corporate income, capital, franchise, or similar taxes payable by Lender with respect to the payments made to Lender hereunder) and all license, filing, and registration fees and assessments and other charges, if any, which may be payable or determined to be payable in connection with the execution, delivery, and performance of this Master Agreement, each Loan Agreement, and each Note or any modification thereof.

Section 21. Performance by Lender of Borrower's Obligations

If Borrower fails to perform or comply with any of its agreements contained herein, or in any Loan Agreement or document related hereto or thereto, and Lender shall itself perform or comply, or otherwise cause performance or compliance, with such agreement, the expenses of Lender incurred in connection with such performance or compliance, together with interest thereon at the Overdue Rate provided for in the applicable Loan Agreement, shall be payable by Borrower to Lender on demand and until such payment shall constitute Secured Obligations secured hereby.

Section 22. Loan Request Right Termination

Without affecting any of Lender's rights, or Borrower's duties, obligations, or liabilities, under this Master Agreement, or any Loan Agreement, or Note, Lender may terminate Borrower's future right to submit Loan Requests pursuant to Section 2 of this Master Agreement, with or without cause, by sending a written notice to that effect to Borrower at Borrower's address specified in Section 19.

Section 23. Miscellaneous

23.1 Survival of Representations and Warranties

All representations and warranties made in, or pursuant to, this Master Agreement, any Loan Agreement, or Note and any documents, instruments, or certificates delivered pursuant hereto or thereto (collectively herein referred to as "Documents") shall survive the execution and delivery of the Documents, and the making of the Loans thereunder, and the agreements contained in Section 20 hereof, shall survive payment of the Notes until all obligations of Borrower to Lender are satisfied in full.

23.2 Modification, Waiver, and Consent

Any modification or waiver of any provision of this Master Agreement, any Loan Agreement, or Note, nor any terms hereof or thereof, or any consent to any departure by Lender or Borrower, as the case may be, therefrom, shall not be effective in any event unless the same is in writing and signed by the party to be charged, and then such modification, waiver, or consent shall be effective only in the specific instance and for the specific purpose given.

23.3 Headings

The headings of the Sections and Subsections are for convenience only, are not part of this Master Agreement and shall not be deemed to affect the meaning or construction of any of the provisions hereof.

23.4 Binding Effect

This Master Agreement and each Loan Agreement, and Note shall be binding upon and inure to the benefit of Borrower and Lender and their permitted respective successors and assigns.

23.5 Complete Statement of Rights

This Master Agreement, and each Loan Agreement, exclusively and completely states the rights and agreements with respect to the subject matter hereof and thereof, and supersedes all other agreements, oral or written, with respect thereto.

23.6 Law Governing

The terms and provisions of this Master Agreement, each Loan Agreement, and each Note and all rights and obligations thereunder shall be governed in all respects by the laws of the State of _____.

23.7 Construction

Any provision contained in this Master Agreement, in any Loan Agreement, or in any Note, or in any agreement or document delivered in connection therewith, or related thereto, which is prohibited or unenforceable in any jurisdiction shall, as to such jurisdiction, be ineffective to the extent of such prohibition or unenforceability without invalidating the remaining provisions hereof, and any such prohibition or unenforceability shall not invalidate or render unenforceable such provision in any other jurisdiction. To the extent permitted by law, Borrower hereby waives any provision of law which renders any provision hereof prohibited or unenforceable in any respect. A waiver by Lender of any right or remedy in any one instance shall not operate as a waiver of such right or remedy in any other instance, and a waiver by Lender of any breach of the terms hereof or Event of Default thereunder shall not be a waiver of any additional or subsequent breach or Event of Default.

23.8 Execution in Counterparts

This Master Agreement and each Loan Agreement may be executed by the parties hereto in any number of separate counterparts, each of which when so executed and delivered shall be an original, but all such counterparts shall together constitute but one and the same instrument.

IN WITNESS WHEREOF, Borrower and Lender have caused this Master Agreement to be executed on their behalf by their duly authorized representatives as of the day and year first above written.

_____
Lender

By:

Title:

_____
Borrower

By:

Title:

Form: I-07a
Disk File Name: I-07a.rtf

LOAN SUPPLEMENT

Form Purpose

A loan supplement to be used in connection with a master equipment security and loan agreement. This form is integrated with Loan and Security Agreement, Form I-07.

Executing Parties
The borrower.
The lender.

See:
Loan and Security Agreement, Form I-07

Exhibit A
Loan Supplement

Loan Supplement No.   ("Loan Supplement")
Dated as of

to Master Loan and Security Agreement,
("Master Agreement")
Dated as of

between

                ("Lender")

and

                ("Borrower")

1. Incorporation by Reference of Master Agreement

The Master Agreement and all documentation attached thereto, or delivered in connection therewith, or pursuant to thereto, including all terms and conditions thereof, are specifically incorporated herein by reference, and made a part hereof, as if set forth at length herein, as the same may from time to time be amended, supplemented, or otherwise modified. This Loan Supplement shall be considered a separate and enforceable agreement incorporating the terms and conditions of the Master Security Agreement and all documentation attached thereto, or delivered in connection therewith, or pursuant to thereto, and is referred to as a Loan Agreement.

2. Lessee

                [Insert name]

3. Lessee Guarantor

                [Insert name]

4. Description of Equipment Lease

                [Insert description]

5. Equipment Description

Qty. Manufacturer Model New/ Used Description Install. Location I. D./ Ser. #   Purchase Cost Per Item Aggregate

[Insert description]

Total Equipment Cost $

6. Loan Principal Amount

The Principal Amount of the Loan to be extended pursuant to this Loan Supplement shall be equal to $, but in no event shall it be less than $, nor shall it be greater than $, and shall be evidenced by a Note.

7. Loan Commencement Date

The Loan Commencement Date for the Note shall be the Loan Closing Date.

8. Loan Term

    8.1 Primary Term

    The Primary Loan Term shall commence on the Loan Closing Date, unless the Loan Closing Date shall not fall on the 1st day of a month, in which case the Primary Loan Term shall commence on the 1st day of the month immediately following the Loan Closing Date, and shall end on the anniversary date thereof   years thereafter.

    8.2. Interim Term

    If the Loan Closing Date does not fall on the 1st day of a month, there shall be an Interim Loan Term.

9. Loan Payment Dates

The Loan Payment Dates with respect to the Loan shall be the   day of each   during the Loan Term, and, in the event there is an Interim Term, any Interim Loan Payment shall be made on the Loan Closing Date, all payments to be payable in lawful money of the United States and in immediately available funds.

10. Loan Interest Rate

    10.1 Loan Interest Rate

    The Note shall bear interest during the Primary Loan Term at a per annum interest rate equal to   % (calculated on the basis of a 360-day year and 30-day month).

    10.2 Interim Loan Term Interest

    The Note shall bear interest during any Interim Loan Term at an interest rate equal to the daily equivalent of the Primary Loan Term Interest Rate.

11. Loan Amortization Schedule

Attached hereto as Annex A is the Loan Amortization Schedule.

12. Loan Proceeds Instructions

Lender shall pay to Borrower the Principal Amount of the Loan by electronic wire transfer in accordance with written wire instructions from Borrower submitted prior to the Loan Closing Date.

13. Cutoff Date

Lender shall not be obligated to make the Loan provided for in this Loan Supplement unless the Loan Closing Date occurs on or before   .

14. Loan Fee

Borrower shall pay to Lender a loan commitment fee equal to _____ on the date of exexcution of this Loan Supplement.

15. Overdue Rate

The Overdue Rate (calculated on the basis of a 360-day year and 30-day month) for the Note shall be a per annum amount equal to two percent (2%) above the Prime Rate (not to exceed, however, the highest rate permitted by applicable law).

16. Loan Prepayment

16.1 Mandatory Prepayment in the Event of Loss

16.1.1 *Event of Loss Prepayment.* In the event that the Equipment or any item thereof subject to this Loan Supplement shall be lost, stolen, destroyed, damaged beyond repair, or rendered permanently unfit for normal use for any reason, or in the event of any condemnation, confiscation, seizure, or requisition of title to or use of any Item of Equipment as to result in the Lessee's loss of possession or use, or the Item of Equipment shall be deemed to have incurred a casualty loss under the applicable Equipment Lease (each of the foregoing being hereinafter called a "Event of Loss"), provided that Lessee is not replacing such Item of Equipment pursuant to any provisions permitting such replacement in the applicable Equipment Lease, Borrower shall make a prepayment on the Note in an amount equal to the sum of:

(i) that proportionate share of the then outstanding Principal Amount of such Note determined by multiplying the outstanding Principal Amount by a fraction, the numerator of which is the Borrower's Purchase Cost of the Item(s) of Equipment which was the subject of the Event of Loss and the denominator of which is the Total Equipment Cost of all Items of Equipment covered by the Loan Supplement to which the Note corresponds;

(ii) all accrued interest, late charges, if any, and any other sums which may be due Lender with respect to the Item(s) of Equipment which was the subject of the Event of Loss, to the date of such payment; and

(iii) a casualty prepayment fee equal to the product of (x) the principal amount prepaid and (y) the product obtained by multiplying 10% by a fraction, the numerator of which will be the number of installment payment dates with respect to such Note remaining after such date of prepayment (including the installment payment date on which such prepayment is made) and the denominator of which shall be the total number of installment payment dates with respect to such Note.

16.1.2 Mandatory Early Lease Termination Prepayment

[If an Early Equipment Lease termination is permitted, this subsection will incorporate the appropriate mandatory Note prepayment provision.]

17. Representations and Warranties

Borrower represents and warrants that:

(a) Its representations and warranties contained in Section 12 of the Master Agreement are true and accurate on and as of the date of this Loan Supplement as though made on and as of such date.

(b) It is not in Default under any of the terms, covenants, agreements, or other provisions of any Loan Agreement, Note, or Equipment Lease, or the Master Agreement, and no Event of Default, or event which with notice, lapse of time, or the happening of any further condition, event, or act would constitute an Event of Default shall have occurred and is continuing thereunder.

18. Term Definitions

The terms used in this Loan Supplement, where not defined herein to the contrary, shall have the same meanings as defined in the Master Agreement.

_____
Lender

By: _____

Title: _____

_____
Borrower

By: _____

Title: _____

Annex A to Loan Supplement No.

[values to be inserted]

Exhibit B

[see Form 1-07b]

Exhibit C

[see Form 1-07c]

Exhibit D

[see Form 1-07d]

Form: I-07b
Disk File Name: I-07b.rtf

PROMISSORY NOTE

Form Purpose

A promissory note to be used in connection with a master equipment loan and security agreement. This form is integrated with Loan and Security Agreement, Form I-07.

Executing Parties
The borrower.

See:
Loan and Security Agreement, Form I-07

Exhibit B
Form of Promissory Note

[Insert city, state where executed, such as New York, New York]

$_____

Date: _____

FOR VALUE RECEIVED, _____ ("the Undersigned") promises to pay to the order of _____ ("Lender") at its office at in lawful money of the United States, the principal sum of _____ DOLLARS ($) and to pay interest in like money on the unpaid principal amount thereof to maturity at the rate of interest of _____ percent (%) per annum, computed on the basis of 360-day year consisting of twelve 30-day months. The principal and interest shall be paid in _____ equal consecutive installments of principal and interest, each in the amount of $ _____, in accordance with the attached Loan Amortization Schedule. The first of such installments shall be due on _____, and each of the remaining installments shall be due on the same day of each _____ thereafter, continuing through _____. Each installment of principal shall bear interest from and after the date due through the date payment is received by Lender at   %.

This Note is one of the Notes referred to in, and is issued pursuant to, a Loan Supplement (the "Loan Supplement"), dated as of _____, by and between the Undersigned and Lender, which Loan Supplement incorporates by reference the terms and conditions of a Master Loan and Security Agreement ("Master Agreement") by and between the Undersigned and Lender, dated as of _____, (the Loan Supplement and Master Agreement are collectively referred to herein as the "Loan Agreement") and the holder hereof is entitled to the benefits thereof. Terms defined in the Loan Agreement are used with the same meanings herein. This Note is secured as provided in the Loan Agreement, and is subject to prepayment only as provided therein. Reference is herein made to the Loan Agreement for a description of the provisions upon which the Note is issued and secured, and the nature and extent of the security and the rights of the holder hereof.

Upon the occurrence of any one or more of the Events of Default specified in the Loan Agreement, the unpaid principal balance of this Note, together with interest accrued to the date of payment, shall be immediately due and payable without notice or demand, although not yet due in accordance with the terms hereof.

The Undersigned hereby waives presentment, demand for payment, notice of dishonor, and any and all other notices or demands in connection with the delivery, acceptance, performance, default, or enforcement of this Note.

In the event that any holder shall institute any action for the enforcement or collection of this Note, there shall be immediately due and payable, in addition to the then unpaid principal balance hereof and any accrued interest, any late charges and all costs and expenses of such action including attorney's fees. The Undersigned and Lender in any litigation (whether or not relating to this Note) in which Lender and the Undersigned shall be adverse parties, waive trial by jury, and the Undersigned waives the right to interpose any setoff, counterclaim, or defense of any nature whatsoever.

This Note shall be governed by, and construed and interpreted in accordance with, the laws of the State of   .

_____
Borrower

By: _____

Title: _____

Loan Supplement No.
Loan Amortization Schedule

(values to be inserted)

Form: I-07c
Disk File Name: I-07c.rtf

ACKNOWLEDGMENT AND CONSENT TO ASSIGNMENT OF EQUIPMENT LEASE

Form Purpose

An acknowledgment and consent of assignment of an equipment lease agreement to be used in connection with a master equipment security and loan agreement. This form is integrated with Loan and Security Agreement, Form I-07.

Executing Parties
The borrower.
The equipment lender.
The equipment lessee.

See:
Loan and Security Agreement, Form I-07

Exhibit C
Acknowledgment and Consent to Assignment of Equipment Lease

Dated: _____

[Insert name and address of Lender]

Gentlemen:

Reference is made to that certain Equipment Leasing Agreement dated as of _____, (the Equipment Leasing Agreement together with all exhibits, attachments, and schedules thereof, and ancillary and related documents are herein referred to as the "Equipment Lease") between _____ ("Lessor"), as lessor, and _____ (the "Company"), as lessee. The Company understands that Lessor and _____ ("Lender") have entered into a Master Loan and Security Agreement, dated as of _____, (the "Master Agreement"), and a Loan Supplement No. _____ dated as of _____, together with all exhibits, attachments, and schedules thereto, and ancillary and related documents thereto (collectively referred to herein as the "Loan Agreement") and that pursuant to the Loan Agreement, Lender shall make one or more loans to Lessor to finance its acquisition of Equipment (as hereinafter defined). In consideration of Lender's financing the acquisition of the Equipment, of the mutual covenants hereinafter set forth, and for other good and valuable consideration, receipt of which is hereby acknowledged, the Company hereby covenants and agrees with Lender as follows:

1. The Company hereby acknowledges and consents to the assignment by Lessor to Lender of all of Lessor's right, title, and interest in, to and under the Equipment Lease, including without limitation the right to receive all remaining rental payments payable under the Equipment Lease and all other monies from time to time payable to or receivable by Lessor under any of the provisions of the Equipment Lease (all such amounts hereinafter referred to as the "Monies"). The items of Equipment subject to the Equipment Lease are referred to hereinafter as the "Equipment."

The Company confirms that as of the date hereof, (a) the remaining term of the Equipment Lease is _____ months, and the Company's remaining rental obligation thereunder is to pay the sum of $ _____ in _____ consecutive installments commencing _____, and ending _____, each in the amount of $ _____ exclusive of applicable taxes.

2. The Company hereby represents and warrants that the documents attached hereto as Exhibit A are true and correct copies of the Equipment Lease, that all dates, amounts, equipment descriptions, and other facts set forth therein are correct (and that the rental amounts set forth therein are exclusive of applicable taxes), and that the Equipment is in its possession and control at the addresses shown in the Equipment

Lease. Further the Company represents and warrants that there are no agreements between Lessor and the Company relative to the Equipment or the lease thereof other than the Equipment Lease, and this Consent.

3. The Company agrees (i) to remit and deliver all rentals directly to Lender at the above address (or at such other address as may be specified in writing by Lender), ABSOLUTELY AND UNCONDITIONALLY, WITHOUT ABATEMENT, REDUCTION, COUNTERCLAIM, OR OFFSET, and (ii) to promptly deliver copies of all notices and other communications given or made by the Company pursuant to the Equipment Lease to Lender at the address shown above at the time as required for such delivery to Lessor, or other parties, under the Equipment Lease. The Company further agrees that (a) it shall not enter into any agreement amending, modifying, or terminating the Equipment Lease without the prior written consent of Lender, and (b) any such attempted agreement to amend, modify, or terminate the Equipment Lease without such consent shall be void.

4. Without limiting the generality of clause (i) of Paragraph 3 above, the Company hereby expressly affirms its understanding that notwithstanding any breach of or default under the Equipment Lease by Lessor, that the Company's obligations under the Equipment Lease are absolute and unconditional, and that the Company's recourse for any such breach by Lessor is solely against Lessor.

5. The Company hereby affirms that all representations and warranties made by it in the Equipment Lease are true and correct on the date hereof with the same force and effect as if made on the date hereof, and that Lender may rely upon the same.

6. The Company hereby affirms its understanding that the assignment made by Lessor to Lender is an assignment of rights, benefits, and remedies only and that Lender has not assumed any duties or obligations whatsoever as lessor under the Equipment Lease, and shall not, now or hereafter, have any duty or obligation as lessor under the Equipment Lease, notwithstanding its receipt of Payments due under the Equipment Lease or its exercise of any other rights and/or remedies of "Lessor" thereunder, and the Company hereby agrees that it shall not now or hereafter look to Lender for performance or satisfaction of any such duties or obligations.

7. The Company will furnish to Lender (a) as soon as available, but in any event not later than 120 days after the end of each fiscal year, its (a) consolidated balance sheet as at the end of such fiscal year, and consolidated statements of income and changes in financial position for such fiscal year, all in reasonable detail, prepared in accordance with generally accepted accounting principles applied on a basis consistently maintained throughout the period involved and certified by certified public accountants selected by the Company and acceptable to Lender; (b), if applicable, as soon as available, but in any event not later than 90 days after the end of each of the first three quarterly periods of each fiscal year, the Form 10-Q report filed by Lessee with the Securities and Exchange Commission for such quarterly period, certified by the chief financial officer of Lessee; and (c) promptly, such additional financial and other information as Lender may from time to time reasonably request.

8. Section ____ of the Equipment Lease is hereby amended by adding the following:
(*Author's Note:* This is to be conformed as necessary.)

9. The Equipment Lease is hereby amended by deleting Section ____ thereof and substituting the following:
(*Author's Note:* This to be conformed as necessary.)

10. The Company agrees to furnish to Lender, before Lender shall make any loan to Lessor pursuant to the terms of the Loan Agreement, (a) the written opinion of counsel for the Company, as to matters contained in paragraphs [____ through ____] inclusive of Lessee's Representations and Warranties set forth in the Equipment Lease, and as to such other matters incident to the transactions contemplated by the Equipment Lease and the Agreement as Lender may request; and (b), if applicable, the Form 10-Q report filed by lessee with the Securities and Exchange Commission for such quarterly period ending ____, in form and substance satisfactory to Lender and certified by the chief financial officer of Lessee.

11. The Company hereby affirms that it shall not voluntarily terminate the Equipment Lease for any reason whatsoever.

12. In consideration of the covenants and agreements made by the Company herein, Lender hereby agrees that so long as no Event of Default (as defined in the Equipment Lease) shall have occurred and be continuing, and the Company shall not be in default of its obligations hereunder to Lender, neither Lender nor any party claiming through or under Lender, will disturb the Company's quiet and peaceful possession of the Equipment and its unrestricted use thereof for its intended purpose under the terms of the Equipment Lease.

13. This Consent may not be changed, waived, discharged, or terminated orally, but only by an instrument in writing signed by the party against which enforcement of a change, waiver, discharge, or termination is sought. This Consent shall be binding upon and inure to the benefit of Lender and the Company and their respective successors and assigns. This Consent shall be governed by, and construed and interpreted in accordance with, the laws of the State of [Insert appropriate state, such as New York].

IN WITNESS WHEREOF, the Company has executed this Consent as of the _____ day of _____ .

_____
Company

By: _____
     (Insert name)

Title: _____

ACKNOWLEDGED AND AGREED:

_____
Lessor

By: _____
     (Insert name)

Title: _____

_____
Lender

By: _____
     (Insert name)

Title: _____

Form: I-07d
Disk File Name: I-07d.rtf

SUPPLEMENT

Form Purpose

A supplement to be used for individual loan takedowns in connection with a master equipment loan and security agreement. This form is integrated with Loan and Security Agreement, Form I-07.

Executing Parties
The borrower.

See:
Loan and Security Agreement, Form I-07

Exhibit D
Supplement

This Supplement is executed and delivered by   ("Borrower") pursuant to the terms of a Loan and Security Agreement ("Loan Agreement") dated as of   , between Borrower and   ("Lender"). Terms defined in the Loan Agreement shall have the respective meanings given them in the Loan Agreement unless otherwise defined herein or unless the context otherwise requires.

1. Borrower hereby confirms that the proceeds of the Loan made this date shall be used to purchase the items of personal property ("Unit of Equipment") set forth below:

Qty.	Model	Mfgrs.	Description	Serial No.	Cost

[Insert equipment information]

2. Borrower hereby represents and warrants that the above described items of personal property have been delivered to it, duly assembled, and are in good working order at: _____.

3. Borrower hereby affirms that the representations and warranties set forth in Section 12 of the Loan Agreement are true and correct as of the date hereof.

4. Borrower hereby affirms that Lender has made a Loan to it for the purchase of the above described Unit of Equipment, which loan is evidenced by a Note, in the principal amount of $ _____ dated _____.

5. Borrower hereby affirms that Lender has a security interest in the items of personal property described above as set forth in Section 9 of the Loan Agreement.

_____
Borrower:

By: _____

Title: _____

Form: m-01
Disk File Name: m-01.rtf

CREDIT APPLICATION

Form Purpose

Equipment leasing company credit approval guideline handout.

ABLE LEASING COMPANY
Lessee Credit Application

Company Information

Legal Name: _____
Trade Name: _____
Address: _____

Telephone Number: (   ) _____
Years in Business: _____
Type of Business (Please Check One):
   Proprietorship___ Partnership (Gen or LP) ___ Corporation ___ Limited Liability Company ___

Description of Business: _____

Reference Credit Information

Bank Reference: _____
Telephone Number: (   ) _____
Account Number: _____
Contact: _____

Trade Reference: _____
Telephone Number & Contact:_____

Trade Reference: _____
Telephone Number & Contact: _____

Trade Reference: _____
Telephone Number & Contact: _____

Owner Information

Name: _____
Address: _____
Social Security Number: _____

Equipment Information

Equipment Description: _____
Vendor: _____
Cost: _____ Financing Term: _____

Form: m-02
Disk File Name: m-02.rtf

CREDIT GUIDELINES—SMALL TICKET

Form Purpose

Equipment leasing company credit approval guideline handout.

ABLE LEASING COMPANY
Lessee Credit Approval Guidelines

Your creditworthiness is the most important consideration in the lessor's decision. If you are aware of any credit problem you've had during your period in business, please bring it to our attention so we may work with you to package your financing and have it presented in the best possible manner. Chances of a subsequent approval are reduced if a problem is discovered after you've submitted your financing package.

To qualify for financing under the ALC Quick Finance Program, your business must meet the following guidelines. If it does not, please call us to discuss your financing. We may be able to obtain an exception if credit augmentation is possible. Remember, we're here to work to get your business financing needs met.

Able Leasing Company will conduct a preliminary "lease acceptability review" before formally submitting a transaction to our Credit Committee to head off potential problems. Very often issues that could result in a turndown can be addressed to facilitate an approval before the application is submitted.

Guidelines

Minimum Time in Business

You must have a minimum verifiable time in business of two years. Three years is required in the case of applications over $25,000 and four years in the case of applications over $100,000.

Existing Banking Relationship

You must have a business bank relationship of at least two years and the bank account must show a minimum low four figure average balance. In the case of transactions exceeding $25,000, the minimum average account balance must be in the low five figures. There cannot be any overdrafts or check returns for insufficient funds.

Trade References

You must provide three significant business trade references, each of whose relationship goes back at least six months. COD trade references will not be acceptable.

Good Personal Credit

Personal credit reports must be forthcoming that contain no derogatory information.

Financial Statements

Financial statements must be supplied for transactions exceeding $25,000. Current assets must exceed current liabilities and, for transactions in excess of $50,000, a minimum equity of $75,000 must be present.

Form: m-03
Disk File Name: m-03.rtf

FINANCING INSTRUCTIONS—SMALL TICKET

Form Purpose

Equipment leasing company finance instruction handout.

ABLE LEASING COMPANY
Financing Instructions

Your application for equipment financing can be processed quickly and your financing will be trouble-free, provided you carefully follow the instructions below. If you have any questions, don't guess. Call us and we'll help.

1. Check Over the Lessee Credit Approval Guidelines

If your business qualifies, go to Step 2. If it does not, we will be happy to explore with you any alternatives or credit augmentation in order for you to obtain financing.

2. Fill Out and Fax Us the ALC Credit Application

The application must be complete or it cannot be processed.

3. Tell Us Now About Any Personal or Business Credit Problems

If you have had, or now have, any credit problem, such as late credit card payments or judgments, describe them on a sheet included along with your credit application.

4. Complete All Paperwork Carefully

When your financing is approved, you will receive the necessary paperwork for documenting the financing. Complete it exactly as indicated and return it to us in the return envelope.

5. Fill Out and Return the Equipment Lease Acceptance Form

When your equipment arrives and you are satisfied that it is operating to your complete satisfaction, fill out and return to us the equipment acceptance-for-lease form included with your financing documentation.

6. Make Sure You Deliver Your Financing Payments On Time

If you don't, it may damage your credit rating.

Able Leasing Company

Fax Number:
Telephone Number:
Address:
24-Hour OnLine HotLine:

Form: m-04
Disk File Name: m-04.rtf

FINANCING LEASE RATE SHEET—SMALL TICKET

Form Purpose

Equipment leasing company lease rate sheet handout.

Lessee Financing Rates and Terms

The Able Leasing Company lease financing rates and terms are as follows:

Transaction Size*	*Lease Term*	
	3 Years	*5 Years*
$1,500 to $4,999	%	%
$5,000 to $24,999	%	%
$25,000 to $50,000	%	%

*Financing for transactions in excess of $50,000 will also be available. Various end-of-lease options will be offered, such as fair market and low fixed-price purchase and renewal options, as well as $1 buyouts. The lease financing interest rates charged will vary with the option chosen; the lowest rates are typically provided by fair market end-of-lease option leases.

Form: m-05
Disk File Name: m-05.rtf

MORTGAGE—INDEMNITY

Form Purpose

A form of mortgage used to secure the obligations of the guarantor of equipment lease agreement obligations.

Executing Parties
The equipment lease guarantor.

See:
Guaranty, Forms g-01 through g-03

Indemnity Mortgage

THIS INDEMNITY MORTGAGE, made this   day of   , by and between
                , (the "Mortgager"), with a place of business at
and   , (the "Mortgagee"), with a place of business at   .

WITNESSETH:

WHEREAS, Mortgagor has requested Mortgagee, as Lessor, to enter into a Lease or Leases [the "Lease(s)"] with respect to certain specified equipment;

WHEREAS, pursuant to Mortgagor's request, Mortgagee has or will enter into the Leases with certain specified lessees;

WHEREAS, in order to induce Mortgagee to enter into the Leases, Mortgagor, by Guaranty dated   , has agreed to guarantee Mortgagee from any loss it may sustain as a result of the Leases, and Mortgagor has agreed to secure the Guaranty by this Mortgage; and

WHEREAS, as a condition precedent to the making of the Leases, Mortgagee has required the execution of this Mortgage for purposes of securing the performance of the terms and conditions of the Indemnity of Mortgagor, and to secure Mortgagee from any loss it may sustain as a result of a Lessee default in any or all of the Leases (the "Mortgage Debt").

NOW, THEREFORE, in consideration of the premises and the sum of One Dollar ($1.00) and other good and valuable considerations, receipt whereof is hereby acknowledged, Mortgagor grants, assigns, and conveys unto Mortgagee, its successors and assigns, all that lot(s) of ground situate in   , State of   , known as   , said lot(s) being more particularly described on Schedule A attached hereto and made a part hereof.

TOGETHER with the building and improvements thereupon and all the rights, roads, alleys, ways, waters, privileges, easements, profits, and appurtenances thereunto belonging or in any wise appertaining, and including any right, title, interest, and estate hereafter acquired by Mortgagor in the Property (defined below) granted herein.

ALSO TOGETHER with and including as part of the buildings and improvements erected on the aforesaid lot of ground all building materials and other chattels on the premises intended to be incorporated in the improvements thereon, and all fixtures, equipment, accessories, and furniture which is attached to or affixed to the buildings and improvements, including kitchen cabinets, hot water heaters, gas and electric ranges, laundry equipment and tubs, medicine cabinets, lighting fixtures, heating plant, airconditioning equipment, piping, tubing, duct work, radiators, storm windows, storm doors, screens, screen doors, window shades and awnings, all of which fixtures, accessories, and equipment now on or hereafter placed upon the lot or lots of ground are hereby declared to be by Mortgagor fixtures and permanent additions to the realty and intended to be included as part of the lot or lots of ground hereby mortgaged.

TO HAVE AND TO HOLD the said lot or lots of ground, improvements, and other property and rights described above (collectively, the "Property") unto Mortgagee, its successors and assigns, in fee simple.

PROVIDED, that if Mortgagor, their heirs, personal representatives, and assigns, shall cause to be paid the Mortgage Debt and interest thereon from the date hereof, and upon the termination, release, or other voidance of the Leases and payment to Mortgagee of all costs, charges, and expenses in connection therewith, without any loss or further liability on the part of Mortgagor, and shall perform all of the covenants and agreements herein on their part contained, then this Mortgage shall be void.

MORTGAGOR HEREBY COVENANTS:

A. To pay, when due, all ground rents, taxes, water rents, assessments, public and other dues and charges levied or assessed or which may be levied or assessed on the Property; and not to permit any lien or encumbrance on the Property except the lien of this Mortgage, any statutory lien of any kind except liens for taxes and benefit charges not then delinquent, or any lien and or encumbrance listed on Schedule B attached hereto.

B. To keep the Property in good order, condition, and repair and to permit Mortgagee to enter upon and inspect the same; to make all proper renewals, replacements, and additions of and to the Property; not to permit or suffer any waste thereof; and not to tear down the improvements or materially change them or permit them to be torn down or materially changed, without the written consent of Mortgagee.

C. To keep the Property insured against loss or damage by fire and such other hazards, casualties, and contingencies as may be required from time to time by Mortgagee, such insurance to be written through an agent or broker selected by Mortgagor in such form and in such companies as may be approved by Mortgagee, and in amounts satisfactory to Mortgagee; to cause a standard mortgagee clause satisfactory to Mortgagee to be attached to such policy or policies providing that all payments thereunder shall be made to the order of Mortgagee as its interest may appear, and, at the request of Mortgagee, to deliver such policy or policies and all renewals thereof to Mortgagee at its place of business, or at such other place as it may designate in writing. All sums payable under such policy or policies shall be paid to Mortgagee and all sums received by Mortgagor on account of such policy or policies shall be paid over promptly to Mortgagee and Mortgagee at its discretion, may apply such sums, in whole or in part, to the repair, restoration, and replacement of the damaged or destroyed Property or toward the payment of the mortgage indebtedness. In the event of foreclosure of this Mortgage or other transfer of title to the Property or any parcel thereof in extinguishment of the Mortgage Debt, Mortgagee is authorized to cancel any insurance policy then in force and the unearned premium shall be applied to the payment of any sums due mortgagee under the terms of this Mortgage.

D. To comply promptly with all laws, ordinances, and regulations affecting the Property or its use.

THE PARTIES HERETO FURTHER COVENANT AND AGREE:

1. Mortgagor warrant specially the Property hereby conveyed and will execute such further assurances thereof as may be requisite.

2. In the event of any default under the terms of this Mortgage or any letter of credit or other documents relating thereto, or in the event a receiver or trustee is appointed for the Property of Mortgagor, or any of them, either in bankruptcy or in equity, or in the event Mortgagor, or any of them, execute a deed of trust of their Property for the benefit of creditors, then the whole Mortgage Debt, at the option of Mortgagee, shall be and become due and payable.

3. It shall be deemed a default under this Mortgage, if, without the written consent of Mortgagee, (a) Mortgagor shall sell, cease to own, assign, transfer, or dispose of all or any part of the mortgaged Property, or (b) the mortgaged Property is abandoned.

4. In the event of any default in any of the covenants of this Mortgage, Mortgagor, in accordance with the general or local rules, regulations, or laws of the State of relating to mortgages, including any amend-

ments thereof or supplements or additions thereto which do not materially change or impair the remedy, do hereby (a) declare their assent to the passage of a decree for the sale of the Property and (b) authorize Mortgagee, its successors and assigns, to sell the Property. Any such sale, whether under the assent to a decree or power of sale, may be made by the person or persons authorized to sell either as an entirety or in such separate parcels and on such terms and at such places and in such manner as it, they, or he may deem advisable.

5. Upon any sale of the Property under this Mortgage, whether under the assent to a decree, the power of sale, or by equitable foreclosure, the proceeds of such sale shall be applied as follows: first, to the payment of all expenses incident to the sale, including a counsel fee of   Dollars ($), for conducting the proceedings if without contest, but if legal services be rendered to the trustee appointed by such decree or to Mortgagee or to the party selling under the power of sale in connection with any contested matter in the proceedings, then such other counsel fees and expenses shall be allowed out of the proceeds of sale as the court may deem proper; and also a commission to the trustee in the amount of (%) percent of the gross sales and a commission of (%) percent of the gross sales to the auctioneer conducting the sale, and also any liens prior to the lien of this Mortgage unless the sale is made subject to such prior liens; second, to the payment of all claims of Mortgagee hereunder, whether they have matured or not, with interest thereon until final ratification of the auditor's report; and third, the balance, if any, to Mortgagor, or to any person or persons entitled thereto, upon the surrender of the Property to the purchaser, less any expenses incurred in obtaining possession.

6. Immediately upon the first insertion of the advertisement or notice of sale, there shall be and become due and owing by Mortgagor, and each of them, to the party inserting the advertisement or notice, all expenses incident to such advertisement or notice, all court costs, attorneys' fees, and all expenses incident to the foreclosure proceedings under this Mortgage and a commission to the trustee of (%) on the total amount of the mortgage indebtedness, principal and interest, then due, and such party shall not be required to receive the principal and interest only of the debt in satisfaction thereof, unless the same be accompanied by a tender of such expenses, costs, attorneys' fees, and commission.

7. If Mortgagee shall incur any expense or expend any sums, including reasonable attorneys' fees, whether in connection with any action or proceeding or not, to sustain the lien of this Mortgage or its priority, or to protect or enforce any of its rights hereunder, or to recover any indebtedness hereby secured, or for any title examination or title insurance policy relating to the title to the Property, all such sums on notice and demand shall be paid by Mortgagor, together with interest thereon at the rate of interest of (%) percent or the maximum interest rate permitted by law, and shall be a lien on the premises subordinate to the lien of this Mortgage, and in any action or proceeding to foreclose this Mortgage, or to recover or collect the debt secured hereby, the provisions of law respecting the recovery of costs, disbursements, and allowances shall prevail unaffected by this covenant.

8. Should Mortgagor fail or neglect to pay any ground rent, taxes, assessments, public or other dues or charges levied or assessed or which may be levied or assessed on the Property or on the Mortgage Debt and interest, when due or to keep the Property in proper repair, or to keep the Property insured as agreed herein, or shall permit any lien or encumbrance upon the Property except as aforesaid, Mortgagee may make such payments or repairs or insure the Property against such loss in such an amount as may be necessary to secure the Mortgage Debt, and any sum so paid shall be added to the principal of the Mortgage Debt and shall bear interest from such time at the rate of interest above stated in Paragraph 7.

9. Should all or any part of the Property be condemned or taken through eminent domain proceedings, all or such part of any award or proceeds thereof as Mortgagee in its sole discretion may determine, in writing, shall be paid to Mortgagee and applied to the payment of the Mortgage Debt and all such proceeds are hereby assigned to Mortgagee.

10. Mortgagee may at any time renew this Mortgage, extend the time for payment of the debt or any part thereof or interest thereon and waive any of the covenants or conditions of this Mortgage, in whole or in part, either at the request of Mortgagor or of any person having an interest in the Property, take or release other security, or any part of the Property, or such other security, grant extensions, renewals, or indulgences therein, or apply to the payment of principal of and interest on the Mortgage Debt any part or all of the proceeds obtained by sale, foreclosure, or receivership as herein provided, without resort or regard to other security, all without in any way releasing Mortgagor, or any of them, from any of the covenants or conditions of

this Mortgage, or releasing the unreleased part of the Property herein described from the lien of this Mortgage for the amount of the Mortgage Debt, and may release any party primarily or secondarily liable on the Mortgage Debt without releasing any other party liable thereon and without releasing the Property subject thereto.

11. Until default is made in any covenant or condition of this Mortgage, Mortgagor shall have possession of the Property. Upon default in any of the covenants or conditions of this Mortgage, Mortgagee shall be entitled without notice to Mortgagor, or any of them, to the immediate possession of the Property and to the appointment of a receiver of the Property to operate the same, without regard to the adequacy thereof as security for the Mortgage Debt, and Mortgagor shall pay all costs in connection therewith, and upon any default, whether or not a receiver be appointed, the rents and profits of the Property are hereby assigned to Mortgagee as additional security.

12. Upon default in any of the covenants or conditions of this Mortgage, any funds on deposit with Mortgagee in the names of Mortgagor or any of them, and all securities and Property of Mortgagor or any of them, in the possession of Mortgagee whether as collateral security or held in a mortgage expense account or otherwise, may be held by Mortgagee as additional security and may be applied to the payment of any sums due Mortgagee under the terms of this Mortgage.

13. The rights, powers, privileges, and discretions specifically granted to Mortgagee under this Mortgage are not in limitation of but in addition to those to which Mortgagee is entitled under any general or local law relating to mortgages in the State of   , now or hereafter existing.

14. Before the full payment of the Mortgage Debt, Mortgagee, in its discretion, may make advances and readvances of funds to Mortgagor and renew, modify, or extend any letter of credit to the extent permitted by law and such sums shall be secured by this Mortgage.

15. The rights, powers, privileges, and discretions to which Mortgagee may be entitled herein shall inure to the benefit of its successors and assigns, are cumulative and not alternative, may be enforced successively or concurrently, and failure to exercise any of them shall not be deemed a waiver thereof and no waiver of any one shall be deemed to apply to any other nor shall it be effective unless in writing and signed by Mortgagee.

16. The covenants, agreements, conditions, and limitations of or imposed upon Mortgagor shall be binding upon their respective heirs, personal representatives, successors, and assigns.

17. The loan secured hereby was transacted solely for the purpose of carrying on or acquiring a business or commercial investment within the meaning of   (cite, if applicable, governing commercial law statute section) of the (cite, if applicable, the appropriate state law).

18. Whenever used herein, the singular shall include the plural, the plural the singular and the use of any gender shall be applicable to all genders.

WITNESS the signature and seal of Mortgagor, the day and year first above written.

_____, Mortgagor

By: _____

                                                          (CORPORATE SEAL)

Title: _____

WITNESS:

STATE OF   , COUNTY OF   , to wit:

I HEREBY CERTIFY, That on this   day of   , before me, the subscriber, a Notary Public of the State of   , in and for the County of   , personally appeared   , who, being by me duly sworn, did dispose and say that deponent resides at   ; deponent is the   of the within named Mortgagor described in and which executed, the foregoing instrument; deponent knows the seal of said Mortgagor; that the seal affixed to said instrument is such corporate seal; that it was so affixed by order of the Board of Directors of said Mortgagor; and deponent signed deponent's name thereto by like order.

AS WITNESS my hand and notarial seal.

Notary Public

MY COMMISSION EXPIRES:

STATE OF   , COUNTY OF   , to wit:

I HEREBY CERTIFY, That on this   day of   , before me, the subscriber, a Notary Public of the State of   , in and for the County of   , personally appeared   , the subscribing witness to the foregoing instrument who, being by me duly sworn, did dispose and say that deponent resides at   ; deponent knows   to be the individual described in, and who executed, the foregoing instrument; that he/she, said subscribing witness, was present and saw him/her execute the same; and that he/she, said witness, at the same time subscribed his/her name as witness thereto.

AS WITNESS my hand and notarial seal.

Notary Public

MY COMMISSION EXPIRES:

State of

County of

RECORDED ON THE   day of   ,

at   o'clock   -m. in Liber

of Mortgages at page   and examined.

Clerk

Please record and return to:

(Insert name and address of Mortgagee)

Schedule A

(description of property)

Schedule B

(liens and/or encumbrances)

Form: o-01
Disk File Name: o-01.rtf

BANK REFERENCE WORKSHEET

Form Purpose

An equipment leasing company lessee bank reference verification worksheet.

Bank Reference Form

FINAL APPROVAL AND CREDIT INFORMATION ON: _____

APPROVED BY: _____ DATE: _____

CREDIT AGENCY RATING: D & B : _____

                                             [   ]: _____

                                             [   ]: _____
YEARS IN BUSINESS: _____

TYPE OF BUSINESS: _____ NET WORTH (if known): _____

BANK INFORMATION	1ST BANK	2ND BANK
DATE CLEARED	_____	_____
NAME OF BANK	_____	_____
BANK OFFICER	_____	_____
CHECKING INFORMATION		
DATE OPENED	_____	_____
AVERAGE BALANCE	_____	_____
RATING	_____	_____
LOAN INFORMATION		
DATE OPENED	_____	_____
INDIV. HIGH AMOUNT	_____	_____
AVG. BALANCE	_____	_____
UNSECURED	_____	_____
SECURED	_____	_____
SECURITY	_____	_____
RATING	_____	_____
BANK COMMENTS	_____	_____
CREDIT APPROVAL		

NOTES_____

Form: o-02
Disk File Name: o-02.rtf

MASTER DOCUMENTATION WORKSHEET/CHECKLIST

Form Purpose

An equipment leasing company master documentation worksheet/checklist.

Master Documentation Worksheet/Checklist

Lessee Name: _____ Lease Application # _____

CREDIT: Check Off Documents Required For Approval   Date: _____ Initials _____

SALES	Req'd	Rec'd		Req'd	Rec'd
Signed Lease	( )		Vendor Recourse	( )	( )
Advance Rental Check	(X)	( )	Purchase Order from Lessee	( )	( )
Signed Delivery Receipt	(X)	( )	Life Ins Policy or Assign	( )	( )
Vendor Invoice		( )	Tax Exemption Certificate	( )	( )
Personal Guarantee	( )	( )	Landlord Waiver *	( )	( )
Corporate Guarantee	( )	( )	Mortgage Waiver *	( )	( )
Corporate Resolution	( )	( )	* Req'd For Vendor Payment		
Credit Info Obtained at Signing	( )	( )			
(Specify)_____	( )	( )			
_____	( )	( )	Other _____	( )	( )

SALES REVIEW

Documents	Process	Complete
Advance Rental Check	Currently dated, payable to Lessor/Agent, Signed	( )
	Company name matches Lessee name	( )
	Amount matches Lease	( )
	Make two copies for file	( )
Signed Lease	No cross-outs, front and back	( )
Lease to Application	Signature name and title match	( )
	Rate and term match	( )
	Monthly rental computed properly	( )
	Lessee name and address match	( )
	Equipment description matches	( )
	Equipment location matches	( )

NOTE: If all documents are received except the Vendor Invoice, pass file to next step.

Performed By: _____ Date: _____

DOCUMENTATION CHECKS

Documents	*Process*	*Complete*
Master Documents	Required Documents as indicated above match	( )
	Application approval terms	( )
	Double-check all documents received and verify sales review	( )
Signed Lease	"Good signature"-Corp. Officer for Corp., Partner for Partnership, LLC Representative Proprietor for Proprietorship	( )
	All copies legible and complete	( )
Delivery Receipt	Signer is same on both documents	( )
Personal Guarantee	Signed without a title	( )
	Home telephone number in file	( )
Corporate Resolution	Signed by Corporate Secretary	( )
	Person authorized in resolution is lease signer	( )
Purchase Order	P.O. sent	( )
	Equipment location and description on P.O. matches signed lease	( )
Purchase Order from Lessee	Made out to Lessor	( )
	Lease term and payments spelled out	( )
	Equipment location and description matches signed lease	( )
Invoice to Signed Lease		
Application	Cost Matches	( )
	Equipment description matches	( )
	Equipment location matches	( )
Invoice	Billed (Sold) to Lessor, not Lessee	( )
	Equipment serial number included	( )
	Extensions and total correct (run tape)	( )
Telephone Verification of Equipment Delivery	Equipment installed and running properly	Date: _____
	Telephone Verification script in folder	( )

Performed By: _____ Date: _____

Lease ready to be signed by credit manager.

___

LESSEE _____

LEASE COST _____ LEASE TYPE ____ TERM _____ RESIDUAL: FMV _____

LEASE NUMBER _____ CUSTOMER NUMBER _____ SALES REP _____

COMMENCEMENT DATE ____ 2ND PAYMENT DUE DATE _____

BOOKING CHECKLIST

Function	Date Competed
Booked into lease register	_____
Thank-you letter sent	_____
Invoicing setup	_____
Invoice for 2nd payment sent	_____
Vendor paid	_____
UCC-1 filed	_____
UCC-1 filing copy received	_____
Insurance received	_____
Lease folder completed	_____

Form: o-03
Disk File Name: o-03.rtf

NEW LESSEE WELCOME LETTER

Form Purpose

An equipment leasing company lessee welcome/thank-you letter.

Executing Parties
The lessor.

[Letterhead of Leasing Company]

(Insert name and address of new lessee)

Re: Lease Number:

Equipment Description:

Dear   :

We would like to take this opportunity to thank you for calling upon us to handle your recent capital equipment lease. We are pleased to have been chosen.

Enclosed is your copy of the Lease Contract, as well as a request for insurance on the equipment. It is EXTREMELY IMPORTANT THAT THIS INSURANCE REQUEST BE FULFILLED IMMEDIATELY PURSUANT TO PARAGRAPH   OF THE LEASE.

All payments are due on or before the due date shown on your rent invoice. A percent (%) late charge, with a minimum of $10.00, will be added to any late payments, to the extent allowed by law.

It is important that you understand paragraph   of your lease contract, which states that you as the lessee are responsible for reimbursing the lessor for all taxes, which includes the property tax related to your equipment, if applicable.

We appreciate this opportunity to serve you and trust that our business relationship will be mutually enjoyable. Please call us for further equipment that you wish to lease.

Very truly yours,

Form: o-04
Disk File Name: o-04.rtf

Tax Notification—Personal Property

Form Purpose

An equipment leasing company lessee personal property tax notification and information memorandum.

Executing Parties
The lessor.

Tax Notification

TAX NOTIFICATION

To: (Insert name and address of lessee)

From: (Insert name and address of leasing company)

    RE: Personal Property Tax

In accordance with Section __ of your equipment lease, you are responsible for all taxes related to your leased equipment.

Personal Property Tax is charged by your state once per year. We are responsible for collecting this tax from you and paying it to the State.

To expedite the collection of the Personal Property Tax, please fill in the information at the bottom of this tax notification memorandum. This will help us insure proper credit to your account and avoid delinquent taxes.

Thank you for your cooperation.

PLEASE RETURN COMPLETED FORM TO US WITH YOUR NEXT PAYMENT.

Company Name: _____

Company Address: _____

Lease Number: _____

County Where Equipment Is Located: _____

Zip Code Where Equipment Is Located: _____

Form: o-05
Disk File Name: o-05.rtf

TRADE REFERENCE WORKSHEET/REPORT

Form Purpose

An equipment leasing company lessee trade reference worksheet.

Trade Reference Worksheet/Report

DATE   _____

LESSEE   _____

INVESTIGATOR   _____

VENDOR/SUPPLIER NAME   _____

PHONE NO.   _____

CONTACT   _____

PRINCIPAL PRODUCTS   _____

                          _____

                          _____

                          _____

PRIME SUPPLIER OF   _____

INVOICE TERMS   _____

OPEN DATE   _____

HIGHEST CREDIT   _____

PAYMENT HISTORY   _____

DISCOUNT   _____

PROMPT   _____

0–30 DAYS   _____

30–60 DAYS   _____

60–90 DAYS   _____

OVER 90 DAYS   _____

COMMENTS

_____

_____

_____

Form: o-06
Disk File Name: o-06.rtf

TRANSACTION SUMMARY WORKSHEET

Form Purpose

An equipment leasing company lease transaction summary worksheet.

Lease Summary Worksheet

[For Transactions of $50,000 or More]

I Name: _____

   Trade Name: _____

   Address: _____

   _____

   Business Type: _____

II Equipment Funding Dollar Amount: _____

III Term: _____ Months

IV Rental:

   Number of Advance Payments: _____

   Total Advance Payment Amount: $ _____

   Number of Periodic Rental Payments:_____

   Periodic Rental Payment Amount: $ _____

   End-of-Lease Equipment Residual Dollar Amount: $_____

   or as a percentage of Equipment Cost: $_____%

V Equipment Description: _____

   Manufacturer: _____

   Model Number: _____

   New or Used: _____

VI Principals/Owners of Lessee

   Name: _____

   Title: _____

Home Addresses: _____

Social Security Number: _____

Background, history:

Name: _____

Title: _____

Home Addresses: _____

Social Security Number: _____

Background, history:

Name: _____

Title: _____

Home Addresses: _____

Social Security Number: _____

Background, history:

VII Lessee Financial Overview:

VIII Guaranties:

IX References:

X Recommendation:

Form: o-07
Disk File Name: o-07.rtf

TRANSACTION WORKSHEET/CHECKLIST

Form Purpose

An equipment leasing company small ticket transaction worksheet/checklist.

Transaction Worksheet/Checklist

LESSEE NAME: _____

LESSOR NAME: _____   APPROVED BY: _____

GUARANTORS: _____

CREDIT AGENCIES: _____

PERSONAL FINANCIALS _____

CORPORATE FINANCIALS _____

TAX RETURNS _____

OTHER _____

SUPPLIERS/VENDORS TO BE PAID:

    Name   Amount

DOCUMENTS & REQUIREMENTS

NAME VERIFICATION: _____

LEASE AGREEMENT: _____

SCHEDULE: _____

D&A CERTIFICATE: _____

INVOICE: _____

ASSIGNMENT: With Recourse _____   Without Recourse _____

GUARANTY: Personal _____   Corporate _____

    UCC FILING: _____

    COMMENTS: _____

    STATE: _____

    COUNTY: _____

    FIXTURE: _____

INSURANCE: _____

LIEN SEARCH: _____

LANDLORD WAIVER: _____

MORTGAGE WAIVER: _____

COLLATERAL PLEDGE AGREEMENT: _____

INDEMNITY MORTGAGE: _____

BILL OF SALE: _____

PHYSICAL AUDIT: _____

SUBORDINATION: _____

Form: o-08
Disk File Name: o-08.rtf

VERIFICATION AND AUDIT WORKSHEET

Form Purpose

An equipment leasing company internal transaction verification worksheet.

Verification and Audit Form

DATE: _____

TIME: _____

LEASE NO.: _____

LESSEE: _____

GUARANTOR: _____

SIGNATORY: _____

TELEPHONE NUMBER CALLED: _____

NAME OF PERSON CALLED: _____

IS ALL THE EQUIPMENT DELIVERED? _____

IS ALL THE EQUIPMENT FUNCTIONING SATISFACTORILY? _____

IS THE VENDOR EXPECTED TO DO ANYTHING FURTHER? _____

IS ALL THE EQUIPMENT ACCEPTED? _____

WHERE WILL THE EQUIPMENT BE LOCATED? _____

IS SIGNATURE ON THE LEASE
AND THE DELIVERY & ACCEPTANCE FORM CONFIRMED? _____

DO THEY KNOW THE LEASE IS NON-CANCELABLE? _____

VERIFIER'S NAME: _____

Form: o-09
Disk File Name: o-09.rtf

EARLY TERMINATION RIGHT/OPTION

Form Purpose

Early lease termination option Rider for short form, net finance master equipment lease agreement. This form is integrated with Lease Agreement, Form l-03.

Executing Parties
The equpiment lessee.
The equpiment lessor.

See:
Lease Agreement, Form l-03

_____

_____ , Lessor

Home Office Address: _____

Phone: (   ) _____

RIDER _____ to Schedule No. ____ , dated as of _____ , to Master Agreement to Lease Equipment,

dated as of _____ , between _____ , Lessor, and

_____ , Lessee.

EARLY TERMINATION OPTION

(a) Provided no Incipient Default or Event of Default has occurred and is continuing, Lessee shall have the right at its option at any time during the respective Lease Terms of the Units described below on not less than 90 days prior notice to Lessor to terminate this Lease with respect to one or more of such Units on the _____ Rent payment date of each such Unit, or on any Rent payment date thereafter ("Termination Date"), provided that Lessee shall have made a good faith determination that each such Unit with respect to which Lessee intends to exercise this option ("Termination Units") is obsolete or surplus to Lessee's requirements. During the period from the giving of such notice to the Termination Date, Lessee, as agent for Lessor, shall use its best efforts to obtain bids for the purchase of such Termination Units by a party or parties other than Lessee or an affiliate of Lessee. Lessee shall promptly certify in writing to Lessor the amount and terms of each bid received by Lessee and the name and address of the party submitting such bid. Subject to Lessor's right to retain such Termination Units as provided in paragraph (b), on the Termination Date Lessor shall sell such Termination Units for cash to the bidder or bidders ("Third Party Purchaser") who have submitted the highest bid for such Termination Units and shall transfer title to such Termination Units to such Third Party Purchaser without recourse or warranty, except that Lessor shall represent and warrant that it owns such Termination Units free and clear of any Lessor's Lien. The total sale price realized upon such sale shall be retained by Lessor and, in addition, on the Termination Date, Lessee shall pay to Lessor the amount, if any, by which the applicable Termination Value of such Termination Units as provided in paragraph (d), computed as of the Termination Date, exceeds the net proceeds of such sale, whereupon this Lease shall terminate as to such Termination Units except as herein otherwise expressly provided. If no sale shall have occurred on the Termination Date as to any Termination Unit, this Lease shall continue in full force and effect as to such Termination Unit.

(b) Notwithstanding the provisions of paragraph (a), Lessor shall have the right at any time up to and including 30 days prior to the Termination Date, within its sole discretion, to elect not to sell any one or more Termination Units to any Third Party Purchaser. In the event Lessor elects not to sell any such Termination Units to such Third Party Purchaser, Lessee shall return such Termination Units to Lessor in accordance with the provisions of Section 8 of the Master Agreement to Lease Equipment designated above, and Lessor thereupon may retain such Termination Units for its own account without further obligation to Lessee under this Lease. In the event of the return of such Termination Units to Lessor pursuant to this paragraph (b), and provided no Incipient Default or Event of Default has occurred and is continuing, all obligations of Lessee with respect to such Termination Units, including the payment of Rent, for any period subsequent to their respective Termination Dates shall cease.

(c) Subject to Lessor's rights as provided in paragraph (b), if as to any Termination Unit the Termination Value exceeds the highest bid or in the event no bids are received by Lessee, Lessee may, at its option, upon notice given to Lessor not less than 15 days prior to the Termination Date, elect to rescind Lessee's notice of termination with respect to such Termination Unit, whereupon this Lease shall continue in full force and effect as though no notice of termination had been given by Lessee with respect to such Termination Unit.

(d) The Termination Value of any Unit shall be that percentage described on Annex A hereto of the Acquisition Cost of such Unit corresponding to the applicable Termination Date of such Unit, plus an amount of money equal to the Rent payment due on such Termination Date.

Unit Description

ABLE LEASING CORPORATION,

Lessor: _____

By: _____

Title: _____

_____ , Lessee

By: _____

Title: _____

Annex A

TO RIDER _____ TO
SCHEDULE NO. ____

TERMINATION VALUE TABLE

The Termination Value of any Unit shall be that percentage specified below of the Acquisition Cost of such Unit corresponding to the applicable Termination Date of such Unit, plus an amount of money equal to the Rent payment due on such Termination Date. [See table on next page.]

Termination Date	Percentage	Termination Date	Percentage	Termination Date	Percentage
0	____				
1		41	____	81	____
2		42	____	82	____
3		43	____	83	____
4		44	____	84	____
5		45	____	85	____
6		46	____	86	____
7		47	____	87	____
8		48	____	88	____
9		49	____	89	____
10		50	____	90	____
11		51	____	91	____
12		52	____	92	____
13		53	____	93	____
14		54	____	94	____
15		55	____	95	____
16		56	____	96	____
17		57	____	97	____
18		58	____	98	____
19		59	____	99	____
20		60	____	100	____
21		61	____	101	____
22		62	____	102	____
23		63	____	103	____
24		64	____	104	____
25		65	____	105	____
26		66	____	106	____
27		67	____	107	____
28		68	____	108	____
29		69	____	109	____
30		70	____	110	____
31		71	____	111	____
32		72	____	112	____
33		73	____	113	____
34		74	____	114	____
35		75	____	115	____
36		76	____	116	____
37		77	____	117	____
38		78	____	118	____
39		79	____	119	____
40		80	____	120	____

Lessee acknowledges receipt of a copy hereof.

_____ , Lessee

By: _____

Title: _____

Form: o-10
Disk File Name: o-10.rtf

PURCHASE RIGHT/OPTION—FAIR MARKET VALUE/FIXED

Form Purpose

A lessee equipment purchase option letter.

Executing Parties
The equipment lessee.
The equipment lessor.

Lessee Purchase Option

[Insert lessee name and address]

Re: Lease Agreement, dated _____,
    by and between (insert name of lessee)
    and (insert name of Lessor)
    Lease No.: _____

TO WHOM THIS MAY CONCERN:

With reference to the above mentioned Lease Agreement (hereinafter the "Lease"), you shall have the option to purchase the equipment described in said Lease, as-is, where-is and without any representation or warranty, at the end of the scheduled term thereof, provided, of course, that there is no default under the Lease and that you have performed all of the terms and conditions of the said Lease.

The purchase price at the expiration of the Lease term shall be (insert, as applicable, "fair market value," or "a fixed price equal to $ _____ " or "a fixed equal to ____ % of equipment cost.") However, you are hereby informed and advised that this purchase option offer is made conditioned upon your signing and returning a copy of this document to our office at the above-mentioned address, together with the _____ , no earlier than one hundred and twenty (120) days and no later than thirty (30) days from the end of the scheduled Lease term. You will also be responsible for any applicable sales tax and agree to sign documentation reasonably acceptable to us to reflect the sale.

Very Truly Yours,

[Insert lessor name]

By: _____

Title: _____

Acknowledged and Agreed to:

[Insert lessee name]

By: _____

Title: _____

Form: o-11
Disk File Name: o-11.rtf

Purchase Right/Option—Fair Market Value

Form Purpose

Fair market value purchase option Rider for short form, net finance master equipment lease agreement. This form is integrated with Lease Agreement, Form l-03.

Executing Parties
The equipment lessor.
The equipment lessee.

See:
Lease Agreement, Form l-03

_____ , Lessor

Home Office Address: _____

Phone: (   ) _____

RIDER _____ to Schedule No. _____ , dated as of _____ , to Master Agreement to Lease Equipment,

dated as of _____ , between _____ , Lessor, and

_____ , Lessee.

Fair Market Purchase Option

Provided that this Lease has not been terminated earlier and no Incipient Default or Event of Default has occurred and is continuing, not earlier than _____ days and not later than _____ days before the end of the Lease Term, or in the event such Lease Term has been extended before the end of any period for which this Lease has been extended ("Renewal Term"), first to expire under this Lease of the Units described below, Lessee may as to all, but not less than all, such Units deliver to Lessor a written notice tentatively electing to purchase such Units at the end of the respective Lease Terms, or any Renewal Terms, as the case may be, for an amount equal to the Fair Market Value of each such Unit at the end of such periods. If no such notice is delivered by Lessee to Lessor within such period, Lessee shall be deemed to have waived any right to purchase such Units. Fair Market Value shall mean the value which would obtain in an arm's-length transaction between an informed and willing buyer-user (other than a lessee currently in possession or a used equipment dealer) under no compulsion to buy, and an informed and willing seller under no compulsion to sell and, in such determination, costs of removal from the location of current use shall not be a deduction from such value. Fair Market Value shall be determined by the mutual agreement of Lessor and Lessee in accordance with the preceding sentence. If Lessee and Lessor cannot agree within 30 days after Lessee's notice of tentative election, Fair Market Value shall be determined by a qualified independent equipment appraiser mutually satisfactory to Lessee and Lessor. If Lessee and Lessor fail to agree upon a satisfactory independent equipment appraiser within 10 days following the end of the 30-day period referred to above, Lessee and Lessor shall each within 5 days appoint a qualified independent equipment appraiser and such appraisers shall jointly determine the Fair Market Value of such Units. If, within 15 days after the appointment of the last of these two appraisers, the appraisers cannot agree upon the Fair Market Value of such Units, the two appraisers shall, within 10 days, appoint a third appraiser and the Fair Market Value of such Units shall be determined by the three appraisers, who shall make their appraisals within 15 days following the appointment of the third appraiser and the average of their three determinations so made shall be deemed to be the Fair Market Value of such Units and shall be conclusive and binding upon Lessor and Lessee. If either party shall have failed to appoint an appraiser, the determination of the Fair Market Value of such Units of the single appraiser appointed by the other party shall be final.

At any time within the 15-day period following the determination of the Fair Market Value of such Units, Lessee may deliver to Lessor a further notice finally electing to purchase such Units. If no such further notice is delivered by Lessee to Lessor within such period, Lessee shall be deemed to have waived any right to purchase such Units. At the end of the respective Lease Terms or Renewal Terms, as appropriate, if Lessee has finally elected to purchase such Units, Lessee shall purchase from Lessor, and Lessor shall sell to Lessee, each such Unit for a cash consideration equal to the Fair Market Value of such Unit, and Lessor shall transfer title to each such Unit to Lessee without recourse or warranty, except that Lessor shall represent and warrant that it owns such Unit free and clear of any Lessor's Lien. All appraisal fees and expenses shall be borne by Lessee.

Unit Description:

_____ , Lessor

By: _____

Title: _____

_____ , Lessee

By: _____

Title: _____

Form: o-12
Disk File Name: o-12.rtf

PURCHASE RIGHT/OPTION—FIXED PRICE

Form Purpose

Fixed price purchase option Rider for short form, net finance master equipment lease agreement. This form is integrated with Lease Agreement, Form l-03.

Executing Parties
The equipment lessor.
The equipment lessee.

See:
Lease Agreement, Form l-03

_____ , Lessor

Home Office Address: _____

Phone: (   ) _____

RIDER _____ to Schedule No. _____ , dated as of _____ , to Master Agreement to Lease Equipment,

dated as of _____ , between _____ , Lessor, and

_____ , Lessee.

Fixed Price Purchase Option

Provided that this Lease has not been terminated earlier and no Incipient Default or Event of Default has occurred and is continuing, Lessee may, upon not less than that number of days' notice specified below before the end of the Lease Term first to expire under this Lease of the Units described below, purchase each but not less than all the Units described below at the end of their respective Lease Terms for cash in the amount specified below. Upon payment to Lessor in full for each Unit, Lessor shall transfer title to such Unit to Lessee without recourse or warranty, except that Lessor shall represent that it owns such Unit and has no knowledge of any Lessor's Lien relating to such Unit.

Purchase Price	Unit Description	Purchase Price as a Percentage of Acquisition Cost	Purchase Price in Dollars	Number of Days' Notice

[Insert information]

, Lessor

By:

Title:

, Lessee

By:

Title:

Form: o-13
Disk File Name: o-13.rtf

Renewal Right/Option—Fair Market Value

Form Purpose

Fair market lease term renewal option Rider for short form, net finance master equipment lease agreement. This form is integrated with Lease Agreement, Form l-03.

Executing Parties
The equipment lessor.
The equipment lessee.

See:
Lease Agreement, Form l-03

_____ , Lessor

Home Office Address: _____

RIDER _____ to Schedule No. _____ , dated as of _____ , to Master Agreement to Lease

Equipment dated as of _____ , between _____ , Lessor, and

_____ , Lessee.

Fair Market Renewal Option

Provided that this Lease has not been terminated earlier and no Incipient Default or Event of Default has occurred and is continuing, not earlier than   days and not later than   days before the end of the Lease Term, or in the event such Lease Term has been extended before the end of any period for which this Lease has been extended ("Renewal Term"), first to expire under the Lease of the Units described below, Lessee may as to all, but not less than all, such Units deliver to Lessor a written notice tentatively electing to extend the Lease as to such Units at the end of the respective Lease Terms, or any Renewal Terms, as the case may be, on the periodic basis described below (not to exceed the aggregate Renewal Term specified below) at the Fair Market Rental of each such Unit as of the end of such applicable periods. If no such written notice is delivered by Lessee to lessor within such period, Lessee shall be deemed to have waived any right to extend the Lease with respect to such Units, Fair Market Rental shall mean the value which would obtain in an arm's-length transaction between an informed and willing lessee (other than a lessee currently in possession or a used equipment dealer) under no compulsion to lease, and an informed and willing lessor under no compulsion to lease and, in such determination, costs of removal from the location of current use shall not be a deduction from such value. Fair Market Rental shall be determined by the mutual agreement of Lessor and Lessee in accordance with the preceding sentence. If Lessee and Lessor cannot agree within 30 days after Lessee's notice of tentative election, Fair Market Rental shall be determined by a qualified independent equipment appraiser mutually satisfactory to Lessee and Lessor. If Lessee and Lessor fail to agree upon a satisfactory independent equipment appraiser within 10 days following the end of the 30-day period referred to above, Lessee and Lessor shall each within 5 days appoint a qualified independent equipment appraiser and such appraisers shall jointly determine the Fair Market Rental of such Units. If, within 15 days after the appointment of the last of these two appraisers, the appraisers cannot agree upon the Fair Market Rental of such Units, the two appraisers shall, within 10 days, appoint a third appraiser and the Fair Market Rental of such Units shall be determined by the three appraisers, who shall make their appraisals within 15 days following the appointment of the third appraiser and the average of their three determinations so made shall be deemed to be the Fair Market Rental of such Units and shall be conclusive and binding upon Lessor and Lessee. If either party shall have failed to appoint an appraiser, the determination of Fair Market Rental of the single appraiser appointed by the other party shall be final.

At any time within the 15-day period following the determination of the Fair Market Rental of such Units, Lessee may deliver to Lessor a further notice finally electing to extend the Lease with respect to such Units. If no such further notice is delivered by Lessee to Lessor within this 15-day period, Lessee shall be deemed to have waived any right to extend the Lease with respect to such Units. All appraisal fees and expenses shall be borne by Lessee.

Unit Description	*Maximum Aggregate Renewal Term*	*Periodic Renewal Term Basis*
	[Insert information]	

, Lessor

By:

Title:

, Lessee

By:

Title:

Form: o-14
Disk File Name: o-14.rtf

RENEWAL RIGHT/OPTION—FIXED PRICE

Form Purpose

Lessee fixed price lease term renewal option Rider for short form, net finance master equipment lease agreement. This form is integrated with Lease Agreement, Form l-03.

Executing Parties
The equipment lessor.
The equipment lessee.

See:
Lease Agreement, Form l-03

_____ , Lessor

Home Office Address: _____

RIDER _____ to Schedule No. _____ , dated as of _____ , to Master Agreement to Lease

Equipment dated as of _____ , between _____ , Lessor, and

_____ , Lessee.

Fixed Price Lease Renewal Option

Provided that this Lease has not been terminated earlier and no Incipient Default or Event of Default has occurred and is continuing, not earlier than   days and not later than   days before the end of the Lease Term, or in the event such Lease Term has been extended before the end of any period for which this Lease has been extended ("Renewal Term"), first to expire under the Lease of the Units described below, Lessee may as to all, but not less than all, such Units deliver to Lessor a written notice tentatively electing to extend the Lease as to such Units at the end of the respective Lease Terms, or any Renewal Terms, as the case may be, on the periodic basis described below (not to exceed the aggregate Renewal Term specified below) for a fixed price (as specified below) with respect to each such Unit as of the end of such applicable periods. If no such written notice is delivered by Lessee to lessor within such period, Lessee shall be deemed to have waived any right to extend the Lease with respect to such Units.

Unit Description	Maximum Aggregate Renewal Term	Periodic Renewal Term Basis	Fixed Price Renewal Rate
	[Insert information]		

_____ , Lessor _____ , Lessee

By: By:

Title: Title:

Form: o-15
Disk File Name: o-15.rtf

SUBLEASE RIGHT/OPTION

Form Purpose

Lessee right to sublease Rider for short form, net finance master lease agreement. This form is integrated with Lease Agreement, Form l-03.

Executing Parties
The equipment lessor.
The equipment lessee.

See:
Lease Agreement, Form l-03

_____ , Lessor

Home Office Address: _____

RIDER _____ to Schedule No. _____ dated as of _____ , to Master

Agreement to Lease Equipment, dated as of _____ , between _____ , Lessor, and

_____ , Lessee.

Lessee Right to Sublease

Provided that no Incipient Default or Event of Default has occurred and is continuing, Lessee shall be entitled without Lessor's consent, and upon 60 days' prior notice, to sublease any or all of the Units to any entity, including without limitation any subsidiary, affiliate, or parent corporation of Lessee, incorporated in the United States of America, but in all cases only upon and subject to all the terms and conditions of this Lease. No such sublease or other assignment of use by Lessee shall relieve Lessee of any of its obligations under this Lease.

Unit Description:

        [Insert unit information]

_____ , Lessor _____ , Lessee

By: By:

Title: Title:

Form: o-16
Disk File Name: o-16.rtf

AUTOMATIC TRANSFER OF TITLE

Form Purpose

Fair market value purchase option Rider for short-form, net finance master equipment lease agreement. This form is integrated with Lease Agreement, Form l-03.

See:
Lease Agreement, Form l-03

_____ , Lessor

Home Office Address: _____

Phone: (   ) _____

RIDER _____ to Schedule No. _____ , dated as of _____ , to Master Agreement to Lease Equipment,

dated as of _____ , between _____ , Lessor, and

_____ , Lessee.

Automatic Transfer of Title

Provided that this Lease has not been terminated earlier and no Incipient Default or Event of Default has occurred and is continuing, immediately upon the end of the applicable Lease Term title to each of the Units described below shall without any further action be automatically transferred to Lessee. Title to each Unit shall be transferred without recourse or warranty, except that Lessor shall, if so requested in writing by Lessee, represent that it owned such Unit immediately prior to the transfer and has no knowledge of any Lessor's Lien.

_____ , Lessor

By: _____

Title: _____

_____ , Lessee

By: _____

Title: _____

Form: o-17
Disk File Name: o-17.rtf

PUT

Form Purpose

A lessor right to force a lessee to purchase equipment subject to lease at the end of the lease term Rider. This form is integrated with Lease Agreement, Form l-03. Care must be exercised in using a put option because it can cause the lease to fail to qualify as a "true" lease for income tax purposes.

Executing Parties
The equipment lessor.
The equipment lessee.

See:
Lease Agreement, Form l-03

_____ , Lessor

Home Office Address: _____

Phone: (   ) _____

RIDER _____ to Schedule No. _____ , dated as of _____ , to Master

Agreement to Lease Equipment, dated as of _____ , between _____ , Lessor, and

_____ , Lessee.

Lessor Sale Option

Lessor may, upon not less than 60 days notice before the end of the Lease Term of each Unit described below, elect to sell to Lessee, and Lessee shall purchase, each such Unit at the end of such Unit's Lease Term in cash for the amount specified below. If Lessor shall make the election provided for in this Rider, the sale shall occur on the day next following the day the applicable Lease Term ends. Upon payment to Lessor in full of the purchase price indicated below, Lessor shall transfer title to each such Unit to Lessee without recourse or warranty, except that Lessor shall represent that it owns such Unit and has no knowledge of any Lessor's Lien. If Lessor exercises this option, it shall upset and prevail over any purchase, renewal, or early termination option Lessee may have under this Lease.

Unit Description	*Purchase Price as a Percentage of Acquisition Cost*	*Purchase Price in Dollars*

_____ , Lessor

By: _____

Title: _____

_____ , Lessee

By: _____

Title: _____

Form: p-01
Disk File Name: p-01.rtf

PROMISSORY NOTE—GENERAL FORM

Form Purpose

A promissory note.

Executing Parties
The borrower.

Promissory Note

$ _____ _____ , 20___

FOR VALUE RECEIVED the undersigned, _____ , a _____ corporation (the "Payor"), having its executive office and principal place of business at _____, hereby promises to pay to _____ , a _____ corporation, having a principal place of business at _____ _____ (the "Payee"), such payment to be made as provided for herein and to be sent to Payee at _____ _____ , or to such other place as the Payee shall hereafter specify in writing thirty (30) days in advance of such change of place, the principal sum of _____ ($_____), in such coin or currency of the United States of America as at the time shall be legal tender for the payment of public and private debts.

1. Interest and Payment.

   1.1 The unpaid principal amount hereof shall bear simple interest from the date hereof at the rate of _____ (__%) per annum.

   1.2 This Note shall be payable in _____ (__), consecutive, equal installments, including principal and interest, as follows:

   (a) The first payment of principal and interest thereon shall be due on _____ , and shall be in an amount equal to $_____, of which $_____ shall be applied toward the outstanding principal balance of the Note; and

   (b) The remaining _____ (__), monthly principal and interest payments shall be due on the _____ (Author's Note: for example, 1st) and the _____ (Author's Note: for example, 15th) of each month thereafter, beginning on _____ , in the amounts set forth on the schedule attached as Annex A hereto and made a part hereof.

   1.3 If any payment of principal and interest accrued thereon is not made on or before five (5) days after the time when such payment is due and payable, then interest shall accrue on such unpaid amount from the date of nonpayment to the date of payment at a simple interest rate equal to _____ (Author's Note: for example, EIGHTEEN PERCENT [18%]) per annum.

   2. Prepayment. At the option of the Payor, this Note may be prepaid in whole or in part at any time or from time to time, without penalty or premium, provided, however, such prepayment may only be made on or after _____ (__) months following the date of this Note stated above. Each prepayment of this Note shall first be applied to interest accrued through the date of prepayment and then to principal.

   3. Modification. This Note may not be modified, or discharged unless paid in full, except by a writing duly executed by the Payor and the Payee.

4. Miscellaneous.

4.1 This Note is secured by _____ .

4.2 The headings of the various paragraphs of this Note are for convenience of reference only and shall in no way modify any of the terms or provisions of this Note, or the Agreement.

4.3 All notices required or permitted to be given hereunder shall be in writing and shall be deemed to have been duly given when personally delivered or sent by registered or certified mail, return receipt requested, postage prepaid, to the address of the intended recipient set forth in the preamble to this Note or at such other address as the intended recipient shall have hereafter given in writing, 30 days in advance, to the other party hereto pursuant to the provisions hereof.

4.4 This Note shall bind the Payor and its successors and assigns.

4.5 The laws of the State of _____ shall apply to this Note.

_____ , Payor

By: _____

Title: _____

Annex A

[Insert debt amortization schedule]

Form: p-02
Disk File Name: p-02.rtf

PROMISSORY NOTE—INTEGRATED

Form Purpose

A promissory note. This form has been integrated with Loan and Security Agreement, Form l-05.

Executing Parties
The borrower.

See:
Loan and Security Agreement, Form l-05

Exhibit B
Promissory Note

$_____

(Insert here City and State)

Dated: _____

FOR VALUE RECEIVED, the undersigned, (insert name of borrower) (the "Borrower"), hereby promises to pay to the order of (insert name of Lender) (the "Lender ") at (insert address of Lender) the principal sum of _____ Dollars with interest on the unpaid balance thereof from the date hereof at the rate of (insert per annum Note interest rate) % per annum, computed on the basis of a 365-day year and a twelve 30-day month.

Past due principal and, to the extent legally enforceable, interest installments shall bear interest equal to _____ % per annum, until paid. Principal of and interest on this Note shall be payable in lawful money of the United States of America.

This Note is issued under and pursuant to a Loan and Security Agreement (Author's Note: See Form l-05 for integrated loan and security agreement form) dated _____ , as amended on _____, between the Borrower and the Lender (the "Security Agreement"), to which agreement reference is made for a statement of the terms and provisions thereof.

A schedule of the installment payments to be made here under which consists of the expected amounts to be paid by the Lessee to the Lender is set forth in the amortization table attached as Schedule A hereto and incorporated by reference herein; such amounts which are paid by the Lessee to the Lender shall be applied first to the payment of accrued interest hereon and then to the payment of the unpaid principal hereof. In addition to the payments set forth on Schedule A, on _____ , a payment of interest only on the Note from the date hereof, in the amount of $_____ shall be due and payable to the Lender.

The principal of this Note may be declared due and payable prior to the expressed maturity date thereof in the events, on the terms and in the manner provided for in the Security Agreement. In the event this Note is accelerated, the unpaid principal balance shall be determined from the schedule annexed hereto. Subject to the provisions of Section 5 of the Security Agreement, the liability of the Borrower is limited to the Units and the assigned income and proceeds from the Lease (as said terms are defined in the Security Agreement).

The provisions of this Note shall inure to the benefit of and be binding upon any successor to the Borrower and shall extend to any holder hereof.

_____ , Borrower

By: _____

Title: _____

Schedule A

Annexed to and made part of Promissory Note dated

in the principal amount of $.

PMT No.	Outstanding Principal	Debt Service	Interest Portion	Principal Portion

Form: p-03
Disk File Name: p-03.rtf

Promissory Note—Confessed Judgment

Form Purpose

A promissory note with a confessed judgment provision.

Executing Parties
The borrower.

$

COMMERCIAL NOTE—TIME

(Confessed Judgment)

Dated: _____ , 20___

The undersigned promises to pay to the order of _____ ("Payee") the sum of
_____ DOLLARS ($ _____) together with interest on the unpaid
principal balance thereof computed at an annual rate (Author's Note: Select [i] or [ii]): (i) which shall float
and which is _____ percent (__ %) above the prime rate as published in the money rates section of the *Wall
Street Journal,* adjusted as of the first day of each calendar quarter; or (ii) which shall be fixed at the rate of
_____ percent (__ %) per annum.

Principal and interest shall be paid in (Author's Note: Select: monthly, quarterly, or semiannually, as applicable) installments, (Author's Note: Select "in advance" or "in arrears") of $_____ beginning on the ____
day of _____ , and each (Author's Note: Select: monthly, quarterly, or semiannually, as applicable) period
continuing on the (first) day of each [Author's Note: Select: monthly, quarterly, or semiannually, as applica-
ble] calendar period thereafter until the principal balance is paid in full. [Author's Note: An alternative could
be that payments shall continue "in accordance with the following schedule:]

(Insert desired payment schedule)

Interest shall be computed on the basis of a 360-day year of twelve 30-day months, and charged for actual
days elapsed.

As used herein, "Obligations" means all indebtedness hereunder and any renewals, extensions, or modifications hereof together with any now or hereafter existing indebtedness of Undersigned to Payee whatsoever.
"Obligor" means undersigned and all endorsers, guarantors and sureties of any Obligation. As security for
the full and timely repayment of the Obligations (in addition to any other collateral), the undersigned hereby
grants to Payee a security interest in all monies, deposits, accounts or credits held by Payee for or owed by
Payee to the undersigned, and, in the event of default or demand hereunder or under any agreement between
undersigned and Payee, such monies, deposits, accounts, or credits may be setoff and applied to payment of
any Obligations.

[Author's Note: Delete if not applicable] This Note and all Obligations are secured pursuant to and entitled
to the benefits of the terms of a certain _____ dated _____ .

The undersigned shall be in default hereunder on the occurrence of any of the following: (a) non-payment
when due of any payment of principal or interest hereunder or of any Obligation; (b) any warranty, representation or statement made or furnished to Payee by or on behalf of the undersigned proving to have been
materially incorrect when made or furnished; (c) the existence of any uncured event of default under the
terms of any instrument or writing evidencing a debt of the undersigned to some one other than Payee; (d)

uninsured loss, theft, substantial damage, destruction, or transfer or encumbrance without fair value in return of any of the undersigned's assets; (e) the institution by or against any Obligor of any proceeding under any provision or chapter of any federal or state bankruptcy, insolvency or other debtor relief law whatsoever, or the appointment of any trustee or receiver for any Obligor or any of its assets; (f) judgment against, or attachment of, property of any Obligor; (g) payee deeming itself insecure; (h) dissolution, merger, consolidation, liquidation, or reorganization of any Obligor; or (i) death of any Obligor. Upon the occurrence of any event of default, Payee at its option may declare any or all Obligations immediately due and payable without notice, presentation, demand of payment, or protest, which are hereby expressly waived by every Obligor. Payee's rights and remedies hereunder are cumulative, and recourse to one shall not constitute a waiver of others. The undersigned shall be liable for all costs and expenses incurred by Payee in connection with collection of the Obligation, including court costs, costs of appeal, and attorney's fees.

In the event this Note or any Obligations are not paid when due or demanded, each Obligor hereby authorizes any attorney at law to appear for them before any court having jurisdiction within the United States or elsewhere and after one or more declarations filed, confess judgment against them, jointly and severally, for the unpaid balance of this Note, any Obligations and interest, court costs, costs of appeal and attorney's fees, such attorney's fees to be equal to twenty-five percent (25%) of the amount confessed, for collection and release of errors, and without stay of execution and inquisition and extension upon any levy on real estate, all of which are hereby waived and condemnation agreed to; and to the extent allowed by applicable law, the exemption of personal property from levy and sale is also hereby expressly waived and no benefit of exemption shall be claimed under any exemption law now in force or which may be hereafter adopted, and further authorizes any attorney at law to confess judgment against them pursuant to all of the terms set forth above for any deficiencies remaining after the collection, foreclosure, realization or sale of any collateral securing the Obligations. or any part thereof, together with interest, court costs and attorney's fees as set forth above.

If any part of this Note is declared invalid or unenforceable, such invalidity or unenforceability shall not affect the remainder of this Note, which shall continue in full force and effect. Any provision that is invalid or unenforceable in any application shall remain in full force and effect as to valid applications.

The undersigned warrants and represents that the purpose of this Note is _____ and that it is a commercial purpose Note.

This Note is executed under seal on the date first above written and shall be governed by the law of the State of _____, without regard to its conflict of law principles.

_____ , Borrower

By: _____   (CORPORATE SEAL)

Title: _____

(Insert address of maker)

Witnessed:

By _____

(Insert name of witnessing party)

Form: p-04
Disk File Name: p-04.rtf

S<small>INGLE</small> I<small>NVESTOR</small> (N<small>ONUNDERWRITTEN</small>)

Form Purpose

An equipment leasing company proposal letter format for a single investor, firm commitment (nonunderwritten) lease financing offer.

Executing Parties
The equipment lessor.

Nonunderwriting Proposal Letter

Date: 20___

Secour Corporation
800 Second Avenue
New York, New York 10017

Attention: Mr. R. Babcox

    President

Gentlemen:

Able Leasing Corporation ("ALC") offers to purchase and lease to Secour Corporation ("Secour") an item of newly manufactured computer equipment on the following terms and conditions:

1. Equipment Description:	The equipment will consist of one (1) new computer, model no. EA-1, manufactured by IXT Computer Corp.
2. Equipment Cost:	Approximately $1 million.
3. Delivery and Payment:	Delivery of the Equipment is anticipated on January 1, 20___, but in no event shall be later than March 1, 20___. ALC shall pay for the Equipment on delivery and acceptance.
4. Lease Term:	Eight years, beginning on delivery and acceptance of the Equipment.
5. Rental Program:	Secour shall remit 32 consecutive level, quarterly payments, in advance, each equal to 4.4000% of Equipment Cost.
6. Options:	At the conclusion of the Lease Term, Secour may (with at least 120 days' prior written notice):
	A. Buy the Equipment for an amount equal to its then fair market value.
	B. Renew the lease with respect to the Equipment for its then fair rental value.
7. Tax Benefits:	The rent is calculated based on the assumption that ALC will be entitled to: A. Five-year MACRS depreciation on the full Equipment Cost, 200% declining-balance switching to straight-line, and B. A corporate income tax rate equal to __%

8. Fixed Expenses: This is a net financial lease proposal and all fixed expenses such as insurance
                            maintenance, and personal property taxes shall be for the account of Secour.

9. Conditions Precedent: This offer is subject to the approval of the Board of Directors of ALC and to the
                            execution of lease documentation mutually acceptable to Secour and ALC.

If the foregoing is satisfactory to you, please indicate your acceptance of this offer by signing the duplicate
copy of this letter in the space provided therefor and returning it directly to the undersigned.

This offer expires as of the close of business on _____, 20___.

Very truly yours,

ABLE LEASING CORPORATION

By: _____
    Vice President

Accepted and Agreed to on this
_____ day of _____ , 20___.

SECOUR CORPORATION

By: _____

Its: _____

Form: p-05
Disk File Name: p-05.rtf

UNDERWRITTEN

Form Purpose

An equipment leasing company proposal letter format for an underwritten, best efforts lease financing offer.

Executing Parties
The equipment lessor.

Underwriting Proposal Letter

Date: 20____

White Airline Corporation
200 Park Avenue
New York, New York 10017

Attention: R. Rosset
            Assistant Treasurer

Gentlemen:

Able Leasing Corporation ("ALC"), on behalf of its nominees, proposes to use its best efforts to arrange a lease for one new Martin RC-75 aircraft for use by White Airline Corporation under the following terms and conditions:

Lessee:	The Lessee shall be White Airline Corporation.
Lessor:	The Lessor will be a commercial bank or trust company acting as owner trustee ("Owner Trustee") pursuant to one or more owners' trusts (the "Trust") for the benefit of one or more commercial banks or other corporate investors (the "Owner Participant"). The Trust shall acquire the Equipment and lease it to the Lessee.
Equipment:	One new Martin RC-75 aircraft.
Cost:	For purposes of this proposal, a total cost of $28 million, plus or minus 5% has been assumed.
Delivery Date:	Delivery of the Equipment is anticipated as of November 1, 20__, however, shall be no later than December 30, 20__.
Interim Lease Term:	The interim lease term shall extend from the Delivery Date until the Commencement Date. For the purposes of this proposal the Commencement Date is assumed to be January 1, 20__.
Interim Rent:	The Lessee shall pay interim rent equal to interest-only on the total cost of the Equipment at an interest rate equal to the Long-Term Debt Interest Rate.
Primary Lease Term:	The primary lease term shall be 20 years from the Commencement Date.
Primary Rent:	From the Commencement Date, the Lessee shall make 40 consecutive, level, semiannual payments, in arrears, each equal to 4.400% of Cost.

Debt Financing: An investment banker acceptable to ALC and the Lessee shall arrange for the private placement of secured notes or similar instruments ("Indebtedness") to be issued by the Lessor for a principal amount equal to 80% of total Equipment cost to certain institutional investors ("Lenders") who may be represented by an indenture trustee or agent bank ("Agent"). This proposal assumes that the Indebtedness shall be amortized in semiannual payments of principal and interest at an 8% per annum interest rate ("Long-Term Debt Interest Rate"), payable in arrears over the term of the lease. In the event that the Long-Term Debt Interest Rate varies from that assumed, the rent shall be adjusted, upward or downward, so that the Owner Participant's after-tax yield and after-tax cash flows will be maintained. The Indebtedness shall be secured by an assignment of the lease and a security interest in the Equipment but otherwise shall be without recourse to the Owner Participant and the Lessor.

Insurance: The Lessee may self-insure the Equipment.

Purchase & Renewal   At the end of the Primary Lease Term, the Lessee may (with 180 days' written notice
Options: prior to the end of the term):

                       A. Renew the lease on the Equipment for its then fair rental value for one five-year period.

                       B. Buy the Equipment for an equivalent price and under similar conditions as rendered by a third party approached by the Lessor and agreed to by the Lessor prior to sale to that third party.

                       If the Lessee does not elect to exercise any of the above options, theLessee shall return the Equipment to the Lessor at the end of the term at amutually agreeable location.

Termination Option: At any lime during the Primary Lease Term, on or after 10 years from the Commencement Date, the Lessee may (with 180 days' prior written notice) terminate the lease in the event the Equipment becomes obsolete or surplus to its needs, on paying a mutually agreed on termination value.

Fixed Expenses: This is a net financial lease proposal with all fixed expenses, such as maintenance, insurance, taxes (other than net income taxes) for the account of the Lessee.

Transaction Expenses: ALC shall pay all transaction expenses, including:

                       1. fees and disbursements of special counsel for the Agent and the Lenders;

                       2. acceptance and annual fees and expenses of the Agent;

                       3. fees and disbursements of special counsel for the Owner Trustee and the Trustor;

                       4. acceptance and annual fees and expenses of the Owner Trustee;

                       5. fees and disbursements in connection with obtaining a ruling from the Internal Revenue Service;

                       6. expenses of documentation, including printing and reproduction; and

                       7. fees and disbursements in connection with the private placement of the Indebtedness.

                       If the transaction is not consummated for any reason, the Lessee shall pay all of the above fees and expenses.

Nonutilization Fee:	Once ALC has obtained equity investor commitments satisfactory to the Lessee, the Lessee shall be liable to ALC for a nonutlilization fee equal to 0.5% of the Equipment cost in the event it does not lease the Equipment in accordance with intent of this proposal.
Commitment Fee:	A commitment fee of 0.5% per annum shall be paid by the Lessee to the equity investors on the outstanding equity investor commitment. The fee shall accrue as of the date investor commitments satisfactory to White Airline Corporation have been obtained, shall run up to the Commencement Date, and shall be payable quarterly, in arrears.
Tax Assumptions:	A. The Rent is calculated based on the assumptions that:

      1. the organization created by the Trust will be treated as a partnership for Federal income tax purposes;

      2. the Lessor will be entitled to seven-year MACRS depreciation on 100% of the Equipment Cost, 200% declining-balance switching to straight-line;

      3. the Lessor will be entitled to deduct interest on the Indebtedness under Section 163 of the 1986 Internal Revenue Code, as amended;

      4. the Lessor will be entitled to amortize the transaction expenses over the Interim and Primary Lease Terms using a straight-line method;

      5. the effective Federal income tax rate of the Owner Participant is __%; and

      6. the Lessor will not recognize any income from the transaction other than from Lessee rental, termination value, stipulated loss value, and indemnity payments payable to the Lessor.

    B. The Lessee shall provide necessary representation relating to the estimated economic life and residual value of the Equipment.

Tax Ruling:	The Lessor plans to obtain a Internal Revenue Service ruling with respect to the tax assumptions stated above. The Lessee shall agree to indemnify for the tax assumptions above. Such indemnity shall remain in effect until a favorable ruling has been obtained.

If the foregoing proposal is satisfactory to you, please indicate your acceptance by signing the duplicate copy of this letter in the space provided therefor, and returning it directly to the undersigned.

This offer expires at the close of business on _____, and is subject to the approval of the Owner Participant's Board of Directors and mutually satisfactory lease documentation.

Very truly yours,

ABLE LEASING CORPORATION

By: _____
   Vice President

Accepted and Agreed to on this
_____ day of _____, 20__ .

WHITE AIRLINE CORPORATION

By: _____

Its: _____

Form: p-06
Disk File Name: p-06.rtf

PURCHASE AGREEMENT ASSIGNMENT—INTEGRATED

Form Purpose

Assignment of equipment purchase agreement rights to an equipment leasing company. This form is integrated with Lease Agreement, Form l-03.

Executing Parties
The equipment lessor.
The equipment lessee.

See:
Lease Agreement, Form l-03

━━

_____ , Lessor

Home Office Address: _____

Phone: (   ) _____

PURCHASE AGREEMENT ASSIGNMENT

PURCHASE AGREEMENT ASSIGNMENT ("Assignment"), dated as of <u>20</u>___, between Lessor and
_____ , a _____ corporation ("Lessee").

WHEREAS, Lessee has entered into one or more purchase agreements identified in Exhibit A hereto (collectively "Purchase Agreement"), true and complete copies of which, as amended to the date hereof, have been initialed and delivered by Lessee to Lessor on or before the execution and delivery of this Assignment, with the manufacturers or vendors identified in Exhibit A (collectively "Vendor"), providing for the purchase by, and delivery to, Lessee of the items of equipment identified in Exhibit A (collectively "Units");

WHEREAS, Lessee desires to lease rather than purchase the Units and Lessor is willing to acquire Lessee's rights and interests under the Purchase Agreement relating to the Units and to purchase the Units, all on the terms and conditions set forth below; and

WHEREAS, Lessor will, subject to certain conditions, pay for each Unit in accordance with the terms of the Purchase Agreement upon delivery to and acceptance by Lessee of such Unit for lease pursuant to the terms and conditions of a Master Agreement to Lease Equipment between Lessor and Lessee, dated as of _____ , <u>20</u>___, and the applicable Schedule identified on Exhibit A (collectively "Lease");

NOW, THEREFORE, for good and valuable consideration, the receipt and sufficiency of which is hereby acknowledged, the parties hereto agree as follows:

1. Assignment. Lessee hereby assign and transfers to Lessor all of Lessee's rights and interests under the Purchase Agreement relating to the Units, including without limitation (a) the right to purchase the Units and to take title to the Units and to be named the purchaser in the bill or bills of sale to be delivered with respect to the Units, (b) all rights to enforce claims against Vendor for damages, losses, liabilities, and expenses arising directly or indirectly out of or in connection with the Purchase Agreement or the Units, including without limitation all guaranty, warranty and indemnity provisions contained in the Purchase Agreement as to the Units, and (c) all rights to compel performance of the terms of the Purchase Agreement. Notwithstanding the foregoing, provided that Lessor has not notified Vendor in writing that an Incipient Default or Event of Default under the Lease has occurred and is continuing, Lessor authorizes Lessee as to each Unit during the

Lease Term of such Unit to exercise in Lessee's name all rights and powers of the purchaser under the Purchase Agreement and to retain any recovery or benefit resulting from the enforcement of any Vendor guaranty, warranty or indemnity under the Purchase Agreement or otherwise; provided, however, that Lessee may not consent to any modification of the Purchase Agreement or any documentation relating thereto without the prior written consent of Lessor.

2. Continuing Liability of Lessee. It is expressly agreed that, anything contained herein to the contrary notwithstanding, (a) Lessee shall perform, and at all times remain liable to Vendor under the Purchase Agreement to perform, all duties and obligations of the purchaser thereunder to the same extent as if this Assignment had not been entered into, (b) the exercise by Lessor of any of the rights assigned hereunder shall not release Lessee from any of its duties or obligations to Vendor under the Purchase Agreement, and (c) the performance by Lessor of any duties or obligations of Lessee to Vendor under the Purchase Agreement shall not release Lessee from any of its duties or obligations to Lessor under this Assignment.

3. Purchase of Equipment; Limitation of Lessor's Liability. Lessor agrees with Lessee, subject to (a) the execution and delivery by Vendor to Lessor of a Consent and Agreement substantially in the form of Exhibit B hereto, (b) the terms and conditions of the Lease, and (c) delivery to and acceptance by Lessee of the Units in accordance with the terms of the Purchase Agreement and the Lease, to pay to Vendor the purchase cost to Lessee of each such Unit. Lessor does not assume and shall not at any time have any obligations or duties to Vendor under or by reason of this Assignment or the Purchase Agreement.

4. Further Assurance. Lessee agrees at any time and from time to time, at the request of Lessor, to promptly and duly execute and deliver any and all such further instruments and documents and take such further action as Lessor may request to obtain the full benefits of this Assignment and of the rights and powers herein granted.

5. Lessee Indemnity. Lessee agrees to indemnify and defend Lessor, its successors and assigns against any and all losses, claims, damages, liabilities and expenses (including without limitation reasonable legal fees) which arise directly or indirectly out of or in connection with this Assignment, the Purchase Agreement or the Units (including without limitation the manufacture, purchase, testing, operation, acceptance, rejection, ownership, shipment, transportation, use, delivery, installation, leasing, possession, storage, return or sale of any Unit); provided, however, that Lessee shall not be required to indemnify Lessor under this Section 5 as to any matter resulting solely from Lessor's willful misconduct.

6. Lessee Warranties and Covenants. Lessee warrants and covenants that (a) the Purchase Agreement is valid, in full force and effect, is not in default, and is and will remain enforceable in accordance with its terms, except as limited by applicable bankruptcy, insolvency, reorganization and similar laws affecting the enforcement of creditor and lessor rights generally, (b) the execution and delivery of this Assignment has been duly authorized, and this Assignment is and will remain the valid and binding obligation of Lessee enforceable against Lessee in accordance with its terms, except as limited by applicable bankruptcy, insolvency, reorganization and similar laws affecting the enforcement of creditor and lessor rights generally, and (c) Lessee has not made and will not make any other assignment of the Purchase Agreement or any part thereof or any of its rights thereunder, all of which are free and clear of any and all liens, encumbrances, rights or claims of third parties whatsoever.

7. Governing Law. This Assignment shall be governed in all respects by, and construed in accordance with, the laws of the State of _____ , without regards to its conflict of law principles.

8. Assignment by Lessor. This Assignment and Lessor's rights, interests and obligations hereunder may be assigned in whole or in part by Lessor without the consent of Lessee. This Assignment shall be binding upon and inure to the benefit of the respective successors and assigns of Lessor and Lessee.

IN WITNESS WHEREOF, the parties hereto have duly executed this Assignment as of the date first above written.

_____ , Lessor

By: _____

Title: _____

_____ , Lessee

By: _____

Title: _____

Exhibit A
PURCHASE AGREEMENTS ASSIGNED

	Purchase Agreement	*Schedule*	*Description*
Vendor	*Date*	*No.*	*of Units*

Exhibit B
PURCHASE AGREEMENT ASSIGNED

CONSENT AND AGREEMENT

For good and valuable consideration, the receipt and sufficiency of which are hereby acknowledged, the undersigned, a _____ corporation ("Vendor"), hereby acknowledges notice of and consents to all of the terms and conditions of the attached Purchase Agreement Assignment ("Assignment"), dated as of _____ , between _____ , Lessor, and _____ , Lessee. The terms defined in the Assignment shall have the same meanings in this Consent and Agreement, Vendor hereby confirms to and agrees with Lessor that (i) all representations, warranties, indemnities and agreements of Vendor under the Purchase Agreement to the extent assigned in the Assignment with respect to the Units shall inure to the benefit of Lessor to the same extent as if Lessor had originally been named the purchaser in the Purchase Agreement, (ii) Lessor shall not be liable for any of the obligations or duties of Lessee under the Purchase Agreement, nor shall the Assignment give rise to any duties or obligations whatsoever on the part of Lessor to Vendor, and (iii) from and after the date of delivery of each Unit or any part thereof pursuant to the Purchase Agreement Vendor will not assert any lien or claim against such Unit or part thereof arising on or prior to the date of such delivery, including without limitation any lien or claim for any work or services performed on or prior to the date of such delivery.

Vendor hereby represents and warrants that (a) Vendor is a corporation duly organized and validly existing in good standing under the laws of the State of _____ , (b) the making and performance of the Purchase Agreement and this Consent and Agreement have been duly authorized by all necessary corporate action on the part of Vendor, do not require any stockholder or other approval, and do not contravene any law binding on Vendor or contravene Vendor's articles of incorporation or by-laws or any indenture, credit agreement or other contract to which Vendor is a party or by which it or its properties are bound, (c) the Purchase Agreement constitutes a valid and binding obligation of Vendor enforceable against Vendor in accordance with its terms, and this Consent and Agreement is a valid and binding obligation of Vendor enforceable against Vendor in accordance with its terms, in each case except as limited by applicable bankruptcy, insolvency, reorganization and similar laws governing the enforcement of creditor and lessor rights generally, and (d) the Purchase Agreement is in full force and effect and no default exists thereunder.

IN WITNESS WHEREOF, Vendor has duly executed this Consent and Agreement as of the _____ day of _____ , 20___ .

_____ , Vendor

By: _____

Title: _____

Form: p-07
Disk File Name: p-07.rtf

PURCHASE ORDER—EQUIPMENT

Form Purpose

An equipment leasing company equipment purchase order.

Executing Parties
The equipment lessor.

Purchase Order No.

VENDOR: _____

SHIP TO: (Insert name and address of Lessee below)

    Description of Equipment   Cost

Confirming Lessee's prior order. Do not duplicate.

INSTRUCTIONS TO VENDOR

Invoice should be mailed to _____ on date of shipment.

INVOICES CANNOT BE HONORED UNLESS THE FULL EQUIPMENT DESCRIPTION INCLUDING SERIAL NUMBERS APPEAR THEREON.

SHOW ON INVOICE:

- SOLD TO—

- SHIPPED TO (Name and address of Lessee)

- FULL DESCRIPTION OF EQUIPMENT, MODEL, AND SERIAL NUMBERS

- OUR PURCHASE ORDER NUMBER

This purchase order is subject to cancellation if the equipment covered by this order is not delivered to and accepted by the Lessee on a Delivery Receipt within 30 days of the date shown below.

THIS PURCHASE ORDER IS SUBJECT TO THE TERMS AND CONDITIONS ON REVERSE SIDE WHICH ARE A PART HEREOF.

DATE: _____

(Insert leasing company name)

By: _____

Title: _____

[Author's Note: The following should be placed on the reverse side.]

TERMS AND CONDITIONS OF PURCHASE

1. No Changes Authorized. This purchase order must be accepted as written. Any increase in price, change in quantities or quality of merchandise ordered or any other change in terms or conditions of this order shall not be binding on the buyer unless such change is agreed to in writing. Delivery must be in accordance with the conditions hereof and unless otherwise specifically noted thereon. Vendor is to deliver the merchandise f.o.b. Lessee's address, destined as thereon indicated.

2. No Charges Authorized. No charges for crating, boxing, packing or drayage, or for unloading, assembling or installing any merchandise will be allowed or payable unless specified herein.

3. Inspection, Acceptance or Rejection. All merchandise shall be received subject to buyer's inspection and acceptance or rejection. The place and time of inspection shall be determined by buyer. Merchandise which is defective or not accepted by Lessee within a reasonable time or otherwise not in accordance with this purchase order may be returned for full credit and Vendor shall assume all transportation and handling charges in connection therewith. Rejected merchandise shall not be replaced except upon buyer's specific instructions in writing to that effect. Any deposit, prepayment or other payment made to Vendor by buyer shall either be refunded to buyer or buyer may, at buyer's option, apply the amount thereof to any other debt or obligation of buyer to Vendor.

4. Risk of Loss. Vendor shall bear all risk of loss of any merchandise covered by this purchase order until physically delivered, installed, inspected and accepted by Lessee at the designated place of delivery, and Vendor shall further bear the risk of loss at all times on rejected merchandise.

5. Delivery to be Made to Lessee. The person, firm or corporation to which the merchandise covered by this purchase order is to be delivered (as indicated herein) has leased said merchandise from the buyer pursuant to a Lease Agreement, and is herein referred to as "Lessee." Lessee is authorized on behalf of the buyer to receive delivery of such merchandise, to inspect, and to accept or reject same. Delivery is to be made promptly, and any delay in delivery requires buyer's prior written approval.

6. Rejection by Lessee. If Lessee shall reject or refuse to accept any merchandise pursuant to this purchase order, buyer shall be deemed relieved of any liability to Vendor under such purchase order as to such merchandise, and all obligations of buyer hereunder as to such merchandise shall upon such rejection or refusal be deemed those of Lessee, with the same force and effect as if Lessee, instead of buyer, had placed this purchase order as to such merchandise, and Vendor in such event, shall look only to Lessee with respect to any liability or obligation hereunder.

7. Cancellation by Buyer. This purchase order may be canceled by the buyer in the event the Lessee is not authorized to enter into the Lease, or the person signing the Lease on behalf of the Lessee is not authorized so to do, or, in the event that the Vendor or any of its agents make any representations to the Lessee inconsistent with the terms or conditions of the Lease, upon which the Lessee reasonably relies.

8. No Assignment by Vendor. Vendor shall not assign this purchase order without the prior written consent of buyer. In the absence of such consent, no such assignment shall be effective, and at buyer's option, shall effect a cancellation of all buyer's obligations hereunder.

9. Patents. Vendor agrees to and does by shipment thereof indemnify, protect, and hold harmless buyer, its successors or assigns and the Lessee and its successors and assigns against all claims. demands, damages, costs or expenses including attorneys' fees) for actual or alleged infringements of any patent covering any merchandise hereby ordered or the use thereof.

10. Fair Labor Assurance. Vendor warrants and represents that the goods ordered hereby have been produced in compliance with the requirements of the Fair Labor Standards Act of 1938, as amended, and with all legislation and regulations, including, without limitation, those governing Fair Employment practices and Equal Employment Opportunity.

11. Warranties by Vendor. Vendor warrants that immediately prior to buyer's purchase Vendor had legal title to the merchandise, title is transferred free from any liens and encumbrances, that the merchandise ordered hereunder will be fit and sufficient for the purpose intended, that it will conform to the specifications, drawings or samples, if any, furnished or adopted by the buyer and will be merchantable, of good quality, and free from defects in material, design or workmanship. No part or plans made according to buyer's design will be sold to any other person, firm or corporation. The foregoing is in addition to and not in lieu of any or all other warranties expressed or implied. All warranties shall run to, inure for the benefit of and be enforceable by both buyer and its lessee, jointly and separately.

12. Excusable Delays. Vendor will not be responsible for delays or defaults in delivery if occasioned by unforeseeable cause beyond the control and without the fault or negligence of tine Vendor; and buyer shall not be responsible for failure to receive or take delivery if occasioned by any like cause or its or Lessee's part.

13. Freight. If the buyer has not indicated any preference for the method of shipment, then the merchandise shall be shipped in the least expensive way.

14. Purchase Price. All quantity, cash or other discounts granted by the Vendor as a direct or indirect result of the purchase herein ordered shall be paid to buyer. Vendor represents and warrants that no payments have been made to the Lessee nor has the Lessee received any other consideration as a direct or indirect result of the purchase herein ordered unless the amount of such payment or the value of Such consideration is deducted from the gross invoice price.

15. Title to merchandise shall pass to buyer only after physical delivery, installation, inspection, and acceptance as provided herein.

Form: r-01
Disk File Name: r-01.rtf

RFQ—DEAL SHEET FORMAT

Form Purpose

An informal lessee request for leasing company lease quotations, incorporating a deal sheet.

Executing Parties
The prospective equipment lessee.

An Informal Deal Sheet Approach

Author's Note: If your company leases a high volume of equipment each year, consider putting together a deal sheet format that can be filled out and attached to a simple lease request cover letter.

Here's a suggested format. If you decide to use a similar format, use the Lessee Proposal Stage Checklist included in this book to ensure you've covered all issues of importance in your deal.

BRIGHT TIME COMPANY
34 Orchard Road
White Plains, New York 10604

(914) 555-0800

May 2, 20___

BY HAND

Ms. Mary Mari
Marketing Vice President
Rapid Leasing Corporation
1425 Money Drive
White Plains, New York 10604

Dear Mary:

We are planning to take delivery on the equipment specified on the attached term sheet during the last week of May. We would be interested in receiving a lease financing quote to determine if leasing is the best alternative for us. Please submit a written quote no later than May 5, 20___.

If you have any thoughts about other structures or benefits that may be beneficial, please include them in your response. Incidentally, we will not accept a brokered transaction and are looking to you to be the actual lessor.

Our decision will be made by May 10, 20___. The lease must be signed no later than May 15, 20___. If you have any questions, my direct line is (914) 555-8795.

Sincerely,

Roger Rogueson
Assistant Manager

BRIGHT TIME COMPANY

TERM SHEET
May 2, 20___

Equipment:	Monitor Sentex Computer System, Model 3 with Excel Payroll Package.
Equipment Cost:	$215, 000 ±15%
Vendor:	Monitor Computer Company
Delivery Date:	May 29, 20___
Lease Term:	3 and 5 year
Rent Quote:	Monthly, in advance, and quarter, in arrears.
Purchase Option:	0% of Equipment Cost
Renewal Option:	Maximum 1st year 25% of primary rent, thereafter year-to-year fair market rental value.
Early Termination Right:	Anytime after first year of base lease term Attach schedule to proposal
Bid Due Date:	May 5, 20___
Award Date:	May 10, 20___

Special Provisions:
1. Transaction to be single investor, non-brokered
2. Lease to qualify as operating lease for accounting purposes
3. Net finance lease
4. Our master lease to be used in the form enclosed. Please identify with proposal any provisions that are not acceptable.
5. A casualty value schedule must be sent with your quote.

Form: r-02
Disk File Name: r-02.rtf

RFQ—INFORMAL

Form Purpose

An informal lessee request for leasing company lease quotations.

Executing Parties
The prospective equipment lessee.

A Less Formal Request for Quotes

Author's Note: In certain situations, as mentioned earlier, a less formal RFQ will do the necessary job. For example, in a $100,000 lease financing, there are fewer issues and negotiating risks. The following letter, although still informal, tells the leasing company what is needed. It states the equipment specifics as well as the lease terms that it is looking for. And it tells when the bids are due and when the decision will be made. It also does not indicate that a lease is the only alternative. To keep your negotiating leverage highest you must leave the door open to a purchase possibility, at least as far as the leasing company is concerned.

BRIGHT TIME COMPANY
34 Orchard Road
White Plains, New York 10604

---

(914) 555-0800

May 2, 20____

BY HAND

Ms. Mary Mari
Marketing Vice President
Rapid Leasing Corporation
1425 Money Lane
White Plains, New York 10604

Dear Mary:

We are planning to take delivery on a Monitor Computer System during the last week of May. We would be interested in having you submit a lease financing quote for our internal purchase/lease evaluation. Please submit the quote in writing no later than May 5, 20____.

The equipment cost is anticipated to be $215, 000. We, however, need some leeway in your bid to cover a cost variance of 15%, up or down. The actual system configuration is a Model 3, Excel Payroll Processing System, sold by Monitor Computer Company. I've enclosed a copy of our vendor equipment purchase order confirmation detailing the equipment specifics. The vendor expects payment in full on the date we accept the equipment for lease.

We would like to see monthly, in advance, and quarterly, in arrears, quotes for three-year and five-year lease terms. We want a 10% purchase option and the right to renew the lease for successive one-year terms, the first term renewal rent not to exceed 25% of the original term rent and the remaining at a rent equal to the fair market rental value. We would also like the right to terminate the lease before the end of the basic term and ask that you submit a schedule of termination values beginning at the end of the first year. Incidentally, we also would like you to submit your casualty value schedule along with your quote.

If you have any thoughts about other structures or benefits that may be beneficial, please include them in your response. Incidentally, we will not accept a brokered transaction and are looking to you to be the actual lessor.

Our decision will be made by May 10, 20___. The lease must be signed no later than May 15, 20___. If you have any questions, my direct line is (914) 555-8795.

Sincerely,

Roger Rogueson
Assistant to the President

Form: r-03
Disk File Name: r-03.rtf

RFQ—LONG FORM

Form Purpose

A long form formal lessee request for leasing company lease quotations.

A Formal Request for Quotes Letter

REQUEST FOR QUOTATIONS

TO

LEASE EQUIPMENT

April 12, 20____

SunTime Corporation is issuing this REQUEST FOR QUOTATIONS (RFQ) to obtain equipment lease bids from perspective lessors. This RFQ is not an offer to contract. SunTime Corporation will not be obligated to lease the specified equipment until a mutually satisfactory written lease has been executed by all parties.

A. *Proposal Request—General*

In accordance with the terms and conditions specified below, SunTime Corporation wishes to receive proposals from equipment leasing companies (Lessors) to provide lease financing for certain data processing equipment.

In the evaluation of each proposal, SunTime Corporation will rely on all written and verbal representations made by each prospective Lessor and each representation will be incorporated into any and all formal agreements between the parties.

No Lessor receiving this RFQ is authorized to act for, or on behalf of, SunTime Corporation prior to the receipt of written acceptance by SunTime Corporation of a satisfactory lease proposal and then only in accordance with the specific terms, if any, of the acceptance.

B. *Proposal Guidelines*

1. Your proposal must be submitted in writing and follow the guidelines in this RFQ. If it does not, it will be rejected.

2. All RFQ requirements must be addressed. Specifically identify any requirements that cannot be satisfied.

3. If you can offer any additional benefits not requested in this RFQ, identify them as "Additional Benefits" and state them in a separate section at the end of your proposal.

4. You must notify SunTime Corporation no later than the Lessor Proposal Intent Notification date specified in the Time Table below if you intend to submit a proposal in response to this RFQ.

5. SunTime Corporation may, without liability and in its sole discretion, amend or rescind this RFQ prior to the lease award. In such event each Lessor offering to submit a proposal will be supplied, as the case may be, with an RFQ amendment or a notification of our intent not to proceed.

6. Your proposal will be considered confidential and none of the contents will be disclosed to a competing Lessor.

7. You shall be responsible for all costs incurred in connection with the preparation of your proposal and any contract(s) in response to this RFQ.

8. Your proposal must be signed by a duly authorized representative of your company.

9. Your proposal must be submitted in triplicate and remain in effect at least until the Lessor Proposal Commitment Cut-off date specified in the Time Table below.

10. Your proposal should be accompanied by (a) a copy of your most recent annual report or financial statements or appropriate bank references with account officer name and telephone number, (b) a description of any material litigation in which you are presently involved, and (c) a statement of any potential conflict of interest, and plan to avoid it, as a result of an award.

11. SunTime Corporation intends to announce its award decision no later than the Award Announcement date specified in the Time Table below.

12. Any questions concerning this RFQ, should sent in writing to:

SunTime Corporation
1823 Third Avenue
New York, New York 11020
Attn. John Peterson
Telephone Number: (212) 754-2367

Any questions and answers which we feel would be of assistance to all Lessors submitting proposals, will be promptly distributed to each.

13. SunTime Corporation may enter simultaneously in negotiations with more than one Lessor and make an award to one or more without prior notification to others we are negotiating with.

14. Any information supplied to you in this RFQ by SunTime Corporation or otherwise by any representative in connection with this RFQ is confidential and may not be disclosed or used except in connection with the preparation of your proposal. If you must release any such information to any person or entity for the purpose of preparing your proposal, you must obtain an agreement prior to releasing the information that it will be treated as confidential by such person or entity and will not be disclosed except in connection with the preparation of your proposal.

15. If you are a selected Lessor, prior to our making the award you will be supplied with a copy of our form lease document(s) for your review. Your response to the acceptability of the document provisions, with exceptions noted in writing, will be a condition precedent to any award.

C. Equipment Lease Requirements

1. EQUIPMENT DESCRIPTION, COST AND TRADE-IN

    a. The equipment will consist of electronic data processing equipment (Equipment) acquired from the following designated vendor(s):

Vendor	Equipment Description	Cost
StarByte Computer Corp.	(1) Model 423 Computer	$1,850,000
Buffalo, NY	(7) Model 3 Remote Ctrs.	350,000
Micro Tech, Inc.	Material Tracking System	150,000
New York, NY		
	Installation:	120,000
	TOTAL:	$2,470,000

    (i) The final cost of the Equipment may vary as much as + (10)% or − (20)%, and your financing offer must permit this leeway without penalty.

b. If you can provide more advantageous financing by supplying equipment you own, have access to, or can acquire through volume discount arrangements with a vendor, please provide the specifics in the Additional Benefits section. If you intend to offer to provide any used equipment, the serial number(s), current location(s) and owner(s) must be stated in your proposal.

(i) Any equipment you offer to supply must be delivered to SunTime Corporation at 937 Secour Drive, Buffalo, New York 11342 no later than the Anticipated Equipment Delivery Date specified in the time table in Section D below and ready for acceptance no later than the specified Anticipated Equipment Acceptance Date. You must provide a firm delivery date commitment with contractual assurances and remedies for failure to meet such date, which should be stated in your proposal.

c. The Equipment will replace equipment under an existing lease of computer equipment and SunTime Corporation would like you to propose an additional financing arrangement which would incorporate the buy-out of that lease. The specifics of the existing lease are as follows:

Lessor: AmerLease Corp.

Lease Term: 7 Years

Lease Start Date: March 1, 20__

Lease Ending Date: February 28, 20__

Monthly Rent: $21,324, in advance

Lease Termination Amount as of August 31, 20__: $397,000

Equipment: StarByte XTRA Material Tracking Computer System

Original Equipment Cost: $1,253,000

Right To Sublease: Yes

Purchase Option: Fair Market

Renewal Option: Year to Year, 90 Days Prior Notice, Fair Market

(i) If you can provide any other arrangement that would be beneficial, such as subleasing the existing equipment to another lessee, please so indicate.

2. ESTIMATED DELIVERY AND ACCEPTANCE DATE

It is anticipated that the Equipment will be delivered and accepted for lease no later than the anticipated delivery and acceptance date(s) specified in the time table below.

3. EQUIPMENT PAYMENT

The Equipment must be paid for by Lessor no later than thirty (30) days following acceptance for lease.

4. EQUIPMENT LOCATION

The Equipment will initially be accepted for lease at our manufacturing plant located at 937 Secour Drive, Buffalo, New York. We must have the right to move the equipment to any location in the United States without the prior consent of Lessor, but upon providing thirty (30) days prior written notice.

5. PRIMARY LEASE TERM

Your proposal must provide offers to lease the Equipment for Primary Lease Terms of five (5) and seven (7) years.

The Primary Lease Terms must run from the later of the Equipment acceptance for lease or payment by Lessor for the Equipment.

6. PRIMARY TERM RENTS

Rent payments must be quoted on a monthly, in advance, and quarterly, in arrears, basis.

The rent payments must be expressed as a percentage of Equipment Cost and be on a consecutive, level basis. The nominal lease interest rate must be provided for each rent quote.

SunTime Corporation shall not be obligated for payment of rent until the Equipment vendor has been paid in full.

7. INTERIM LEASE TERM

No Interim Lease Term will be permitted that Requires payment of interim rent.

8. INTERIM RENTS

No Interim Lease Term rent payments will acceptable.

9. OPTIONS

a. SunTime Corporation must have the option to renew the term of the lease year to year for a total of three (3) years, on a fair market value basis. Offers providing for a fixed-price renewal will also be considered. Any fixed price offers should be included in an "Additional Benefits" section at the end of the Lessor's proposal.

b. Lessee must have the right to purchase the Equipment at the end of the Primary Lease Term and each Renewal Term for its then fair market value. Offers providing for the right to purchase for a fixed percentage of Equipment Cost will be given favorable consideration and should be included in an "Additional Benefits" section at the end of the Lessor's offer.

c. SunTime Corporation must have the right, beginning as of the end of the first year of the Primary Lease Term, to terminate the Lease prior to the end of the Primary Lease Term, or any Renewal Term, in the event the Equipment becomes obsolete of surplus to SunTime Corporation's needs.

(i) In the event of an early termination, SunTime Corporation shall have the right to arrange for the sale or re-lease of the Equipment. Any proceeds from the sale, or anticipated proceeds from the lease, of the Equipment shall reduce any termination penalty payment required.

(ii) A schedule of early termination values must be included with your proposal.

d. SunTime Corporation must have the right to upgrade the Equipment, by adding equipment or replacing components, at any time during the term of the lease and Lessor must provide financing for such upgrade for a term coterminous with the term remaining during the upgrade period at a financing rate which will not exceed Lessor's transaction nominal after-tax yield.

10. INSURANCE

The Equipment shall be self-insured.

11. CASUALTY VALUE SCHEDULE

A schedule of casualty values, expressed as a percentage of Equipment Cost, for both the Primary Lease Term and any Renewal Term(s) must be submitted with your proposal.

12. TRANSACTION FEES

Lessee will not pay financing commitment or nonutilization fees.

13. ACCOUNTING CLASSIFICATION

Preference will be given to a Lease which qualifies as an operating lease under the applicable accounting guidelines.

14. SINGLE SOURCE PREFERENCE

Preference will be given to Lessors who intend to provide 100% of the funds necessary to purchase the Equipment over those who intend to leverage the purchase with third-party debt. Your proposal must disclose your intent.

(a) In the event you determine it would be advantageous to propose a leveraged lease financing structure, it should be submitted assuming a long-term debt interest rate of 6.75% per annum. In addition, the following terms will apply:

(i) Our investment banker, Chicago First Corporation, will be responsible for securing the third-party leveraged lease debt at a rate satisfactory to SunTime Corporation, within our sole discretion.

(ii) You must provide assurance that the lease will qualify as a true lease for Federal income tax purposes under the current tax rules and guidelines.

(iii) You must state whether your proposal is on a best efforts or firm basis; preference will be given to those on a firm basis.

(iv) At the time of submission of your proposal you must be prepared to identify all lease participants (with contact name and telephone number), including each identified equity and debt participant, so they may be called immediately for verification in the event you are the successful bidder.

15. BROKER DISCLOSURE

We will give a preference to lease offers from principal funding sources who do not intend to re-sell or broker the transaction. In the event that you do not intend to act as a principal and purchase the equipment for your own account, you must disclose that in your proposal.

16. EXPENSES

Lessor shall be responsible for payment of all fees and expenses of the transaction, other than Lessee's own direct legal fees in connection with documenting the lease transaction, including fees and expenses incurred in connection with the arranging, or documentation, of the Equipment Lease.

D. *Time Table*

SunTime Corporation will adhere to the following time schedule in connection with evaluating submitted proposals, making the award decision and negotiating the equipment lease document(s):

Action	*Date*
Lessor Proposal Intent Notification Due	
Lessor Proposals Due	
Lessor Proposal Commitment Cut-Off	
Lessor Notification of Initial Qualification	
Form Lease Document(s) Sent to Qualified Lessor(s)	
Lessor Response to Form Lease Document(s)	
Lessor(s) Selection	
Award Announcement	
Lease Negotiations—Start	
Lease Signing	
Anticipated Equipment Delivery	
Anticipated Equipment Acceptance For Lease	

Form: r-04
Disk File Name: r-04.rtf

RFQ—SHORT FORM

Form Purpose

A short form formal lessee request for leasing company lease quotations.

Request for Lease Quotation

THE MIDEASTERN RAILWAY CORPORATION

Lessee:	The Mideastern Railway Corporation.
Equipment:	Model 6 RD-10, 23,000 hp. diesel locomotives (est. unit cost—$525,000), manufactured by Arcane Locomotive Corp.
Estimated Total Cost:	$3,150,000
Equipment Delivery:	February, 20___—Two units March, 20___—Two units April, 20___—Two units
Equity Contribution & Commitment:	Not less than 20% of cost. The equity investor(s) must agree to buy equipment with a maximum equipment cost up to $3.5 million.
Interest Rate Assumptions:	7 3/4%, 8%, 8 1/4%.
Agent for Debt Placement:	Samon & Smith Co.
Attorney for Long-Term Lenders:	Carr, Swift & Moore, subject to agreement of the long-term lenders.
Structuring of the Transaction:	15-year net finance leveraged lease with semiannual, in arrears, level payments. Any other proposal format will be considered provided a bid as requested has been submitted.
	The lessee must have three two-year fair market rental renewal options. A fair market purchase option at the end of the initial term and each renewal term should also be provided. The lessee will give a letter stating that, in its opinion, the locomotives will have a useful life exceeding 18 years and a residual value equal to 20% of the original cost at the end of 15 years.
Delivery Cutoff Date:	The cutoff date for the equipment deliveries will be July 1, 20___. All equipment not delivered before this date will be excluded from the transaction unless the lessor and the lessee agree to extend such date.
Expenses:	All expenses of the transaction, including rating fees and the investment banking fees, will be borne by the lessor.
Security:	The lessee's lease obligations will be unconditionally guaranteed by The Eastern Railway Company. The Mideastern Railway Company is a wholly owned subsidiary of The Eastern Railway Company.

The long-term debt will be secured by an assignment of the lease. An agent bank will be selected by The Eastern Railway Company and Samon & Smith Co. after the long-term debt is placed. The long-term debt will be noncallable except for casualty occurrences.

Indemnification: Preference will be given to bids with minimum indemnification. All indemnification requirements must be precisely stated in the proposal.

Interim Rentals: All quotations must assume not more than three equity closing dates and provide interim rents from such dates to July 1, 20__, the beginning of the primary lease term. Interim rentals will be equal to the daily equivalent of the long-term debt interest rate.

Casualty Values: All bidders must provide a schedule of casualty values, expressed as a percentage of original cost, both for the primary lease term and any extensions thereafter. The method of calculating the casualty values must also be supplied.

Insurance: The equipment will be self-insured.

Please mail us your proposal in writing postmarked no later than _____. Your proposal must be on a "firm" basis and at the time of submission you must be prepared to identify the investor source(s) so that they may be contacted immediately by telephone for verification in the event you are the successful bidder.

Form: s-01
Disk File Name: s-01.rtf

LESSEE CREDITOR

Form Purpose

A subordination agreement for use by a leasing company in obtaining a lessee creditor waiver of any potential claims against the leased equipment.

Executing Parties
A lessee creditor.

Subordination Agreement

The undersigned hereby waives any interest in the below described equipment currently owned by
(Lessor).

[Equipment description]

[Insert creditor's name]

By: _____

Title: _____

Date: _____

Form: t-01
Disk File Name: t-01.rtf

TIME TABLE—DEAL SCHEDULE

Form Purpose

A lessee-prepared deal time table to keep an equipment lease deal on track from lease proposal to document closing.

Time Table

(Insert name of lessee) will adhere to the following time schedule in connection with evaluating submitted proposals, making the award decision, and negotiating the equipment lease document(s):

Action	Date
Lessor Proposal Intent Notification Due	
Lessor Proposals Due	
Lessor Proposal Commitment Cut-Off	
Lessor Notification of Initial Qualification	
Form Lease Document(s) Sent to Qualified Lessor(s)	
Lessor Response to Form Lease Document(s)	
Lessor(s) Selection	
Award Announcement	
Lease Negotiations— Start	
Lease Signing	
Anticipated Equipment Delivery	
Anticipated Equipment Acceptance for Lease	

Time Table Action Category Explanation

Lessor Proposal Intent Notification Due

The date when each leasing company receiving the RFQ must indicate its willingness to submit a lease offer. Typically, I set a date one week following the delivery of the RFQ to prospective bidders.

Lessor Proposals Due

The date when all lessor proposals are due. Use a date which will provide adequate lead time to have the transaction re-bid, get the equipment delivered and operationally accepted, and cover any unforeseen delays.

Lessor Proposal Commitment Cut-Off

The date through which the lessor must keep its proposal available for acceptance by the lessee. I set a date which will provide adequate time to review all proposals, with a margin for comfort.

Lessor Notification of Initial Qualification

The date when the lessee will make the preliminary lease award, subject to acceptance of the lessee's form lease documents. Set a date you're comfortable with.

Form Lease Document(s) Sent to Qualified Lessor(s)

The date when the lessee's form lease documents will be sent to the preliminary selected lessor(s) for review and comments. The date is typically one shortly following the Lessor Notification of Initial Qualification Date.

Lessor Response to Form Lease Document(s)

The date when the initially selected lessor(s) must submit comments to the lessee's form lease documents. Typically, I like to give a lessor two weeks to review the form lease agreement and respond.

Lessor(s) Selection

The date on which you will make the final winning lessor(s) selection. Set a date which will give you adequate time to review with your lawyers the lessors' form lease agreement responses.

In certain situations, it may be a good negotiation approach to select three lessors—specifying a first place, second place, and third place award and simultaneously telling all three that if negotiations break down with the first place lessor, you will immediately begin negotiations with the second place lessor and similarly, if necessary, with the third place lessor.

Award Announcement

The date when all lessors will be notified of your lessor selection decision. Typically, I set a date one to two business days after the Lessor(s) Selection Date.

Lease Negotiations—Start

The date when negotiation will begin with the winning lessor. I usually set a date three to five business days following the Award Announcement date.

Lease Signing

The date when you expect all lease negotiations to be concluded and the lease documents to be signed by all parties. The date you set will depend on the complexity of the lease financing. A simple transaction can be documented in one week, while a complex leveraged lease transaction may take three months. Seek the advice of experienced legal counsel in setting this date.

Anticipated Equipment Delivery

The date when the equipment is anticipated to arrive on the lessee's premises.

Anticipated Equipment Acceptance for Lease

The date when the lessee expects to accept the equipment for lease. This date should allow sufficient time to ensure that the delivered equipment is operationally acceptable.

Form: v-01
Disk File Name: v-01.rtf

PROGRAM AGREEMENT

Form Purpose

A vendor program agreement providing for an arrangement in which a leasing company will purchase equipment leases entered into from time to time by a equipment vendor with its customers.

Executing Parties
The equipment lessor.
The equipment vendor.

─────────────────────────────

Dealer Program Agreement

DEALER PROGRAM AGREEMENT

THIS AGREEMENT is made as of the ____ day of _____ , by and between Able Leasing Company, a _____ corporation having a place of business at _____ _____ ("ALC"), and _____ ("Dealer"), a _____ corporation, having a place of business at _____ _____.

WHEREAS, ALC and Dealer contemplate engaging in a program ("Program") in which Dealer will, in the ordinary course of its business, lease personal property to retail Lessees (singularly, "Lessee"), which leases will be upon such terms and conditions as are acceptable to ALC; and

WHEREAS, the Program contemplates the sale and assignment from time to time by Dealer to ALC of such leases and all of Dealer's right, title and interest in and to such personal property, without recourse, except with regard to Dealer's (i) representations, warranties and covenants, and (ii) repurchase obligations, all as provided in this Agreement.

NOW THEREFORE, for good an valuable consideration, the parties hereto agree as follows:

1. OFFER OF LEASES

(a) Submission of APSs. Dealer may from time to time, offer lease application packages ("APS") to ALC for approval and, upon acceptance by ALC, the related Leases and property for purchase by ALC. The APS Dealer submits to ALC shall be in such form and contain such information and be evidenced by such documents as ALC may supply or otherwise require.

(b) Terms. The APS submitted to ALC shall provide for such rentals, rental periods, charges and residual values, if any, as are acceptable to ALC in its sole discretion from time to time.

(c) Approval or Rejection. ALC shall not be required to approve any APS submitted by Dealer. ALC may condition approval as to any APS on the Lease containing various specified and required terms. ALC shall advise Dealer within a reasonable period of time as to whether the APS has been accepted or rejected and, if accepted, upon what conditions.

(d) Documents, Records and Reports. ALC shall have access to all records of Dealer for any Lease which ALC shall have purchased from Dealer.

(e) The Terms, Leases and Property. As used in this Agreement, "Lease" means the lease agreement and other related documentation which evidences the obligation of a lessee ("Lessee") to pay to Dealer the monthly rentals and other sums due for the leasing of the property, and may include the obligation, if any, of another person or persons to pay to Dealer the residual value of such property upon termination or expiration of a

Lease. The term "property" shall be deemed to include all equipment, accessories, and accessions in any way attached to or pertaining to the use or operation of the leased property.

2. ASSIGNMENT AND DEALER'S RESTATEMENT OF WARRANTIES, REPRESENTATIONS, AND COVENANTS.

(a) Assignment. Dealer hereby agrees to sell, assign, transfer and set over to ALC all of its right, title, and interest in and to each Lease and the property covered thereby. ALC hereby agrees to purchase each such lease and the property covered thereby as are acceptable to ALC and conform by signing and delivering an approved Lease to ALC, shall thereupon be deemed to restate to ALC with regard to that Lease all of Dealer's representations, warranties and covenants as are provided in this Agreement.

(b) Breach of Warranties. All Leases purchased from Dealer by ALC will reflect Leases made in the ordinary course of Dealer's business. Dealer represents that it has no knowledge of any breach by Dealer or by the manufacturer of the property covered by such Leases of any warranties or representations made to the Lessees, or of any breach by any of the Lessees of any warranties, representations, covenants, promises or obligations of any of the Lessees to the Dealer as provided in the Lease. In addition, if a Lessee asserts against ALC a claim or defense which the Lessee may have against the Dealer which arises out of the ownership, use, possession, operation, control, maintenance or repair of the property covered by the Lease, Dealer shall indemnify and defend ALC for the entire amount of ALC's loss, cost and expense. The liability shall be in addition to any liability Dealer may have under Paragraph 3 below.

3. DEALER'S FURTHER WARRANTIES, REPRESENTATIONS, AND COVENANTS

To induce ALC to acquire Leases, Dealer warrants, represents and covenants and, so long as any Leases purchased by ALC hereunder remain unpaid in whole or in part, continues to warrant, represent and covenant that, at the time of assignment of any Lease to ALC as to all acts and conditions required to be completed by or to exist at such time and, as to all acts required to be performed and conditions required to exist thereafter, with respect to that and each Lease acquired by ALC pursuant to this Agreement: (1) (a) the Lease and related documents are valid, (b) they represent the obligation of a bona fide Lessee, and (c) the documents supporting the transaction and the signatures thereon are genuine; (2) all amounts stated in the Lease are true and correct; (3) the description of the property and related accessories, equipment and accessions is complete and correct; (4) other than the Lease, no agreement has been or will be entered into between the Lessee and Dealer or any other person with respect to the financing or leasing of the property; (5) Dealer shall have full responsibility to assure ALC receives full and complete title: (6) if the transaction involves the leasing of new or used property for which title is evidenced by a Certificate or Document to Title and with regard to which a security interest is or may be perfected pursuant to a title encumbrancing law, Dealer shall have obtained, or caused an APS to be filed for such Title Certificate or Document with ALC ownership or security interest, as applicable, duly noted thereon and/or, if appropriate, the applicable financing statement(s) or security agreements have been duly filed with the appropriate filing office(s); (7) the form, terms and execution of the Lease and all related documentation and Dealer's activities in originating the Lease and documents supporting the Lease and the actual leasing of the property giving rise to the transaction each comply with all applicable federal, state and local laws; (8) to the best of Dealer's knowledge, all of the information contained in the Lessee's APS submitted to ALC is true and correct; (9) ALC has been named as a loss-payee and/or second beneficiary on a policy or policies of insurance covering all such risks and with such amounts of coverage and such insurers as are reasonably acceptable to ALC, and such insurance coverage shall be in force at or prior to the delivery of the property to the Lessee; and (10) Dealer and its affiliates currently hold and at all material times shall hold in good standing, any and all federal, state and local licenses and other regulatory approvals required to enable Dealer lawfully to originate and assign the Leases contemplated hereby.

4. COMPENSATION

ALC shall pay to Dealer a purchase price ("Purchase Price") for each Lease purchased by and sold and assigned to ALC, as specified in ALC's approval of an APS, or otherwise as agreed upon by the parties.

5. COLLECTION

ALC or its assignee shall collect payments on all Leases purchased from Dealer, unless the parties to this Agreement mutually agree otherwise. ALC may request Dealer to make reasonable efforts to arrange for the release or disposition of repossessed property. Dealer will not, without ALC's written consent: (1) grant any extension of time or payment; (2) compromise or settle any Lease for less than the full amount owing; (3) release, in any manner and Lessee or guarantor; or (4) sell, release or dispose of the property or any other collateral for the Lease for less than the unpaid balance due under the Lease (including, if applicable, the residual value of the property as provided in the Lease).

Unless with ALC's prior approval, all payments on Leases which may be received by Dealer shall be received in trust and immediately paid to ALC in the form received, except for necessary endorsement(s), without intermingling them with the Dealer's funds. Dealer appoints ALC and each of its officers as the Dealer's attorney-in-fact, without any right of revocation and with full power of substitution, to endorse the Dealer's name upon any notes, checks, drafts or other instruments for the payment of money received by ALC which are payable to Dealer with respect to Leases. Repossessed Property and other collateral held by Dealer will be in trust for ALC and kept apart time, by notice to Dealer, required that any such property or collateral be surrendered directly to ALC.

6. NONRECOURSE ASSIGNMENT DURING LEASE TERM; REPURCHASE OBLIGATION

Dealer's sale and assignment of any Lease to ALC shall be without recourse during the entire term of the Lease, except the Dealer shall remain personally obligated: (i) to repurchase the Lease and the property covered thereby on demand of ALC if, in ALC, reasonable judgment, any of Dealer's representations, warranties and covenants as to such Lease shall have been breached, and to pay to ALC all sums then due under the terms of the Lease as if the Lease were actually paid in full by a Lessee in default, and (ii) at the end of the Lease term, to repurchase the Lease and the property from ALC for the residual value as provided in the applicable APS for the Lease. ALC shall, upon any such repurchase by Dealer, provided such endorsement and cooperate with Dealer in effecting such transfers of title or security as Dealer may reasonably request or require.

Notwithstanding anything contained in the immediately preceding paragraph to the contrary. Dealer may elect not to purchase a Lease and the property covered thereby from ALC at the end of the Lease term and will be absolved of and from any personal obligation therefore if Dealer, within 10 days after the end of the Lease term, advises ALC of such election and pays to ALC the sum of $_____ .

7. ADDITIONAL LIABILITIES AND INDEMNITIES

Dealer shall promptly fulfill and perform all obligations on its part and agrees to enforce, assert and exercise, and cooperate with ALC in so doing any right, power or remedy conferred on it by any Lease or related document or under this Agreement. The purchase by ALC of any Lease shall not be deemed an assumption by ALC or an imposition on ALC, of any Dealer obligation under the Lease or any other Dealer agreement with the Lessee, which lease shall be and remain enforceable by the Lessee solely against Dealer. Dealer agrees to indemnify and hold ALC harmless from and against any and all loss, damage and expense, including attorney's fees reasonable in amount, which ALC may suffer, incur, be put to, pay or layout by reason of Dealer's actions or omissions to act, except where specifically attributable solely to directions from ALC given in writing. ALC similarly shall indemnify and hold Dealer harmless against such loss, damage, and expense which Dealer may suffer, incur, be put to, pay or lay out by reason of any action taken by Dealer on behalf of ALC for collection, repossession, release or resale where Dealer relied upon incorrect information from ALC and Dealer was not negligent under the circumstances.

8. RELATIONSHIP

This agreement shall not create an employer–employee relationship, it being the contemplation of the parties that all acts performed by Dealer in carrying out the provisions of this Agreement shall be those of an independent contractor. Except for acts performed by Dealer at ALC's express direction, ALC shall not be responsible for the acts of Dealer, its officers, agents or employees.

9. TERMINATION

(a) Dates. This Agreement shall become effective as of the date first written above, and shall remain in effect until terminated by either party on giving ninety (90) days written notice to the other of its intention to terminate at its respective address above, or to any address which such party shall have specified on the ninetieth (90th) day after the day on which such notice is mailed by Certified Mail, Return Receipt Requested; provided however, that if any event occurs which materially affects the ability of Dealer to lawfully honor its obligation to ALC under this Agreement, ALC may terminate this Agreement effective immediately.

(b) Rights on Termination. Upon the effective date of any termination except with regard to Dealer's warranties, representations and covenants, or any indemnification and/or repurchase liability of Dealer incident thereto or otherwise contained under the provisions hereof or the Lease, all of which shall survive this Agreement, Dealer shall have no further obligation to ALC under this Agreement except to cooperate with ALC in any action in which ALC becomes a party or if ALC requests collection assistance on delinquent Leases.

10. FORMS

ALC will in no way be responsible for the validity, legality or sufficiency of any form of Lease or other documents which the exception of forms provided by ALC.

11. MODIFICATION, BINDING EFFECT, AND GOVERNING LAW

No modification, rescission, waiver, release, or amendment of any provision of this Agreement shall be made except by written agreement signed by duly authorized officers of the parties hereto. This Agreement is binding upon and shall inure to the benefit of the successors and assigns of the parties hereto. However, Dealer may not assign this Agreement without the prior written consent of ALC. This Agreement shall be construed under the laws of the State of _____ , as amended from time to time.

12. In the event of an early payout or default by Lessee, any unearned commissions, as determined by the rule of 78 payoff method, shall be refunded to ALC within 30 days of written request by ALC.

13. All commissions over _____% shall be shared equally with ALC at the time of funding.

DEALER

By: _____

Its: _____

ABLE LEASING COMPANY

By: _____

Its: _____

Form: v-02
Disk File Name: v-02.rtf

REMARKETING AGREEMENT

Form Purpose

A vendor program agreement providing for an arrangement in which a leasing company will purchase equipment leases entered into from time to time by a equipment vendor with its customers. In this case the equipment vendor has a captive leasing company (the "initial lessor") that initiates the leases which will be sold off to a third-party equipment leasing company ("Credit Funding Corporation").

Executing Parties
The equipment lessor.
The equipment vendor.
The equipment vendor's captive leasing company.

See:
Assignment of Lease Forms

Vendor Remarketing Agreement and Reserve Agreement

THIS AGREEMENT entered into and made effective this ____ day of _____ , 20__ , among (insert name of vendor), a _____ corporation, with its principal office at _____ ("Vendor"), (insert name of initial lessor) a _____ corporation, with its principal office at _____ ("Lessor") and CREDIT FUNDING CORPORATION, a _____ Corporation, with its principal place of business at _____ ("Credit Funding").

WITNESSETH:

WHEREAS, Vendor is engaged in and provides equipment and support services to Merchants (as defined hereinafter) with respect to electronic bank card processing; and,

WHEREAS, Lessor is engaged from time to time in the business of leasing Vendor's electronic credit card authorization and related equipment to customers of Vendor; and,

WHEREAS, Credit Funding is in the business of financing equipment leases and the underlying equipment by taking an assignment of all right, title and interest in such leases, their non-cancelable lease payments and the equipment subject to such leases; and,

WHEREAS, (i) Vendor and Lessor desire to establish a program with Credit Funding in which Lessor will assemble and remit Leases to Credit Funding executed by Vendor's customers, providing for the lease of equipment for use solely by Customers (as defined hereinafter), and (ii) Credit Funding will review such leases and accept assignment and fund those leases which, in the sole discretion of Credit Funding, meet the reasonable independent credit standards of Credit Funding.

NOW, THEREFORE, in consideration of the foregoing, and of the representations, warranties, covenants and agreements hereinafter contained, and to induce Credit Funding to accept assignment and fund Leases with Customers, the parties hereto agree as follows:

ARTICLE 1—DEFINITIONS

Section 1.1. Definitions. As used in this Agreement, the following terms shall have the following meanings (such meanings to be equally applicable to both the singular and plural forms of the term defined):

1.1. ASSIGNMENT DOCUMENTATION shall mean a duly executed assignment of lease agreement from Lessor acceptable to Credit Funding in its sole discretion, financing statements sufficient under the Uniform Commercial Code in form satisfactory for filing in the appropriate a jurisdiction when requested by Credit Funding, and any other documents, instruments and ably required by Credit Funding.

1.2. COLLATERAL shall mean (i) all of Vendor's and Lessor's right, title and interest in and to all accounts, deposit accounts, money market accounts, money, and deposits which are now or hereafter held by, assigned, pledged to or otherwise restricted on behalf of Credit Funding, its successors or assigns, (ii) any Reserve Account and the funds represented by any Reserve Requirement, all rights to payment and connection therewith, all sums or property now or at any time hereafter on deposit therein, together with all earnings of every kind and description which may now or hereafter accrue thereon, (iii) any Commitment Reserve Account and the funds, leases and equipment related thereto and, (iv) any Security Leases, and the rights and funds related thereto or arising therefrom; and (iv) all proceeds, and interest thereon, of the foregoing.

1.3. COMMITMENT RESERVE ACCOUNT shall be as defined in Section 4.3 hereof.

1.4. CUSTOMER shall mean a Merchant and any lessee, debtor, guarantor, borrower or other person, partnership, corporation or other entity which executes or becomes obligated to Lessor pursuant to a Qualifying Lease (or any part thereof).

1.5. CUSTOMER DEFAULT shall mean any breach by a Customer of any obligation, covenant, duty, condition, or agreement with respect to any Qualifying Lease including, without limitation, failure to timely pay rent or other sums when due, failure to return the equipment, or failure to keep the equipment properly insured, which breach shall occur and continue for a period of sixty (60) days following notice in writing from Credit Funding to Customer specifying the default and requesting that it be cured or fully corrected within such time.

1.6. DEFAULTED LEASE shall mean any Qualifying Lease with respect to which any one or more of the following shall have occurred: (i) a Customer Default shall occur, or (ii) Credit Funding is unable to timely recover, or reasonably believes it will be unable to recover, its Unamortized Net Investment with respect to a particular Qualifying lease.

1.7. DEFAULT PERIOD shall be as defined in Section 5.1 (a) hereof.

1.8. EQUIPMENT shall mean all equipment or machinery and other personal property which is the subject of a Qualifying lease including, without limitation, credit card authorization and processing equipment.

1.9. LEASE shall mean a lease of Equipment by Lessor to a Customer and all other documents and instruments relating thereto or executed in connection therewith (other than Vendor's Merchant Processing Agreement), including, without limitation, any personal guarantee, corporate guarantee, certificate of acceptance (or other instrument whereby customer acknowledges acceptance of the equipment), corporate resolution or financing statement.

1.10. MERCHANT shall mean any seller of goods, services, or both, who is a customer of Vendor.

1.11. OBLIGATIONS shall mean (i) all sums, payments, monies, rents and other amounts due or to become due from Vendor and Lessor to Credit Funding, now existing or hereafter arising, and (ii) all agreements, warranties, duties, obligations and covenants of Vendor and Lessor to Credit Funding pursuant to this Agreement or otherwise.

1.12. PRESENT VALUE shall mean the total sum of all future rent payments, due and unpaid discounted to present value using a ten percent (10%) per annum interest rate, or such other per annum interest rate as shall be mutually agreeable to the parties.

1.13. PURCHASE PRICE with respect to a Qualifying Lease shall mean the Present Value of the regular monthly non-cancelable rent payments due and unpaid.

1.14. QUALIFYING LEASE shall mean a Lease with a Customer which has been approved by Credit Funding for financing in its sole discretion, and which has been sold and assigned to Credit Funding pursuant to the provisions of this Agreement.

1.15. RESERVE ACCOUNT shall be as defined in Section 4.1 hereof.

1.16. RESERVE REQUIREMENT shall be as defined in Section 4.1 hereof.

1.17. SECURITY LEASES shall be as defined in Section 4.3 hereof.

1.18. SUBSTITUTE LEASE shall mean a Lease or sublease with a Customer which replaces a Defaulted Lease upon approval by Credit Funding in its sole discretion as a Qualifying Lease.

1.19. UNAMORTIZED NET INVESTMENT shall mean the sum of all accrued and unpaid rent payments discounted to present value at an interest rate equal to the simple interest lease rate on the Qualifying Lease, calculated monthly in arrears, plus all rents accrued and not yet paid, and all other sums due Credit Funding or its equipment lease lender with respect to a Qualifying Lease or a Defaulted Lease, including accrued interest on unpaid rent payments.

ARTICLE II—ASSIGNMENT OF LEASES

Section 2.1. Sale of Equipment to Credit Funding. Lessor agrees to sell and does hereby sell, assign and transfer to Credit Funding the equipment described in each Qualifying Lease. Vendor and Lessor warrant to Credit Funding with respect to each sale of equipment (whether or not separately documented) that Lessor has good and marketable title to the equipment free and clear of all liens, claims and encumbrances; that Lessor has the right to sell, transfer and assign the equipment to Credit Funding; and that Credit Funding is obtaining good and marketable title to the Equipment free and clear of all liens, claims and encumbrances, except those arising through or from Credit Funding.

Section 2.2. Assignment of Lease Rights and Obligations.

(a) Lessor agrees to use its best efforts to present or cause to be presented Leases with Customers to Credit Funding from time to time in accordance with this Agreement which will qualify as Qualifying Leases whose aggregate monthly Purchase Price shall equal _____ dollars ($ _____) provided, however, Lessor will supply Credit Funding over the initial first year term of this Agreement Qualifying Leases whose aggregate Purchase Price equals at least _____ dollars ($_____), together with such credit information, credit reports and other documentation as Credit Funding shall reasonably request. Upon receipt of all such information, Credit Funding shall promptly approve or disapprove each Lease for funding. Credit Funding shall have the right to approve or disapprove each Lease in its sole discretion in accordance with independent credit standards acceptable to Credit Funding. Upon proper completion and delivery to Credit Funding of Assignment Documentation for each Qualifying Lease, and other relevant documentation, Credit Funding shall pay to Lessor the Purchase Price less the Reserve Requirement and less any other sums due Credit Funding from Vendor or Lessor under this Agreement. Credit Funding does not by this Agreement or otherwise assume any of the obligations of Vendor or Lessor or any other party under the leases, and Credit Funding shall not be responsible in any way for the performance by Vendor or Lessor or any other party of the terms and conditions of the Qualifying Leases.

(b) In the event Credit Funding determines that any Qualifying Lease with respect to which the Purchase Price has been paid is not as represented by the credit or documentation information supplied by Vendor or Lessor at any time prior to and including two (2) months following payment of the Purchase Price (the "Review Period"), Credit Funding shall so notify Vendor and Lessor in writing at which time Lessor shall within five (5) business days after the receipt of such notice pay Credit Funding, or its designee, less any rent payments received by Credit Funding, or its designee, an amount equal to the Purchase Price, plus in the event of a material misrepresentation a fee equal to seventy-five dollars ($75.00) per lease.

Section 2.3. Assignment Documentation. With respect to each Qualifying Lease, Lessor agrees to execute or cause to be executed and delivered to Credit Funding, the originals of the Qualifying Leases and all Assignment Documentation prior to payment of the Purchase Price by Credit Funding. The terms and conditions of the Assignment Documentation shall supplement the terms and conditions of this Agreement. Credit Funding shall have the right, if applicable, to stamp or mark each Qualifying Lease and all Assignment Documentation to clearly and conspicuously state that it is subject to the security interest of Credit Funding, in such form and with such language as Credit Funding may desire. The originals of such Qualifying Lease and all Assignment Documentation shall be maintained in the possession of Credit Funding.

Section 2.4. Security Interest. As security for (i) the payment, and performance, of the obligations and all other present and future indebtedness, liabilities and obligations of Vendor and Lessor to Credit Funding, whether arising hereunder, or under the Assignment Documentation, or under any other document or instrument executed in connection with the transactions contemplated hereunder or otherwise, including indebtedness of every kind and description, direct or indirect, absolute or contingent, due or to become due, now existing or hereafter arising, and (ii) Vendor's and Lessor's obligations and liabilities arising out of its covenants, warranties and representations contained herein, or in any other document or instrument executed in connection with the transactions contemplated hereunder, Lessor hereby pledges, assigns and grants to Credit Funding a priority security interest in the Collateral free and clear of all liens, claims and encumbrances except those arising through or from Credit Funding. If any deposit or account constituting Collateral is evidenced by a certificate of deposit or is otherwise subject to Article 9 of the Uniform Commercial Code, the foregoing security interest shall be construed as a grant of a security interest subject, to the extend applicable, to the Uniform Commercial Code as enacted in the State of _____ .

Section 2.5. Payment of Rent Directly to Credit Funding. Lessor shall cause all rental and other payments assigned to Credit Funding pursuant to Qualifying Leases to be made by electronic funds transfer directly to Credit Funding when received, and, to that end, to have caused each Customer to sign an authorization giving Lessor or its designees and assigns the right and power to authorize such transfers to be made. If any Customer has not signed such an authorization, the lease to such Customer shall not constitute a Qualifying Lease under any circumstances and Credit Funding shall have no obligation to consider funding such lease. All electronic transfers of payments shall be made to an account designated by Credit Funding. Lessor hereby irrevocably designates Credit Funding as attorney-in-fact to direct the electronic funds transfer as to each Qualifying Lease and Lessor shall cause each Lessee to be notified of the assignment of rent payments to Credit Funding.

Section 2.6. Financing Statements. Upon written request by Credit Funding Lessor agrees to execute and provide Credit Funding with commercially standard UCC financing statements covering the Collateral, which Credit Funding is authorized to file upon receipt. Lessor agrees that it will, at its expense, execute such additional financial statements, endorsements, continuation statements and other documents in connection therewith and do such other acts and provide such further assurances as Credit Funding may from time to time reasonably request to establish and maintain a first lien priority security interest in the Collateral free and clear of all liens, claims and encumbrances, except those arising through or arising from Credit Funding, and preserve and protect Credit Funding's interests acquired herein. At the option of Credit Funding and upon notice to Lessor, Credit Funding may sign any financing statements on behalf of Lessor (directly in the name of Lessor or in the name of Credit Funding on behalf of Lessor) and file the same, and Lessor hereby irrevocably designates Credit Funding, its agents, representatives and designees, as agents and attorneys-in-fact for Lessor for this purpose. In the event that any re-recording or re-filing thereof (or the filing of any statement of continuation or assignment of any financing statement) is required to protect and preserve such lien or security interest, Lessor shall, at Credit Funding's written request, and at its sole cost and expense, cause the same to be re-recorded or re-filed at the time and in the manner requested by Credit Funding

Section 2.7. Quarterly Accounting. Lessor agrees to provide, or cause to be provided, Credit Funding with a quarterly (or monthly, if requested by Credit Funding), accounting of all Qualifying Leases within thirty (30) days following the last day of the immediately preceding calendar quarter (or month, if applicable), commencing on _____ , 20___ .

Section 2.8. Taxes and Reporting. Lessor agrees to report, file, and pay promptly when due as required by statute or regulation to the appropriate taxing authority, indemnity, defend, and hold Credit Funding, and any of its assignees, harmless from any and all taxes (including sales, use, property, transaction, and gross receipts), assessments, license fees and governmental charges of any kind or nature, together with any penalties, interest or fines relating thereto that pertains to a Qualifying Lease, the equipment, its lease or rent or other sums due thereunder. On all such reports or returns required hereunder, Lessor shall show the ownership of the equipment by Credit Funding or, if requested, its designee. Upon written request by Credit

Funding, Lessor agrees to remit such taxes to Credit Funding and First Street shall remit such taxes so collected by Credit Funding to the appropriate taxing authority.

Section 2.9. Licenses, Permits, Consents and Approvals. Vendor and Lessor have or will obtain all licenses, permits, consents, approvals, authorizations, qualifications and orders of governmental authorities required to enable them to continue to conduct their business as presently conducted and will be duly qualified to conduct business in each and every state in which they enter into a lease transaction. Vendor and Lessor have duly filed and shall continue to timely file with the appropriate federal, state, local and other governmental agencies, all tax returns, information returns and reports required to be filed by them and their subsidiaries, have and will continue to pay or cause to be paid, in full or make adequate provision for the payment of all taxes (including taxes withheld from employees' salaries and other withholding taxes and obligations), interest, penalties, assessments or deficiencies shown on such returns or reports to be due to any taxing authority, including but not limited to all sales, use, transaction, property taxes which may be due or become due for all equipment subject to a Qualifying Lease, whether assessed against Lessor or Credit Funding. All claims for taxes due and payable by Lessor have either been paid or are being contested in good faith by appropriate proceedings. Vendor and Lessor warrant that neither is a party to, nor are they aware of, any pending or threatened action or proceeding, assessment or collection of taxes by any government authority. Credit Funding reserves the right at any time to enter the business premises of Vendor and Lessor and to inspect and audit the appropriate books and records of Vendor and Lessor to verify and assure compliance with all applicable regulations and the provisions of this Agreement, including, but not limited to, sales, use and property tax regulations.

Section 2.10. Advances by Credit Funding. At its sole option, and without any obligation to do so, Credit Funding may discharge or pay any taxes, liens, security interests (other than the lien or the security interest of Credit Funding contemplated in this Agreement or liens arising from acts or omissions of Credit Funding), or other encumbrances at any time levied or placed on or against the Collateral or Vendor or Lessor in breach of this Agreement, and may pay for insurance on the Collateral, and may pay for its maintenance and preservation. Vendor and Lessor agree to reimburse Credit Funding on demand for any such payment made, or expense incurred, pursuant to the foregoing authorizations, and such advances shall be deemed additional obligations secured by the Collateral.

Section 2.11. Commitment Paid to Credit Funding. Vendor shall pay to Credit Funding upon the execution by Vendor of this Agreement a non-refundable commitment fee equal to _____ dollars ($_____). Neither Vendor nor Lessor shall be obligated to pay any other fees, including attorney's fees, or expenses in connection with this Agreement unless otherwise expressly stated herein.

ARTICLE III—TERM

Section 3.1. Term. The initial term of this Agreement shall be one (1) year from the date hereof. Unless either Vendor or Lessor notifies Credit Funding or Credit Funding notifies Vendor or Lessor not later than one hundred twenty calendar (120) days prior to the expiration of the initial or any renewal term that it does not wish to renew this Agreement for a subsequent term, this Agreement shall automatically renew for additional terms of one (1) year upon the same terms and conditions. The foregoing notwithstanding, all rights and obligations of the parties herein to each with respect to Qualifying Leases assigned to and funded by Credit Funding during the time this Agreement is in force, and all representations, warranties and covenants of Vendor and Lessor, shall survive any expiration or earlier termination of this Agreement. Notwithstanding the foregoing, Credit Funding may terminate this Agreement, in whole or in part, at any time in the exercise of its rights and remedies upon an Event of Default hereunder.

ARTICLE IV—RESERVE ACCOUNT

Section 4.1. The Reserve Account. Credit Funding agrees to deposit into and maintain in a restricted Reserve Account in the name of Lessor an amount equal to ten percent (10%) on Qualifying Leases calculated on the Purchase Price of each Qualifying Lease (such sum hereinafter is referred to as the "Reserve Requirement"). Credit Funding may hold back and deduct the Reserve Requirement from the proceeds due Lessor from Credit Funding for each Qualifying Lease. Credit Funding and Lessor agree that they will not withdraw or attempt to withdraw funds from, terminate, deplete, pledge, hypothecate, assign, grant a security interest or permit a lien to attach to the Reserve Account, except those permitted pursuant to this Agreement

Section 4.2. Distribution from Excess Funds. Credit Funding and Lessor recognize that as Customers make lease payments, the Unamortized Net Investment in its portfolio of Qualifying Leases may decline. Provided Credit Funding has a favorable loss experience as set forth below with respect to Qualifying Leases, the amount of funds on deposit in the Reserve Account may exceed the Reserve Requirement. Credit Funding will review the Reserve Account and its loss experience quarterly, and provided that each and every one of the following conditions has occurred and is continuing, Credit Funding shall distribute to Lessor the funds in the Reserve Requirement:

(a) Credit Funding actual cumulative Customer default experience (without regard to recovery) has been less than the Reserve Requirement (for purposes of determining Credit Funding default experience, Substitute leases will be excluded); and

(b) No event of default has occurred on the part of Vendor or Lessor and continued uncured for a period of sixty (60) days following notice in writing from Credit Funding specifying the default and requesting that it be cured and fully corrected within such time.

Section 4.3. The Commitment Reserve Account. Lessor and Vendor agree as a condition precedent to the purchase by Credit Funding of any Qualifying Leases to assign all right, title and interest to Qualifying Leases, and related equipment and proceeds, with a total Purchase Price of not less than four hundred thousand dollars ($400,000.00) to Credit Funding or its designee (the "Security Leases") as security for the reasonable performance by Vendor and Lessor under this Agreement. The Security Leases shall be re-assigned to Lessor at the end of one (1) year from the date of assignment to Credit Funding, or its designee, if Vendor and Lessor have reasonably complied with their obligations under this Agreement.

ARTICLE V—DEFAULTED LEASES

Section 5.1. Substitution Procedure. With respect to any Defaulted Lease, upon written request of Credit Funding, Lessor, at its sole expense, agrees promptly to perform the following:

(a) Upon notice from Credit Funding or actual knowledge on the part of Lessor that a lease constitutes a Defaulted Lease, whichever shall first occur, Lessor shall (i) take immediate steps to replace the Defaulted Lease with a Substitute Lease of equal or greater present value than the Unamortized Net Investment of the Defaulted Lease and (ii) pay to Credit Funding within ten (10) days following the receipt of such notice seventy-five dollars ($75.00). Lessor shall not be obligated to replace a Defaulted lease with a Substituted Lease if a Qualifying Lease becomes a Defaulted Lease as a result of events occurring following two hundred and forty (240) days following the date of payment by Credit Funding of the Purchase Price (the "Default Period"). If the Present Value of the Substitute Lease exceeds the Unamortized Net Investment of the Defaulted Lease, Credit Funding will refund the excess present value to Lessor after first deducting all fees, costs and interest due with respect to the Defaulted Lease due on the Substitute Lease. Lessor shall take all steps necessary to assign the Substitute Lease and underlying equipment to Credit Funding within sixty (60) days from such notice or actual knowledge. Upon approval by Credit Funding in its sole discretion, the Substitute Lease shall thereafter constitute a Qualifying Lease hereunder. Lessor shall only be permitted under this Agreement to make one lease substitution in the case of a Defaulted Lease.

(b) A Substitute Lease may be for the same equipment originally leased under the Defaulted Lease or for like equipment of at least equal value as the equipment under the Defaulted Lease.

(c) Lessor's obligation to substitute such Defaulted Lease hereunder shall not be subject to or diminished by any defense, counterclaim, or set-off which it may have or claim to have against Credit Funding and shall also not be conditioned on Credit Funding first having obtained a judgment against the Customer or otherwise proceeding against the Customer. Credit Funding may, but shall not be obligated to proceed in any manner against the Customer or the applicable leased equipment.

(d) Upon approval and assignment of a Substitute Lease by Credit Funding, Credit Funding shall return to Lessor the originals of each lease corresponding thereto which constitute a Defaulted Lease, and all Assignment Documentation associated therewith.

(e) Should Lessor fail to substitute a Qualifying Lease or if the applicable Substitute Lease becomes a Defaulted Lease, Credit Funding may debit the Reserve Account for the Unamortized Net Investment in the

Defaulted Lease. If the Reserve Account contains insufficient funds to satisfy the Unamortized Net Investment in the Defaulted Lease, Credit Funding may collect from the Collateral described in Section 1.2. hereof upon sixty (60) days written notice to Lessor of its intention to do so, and Lessor's failure to sufficiently replenish the Reserve Account within said sixty (60) days.

(f) In the event the Collateral described in Section 1.2 is insufficient to Satisfy the any Defaulted Lease, then upon written demand by Credit Funding, Lessor shall pay to Credit Funding such amounts within ten (10) days, as the Purchase Price of said Defaulted Lease.

(g) In the event Lessor fails to pay Credit Funding in accordance with Section 5. 1.(f) above and upon written notice to Vendor, Vendor shall pay the amount specified by Section 5. l.(f) within ten (10) days after receipt of written notice from Credit Funding.

ARTICLE VI—VENDOR'S AND LESSOR'S REPRESENTATIONS AND WARRANTIES

Section 6.1. Warranties and Representations. Vendor and Lessor hereby represent, warrant and covenant the following to Credit Funding:

(a) With respect to each lease sold hereunder during the term of the lease, Credit Funding or its assignee, is and shall remain (except for acts or omissions of Credit Funding) the sole owner of the lease and equipment leased thereunder, which are and will remain free and clear of any lien, security interest, mortgage, charge, or encumbrance (except for a security interest granted by Credit Funding, its successors and assigns and the Lessee's leasehold rights in the equipment).

(b) This Agreement, the sales and assignments of Qualifying Leases and underlying equipment to Credit Funding (and any sales and assignment of the Qualifying Leases from Vendor to Lessor), the Qualifying Leases and all other documents now or hereafter executed by Vendor and Lessor pursuant to the terms hereof, are and shall be enforceable in accordance with their respective terms, except as they may be limited by bankruptcy, insolvency or other similar laws affecting enforcement of creditors' rights in general.

(c) At the tine of the sale or assignment of any lease and underlying equipment to Credit Funding, the equipment thereunder shall have been delivered to and accepted by the respective Lessee under the lease. The equipment shall not be or suffered to be wasted, misused, abused or to deteriorate, except for ordinary wear and tear, and will not be used in violation of any law, ordinance or regulation of any governmental authority insofar as it adversely affects the value of the respective lease, equipment or the security interests granted hereunder. Vendor and Lessor will during the Default Period (or will cause the Lessees to) maintain, preserve, protect and keep the equipment under each Qualifying Lease in good repair, working order and condition and from time to time, will make all repairs, renewals, replacements, additions, betterment and improvements to the equipment as are needed and proper, at Vendor's and Lessor's sole cost and expense.

(d) Neither Lessor, Vendor nor any Lessee are in default under the leases as of the date of payment of the applicable Purchase Price. The Lessees under the Qualifying Leases have no claims, defenses, set-offs or counterclaims against Lessor or Vendor under such leases. Vendor and Lessor shall indemnify, defend and save the Credit Funding harmless of and from all costs, expenses, losses, claims, damages, attorney's fees and expenses, suits and liabilities arising out of or incurred by Credit Funding as a result of any claims, defenses, set-offs or counterclaims raised or asserted by any Lessee under any lease arising by, through or under Lessor's or Vendor's acts or omissions.

(e) With the exception of a lease which constitutes a Defaulted Lease, neither Vendor nor Lessor will repossess or consent to the return of any equipment prior to the scheduled expiration of the lease term without the prior written consent of Credit Funding.

(f) Neither Vendor nor Lessor will cause the Collateral to be sold, transferred, assigned, encumbered, pledged, hypothecated, or disposed of, without the prior written consent of Credit Funding. Credit Funding recognizes that certain Customers may sell or transfer their business and the new owner may sublease the equipment from the Customer. Credit Funding shall allow such subleases, subject to satisfactory credit review.

(g) Each lease delivered by Lessor to Credit Funding shall be the original counterpart of such lease and shall be the sole counterpart deemed chattel paper under the Uniform Commercial Code as enacted in the State of _____ , and effective to transfer Lessor's rights as Lessor to be assigned herein and therein.

(h) Vendor will punctually perform and observe all of its obligations and agreements contained in any servicing or processing agreements made with respect to the Qualifying Leases. Vendor, Lessor and Credit Funding will immediately notify the other of any default by any party under the Qualifying Leases of which it becomes aware.

(i) Lessor will not declare a default under or exercise any remedies under the Qualifying Leases or enter into or permit any cancellation, termination, amendment, supplement or modification of or waiver with respect to such leases or give any consent or approval as to any matter arising out of such leases, and any such attempted declaration, exercise, cancellation, termination, amendment, supplement, modification, waiver, consent or approval shall be void and of no effect unless the Lessor shall have received the express prior written consent thereto from Credit Funding.

(j) Vendor and Lessor are corporations duly organized, validly existing and in good standing under the laws of the State of _____ . Vendor and Lessor shall do all things necessary to maintain and preserve their corporate existence.

(k) Each lease to be assigned to the Credit Funding shall be a valid and genuine lease, and in all respects what it purports to be.

(l) There are and shall not be any agreements, undertakings or other documents relating to the leases hereinafter assigned to the Credit Funding which are not contained in such leases.

(m) Vendor and Lessor will keep true books of records and account in which full and correct entries will be made of all its business transactions, and which reflects in such financial statements adequate accruals and appropriations to reserves, all in accordance with generally accepted accounting principals.

ARTICLE VII—TERMINATION

Section 7.1. Default by Vendor and Lessor. Vendor and Lessor shall be in default hereunder upon the occurrence of one or more of the following ("Event of Default"):

(a) Vendor or Lessor fail to pay any amount when due hereunder to Credit Funding or its assigns;

(b) Vendor or Lessor shall fail to pay or perform any of its obligations or any other obligations hereunder or shall breach or default in the due observance or performance of any other term, covenant, warranty or representation contained herein, in the assignments of the leases to Credit Funding, or in any other document or instrument executed in connection herewith;

(c) a receiver, liquidator or trustee is appointed for Vendor or Lessor or any of their assets or properties;

(d) any proceeding under any state or federal bankruptcy or insolvency laws is instituted against Vendor or Lessor, and such proceeding is not dismissed, vacated or fully stayed within sixty (60) calendar days;

(e) any property of Vendor or Lessor is attached, levied upon, or seized under any judicial process which could materially and adversely interfere with the operation of Vendor's or Lessor's business;

(f) Vendor or Lessor shall file a petition for relief under the bankruptcy laws including, without limitation, a petition seeking for itself any reorganization, readjustment, liquidation, dissolution or similar arrangement under any present or future bankruptcy statute, law or regulation, or a petition to take advantage of any insolvency laws, or make an assignment for the benefit of creditors, or admit in writing its inability to pay its debts as they become due;

(g) Vendor or Lessor shall sell, transfer, assign, pledge, encumber, hypothecate, grant a security interest, or dispose of the Collateral, without the prior written consent of Credit Funding;

(h) any warranty, representation, financial statement, covenant or agreement made or furnished to Credit Funding by or on behalf of Vendor or Lessor is false or misleading in any material respect when made or furnished;

(i) Vendor or Lessor default under or otherwise has accelerated any material obligation including, but not limited to, credit agreements, loan agreements, conditional sales contracts, lease indentures or debentures, or Vendor defaults under any agreement now existing or hereafter made with Credit Funding or its assignees;

(j) the breach or repudiation by Vendor or Lessor or any party to any subordination, waiver, or other agreement running in favor of Credit Funding obtained in connection with this Agreement or a Qualifying Lease;

(k) if the validity or effectiveness of any Qualifying Lease of its assignment by Lessor or to Credit Funding shall be impaired.

Section 7.2. Default by Credit Funding. Credit Funding shall be in default hereunder upon the occurrence of one or more of the following ("Event of Default"):

(a) Credit Funding falls to pay any amount when due hereunder to Vendor or Lessor; or

(b) Credit Funding shall fail to pay or perform any of its obligations to Vendor or Lessor hereunder, or shall breach or default in the due observance or performance of any other term, covenant, warranty or representation contained herein, in the assignment of the leases to the Credit Funding, or in any other document or instrument executed in connection herewith.

Section 7.3. Notice and Right to Cure. In the event an Event of Default occurs and continues for a period of thirty (30) days following notice in writing to the other party or parties, as the case may be, specifying the default and requesting it be cured or fully corrected within such time, this Agreement may be terminated, without further notice or action of any kind.

Section 7.4. Rights Upon Default. Upon the occurrence of an Event of Default under this Agreement which is not cured in accordance with the terms herein, Vendor and Lessor or Credit Funding, as the case may be, against whom the default has occurred, may recover any amounts owing to it pursuant to this Agreement and may:

(a) terminate this Agreement without further notice or demand of any kind;

(b) seize, appropriate, apply and set-off (as such term is defined in the Uniform Commercial Code of the State of _____) any and all items of Collateral against any amounts owing to Credit Funding by Vendor or Lessor;

(c) institute legal proceedings against the other party or parties at law or in equity; or

(d) exercise any and all rights and remedies available to it under this Agreement, the assignments of the leases and all other documents and instruments executed in connection herewith.

Section 7.5. Remedies not Exclusive. No remedy referred to in this Agreement is intended to be exclusive, but each shall be cumulative, and shall be in addition to any other remedy referred to above or otherwise available by statute, at law or in equity, and may be exercised from time to time and any number of times. In addition, Vendor and Lessor agree that they shall be liable for any and all unpaid obligations or additional sums due hereunder, before, after or during the exercise of any of the foregoing remedies. If Credit Funding or its assignee employs counsel to represent Credit Funding, or its assignee, in any litigation, dispute, suit or proceeding in any way relating to the leases assigned to Credit Funding (excluding enforcement and collection with respect to the Qualifying Leases), or conflicting claims of third parties to all or any portion of the Collateral, or the sums advanced or paid to Vendor or Lessor hereunder, or any provision of this Agreement or of the Assignment Documentation, or other documents arising out of the transactions contemplated herein or to enforce any term of this Agreement, the Assignment Documentation, or documents arising out of the transactions contemplated herein, then Vendor and Lessor shall pay on demand all of Credit Funding's reasonable attorney's fees arising from such services and all expenses, costs, court costs and charges relating thereto.

ARTICLE VIII—GENERAL PROVISIONS

Section 8.1. Notification. Each party shall promptly notify the others of any suit or threat of suit of which that party becomes aware (except with respect to a threat of suit one party might institute against the other) which may give rise to a right of indemnification. The indemnifying party shall be entitled to participate in the settlement or defense thereof and, if the indemnifying party elects (and demonstrates to the satisfaction of the indemnified party the financial ability to promptly honor its obligation to indemnify), to take over and control the settlement or defense thereof with counsel satisfactory to the indemnified party. In any case, the indemnifying party and the indemnified party shall cooperate (at no cost to the indemnified party) in the settlement or defense of any such claim, demand, suit or proceeding.

Section 8.2. Indemnification. In addition to such obligations of indemnification as may be provided elsewhere in this Agreement, Vendor and Lessor as a unit and Credit Funding hereby also agree to indemnify, save and keep harmless each other and their successors and assigns from and against any and all losses, damages, penalties, injuries, actions and suits, including litigation costs and attorney's fees of whatsoever kind and nature directly and indirectly arising by reason of breach or default of any term, condition, representation, warranty or agreement set forth in this Agreement or by reason of any improper act or omission to act in relation to the subject matter of this Agreement. The foregoing indemnity shall continue in full force and effect notwithstanding the expiration or earlier termination of this Agreement.

Section 8.3. Disclosure. Each party shall promptly notify the others of any action, suit or proceeding, facts or circumstances, or the prospect or threat of the same, which might materially adversely affect that party's ability to perform this Agreement. Each party represents and warrants to the others that there are no suits, actions, or legal, administrative, arbitration, or other claims or proceedings or government investigations which are pending or which have been made against that party or its parents or affiliates, or its officers, directors or employees or, to the knowledge of that party, threatened against Vendor, Lessor or Credit Funding, as the case may be, or its parent or affiliates, or its officers, directors or employees, which might materially adversely affect the financial condition of Vendor, Lessor or Credit Funding, or its ability to observe or perform its obligations under this Agreement.

Section 8.4. Compliance with Laws. Each party hereby represents and warrants to the others that it is familiar with the requirements of all applicable laws and regulations and covenants and agrees that it will comply with all such laws and regulations, as well as all other applicable laws and regulations in the performance of this Agreement. The parties each agree to comply with all applicable statutes, rules, regulations, orders and restrictions of the United States of America, foreign countries, states and municipalities, and of any governmental department, commission, board, regulatory authority, bureau, agency, and instrumentality of the foregoing, and of any court, arbitrator or grand jury, in respect of the conduct of its business and the ownership of its properties, except such as are being contested in good faith.

Section 8.5. Relationship of the Parties. The parties acknowledge and agree that in performing their responsibilities pursuant to this Agreement they are in the position of independent contractors. This Agreement is not intended to create, nor does it create and nor shall it be construed to create, a relationship of partner or joint venture or any association for profit by and between Vendor or Lessor and Credit Funding. Neither Vendor nor Lessor are agents of Credit Funding, and Credit Funding is not an agent of Vendor.

Section 8.6. Further Assurances. Within five (5) business days following written notice by Vendor or Lessor or Credit Funding, as the case may be, each party shall produce and make available for inspection by the others, or its officers and agents, at the business premises of the other, such hooks and records of Vendor and Lessor or Credit Funding, as the case may be, shall deem reasonably necessary to be adequately informed of the business and financial condition of Vendor and Lessor or Credit Funding, or its ability to observe or perform its obligations hereunder. Vendor agrees to execute and deliver such other or additional documents as may be requested by Credit Funding from time to time hereafter which are necessary or desirable to effectuate the intent of this Agreement.

Section 8.7. Assignment, Benefit and Binding Effect. This Agreement may not be assigned or transferred by Vendor. Credit Funding may freely assign or transfer its rights and privileges hereunder. This Agreement shall be binding upon Vendor, Lessor and Credit Funding, and shall inure to the benefit of and be enforceable by the Credit Funding successor and assigns (hereinafter "Assignee"). Any Assignee of Credit Funding may reassign its rights and interests hereunder.

Section 8.8. Continuation of Corporate Condition. Vendor and Lessor represent and warrant that neither shall, where Credit Funding's rights and interests are diminished or impaired: (i) merge into, consolidate with or be acquired by an unrelated entity, or sell or otherwise dispose of all or substantially all of its assets or any of its assets except in the ordinary course of its business; (ii) make any material change in capital structure or operations which might in any way adversely affect the ability of Vendor or Lessor, as the case may be, to make payment or perform its obligations to Credit Funding hereunder; or (iii) knowingly enter into or continue to be a party to any transaction, which materially or adversely affect its business, operations, assets or conditions (financial or otherwise) or Vendor's or Lessor's ability to make payment or perform its obligations to Credit Funding hereunder. Vendor's and Lessor's principal place of business and chief executive office is at _____ . Vendor and Lessor will notify Credit Funding promptly should the location of such principal place of business and chief executive office change.

Section 8.9. Notices. All notices, requests, demand and other communications hereunder shall be in writing and shall be deemed to have been duly given if delivered or mailed by certified mail or confirmed facsimile transmission;

if to VENDOR:

with a copy to:

if to LESSOR:

with a copy to:

if to Credit Funding:

with a copy to:

Section 8.10. Waiver. None of the parties shall be deemed to have waived any of its rights, powers or remedies hereunder unless such waiver is approved in writing by the waiving party and signed by a duly authorized officer of the waiving party. No course of dealing between the parties hereto any failure or delay on the part of Credit Funding or Vendor or Lessor in exercising any rights or remedies hereunder shall operate as a waiver of any rights or remedies of Credit Funding or Vendor or Lessor, and no single or partial exercise of any rights or remedies hereunder shall operate as a waiver or preclude the exercise of any other rights or remedies hereunder. No modification or waiver of any provision of this Agreement and no consent by Credit Funding or Vendor or Lessor to any departure therefrom by Credit Funding or Vendor or Lessor shall be effective unless such modification or waiver shall be in writing and signed by duly authorized officers of all parties, and the same shall then be effective only for the period and on the conditions and for the specific instances and purposes specified in writing. No notice to or demand on Credit Funding or Vendor or Lessor in any case shall entitle Credit Funding or Vendor or Lessor to any other or further notice or demand in similar or other circumstances.

Section 8.11. Amendments. This is the only Agreement between the parties. The terms and conditions of this Agreement may be altered, modified, or waived only by a written agreement, signed by all of the parties to this Agreement.

Section 8.12. Construction. The captions contained in this Agreement are for the convenience of the parties only and shall not be construed or interpreted to limit or otherwise define the scope of this Agreement. This Agreement shall not be deemed to have originated with any particular party hereto.

Section 8.13. Counterparts. This Agreement may be executed and delivered by the parties hereto in any number of counterparts, and by different patties on separate counterparts, each of which counterpart shall be deemed to be an original and all of which counterparts, taken together, shall constitute but one and the same instrument.

Section 8.14. Time is of the Essence. The parties agree that the time is of the essence as to all rights, obligations and duties under this Agreement.

Section 8.15. Additional Documents. Subsequent to the execution of this Agreement, the parties agree to execute and deliver such further documents, instruments, certificates or notices as any other party shall reasonably request which are necessary or desirable to effect complete consummation of this Agreement.

Section 8.16. Non-Exclusivity. The parties hereto acknowledge that this Agreement is not exclusive and any party may market or fund leases and leasing programs separate from this Agreement with other persons.

Section 8.17. Severability. In the event that any part of this Agreement is ruled by any court or administrative or regulatory agency to be invalid or unenforceable, then this Agreement shall be automatically modified to eliminate that part which is affected thereby. The remainder of this Agreement shall remain in full force and effect.

Section 8.18. Survival. All representations and warranties shall survive the execution and termination of this Agreement. Each representation, warranty and covenant of Vendor and Lessor contained in this Agreement or Assignment Documentation shall be deemed remade by Vendor and Lessor as of the time of acceptance by Credit Funding of each Qualifying Lease and payment of the Purchase Price by Credit Funding and shall be deemed remade by Vendor and Lessor as to each Qualifying Lease.

Section 8.19. Governing Law and Jurisdiction. This Agreement shall be interpreted and construed in accordance with the laws of the State of _____ . The parties expressly agree that any suit between the parties in connection with this Agreement shall be filed and venued in the County of _____ located in the State of _____ with respect to any dispute, proceeding or action arising from this Agreement.

Section 8.20. Legal Authority. Each of the parties represents and warrants to the others that all consents and approvals necessary to the validity of this Agreement have been duly obtained, and that this Agreement does not conflict with any provision or any document or agreement binding that party or its property or affairs. Each party hereto further specifically represents and warrants to the other party hereto that: (i) the making of this Agreement is duly authorized on the part of such party and that upon its due execution by the other party hereto, it shall constitute a valid obligation binding upon, and enforceable and against such party in accordance with its terms; (ii) neither the making of this Agreement nor the due performance hereof by such party shall result in any breach of, or constitute a default under, or violation of, such party's certificate of incorporation, bylaws or any agreement to which such party is a party of by which such party is bound; and (iii) such party is duly incorporated and in good standing in its state of incorporation and is in good standing in any jurisdiction in which it owns properties or is carrying on business (except Credit Funding shall not be deemed to be carrying on business in any jurisdiction by virtue of its purchase of Qualifying Leases from Vendor).

Section 8.21. Entire Agreement. This Agreement represents the entire understanding among Vendor, Lessor and Credit Funding with respect to the matters contained herein.

IN WITNESS WHEREOF, each party has caused this Agreement to be executed on its behalf by its proper officer thereunder duly authorized, as of the date first written above.

(Insert name of Vendor)

("Vendor")

By: _____

Its: _____

(Insert name of initial lessor)

("Lessor")

By: _____

Its: _____

CREDIT FUNDING CORPORATION

("Credit Funding")

By: _____

Its: _____

Addendum

Parties agree and understand that insurance obligations referenced in Paragraphs 1.4 and 2.10 may be imposed. Credit Funding shall exercise its best efforts to avoid the imposition of insurance costs. In the event insurance is deemed necessary by Credit Funding, and Credit Funding intends to enforce its right under a Qualifying Lease to require the lessee to purchase insurance as specified in the Qualifying Lease, then in the event the lessee does not purchase such insurance the failure to do so will not be deemed a Customer Default if (i) Vendor or Lessor provides on behalf of the lessee the applicable insurance at its own cost, or (ii) Credit Funding provides the applicable insurance and Vendor or Lessor reimburse Credit Funding in full for the cost of providing such insurance, provided, however, in no event shall Vendor or Lessor be required to pay in excess of ____ dollars ($____) per Qualifying Lease per year during the term of such lease for such insurance cost.

(Insert name of Vendor)

("Vendor")

By: _____

Its: _____

(Insert name of initial lessor)

("Lessor")

By: _____

Its: _____

CREDIT FUNDING CORPORATION

("Credit Funding")

By: _____

Its: _____

Form: w-01
Disk File Name: w-01.rtf

Worksheet—Lease Proposal Evalution

Form Purpose

A lease proposal summary response sheet to enable a lessee to easily evaluate lessor offers. Typically, leasing company offers have different formats. Digging through each can take work. To simplify your job, you can include with your RFQ a Summary Response Sheet for the lessor to complete and return with its proposal. The sheet should list, in an orderly and clear fashion, every key review item so a quick look will tell you whether the proposal is in the ball park.

This summary response form must be tailored to your company. You can use the Lessee Proposal Stage Checklist, Form c-01, to identify what should be included for your particular needs.

See:
Request for Lease Quotations, Forms r-01 through r-04
Lessee Proposal Stage Checklist, Form c-01

Proposal Summary Response Sheet

Leasing Company Information:

    Name: _____

    Address: _____

    _____

    Deal Contact: _____

    Telephone No.: (   ) _____

Equipment Cost (± 15%):_____

Lease Term: Lease Rate Factor (As a % of Cost)	Payment Mode (Monthly, In Arrears, Etc.)	Interest Rate (Nominal)
3 Years	_____	_____
5 Years	_____	_____

Purchase Option (Check One)

    _____ FMV

    _____ Fixed Price (___% of Equipment Cost)

Renewal Option (Check One)

    _____ FRV, For ____ Years, Every ___ Year(s)

    _____ Fixed Price, (___% of Primary Rent, Every __ Year(s))

Early Termination Option (Schedule of Values attached __ Yes, __ No)

_____   Not Available

_____   Available, Beginning the ___ Year of the Lease Term

Upgrade Financing Option (____ Yes, _____ No)

State Future Lease Rate Determination Basis if Upgrade Financing Not Fixed at Award (Adjustment so Lessor Can Maintain Nominal After Tax Yield, Pre-Tax Yield, etc.) _____

Casualty Schedule Attached (____ Yes, ____ No)

Transaction Structure (Check One)

Single Investor   ____

Leveraged Lease   ____

Lessor Offer: (Check One)

Brokered   ____ (___ Best Efforts, ___ Firm)

Principal Lessor   ____

Lessor Financial Statement Attached (___ Yes, ___ No)

Subject Index

Note: Italicized page numbers indicate illustrations.

Forms Index

Note: Form file names appear in brackets; access CD files by adding the extension .rtf.